CASEBOOK IN SOCIAL PROCESSES

CASEBOOK

in SOCIAL

PROCESSES

Eugene L. Hartley
Professor of Psychology
The City College of New York

Gerhart D. Wiebe
Partner, Elmo Roper and Associates

Thomas Y. Crowell Company, New York

ESTABLISHED 1834

To HELEN *and to* RUTH

Manufactured in the United States of America
By Vail-Ballou Press, Inc., Binghamton, N. Y.
Designed by Andor Braun

PREFACE

EXCEPT for the introductory pages and the several paragraphs of orientation which precede each chapter, the contents of this book come entirely from official records of hearings conducted by committees of the Senate or the House of Representatives of the United States. Among these excerpts you will find the vision and eloquence of some of our statesmen as they discuss topics of international scope, the unusually concise testimony of experts and prominent authority figures, and you will find the verbatim, and often pungent, statements of private citizens as they inform their governmental representatives of the problems and perplexities they face in their local situations. You will find wisdom and insight regarding social processes, and in some passages you will note the absence of these qualities. You will find the diversity of values and the range of sophistication that bear on our legislators as they consider social problems.

In selecting these materials, no attempt has been made to illustrate "right" or "wrong" approaches to human interaction. The editors have deliberately attempted to avoid emphasis on any particular theoretical orientation or school of thought. The guiding idea in selecting and editing the content of this volume has been to bring the student of social science into contact with social science problems and processes as they appear in the deliberations of our Federal Government.

Accommodation and compromise are characteristic of democratic government. But it is also true that governmental decisions are binding. Consequently, the give-and-take in legislative hearings has a special vitality and a basic validity. Statements are "on the record" and will be preserved in government archives. Participants attempt to be as effective as possible in promoting the ends in which they believe.

The honor of participating in the deliberations of the Federal Government, the possibility of exerting great impact on crucial decisions, and the almost inevitable press of time, all tend to bring

v

out what each participant considers to be his most effective, most pertinent, most important contribution in the given situation. Such factors as these operate to lend a special authenticity, an air of consequence, to what people say to each other and how they inter-act in the highly charged circumstances that characterize congres-sional deliberations. Finally, the members of the Senate and of the House, by their very presence in these bodies, are demonstrated to be experts in the practical mechanics of social processes in our society.

It is the editors' hope that students of the social sciences will find stimulation and a broadening experience in this contact with social processes as they are perceived, discussed, and also acted out in congressional hearings. We also hope that as a result of such broad-ening, future contributions from the social sciences may have even greater impact than they now do in the search for solutions to the problems confronting our nation and the world.

CONTENTS

INTRODUCTION

ONE NEED NOT be committed to a philosophy of *resistential-ism* (defined as the systematic examination of the "innate cussed-ness of things") to recognize the validity of Dr. Frank Miller's observation that "the techniques and procedures which seem so eminently logical and practical as [the student] hears them in class, or reads success stories in professional journals, may not perform as expected in the usual messy and confused real-life situation." [1] Perhaps the most difficult task for the teacher in the behavioral sciences is to help the student understand properly how the chapters of his textbooks are walking around in people. A valuable aid in achieving such understanding is the case method of instruction.

The case method has long been used in teaching at the graduate level, in medical schools and law schools, in schools of business and of social work. When properly developed, it is capable of playing a significant role in undergraduate instruction as well; es-pecially when teachers and students are on guard lest the course objectives be missed. Case discussion is *not* "a bull session for academic credit"! Through case analyses, abstract principles are observed in a concrete setting; skills can be developed in analyzing the complexities of real-life situations and discovering the applica-ble principles. Since much of "learning" involves changed per-ceptions, the classroom discussion of cases helps the participants resolve the conflicts between old and new emphases. Case discus-sion requires participation by the students rather than lengthy presentations by the instructor — an active rather than a passive approach to learning. The intrinsic interest of the cases, the chal-lenge of an unsolved problem of concern in the community, estab-lishes far greater motivation for most participants than reviewing solved problems and completed research.

It should be recognized, however, that the case method is no

---

[1] Frank B. Miller, " 'Resistentialism' in Applied Social Research," *Human Organization*, XII (Winter, 1954), 5.

panacea. Among the faculty as well as among the students there
will be those who find it uncongenial. Some teachers will be dissatisfied by the data not available in the cases, and impatient
with the initially slow pace of student development. Students will
feel the instructor is "holding out" on them, not giving the right
answers nor telling them when their contributions are wrong.
Both, if accustomed to traditional lecture and recitation methods,
will exert pressures on one another which may lead to a breakdown of group discussion. Well-executed case discussion, however, provides a setting in which the student can grow in his assimilation and integration of new principles, orientations, and
facts; he will also develop a maturity and depth in relating these
learnings to the social milieu.[2]

In using the case method to teach social psychology, the instructor will have to adopt a procedure appropriate to the background of the students and the major objectives of the course.
The essential facts and principles of the field are generally available in texts, and reports of significant researches are equally accessible. The student may be asked to go from the concrete material
of the cases to more abstract treatments in texts and research
studies; or it may be preferable to start with the abstractions and
ask the students to apply them (find illustrations for them) in
the cases. Analyses of the cases might be followed by relating the
findings to other cognate disciplines, by research designs for testing the hypotheses proposed in the analyses, by "solutions" of the
problems in the form of proposals for social action.

When studying social psychology by using cases, the student
will have to prepare thoroughly for participation in class discussions. It is not enough simply to read the case through in order
to follow the presentations of others; he should be able to contribute constructively to the discussions. The following suggestions
may be helpful:

1. Read the case and become thoroughly familiar with the
   nature of the problem, the facts available, and the per-
   spectives of the people involved.
2. Where necessary, translate the problem into a form which
   involves the behavior of people. This may require the
   transformation of a problem into a series of problems.

[2] A good general reference for teachers and students is Kenneth R. Andrews,
ed., *The Case Method of Teaching Human Relations and Administration; an
Interim Statement* (Cambridge: Harvard University Press, 1951).

3. Outline an analysis to account for the behavior identified in 2.
4. Check your analysis against the data in the case, noting evidence which supports your analysis, evidence which runs counter, and points made for which there is no evidence.
5. Consider alternatives to your analysis, and the evidence pro and con in the case.
6. Search texts and the research literature to find general documentation for your analyses in terms of broader theory and findings in systematic studies of similar or related problems.
7. Try to assess the degree of confidence that is reasonable for the various points in your analyses, identify those that represent practical certainty, those that are very tentatively proposed, and those that are intermediate between these two extremes. (Perhaps after a while a five-point scale of confidence can be used.)

Depending on the interests and objectives of the individual student and the particular course, the list can be continued in various ways. How might the same problem be analyzed from a different theoretical point of view? What other disciplines could contribute to our understanding of the general problem? What kinds of data would we need to increase the confidence in the key hypotheses? How might such data be secured? What kinds of social programs seem indicated for purposes of improving the situation? Are data available to support the action program recommended?

In the give-and-take of case discussion, "to take" is as important as "to give." Listen to what others propose, and test new ideas against the available evidence rather than on the plane of whether or not they are in line with your views. And remember there is frequently a great difference between what you hear and what another person actually says. In a discussion you can disagree with someone without necessarily attacking him, so you must not feel defensive if someone disagrees with a contribution you make. Divergent contributions can frequently be synthesized into an analysis that is more adequate than that of any one contributor.

This volume does *not* give a good picture of what our country is really like. We have selected materials to contribute to the learning of social psychology and in doing so have relied on discussions of "problems" rather than a properly balanced list of topics.

We realize that the "individual" material is often too brief or too superficial to do more than hint at what might be involved. For a variety of reasons, we feel that it is preferable to use these data rather than the fuller material taken from psychological research files. The latter have the advantage of "fullness" but the disadvantage of having the data collected within the explicit or implicit frame of reference of the worker. Here we are dealing, for the most part, with the offerings of individuals as *they* see the nature of the problem with hypotheses about what might be useful socially, perhaps, but certainly not deciding what to present on the basis of some special psychological theory. The material, in some cases, because it is obviously sketchy, may encourage students to initiate data-collecting activities which may well contribute to the formulation of significant research studies in these fields.

The case materials in this volume have been chosen because we consider them excellent in aiding undergraduate students to approach the study of social psychology in the community context. That the material comes from the committee rooms of our national legislature assures the reader of its authenticity. The inclusion of biased observations and special pleading serves to sample the views people are willing to place on the record. In each case we have tried to include a general orientation on the problem as it was viewed by the congressmen, and protocols to represent selected individuals. Where portions of the record have been deleted in order to maintain our emphasis on the more "social-psychological" materials, we have indicated this, and the reader can refer in the libraries to the full texts.

It is our sincere hope that this volume will contribute to an acceleration of social science research on the problems confronting our national community, as well as to an increased appreciation of the legislative process and a more alert, better informed, more actively participating citizenry.

The editors will welcome suggestions for improvement of the inclusions in future editions, and discussions of effective class use of the approach.

1.

The Star-Spangled Banner

THE STUDY OF SYMBOLS HAS PLAYED A PROMINENT ROLE IN the development of psychology. A proper understanding of the nature and functioning of symbols has been involved in the analysis of thinking and problem solving as well as in personality study. A sound understanding of symbols is necessary for the study of communication processes; and very often the study of intergroup relations is made through the examination of common symbols for out-groups (stereotypes).

The following section deals with a national symbol, our national anthem. Such symbols have played a very important part in reinforcing group solidarity, reaffirming deep-rooted loyalties, and providing a convenient and almost tangible way of representing many complex and subtle feelings and aspirations. About our flag, as a national symbol, there has developed a code not only for formal standardization of its appearance, but also for the manner in which it is to be treated: how it is to be displayed, when it should not be displayed, how it is to be carried in relation to other standards, how it is to be saluted, and so on. No similar code has been developed for the anthem despite its equivalence from many points of view.

The hearings from which these records have been taken were occasioned by the introduction of legislation designed to standardize an official version of "The Star-Spangled Banner." Great interest was expressed in this legislation and the congressmen were deluged with mail. This popular concern is indicative of the importance of such symbols in the general social process as well as in scientific analysis.

Suggested Discussion Questions

How can you account for the widespread interest in this legislation? How can you account for the attitudes of those who think the text and/or music should not be changed? How can you account for the attitudes of those who think some slight changes might be desirable? Can these two groups be compared and differentiated with respect to their patriotism or love of country? How would they compare with respect to other variables? In the exchanges between Mr. McNamara and Mr. Whitener, was there "good communication"? What were some of the evidences of difficulty? What were the bases for the difficulty?

THE STAR-SPANGLED BANNER

HEARINGS *before Subcommittee No. 4 of the Committee on the Judiciary, House of Representatives, 85th Congress, Second Session*

WEDNESDAY, MAY 21, 1958

Washington, D.C.

THE SUBCOMMITTEE MET at 10 a. m., pursuant to call, in room 346, House Office Building, Hon. E. L. Forrester presiding.

Present: Messrs. Whitener, Robsion, Nimtz, and Smith.

Also present: Murray Drabkin, counsel.

Mr. FORRESTER. The subcommittee will come to order.

Mr. Counsel, will you take notice of the fact that a quorum is present at this meeting of Subcommittee No. 4 of the House Judiciary Committee.

This morning's hearings concern a number of bills to provide a standardized version of The Star-Spangled Banner. These bills are:

House Joint Resolution 17 and House Joint Resolution 558 by Congressman Broyhill; House Joint Resolution 517 by Congressman Dorn; H. R. 10542 by Congressman Kearns; and H. R. 12231 by Congressman Zelenko.

[. . . . .]

Mr. FORRESTER. The purpose of these hearings is to consider the contentions that after 140 years there is still no single standard authorized version of our national anthem; and, if that be true, to determine whether a single version should be adopted, and, if so, what it will be; also to consider suggestions concerning whether any change in the musical score or range will be helpful and conducive to a wider use of our anthem.

Certainly this subcommittee approaches this hearing with reverence and affection. We realize that this is a responsibility we

7

must assume and a decision we must make that will be in harmony with the heartbeats of all good Americans.

We are engaged in a busy and oftentimes controversial session of Congress. We are pressed for time and we must make every minute count. To that end we ask the cooperation of all witnesses. Nevertheless, we realize that half a hearing is worse than no hearing at all. We expect to be fair to all sides.

I do not know how much time we are going to have to consume in these hearings. I do hope that we will have the cooperation of all of these witnesses because, seriously, this subcommitee had to debate whether or not we had sufficient time to undertake hearings, on matters of such interest and a matter which is bound to be sacred and dear to the hearts of all of our people.

We intend to do the very best we can. We certainly do expect to give everyone an opportunity, just as far as we possibly can, to hear their side.

[. . . . .]

Mr. FORRESTER. . . . Mr. Counsel, I believe we have statements that have been sent us by mail.

Mr. DRABKIN. Mr. Chairman, we have a considerable number of statements. If you would like, I can turn them over to the reporter for inclusion or would you like me to read off the contributors?

Mr. FORRESTER. I think it might be well if we can, if it is not too time consuming, to identify for the record the various statements, so that we may specifically order that they be made a part of the record.

Mr. DRABKIN. We have statements here from Dr. Harold W. Arberg, music adviser of the Special Services Division, Office of the Adjutant General, Department of the Army and Hon. Elmer J. Holland, Member of Congress from Pennsylvania.

Mr. FORRESTER. Both of the statements that have been described are ordered made a part of the record.

[. . . . .]

(The statements referred to follow:)

STATEMENT OF DR. HAROLD W. ARBERG CONCERNING BILLS RELATING TO THE ADOPTION OF A SPECIFIC VERSION OF THE STAR-SPANGLED BANNER AS THE NATIONAL ANTHEM OF THE UNITED STATES OF AMERICA

Mr. Chairman and members of the committee, I am Dr. Harold W. Arberg, music adviser of the Special Services Division, Office of The

Adjutant General, Department of the Army. The Department of the Army has been designated as the representative of the Department of Defense on this legislation.

I have a brief prepared statement which I would like to present to the committee.

The Department of Defense is in accord with the objective of the bills to adopt a specific version of the words and music of The Star-Spangled Banner as the national anthem of the United States of America. It believes, however, that the selection of the words and music is a matter of broad national interest and prefers to leave such standardization to the discretion of the Congress.

I appreciate this opportunity of appearing before the committee and shall be happy to answer any questions you may have.

STATEMENT OF HON. ELMER J. HOLLAND, A REPRESENTATIVE IN CONGRESS FROM THE STATE OF PENNSYLVANIA, IN BEHALF OF MRS. CLARISSA B. NICHOL REGARDING COPYRIGHTED VERSION OF THE STAR-SPANGLED BANNER

Mr. Chairman, and members of the committee, you have under consideration House Joint Resolution 558, introduced by Congressman Broyhill, which requests the adoption of a specific arrangement of The Star-Spangled Banner as the national anthem of the United States of America.

In this Resolution 558, there has been given a copy of the score written in B flat.

In 1943, this exact version of our national anthem was arranged by Mrs. Clarissa B. Nichol, copyrighted and published in book form. The publisher was Volkwein Bros., Inc., of Pittsburgh, Pa.

Since that date, 1943, this version and the book have been used by the music department of the Pittsburgh public schools and by schools throughout the Nation and in our Territory of Hawaii.

The book has been revised this year, 1958, and is about to be released by the publisher with The Star-Spangled Banner as arranged and copyrighted by Mrs. Clarissa B. Nichol.

Identical notes have been used and the only difference in the arrangements suggested by Mr. Broyhill's resolution — and that copyrighted by Mrs. Nichol — is in the rhythm. You can see this in measures 5, 7, 11, 13, 15, 17, 21, 25 and these changes are very minor, such as the holding of an eighth note, thereby making the following note a sixteenth, etc.

I think it is only fair that this committee take Mrs. Nichol's arrangement under consideration. The years that her copyright of this version have been in effect, the many schools using this version, and the money invested by Mrs. Nichol in her new book that is being published soon — all these points should be considered.

Mrs. Nichol resides at 1217 Dillar Avenue, Pittsburgh, Pa. She has been and still is a teacher and music educator in the Pittsburgh schools since 1914. She has taught all grades from elementary through college. Since 1940 she has written and published music for the use of the schools and the children. She is a native-born Pittsburgher and, I am proud to say, a resident of the 30th District of Pennsylvania which I represent.

We, in Pittsburgh, are proud to have the arrangement similar to that of Mrs. Nichol's chosen for adoption — but — we feel that the very minor changing of the rhythm is not sufficient to take away from Mrs. Nichol the honor that is due her. We feel that recognition should be given to her and her work.

Mrs. Nichol has been a life member of the Federation of Music Clubs, which is sponsoring the version introduced by Congressman Broyhill, and she is chairman of the Young Artists and Students Musicians Auditions.

There will be a great amount of prestige and honor taken from Mrs. Nichol if her copyright version is not considered and substituted for the arrangement now before this committee for approval.

I ask that you amend this resolution and place Mrs. Nichol's arrangement in its place.

[. . . . .]

Statement of Hon. Joel T. Broyhill, a Representative in Congress from the State of Virginia

Mr. BROYHILL. Mr. Chairman, my name is Joel T. Broyhill, Member of the House of Representatives from the 10th Congressional District of Virginia. I have a prepared statement, which has been submitted to the counsel. I would like to have it made part of the record, and in order to conserve the time of the committee, I will just briefly touch upon some of the high spots.

(Mr. Broyhill's prepared statement follows:)

[. . . . .]

Here is the poem taken directly from House Joint Resolution 558, reproduced with only the remaining singing guide hyphens omitted:

"O say can you see, by the dawn's early light,
    What so proudly we hailed at the twilight's last gleaming,
    Whose broad stripes and bright stars through the perilous fight,
    O'er the ramparts we watched, were so gallantly streaming?
    And the rocket's red glare, the bomb bursting in air,
    Gave proof through the night that our flag was still there,
    O say does that star-spangled banner yet wave
    O'er the land of the free and the home of the brave?

"On the shore dimly seen through the mists of the deep,
Where the foe's haughty host in dread silence reposes,
What is that which the breeze, o'er the towering steep,
As it fitfully blows, half conceals, half discloses?
Now it catches the gleam of the morning's first beam,
In full glory reflected now shines in the stream,
'Tis the star-spangled banner — O long may it wave
O'er the land of the free and the home of the brave!

"And where is that band who so vauntingly swore,
That the havoc of war and the battle's confusion
A home and a Country should leave us no more?
Their blood has washed out their foul footsteps' pollution.
No refuge could save the hireling and slave
From the terror of flight or the gloom of the grave,
And the star-spangled banner in triumph doth wave
O'er the land of the free and the home of the brave.

"O thus be it ever when free men shall stand
Between their loved homes and the war's desolation!
Blest with vict'ry and peace may the heaven rescued land
Praise the Power that hath made and preserved us a nation!
Then conquer we must, when our cause it is just,
And this be our motto — 'In God is our trust.'
And the star-spangled banner in triumph shall wave
O'er the land of the free and the home of the brave."

Further Provisions of House Joint Resolution 558

Another prominent advantage of House Joint Resolution 558 is its section (c), which gives four major directions for the use of the anthem by the public. I know such instructions will be welcomed by everyone who has occasion to be in charge of an event where the anthem is played.

The four guides point out, first, that keys other than the traditional one in the bill may be used as different renditions require different keys; second, it is not necessary to always sing all four stanzas; third, the music in the bill is a basic model for arrangements rather than a rigid restriction; and fourth, the anthem should always be performed in a respectful manner.

Patriotic Organizations Notified

I would like to submit herewith for your committee records a copy of a letter which I sent to some 36 patriotic organizations during the latter part of March this year. I have faithfully tried to keep all patriotic organizations abreast of the developments in this matter in view of the intense interest they have displayed. The letter reads as follows:

"It is indeed a pleasure to inform you that the House Judiciary Committee has scheduled hearings for May 21 for the purpose of selecting an official version of the words and music for our national anthem. This action greatly enhances our prospects of ending the many conflicts concerning the poem and the melody which have come about in The Star-Spangled Banner since it was first written on September 14, 1814.

"As you were informed in previous correspondence, the law passed in 1931 to establish our national anthem did not attempt to settle the many variations then in existence. Now the opportunity is available to end the confusion.

"However, this is a busy year for Congress. The Judiciary Committee could reserve but 1 day for hearings. Further, there is only a short space of time after May 21 to obtain passage in the House and for committee and floor action in the Senate. The bill will become void unless it is sent to the President for signature by the end of the 85th Congress in July or August.

"It is, therefore, necessary that the interested groups reach accord in their wishes in this matter so that a lengthy controversy will not delay or prevent action by Congress. It is with this thought in mind that I am writing to ask the cooperation of your organization. I hope that I may serve as your coordinator to work with you and the other groups so that any questions may be answered and any necessary changes might be worked out in advance of committee hearings.

"I would like to respectfully suggest that you plan to submit any resolution or statement to the committee well in advance of May 21. I hope you will consult with other patriotic or music organizations and with me as you study the matter. If your organization develops a strong position on one point, perhaps further information may clear away the difficulty before a deadlock is precipitated.

"Certainly, in dealing with our beloved Star-Spangled Banner, we should never have a controversy. It is not something to be decided by majority vote but rather by unanimity. I would not feel that I could properly testify before the Judiciary Committee in the face of any major opposition views. But I would thoroughly enjoy the opportunity to take part in this endeavor as one of the many asking Congress to declare an official version. I am certain that you and your membership would have similar feelings.

"Because of this, I have made an intensive study of the historical background of the famous poem by Francis Scott Key. My new bill, House Joint Resolution 558, was prepared with exceeding carefulness to carry out Key's original thoughts. The melody has also been given deep and respectful attention by a fine group of well-known musicians representing the National Music Council. It is legislation which I am confident is worthy of selection by Congress. A copy is enclosed for your consideration along with a statement giving a detailed explanation.

"However, I am not dogmatic in support of House Joint Resolution 558. If a suggestion for change should arise, I would be pleased to learn of it and to discuss it at length. If the interested groups reached accord on a change, I am sure the bill could be easily amended in committee, and I would certainly not object to this.

"Please give your kind attention to a thorough review of this matter and let me know if I may be of service to you in any way to facilitate your work. I look forward to our association during this wonderful endeavor to clear away the confusion regarding our national anthem, The Star-Spangled Banner.

"With best wishes, I am,
   "Sincerely,
                                        Joel T. Broyhill,
                                        MEMBER OF CONGRESS"

The above letter was sent to the following organizations:

Society of the Cincinnati
National Society of Colonial Dames of America
Daughters of the American Revolution
Catholic War Veterans
The American Legion
Veterans of Foreign Wars of the U. S.
American Veterans of World War II
Maryland Historical Society
National Society of the Sons of the American Revolution
Freedom Hill Society of Children of the American Revolution
General Society, Sons of the Revolution
American Coalition of Patriotic Societies
Disabled American Veterans
Boy Scouts of America
National Music Council
Women of the Army and Navy Legion of Valor of the U. S. A.
National Society Dames of the XVLI Century, N. Y. State Society
National Society of New England Women
National Society, Women Descendants of the Ancient and Honorable Artillery Company
Dames of the Loyal Legion of the United States of America
United States Army Mothers
The Wheel of Progress
Navy Club of the United States of America Auxiliary
National Society, Patriotic Women of America, Inc.
National Society, Guardians of American Heritage
National Society Daughters of the Union, 1861–1865, Inc.
National Society for Constitutional Security
National Service Star Legion, Inc.

Gold Star Wives of America, Inc.
The Colonial Dames of America
National Society Daughters of the American Revolution
National Society Congress of States, Inc.
Ladies of the Grand Army of the Republic
National Society Daughters of the Revolution
The United States Flag Committee
American Heritage Magazine
Daughters of the American Colonists
Sunnyside Womens Club
The American Society for the Preservation of Sacred, Patriotic,
  and Operatic Music.
[. . . . .]

Mr. BROYHILL. The chairman has already very thoroughly
outlined the objectives of this legislation, and I would like to first
of all personally thank the chairman and the committee for taking the time from what I know is a very busy, pressing schedule
to consider this very important legislation. I believe many of the
patriotic organizations throughout the country will join with me
in expressing our appreciation to the committee.

Most certainly it is a very serious matter when we do not have
an official, designated, set version of our beloved national anthem.
That has caused a great deal of confusion in the past. I do hope,
Mr. Chairman, as you touched upon earlier, that we are able to
expedite these hearings and that we can eliminate any controversy
and confusion in trying to designate an official version.

I am certain that there will not be any great competition among
the various bill sponsors. Our basic objective is identical and that
is to get a specific, designated version.

At the outset, Mr. Chairman, I should also like to emphasize
that neither one of my bills, House Joint Resolution 17 and House
Joint Resolution 558 — and I say this with emphasis — was intended
to change or alter or subvert our national anthem in any way.
The primary purpose of that legislation, of both of those bills —
and I imagine all of the bills introduced by my colleagues — is to
designate one specific, official version.

House Joint Resolution 558 is a perfected bill, more or less an
amendment to House Joint Resolution 17. House Joint Resolution
558 is the one I am actually urging the committee to consider this
morning.

I first got into this matter back in 1955 when a high school class over in northern Virginia asked me to perform a very reasonable, very simple task, and that is to send them a copy of our official national anthem. We took that to be just like hundreds of other requests, and started to process it. We found it was a very difficult request to fulfill. There was no such item as an official version of our national anthem.

We did learn, however, that the Congress in 1931, by Public Law 823, an official act, designated The Star-Spangled Banner as the national anthem, with that statement being the complete language in the bill at that time. It did not spell out what was meant by The Star-Spangled Banner.

As we got further into the matter we found that most of this confusion started back at the time that Francis Scott Key wrote The Star-Spangled Banner, on September 14, 1814. There is a little confusion in the historical fact there, in that some state Francis Scott Key wrote only a few notes when he was out on the prison ship. Then he came back to his hotel room and wrote out the complete verses of The Star-Spangled Banner. He turned one handwritten copy over to a printer and it was set in type by a 14-year-old apprentice.

In printing that broadside that same day, the apprentice made many errors, and introduced many changes or variations in Francis Scott Key's original text. One of the more common errors is the capitalizing of many of the words that should not have been capitalized.

Then it is alleged from some quarters that Francis Scott Key on that same day wrote another copy — the Maryland Historical Society may disagree on this — but he wrote another copy which he turned over to his brother-in-law, Judge Nicholson, of Baltimore. Whether or not it was the second or first copy he wrote that day, the only copy we know to be truly original is the copy in Francis Scott Key's own handwriting which is in the possession of the Maryland Historical Society at this time.

As far as the conflicts in the music are concerned, that is a little more difficult to trace because that was written years before The Star-Spangled Banner was written. There have been many changes to that music over the period of years. However, a development did take place back in 1918, which did, as a result, establish the two most familiar versions that we know today.

In 1918 there were two committees organized. One adopted the so-called service version. It was a committee of 12, arranged by the War Department, to write a version of The Star-Spangled Banner to be used in the Army and Navy songbooks.

At the same time, at the request of the United States Office of Education, another committee was organized, consisting of Will Earhart as chairman, Walter Damrosch, Arnold Gantvoort, O. G. Sonneck, and John Phillip Sousa, that came up with another version. That is known today as the education version.

There are slight variations and deviations in those two versions that were adopted at that time. When I introduced my first bill I used that education version because I thought it was the closest to what might be considered an official version.

Incidentally, my first bill on this subject was introduced back in 1955 as House Joint Resolution 341. It was reintroduced as House Joint Resolution 17 in January 1957, the first day of this Congress.

House Joint Resolution 341 was the first bill to my knowledge that ever contained music that was ever introduced in the Congress of the United States. It caused quite a bit of confusion and controversy in that that education version was unacceptable to so many people in this country. One glowing error is the fact that the version eliminated the third stanza. Another error is the fact that the word "power" was in the lower case, not capitalized, and many organizations certainly felt that as a reference to God it should be capitalized.

To add to the confusion of this problem, when the committee asked for a report from the Department of Health, Education, and Welfare, which is the successor to the Department of Education, they submitted the following report:

Many versions of The Star-Spangled Banner are being used at the present time and this Department feels that there is a need for a simple, direct, and unadorned version of our national anthem which would be recognized as an official version.

To this extent we favor the intent of the resolution.

At that point, we are all right. There is no disagreement. Then they come along in their next paragraph and say as follows:

However, we are unable to recommend favorably concerning House Joint Resolution 17. Although this Department is not prepared to suggest an official version, it is our view that the version presented in the resolution is unsuitable. The first four lines of the music on page 2 consist of a melody line with piano accompaniment. The two lines of music on page 3 are given in four-part harmony with piano accompaniment. The Department feels an official version of the national anthem should be uniform in its presentation.

Here we have a report, Mr. Chairman, from an agency of the executive branch of our Government, objecting to a version that was contained in a bill, which was their own version, which they or their predecessor designated as the most official version of The Star-Spangled Banner back in 1918. However, I do agree with the Department of Health, Education, and Welfare in the second instance. I also disagree with the actual version that is contained in House Joint Resolution 17. I go back again to repeat, the main intent of the legislation was to designate an official version. I am not trying to write the language of The Star-Spangled Banner myself and I am sure no other sponsor of legislation is attempting to do that.

With all the confusion that has developed, we did attempt to go back into history and spent a lot of study and time toward preparing a version that we could suggest, and recommend to the committee as one to adopt, and one that would cause a minimum of controversy and confusion. If there is any controversy and confusion in designating the official version of The Star-Spangled Banner certainly I for one realize what the position of this committee would be. We felt the best method to use would be to go back to the oldest known handwritten copy, or the oldest copy in Key's own handwriting. That is the copy in the possession of the Maryland Historical Society.

Very briefly, Mr. Chairman, I would like to pass out these handwritten copies to the members of the committee so that they can see some of what we feel are errors in his original handwriting and a few minor changes we made from his original text when we actually incorporated that into this House Joint Resolution 558.

Mr. FORRESTER. Did the gentleman say he thought Mr. Key made some errors?

Mr. BROYHILL. Let me correct that, Mr. Chairman. There were, I think, grammatical errors in Key's original text there that we changed and corrected. We did not make any change in his actual language, the language of the handwritten copy itself.

Just very briefly I would like to point out the minor changes that we made in this original handwritten copy.

House Joint Resolution 558 differs from the Maryland manuscript in a number of minor ways. Keys used apostrophes in lieu of "e" in many words and he used the ampersand in lieu of "and." These have been altered to agree with modern usage in House Joint Resolution 558.

Further, four other changes have been made as follows:

The word "home" in the second line of the fourth stanza has been pluralized and a comma added after the word "fight" in the third line of the first stanza. Both are grammatical corrections. The word home is pluralized in all other of Key's handwritten scripts now in existence.

The word "footstep's" in the fourth line of the third stanza has been changed to "footsteps'" as the apostrophe properly belongs after the "s" to show plural possessive.

The word "power" in the fourth line of the fourth stanza has been capitalized. Although all three of Key's handwritten copies use the small "p," the change has been made in response to many requests from interested citizens who feel that Key meant this as a direct reference to God.

Other than these necessary corrections, House Joint Resolution 558 is a word for word, painstakingly checked, duplicate of Key's original. Proofs were requested from the Government Printing Office prior to printing of the bill, 20 errors were found in the first proof and a total of 4 succeeding proofs were required before the bill could be printed.

In coming up with what we feel is an acceptable version insofar as the music is concerned, I invited many musical organizations to share in establishing our national anthem by submitting their recommendation to the Judiciary Committee. Among them were the United States Army, Navy and Air Force Bandsmen's Association, Inc., the United States Marine Band, the National Music Council, the American Society of Composers and Publishers, and the United States Naval School of Music.

Incidentally, the National Music Council is a congressionally chartered organization. We asked them to study this matter for us, and come up with a recommendation of a simple, plain, unadorned version, that we could recommend to the committee. The council accepted this invitation and they appointed a committee back, I think, in 1955.

Mr. HILL. 1956.

Mr. BROYHILL. In 1956 they appointed the committee and Mr. Hill, head of the Music Reference Service of the Library of Congress was made the chairman. They put a lot of work, time, and study into this problem. They submitted the various suggestions throughout the organization, published it in their bulletins, and asked for comments in order that they could get a complete, unanimous agreement from the council as to what should be the language of House Joint Resolution 558.

They have come up with a finally perfected version. We have it incorporated in House Joint Resolution 558. I understood the council officially has not adopted it yet because they will not meet until the latter part of this month. But there is no question about their approving that version.

Mr. Chairman, I have in this prepared statement a copy of the poem itself, to show the way we have worded the poem, punctuated it, hyphens, dashes, et cetera, how easily it can be lifted out of the resolution and used as a separate poem in the event any organization asks for a copy of the poem without the music.

There are other provisions of House Joint Resolution 558 which I think the committee would be interested in, and that is the part on page 3, designated in the bill as "section C."

There are 4 points that are suggested there as guides in the playing of our anthem.

First, that the keys, other than the traditional one in the bill, may be used. Different rendition require different keys; second, it is not necessary to always sing all four stanzas; third, the music in the bill is a basic model for arrangements, rather than a rigid restriction; and fourth, the anthem should always be performed in a respectful manner.

Mr. Chairman, we notified 39 patriotic organizations about this legislation, and asked them for suggestions and comments. We sent each of those 39 organizations a very lengthy and detailed letter explaining what was going on. A copy of that letter is included in my statement. We have heard from all these organizations, and I know the committee counsel has also received statements that he referred to earlier this morning that have been filed and made a part of the record.

I have listed these 39 organizations in my statement.

I have also contained in my prepared statement excerpts from these letters I have received from these many organizations who are supporting the language of House Joint Resolution 558.

I also have contained in my prepared statement a detailed analysis of the problems with which this National Music Council Committee were confronted in trying to come up with this simple, plain,

unadorned music to be designated as the official version of The
Star-Spangled Banner.

[. . . . .]

Mr. SMITH. I want to commend Mr. Broyhill for all his work.
It was a very able presentation. As an old reed man I rather enjoyed it.

Mr. FORRESTER. I would like to ask a few questions of the
gentleman.

I was impressed with the gentleman's statement to the effect that
quite a bit of confusion had arisen. I did not know of any confusion. I just wonder if the gentleman would elaborate and tell
us what this confusion is.

Mr. BROYHILL. There are 262 copyrighted versions of The
Star-Spangled Banner on file with the Library of Congress. There
are hundreds of variations in the words. For example, "bombs"
bursting in air versus "bomb" bursting in air.

Mr. FORRESTER. As I understand it, the fact that there are
many copyrights and the fact that there are many differences in
words have caused confusion.

Mr. BROYHILL. Yes.

Mr. FORRESTER. To whom?

Mr. BROYHILL. If you are teaching an elementary school class
the words of The Star-Spangled Banner, what words would you actually use? I mentioned the plural and singular question in the
word "bomb." In Key's handwritten version it is singular but a lot
of organizations sing it plural.

"Bright stars" and "broad stripes" are reversed in many printed
versions.

Mr. FORRESTER. Could that actually create any confusion?

Mr. BROYHILL. Maybe confusion is too strong a word, Mr.
Chairman. If the national anthem is going to mean anything, if the
Congress thought enough of a national anthem to designate a certain title to be our national anthem, we should spell out under that
title what we mean by the phrase "Star-Spangled Banner" because
unless we pin it down it is possible — this may sound extreme —
it is possible over the period of years we may get changes in the
words. There are many desiring changes. For instance, the words
"when our cause is just," many people feel it should be "since our
cause is just." Those things could creep into the teaching of The
Star-Spangled Banner over the years. The Congress should spell
out what it means by Star-Spangled Banner and prohibit any

change from that official national anthem. It is not a question of confusion as it is a patriotic thing and we should not permit any confusion or ambiguity whatsoever when the Congress said in 1931 The Star-Spangled Banner would be our national anthem.

[. . . . .]

Mr. FORRESTER. The gentleman is familiar with the fact there is a controversy and no matter what we do we will not settle that controversy. We know there are some religious organizations who insist that certain words be capitalized.

Mr. BROYHILL. I think the word "controversy" is a little strong to be used there. There are variations to our national anthem, very few people know that these are variations because they do not know what the actual official wording of The Star-Spangled Banner is. I do not think it is controversy so much as that there are many variations. Most people who see any copy of The Star-Spangled Banner think it is The Star-Spangled Banner and there are no variations. It is not so much controversy as there are variations. If we do not pin it down we might go away from this official document of Francis Scott Key to where we might not recognize the original words of the song. There are some words in Key's original document that some people think should be changed. They do not like the words "foul footsteps' pollution," et cetera. You might find some organization deleting it over a period of years. We might not recognize the original national anthem 50 years from now.

Mr. FORRESTER. I do not doubt that. There might be some people who would want to change Mr. Key's brain child. This subcommittee naturally would like to take that under consideration whether we wanted to deliberately change something that Mr. Key wrote in the excitement of battle and something that has survived through the ages, or whether or not we want to accept parts of it and reject parts of it. The gentleman can see we have a big question here.

I want to ask this question, and it is something I will ask counsel to go into more fully. On this particular version who did you say was the author of this version?

Mr. BROYHILL. The author of this version?

Mr. FORRESTER. Yes.

Mr. BROYHILL. I introduced the bill. The words, except for those few minor changes in grammar and punctuation, are the identical words from the oldest known manuscript in Key's own handwriting written the day of his inspiration. The music is the result of months of work and effort on the part of this committee that was created by the National Music Council of topflight musicians and has been approved through bulletins and circulations and what not by the National Music Council.

Mr. FORRESTER. Do they have a copyright?

Mr. BROYHILL. They do not have a copyright.

Mr. FORRESTER. What would happen if we did adopt this version? Would they proceed then to copyright it?

Mr. BROYHILL. The committee consists of all lawyers. I am not a lawyer, Mr. Chairman.

Mr. FORRESTER. It poses a serious question to me. It should be determined.

Mr. BROYHILL. It is public property. It is in the bill. There is no claim from the National Music Council on that.

Mr. FORRESTER. We want to get that spelled out. We want to know if some act of ours is going to give some particular person the opportunity to make millions of dollars.

[. . . . .]

Statement of Hon. Francis E. Dorn, a Representative in Congress from the State of New York

Mr. DORN. Mr. Chairman, members of the committee, and others, I am Congressman Francis E. Dorn, representing the 12th Congressional District of New York. I want to congratulate first the chairman of the committee and the committee itself for giving so much time to this matter which I consider to be very important. The chairman brought out very pointedly the need of an exact version of The Star-Spangled Banner when he noted that if there was a law providing that the Ten Commandments must be recited in all the schools of the Nation there would be as many versions of the Ten Commandments as there are different sects and different ideas in the country.

As the chairman pointed out, there is a controversy over the words and also the music of The Star-Spangled Banner. This is shown clearly in the report on the proposed official version of The Star-Spangled Banner by Mr. Richard S. Hill, chairman of the committee of the National Music Council. With reference to the words he said:

A good many corruptions have crept in during the course of the years. Someone who did not realize what a political realist Key actually was has attempted to substitute "since" for "when" in the phrase "when our cause it is just" and Key himself apparently forgot his more stirring "the perilous fight" and substituted in his three manuscripts "clouds of the fight."

In other words, if Key himself in his various manuscripts had different versions it would be apparent that throughout the United States there are different versions at the present time. I do think this committee can settle this question and have a specific Star-Spangled Banner so that in New York they will not be singing it one way and California or New Mexico singing it in another. It is very important that the words and music of The Star-Spangled Banner be specifically set forth by this committee.

[. . . . .]

Mr. WHITENER. That is exactly the point I was trying to make a while ago. If you have an official version by a congressional act, and a band played another tune or another version of it, we may well have a situation at a given time where you folks from Brooklyn and we folks from the mountains of North Carolina would act differently; one crowd would be standing and the other sitting, just like they would if they played Dixie.

Mr. DORN. No. I think that is drawing the matter too close and too fine, because we both recognize, I am sure, both the words and the music, because all through our history there have not been any serious diversions from The Star-Spangled Banner as it exists. There have been little, minor changes, and the idea is to settle the words once and for all.

Mr. WHITENER. I am sure you have done a lot of research on this thing. Is there an official version of The Marseillaise in France, God Save the King — or Queen, as the case might be — in Britain?

Mr. DORN. I have not compared our national anthem to any of the national anthems of the other countries, but I would be glad to find out and let you know at subsequent hearings.

Mr. WHITENER. Is it your idea that if we adopt an official version the FBI might go around seeing if folks are playing the official version?

Mr. DORN. Of course not. Now I think you are being facetious.

Mr. FORRESTER. Let's not have any argument.

Mr. WHITENER. In the present ——

Mr. DORN. We are not arguing, Mr. Chairman. We are discussing the situation, I am sure. But I do feel, without any question, that ——

Mr. FORRESTER. I do not think the gentleman meant to say the question was facetious.

Mr. DORN. We understand one another. We are old friends, Mr. Chairman.

Mr. WHITENER. We debated on the networks once. I am serious about this. If we adopt an official version, then that is the legal version.

Now, suppose there is a band leader in Big Stone, Tenn., who just says, "I am not going to play that and my students in this school are not going to play this official version," and some President says, "By golly, he is going to play it. We will regulate the schools. We will send the airborne down there. We will take care of him."

Mr. DORN. If something is to be done a certain way, and that is The Star-Spangled Banner, you can play it any other way you want but then it would not be The Star-Spangled Banner. It will be his idea of The Star-Spangled Banner. There are no penalties for playing it another way. Of course there never would be. It is merely when you are playing your national anthem the Congress has said, "This is what we say is the national anthem." We say, "If you play it some other way, we are not telling you you are doing anything wrong, but we are saying this is the national anthem."

There are no penalties for playing it any other way, just the same as somebody could, of course, right now, and could subsequently, label something else, a completely different work, The Star-Spangled Banner.

Mr. WHITENER. Should there not be some freedom of music as well as freedom of speech and freedom of the press?

Mr. DORN. From what you are saying, is there a freedom of saying what the Ten Commandments are? I think the Ten Commandments are pretty well set. We are not saying anything more than this is the music of The Star-Spangled Banner, these are the words of The Star-Spangled Banner. Play whatever you like, say whatever you will, but if you are going to play the national anthem of the United States, this is it. If you are going to play something else, that is not the national anthem of the United States.

That is what we want to have set forth exactly, so that people will have a very definite form of the national anthem.

Mr. WHITENER. But the people have very definite ideas about the national anthem. I am sure you remember that a few months ago one of our major radio networks — I am not a musician, but I recognized what they were doing — had as their tone signal and signal breaks, "Oh, say can you see." They did that about 2 or 3 weeks, and suddenly they stopped. They are using a different tone signal now.

I did not see anything in the press about it, but I am sure that many folks felt as I did, that they were misusing the national anthem. Apparently it was the pressure of the public that caused them to change.

If that is true, if my presumption is true, certainly — I am not going to say you are facetious, but if somebody would start playing, well, Hound Dog, and call it The Star-Spangled Banner, the revulsion of the public would be so great that that fellow would probably never want to hear either tune again.

Mr. DORN. You are so right.

[. . . . .]

Mr. FORRESTER. Gentlemen of the subcommittee, it is now 10 minutes to 12 o'clock. I am sure there was not any member of the subcommittee impressed with the suggestion that we could get through with these hearings in the course of 2 hours, although we have been assured we would. I think experience causes us to know differently from that.

We do have a bill on the floor today which deals with the admission of Alaska to the United States. It may be that some members of this subcommittee feel their presence is required on the floor. If they do not, however, in the interest of dispatch and in consideration of the number of witnesses who are present here who must have traveled some distance, and to whom a delay would work a serious inconvenience, I am wondering if we could get permission from the House to sit during general debate, reconvening at 2:15. I wonder if we could do that.

Mr. Whitener?

Mr. WHITENER. I am rather interested in what is going on over there.

[. . . . .]

Mr. FORRESTER. The gentleman from California, Mr. Smith, told me he would be available. Mr. Nimtz?

Mr. NIMTZ. I will be available.

Mr. ROBSION. Mr. Chairman, in the meanwhile, of course, our

colleague, Mr. Zelenko, is here, and I suggest we proceed to hear him.

Mr. FORRESTER. I had intended to do that, but I thought perhaps we might get the situation cleared up in order that these other witnesses might know when they are going to have an opportunity to appear. I wanted to do that for their convenience to the maximum.

Counsel has just advised me that this room will be available this afternoon. We have to inquire about that because we have a large number of committees, and sometimes they want these rooms at particular times.

If it is agreeable — and, as I understand, it is — we will reconvene at 2:15 this afternoon.

We have a few minutes remaining, and while we do not want to press you, Congressman, but want to give you full hearing, we will permit you to proceed at this time, if it is in harmony with your wishes, and will continue hearing you when we reconvene again.

Statement of Hon. Herbert Zelenko, a Representative in Congress from the State of New York

Mr. ZELENKO. Thank you very much, Mr. Chairman. My statement, of course, will take more than a few minutes. Of course, as the chairman pointed out, the question of Alaskan statehood is very important. I appreciate the chairman's reconvening at 2:15. I do have some out-of-town witnesses.

I would like to proceed with my presentation in order before the out-of-town witnesses come in. In the event of a roll call I would appreciate permission to leave for the floor to vote.

Mr. FORRESTER. We can relieve the gentleman on that, because if he gets caught in a roll call, we all will.

[. . . . .]

Mr. FORRESTER. The Chair understands that one of the most beloved ladies in this country is present in this audience today. I want to profusely apologize to her for not having recognized her heretofore. I have never had the opportunity of meeting her personally, or even of having a good look at her, but many times have I heard her sing The Star-Spangled Banner, and on each occasion I received a thrill to the very depths of my soul.

Some people may find it a little hard to sing the national anthem, but that young lady has found it no trouble whatever.

Gentlemen of the subcommittee, I understand that Miss Lucy Monroe is in this audience. If she is, would she please stand up and permit herself to be seen? [Applause.]

I am sure the gentlemen will pardon me for interrupting.

Mr. ZELENKO. I welcome the opportunity to introduce her because Miss Monroe is here to testify on behalf of my bill. I think what took place is more eloquent than any words I can utter.

I think one of the most important phases of this hearing is the educational feature, the patriotic feature, and particularly that relating to the children, what will we teach them as our official version. It comes back to Congressman Broyhill's original request: Of course, some people for one reason or another may deviate from the words or the music; it will make them no less patriotic. If we do adopt an official version it will not be a penal or civil statute. It will be "This is what we of the United States consider our official version," whoever sings it, whoever says it, in whatever way, if they sing it with good heart, we welcome it and we listen to it.

[. . . . .]

On the question of the music — and I direct myself particularly to the music — it is well to hear a band play, it is well to hear a trained singer like glorious Miss Monroe, but the anthem itself is not something to be looked at and to be viewed as a picture or a masterpiece. It is something that I want to be able to sing, that you want to be able to sing, and that a child should be able to sing.

Now, we come down to this point: What about the music?

People have written to me, and I assume to the chairman, "Don't touch anything, don't make any changes, don't make things easy. If it is tough to sing The Star-Spangled Banner; leave it that way. That will bring us back to our pioneering heritage," but I might point out that the very people who wrote in that vein did not write with a quill pen but they did with a ballpoint and the very people who editorialized against change and said, don't make it easy, I am sure did not set the type by hand.

People talk of the traditionalism of the music. Unfortunately for us, and maybe it is good we do not know too much about it, the music of the Star-Spangled Banner has uncertain antecedents. I have covered that in my statement. The words are American. They are just as American as the land. Our flag is American, our Pledge of Allegiance is American.

[. . . . .]

I take up in my statement the origins of the music. There was a drinking and convivial society in England, I think Boswell and Johnson belonged to it. I think they called it the Anacreontic Society. They had a song dedicated to a Greek god something like what I pronounce, I cannot say it too good. They used to meet. They had ribald lyrics to the song. That song was brought to this country and before it was known as The Star-Spangled Banner and before Francis Scott Key adopted it someone used it in a song called Adams and Liberty and they changed it to Jefferson and Liberty. It had a number of different versions, all of which are taken up in my statement. The music was adopted by Francis Scott Key from this song which had acquired some sort of patriotic tone, having been adopted from the English song.

With antecedents that way — and no derogation meant by the fact that it did come from England — it was a drinking song and traditionally I say it was a good one.

Mr. FORRESTER. Has the gentleman ever heard the story about Reverend Sam Jones of Georgia and a gambler who wanted to give the church some money?

Mr. ZELENKO. I would like to hear the Chairman tell it.

Mr. FORRESTER. The gambler asked him if he would take a thousand dollars of money won at the gambling tables and use it for the church. He says, "Yes, it has served the devil long enough. Let's give the Lord a chance to use it." Maybe that was what Mr. Key had in mind at the time, if that be the true origin of the music.

Mr. ZELENKO. Frankly, research further on the subject showed Mr. Key tried to adopt his lyric poem, in the nature of a prayer, to something of a stirring nature. I think it may have come about by accident. He adopted it from Adams and Liberty, Jefferson and Liberty. This song had those names.

I bring this out because the people say do not tamper with tradition but there is not anything in the nature of tradition in the music or sacred in the music as such. I would be the last one to try to change it.

What I am attempting to do with this bill is to in view of the fact we may do something about it here, we may create what is an official version, to do as little as possible but yet make the song singable by the average child and the average nonsinger.

In this version, as will be explained by the man who arranged it, even a professional singer or an orchestra may continue with what we know as the conventional version and would not have to change the music. But the average person will be able to sing this song and

it involves a lowering of several of the notes in the very high registers.

[. . . . .]

I found out about this version through an article in one of the
great newspapers of the country. I became acquainted with the
man since then who drew it. I wanted to be sure that If I am going
to adopt his musical version I want to be sure the man was a good
American, too. I found out — he is going to be here as a witness —
he has tremendous musical background, musical director for two
of the greatest networks of the country. He was a combat veteran
of World War II and was decorated. That satisfies me. Since that
time since I introduced the bill there has been a lot of publicity.
There were about 75 editorials in papers all over the United States
just on this particular bill. May I say without going into it at this
time — I will not even read the quotations from the favorable
editorials — but I do mention that a New Orleans paper covered it.

Mr. FORRESTER. We will take a recess and reconvene as nearly
at 2:15 as is possible subject to the ringing of that bell requiring
our presence on the floor.

[. . . . .]

THURSDAY, MAY 22, 1958
Washington, D.C.

THE SUBCOMMITTEE MET at 10 a. m., in room 304, Old House
Office Building, Hon. E. L. Forrester presiding.

[. . . . .]

Mr. ZELENKO. If it meets the pleasure of the committee, I
would like to interrupt my testimony to permit one of my witnesses
to make a very short statement. That is Miss Lucy Monroe, who has
to go back to her own affairs. With the permission of the Chair,
I should like to call her at this time.

Mr. FORRESTER. Congressman, I cannot conceive of anybody
objecting to that. We will let her come around.

We will be glad to hear from you.

Statement of Miss Lucy Monroe, New York, N. Y.

Miss MONROE. I thank you very much for your generous
welcome yesterday. I would like to thank this honorable committee
for extending this time to me to speak on behalf of H. R. 12231. My

name is Lucy Monroe. I reside in New York City. I am a concert
singer and I specialize in singing The Star-Spangled Banner, having done so over 5,000 times, at baseball games, public events,
Government functions, in every State in the Union, all over Canada
and all around the world, including Korea, Formosa, Okinawa, and
Japan. I have sung our national anthem at affairs sponsored by the
United States Government, the State of New York, the city of New
York, almost every charity, as well as governments of foreign countries where their programs have been dedicated to Americans. No
one has more respect and love for our national anthem than I. In
my opinion, to alter the poem would be unthinkable, since it is
part of our tradition and our history. But there can be no denying
that the melody of the old English tune is difficult for an untrained
voice.

I have never considered The Star-Spangled Banner a solo and
have always asked people to join me in singing, as the song belongs
to all of us. Almost always, even in huge fields like Yankee Stadium
where I sang before every game, audiences have difficulty with
the high notes in the middle section and again in the phrase before the end. The people want to sing "our song" well, but rather
than not make the high notes, some of them do not sing at all.
This is a sad situation indeed, but I have seen it many times. I
feel strongly that the basic melody should not be altered and Mr.
Paul Taubman's proposed version would make only the smallest
changes, leaving the tune as beautiful and stirring as it has always
been. These changes, which are harmonic ones, would give the
song an added richness of sound and would allow all of us to join
in with greater assurance and joy. The more participation, the
more identification, and an even greater love for The Star-Spangled
Banner, our glorious national anthem. Thank you.

Mr. FORRESTER. Does that conclude your statement?

Miss MONROE. Yes.

Mr. FORRESTER. Are there any questions?

Mr. WHITENER. No questions.

Mr. FORRESTER. Mr. Smith.

Mr. SMITH. On the wording, all the times you have sung this
song now, have you found that people are confused in the words
and lots of times maybe they do not know a set wording so that
everybody sings the same words?

Miss MONROE. It is hard for me to notice that as much as it
would be their difficulty in following the tune. During the Second

World War I used song sheets and therefore they had the words in front of them. I think it is possible that people do not know the words as well as they should, perhaps. In my opinion the fourth verse is the strongest of the four verses but you cannot use that without using the first verse first. The two are too long.

Mr. SMITH. Do you feel the words of the first verse should be the same throughout the United States so that every school child who learns it would sing the same words to the piece if they all went any place else and engaged in singing?

Miss MONROE. I do agree we should have one set of words.

Mr. SMITH. You think we should have a basic melody everybody should follow?

Miss MONROE. Yes, I feel we should not alter the basic melody as we hear it now and this change that is proposed would make the orchestrations and accompaniments unchanged. This would be a harmonic change to drop the melody a third in a few bars and voices that could not go up would remain lower and those who can, a voice such as mine and others who can sing far better than I can, go on up.

Mr. SMITH. Do you think most of the people, most Americans, actually know the words to The Star-Spangled Banner?

Miss MONROE. Yes sir; I think they do. It is possible that one of our historical societies might do more perhaps to acquaint the public, not in the schools but grownups, perhaps through some sort of campaign.

Mr. SMITH. Thank you.

Mr. FORRESTER. If there are no further questions, thank you. We are glad to have heard from you and have the benefit of your views.

Miss MONROE. Thank you, Mr. Chairman.

[. . . . .]

Statement of Paul Taubman, Musical Director, National Broadcasting Co. Television, and Columbia Broadcasting System Television

Mr. TAUBMAN. Mr. Chairman and members of the committee, I wish to thank this honorable committee for giving me the time on behalf of H. R. 12231 and also to extend my appreciation to Congressman Herbert Zelenko for incorporating my musical arrangement in his bill.

My name is Paul Taubman. I am presently engaged as musical director on both the National Broadcasting Company Television and the Columbia Broadcasting System Television conducting the music for some 17 network programs each week. In addition, I am the producer and moderator of a radio show heard on the NBC radio network called The Man Behind the Song, which deals with the men and women who have written our great heritage of American songs.

My early musical studies were on the piano and cello. I went on to further my musical education at the Julliard School of Music and later at the New York University. I appeared on radio as early as 1921 and my experience as a pianist, organist, cellist and conductor, both orchestral and choral, encompasses nearly every phase in the field of musical endeavor.

I am a member of the American Society of Composers, Authors, and Publishers and also a member of Local 802 of the American Federation of Musicians.

I served in the United States Army with the 63d Infantry Division from 1943 to 1946.

It was during my Army service that I became even more aware of the contention that I had held for many years, namely, the difficulty most people have in singing our national anthem, The Star-Spangled Banner. I observed that whenever a group of soldiers on march, or during a rest or recreational period raised their voices to sing any of the service songs or the popular songs of the day, they sang with great enthusiasm and abandon. However, when the occasion arose to sing our national anthem, just the reverse held true. Those men who happened to remember the words invariably would lower their voices, perhaps sing an octave lower, especially during the phrases that soar to the high register, or hum quietly to themselves. Others would remain mute, some just move their lips looking sheepishly ahead, while others would stop singing entirely after a few moments.

In giving this problem further consideration, I observed that at every gathering of either men, women, or children, whenever they stood erect to sing The Star-Spangled Banner, the same thing happened that I had found in the Army. The reason for this is not very difficult to explain.

Francis Scott Key, in setting his stirring, inspirational poem to music, was probably not aware that an octave and a half is much too difficult for most of us to negotiate vocally. It is interesting to note that no modern songwriter would dare go beyond an octave and 2 or possibly 3 notes because he knows that his song would never receive public acceptance due to the wide vocal range. Even professional singers have difficulty singing the octave and five-note range of our national anthem. I have seen spectators at baseball games smiling or giggling amusedly at some professional soloists who haven't quite made the high notes in the phrases "The rockets red glare" and "O'er the land of the free." Instead of instilling the people with great patriotic pride and fervor, just the opposite takes place.

Personally, I feel that our Star-Spangled Banner is a beautiful national anthem. I truly believe that when Francis Scott Key set his lyrics to the old English air which was the tune for To Anacreon In Heaven, Thomas Paine's Adams and Liberty and numerous other popular songs of the times, his was the best wedding of words and music of all.

I wish to point out that Francis Scott Key made many changes in the melody of the old English air himself, and the tune of The Star-Spangled Banner as we know it today is quite different from the original.

If only he had made just a few more minute changes, so that the range of the tune would not be so extremely difficult to sing, and consequently enable all of us to sing it.

Which leads me to try to explain to you in committee what I have done to enable everyone to sing the Star-Spangled Banner. I firmly believe that if everyone could comfortably sing all the notes, then our national anthem would be sung much more often at all public functions and gatherings as it should be, and very soon every American would learn all the words and take great pride in singing himself rather than being a mere listener.

What I have done is simply the following: Beginning with the phrase "And the rockets red glare, the bombs bursting in air," I have merely lowered each note a minor third. Also in the phrase "O'er the land of the free," I have done the same thing, lowered each note a minor third.

I am sure the committee realizes that it is difficult to demonstrate a musical change without a musical instrument; however, my changes are so minute I hope that I have made myself clear. It is important that I make the following point clear. I have in no manner, shape, or form changed the rhythmic pattern or the melodic pattern of the melody as we presently sing it. Also, the words and the harmony have not been changed; in fact, those professional singers and people of better than average voice who will still elect to sing the high notes can very well do so and thereby add a rich harmony to the two most inspiring phrases of the anthem. Also, I recommend we retain the key of B flat.

In summing up, may I respectfully submit, that all I have done is in a very minute manner changed a very few notes in the two very difficult high phrases of our national anthem, in order that every American man, woman, and child can proudly join in the singing of our beloved Star-Spangled Banner, I thank you.

[. . . . .]

Mr. FORRESTER. I also have a statement from Mr. Arthur Fisher, Register of Copyrights, dated May 7, 1958, in which he gives his opinion respecting the copyright law, where a bill has been enacted into law and published and which is subject to the inspection of the subcommittee.

(The statement from Mr. Fisher follows:)

COPYRIGHT OFFICE,
THE LIBRARY OF CONGRESS,
Washington, D.C., May 7, 1958

Hon. Carroll D. Kearns,
House of Representatives,
Washington, D.C.
(Attention: Miss Aker:)

DEAR MR. KEARNS: Your recent inquiry to the Legislative Reference Service of the Library concerning the number of copyrighted versions of the Star-Spangled Banner has been referred to this Office for reply.

A search of our records from 1898 through March 7, 1958, disclosed approximately 262 registrations for musical compositions entitled the "Star-Spangled Banner." These include all manner of arrangements, adaptations, and other versions.

With respect to the further question asked by your Office; namely, is there any rule that forbids bills passed by Congress from being copyrighted; section 8 of the copyright law (17 U. S. C.) provides that "No copyright shall subsist in any publication of the United States Government, or any reprint, in whole or in part, thereof." It would seem that a bill enacted into law and published, would thereby become a publication of the United States Government as to which copyright is prohibited.

Sincerely yours,

Arthur Fisher,
REGISTER OF COPYRIGHTS

[. . . . .]

Statement of Mrs. Charles Carroll Haig, Representing the National Society of the Daughters of the American Revolution

Mrs. HAIG. Mr. Chairman and members of the committee, the following resolution was adopted by the 67th Continental Congress, National Society, Daughters of the American Revolution:

Whereas, legislation has been introduced in the present Congress proposing objectionable and unnecessary changes in the text of our National Anthem, The Star-Spangled Banner;

Resolved, That the National Society, Daughters of the American Revolution urge Congress to oppose the consideration of any change or abridgment of words or music of The Star-Spangled Banner.

REMARKS

In 1916 the customary and traditional words and music of The Star-Spangled Banner were publicly introduced by the Secretary of War, the Secretary of the Navy, and approved by President Wilson.

In 1931 this version of The Star-Spangled Banner was declared the national anthem when President Hoover signed Public Law 823, which in our opinion is adequate.

Any further legislation might result in weakening or liberalizing amendments, the result of which could be a lessening of reverence in performance.

Wisdom dictates that no action should be taken.

Thank you, Mr. Chairman.

Mr. FORRESTER. Thank you, ma'am.

Let us see if there are any questions.

Mr. WHITENER. That is a fine organization you represent.

Did you say that there was a version approved by President Wilson?

Mrs. HAIG. No, the customary and traditional words and music of The Star-Spangled Banner were publicly introduced by the Secretary of War, Secretary of Navy, and approved by President Wilson.

Mr. WHITENER. In your view and in the view of your organization, that gave us an official version which the 1931 statute referred to?

Mrs. HAIG. Under President Hoover, yes. In Public Law 823 we feel ——

Mr. WHITENER. Do you have a copy of the version that you say was approved by the President?

Mrs. HAIG. No, I do not have a copy but I can get it for you. I can get it from the national defense office of our society. I believe that they have it. I will be glad to get it and file it with the subcommittee.

Mr. WHITENER. If the lady could do that, I would like to request the chairman to have it go into the record when it is submitted.

Mr. FORRESTER. If and when it is submitted by Mrs. Haig, it is now ordered that it shall be made a part of this record.

Mr. WHITENER. That is all.

[. . . . .]

Mr. WHITENER. You have been faithful in your attendance here and you have heard the testimony.

Do you feel at this time, based upon the testimony here, where there are apparently so many different versions of The Star-Spangled Banner, do you still feel that this resolution is correct or that your organization could give it further consideration at this time?

Mrs. HAIG. Personally, I feel, and I think that judging from the resolution, we do not want any change made. We can see no necessity for a change. We have been going along all these years and I think The Star-Spangled Banner is singable, in spite of what people say. I am a musician, and I have led singing for children and for young people and for older people and if you want the key of The Star-Spangled Banner lowered, you can always have your accompanist, or someone, see to it that it is transposed to a little lower key to fit the occasion. I have in my possession two keys right now, and it does not go up as high as the "F" as they usually sing it. You know there are a lot of people who cannot carry a tune anyway. They could not sing anything, even a hymn. Just because you have an authorized or revised standard version, or official version, that does not mean the audience will be able to sing it.

I think we have permission to have the publishers put it in the various keys, and I think that is all that is necessary.

Mr. WHITENER. Assuming that the music is kept as it is ——

Mrs. HAIG. It is a thrilling, stirring thing, and it absolutely thrills you every time you hear it. Those higher notes do add to it. I know that the version I heard when they did change those few notes, 3 or 4 notes, on the "rockets red glare" and so forth, it did not have the same appeal or the same inspiration back of it.

Mr. WHITENER. Assuming that we keep the music identical ——

Mrs. HAIG. And the words identical.

Mr. WHITENER. Do you think we should authorize the words as Mr. Key allegedly wrote them and make that a suggested authorized version?

Mrs. HAIG. I think they should definitely be as Mr. Key wrote them. I thought Public Law 823 made the words that Mr. Key wrote official. Did it not?

Mr. WHITENER. I do not know that I can answer that. It is rather short and I think possibly that was the intention.

Mrs. HAIG. I thought that was the intention.

Mr. WHITENER. Thank you, Mrs. Haig.

Mr. FORRESTER. Mr. Robsion?

Mr. ROBSION. If there are some grammatical errors in the wording, as Mr. Key wrote them, would you find any objection to correcting those grammatical errors in the official version of The Star-Spangled Banner?

Mrs. HAIG. Yes, because I feel that he was inspired to write it and wrote it under terriffic strain. That is what makes it so fine and so wonderful. I think it is a tradition that we should have the anthem as written by Mr. Key. We have been taught it and our children have been taught it and we should have it the way it is. I do no believe in changing it at all. I do think the word "power" should be spelled with a capital "P" but I think it is in some of his versions. We speak of the "power of God." We speak of God Himself and not the power of God. We are speaking of God and "praise the power that has made and preserved us a Nation." That is God Himself.

Mr. ROBSION. You feel it should not be changed from the way he wrote it, even though there are grammatical errors, but you do want to change the capitalization of "P"?

Mrs. HAIG. It was changed in one of his versions.

Mr. ROBSION. Which of these versions do you want to accept?

Mrs. HAIG. The ones we have been using all the time. I think that is capitalized there. I do not believe in any change. That is all.

Mr. FORRESTER. Mrs. Haig, I would like to ask a question or two.

As I understand you, you think that we ought to accept what Mr. Key said?

Mrs. HAIG. Yes.

Mr. FORRESTER. That song would be all. We should reject the idea completely that we are operating on Mr. Key's brainchild and should just proceed on that premise and spurn Mr. Key's version unless we are going to follow Mr. Key?

Mrs. HAIG. I would not say that. I would not say that I wanted anything spurned. I want the anthem to remain as it is in text and music.

Mr. FORRESTER. Let me ask you this: Throughout these hearings there have been some statements made so far that have not been challenged in the record. Those are things that I do not know about and maybe you do. If not, maybe some other witness here might know something about them.

One of the statements has been made that the music or the melody was taken from an old English drinking song. Is that a matter beyond the realm of dispute?

Mrs. HAIG. I could not answer that but we have been taught that it was Anacreon. I do not know how they pronounce it. As I understand that, that was the way it was originally obtained.

Mr. FORRESTER. Let me ask you this question: There have been statements made in this record, and so far as I know they have been unchallenged, that one of the printed versions which appeared in the newspaper — I believe it was in Baltimore, they said it was a work of a 13-year-old printer's devil who was very careless with the use of his capital letters.

Is that historically true? Is that accepted or is there a little argument about that?

Mrs. HAIG. I am sorry that I cannot answer that. Perhaps the Maryland people can.

Mr. FORRESTER. To me that is a matter of some interest.

Mrs. HAIG. It is.

Mr. FORRESTER. I would like very much to know whether a careless act on the part of a 13-year-old was responsible, or whether or not it actually represents the version, as Mr. Key had delivered it over to that newspaper.

I think that is important.

Mrs. HAIG. Yes; it is.

Mr. FORRESTER. Any further questions?

Mr. WHITENER. May I make this observation. You made another point, did you not, in your statement, and I think perhaps it is a very key point, that your society fears that if any bill is put into debate on the floor of the House, that something could happen in the form of amendments which would bring about very unfortunate results from your standpoint?

Mrs. HAIG. Yes.

Mr. WHITENER. So you are just as apprehensive about that as you are of adopting a version by the committee? You would be in favor of the Wilson version, you might say?

Mrs. HAIG. Yes.

Mr. WHITENER. The gentleman from Kentucky mentioned something about correcting typographical or grammatical errors. You folks further take a position that if we struggled along ungrammatically for all these many years, we might do it a little while longer without injury; is that right?

Mrs. HAIG. I think we have gotten along very well with the anthem like it is. I think it has inspired us and has helped us to realize that we have a wonderful anthem and beautiful music. I do not see any reason we have to change any of the text.

Mr. WHITENER. You are not too concerned about whether there is a hyphen between the words "star spangled"?

Mrs. HAIG. No, because in those days they might have written it that way. It is like the word "ha'led." I think we used to use an apostrophe quite often.

Mr. WHITENER. What might be considered ungrammatical in one area of the United States might not necessarily be ungrammatical in another area; is that true?

Mrs. HAIG. Yes.

Mr. FORRESTER. Any questions, counsel?

(No response.)

Mr. FORRESTER. Thank you, Mrs. Haig.

Mrs. HAIG. Thank you very much, Mr. Chairman.

Mr. FORRESTER. The next witness is Mr. Francis J. McNamara, assistant director, national legislative service, Veterans of Foreign Wars.

Would you come around and be seated, please?

We will be glad to hear from you, Mr. McNamara.

Statement of Francis J. McNamara, Assistant Director,
National Legislative Service, Veterans of Foreign Wars

[. . . . .]

The VFW endorses the idea behind all these bills. Many different versions of The Star-Spangled Banner have been published since the poem was written by Francis Scott Key in September 1814. We believe that, to prevent further corruption of our anthem and confusion about its words, an official text should be adopted. We insist, however, that that text be Francis Scott Key's own poem and not an altered version of it written by someone else.

[. . . . .]

MANNER OF PLAYING THE ANTHEM

Section (c), paragraph 3, of the Broyhill bill states that "strange and bizarre harmonizations" of the national anthem "should certainly be avoided."

Paragraph 4 of the same section provides that the anthem "should always be performed in a manner that gives it due honor and respect."

Both H. R. 10542 and H. R. 12231, the Kearns and Zelenko bills, provide that the anthem be played "in a dignified manner, reflecting the meaning of the words thereof."

We completely endorse the purpose of these provisions, but suggest that the committee give thought to strengthening them so that they actually forbid certain types of renditions of the anthem and provide a penalty for violation of such a ban.

There are reports and claims that some musicians object to our anthem because they cannot "swing" it and it is not adaptable to a "jazzed-up" rendition. We believe that any swinging or jazzing up of the national anthem of this country is disrespectful, inappropriate, and abusive, and should be barred. It is possible some musicians would claim that their swing or jazz method of treating songs is neither "strange" nor "bizarre" and that, in playing The Star-Spangled Banner in such style, they were not performing it in a manner that was undignified or that denied it "due honor and respect." For this reason we recommend that whatever bill is adopted by this subcommittee be worded so as to forbid, in the same manner as abuse of the flag is forbidden, any "jazzed-up," "swing," or other form of temporarily popular, fad music treatment of The Star-Spangled Banner.

House Joint Resolution 517, the Dorn bill, says nothing about the manner in which The Star-Spangled Banner should be performed. This, we believe, is a deficiency which should be corrected before it could be endorsed.

[. . . . .]

Following is the exact text, including spelling and punctuation, of the original version of the poem known as The Star-Spangled Banner as it was written by Francis Scott Key in 1814. This is based on the version in Key's own handwriting, now in possession of the Maryland Historical Society.

The Star-Spangled Banner

O say can you see, by the dawn's early light,
What so proudly we hail'd at the twilight's last gleaming,
Whose broad stripes & bright stars through the perilous fight
O'er the ramparts we watch'd, were so gallantly streaming?
And the rocket's red glare, the bomb bursting in air,
Gave proof through the night that our flag was still there,
O say does that star-spangled banner yet wave
O'er the land of the free & the home of the brave?

On the shore dimply seen through the mists of the deep,
Where the foe's haughty host in dread silence reposes,
What is that which the breeze, o'er the towering steep,
As it fitfully blows, half conceals, half discloses?
Now it catches the gleam of the morning's first beam,
In full glory reflected now shines in the stream,
'Tis the star-spangled banner — O long may it wave
O'er the land of the free & the home of the brave!

And where is that band who so vauntingly swore,
That the havoc of war & the battle's confusion
A home & a Country should leave us no more?
There blood has wash'd out their foul footstep's pollution.
No refuge could save the hireling & slave
From the terror of flight or the gloom of the grave,
And the star-spangled banner in triumph doth wave
O'er the land of the free & the home of the brave.

O thus be it ever when freemen shall stand
Between their lov'd home & the war's desolation!
Blest with vict'ry & peace may the heav'n rescued land
Praise the power that hath made & preserv'd us a nation!
Then conquer we must, when our cause it is just,
And this be our motto — "In God is our trust,"
And the star-spangled banner in triumph shall wave
O'er the land of the free & the home of the brave.

Mr. WHITENER. Mr. McNamara, as I understand your position, it is: First, that there ought to be some sanctity attached to the words of Francis Scott Key. You are not too much concerned with the music as long as they do not jazz it up. Second, you want to make it a crime for anybody not to play it like the VFW, or this committee, or somebody else, thinks it ought to be played?

Mr. MCNAMARA. I did not say exactly that, Mr. Whitener. Not as we think it should be played, but in any manner that would be disrespectful.

Mr. WHITENER. You say that your organization is opposed to certain of these versions?

Mr. MCNAMARA. Yes.

Mr. WHITENER. You are concerned about where the apostrophes are and certain things of that sort?

Mr. MCNAMARA. Yes.

Mr. WHITENER. I wonder if in examining these bills, you folks observed that on the one you seemed to favor most they do not even mention the name of Francis Scott Key or James Stafford Smith?

Mr. MCNAMARA. I had not noticed that.

Mr. WHITENER. It certainly is not your intention to disavow any connection which Francis Scott Key had in giving us this national anthem?

Mr. MCNAMARA. No, sir; it is not.

Mr. WHITENER. I notice something in looking at some of these bills. In looking at the Kearns proposal, he says, at the top of the music, "Music attributed to John Stafford Smith."

Then we have Mr. Taubman's version and his name is bigger than anybody else's, but he just indicates that John Stafford Smith wrote the music.

Then Mr. Dorn and Mr. Broyhill completely disassociate the bill from Francis Scott Key or James Stafford Smith.

Mr. MCNAMARA. On that point, sir, it would be our position, I am sure, that we would want Francis Scott Key's name in the bill.

Mr. WHITENER. It is apparent here that their names are not mentioned.

Mr. MCNAMARA. Yes, sir. The reason we ——

Mr. WHITENER. I am a member of a post of the VFW and I think that the average member of my VFW post would be just about as concerned that we continue to give the real author the credit for this matter, as he would be about whether an apostrophe was in the wrong place.

Mr. MCNAMARA. I agree with you on that. It is something that I overlooked in reading these bills. Our staff overlooked that. I take it for granted that everybody knows that Francis Scott Key wrote The Star-Spangled Banner. We did not realize his name was missing from the bills and we would want it inserted.

Mr. WHITENER. If this were the official version, and if we are going to follow your suggestion that we lock somebody up if he is not observing that version, if somebody printed it with the name of Francis Scott Key in it, he would be violating the criminal statute that you advocate, would he not?

Mr. MCNAMARA. The criminal statute we advocate is not that if somebody printed the version — if the Congress adopted a version without Francis Scott Key's name in it, and somebody printed it with his name —

Mr. WHITENER. That would be a violation of the law?

Mr. MCNAMARA. The violation I was referring to, sir, was a violation of the type that showed disrespect for the national anthem.

Mr. WHITENER. Let us think about that a little. I happen to belong to one church and some of my colored friends can take a song that we sing in my church and, I think, sing it much more beautifully than we do. It does not necessarily sound the same as we sing it and certainly you would not say that their rendition of it was a strange and bizarre rendition. It is a perfectly natural rendition for a spiritualistic service. While I am not injecting race into this thing, I imagine that I can find in my area, and probably right here in Washington, a colored male or mixed quartet that would sing The Star-Spangled Banner differently from the manner in which the Air Force Male Chorus would sing it. They would sing it with as much feeling and with as much love of country, and perhaps with more beauty, than any others.

If you are going to follow your recommendation, some FBI man sitting out there might say that that is a strange and bizarre rendition and they violated the law.

Mr. MCNAMARA. That is not our intention. I agree with everything you just said. As a matter of fact, I believe the Broyhill bill does say that there can be —

Mr. WHITENER. They got around to mentioning Francis Scott Key on page 3.

Mr. MCNAMARA. He does permit some variation in the manner in which it is played. The only thing we are concerned about is the rendition of it in what would be called a swing style or jazzed-up version, which would be disrespectful. We are not quibbling about every slight variation.

Mr. WHITENER. Suppose he does not think that he is being disrespectful? That is his natural way of singing.

Mr. MCNAMARA. Sir, I would say in response to that, that there are certain limitations beyond which a man's subjective views are not acceptable. A man may think he may not be disrespectful if he tears down that flag over there, but that does not mean that he should be permitted to do so.

Mr. WHITENER. If I stood up here now and sang The Star-Spangled Banner, we would all agree that would be a strange and bizarre rendition. That is my point.

I may be perfectly sincere in trying to sing it. I just do not like your suggestion about the force of criminal law, because I do not believe that the rank and file of our people would be in favor of that.

Mr. MCNAMARA. We have different views on that, sir.

Mr. WHITENER. I do not mean to take up so much of your time, but the lady from the DAR just said that in 1916 the Secretaries of the military branch of the Government submitted to President Wilson a version and that the President approved that and then in 1931, when Congress enacted this bobtail law everybody got upset about it and apparently the Congress referred to the version which had the imprimatur of President Wilson.

Mr. MCNAMARA. It is my understanding that at the time Public Law 823 was adopted in 1931 the Marine Band actually appeared here and played The Star-Spangled Banner. On the basis of legislative intent, I think there is no question that that was the version which was meant to be the official version. However, it is not in the law.

Mr. WHITENER. Who has that version? Where is it now?

Mr. MCNAMARA. The services version, the so-called services version ——

Mr. WHITENER. Not a single one of these bills has that version.

Mr. MCNAMARA. I believe that in the Kearns bill, the music is the same as that. From the way I understand the hearings that preceded this one, Representative Kearns, in his bill, has the services music.

The Star-Spangled Banner 45

Mr. WHITENER. The Kearns bill said that Mr. Kearns wrote The Star-Spangled Banner; did it not? It says, "Revised standard version, by so-and-so" and the Honorable Carroll Kearns, Congressman from Pennsylvania. He says in his bill that he wrote it.

You do not feel that we owe John Stafford Smith any recognition that he wrote the music?

We can change the music to suit ourselves?

Mr. MCNAMARA. We have no objection certainly to giving him credit for the music in the bill. I think it would be only fair in any bill.

Mr. WHITENER. His music does not have the same degree of sacredness as Key's, as far as the VFW is concerned?

Mr. MCNAMARA. There is a difference in importance, I would say. Key wrote this as a poem, a patriotic one, that has been made our national anthem. It so happens that this other song had been written previously and when The Star-Spangled Banner was written, the music could be fitted to it.

As a matter of fact, there is reason to believe that Key had this song Anacreon in Heaven in mind when he wrote The Star-Spangled Banner.

Mr. WHITENER. Do you think that anybody is being hurt, or the country is being hurt, or there is any lack of respect for the national anthem at present?

Mr. MCNAMARA. No, sir; I do not.

Mr. WHITENER. That is all.

Mr. FORRESTER. Any questions, Mr. Smith?

Mr. SMITH. I personally think Mr. McNamara has presented a very detailed statement. I do not agree with the suggestion made relative to punishment but I think the VFW should be commended for bringing this statement here in detail. I want the record to show it.

[. . . . .]

Statement of Mrs. William D. Leetch, Secretary, American Coalition of Patriotic Societies

Mrs. LEETCH. Good morning, and thank you for your courtesy. I am Mrs. William Leetch, secretary of the American Coalition of Patriotic Societies. I would like to make a general statement first to say how much I have really benefited by what I have learned here and the argumentation has been extremely interesting and beneficial and I thank the chairman for his observations, with which we most heartily agree.

Possibly some things in this statement might be altered had we heard all of it from the beginning before the statement was written, but in general I want to say that our office has been swamped with mail on this subject. It has excited more interest, perhaps, than what we consider on the scene here more important national issues.

Mr. FORRESTER. May I interrupt, please?

Mrs. LEETCH. Yes.

Mr. FORRESTER. I would like to say that is also the experience of this subcommittee. We have Alaska statehood, we have mutual security, we have the most controversial problems before this Congress that we have had in many, many years. But so far as my mail is concerned I have had more letters on this particular thing.

Mrs. LEETCH. So has Mr. Broyhill and the sponsors of these other resolutions, I can assure you. Hence the change made in his original bill.

Mr. WHITENER. The burden of my mail is that we should not change.

Mrs. LEETCH. That is the burden of the mail of the patriotic societies as expressed through their letters from members. The other thing is they want no change or abridgment and the American Coalition adopted a resolution to that effect. There are a hundred patriotic societies cooperating with the American Coalition and, represented by their delegates at the annual convention, they voted for no change. They would however, go along with a capital "P" in Power.

The American Coalition adopted a resolution at its 28th annual convention January 1958, expressing opposition to changes or abridgment of the national anthem. My remarks are my own.

The proposed resolutions to adopt a specific, official, or revised standard version of the national anthem are not the outgrowth of ideas of the hereditary societies. None were consulted. They were asked to support various resolutions after the texts were printed. A fraternal organization backed Senator Bridges and Mr. Dorn's joint resolution in an effort to restore the third stanza omitted from Mr. Broyhill's first House Joint Resolution 17 and to capitalize the letter "P" in the word "Power." Patriotic societies would subscribe to this latter change from Key's original manuscript to conform to present-day custom when referring to the Deity.

The gentleman from the Historical Society of Maryland pointed out Key was a religious man who had even considered going into the ministry. If there is to be a change perhaps that would be the least harmful change.

We do not think the ampersands, apostrophes, and commas need to be changed. After all, we do not sing them. We like the quaint form as authentic and real as any other early American historic document or piece of furniture. It should be as lasting. We prize it the way it is, for what it is. However, the words and music were printed and sold at Carr's Music Store in Baltimore, Md., in 1814. Speaking of the words only, Mr. James W. Foster, director of the Maryland Historical Society, owner of the original copy in Key's handwriting, declared them to be satisfactory. This early printing capitalizes the letter "P" for Power, capitalizes "S" for Star-Spangled Banner and retains the word "home" without the plural "s" as in Key's original. It adds an exclamation point after "O!" and changes the ampersands to "and." Why would not this first printing be a satisfactory compromise official version to satisfy the critics of the original?

Key's poem breathes the spirit of patriotism without which we would have had no country. We think it certain the word "home" means "homeland" and should be retained. The poem bespeaks pride in a great victory of American independence and self-reliance, the thinking of Key's whole generation. No one can rightly read between the lines and see any glimpse of what the sponsor of one of these bills calls, "a democratic ideal of the brotherhood of mankind" and we do not want that misconception influencing a change.

Apparently the first bills originated with the Department of Health, Education, and Welfare and its Office of Education which the State Department says is the chief channel of UNESCO propaganda into the Nation's schools (UNESCO Story, Department of State Publication, 3931, p. 46), and with the National Music Council, a UNESCO affiliate, and especially with its chairman for this undertaking, Mr. Richard S. Hill, Head, Music Reference Section, Library of Congress. Mr. Hill was a candidate for a bachelor of literature degree at Oxford University. This perhaps accounts for his reported concern lest the third stanza of our national anthem offend the British and so left it out. This is puerile in our opinion. It should also be pointed out that not all the members of the National Music Council claim to be musicians. Some are publishers, merchants, piano tuners, and manufacturers.

The American Legion, the Veterans of Foreign Wars and other patriotic society researchers have documented the studied attempt on the part of many leaders, especially educators, with the help of the United Nations Educational, Scientific and Cultural Organization (UNESCO) to play down nationalism and patriotism for something alleged to be more ennobling — internationalism. In this connection we do not think any attempt should be made to suggest which stanzas shall be sung as in Mr. Broyhill's second bill, still toward the elimination of the third stanza. Cannot some independence of choice be left to the people who are going to do the singing?

If we are to have an official publication, the opportunity should be seized upon to write in protective language to insure against abuse or distortion in more specific language as to "reasonable latitude" and "on the other hand" which seems to negate what goes before. A musical trade magazine is campaigning for a new national anthem because "you cannot swing The Star-Spangled Banner," and they write ungrammatically and thoughtlessly, "it don't mean a thing," which in itself is a sad commentary on our educational system. Any law should include such a prohibition and might profitably include a brief history of the composition, so that it will mean something.

The conventional key of B-flat is used in all but one of the proposed bills. This key is the one that has caused most criticism as being unsingable. However, there are already 262 registrations for musical compositions entitled "The Star-Spangled Banner," according to the Register of Copyrights, Mr. Arthur Fisher, in a letter dated May 7, 1958. Musicians have already arranged the score to meet any exigency. Our musician members tell us that the key of A-flat is easy for both men and women's voices and argue that an official version should be in this lower key, with all others permitted.

After listening to recordings of the proposed musical scores here, we have concluded that the music is played with little or no thought of the inspiring words. Somewhere there must be a music lover of the anthem who has the divine spark of enthusiasm and imagination to interpret the words and write in the symbols musicians say are necessary, in order to create an inspired, thrilling rendition. Anything less would be a pity to call official. Mr. Kearn's bill in A-flat is disappointing in this respect. You might go to sleep standing up on that one.

Patriotic societies are keenly aware that the pledge of allegiance to the flag set to music by Irving Caesar, whose leftist record was established by the House Committee on Un-American Activities, was slipped through the closing hours of the 84th Congress and copyrighted and he and ASCAP are getting the benefit of free advertising via Government Printing Office on a beautifully illustrated flag folder at taxpayers' expense.

We are certain this committee is aware of the possible misuse and possible profit or benefit to some that might come out of this effort, and that you seek to prevent it. The increasing neutrality of world powers may force the United States to pick up the thread of patriotism and independence where it was dropped and go forward toward relative self-sufficiency where lies our real strength. The spirit of the national anthem will be the springboard for this long overdue revival of patriotism. Let us preserve it an inspiration in our need.

[. . . . .]

Mr. WHITENER. Mr. Chairman, I wonder if the committee would indulge me to call Mr. Hill back for one or two questions?

Mr. FORRESTER. Yes, we certainly will.

Mr. WHITENER. Would you restate your name and position at the Library of Congress?

Mr. HILL. Richard S. Hill, head, Reference Section, Music Division, Library of Congress.

Mr. WHITENER. Mr. Hill, have you done some research on the nature of the society in England to which this song has been attributed originally?

Mr. HILL. Yes, sir. Considerable information has developed partly through my own efforts and partly through that of others which supplements the very important report which Mr. Sonneck, the Chief of the Music Division of the Library of Congress, prepared and published in the Government Printing Office in 1914. According to those findings, it now begins to look very much as if John Stafford Smith had nothing whatsoever to do with the actual composition of the tune. He did write an arrangement in 1799, it turns out. When the discussion first started, nobody had dated the collection in which the arrangement appeared and it was thought to be much earlier than it was. In fact Mr. William Chappel of an important publishing house in London was under the impression that it was the earliest publication of the tune and he assumed, therefore, that the tune was to be attributed to John Stafford Smith. This was in 1783. Except for that one publication, Smith, who lived until 1836, never made any claim to the tune, only to his harmonization or arrangement of that tune. It so happens that Mr. John Stafford Smith also made a three-part arrangement of God Save the King, but since the history of that tune is better known, nobody has ever ascribed it to Mr. Smith. Since 1873, however, they have continually ascribed the Anacreontic song to John Stafford Smith, and it appears in that form in many collections.

It is also ascribed to Samuel Arnold, who was the conductor of the orchestra of the Anacreontic Society. I might say that the Anacreontic Society is somewhat slandered when it is called a drinking society.

Mr. WHITENER. That is the point I wanted to go into.

Mr. HILL. Yes. Very little is actually known about it in a documentary fashion until you get down to a year or two before the society was finally disbanded. However, it turns out that it must have been rather important as an organization from a sociological point of view. Before 1750 it was quite common for a nobleman to support an orchestra in his own home. There were no public concerts whatsoever except for an occasional one put on by a church or some organization but no regular symphony concerts anybody could go to. By the end of the 18th century, such private orchestras were a little expensive, and noblemen and people with reasonable wealth felt they should combine and have an orchestra together. They did not want the hoi polloi in their concerts. They wanted them for themselves. Therefore, they organized a society — the Anacreontic Society — and Samuel Arnold was conductor of their orchestra which was one of the shining lights in the musical world of London at the time.

When Haydn came to visit London — he was brought there to conduct some of his own music — he was taken to a meeting of the Anacreontic Society where they made much of him and played for him one of his symphonies; he was very much impressed and pleased with it and then went on his way.

Each session of the Anacreontic Society took place approximately once every 2 weeks in the wintertime, and there were usually from 12 to 14 meetings during the season, each meeting consisted of a concert that lasted about 4 hours. They met at 4 o'clock and listened to the music until around 8 o'clock. At that time they went to the next room and enjoyed what was called a cold collation, together with a bowl of punch.

The 18th century was not a particularly sober century and particularly in England was this true. I have no doubt that the gentlemen imbibed, but nonetheless the function of the Anacreontic Society was not that of a drinking society. It was an orchestral society and there was a matching choral society called the Noblemen's and Gentlemen's Catch and Glee Club which was formed slightly earlier and lasted considerably longer than the Anacreontic Society.

Mr. WHITENER. Basically the society was a musical organization and if there was any drinking it was a matter which was incidental to the main purpose?

Mr. HILL. The word "Anacreon" is definitely of the convivial sort. The word "convivial" is usually used.

The couplet at the end of each stanza, similar to our Star-Spangled Banner to the couplet "land of the free," and so forth ends with:

[. . .] while snug in their clubroom they jovially twine the myrtle of Venus with Bacchus' vine.

This was sung after they retired from their concert and went on to their supper and drinks. In that sense, it was a drinking song and there is no sense in trying to clean up the thing. Actually, there is considerable evidence now that the tune goes back earlier than the use made of it by the Anacreontic Society. There are quite a few points that get so highly technical that I hate to venture into them at this particular time when it is not too much to the point.

There is quite a lot of evidence to show that Ralph Thompson wrote the words to the Anacreontic Song to go with the preexisting tune, which is one of the reasons we end up with some of the strange combinations of words and melody that you get in his version of the song.

Mr. WHITENER. That is all.

Mr. FORRESTER. I agree with the gentleman to this extent: Very candidly, I have never understood just why the question of being a drinking song was injected into this. I thought that was excess baggage at the time. Inasmuch as it was injected, however, I thought that this might be sometime later read by someone and that they might give us credit for doing a little more than we did and they might figure that we really had gotten down to it and scuttled the truth.

Maybe we had better see what we can do toward determining the truth.

As I understand the gentleman, actually this music, or this tune, antedated this society that you are talking about, whether it was for convivial purposes or social purposes or whatnot.

Mr. HILL. There are indications in the shape of the tune itself. Mr. Sonneck mentions the possibility that it was written for what is known as a valveless horn or trumpet. He was thinking of it in terms of a hunting song. The melody has turned up in one manuscript but, unfortunately, not early enough to be used as definitive evidence associated with a military regiment from Ireland. The point is that the shape of the tune itself is eminently fitted to be played on a trumpet which has no valves.

Now you get into the technical aspect of this.

A trumpet in those days consisted of a long tube wound around on itself to make it simpler to handle. Since it lacked the three valves or pistons of the modern trumpet, one could not play many of the notes in our normal scale. One could only play those notes which are made when the tube of the trumpet vibrates as a whole, or as an even half, or as a third, or as a fourth. This means that what you get out of it is not unlike a bugle call. It starts out like a bugle call but because of the difference in manufacture and the longer tube, you can go higher than with a bugle and eventually the notes that you perform are close enough together so that you get a scale passage.

In The Star-Spangled Banner, the opening part is largely in the lower octave where the main notes fall on the tonic triad — that is, the bugle tones. But the only range in which a trumpet can play a straight diatonic scale is in the half-octave above this bugle range, and up there one can play straight along — C, D, E, F, and G. Thus, when the composer of our tune wanted a smooth melody without leaps, he necessarily had to use this upper range. This may very well be why the smooth middle section of the melody is so hard to sing — it had to be placed high since that was the only range in which a trumpet could play a smooth melody — whereas when disjunct intervals were sufficient for the composer's purpose the melody could climb around on the arpeggio of the lower octave. Only some half dozen notes, all of them passing tones, would have to be altered in the 18th century form of the melody to make it perfectly practical for performance on the valveless trumpet. Because of this, there is a growing feeling that quite possibly the tune actually had a military origin rather than the Anacreontic Society origin that is usually ascribed to it.

This is still very much in the argumentative stage and has never been settled.

Mr. FORRESTER. As I understand from your testimony and from your research, this tune which was adapted to The Star-Spangled Banner antedates the creation of this society or organization which has been referred to as a drinking society?

Mr. HILL. Yes.

Mr. FORRESTER. That being true it follows that your conclusion must be that the tune having been taken from a drinking song actually is incorrect; is it not?

Mr. HILL. Yes, if you could ever prove this prior origin.

Mr. FORRESTER. In other words, by that process of reasoning, 50 or 75 years from now, history may malign Sweet Adeline?

Mr. HILL. Yes, sir.

Mr. FORRESTER. That is the one that down my way, when the boys get to drinking, their minds go automatically.

I believe that the gentleman told me that there are one or two points that he wanted to touch on briefly.

Mr. HILL. Yes.

I have been very much impressed with the discussion here about the real basic complexity of the documents involved in this case. I cannot really understand why so many people have failed to notice the fact that there are differences because this is something that has been on record for a long while. It is not something that anybody in modern times has made up.

For instance, Mr. Sonneck, in writing his report, which was a Government publication published in 1914 by the Government Printing Office, listed Key's four manuscripts. He also threw in one other which is not actually by Key.

I might parenthetically interrupt myself here to say that this document in Joseph Muller's book is actually a manufactured product that does not correspond fully to any of Key's autographs.

In 1864, the Sanitary Commission organized a fair in Baltimore. Like the modern Red Cross, the Commission cared for the wounded on the battlefields, and needed to raise funds to support its work. In conjunction with that fair, a handsome collection of facsimiles, called Autograph Leaves, was prepared for sale to help raise those funds. A facsimile of The Star-Spangled Banner was given as the first item in the volume, followed by facsimiles of the

handwriting of Abraham Lincoln and any other important historical and artistic documents which the editors could assemble.

Mr. Sonneck was apparently under the impression that this
facsimile was produced by photolithography, and since he knew
of no Key autograph that had the exact characteristics of this
facsimile, he hypothecated the existence of a fifth autograph which
had since gone astray. It would now seem that the facsimile was
produced by carefully drawing the text on a lithographic stone by
hand, since while using this method slight alterations could be
introduced. Actually the text of the four stanzas of the poem correspond exactly with the autograph Key wrote out for General
Keim and which is now in the Pennsylvania Historical Society.
The facsimile could be laid on the top of the Keim autograph and
the two would correspond in every detail, every flange of every
letter. It would be quite impossible for any normal individual to
write out such a document twice on different occasions, and still
have both copies coincide so exactly in every respect. Presumably
the lithographer carefully copied out the text for his facsimile
from the Keim autograph.

He could take the signature from the same source, but here the
similarity between the two documents ends. To generalize the
effect, the lithographer omitted the dedication at the foot of the
page "To Gen. Keim." But on the other hand, the Keim autograph
lacked a title, and this the lithographer obviously needed. He got
it by copying out the phrase: "The Star-Spangled Banner" from the
seventh line of the second stanza of the poem itself. One can easily
compare the two and see that the correspondence is exact, even to
the twisted curve at the bottom of the "g." As a consequence, Mr.
Sonneck's problematical fifth autograph can safely be forgotten.

What is more, it would obviously be unsafe to use either the
facsimile in Autograph Leaves or Mr. Muller's facsimile of this
facsimile as an argument as to how Key might have written the
title had he chosen to write it. One should not forget that the title
Key gave his poem in the first place was "The Defence of Fort
McHenry." All of the early printings bear this title, and it was
only later that the catchy phrase from the body of the poem was
extracted and put at the head. The shift took place in Baltimore
weeks after Key had returned to his home in Georgetown, and
although there can be no question that he accepted the change
in title, he was apparently not himself responsible for it.

To come back to this business of the various versions, Mr. Sonneck wrote in 1914, after citing his five manuscripts:

There may be other copies, but these five are sufficient for the purpose of showing the changes Francis Scott Key himself made in his poem. The different versions, would, as often happens in such cases, be used by different compilers. In the course of time, verbal inaccuracies would creep from one songbook into the other. Also the compilers themselves have sometimes felt justified in improving Key's text. The result of all of this has been, of course, that gradually Key's text became unsettled. As early as 1872, Preble marked the verbal differences between certain different versions and since then surely the confusion has not decreased. Hence, very properly the cry for an authoritative text has been raised [. . .].

Mr. Sonneck formulated that statement in 1914, but nevertheless the situation remains very much the same to this day. The point may be demonstrated by a letter received in the normal course of business at the Library. Essentially it is a request for an official version of the national anthem for use in the Handbook of the Boy Scouts of America. The Boy Scouts have been mentioned earlier in these hearings by Mr. Broyhill because, when the Library was unable to supply something that does not exist, the writer of the letter was referred to Mr. Broyhill's office. In part to complete the sequence, but almost more because the writer of the letter states his problem so convincingly, a transcript of the original letter should make a pertinent addition to these records.

The letter was addressed to the Library of Congress, Washington, D. C., and reads:

In working on a revision of the Scout Handbook, I have had occasion to compare the version in the handbook of The Star-Spangled Banner with other versions and have so far come up with eight different versions, all of them differing from each other and from Francis Scott Key's own handwritten version.

In the first line of the first verse, for instance, I have found:
"O say can you see   O! say, can you see,   Oh; say, can you see"
In the second line:
"hail'd   hailed   gleaming (comma)   gleaming? (question mark)"
In the third line:
"through   thro'   thro"
In the fourth line:
"watch'd   watched (no comma)"
In the fifth line:
"rocket's bomb (singular, Key's own version)   rockets' bombs"

In the sixth line:
"through   thro'   thro   still there,   still there;   still there."
In the seventh line:
"O say does   O! say does   Oh! say, does
"that star-spangled banner (Key's own version)   the Star-Spangled
Banner"
I could go on, but this will suffice to describe our dilemma.

We would appreciate it greatly if you will be kind enough to send us
a copy of the official version of the Star-Spangled Banner — as approved
as our national anthem.

Also kindly inform us of the official choice of the following:
"the flag of the United States   The Flag of the United States
"our flag   our Flag"
Thanking you for your cooperation, I am,
　　　Sincerely yours,
　　　　　　　　　　William Hillcourt,
　　　　　　　　　NATIONAL COUNCIL, BOY SCOUTS OF AMERICA

This is merely a sample of a type of letter which the Library
receives in quantity. In addition to the purely textual inquiries,
the story of The Star-Spangled Banner has many other ramifica-
tions, and in the course of time letters touching on most of them
have been received. In the beginning, I probably had as little
knowledge of the subject as the average citizen, but it is part of
my job to answer letters in this field, and in simple self-defense
it rapidly became necessary to familiarize myself thoroughly with
all the documents and their interrelations. Before long, the study
became fascinating in itself. This was particularly true during the
war when the correspondence regarding The Star-Spangled Banner
was naturally far greater than it is now. At the present time, I
doubt if the Library receives an inquiry much oftener than once
a month, but during the war the rate was closer to a dozen letters
a week, if not two dozen. And the letters came from all sorts of
people — private individuals, schoolchildren and schoolteachers,
sometimes official organizations, and so forth.

Under current legislation, the only practical solution to inquiries
about the text of the anthem was to refer the inquirer to Key's
original manuscript as preserved in the Maryland Historical Society. We made no attempt to choose between the music of the
two 1918 versions as established by the 2 committees, but suggested
that the inquirer consult both the education and service versions.
Both versions have points in their favor, but on the other hand
both leave out the third stanza completely, and this must be sup-

plied from some other source. Of the two, the education version perhaps has an edge over the service version, since the text of its three stanzas seems to have been more carefully edited (I suspect by Mr. Sonneck), whereas the service version has a text that was apparently tossed together from whatever the committee had at hand.

Possibly this is a good and sensible answer to such inquiries, but for myself I have never felt completely comfortable about telling some poor schoolteacher out in Kansas or Missouri or Georgia, or anyplace else, that she should go forth and buy a copy of a manuscript plus the two 1918 editions of the anthem, and establish a proper version of the national anthem for herself. For one thing, although those three documents would supply her with quite a few variants between which she might choose, she would still not have sufficient evidence for making a sensible and informed choice. Besides, if I read these letters correctly, none of the people that write them are in the least interested in undertaking an extended piece of research. They have run into a conflict between versions, and merely want to be told which is right. In such a confused state of affairs as we have at present — a confusion to which Key himself has contributed — there can obviously be no such thing as a right reading, unless Congress says it is. Thus what seems to be needed is a version, carefully arrived at, that can be considered as a sort of norm. As far as I am concerned, it makes relatively little difference what the exact details are that finally go to make up that norm, although naturally it would be best to have a sound version that can be justified from all points of view, rather than to trust either to ignorance or prejudice. The main thing, however, is to have something so that one can settle the problems of those poor people who want guidance. Certainly, it should not be a question of forcing anybody into anything. Anybody who prefers to be different should have that privilege. In this country, it should not even be necessary to make such an affirmation.

But equally those who want guidance and need help should be able to get it. Even the Bible appears in authorized versions. The versions may vary according to the denominations authorizing them, and the Catholics have a different Bible than the Protestants. Nonetheless, each denomination seems to have a particular version of the Bible to which it gives its stamp of approval. Well, if countries can be compared to religious denominations, there is certainly room here for large differences of opinion. And if the

British can have an authorized version of God Save the Queen and the French have a standard version of La Marseillaise, I would suppose that it would be entirely proper for us to have an authorized version of our own national anthem.

Thank you.

Mr. FORRESTER. Thank you, sir.

Mr. NIMTZ. The gentleman has made a great contribution to this hearing and has given us an excellent basis for action and he has expressed my feelings well. He has expressed my opinion as to why we need to do something on this subject, Mr. Chairman.

2.

Brainwashing

THE STUDY OF ATTITUDES HAS LONG BEEN FOCAL IN THE analysis of social behavior. With the increasing reluctance to account for individual differences in social attitudes on the basis of native dispositions, attention has tended to focus on the dynamics of the learning process itself. For social psychologists, however, the general problem of socialization assumes more importance than the controversies among the exponents of different learning theories. Along with the study of the normal growth and learning processes, many experimental studies of attitude change have been undertaken.

The limits imposed on ethical research workers are, of course, not recognized by agents whose mission is to create change during times of war and stress. During the Korean conflict, some of the procedures applied to captured United Nations personnel gave rise to the term "brainwashing." Upon the release and repatriation of these individuals, it was possible to study attitude stability and change under conditions of extreme pressure. Though the reconstruction of the procedures used makes it clear that we are not dealing with the neat data of an experiment and that many variables are uncontrolled, nevertheless we can learn much by examining the procedures and their apparent successes and failures. The results of such analysis should contribute not only to our understanding of the nature of attitudes, but to a variety of applied problems. Among the latter are military problems in developing ways to increase resistance to such tactics in the event of future emergencies; and civilian problems such as emotional re-education in psychotherapy and in dealing with attitudes toward health practices in the general community.

Suggested Discussion Questions

What seem to be the major psychological principles of attitude change used in the two forms of brainwashing? How is the relation of the individual and the group related to the techniques used and their effectiveness? Is the group a hinderance to compliance with the interrogator or is it capable of being an aid? What determines how the group will function? What "individual" factors contribute to variation in the way individuals respond to the treatment used? How is knowledge of the methods used in interrogations likely to increase resistance to compliance? How will the "Code of Conduct" contribute? If brainwashing is such a complex process and can be resisted for such a long time, why is it that ordinary commercial advertising is effective?

COMMUNIST INTERROGATION, INDOCTRINATION AND EXPLOITATION OF AMERICAN MILITARY AND CIVILIAN PRISONERS

REPORT, *Submitted by Mr. McClellan, of the Committee on Government Operations, Made by Its Permanent Subcommittee on Investigations, United States Senate, 84th Congress, Second Session*

DECEMBER 31, 1956

Washington, D.C.

Introduction

What is brainwashing? Were the American prisoners of war in North Korea brainwashed? Has the Department of Defense taken any action to prepare American soldiers for such treatment as their Chinese captors inflicted? These were some of the pressing questions confronting this country and which led to an investigation and hearings by the subcommittee.

Brainwashing is a loose term difficult if not impossible to define with exactness. It means many things to many people. It has been interpreted by some to be a mysterious and irresistible type of treatment based on certain psychological knowledge possessed by the Communist countries. To others it is continuous interrogation of prisoners, and to still others brainwashing is a misnomer for certain police practices that have existed for many years. Through the subcommittee hearings we attempted to portray the type of treatment received by our prisoners of war from the Communists which is popularly known as brainwashing. We hope that through these hearings and this report the American public will have a better understanding of the Communist methods of interrogation and indoctrination. How these methods originated, what are the purposes, how they are applied, how much success is achieved, are questions for which the subcommittee has attempted to find some answers. We feel that it is only through an understanding of this problem that we can hope to meet and solve it. Ignoring it, pretending it does not exist because what is revealed may be embarrassing, can lead only to disaster.

[. . . . .]

Civilian Prisoners

Dr. Harold G. Wolff, professor of medicine in charge of the department of neurology, Cornell University, who was head of a group of 20 civilian military scientists, has made an exhaustive study of the methods and procedures used by the Communist state police in the interrogation and indoctrination of persons regarded as enemies of the state. He testified that the methods used in Communist countries have their roots in secret-police practices which go back for many years. These practices, commonly referred to as "brainwashing," have become refined and developed in the 20th century as a result of many years of trial and error. Russia by the 19th century had developed a highly organized, effective, and powerful secret police.

Many of the techniques used today came into existence in some form at that time. The method of arrest, the development of the personal dossiers on individuals, the use of repetitive interrogation and the isolation technique find their origin or owe their developments to the Russian secret police.

The 20th century brought forth a development and refinement of these techniques.

[. . . . .]

EASTERN EUROPEAN OR RUSSIAN SYSTEM

Testimony revealed that a *political* criminal, that is, *any person who is a threat to the Communist Party or to the state,* is subject to the following system in Russia: The KGB, which is the state police, decides who threatens the party or the state. Once a person is arrested, he is deemed to be guilty. There is no hope for acquittal or vindication, as under this system judgment is made as to his guilt prior to his arrest. His case cannot be settled until a confession has been prepared which must be signed by both the prisoner and the interrogating officer.

Dr. Wolff furnished a typical timetable with regard to an individual accused of a political crime:

1. Suspicion.
2. Accumulation of evidence by surveillance and informers which takes approximately 4 weeks.
3. Arrest and detention resulting in isolation and interrogation which embraces a period of approximately 7 or 8 weeks.
4. Confession (12th week).
5. Punishment.

Thus, the Russian system generally allocates a period of a few weeks to several months, during which time the interrogator must obtain a confession from the prisoner. The emphasis in Russia is placed on interrogation and not on indoctrination as it is in the Chinese system.

During the first period when the KGB is deciding about an individual he is under suspicion and close surveillance. This period usually lasts about 4 weeks. The party has decided that this man is a political enemy of the state, and it is trying to collect evidence against him. The individual, becoming aware of the investigation and the surveillance, grows anxious and fearful. The suspect becomes worried and filled with apprehension.

When sufficient evidence has been collected by an interrogator, the person is arrested. This is effected quietly, usually in the middle of the night. The subject is not told the reason for his arrest. He is merely informed that he has committed some crime against the state and he knows what he has done. As a matter of fact, during the entire period of his imprisonment he may not be informed of any charges.

For a period of time, usually 3 to 6 weeks, he is detained in complete isolation. This is a very fearful experience. His room is small, being approximately 6 by 10 feet. The light is apt to be burning in the ceiling at all times. He has no contact with anyone other than the guard. He has no opportunities to consult with anyone. Often he may sleep only with his hands exposed outside the covers, lying rigidly on his back and then only at fixed hours. Toilet arrangements are inadequate and are arranged to disgust and em-

barrass the prisoners. His cell may be purposely a little too cold
or a little too hot. Many foreign nationals find the food distasteful,
although it is adequate according to Russian standards. The prisoner may be caused to stand in one position for up to 20 or 22
hours in which case he gets very severe joint and muscular pains.
He is allowed only a short time for washing up. Sometimes he must
eat with no utensils or must sit in a fixed position. If the prisoner
has behaved in what is deemed an uncooperative manner, he may
be allowed toilet privileges only at arbitrary and fixed times.

What is the effect of all this? The prisoner initially goes through
a period of being bewildered, demanding explanations, wanting to
see people, and complaining. This lasts for a few days when he
becomes more and more depressed and humiliated. He is bothered
by anxiety, sleeplessness, boredom, fatigue, and hunger. After about
the third week he usually experiences intense fatigue, drowsiness,
and craving for companionship. Gradually, his period of isolation
develops in him a feeling of despair. Living in the filth of his prison
with no activity often creates delusions and hallucinations. He has
a great need for companionship, a great need to talk.

Now the work of the interrogator begins. The interrogator is
usually a young man in his 20's or 30's who has no special training
in psychology, psychiatry, neurophysiology, or any of the so-called
scientific mind-study procedures. He has very little formal education beyond high school. However, he has had some formal training
in being an interrogator and most importantly he is an individual
with strong convictions about communism.

The interrogator has his own problems. He must obtain a confession from the prisoner, and that confession must have certain
elements of plausibility. At the same time he realizes that the
prisoner is probably not guilty of the severe crimes to which he,
the interrogator, is attempting to obtain a confession. However,
he rationalizes his own conduct on the ground that he is serving
communism and the state.

The first thing the interrogator does is to befriend the prisoner.
He reviews the prisoner's life history in great detail, asks about all
sorts of personal incidents in his early life. From the beginning he
persuades the prisoner that his sole aim is to help him. He tells
him they know everything already and if he will cooperate and confess they can close this case. The prisoner is anxious to talk. The
interrogator is never completely satisfied with the information

that he receives and asks for more and more. Unimportant incidents in the life of the prisoners are gone into in great detail. Any discrepancy in the life story of the prisoner is interpreted as the prisoner being unfriendly and attempting to mislead and lie to his friend the interrogator.

In stage 2 of the interrogation, episodes and incidents of the life history of the individual which the interrogator has now learned are used to harass the prisoner. He becomes upset and disorganized. At this point the interrogator may threaten to withdraw his interest or may use punitive methods against the prisoner. Punishment by the interrogator may be causing him to stand or sit in certain positions. The prisoner strives to please the interrogator and becomes increasingly suggestible. The prisoner then is alternatively rejected and befriended, which over a period of time causes a severe mental strain. It must be borne in mind that during this whole procedure the only contact that the prisoner has with any person is his interrogator. An important and vital personal relationship has been established for the prisoner.

Now starts stage 3. The interrogator continues talking to the prisoner, suggesting half-truths and urging upon him that the only possible and correct solution is for him to confess. This particular technique is repeated until such time as the conversations between the interrogator and the prisoner convinces the latter that he should do as his interrogator suggests. The prisoner has become more and more amenable. He is tired, alone, and has no one to support him. He rationalizes and accepts half-truths. With this rationalization he signs a confession and immediately is allowed rewards. He is permitted to sleep, to rest, and he is given better food. If, after this period of time, he recants on his confession, the case is reopened and he is again subjected to the entire series of treatments.

The primary work of the interrogator has been to convince the prisoner that what he has done is a crime. With the advent of a successful confession the subject is now ready for trial and punishment.

Testimony was received that well over 90 percent of the persons subjected to this treatment give confessions. There are those who never get to trial because they do not confess. These individuals are arbitrarily dealt with by the Russians or allowed to remain in detention for an unspecified period.

Testimony revealed that the Chinese have adopted the methods used by the Russians with some modifications. The most important of these are as follows:

1. Under the Chinese system the timetable is quite different, as there is an attempt to produce a long-lasting change in the basic attitude and behavior of the prisoner. Thus, indoctrination plays a very important part in the Chinese methods.

2. The prolonged isolation as used in Russia is not used in China. The Chinese emphasis is on group interaction as distinct from private isolation. Thus, in China, a prisoner is generally in a cell with 6 to 8 other political prisoners.

3. The Chinese use public self-criticism and group criticism for indoctrination as well as the use of diary writing as distinct from verbal discussions for the prisoner to give his autobiography.

These are the main differences. However, there are some variations in detail. In China, after the period of surveillance and preparation for arrest, the individual is seized under most dramatic circumstances. The arrest is generally made by armed troops with a great amount of furor, and the prisoner is immediately taken before three judges who are also interrogators. At this time the prisoner gives them certain information.

Because of the lack of facilities the prisoner may be subjected to so-called house arrest where he is kept under guard in his own home for weeks. Throughout this period of house arrest he is exposed to a certain amount of Communist indoctrination.

Ultimately, he is taken to a detention house where he generally is placed in a cell with 6 or 8 other political prisoners. This group is intensely competitive in attempting to bring to the newcomer evidences of his inadequacies and defects. He is exposed from morning until night to this hostile group which engages in self-criticism. He must participate. The prisoner has no privacy. The constant pressures leave him feeling defeated, humiliated, mentally dull, with a great need for talk and kindness. While he is rejected, reviled, humiliated, and brutalized by his fellow prisoners, he undergoes feelings of emotional nakedness and helplessness.

During this period of time the prisoner is also subjected to interrogations by an interrogator. The writing of diaries and autobiographic material is one of the methods used by an interrogator in obtaining information. Such writings are rejected numerous times. After a session with the interrogator the attitude of his fellow prisoners might be guided by the prisoner's appearance. Thus, if he is manacled the group bear down on him in an attempt to persuade him to change his attitude and confess. In many cases, the group of fellow prisoners may beat him. There is increasing dejection, fatigue, sleep loss, pain, hunger, weight loss, mental dulling, and confusion. He is subjected to constant reading, discussion, and repetition of Communist material. All during this period of time he has intermittent sessions with one or more interrogators. He loses his capacity for making sharp discriminations.

As a result of this constant treatment the prisoner ultimately prepares a confession. Its preparation to meet the demands of the interrogrator is extremely difficult. On many occasions the confession is rejected by the interrogator. A new confession must be prepared. This might be rejected. Actually, various confessions might be prepared from 3 to 6 times. Finally, by rationalization and partial beliefs he is able to properly prepare a confession which is accepted. During this entire period of time he must continue his study and discussion of Communist materials. He is now tried and punished. His imprisonment may have already lasted for an unusually long period of time, as much as 5 years. Unlike the Russian system, he may be given credit for his pretrial detention when he is officially tried and sentenced.

The timetable as to Chinese prisoners is vastly different from that of the Russians. They are not only interested in getting a satisfactory confession, but they want to produce a different ideological attitude. They, therefore, through this rather long and arduous treatment attempt to convert the prisoner to communism.

The Chinese interrogators are generally far less experienced and less knowledgeable about American and European people than the Russians.

As soon as individual prisoners are released they, rather quickly, fall into a place in society not very different from that which they originally held. The effects of the imprisonment are transient, and the released prisoner nearly always rejects communism and all those connected with it.

Dr. Wolff testified that it was his conviction that knowledge of the process and the steps involved in either the Russian or Chinese system is the most effective weapon against them.

[. . . . .]

Army

An example that even the worst of Communist treatment could be resisted is the case of Capt. Theodore Harris who testified before this subcommittee.

On July 4, 1952, Harris' aircraft was shot down. As a result, Harris was in a severe state of shock and was very badly burned around the face, hands, mouth, throat, and back. The skin on his face was burned off. Within a short time he was captured by the Chinese Communists.

For a period of several days until he reached the hospital compound in Pyongyang, Korea, he was in extreme pain because of virtually no medical attention. Maggots infested his burns and entered his ears and nose until his mental processes were being affected. Ultimately he was treated by a Chinese doctor. He remained in the hospital for approximately 5½ weeks before his captors felt he was strong enough to be interrogated.

He was then taken out and placed in a trench, dug on the side of a hill about 2½ to 3 feet wide, and about 6½ feet long. His interrogations now began and were virtually constant. The first interrogation ended after 5 weeks when the interrogator became angry and struck Harris on the side of the head with a board. Harris lost his temper and struck the interrogator, and as a result was put in handcuffs the rest of the day. The next morning he was taken out and instructed to dig a hole in the ground about 3 feet deep, the size of a grave. They then told him he had a choice of either signing a confession that he had been dropping bacteriological bombs on North Korea and agreeing not to strike any officers, for which they would let him go, or otherwise they would shoot him. He agreed not to strike any of their officers provided they didn't abuse him, but refused to sign a confession. They then put him before a firing squad but when they pulled the triggers their weapons were empty.

A new interrogator appeared on the scene, and he lasted approximately 2 months, at which time he flew into a rage and had Harris put in handcuffs. During one period of time Harris was shackled for 30 days. On another occasion he was handcuffed behind his back for a period of 2 or 3 weeks. It should also be noted that during the entire period of time he was a prisoner of war, namely, 14 months, he was in solitary confinement. Except for the initial period that he was hospitalized he received no medical attention other than that administered by a corpsman who would come around once a week and take off his old bandages and replace them with fresh ones. While the interrogations were going on in the trenches, Captain Harris was forced to sit on the floor with his feet in front of him constantly. The only time he was allowed to walk was to go to the latrine.

On one occasion during the winter he was moved to a lean-to outside a Korean house. The temperature was 20 or 30 below zero. He had been furnished with a regular POW Chinese winter uniform, but this was not sufficiently warm against the intense cold. His toes and fingers became frostbitten, and no adequate medical attention was afforded him.

The food was rotten, and, in fact, often inedible. On one occasion Harris, because he resented the type of questions he was being asked, went on a hunger strike which lasted for 12 or 13 days. His Chinese captors ended the strike by agreeing not to ask him any more bacteriological questions. This agreement the Communists honored for one month.

In January he was blindfolded, handcuffed, and taken on a long trip. He later learned that he had been transferred across the Yalu into Manchuria. After arriving at their destination, Harris was placed in a prison which was quite different from that in which he had been. He was given bedding, placed in a large cell, 20 by 30 feet, and was cleaned up. For the next 6 weeks he was interrogated daily, but more on a formal basis with a recording clerk present. The questions didn't vary from those previously asked, but the food and quarters were better. Occasionally they would vary the heat in his cell from over 100° down to about 30° below zero.

On one occasion, after a Chinese guard had wiped his feet on Harris' clothes, Harris struck him. For this Harris was handcuffed and placed in a box which was about 30 inches square. He was forced to sit in it for approximately 9 hours, and was temporarily paralyzed when he was removed. They then took him out of the box and handcuffed his arms to his ankles where they left him for 3 or 4 days, following which they handcuffed him in a conventional manner for about 6 weeks.

About the latter part of March he was transferred into an old prison where the cell was very small. He was informed that he was to stand trial for his criminal activities. The so-called trial lasted about 6 weeks. Actually the trial was very little more than normal interrogation. He was allowed no counsel. He had no witnesses appear against him. They finally told Harris he had been found guilty and would be sentenced at a later date.

While in this particular cell after a guard had been goading him, Harris punched him in his nose and broke it. This time he was placed in the same box for approximately 16 hours. While so imprisoned, they pounded on the lid all of the time. When they finally took him out, he could not walk and his mind was dazed.

Afterward he was returned to his original prison, where conditions improved. He was furnished a grass mattress, clean clothes, and given smoking material. The food was comparatively good, much better than it had been. He was furnished much literature. During this period, about every 2 weeks he was permitted to take a bath, and once a week he was allowed to wash his clothes.

When he was informed that he was to be repatriated, he recognized voices of his crew who were apparently in the same prison. He had not seen or conversed with any of his crew members during the entire time of his ordeal. They were placed on a train and taken to Kaesong. There he not only refused to sign a document that they read wherein he admitted to engaging in bacteriological warfare, but he demanded a copy of it, which they refused to give him. The next morning the trucks arrived to take the prisoners to Panmunjong. Harris at this time informed his interpreter that he was not leaving until he got a copy of the statement with which the Chinese confronted him. The other prisoners left, but Harris just stayed where he was. After some time and after breaking the windshield of a jeep into which the Communists were trying to force him to take him back to the United States lines, he was bodily removed in a truck where five Communist soldiers sat on him and finally dumped him into the United States zone.

COMMUNIST INTERROGATION, INDOCTRINATION AND EXPLOITATION OF AMERICAN MILITARY AND CIVILIAN PRISONERS

HEARINGS *before the Permanent Subcommittee on Investigations of the Committee on Government Operations, United States Senate, 84th Congress, Second Session*

JUNE 19, 20, 26, 27, 1956

Washington, D.C.

[. . . . .]

Testimony of Maj. William E. Mayer, Medical Corps, United States Army, San Antonio, Tex.

The CHAIRMAN. Major, state your name, place of residence, occupation or profession, please.

Major MAYER. Dr. William E. Mayer, Major, Medical Corps, United States Army. I live in San Antonio, Tex. I am permanently assigned to the faculty of the Army Medical Service School where I teach psychiatry. I am temporarily assigned at the Continental Army Command Headquarters at Fort Monroe, Va., for the purpose of assisting in the preparation of doctrine relating to the teaching of the Code of Conduct.

The CHAIRMAN. How long have you been in the military service?

Major MAYER. Thirteen years.

The CHAIRMAN. All right, Mr. Counsel, you may proceed.

Mr. KENNEDY. Major Mayer, you have been working, have you not, with some of the prisoners who came back from the conflict in Korea?

Major MAYER. Yes, sir.

Mr. KENNEDY. You did some of the interviewing, did you not?

Major MAYER. Yes, sir.

Mr. KENNEDY. Will you outline some of your background in that field, briefly?

Major MAYOR. My attention to this problem began when it became possible that there would be a prisoner exchange of sick and wounded. That is at the time of Operation Little Switch, which Captain Cumby described yesterday. At that time I was placed on a board called the Joint Classification Board in Japan, set up for the purpose of both conducting and reviewing and supervising the interrogations and examinations of all people recovered from the Communists in Korea.

Subsequently, I served in the same capacity as the medical member of a board set up to supervise the examination and inquiries of all the United States and U. N., with the exception of British, personnel repatriated during operation Big Switch, the principal prisoner exchange. I continued this study of data that we derived from those studies and in addition in connection with this, in order to provide material of value within the military, I reviewed much of the literature available written by and about prisoners of war from World War II, to give us a basis of comparison and I have interviewed a number of them.

Mr. KENNEDY. Supplementing what has been said already, do you have any information regarding the method used by the Chinese Communists and North Koreans in interrogation and indoctrination of American prisoners of war?

Major MAYER. Yes, Mr. Kennedy, I think I can possibly throw light on the entire process from a slightly different point of view. I should like to explain what that is.

First of all, I am concerned, as is every member of the medical service, with the implications of Communist handling of these prisoners from the standpoint of what it does to the man himself, what effect it has on him. Our primary mission is to conserve his well-being. So we have examined the whole procedure from the standpoint of its effects on him insofar as it is possible.

Secondly, however, my principal area of concern has been with the military implications and fairly strictly limited to the military implications of Communist handling of prisoners in relation to how these methods affect our fighting strength and in relation to what advantages the Communist method gives him in the battle which is represented by a prisoner of war camp.

We have heard from Dr. Wolff a magnificent discussion of Soviet methods in the police state, particularly as they relate to the individual state criminal and the adaptations the Chinese have made of this same procedure. I would like to emphasize that one of our initial findings was that while the war criminal, individual criminality subject did come up, and was introduced by the Communists in their handling of Americans, in spite of this the handling of these people by and large was not exactly similar to the methods Dr. Wolff described but was clearly derived from those, some of them very ancient police methods.

Mr. Hunter's interesting exposition of the Communist indoctrination procedure also throws a good deal of light on what actually was done to Americans, however, with certain qualifying remarks.

For example, he talked a good bit about hunger and fatigue. These undoubtedly affect behavior and can affect behavior very profoundly. In fact, many ordinary, well-adjusted people react emotionally if they miss a meal. You multiply this by hundreds of instances and by a generally inadequate diet such as Dr. Anderson described, and you can imagine what the effect is.

These things were factors in Korea in whatever happened to the American soldier, unquestionably. However, to be realistic about the whole situation and to put it into its proper perspective it is necessary to remember that this is probably going to be the case against the Communist enemy. There is certainly no indication that he is going to start giving people plenty of food and the kind of good treatment we give them. Secondly, it is undeniable that in Japanese and German POW camps the inadequacy of the diet, the terrible conditions of working in coal mines, on road gangs, and so on, particularly in Germany, were comparable at least to these elements of hunger and fatigue among the Korean prisoners.

Also, the subject of the use of drugs and of hypnosis and of the Pavlov conditioned reflex have been introduced here. Our findings based upon what now amounts somewhere between 800 and 1,000 complete files of intelligence and medical data on returned United States and U. N. prisoners indicates that drugs and hypnosis were not in the Korean POW camps significant factors in the handling of these soldiers.

Relative to the Pavlov conditioned reflex which does play a part in human learning, it is dangerous, I believe as a psychiatrist, to overemphasize this kind of human learning. We can demonstrate the conditioned reflex even in the unborn child. It certainly has been demonstrated on all kinds of laboratory animals. Dr. Pavlov, when he described it, pointed out how inconsistent this response is, how easy it is to extinguish. I would merely like to add a cautionary word relative to the Pavlovian conditioned reflex, namely, that its use or its absence, neither, says anything about the inevitability of succumbing to something that the Communists have.

I would like to try to avoid any implication that they have something magical because that is what Pavlov sounds like, or something you can't resist, because that is what Pavlov sounds like. That simply isn't true.

One other thing that was mentioned was destruction of the mind and the word "insanity," which is not a medical but legal term, was introduced several times. This issue was fought out at great length in relation to at least one trial that I know of, and it is an important one, because this, too, lends credence to the idea that the Communists have something which can destroy people's minds and drive them insane and relieve them of their personal responsibility for their actions. This, too, I don't believe to be true in any sense in this restricted environment of the Korean prisoner of war camp.

I am not talking about the rest of the Communist world.

Mr. Hunter did say something about tenseness, which, as a psychiatrist, I call anxiety. Whatever you call it, this is a tremendously important factor in determining what behavior is going to be. Every prisoner of war is anxious. He comes ultimately to a realistic realization that the captor can do anything he wants to him. He is relatively defenseless. He is unarmed, certainly, in the face of a captor who may exercise any form of brutality. No prisoner ever really forgets this. To a lesser extent we see the same kind of anxiety among prisoners in county jails and in penitentiaries.

Captain Cumby emphasized the minimal use of physical torture. It was quite natural, therefore, to turn to a consideration of mental torture. I think this needs some defining. I don't know exactly what mental torture is. Certainly a great many mental patients who come to me, particularly in a combat zone, who are emotionally disturbed and who feel that they can no longer function for some reason, describe things that to them are torture of a mental sort. For example, the separation from their home and their family. Sometimes it is the food. Sometimes it is what they consider to be a punitive superior. These things to different men constitute mental torture.

If I am right in assuming that by mental torture is implied a system of actively terrorizing people, of trying to create in them horrifying images of what might occur if they don't absolutely toe the line, I don't think we can say properly that mental torture in this horrendous atmosphere was a very important nor a necessary part of the Communist method for handling prisoners.

I have said a great deal about what it isn't. I would like to try to point out as simply as possible some of the important things that the Communist handling of prisoners does involve.

Dr. Segal this morning talked about dividing and conquering, and certainly every opponent in history who wants to conquer has tried some variation of this and the Communist is no exception to this. However, there is a limit on how many solitary confinement cells you can build for prisoners, and if you can possibly divide them without physically isolating them from one another you have accomplished a miracle, certainly a great achievement.

So they set out — again I am talking from this somewhat provincial point of view of applied psychiatry — they set out to isolate them from one another just as effectively as if they were in cells. The informing that you have heard about was part of this. As Dr. Anderson pointed out, any figure that you give about informing is likely to be misleading, because informing in these camps was given an entirely different atmosphere. You will recall that someone has described the reception of the prisoner by the Chinese that frequently he was received in a more or less benign fashion. He was told that they were glad to have him, glad to have liberated him from the clutches of the Wall Street warmongers, glad that he was free from further dangers on the battlefield, that they would demand nothing of him, that they weren't going to mistreat him, that they merely wanted to give him a chance to learn the truth as they understand the truth to be.

This goes further than just mere propaganda. This begins to alter the soldier's preconceived idea about the captor in a significant way, and a relationship begins to develop between the prisoner and the captor which is somewhat new from the standpoint of our previous experiences with how prisoners feel about those who catch them.

In line with this rather privileged and more secure, unusual relationship, seemingly, between the captor and the prisoner, the prisoners were encouraged to talk about themselves principally, secondarily about others, not as an exercise of some vindictive, punitive police state. It was always interposed as talking about your own activities or the activities of other people. It was always interpreted as a worthwhile service to the people, you see. This was an evidence of your increased civic consciousness in the sense of civic responsibility.

So much informing, if you can even call it that, was simply the unwitting dissemination of material by prisoners who were in a very real sense seduced into this since it was called something else and it wasn't done in a bitter or vituperative manner. Had the original stages of informing led to severe punishment of other prisoners, the informers would have suffered the same fate as in previous wars. Men who have been informed upon or their friends would have ganged up on the informers and destroyed them. This has been almost invariably true.

The informer holds the lowest rung of our social hierarchy. But people didn't ordinarily suffer when some of this information came out beyond being required to have one of these walking conferences or a heart-to-heart chat with one of the Chinese instructors, who generally begged him to try to see the error of his ways and improve his sense of responsibility for the welfare of the group. That was misleading. Ultimately, of course, it was possible as a result of informing for serious things to happen, but by then the whole process had gone too far. It was typified by the statement by many returnees, "While there was a lot of informing, they seemed to know everything we were doing and sometimes I even had the feeling they even knew what I was thinking, but I don't know who was informing."

As Dr. Anderson clearly pointed out, sometimes you were informing on yourself, sometimes on others with nothing punitive intended. This wasn't a renunciation of principle on the part of the man who did it.

Another method of isolating these people from each other was through their selection of mail, which you have also heard described. This effectively separates people one from another by shearing away what ordinarily serves as a common basis for unified effort and unified activity. When two soldiers get together and compare their letters from home about their kids and about their family and about their house, this has a unifying effect. This binds men closer together. But when your letters are restricted to letters very often which announce some major or minor domestic crisis, when your letter turns out to be a notice from a collection company, or what a soldier calls a "Dear John" letter, this isn't the kind of thing you get together with your buddy and talk about. Consequently, men were deprived of this common emotional basis for sticking together.

They also used this control of the mail to make men feel that what the Communist says about capitalism and what it does to its members was demonstrably true, in this respect: It said that our system of free enterprise leads to selfishness, grasping, caring only for what is in it for you, little regard for another individual, especially if he is not there. They said, "Your people at home have forgotten about you. They don't really care about you." What little mail you got was likely to bear this out. Of course this helped make men feel that they were alone and abandoned and isolated.

The self-criticism meeting is still another step and an important one psychologically.

Senator MCCARTHY. May I interrupt at this point? By control of the mail, you mean censorship?

Major MAYER. Yes, sir. Not only censorship, Senator McCarthy, but withholding of mail, allowing only certain letters to go through. In other words, not just censorship in cutting things out. It was interesting that they routinely did not allow a photograph to come through. A man might get an intact letter in which it said "Here is a picture of me and the kids." No picture. This was almost invariably true, because they didn't want this kind of reminder. They didn't want to give him supports of an emotional kind. It is a diabolical kind of censorship and it is bound over a period of time to be extremely effective.

They cut these people apart, making them isolated and thus obviously much more helpless by this self-criticism which has received a good deal of attention. I think even Mr. Molotov published a self-criticism only a few months ago.

The self-criticism is not so different from the exhortation of your minister to look inwardly and see what you have not been doing that you should have been doing, and vice versa, except that like everything in the Communist state, it is collectivized. You are gathered together in a group frequently for a self-criticism meeting. Some of the Chinese prisoners that we captured on the front lines told us this was being done in the Chinese army, right within the combat unit, that they had self-criticism meetings. This was certainly done among the prisoners.

In a self-criticism meeting, which resembles in some ways group psychiatric treatment, group psychotherapy, in this meeting you examine and criticize your defects of attitude or of character or of behavior in terms of the standards which are often impossibly high, which are stated to be the ideal standards of a people's state.

First, this seems or seemed at least to many of our soldiers to be a kind of a joke, kind of ridiculous, but inevitably over a period of time something occurs when you do this. This is why in this group psychotherapy, in the treatment of patients, we control such sessions very carefully. What would happen otherwise is that eventually you begin to run out of superficial or joking things to talk about. Eventually you begin to talk about beliefs I have which maybe you can't support logically but which you nonetheless have.

You begin to talk about rather personal things. You may even begin to talk about your family and how they developed your attitudes. Pretty soon you do indeed feel naked and vulnerable, and you are not quite so sure that your listeners are as friendly as you once thought. You have the feeling that you have talked too much, you have gone too far. They know too much about you.

This produces not only the tendency to withdraw from other people, but a real feeling of guilt and a feeling of anxiety which you can't pin down and therefore you can't solve. You don't know exactly what you are guilty about, but you do know you have this feeling which is very unpleasant. This, of course, as Dr. Wolff pointed out, is one of the factors that makes people vulnerable to Communist pressure. The individual with a sense of guilt.

One other thing about the self-criticism. Oral self-criticisms are one thing, but a frequent next step was to say, "You have now said this. We want you to write it out. There can be no harm in this. You have said it publicly in front of witnesses. So write it down, not an essay on it exactly, but describe it in writing and sign it." These were carefully picked up. Of course they found their way into the dossier that was kept on each man. Self-criticism might be for something minor, selling a turnip, let us say, but 100 self-criticisms — and this was somehow communicated to the prisoner — might eventually add up to enough to constitute a real indictment of you as a war criminal, you see, or certainly at least as not a worthwhile member of the people's democracy.

Senator MCCARTHY. May I interrupt again at this point. I read once about the attempts to induce a man to sign a confession, and after he signed the confession he would then be told he was no longer a prisoner of war, but he was treated as a war criminal. How much of that was there, if you know?

Major MAYER. Not very much.

Senator MCCARTHY. There was not too much of that?

Major MAYER. No, sir; although it happened enough that a great many people knew about it. So it is the kind of thing that undoubtedly affected people, but you can't say exactly how much it affected people.

Senator MCCARTHY. In other words, if I understand it, as I get it from reading various articles, they would promise a man special consideration if he would sign a confession, and once he signed the confession about germ warfare or something along that line, he was then told "You are no longer a prisoner of war, you will now be treated as a war criminal."

Major MAYER. Which of course means you have none of the protections of a POW. I believe this was true, Senator, in relation to the people who are handled individually or specially. These people were mostly not in the Army. My data, perhaps I should emphasize this, is almost entirely restricted to Army plus about 300 U. N., other than United States. It is not drawn to any significant degree at all from the experiences of Air Force people or any other group.

Senator MCCARTHY. You would not have any idea how many times this occurred, I suppose?

Major MAYER. No, sir. There may be someone in a subsequent hearing who will have direct access to that information.

Senator MCCARTHY. Thank you.

Major MAYER. Yes, sir.

The educational program has been well described. I would like merely to add to its previous description that this education program is not just to disseminate information. Obviously, by the results which have been described by, for example, Dr. Segal, it isn't very effective in selling people ideas or at least political philosophy. It certainly didn't succeed in turning Americans into Communists. But the education program psychologically is a step beneath that, a step deeper into the individual, by devaluing those values which really are the strength of a democratic nation, the dependability of the individual and his right to function as an individual and his sense of individual responsibility. By devaluing these things, one takes away or whittles away at personal character traits which otherwise could defend a man in this situation.

In other words, having nothing to do with politics, having to do with the immediate reality of being in a POW camp. If you no longer think that American principles of fair play and of intense personal loyalty and of speaking your mind individually — that these things are no longer so important, then ——

Senator MCCARTHY. I hate to interrupt the witness too often, because he is a very intelligent witness, but I would like to get some additional comment in this connection.

I understand that the Turkish soldiers deviated practically not at all. Is that right?

Major MAYER. Yes, sir; that is correct.

Senator MCCARTHY. Regardless of what type of mental or physical torture was inflicted, we have practically no record of any Turkish soldier deviating.

Major MAYER. That is correct, sir, and we interrogated them all.

Senator MCCARTHY. How about the Marine Corps? I ask that as a Marine.

Major MAYER. As a former Marine psychiatrist ——

Senator MCCARTHY. There isn't such a thing as a former Marine.

Major MAYER. I agree. Among the Marine ground troops held prisoner — and I must point out that I have had access to only probably less than 60 of their complete reports — among these men the incidence of giving in to Communist pressures was almost — well, it certainly was extremely low.

Senator MCCARTHY. That might indicate, taking the Turkish troops and the Marine troops, that the indoctrination and the esprit de corps had a tremendous amount to do with whether or not they would give in; right?

Major MAYER. I think most emphatically, Senator. There are other factors involved, surely, but here is one factor that we think is undeniable and it is something we can work on in any branch of the military service and something we can work on in fact throughout the whole society. I would like to come to that in a couple of minutes, If I may.

Senator MCCARTHY. I understand that there were only 230 Marines captured during the entire Korean war; is that correct, if you know?

Major MAYER. The figure to the best of my recollection is approximately 231. That may be 10 numbers off one way or the other.

Senator MCCARTHY. I am not here now to extol the virtues of the Marine Corps over the Army, because I have a tremendous respect for all the boys who serve in the Army, but how do you account for the much lower percentage of Marines and Turkish soldiers who surrendered as compared to the percentage of Army boys? Was that the result of the indoctrination they got during training or the esprit de corps?

Major MAYER. I think there are a number of possible factors in this, Senator, although training, esprit de corps, and the quality of leadership and discipline in particular are, we believe, of critical importance in preparing a man to stand anything that the Communist tries to do, in fact, that any enemy tries to do to him, whether on a battlefield or in a POW camp.

Senator MCCARTHY. The chairman just mentioned a point which I think is very important, the fact that all of the Marines are volunteers might also have some effect, I assume.

Major MAYER. I have some interesting data on that, Mr. Chairman. When I was a psychiatrist in the First Marine Division in Korea this was largely true, yes. Most Marines have volunteered. If you pick apart the reasons why they volunteered, sometimes the reasons are fairly simple ones or immature reasons. Nonetheless they are voluntarily in this situation, and this undoubtedly makes them a good soldier.

The CHAIRMAN. I did not quite understand that.

Major MAYER. They are voluntarily in the position of being committed to be a Marine, and therefore this can help them to become better soldiers. On the other hand, we in Korea did serve with drafted Marines. We had drafted Marines in the Marine division.

The CHAIRMAN. Did they elect their branch of the service after they were drafted?

Major MAYER. I don't believe this was true, sir.

The CHAIRMAN. I was just inquiring. Or were they assigned to fill in?

Major MAYER. They were assigned, sir. Most of them were of Puerto Rican extraction and had come from New York. Many of them spoke very little English. I merely want to say about these drafted Marines that they became quite good Marines. So you can't write it all off just by the mere fact of their being volunteers.

The CHAIRMAN. I did not think that was a factor exclusive unto itself that might control, but it just occurred to me that one who volunteers to serve in the military has possibly weighed the responsibilities and obligations, and he more readily can be indoctrinated than one who perhaps is drafted. This is no reflection upon those who are drafted. Many who are drafted have purposes or ambitions in life. They have a different code. Their career and plans are disrupted or interrupted for a brief time in the military, whereas the voluntary Marine has chosen that for at least his immediate occupation. Therefore, some may be drafted who are reluctant to go in the first place. In other words, they have not that buildup of character and resistance to conditions that maybe the Marine volunteer who chooses that profession would naturally have by reason of his stronger conviction about it.

Major MAYER. I agree wholeheartedly, although I believe that even among drafted citizens, with more emphasis upon the service aspects of being in the service on the part of the public in general, we would get something that more closely approaches, even in the men who have been drafted, an attitude that while he didn't initiate the act, he voluntarily and wholeheartedly puts himself into it.

The CHAIRMAN. I am sure most of those who are drafted do that.

Major MAYER. Yes, sir.

The CHAIRMAN. I am sure the majority of them do. But I can appreciate that in a draft you occasionally bring somebody in who is very reluctant and unhappy about it in the first place, and unless he actually gets in combat where he has to defend himself, he is a little bit lukewarm about the training and discipline and all of the other things associated with military life.

Senator MCCARTHY. May I say, Mr. Chairman, that I did not bring up this question of the Marine Corps and the Turkish soldiers for the purpose of comparing them with our excellent Army. It is merely because we are here studying what can be done to prevent defectees in some future war, and I thought we should at some time try to find out why, for example, none of the Turkish soldiers and none of the Marines defected. I understand three Marines were tried, but all were found not guilty, and not a single Marine prisoner defected. So I think it might be well for the military to examine the different type of training and to determine, if possible, how we can prevent as many defectees as possible in a future war. It was not just because I was in the Marines that I was bringing this up.

The CHAIRMAN. I think at this point I would like your comment — or perhaps you would rather wait until you have concluded your formal presentation — about what we are doing now in the military. What lesson have we learned from this and what are we doing about it? That is the important conclusion to this.

Major MAYER. I should like to comment on that, sir, if I may wait just a moment or two.

Mr. KENNEDY. May I say something in regard to your statement, Senator McCarthy? During the course of the study which we have been making together with the Army they have been most cooperative so far as turning over records and making people available. As far as we can find, they are realistic enough to see that there are certain problems. I think they are aware of certain facts which are coming out in these hearings which perhaps are not most favorable to certain people or certain branches of the service, and they are trying to take steps to correct them. I think that before they have finished they are going to outline what steps they have been taking and are taking.

Senator MCCARTHY. I am sure you are right, Mr. Kennedy. They are taking whatever steps they think are necessary. I am sure that these hearings will help.

I should like to take up with the chairman a matter which he may not wish to decide now. I think we should make a part of this record the hearings which we held about 2 years ago, I believe, in which we introduced a sizable number of the books used to indoctrinate soldiers, some of which were just rank and complete Communist propaganda. We had them as part of the record then, and I think they should be put in this record to make it complete. I do not wish to ask the chairman to rule on it now, but I should like him to look over the books which we now have in his committee and decide whether or not they should be put in this record. I think indoctrination by the type of books which we found were being used may have had a considerable effect on many of the soldiers who defected.

As I said, I am not asking for a ruling at this point.

The CHAIRMAN. I assume that the books which the Senator refers to are already on file.

Senator MCCARTHY. Yes; they are.

The CHAIRMAN. We will give proper consideration to that later. I will say at least that some of the books are not conducive to making American soldiers more patriotic, and this committee

severely condemned their use where those were found. Of course
you have in mind, I am sure, that much corrective action has taken
place since, just as we expect to occur as we explore and develop
the facts in connection with how our prisoners of war were treated,
how they responded, the defections which came about. We are
learning from our experience of the past and expect to take every
corrective measure indicated to be necessary or proper to prevent
a recurrence in the future.

Senator MCCARTHY. May I say, Mr. Chairman, in fairness
to those in charge in the Army that while I have no proof of it, I
have been informed that they have withdrawn many of the books
that were introduced before the committee at the previous hearings.

The CHAIRMAN. All right, you may proceed, Major.

Major MAYER. Up until now I have been discussing some of
the things we heard about before in the context of isolating people
psychologically from one another in an attempt to make them alone
and helpless. The next logical area to examine is, Did it work? Was
it effective? What was achieved by doing this? This must be done
with any enemy weapon, whether that weapon is made of metal
or whether it is a technique or a set of techniques like this.

In relation to this it is necessary to review just momentarily
what the Chinese objectives were in the whole program. I wish
to second most emphatically Major Anderson's contention that all
desires to communicate ideas and develop propaganda to the contrary notwithstanding, the Chinese principal objective was the
control of the prisoners. It is dangerous to have several thousand
enemy soldiers behind your lines even when they are not armed.
The Germans found that out. The Japanese found it out. Americans in captivity are notably difficult to control.

So, in terms of this objective, did the Chinese accomplish what
the program primarily, in my opinion, was designed to accomplish?

They did to a degree to which you cannot assign a precise value.
However, it appears that it was possible in North Korea to maintain security in the prison camps holding Americans with less expenditure of enemy military strength than we expected them to
have to expend to control these people. In other words, it didn't
take as many guards or as many guns or as many barbed wire
fences. That is important to us from the standpoint of simple military operations.

As far as their selling ideas, getting acceptance of communism
by Americans, one can only speculate about this. You certainly

can't assign degrees of acceptance of Communist indoctrination, particularly from a man's own statements if he is under the emotional stress of just coming out of a prison camp and is being questioned by an Intelligence agent. It is impossible to get anything except a wild guess at best. It is my impression that, as Dr. Segal pointed out, they were extremely unsuccessful in selling the ideas. They did, however, accomplish the production of a certain amount of propaganda material and they did, I repeat, manage to control these men with less expenditure of troops and materiel on their part than we think would have been ideal.

You heard all kinds of discussions of what the results are in terms of resisters and collaborators. I don't honestly think that is our area of principal interest, at least not in my particular field of endeavor. I am interested in the 80 percent that they said were in the middle. I am interested in the average soldier, if there is such a thing, the ordinary fighting man who finds himself in this situation, who is not a hero of the Nathan Hale variety and is not an out-and-out opportunistic informer or collaborator. You will find a few such people in any large collection of men.

The CHAIRMAN. Do you mean we are not interested in the defectors?

Major MAYER. I am interested, sir.

The CHAIRMAN. I did not quite get the significance of that.

Major MAYER. I mean that my primary area of concern is with the large general group in the middle rather than either of the two extremes. In considering the future welfare of soldiers in the American Army in this situation this is going to be the majority. These are the people that possibly the most can be done with. These are the ones who deserve a good deal of our attention. I don't mean that the others are inconsiderable. I just mean that this is where I have focused my principal interest in terms of corrective measures.

Senator MCCARTHY. Could I interrupt to ask a question which I asked a witness this morning? I should like to ask you the same question, if I may. Am I correct in the assumption that the vast majority of the men who served in Korea — Army, Navy, Marine Corps, Air Corps — proved themselves really good Americans, good soldiers, and that the group who defected or did not come through were just an infinitesimal part of the military?

Major MAYER. You are certainly correct in saying that the great majority of Americans ——

Senator MCCARTHY. So, as a whole there is no reason that we cannot be proud of the military conduct in Korea.

Major MAYER. Yes, sir; we can be proud of the behavior in Korea, but we have to recognize what lessons are still involved, because no matter how well they did, we would like ideally, if we are going to have to fight this enemy, to do even better. Otherwise there would be no point in improving any of our weapons.

With this large central group, the 80 percent you have heard described before, we came across a number of things which we would like to correct from the standpoint of the welfare of the soldier himself. For example, we found that apparently they had some difficulty in developing close buddy relationships. We would like to see these relationships as we have in previous wars, because they give strength to the soldier. They protect him. They help keep him alive. The more and the better your buddy relationships are, the more strength you have against any threat.

Secondly, we would like to see active and continued resistance on the part of soldiers who are in enemy hands. Our new code of conduct says almost at the very beginning, "If I am captured by an enemy I will continue to resist." This, of course, is the mission of the soldier, whether he is in a POW camp or on the battlefield.

We would like to see more engineered escapes. We would like to see a continuing, active program to get people out, because not only does this demoralize the enemy but it does good things even for the men who don't escape. It does good things for the emotional life of the man left behind in camp. For every man who escapes, the fellow left behind escapes just a little bit. At least he knows there is somebody going home who is going to fire up the people about what is happening to us. Maybe it will hasten our repatriation. So we would like to see that.

The CHAIRMAN. What are the chances of escape?

Major MAYER. The chances of escape, Mr. Chairman, are related very closely to the presence or absence of escape groups. Escape as a solitary individual pastime is doomed to almost certain failure. However, even under the conditions existing in Korea, with the escaping prisoner being surrounded by people of a different race and therefore he is more easily recognized, even there it is conceivable. Based upon what Americans have done in previous wars in similarly difficult situations, if enough people work on the preparation and enough people cover up his movements, if enough people are engaged in the escape committee, it is conceivable that a man can escape. In fact, we expect escapes to occur in this fashion.

The CHAIRMAN. Did they succeed in escaping from our compounds?

Major MAYER. I am not qualified to answer that in any quantitative sense, sir.

The CHAIRMAN. I can appreciate this one point which is made. I don't know how tremendously important it is, but, of course, the more resistance the more threat of escape, the more danger of escape that the prisoners can create, the more it taxes the strength, the manpower, and so forth, of the enemy, and thus insofar as combat that many troops are neutralized, so to speak. They are occupied with something other than on the front line killing. Taking it overall, I don't know how big a factor it would be, but I assume that in war everything that taxes, obstructs, or hinder the enemy from putting his maximum force of destruction where our troops are, which detracts from it to any extent, therefore helps the cause.

Major MAYER. Absolutely; but also it is important for what it does to the prisoner himself.

The CHAIRMAN. To the man himself.

Major MAYER. Even if no escape ever actually takes place, the constant sustained activity — you remember Mr. Hunter said something about keeping your mind busy — is a good defense against the best the Communists have. Escape and preoccupation with it is an important part of it.

Senator MCCARTHY. If I may interrupt again, Mr. Chairman, there is a big difference, of course, between urging your soldiers to try to escape when the enemy is following the Geneva Convention rules of warfare. You know if a man is apprehended he will not be mistreated so badly. But as far as the North Koreans were concerned, as far as the Japanese were concerned, frankly I would not have advised any of my men to try to escape. Am I right in that?

Major MAYER. Certainly it is a point very well taken. The Japanese used to threaten, for example, if 1 man did escape they would shoot 9 others. This has a deterrent effect on escapes, but not a total deterrent effect. I can't believe that we can ever retreat from the position that one of the primary duties of the soldier who is for the moment held captive is to try in some way to escape. This is an opinion.

The CHAIRMAN. That has to be left up to the soldier.

Major MAYER. Yes, sir.

The CHAIRMAN. He should not be directed to try to escape because it might mean immediate death not only to himself but to some of his fellow prisoners. It is something which has to be left to his discretion after he has been properly trained and indoctrinated and has become a good soldier. When he is on his own like that he certainly has to be the final judge.

Major MAYER. This emphasizes the fact that escape has to be done as an organized community effort, that it cannot be just the isolated efforts of individuals.

The CHAIRMAN. All right; let us go ahead.

Mr. KENNEDY. Major, on the question of the participation or cooperation with the Communists are you using the figure 15 percent or have you used in the past a larger figure? I want to get it straight now for the record.

Major MAYER. I have in the past said that the total number of people that the Communists managed in one way or another to get to engage in activities ultimately detrimental to the prisoner himself or to the country was probably closer, in my opinion, to 30 percent. Based on this, 15 percent were the hard core that we have heard described several times before. From the point where one is completely cooperative with the enemy to the point where he does absolutely nothing is not just one big jump. It is a series of little steps. It is possible, therefore, to have an opinion as to the seriousness of any given amount of cooperation. It seemed to me that an additional 15 percent beyond the hard core were active enough in what the Communists wanted them to do, like the study group.

Mr. KENNEDY. Major, isn't that other 15 percent one of the problems or difficulties, and to a lesser extent those who did not participate or those who did not resist? Isn't that group one of the biggest problems that we have to face?

Major MAYER. Yes.

Mr. KENNEDY. I wanted to make sure we understood that that is one of the difficulties. I don't think we should pass over it as just the 80 percent, but this other group which did participate and did cooperate.

The CHAIRMAN. The Chair will have to announce at this time that a quorum is not present, and therefore you may proceed and make a statement for the record. If later a quorum returns, we can then verify what you now say under oath.

Mr. KENNEDY. Mr. Chairman, if you are going to have to leave shortly, we have one other witness who has to leave the city. How long will you be, Major?

Major MAYER. I was going to leave tonight. You mean how long here? Just a very few minutes.

Mr. KENNEDY. We have another witness also.

The CHAIRMAN. The Chair has to go to a conference at 4 o'clock, a meeting of conferees on the public works appropriation bill. I have a little interest in the outcome of that conference, and I think I had better be present to look after that interest.

All right, go ahead, Major. We will proceed as expeditiously as we can.

Major MAYER. In relation to what you were just asking about, Mr. Kennedy, invariably the question arises, Did this experience in Korea reveal that there was something defective about Americans or that our people can't stand up to the Communists? I wish to say emphatically that this is not what the Korea experience showed at all. It did, however, point out for us areas for maximum effectiveness of our fighting forces in any future conflict, particularly against a Communist enemy — areas that, however good they are now, desirably could be strengthened. This is what the Code of Conduct in the military service attempts to do.

We know in studying combat soldiers and what makes them fight and why they break down during battle that there are certain factors which defend a man against terror and anxiety and being unable to go on in the face of this terrible threat of being dismembered or killed in battle. These factors are pretty simple, and they are classical. They are not the private property of the psychiatric department.

They include certainly adequate, firm, consistent, predictable leadership.

They include a definite, well-defined system of discipline, and by this I do not mean punishment. I mean the kind of discipline that is internalized, a system of values, as Mr. Hunter talked about and as Dr. Wolff even suggested, the kind of discipline that arises from within the individual and makes it possible for him to function effectively as a member of a group and as actually a member.

We know that the sense of group identification, of belonging, is extremely important in defending a man against fear and anxiety in battle. We know that morale and esprit de corps are essential. We know that his training and his knowledge of the situation of the enemy can defend him.

The Code of Conduct simply reemphasizes, in relation to each of those things I have mentioned, what we have been trying to teach all along. The Code of Conduct, although it uses the language of a prisoner of war, talks about loyalty to other individuals. It talks about continuing to resist. By executive order of the President it states, "I will try to escape and assist others to escape." The Code makes other statements, such as keeping faith not only with one's comrades but with the United States of America in prohibiting any statement which would hurt the United States.

The CHAIRMAN. Perhaps a copy of that should be supplied for the record.

Major MAYER. Yes, sir. I have a copy right here which belongs to the judge.

The CHAIRMAN. I think it might be printed in the record at this point for the information of those who read the record.

(The document referred to follows:)

CODE OF CONDUCT

FOR MEMBERS OF THE UNITED . STATES . ARMED FORCES

I

I am an American fighting man. I serve in the forces which guard my country and our way of life. I am prepared to give my life in their defense.

II

I will never surrender of my own free will. If in command I will never surrender my men while they still have the means to resist.

III

If I am captured I will continue to resist by all means available. I will make every effort to escape and aid others to escape. I will accept neither parole nor special favors from the enemy.

IV

If I become a prisoner of war, I will keep faith with my fellow prisoners. I will give no information or take part in any action which might be harmful to my comrades. If I am senior, I will take command.

If not, I will obey the lawful orders of those appointed over me and will back them up in every way.

V

When questioned, should I become a prisoner of war, I am bound to give only name, rank, service number, and date of birth. I will evade answering further questions to the utmost of my ability. I will make no oral or written statements disloyal to my country and its allies or harmful to their cause.

VI

I will never forget that I am an American fighting man, responsible for my actions, and dedicated to the principles which made my country free. I will trust in my God and in the United States of America.

Major MAYER. In summary I would like to say that this Code of Conduct, which is new as a document, is simply a restatement of the very things we have been trying to teach and emphasize in the military all along. The Korean experience more than anything else has emphasized the fact that these things need continuous and increasing attention on our part. So we are attempting to do this, not just in reading people a Code of Conduct, but every branch of the military service has devised a program of formal instruction, a program of field instruction, not just to teach people how to be prisoners but how to be the kind of soldier who will also be a good prisoner on the basis of these same principles.

One thing needs to be said in addition, and it was said by the men who drew up the Code of Conduct and by many others who have reviewed this. We don't pretend that we can teach the elements of character within the limits of the military service strictly. We can't teach a man about loyalty or dedication to a cause or continuing to resist in the face of adversity, unless he has within him from his previous 18 years of education, particularly in his home, some understanding of those same values. Those values basically are moral and ethical principles. They are not things restricted to fighting a war. They are things which give the country its strength as it is. We are trying to teach it within the service, but we need a great deal of help, mostly from parents, and public attention to this code.

The CHAIRMAN. In other words, if they have had the proper training at home, if it has been instilled in them from childhood, you have much better material to work with in making the kind of soldiers that we need and that we desire.

Major MAYER. Yes, sir; because in any future conflict, particularly against a Communist enemy, if he further refines and further develops his techniques, which is predictable, and if we don't take the lessons from the battlefield of the Korean war, then particularly if we are engaged in a general war, if he can manage to isolate these people from one another and neutralize them and not have a problem holding them and extracting information from them, this can be an extremely serious fact from the standpoint of the consequences militarily.

The CHAIRMAN. Thank you very much, Major.

I hope we may be able to get through the next witness. Will you come around, please?

Mr. KENNEDY. Major Panell.

The CHAIRMAN. Major, will you be sworn? You do solemnly swear that the evidence you shall give before this Senate investigating subcommittee shall be the truth, the whole truth, and nothing but the truth, so help you God?

Major PANELL. I do.

Testimony of Maj. Marion R. Panell, Artillery, United States Army

The CHAIRMAN. Be seated, Major Panell. Will you state your name, your place of residence, your occupation, how long you have been in the service, and what your duties are at the present time?

Major PANELL. Marion R. Panell, major, Artillery, United States Army. I am presently assigned to the Assistant Chief of Staff, Intelligence, at the Pentagon. I have been in the Army for 16 years, and I am presently residing in Baltimore, Md.

Mr. KENNEDY. You are in Army Intelligence, are you?

Major PANELL. Yes, sir.

Mr. KENNEDY. One of your duties in the past has been to interrogate all the United Nations troops who fought in Korea, other than American and British; is that correct?

Major PANELL. That is not entirely correct. While in Japan I served on two joint boards of the Army, Navy, Air Force, and Marine Corps, which processed the results of the interviews and interrogations of all the American prisoners of war who were returned to Japan and all of the United Nations prisoners of war who were returned, with the exception of the British.

Mr. KENNEDY. Then you have examined the records of all the prisoners of war other than the British; is that right?

Major PANELL. That is correct.

Mr. KENNEDY. Specifically were you working on the other United Nations troops who fought in Korea and were captured?

Major PANELL. No; I was not working specifically on that.

Mr. KENNEDY. You did work with their records.

Major PANELL. Right; and I did examine in detail the record of each returned United Nations prisoner of war.

Mr. KENNEDY. Will you give us the number which you have examined?

Major PANELL. During the first sick and wounded exchange there were approximately 14 Turkish prisoners. During the general prisoner exchange, referred to as "big switch," there were 299 Turkish prisoners returned, 40 Filipinos, 22 Colombians, 12 French, 2 Greeks, 2 Netherlanders, and 1 Belgique, a total of 307 prisoners other than United States and British.

Mr. KENNEDY. Did you find from an examination of their records that these prisoners were subjected to the same kind of indoctrination and interrogation that the United States prisoners were?

Major PANELL. As far as we could determine, all these prisoners were subjected to the same treatment, lived under the same conditions, and were subjected to the same indoctrination and interrogation procedures.

Mr. KENNEDY. Major, was there one particular group which stood out as far as resisting the interrogation and indoctrination of the Communists?

Major PANELL. There was. Actually I think there were 2 groups that stood out, although 1 group, the Turks, being in the number that they were, are the only one from which I think we can draw a comparison to the conduct of our own prisoners of war.

Mr. KENNEDY. What was the second group?

Major PANELL. The second group that I remember specifically were the 22 Colombians.

Mr. KENNEDY. They did very well also?

Major PANELL. Yes; as far as we could determine, in the degree of acceptance of indoctrination or cooperation.

Mr. KENNEDY. Would you tell us a little bit about what you found as far as the Turks were concerned?

Major PANELL. I said the Turks were subjected to the same conditions that our people were, and I think that is accurate. These 229 were captured in two increments. Roughly one-half of them were captured in November of 1950, and the second half were captured in April of 1951. So they were in prison with our people at the same time that we had a very high death rate. They were on the same so-called death marches that some of our people were on. During both experiences they had a very high survival rate. In fact, on one march it is alleged that we lost about a man a mile, as it was referred to. I think it was about a 90-mile march, and about 90 Americans died during the course of this march. I believe there were approximately 900 Americans in that group, so approximately 10 percent of them died during the course of the march. There were 100 Turks who made the same march, and no Turk died.

Also I might mention that, although I do not have any specific figures, the large majority of the Turkish prisoners who were captured were wounded. Although I have nothing to compare it to, I believe probably a larger percentage were wounded than our own people.

Mr. KENNEDY. They were wounded prior to capture? Is that the point?

Major PANELL. Yes. After both groups went into temporary camps where we had a very high death rate between October of 1950 and, I believe, approximately the 1st of September 1951, no Turk died or is known to have died during that time, although at one camp it was reported by various prisoners that we had about 1,600 Americans die in that one camp. I think this can be attributed to several factors. One is that the Turks were possibly in better physical condition than our people. Their unit was no doubt one of their best because it was a brigade which represented their country, whereas we had initially in Korea the troops that were immediately available, that had to be pulled out of other duty, occupation in Japan, and put in piecemeal into Korea. It was from this group that the majority of our people were captured.

The CHAIRMAN. Major, have we learned the lesson to keep our men trained and to keep them in physical condition?

Major PANELL. I hope we have.

The CHAIRMAN. Were they in this instance?

Major PANELL. Initially I don't believe they were, sir.

The CHAIRMAN. So you attribute part of the loss of life to that very fact.

Major PANELL. I think there is no doubt about it.

Mr. KENNEDY. Is there any other factor that you want to mention in connection with that?

Major PANELL. Yes. The Turks had a very high esprit de corps. They were very much concerned with the health and welfare of each other. If one Turk happened to get sick he was babied and nursed back to health by his fellow prisoners.

Another thing is that they live in their army under a very rigid disciplinary system whereby the line of authority goes from the top down to the lowest man. Whoever happens to be the ranking individual in the group assumes command, and there is no question about it. Although the group may be all privates, the man who has been in the army the longest or the oldest person, one of them assumes command and the other people recognize that command authority.

A little bit of it may be attributed to the fact that these people knew that if they didn't follow the orders of this individual in charge, when and if they were repatriated they would have to answer for their failure to do so.

Another factor, I think, is the fact that in their own country they had probably lived a little closer to the earth than we had, for instance. Because their native life is a little more primitive generally than ours, I think maybe they are just a little bit more rugged. They recognized the fact that they could supplement the diet which Dr. Anderson mentioned. They supplemented it by boiling various herbs, weeds, and so forth, which I think possibly contributed to their high survival rate.

They were subjected to the same indoctrination program. They attended forced indoctrination lectures. There was a language barrier. As far as we could determine, the Chinese had only one well qualified, fluent Turkish linguist, who was of Turkish descent and whom the Turks had very little respect for. Apparently they paid no attention to his lectures. He didn't accomplish much. As far as could be determined, they didn't accept to any appreciable degree the ideology that was being preached.

It must be kept in mind also that this whole program was more a hate-America campaign, and certainly it was not a hate Turkey program. So they might have had a little less interest in it than our people.

Mr. KENNEDY. Was their degree of cooperation or collaboration, or whatever word you wish to use, with the Chinese Communists or the North Korean Communists slight or negligible?

Major PANELL. There were two Turkish prisoners who were accused fairly universally by their own fellow prisoners of having cooperated.

Mr. KENNEDY. Just two out of the group?

Major PANELL. There were a few more who were accused by one or two individuals, but universally only two.

Mr. KENNEDY. What was the degree of cooperation that these two had given to the Communists?

Major PANELL. These people participated in the preparation of a petition. Actually we considered it pretty minor. They signed a statement, a sort of self-criticism statement, in which certain derogatory or uncomplimentary remarks were aimed at their Government. It was something that I certainly would not generally consider to be very serious. However, after reading this before the assembled Turkish prisoners, these two were completely ostracized by the group.

Mr. KENNEDY. By the rest of the Turks?

Major PANELL. By the rest of the Turks. When they were repatriated, after they were brought back to Tokyo, these two particular Turks asked for and received from the Americans protective custody against their own fellow prisoners. They were repatriated to Turkey. At least they got on the ship and started to Turkey and I have often wondered if they did get back to Turkey.

Mr. KENNEDY. There was that much hatred and feeling toward those acts on the part of the rest of the prisoners.

Major PANELL. That is right.

Mr. KENNEDY. To what do you attribute that, Major?

Major PANELL. Of course their discipline and their esprit de corps certainly were factors. Another thing. They had lived next door to communism. Possibly they didn't know too much about it from the theoretical standpoint, but certainly they had seen it in operation. They had no use for it. I think those were the primary factors. They just did not buy it.

While the Turks were incarcerated they pretty well flaunted the authority of the Chinese captors. They broke rules. They refused to obey actually pretty reasonable requests. They just refused to cooperate in any way, to the degree that eventually the attendants left them pretty much alone. In fact, I think it was generally believed that they were a little bit afraid of them because they stuck together as a group and resisted as a group. A lot of them underwent a degree of punishment, having to stand out and face the sun for a long period of time, or stand on rocks or sticks or stand out in the cold, and so forth. Things that are commonly referred to as brutality were inflicted on them for breaking the camp rules and regulations.

The other group that made an impression on me was the group of Colombians, although there were only 22, certainly not enough to make an accurate comparison with the Americans or the British or any other large group. There again of course there was a little bit of a language barrier because these were Spanish-speaking people, and the Chinese had few, if any, fluent Spanish linguists to deal with these people. So they had to rely on English-speaking Filipinos or in some cases some of our people who also spoke Spanish, to relay their messages to these Colombians.

These people were 100 percent devout Catholics. From all appearances they did not succumb to the indoctrination and seemed to hold on to their religious beliefs, which I believe certainly was a factor, and I believe that any person who had a similar belief or hold on anything would have resisted equally well. The result would have been the same with any person with strong family ties or any person who was strongly patriotic. Their lack of cooperation was certainly noticeable.

Mr. KENNEDY. Major, from examining the files of our troops and also those of the Turks and Colombians who had resisted, did you come back with any ideas as to our training or as to what could be or should be done in the field?

Major PANELL. Yes, I think I did. I think anyone in the same circumstances would have. I believe a lot of our people who were captured initially had no strong unit identifications. They had been in the unit for a small period of time and hadn't had an opportunity to train on maneuvers and really become a part of the team. During the last war and up to the Korean conflict we have used a system of individual replacements within the unit, so eventually there is nobody left in the unit who was in it originally. They don't become attached to the unit, as do the Turks and the British, for instance, who use a unit rotation system. Since that time, as is commonly known, we have adopted the divisional and large unit rotation system. When we replace a division overseas, we replace it with an entirely new division and bring the old division back to the States, which I think is partly an outgrowth of our experience in Korea. I think it will aid immeasurably in creating the pride of unit and strong unit identification.

Mr. KENNEDY. Having some attachment to some person or some group or organization, or whatever it might be, you think is a major factor.

Major PANELL. Yes, I do.

Mr. KENNEDY. Have you anything else on this whole situation?

Major PANELL. No, I have not.

The CHAIRMAN. Thank you very much, Major.

[. . . . .]

EXHIBIT NO. 18: COMMUNIST PATTERNS OF
COERCIVE INTERROGATION

By Albert D. Biderman, Intelligence Methods Branch, Air Force Personnel and Training Research Center, Air Research and Development Command, Maxwell Air Force Base, Ala., April 1955.

Introduction

Terror is a paramount Communist weapon of conquest and control. A major objective of the Communists is to create the fear in the minds of their opponents that they possess mysterious, irresistible techniques for bending individuals to their will. Speculations about the extortion of false "bacteriological warfare confessions" from American airmen in Korea and about similar events have helped foster this fear. Labels such as "brain washing" and "menticide" reinforce the impressions of mystery and awe relating to Communist techniques of coercion.

In actuality, the means by which Communists extort false confessions or other compliance from persons under their power are neither new, mysterious, nor always irresistible. The various devices of coercive interrogation employed by the Communists have been known and used for centuries. They are based primarily on simple, easily understandable ideas of how an individual's physical and moral strength can be undermined, rather than upon subtle or startling psychological theories, Pavlovian or otherwise. Without ever capitulating, numerous individuals have withstood for months and even years the most determined Communist efforts to wring false statements from them and have survived to tell of their experiences.

This does not mean that men who have capitulated to such coercion, even after very short periods of time and seemingly slight duress, are weaklings, cowards, or fools. Cases of completely successful resistance to the most skilled and determined coercive interrogation represent spectacular feats of courage, endurance, and resolution. Not infrequently, extraordinary intelligence and insight have contributed as well. Sometimes, however, successful resistance is attributable as much to blunders of the inquisitors as to the singular strengths of the victim. For despite the fact that the Communists apply measures for inducing compliance in a more artfully calculated manner than has been encountered before, they are neither all-knowing nor all-powerful even when dealing with a seemingly powerless victim.

The impression that the Communist coercive methods create a zombie-like creature is a false one. Victims are not stripped of all independent will, of consciousness of what they are being forced to do, or of all ability to continue attempts at resisting and evading the demands of their captors. Men are seldom "broken," as in theory a horse can be, so that they cease all attempts at resisting the demands of their masters. Their physical and moral strength may be so enfeebled that the amount of resistance and evasion to successive demands may appear insignificant in relation to the enormity of the acts they are compelled to commit. But however feeble the ability, the will to resist remains and reasserts itself as strength and means are found. Thus, one of the Air Force officers whom the Chinese Communists exploited most extensively for bacteriological warfare propaganda can be seen in the Communist film of his "confession" indicating to the world, by gesture, that he has his "tongue in his cheek." A recent analysis of the notorious Soviet purge trials of the late 1930's provides an extensive analysis of the veiled language the victims used in their "confessions" and in cross-examination to communicate what their real thoughts and feelings were.[1]

There are several reasons for stating the above considerations, and for giving the description of Communist coercive methods which follows.

First of all, false notions should be combated which exaggerate the power of Communists over men and which contribute to the terror on which the Communists rely.

Secondly, the aura of mystery and dread which has long been associated with these methods is in itself a major factor in their effectiveness. The anxieties the victim may already have at the moment of his capture, from what he has heard about "brain washing" and the like, may be sufficient in themselves to weaken his ability to resist, with no particular effort from his captor needed. Disseminating realistic information may thus aid any who may fall into Communist hands in the future.

Thirdly, this is indeed a matter in which "to be forewarned is to be forearmed." The Communists place great reliance on the poor under-

---

[1] Nathan Leites and Elsa Bernaut, *Ritual of Liquidation* (Glencoe, Ill., The Free Press, 1954).

standing of the victim of what is happening to him. Deceiving, tricking, and confusing the victim are important. It is also significant that certain individuals have maintained their moral strength under Communist interrogation and in similar stress situations by virtue of their ability to understand their experiences in a detached manner.[2]

The description of Communist coercive methods, below, attempts to contribute to an understanding of the measures used by Communists to induce compliance from an individual prisoner. It is possible to do this since Communists, the world over, utilize a mode of pressuring the individual which is identical in its essentials and even in many of its details wherever and whenever used. Its application varies only slightly from place to place, from time to time, and from objective to objective. Soviet Russian secret police, Chinese Communist interrogators in Korea, and satellite purge trial "investigators" have all employed essentially similar methods. Slight variations make the techniques adaptable to such objectives as: extracting information from reluctant POW, extorting "confessions of guilt," making forced laborers more tractable, converting honest men into spies and false informers, or keeping domestic populations in line.

The dispassionate, generalized kind of description attempted here cannot substitute for the appreciation of the feelings experienced by a victim which only the personal accounts of the most insightful, honest, and eloquent victims provide. For anyone whose life involves the potential hazard of falling into Communist captivity, as is true of all Air Force combat personnel, the reading of such an account is recommended.[3] Not recommended are accounts motivated by desires for self-justification and self-glorification, or laden with bitterness, vengeance, and propaganda, as many unfortunately but understandably are.

For the present purposes, different emphasis are required than in treatments of the same subject which aim primarily at informing the world of the monstrous barbarity of the Communist system. Probably no other aspect of communism reveals more thoroughly its disrespect for truth and the individual than its resort to these techniques. This, at the same time, is a demonstration of the fundamental weakness and insecurity of the

---

[2] Good examples are: Alexander Weissberg, *The Accused* (New York, Simon & Schuster, 1951); Anton Ciliga, *The Russian Enigma* (London, Labour Book Service, 1940); Elie A. Cohen, *Human Behavior in the Concentration Camp* (New York, W. W. Norton & Co., 1953); Bruno Bettelheim, "Individual and Mass Behavior in Extreme Situations," *Journal of Abnormal and Social Psychology*, XXXVIII (1943), 417–452. A view contrary to that expressed here is held by some former victims. See, for example, Gustav Herling, *A World Apart* (New York, Roy Publishers, 1951), p. 91.

[3] See works cited above, as well as the following: Maj. Gen. William F. Dean, *General Dean's Story* (New York, Viking Press, 1954); F. Beck and W. Godin, *Russian Purge and the Extraction of Confession* (New York, Viking Press, 1951); Z. Stypulkowski, *Invitation to Moscow* (London, Thames and Hudson, 1951).

Communist enemy — his unprecedented need to coerce the individual will, to falsify truth, and to attempt to reshape it and the individual man into that mythical world in which communism alone could thrive. No more important purpose could be served than to bring these facts home to the peoples of the world. To do this, the most brutal, ugly, and insane examples ought to be portrayed vividly.

This study, however, seeks to show that Communist attempts at individual coercion can be and ought to be resisted, and it is hoped that this paper will provide information which may help future victims resist. One important principle that requires emphasis here is that Communist purposefulness frequently limits Communist brutality. Although the Communists will attempt to utilize the anxiety which their notorious brutality has almost universally instilled, many interrogation victims will never be physically exposed to violence, even though they refuse to capitulate. The reasons for this vary, but an important one is that the Communists have learned that physical violence more frequently than not stiffens the resistance of the American prisoner, rather than the reverse.

Another significant principle which should be emphasized here is that communism assumes many disguises. At various times and places, it may seek to achieve its purposes by representing itself as a kindly, solicitous, smiling creature — at others, it may wantonly display its brutality in all its nakedness. Some prisoners have encountered communism in both guises; others in only one or the other. Many have been impressed by its abilities as a quick-change artist. Anyone falling into its hands should be well prepared to encounter communism in any of the forms it assumes — not even excluding indignant denials that it is communism at all.

The outline below is restricted to those measures which are used to undermine the resistance of the victim. This omits the positive, primarily verbal, measures which are used to fashion the victim's compliance in the manner desired for particular objectives; i. e., the verbal content of the interrogations themselves. A more extensive treatment than is possible here would be required to depict the plays on meanings, the verbal tricks and traps, the endless repetition of questions, the special language of Communist interrogation.

The material presented here is an outgrowth of a larger classified study of Communist exploitation of USAF prisoners of war being conducted jointly by the Officer Education Research Laboratory of the Air Force Personnel and Training Research Center and by the Evaluation Staff of the Air War College. While considerable reliance in preparing this outline has been placed upon the reports by USAF personnel who were POWs of the Communists in Korea and Manchuria, a rather extensive review has also been made of the experiences of others who have been subjected to Communist coercive interrogations. Included were accounts by World War II POWs of the Soviets, Soviet and satellite purge trial victims, and slave laborers. While this review indicated that the full repertoire of exploitative techniques was used against Americans during the Korean war, relatively few POWs encountered them in their most skilled, intensive, and refined form. The North Koreans had comparatively few trained personnel for the effort. The Chinese Communists during the later stages of war were in some respects restrained in their methods by the likelihood of a truce and the necessity for repatriating prisoners.

It is likely that Americans who fall into Communist hands in the future will encounter captors who are better prepared. Perhaps the captives, too will be better prepared to thwart the captor.

Outline of Basic Communist Techniques of Coercive Interrogation

The major categories below are each essential elements of the Communist techniques for forcing false confessions, "self-criticisms," information, and other collaboration from reluctant prisoners. The major purposes believed to underlie the use of each element is given. Each general technique may take one or several of the various forms indicated. Almost all victims will encounter every one of the general techniques in some form or other. The success of the entire interrogation, however, frequently depends upon the careful combination of the specific kinds of stress into a pattern adapted to the particular victim and the particular objective. The selection and timing of the specific forms of the techniques are varied— apparently in accordance with estimates of the temperament and weaknesses of the subject, the nature and degree of his resistance, the character of his interrogator, the significance and urgency of the collaboration sought, and variations from time to time and place to place with regard to the overall policies governing the treatment of prisoners. Both the prisoner's compliance and the cessation of the interrogation process without any compliance have occurred after the application of only the mildest of these measures. On the other hand, many prisoners have had "the whole book thrown at them."

1. *Isolation*   Purposes: To develop an intense concern with self; to make the victim dependent on the interrogator; to eliminate support of the victim's resistance, including mutual encouragement, praise, and blame from his fellows in terms of the moral standards of his own group.

(*a*) Complete solitary confinement: The prisoner is held for a prolonged period with no social contact whatsoever — not even with enemy personnel.

(*b*) Complete isolation: The prisoner is held with no contact with his fellows. The prisoner may live alone or together with his interrogator or with a guard.

(*c*) Semi-isolation: Two prisoners (less frequently, 3 or 4) under similar pressure are isolated from all others for prolonged periods. Frequently, one of the pair is regarded as more disposed to capitulation and hence likely to influence his partner in that direction.

(*d*) Group isolation: Small groups of prisoners (8 to 30) are held under extremely crowded and difficult conditions, with no communication outside the group. Individual prisoners are periodically pulled out for periods of intensive interrogation in complete isolation. Scarcity of space, food, and clothing are calculated to promote destructive competition and dissension among the group. Frequently, harsh punishments are inflicted for "violations of rules," which not only are expected to condition cooperation but are also calculated to alienate the members of the group from one another and to provoke fear of informers.

2. *Monopolization of Attention*   Purposes: to fix the prisoner's attention upon his immediate predicament and discomforts.

(*a*) Physical isolation: The prisoner is held in a small, bare, windowless cell — sometimes in complete darkness.

(*b*) Other restrictions of sensory stimulation: The captors strive for control over the sights, sounds, and feelings that the prisoner experiences. Potentially gratifying or diverting sensations are reduced by denying the victim materials for reading, writing, or diversion; restricting the pleasure of movement by forbidding exercise or even, in some cases, any deviations from a fixed posture; serving monotonous food; etc. Exceptions are experiences which may orient the thoughts of the victim in accordance with some Communist purpose. Examples are the provision of the prisoner with Communist reading material as the only escape from boredom or worry; the hearing of real or feigned cries of anguish of another victim; a visit from a "friendly" interrogator; etc.

(*c*) Prolonged interrogation and forced writing: The thought and attention of the prisoner are concentrated in the manner sought by the captor through prolonged interrogation and through forced writing and rewriting of answers to very general questions. (See also 3 (*f*), below.)

3. *Induced Debilitation, Exhaustion*   Purposes: To weaken mental and physical ability to resist.

(*a*) Semistarvation: Rations restricted to minimum necessary to maintain life.

(*b*) Exposure: Subjection to intense cold, intense heat, or dampness.

(*c*) Exploitation of wounds and induced chronic illness: Dysentery, colds, skin disorders, and other chronic illnesses which do not present immediate threats to the life of the prisoner are allowed to progress unchecked to keep the individual in a state of intense discomfort and debilitation. Wounded prisoners may be told they can be treated only after completing the interrogation.

(*d*) Sleep deprivation: The victim is robbed of sleep when he is forced to attempt to rest in uncomfortable positions, with a minimum of protection from cold, and on a hard, vermin-infested floor or platform. Sleep is frequently interrupted by waking prisoners for interrogation or a "bed-check."

(e) Prolonged constraint: Long periods of forced sitting or standing at attention or in other strained positions; confinement in a box, hole, or shackles permitting only painful, unnatural postures.

(f) Prolonged interrogation or forced writing: Persistent interrogation for many hours each day over a period of weeks or months; round-the-clock "conveyor belt" interrogation by successive interrogators; weary-ing, forced writing and rewriting of answers to interminable repetitious questions. (See also 2(c), above.)

4. *The Cultivation of Anxiety and Despair*   Purposes: To develop dis-organized and irrational responses; to make compliance appear trivial in relation to the victim's peril; to make eventual compliance appear in-evitable, with not even death possible as an avenue of escape. (See also 5, below.)

(a) Threats of death: In addition to verbal threats, prisoners are forced to dig their own graves; undergo or observe fake executions; and to endure trial and sentencing to death by fake tribunals.

(b) Threats of nonrepatriation: Prisoners are told they will never be repatriated unless they comply.

(c) Threats of punishment as a "war criminal": Prisoners are told that they will be considered "war criminals" until they comply; that they will be tried as "war criminals"; that they will be turned over to the civilian population for punishment.

(d) Threats of endless isolation: Prisoners are told that the interrogators are not in a hurry; that they will be held continuously in isolation and con-stantly interrogated until they capitulate.

(e) Vague threats: Threats may sometimes be vague, either when the interrogator is veiling his threats in an attempt to maintain the fiction that he has a benevolent interest in the prisoner, or when he is attempting to convey the impression that a fate more terrible than words can express is in store for the prisoner if he persists in resisting.

(f) Threats against prisoner's family: Some Korean war prisoners were told that injury would be inflicted on their families by the Communist underground in the United States if they did not cooperate.

(g) Mysterious changes of treatment or place of confinement: The POW may frequently be moved from place to place, either temporarily or permanently ("with belongings") with no explanation as to the reason for the move. The objective appears to be to make the prisoner anxious regarding the consequences of the move. Great changes in treatment occur for no apparent reason.

(h) Changes in questioning and interrogators: Interrogations frequently take new and puzzling directions. Interrogators may frequently be changed.

5. *Alternating Punishments and Rewards*   Purposes: To "condition" the victim to comply; to hinder adjustment to privation; to indicate possibilities of "a happy future" in captivity.

(*a*) Occasional "favors": Almost never do the Communists allow the treatment of the prisoner to be completely negative in tone for any long period of time. Even when the most extreme deprivations are being inflicted, the prisoner may well receive his customary tobacco ration; a surprisingly good meal; some liquor in celebration of an American holiday; solicitous inquiries from his tormentor; etc. The intent is probably to convince the prisoner that the Communists are really "good people," to remind him of how pleasant things can be, and to prevent him from completing an adjustment to "doing without" various comforts.

(*b*) Extreme fluctuations of interrogators' attitudes: Interrogators will frequently switch from a calm or kindly manner to violent excoriations of the prisoner. Frequently, different interrogators will take different attitudes. One, sometimes appearing as of higher authority, will pretend to be the prisoner's benefactor who does not quite approve of the methods of his subordinates.

(*c*) Promises of improved conditions: Prisoners are told that they will be given regular POW status, that their isolation will end, that they will receive mail, good food, medical attention, etc., if they comply with the interrogator's demands.

(*d*) Special promises: POW may be promised special jobs or privileged status as rewards for cooperation.

(*e*) Rewards given for partial compliance: Most improvements of the prisoner's conditions are represented as a reward for cooperativeness. Short of complete capitulation, and generally even then, rewards are trivial — cigarettes, a blanket, somewhat better food, or merely a good word from the interrogator.

(*f*) Tantalizing: Prisoners may be shown rewards (e. g., good food, pictures of other POWs at play, or a well-fed and well-groomed POW may be brought in), which they are told will be given to them if they cooperate. Cigarettes may be given in quantity, but matches withheld. Tasty food may be given, but in miniscule quantities.

6. *Demonstrating "Omnipotence" and "Omniscience" of Captor*   Purpose: To suggest futility of resistance.

(*a*) "Omniscience": Painstaking efforts are made to collect minute facts about the prisoner, his unit, his friends, and his previous life, generally. This information is fed to the prisoner to bolster the interrogator's assertions: "We know all about you!" Useful information for this purpose is gained from fellow prisoners; information given by the prisoner himself in previous interrogations and questionnaires; letters the POW has written or received; and United States newspapers and radio broadcasts. The interrogators attempt to create the impression that they already know the answers to all the questions they ask and that the interrogation is "a test of the cooperativeness and veracity of the prisoner." Subjects are constantly accused of lying and being caught in lies.

(*b*) "Omnipotence": The prisoner is shown evidence, real or false, that other POWs have capitulated — especially those with whom the subject is acquainted. Other POWs may be forced to tell him that resistance is futile. Interrogators behave at all times as if cooperativeness on the part of the subject is taken for granted. Refusals are reacted to with feigned surprise. Noncooperation is treated as a strange and foolish aberration. Interrogators may make frequent mention of the might of the Communists. Many heavily-armed guards are in evidence. Strict obedience to many rules is required of the prisoner. (See also 8, below.)

7. *Degradation*   Purposes: To make capitulation appear less damaging to self-pride than the indignities and debasement inflicted because of resistance; to reduce the prisoner to simple, "animal level" concerns.

(*a*) Personal hygiene prevented: Facilities for maintaining bodily cleanliness are withheld; combs and shaving equipment are taken away; in extreme instances the individual may be forced to live in his own filth.

(*b*) Filthy, infested surroundings: The problem of personal sanitation is aggravated by the deliberate choice of filthy, vermin- or rodent-infested places of confinement.

(*c*) Demeaning punishments: Slapping, ear-twisting, and other degrading, but physically mild, punishments may be inflicted.

(*d*) Insults and taunts: Interrogators verbally abuse the prisoner. An insult which appears to affect the prisoner will be repeated, e. g., information regarding the personal life of the prisoner which the interrogators possess from other sources will be distorted so as to cast aspersions against his own or his wife's morality; an ailment complained of may be falsely diagnosed as venereal disease.

(*e*) Denial of privacy: Prisoners may be subject to constant surveillance; if vulnerable to embarrassment, they may be forced to perform private functions in public.

8. *Enforcing Trivial and Absurd Demands*   Purpose: To develop habit of compliance.

(*a*) Forced writing: Most POWs are required to write and rewrite answers to numerous questions — frequently, exceedingly trivial questions. They are given only very general instructions and forced to rewrite answers over and over again until "an acceptable" version is completed. In this way, the tendency to seek to understand and satisfy the interrogator's wishes is fostered.

(*b*) Enforcing rules: Numerous rules are stipulated (and punishments are given for violations of rules which have never been stated). These rules may even include the position which is to be assumed when sleeping, the prisoner being awakened if he changes position. Permission may be required from the interrogator or guard for the performance of almost any act; to stand up, sit down, sit in the sun, wash, or go to the latrine.

(c) "Upping the ante": Either at the outset of an interrogation, or when faced with resistance to a consequential demand, the interrogators will pretend that all the prisoner needs to do to end the interrogation is to comply with a relatively trivial demand. In seeking a false confession, for example, the interrogator may ask a resistant prisoner to write a denial of the accusation, then successively more and more detailed denials, and finally, to eliminate all the negative statements in the denial, thus changing a "denial of charges" to a "confession of their truth." Similarly, in attempts to extract true information from prisoners who maintain a rigid silence, the interrogator indicates that no information is required from the prisoner, but that some simple statements are needed from him "for the record" or to "insure that you are a pilot and not really a spy," etc. The interrogator may plead with the prisoner not to remain endlessly in solitary confinement, or "be shot as a spy" because of such a trivial matter.

Supplementary Comments

Violence and Torture   Physical violence and torture have not been included in the above list, despite their frequent use by the Communists. This omission is intended to emphasize the fact that physical torture is not an essential part of the Communist repertoire. The available evidence suggests, in fact, that torture may intensify, rather than weaken, the resistance of the prisoner and that more skillful and experienced Communist interrogators avoid its use.

POWs of the Communists are apt to encounter physical violence as a coercive measure, however. This seems especially likely to occur (a) when a prisoner displays unusually intense fear when threatened with violence; or (b) when the interrogator is poorly trained, inexperienced, or sadistically inclined.

POWs of the North Koreans, especially in very early stages of the war, were more likely to encounter crude torture methods than the more calculated techniques described in the above outline.

Self-inflicted Pain   Increased understanding of the patterns described above can possibly be gained by noting one characteristic of these techniques: The emphasis in the pattern is on the individual doing things to himself, rather than on things being done to him.

The assertion that physical violence is not an essential element of these Communist techniques should be qualified accordingly. In a way, it would be more accurate to say that external violence — external torture — is not essential to the pattern, and in fact, seems to conflict with it. Self-inflicted torture is a frequent part of the pattern, however. Requiring the individual to stand at attention for extremely long periods or to assume other strained, painful positions is the typical form this takes.

Self-inflicted pain has distinct advantages for rendering the subject cooperative.

In the simple torture situation — the bamboo-splinters technique of popular imagination — the contest is clearly one between the individual and his tormentor. Can he endure pain beyond the point to which the interrogator is able to go in inflicting pain? The answer, from the standpoint of the interrogator, is all too frequently yes.

Where the individual is brought to inflict pain on himself, however, as when he stands for long periods at attention, an intervening factor is introduced. The immediate source of pain is not something the interrogator is doing to the victim, but something the victim is doing to himself. The contest becomes one of the individual against himself. The motivational strength of the individual is likely to exhaust itself in this internal struggle.

Bringing the subject to act against himself has other advantages to the interrogator. As long as the subject can be brought to do this, there is no showdown on the actual ability of the interrogator to injure the subject. Although a few former victims assert that they continue self-inflicted tortures out of pride, most have felt that something worse would happen to them if they disobeyed the interrogator's orders to assume some pain-producing position. More frequently than not, the extent to which the interrogator was willing or permitted to inflict physical punishment actually was very limited. In most of the Korean and Manchurian POW situations, it appears to have been limited to cuffs, slaps, and kicks. Frequently, it seems to have been limited to shouted threats and insults. Returnees who have undergone long periods of sitting or standing assert that no conceivable experience could be more excruciating.

A corresponding advantage of self-inflicted torture from the standpoint of the interrogator is that it is consistent with formal adherence to the mythical principles of legality and humaneness important to the Communists. These principles are important in the interrogation situation itself; for example, in facilitating the adoption of a positive attitude by the subject toward the interrogator and the forces he represents. Adherence to these principles protects the interrogator from potential punishment at some future time for mistreating prisoners. There also is considerable propaganda advantage when victims are released if to be truthful they must admit that no violence was actually used against them.

As a reading of the outline of coercive techniques will disclose, this emphasis on having the subject do things to himself, as against things being done to him, is not confined to the matter of physical punishment. The techniques, in general, seem to strive for a maximum enlistment of the subject's energies in the encounter. The environment of the prisoner is structured so that it is next to impossible for him to avoid thinking about things the interrogator wishes him to think about. He is led to ask himself the questions of fact that are of importance to the interrogator. He himself must figure out what his crime was. He is brought to develop in his own mind the consequences of continued resistance. His own pride is the measure of the degradation he suffers. And, as is explained later, his own guilt is likely to become the key factor in the outcome.

Ideological Appeals An almost universal feature of Communist interrogations is the frequent injection of political and moral arguments. Appeals are made for the cooperation of the prisoner on the seeming assumption that he accepts the Communist viewpoint of the matter at issue. Almost all interrogations feature attempts by the interrogator to arouse the class consciousness, the "love of peace," or some similar attitude of the prisoner as a basis for securing his cooperation. This aspect of interrogation is necessary to the Communists when a confession is sought for propaganda use, since the confession must include expressions of repentance and other ideological references to fit its propaganda objective. In the case of interrogations of American POWs by the Communists, when the interrogation objective was true information, the use of these Communist political appeals generally seemed to hinder the attainment of the objective. The alien political appeal generally intensified the prisoner's determination to resist. Not infrequently, it made the interrogator appear a ludicrous figure for believing in obvious absurdities.

Mind Reform It should be pointed out, however, that much of the interrogation which captives of the Communists experience is oriented toward gaining their total submission, rather than any single act of collaboration. As Communist interrogators put it: "You do not have the correct attitude. I am trying to help you adopt the correct attitude. You must change your attitude." The correct attitude, of course, involves viewing everything from the Communist political and moral perspective. It involves not only submitting to the expressed demands of Communist authority, but learning to act in terms of correct anticipations of what its demands will be. This is the broader concept of mind reform as it figures in the coercive interrogations of individuals. Analogous measures are applied to groups within Communist society and, through mass campaigns, to the society as a whole.

Much concern has been aroused by instances of victims of Communist coercion continuing to show an apparent acceptance of Communist political and moral beliefs for varying periods after they have been freed from coercion. Not even in cases where individuals had some earlier predisposition to Communist ideology is it readily comprehensible to many how these victims could have any feelings other than hatred for everything for which the perpetrators of the abominable outrages against them stood.

It is not the intention here to suggest that the behavior of these individuals, or human behavior, generally, is other than an exceedingly complex matter. Nonetheless, it is felt that a basic, readily understandable explanation of succumbing to mind reform exists. This is a principle upon which communism, and all states based upon terror, rely for whatever mobilization of the wills of their subjects they can secure. Communist terror confronts the individual with a choice between external punishment if he does or thinks what he regards as right, and internal punishment (guilt) if he begins to do or think as the Communists demand. One way out, of course, is for him to change his conscious ideas of what is right and wrong to accord with that of the Communists. The heavy emphasis in Communist coercive interrogation upon moral arguments attempts to provide the victim with a new moral justification for his behavior.

Paradoxically, the more morally outrageous the Communist demand, the more intense is the conflict for the individual when, as is almost inevitable under intense duress, he contemplates the possibility that he may be forced to comply. Similarly, the firmer the moral convictions of the victim, the greater is the internal torment during the effort to continue resistance.

In different cases, the moral rationalizations of unwilling compliance are of varying degrees of intensity. In some instances, reconciling the conflict may require only superficial rationalizations. In others, only by repressing intensely held values can the individual avoid what for him is intolerable self-reproach. How fundamental a self-delusion is required depends upon the nature of the demands made upon the victim by the Communists, upon the thoroughness and skill of the coercive tactics employed against him, and upon his own personality. Some have been able to regard each particular demand for collaboration separately and merely had to convince themselves that their submission was really of no particular consequence. Thus, some victims of pressure for false germ warfare confessions during the Korean conflict assured themselves that the confessions they gave the Communists were not really of any value and there was consequently nothing morally wrong with playing along to escape further duress. Others, faced with demands they could not regard as other than intensely repugnant, could not escape remorse through so easy a rationalization.

In the latter event, there were three possible outcomes. Some continued to draw sufficient strength from their self-esteem to continue resistance. Others, though brought to capitulate, were able to accept and live with their feelings of guilt. For others, only a reversal in consciousness of ideas of right or wrong could make their capitulation appear tolerable.

Recovery of true consciousness in the last type of case has frequently occurred as soon as the source of terror has been removed. In a very few cases, including the much publicized two most thoroughly brainwashed recently released by the Chinese Communists, recuperation is slower.

To the extent that the discussion here is sound, three kinds of solution to the individual's problem exist. Guilt can be minimized. Guilt can be accepted. Guilt can be avoided. All are possible. All are defensible.

Guilt can be minimized where the demands upon the individual are indeed of trivial importance in relation to the costs of resistance. Not infrequently, demands made by the Communists can legitimately be regarded as such. As has been pointed out above, pressing trivial demands is one of the Communist techniques. Vainglorious behavior in such circumstances may eventuate in inglorious consequences. When demands are not trivial, guilt can also be reduced by the recognition that better men than oneself have had to bend before Communist pressures.

Judgments of one's own behavior are made in terms of one's own standards, however. Where an individual feels that he has yielded too much or too readily, and feels compelled to judge himself harshly in terms of his standards, insight into the dangers of deluding himself to escape this judgment may help protect him from a more devastating outcome.

The most desirable solution for the individual, and for what he represents, is the avoidance of guilt by resisting all efforts to force him into behavior contrary to his beliefs.

This paper assumes that an understanding of both the external and internal pressures it has sought to describe will increase the ability of captives of the Communists to attain this most desirable solution.

3.

The Small Farm

THIS IS AN ERA OF SOCIAL CHANGE. TECHNOLOGICAL INNO-
vations have transformed the means of production,
transportation, and communication. Corresponding modifications have developed in related social behavior. Social
innovations, however, are often more difficult to accept
than technological changes. Resistance to change can be
found in the many social forms that persist in the face of
apparent obsolescence and the threat of economic failure.
The status of the family-sized farm on the current American
scene illustrates many of the major forms of resistance to
change.

The men who maintain small farms find themselves confronted by a paradox: apparently government regulation is
needed to preserve an autonomous way of life. There is the
traditional belief in the farm as being the best place to raise
children, yet there is no future for the children on the farms.
Conflicts and compromises characterize the adjustments. As
cities expand and means of transportation improve, many
farmers find it necessary and possible to take jobs in industrial
centers and become only part-time farmers. Such adjustments
give rise to the conflict between the values of organization

into unions for the industrial worker and the tradition of the autonomy and self-sufficiency of the farmer.

In studying the family farm, it is clear that the psychology of adjustment to change, the integration of value conflicts, and the importance of the emotional meaning of farming are as significant as more abstract economic considerations.

Suggested Discussion Questions

Why do farm families leave their holdings? What are the problems that confront the small farmer as he sees them? With what socio-economic class does the small farmer identify, or with which class do his values seem to be most congruent? What status position do farmers hold in the general national community? How does such a status position integrate with the farmers' values? What status mobility patterns are there? Are the farms failing because of the personal inadequacies of the farmers? Why do children want to be farmers even when they see their parents failing?

THE FAMILY-SIZE FARM

REPORT *of the Subcommittee on Family Farms of the Committee on Agriculture, House of Representatives, 84th Congress, Second Session*

AUGUST 1, 1956

Washington, D.C.

AMERICA'S HERITAGE

The free-enterprise system grew out of an early dream of a nation sustained chiefly by and for devout, free, independent, and home-owning farmers.

With its roots planted in this dream, the United States has become the envy of the world, in its strength, love of liberty, and in its standard of living. Whether such a nation might have grown from a different beginning can be answered only in the failure of history to disclose a comparable triumph of human vision and longings elsewhere or under other conditions and circumstances.

All students of the growth of the American civilization seem in agreement that the family farm established the economic foundation for the liberties and the enterprise, and the national conscience, that are the heritage of the United States.

The relationship of the family farm and the character of the American Government was well stated by Daniel Webster, who said:

Our New England ancestors brought thither no great capitals from Europe; and if they had, there was nothing productive in which they could have been invested. They left behind them the whole feudal policy of the other continent. [. . .] They came to a new country. There were as yet no lands yielding rent, and no tenants rendering service. The whole soil was unreclaimed from barbarism. They were themselves either from their original condition or from the necessity of their common interest, nearly on a level in respect to property. Their situation demanded a parceling out and division of the land, and it may fairly be said that this necessary act fixed the future frame and form of their government. The character of their political institutions was determined by the fundamental laws respecting property. [. . .] The consequence of all these causes has been a great subdivision of the soil and a great quality of condition; the true basis, most certainly, of popular government.

Disturbing reports have come from the broad agricultural domain of America, telling of increasing numbers of farm families leaving the soil because of the deterioration of their competitive position, with their acreages becoming consolidated by purchase into larger holdings where hired labor supplants the family unit enterprise.

Believing this to be the concern of the Congress and of all the people, Chairman Harold D. Cooley of the House Committee on Agriculture on August 5, 1955, appointed a Family Farms Subcommittee, under the chairmanship of Representative Clark W. Thompson of Texas, and he assigned this subcommittee this specific duty:

To make a special study of the ways and means to protect, foster, and promote the family farm as the continuing dominant unit in American agriculture, with special attention to the manner in which we can adjust our farm programs to accommodate the convenience, productivity, and prosperity of the family farm unit.

This is the final report of the Family Farms Subcommittee to the 84th Congress.

Scope of Study

The subcommittee went directly to farmers to hear in their own locations and in their own words the cause of their distress and the extent of their thoughts that might suggest remedy.

For this on-the-ground study the areas where the problem is now more acute were selected. Traveling some 3,000 miles, most of this across country by bus, the subcommittee held sessions at Hallettsville, Tex.; LaGrange, Tex.; Texas A. & M. College at College Station; Louisiana State University at Baton Rouge; at Troy, Ala.; Fulton, Miss.; Pulaski, Tenn.; Raleigh, N. C.; and at Abingdon, Va. There were special conferences with farmers and their leaders at Schulenburg, Tex.; Columbus, Miss.; Andalusia,

Ala.; Greenville, Ala.; Town Creek, Ala.; and at Virginia Polytechnic Institute, Blacksburg, Va.

The subcommittee in effect took the Congress to the small farmers and to others interested in their problems who cannot come to Washington to tell their story and present their views.

Subsequently, the subcommittee held hearings in Washington, to receive the views and suggestions of the general farm organizations on family farm problems.

Statement

From the direct association of its members with farmers, in these rural travels, from the hearings in Washington, from study of information in the Department of Agriculture and of other inquiries into the problem, and from an awareness of the source of the Nation's vitality in its beginning and growth, this Subcommittee on Family Farms finds:

1. There is a deterioration of the economic structure of the family farm, already manifest in the disappearance of thousands of small family-operated farm units.

2. Remedy will require action by the Federal Government, in close cooperation with farmers and their organization and community leaders.

3. The answer ultimately must be the decision of the American people — urban and rural people alike — on the fundamental question whether the Nation can afford to risk the consequences of a decadence of the basic rural system that pioneered and for so long a time has nourished the American economic, social, and political order.

This subcommittee impresses particularly upon all thoughtful persons, in these circumstances, the place of the family farm in the free enterprise system.

Small, independent business is in a relative position.

FREE ENTERPRISE

It is appropriate then to stress that the free enterprise system, in the natural aspirations for individual achievement by a free people, has two prime motivations. They are:

1. Profit, which is a primary dimension of the individual and family standard of living.

2. The hope of people working for others, particularly those of

younger ages, that with diligence and frugality some day they may own their own farms or their own businesses. This is an American aspect of every man's desire to be his own boss.

This subcommittee is convinced that by the proportion the Nation permits a lessening of the number of opportunities for venture into individual enterprises — for one to own his own farm or his own business — then by an even larger measure will the free enterprise system be weakened. Free enterprise is the spirit of the frontier. The frontier must be kept open for men to venture into, and to achieve independence in, individual and family enterprises.

The self-interest of those who have a stake in the American system — and that is all Americans — requires this.

SPIRITUAL, SOCIAL, AND POLITICAL VITALITY

Moreover, this subcommittee by its intimate studies is persuaded that, beyond all other notice and regard, the agricultural order in the family unit pattern must be considered especially for the spiritual, social, and political vitality it has contributed to our civilization.

A lessening of this vitality already is manifest in the shapes of an alarming growth in juvenile delinquency in urban areas, of crime, of the disappearance of many rural churches, of decaying little towns, or neglect of community loyalties and pride, and perhaps a lack in many places of the full satisfaction of a free trade in friendship and common purpose.

The Committee for Economic Development, an organization of the Nation's top business leaders, has this to say:

America came to greatness from her "grassroots," and it is from life in small communities that strength must continue to flow and nourish our country toward greater accomplishment which can be shared by all. The hope of America is not that our huge cities shall become more vast — it is rather that the small communities shall consolidate their opportunities to grow and become better, more interesting places for our people to live in and prosper. In the final analysis, our Nation is just one community added to another until the splendid total makes us what we are.

Much valuable information was accumulated by subcommittee members, during their travels, through personal conversations not reflected in the record, but incident to meetings in the various communities.

In Texas it was noted that many clergymen were in attendance.

They seemed particularly aware of the problems of the family farmers, and several testified beneficially. When a committee member remarked to a clergyman that it was gratifying to note their interest, the clergyman replied that his church regarded it as of paramount importance to keep its members in rural communities. Here, he said, family and home life flourish without the distractions of the big cities. Here young people are raised in healthful family environments. Here the men of the family were not apt to join in activities of a kind which, although they might be necessary to city life, would weaken the bond between a pastor and his parishioners.

The Special Committee to Study Problems of American Small Business, created by the 79th Congress, studied the family farm in its relationship to free enterprise and its influences upon community life and the democratic institutions. The summary and findings of the special committee are deeply related to the studies of this Family Farms Subcommittee, and merit a place in the body of this report. This matter follows:

Whether industrialization of farming is a threat not only to the family farm, but also to the rural society founded upon the family farm, is the specific subject of the present report. The purpose of this study is to test by contemporary field research the historic hypothesis that the institution of small independent farmers is indeed the agent which creates the homogeneous community, both socially and economically democratic.

The present inquiry consists of a detailed analysis and comparison of two communities, one where agricultural operations are on a modest scale, the other where large factory-like techniques are practiced. Both communities lie in the fertile southern San Joaquin Valley in the great Central Valley of California, where highly developed and richly productive agriculture is characteristic. Limitations of time and resources dictated that no more than two communities be studied. Numerous other pairs might have been chosen which doubtless would have yielded comparable results.

The two communities studied here naturally vary in some degree with respect to proportions of surrounding lands devoted to this or that crop, with respect to age, to depth of water lift for irrigation, etc., as well as with respect to the scale of the farm enterprises which surround them. Controls as perfect as are possible in the chemist's laboratory are not found in social organizations. Yet the approximation to complete control achieved by selection of the communities of Arvin and Dinuba is surprisingly high. Other factors, besides the difference in scale of farming, which might have produced or contributed to the striking contrasts of Arvin and Dinuba have been carefully examined. On this basis the conclusion has been reached that the primary, and by all odds the factor of greatest weight in producing the essential differences in these two communities, was the characteristic difference in the scale of farming — large or small — upon which each was founded. There is every reason to believe that the results obtained by this study are generally applicable wherever like economic conditions prevail.

Certain conclusions are particularly significant to the small-business man, and to an understanding of the importance of his place in a community. Not only does the small farm itself constitute small business, but it supports flourishing small commercial business.

Analysis of the business conditions in the communities of Arvin and Dinuba shows that:

1. The small-farm community supported 62 separate business establishments, to but 35 in the large-farm community: a ratio in favor of the small-farm community of nearly 2 to 1.

2. The volume of retail trade in the small-farm community during the 12-month period analyzed was $4,383,000 as against only $2,535,000 in the large-farm community. Retail trade in the small-farm community was greater by 61 percent.

3. The expenditure for household supplies and building equipment was over three times as great in the small-farm community as it was in the large-farm community.

The investigation disclosed other vast differences in the economic and social life of the two communities, and affords strong support for the belief that small farms provide the basis for a richer community life and a greater sum of those values for which America stands, than do industrialized farms of the usual type.

It was found that:

4. The small farm supports in the local community a larger number of people per dollar volume of agricultural production than an area devoted to larger scale enterprises, a difference in its favor of about 20 percent.

5. Notwithstanding their greater numbers, people in the small-farm community have a better average standard of living than those living in the community of large-scale farms.

6. Over one-half of the breadwinners in the small-farm community are independently employed businessmen, persons in white-collar employment, or farmers; in the large-farm community the proportion is less than one-fifth.

7. Less than one-third of the breadwinners in the small-farm community are agricultural wage laborers — characteristically landless, and with low and insecure income — while the proportion of persons in this position reaches the astonishing figure of nearly two-thirds of all persons gainfully employed in the large-farm community.

8. Physical facilities for community living — paved streets, sidewalks,

garbage disposal, sewage disposal, and other public services — are far greater in the small-farm community; indeed, in the industrial-farm community some of these facilities are entirely wanting.

9. Schools are more plentiful and offer broader services in the small-farm community, which is provided with 4 elementary schools and 1 high school; the large-farm community has but a single elementary school.

10. The small-farm community is provided with three parks for recreation; the large-farm community has a single playground, loaned by a corporation.

11. The small-farm town has more than twice the number of organizations for civic improvement and social recreation than its large-farm counterpart.

12. Provision for public recreation centers, Boy Scout troops, and similar facilities for enriching the lives of the inhabitants is proportioned in the two communities in the same general way, favoring the small-farm community.

13. The small-farm community supports two newspapers, each with many times the news space carried in the single paper of the industrialized-farm community.

14. Churches bear the ratio of 2 to 1 between the communities, with the greater number of churches and church-goers in the small-farm community.

15. Facilities for making decisions on community welfare through local popular elections are available to people in the small-farm community; in the large-farm community such decisions are in the hands of officials of the country.

These differences are sufficiently great in number and degree to affirm the thesis that small farms bear a very important relation to the character of American rural society. It must be realized that the two communities of Arvin and Dinuba were carefully selected to reflect the difference in size of enterprise, and not extraneous factors. The agricultural production in the two communities was virtually the same in volumes — $2\frac{1}{2}$ million per annum in each — so that the resource base was strictly comparable. Both communities produced specialized crops of high value and high cost of production, utilizing irrigation and large bodies of special harvest labor. The two communities are in the same climate zone, about equidistant from small cities and major urban centers, similarly served by highways and railroads, and without any significant advantages from non-agricultural resources or from manufacturing or processing. The reported differences in the communities may properly be assigned confidently and overwhelmingly to the scale-of-farming factor.

The reasons seem clear. The small-farm community is a population of middle-class persons with a high degree of stability in income and tenure, and a strong economic and social interest in their community. Differences in wealth among them are not great, and the people generally associate together in those organizations which serve the community. Where farms are large, on the other hand, the population consists of relatively few persons with economic stability, and of large numbers whose only tie to the community is their uncertain and relatively low-income job. Differences in wealth are great among members of this community, and social contacts between them are rare. Indeed, even the operators of large-scale farms frequently are absentees; and if they do live in Arvin, they as often seek their recreation in the nearby city. Their interest in the social life of the community is hardly greater than that of the laborer whose tenure is transitory. Even the businessmen of the large-farm community frequently express their own feelings of impermanence; and their financial investment in the community, kept usually at a minimum, reflects the same view. Attitudes such as these are not conducive to stability and the rich kind of rural community life which is properly associated with the traditional family farm.

THE CONDITION

An understanding of the cause and condition of the strain upon the family farm is essential to any discussion of remedy.

There are a number of definitions and concepts of the family-type farm. One definition the subcommittee heard is this: The family-type farm generally might be considered a farming operation in which managerial decisions are made by the farmer and most of the physical work in the production of the farm enterprise — exceptions would be made in harvest operations — is done by the members of the farm family living on the farm. It should be large enough to provide a reasonably full-time job for the operator, and sufficient income for the farm family.

Family farms long since have shifted to production for exchange rather than production primarily for the family's own use. In this process the capacity for self-sufficiency on the farm has waned. The fast mechanization of agriculture has made capital as important to the farmer as to the industrialist and cash income as essential to the family on the land as to the worker in the factory.

This transition rendered farmers increasingly vulnerable, in their forced reliance on the uncertainty of the prices in the market places. Industrialists make their own prices for the things they produce, to reflect their costs and profits; industrial workers are organized to improve and protect their wages; whereas farmers still must sell primarily in auction markets, usually on terms dictated by the buyers.

Thus exposed to the unrestrained play of economic forces, agriculture in the late 1920's was caught in a downward spiral of prices. Then, much as today, there was prosperity in the rest of the economy, and the farmers' worsening circumstances attracted only limited notice. But, when the whole economy entered into the great depression, the Nation became aware of the importance of agriculture to the well-being of all our people.

It was then that the farm program came into being.

In the operation of this program, and due largely to an expanding economy during the war and postwar periods, the cash receipts of farmers increased from $4,735 million in 1932 to more than $30 billion.

The improvement in farm income created a great market for things produced in the towns and cities. This made jobs and kept factory wheels turning. Rural people were able to buy the conveniences and comforts that previously had been within the reach only of city and town people. The REA took electricity to the farm homes. Farmers were able to mechanize and apply the new sciences including the use of more and improved plant foods. Farmers, with the means to do it, used their new resources and their energies to restore and conserve the soil. Farmers' capacity for production of food and fiber was vastly increased and, in each of the 11 years, 1942 to 1952, inclusive, farm income was at or above 100 percent of parity.

But now agriculture is subjected again to a deepening recession.

While the rest of the population enjoys unprecedented prosperity, the farm economy declines year by year. In 1955 the per capita income of people on farms went down to $860, while the per capita income of nonfarm people climbed to $1,922; and of the $860 per capita income for farm people, approximately one-third was derived from nonfarm sources such as pay to farmers who take part-time employment in town.

THE CAUSE

The subcommittee emphasizes that these new strains and hardships in the agricultural economy cannot be attributed to any failing or fault of farmers, but they derive principally from the abundance of food and fiber built up in response to the policy of Government which, at the outbreak of the Korean conflict, suspended all crop controls and called for all-out production. This was an essential and proper policy related directly to the safety of the

Nation, and farmers responded with a great outpouring and mobilization of food and fiber.

But the Government, since the end of the Korean conflict in 1953, has not extended to agriculture the considerations which were provided for industry.

Agriculture was geared by Government policy to meet a worldwide threat of communism. The same was true of industry. But industry has operated on a cost-plus contract basis, enjoying guaranteed profits on Government business; it has received special tax considerations; and was awarded billions of dollars for reconversion from emergency production. Industry has been protected against the competition of surplus war and defense material. Trucks and cars, and other Government-owned industrial surplus goods have been kept off the normal competitive markets. Industrial war plants have been recognized as surplusage, and charged off to war. Conversely, farmers have been forced to carry a large burden of their costly changeover to more normal production. The presence of the abundant stores of food and fiber, produced in farm operations attuned to emergency, has depressed farmers' prices and has caused severe hardships by cutbacks in crops in the effort, approved by farmers in their own elections, to eliminate the surpluses. The costs of price supports on these stored commodities are charged to the farm program, and not to war or defense, as in the case of industry's production of guns, planes, and the vast number of other items that never were used in combat or moved up to a firing line.

Thus protected, and in an expanding economy, industry is prosperous: thus unprotected, despite the expanding economy, agriculture has moved into a deepening recession.

The subcommittee recognizes, of course, that all the problems of agriculture are not of emergency or recent origin. The advance of technology — the mechanization of farms and the application of new sciences — has rendered the land more productive. These advances, while assuring the total population an abundance of food and fiber at less and less cost, in relation to individual income, have worked in one critical respect to the disadvantage of the institution of farming. One farm worker today produces food for 20 persons, while as late as 1930 a worker in agriculture provided food for only 10 persons. The output per farm worker has doubled in 25 years. Fewer persons are required in agriculture as efficiency advances, and there is the ever-present threat that the increase

in mechanization will bring greater industrialization into agricultural production, with economic resources being concentrated into
fewer and fewer hands.

[.   .   .   .   .   ]

This subcommittee went behind the statistics to study the human equation in the disappearance of the small family farms.
The testimony of farmers and the association with them disclosed
an area in the national economy where free enterprise is sup-
pressed, where effort is without due reward and where the opportunities are but few for sons to follow in the footsteps of their
fathers, to venture into individual and family enterprises upon the
land.

Bureau of the Census and Department of Agriculture statistics
show that 600,000 farm units vanished between 1950 and 1954.
The decline in farms during this 4-year period thus was almost
twice the total in the 20 years 1920–40. The disappearance of
farms in recent years has taken place among those of 259 acres and
less. Conversely, there has been a marked increase in the number
of farms of more than 260 acres.

[.   .   .   .   .   ]

GENERAL FARM ORGANIZATIONS SPEAK

The thesis of the foregoing textual matter of this report was
set forth primarily on the basis of the subcommittee's direct association with farmers, in its rural travels and study.

Subsequently the subcommittee, sitting in Washington, heard the
views of the general farm organizations: the American Farm Bureau Federation, the National Council of Farmer Cooperatives, the
National Farmers Union, and the National Grange.

We sought from these organizations and their staffs specific
remedies to promote the stability and prosperity of family-unit
farms. We received valuable suggestions from each. But we observed a diversity of views and persuasions abiding among these
organizations that, if not mediated and resolved, might delay indefinitely the effectuation of a program essential to protect family
enterprise in agriculture from the growing trend toward concentration of land into larger holdings and factory-type operations.

Conclusions and Recommendations

A farm program must be measured by its usefulness in buying values for all the people of the United States. These values in

agriculture embrace chiefly: (1) An abundance of food and fiber for the great consuming populations; (2) a solid base under the total economy of the Nation, by maintaining a fair return to the producers of food and fiber; (3) a healthy and vigorous free enterprise system, where opportunities remain open for individual venture with the hope of due reward; and (4) a perpetuation of the rural family and community order that is indispensable as a source of spiritual, social, and political vitality in a growing nation.

The major dimensions of these values are in direct proportion to the duration and circumstances of the family farm as the basic unit of agriculture.

It is recognized that any discussion of the family-type farm is easily associated with affection and sentiment, and perhaps emotion, because of the long identity of this rural order with the fundamental values. This is not to manifest or intimate, however, that this rural order can be maintained solely for the values heretofore supplied. The hard test now is in the growing competition within agriculture due substantially to technical evolution. It is the judgment of this subcommittee that the family system in farming, in adequate production units, can continue to be the most efficient, the most economic, and the most satisfying operation in a prosperous agriculture.

This subcommittee concluded that the Nation's farm program must begin with the family farm; that the program should not promote the "factory in the field" type of farming, for, except in a few specialized operations, there are no values for the Nation in substituting a hired labor agriculture for the independent family farm; that specific emphasis must be placed upon the development of our smaller farms into adequate units with resources sufficient for economic production; and that the rights of tenants as well as those of landowning farmers must be protected.

[. . . . . .]

Vocational Education Vocational instruction should be available, both in formal schooling and on the farm. Vocational instruction should begin in the seventh or eighth grade rather than be delayed to the high-school period, and it should include industrial subjects as well as agriculture, in order to gain the interest and convey the scopes of opportunities at an earlier age. Since 2 or 3 out of 4 rural youngsters are destined to settle into urban and industrial employment, the vocational education of rural schools definitely should embrace elementary training in urban pursuits. This applies especially to areas of small farms, since these are the sources of the largest youth migrations to urban employment. There needs to be established in land-grant colleges and vocational schools more detailed emphasis on teaching future vocational teachers, supervisors, and county agents, especially in the practical operation of mutual and efficient marketing by family-unit farms.

Industry Establishment of a national policy on the widest possible dispersal in the location of industry, both in Government defense plants and in private industry. This is not only a matter of good sense in national defense, but the placement of industry in rural areas will find a wealth of sturdy manpower. Despite lack of experience and training in industrial operations, the great majority of rural people have shown they acquire industrial skills quickly. The social conditions under which people live and raise their children in rural or community areas are far superior to those existing where increasing city populations are pressed into more and more crowded environments. Moreover, there is a distinct advantage to industry and workers in the rural community, where managers and employees attend the same churches, their children associate in the same schools — in brief, where the community spirit discourages the frequent antagonisms associated with concentrated industrial areas.

[. . . . .]

Leadership A program should be encouraged by the Department of Agriculture to provide trained leaders in community organization. Democracy finds its meaning in the community. Programs for economic improvement can be put into effect far more quickly and beneficially in organized rural communities. Local initiative and cooperation are imperative in programs directed at improving the economic position of the family farm. The greatest hope for the future lies in interest in and emphasis upon rural youth organizations. Rural churches, the Extension Service, the schools, and other organizations and activities are making great contributions. The leadership essential to the solutions sought in this study and recommendations of this report now is coming from the ranks of rural youth.

THE IMPORTANCE OF UNDERSTANDING

Finally, this subcommittee emphasizes that the paramount need today is unity of purpose in agriculture and better understanding between farmers and their customers in the towns and cities. The interests of our great rural and urban populations are one and the same. They are intermixed and inseparable. The farmer's problem is everybody's problem. It is important to the well-being of rural and urban people alike, as it is a matter of simple justice, that farm families should share fairly in the fruits of free enterprise, which is the heritage and pride of all Americans.

[. . . . .]

THE FAMILY-SIZE FARM

HEARINGS *before the Subcommittee on Family Farms of the Committee on Agriculture, House of Representatives, 84th Congress, First and Second Sessions, and 85th Congress, Second Session*

MONDAY, JULY 16, 1956

Washington, D.C.

Statement of Hon. Lester Johnson, a Representative in Congress From the State of Wisconsin

Mr. JOHNSON. Mr. Chairman, several bills have been referred to this subcommittee on proposals for a family-farm policy act. Among the bills referred to the subcommittee is one I introduced. I refer to my bill, H. R. 2000.

I am very much concerned about certain trends which I believe are not favorable to the present and future economic plight of our family-type farmers. Therefore, rather than speak specifically on my bill, I wish to discuss the basic principles involved in all of the proposals that are similar to those embodied in my bill.

I earnestly urge the subcommittee to consider the bills referred to it and report out a bill which states clearly that it is the policy of our Government to preserve and strengthen the economic position of family-type farmers. Also, in keeping with this philosophy, I believe Congress should enact all necessary legislation to implement a Federal family-farm policy.

I shall not burden the subcommittee with a historical review of congressional concern with legislation pertaining to family farmers. Suffice to say, from the days of the First Congress down to the present session, the subject of farm legislation has been considered in almost every Congress. A considerable body of farm legislation has been passed by Congress since our Government was founded, but not all of the legislation has been beneficial to family-type farmers.

For example, I am sure that a careful study would reveal that some of our price-support legislation has been more beneficial to large or corporation farmers than it has to family farmers. The question of price supports is not at issue in the present discussion, but I do mention it for the purpose of emphasizing the need for a family-farm policy act and other legislation to implement a family-farm program by the Government.

The members of this subcommittee I know are aware of the fact that there was a drop of 242,000 family-type farmers in the period from 1950 to 1954. I was amazed to learn that in the ninth district of Wisconsin, which I represent, there were nearly 2,600 less farmers operating in 1954 as compared to 1950.

The great majority of farmers in my district — and that is true for the entire State of Wisconsin — are family-type farmers. While there is no threat at the present of the growth of corporate farming in my district and Wisconsin, our farmers are faced with problems that could leave the door open for corporation farms to take over in the future.

This is a trend that I wish to halt, and the time to apply the proper economic remedies is now through enactment of a family-farm policy act and the other legislation needed to implement the act in the way of adequate credit at reasonable rates and a price-support program designed for family farmers.

In the light of unrest among the agrarian people in many nations throughout the world, I need not tell the members of this committee that the most fertile seedbeds for Communist agitators is in those countries where the farm population is landless and the bulk of the land is owned by a few large landowners.

We, in the United States, have always considered our family farmers an essential part of the backbone of our democratic system. Family farmers, however, are not faring too well at present, and the future does not look too well for family farmers.

It is for these and many other reasons — most of which I am sure the committee has considered — that I urge the subcommittee to report out a farm family policy bill.

I wish to thank the members of the subcommittee for the privilege of appearing before you and for your kind attention on this matter.

[. . . . .]

SATURDAY, FEBRUARY 18, 1956
Abingdon, Va.

Statement of G. B. Parks, President, Smyth County Farmers' Union

Mr. PARKS. Mr. Chairman, and members of the committee, and ladies and gentlemen, I would like for you to take a good look at me. I am one of those small, inefficient farmers, as you have heard so much about. I am unable to make any money for the last couple or 3 years, and not enough to amount to anything. I am a small farmer. My father and I operate a farm in partnership, 5 miles southeast of Chilhowee.

I am also a veteran of World War II, serving 7 years. I served in the CBI theater of operations, flying a total of 300 combat hours in bombing missions over Mandalay, Rangoon, and various other places in Burma.

While I was in the service I used — I am one of those persons whom you heard a lot about, that you can take the boy out of the country but you can't take the country out of the boy. Well, I am one of those persons, and I thought a lot about farming while I was away from home and made a lot of plans as to what I would like to do, and hoped to do when I got back to the United States, which I am very fortunate that I got back.

So I came back after the war and went back to the farm where I had been born and raised. My father's health had been bad during the war and also labor was a little hard to get at that time, so the farm was run down quite a lot. So my father and I got together and decided that we would go into the cattle business.

We only had about four head at that time. I believe there were 2 cows and 3 yearlings, and 1 of those was a steer.

We sold the steer and bought another heifer. That is the way that we have built our cow herd up to today to where we did have around fifty-some head of cows.

Of course, when the market broke, we were in a position at that time to make some money, just about the time that things broke.

All these years that prices were high, they weren't too high, I didn't think, because at the time that I got out of the service, I remember that I could buy my gasoline, I could buy a tractor, anything I needed to operate my farm, I could buy it much less and much cheaper than I could buy it today; and I've got to take a much smaller price, a much smaller price than I had to take at that time for my cattle.

Of course, as I have said before, just as I left the service everything was run down; we had no machinery and things looked prosperous.

My father and I went to the bank and borrowed money, bought machinery, and equipped our farm to where we had a very efficient operation at that time, and got along very well. We could sell grain, corn, anything that we raised. We didn't get rich off of it, but we could pay our expenses. And now, the way the situation is at the present time, I don't know how other farmers are, or what kind of shape they are in — I have had some to tell me that they were doing fine. I had one farmer tell me last week that he made more money than he had ever made — it was the first year that he had ever had to pay income tax. I said, "Mister, I would sure love to have your recipe."

The CHAIRMAN. Did he give it to you?

Mr. PARKS. No sir. He wouldn't let me in on the secret.

The CHAIRMAN. I would like to interrupt you and tell you this. You are telling a story that this committee has heard time and time again. Unfortunately, there are tens of thousands of young men caught in the same situation that you are in, and that is what makes our problem so great, that it is actually terrifying us.

To think of the great contribution you made in time of war, and then to come back and find yourself in the pitiful plight that you are in now, is something that should attract the entire Nation, not only this committee and this community, it is nationwide.

I believe that this committee has found it to be that way.

If you have any suggestions to make to the committee, as to how, by Federal legislation, we may improve the situation, I know the committee would like very much to have it.

I have friends in my home county, young men just like you, who are facing the same distressing problems that you are facing, and at the moment, they cannot make a go of it. Like yours, their situations are just hopeless.

Mr. BASS. Mr. Chairman, may I ask a question here?

Mr. JENNINGS. Mr. Bass.

Mr. BASS. You are probably a young man of 35 years old, in that neighborhood, somewhere, are you not?

Mr. PARKS. That is right.

Mr. BASS. How many other men your age in your age-group still live on the family farm and try to make a living, say, in your civil district?

Mr. PARKS. There aren't but very few, sir.

Mr. BASS. Almost all of them have had to leave?

Mr. PARKS. All of them haven't left, but a large majority of them have. They either have left the farm or they have gone into the cities to find employment to supplement their income on the farm. That I will have to do if something doesn't turn up.

Mr. BASS. Actually, of the men in your age-group in your community, very few operate a family-type farm and make a living off it today; is that not correct?

Mr. PARKS. That is right — where I live, sir.

The CHAIRMAN. When you went into the farming business, you mortgaged your future to equip yourself for a life on the farm. That is what happened to you?

Mr. PARKS. Yes, sir. As to the way the situation looked at the time, it looked very promising, and I tried not to be extravagant; I try to farm to the best of my ability. I attended agricultural on-the-job training for veterans and tried to gain all the information that I could. I took Blacksburg's recommendations, practiced farming, and sowed the ladian clover orchard grass, which are new things in my section.

I tried to do the job the way it should be done. I see now where I made some mistakes. I probably went into it a little heavy. If I had not used as heavily on fertilizer, probably if I kept the old team of mules we had, and probably I couldn't have farmed as much, but I don't believe I would have been as hard up as I am today.

The CHAIRMAN. At that time, when you were doing that, the national and all the leaders of Government were encouraging you and almost begging the farmers to produce; is that not right?

Mr. PARKS. That is right, sir. How well I remember. When I was in India and about ready to come back to the States, you know, they sent us a lot of newspapers to USO clubs, and I would sit around and read these papers, and farm magazines was my specialty, and I remember reading articles in these magazines encouraging the young farmers to come back to the farm, and I imagine some of you people have read the same things.

Mr. JOHNSON. One question.

Is your land mostly in grass and small grain?

Mr. PARKS. Mostly. We try to farm enough to raise our own feed.

Mr. JOHNSON. Can you see where a soil-bank program that is going to take a certain number of your acres — I think the chairman got a letter as to what they intend to pay on grass out of production. Do you see where that is going to help you?

Mr. PARKS. The way I understand the soil-bank program, I don't see where it is going to help me any — it may help other individuals — but it is not going to help me.

[. . . . .]

FRIDAY, FEBRUARY 3, 1956
Raleigh, N.C.

Statements of Walter M. Benson and Iris Benson, His Wife, Farmers, Clayton, N. C.

Mr. BENSON. She finally came up.

Mrs. BENSON. I was afraid he would say something wrong.

Mr. BENSON. Mr. Chairman, we are on a 62½-acre farm with 4¹⁄₁₀ acres allotment, 3 acres cotton allotment, 3 acres wheat allotment, 21 acres corn allotment.

In addition to that we rent 2 acres adjoining farms of tobacco. We have 7 head of cattle, and a year ago we carried 14 head of brood sows, and we are in pretty bad shape.

At this meeting I learned a lot, and most everything I had in mind to say has already been said, but I do want to bring out the flexible scale.

In other words, we have heard for the last 3 years of the flexible scale, and I want to bring to your attention that it is my opinion — I speak only from this person himself — that our commodities have always been on a flexible scale, because in December you take pork, eggs to market, and eggs is a good price, and then just 3 months later its value may be half of what it was.

Of course, hogs is low during December, and higher maybe in the summer.

What I would like to bring out is a better marketing situation, something standarized for the 12 months period, not only the 3 months or 2 months.

Of course, we have got support prices, and I am proud of it.

We've got cooperation, but we want a market that we can carry our produce down to each month of the year and evaluate it at the same dollar.

A fair return is what I would like to see the small farmer get, in our community, in your community, and I want laws passed for one and for all. In other words, I am not selfish, but we are in a strain with a surplus. The surplus situation you see, is a big surplus. You read some people advocate no surplus at all, if we could get it. Well, I am not one of them. I want to bring out the soil-bank program.

In other words, instead of the soil-bank program I would prefer having a farmers' bank program, in other words, the little farmer, in other words, we may do good by the soil conservation, these bank programs, but I do think these little farmers should have a bank program of their own, to maintain a better marketing situation, a better price.

That is what we need on Johnston County. I am from Clayton.

Mr. ABERNETHY. What you are trying to say is that what you little fellows need is something to bank? That is what you mean, is it not?

Mr. BENSON. We speak of the soil-bank program.

Mr. ABERNETHY. That is right.

Mr. BENSON. And I want a farmer's bank program.

Mr. ABERNETHY. To have something to bank.

Mr. BENSON. That is right. To conserve the soil is wonderful, but I think conserving the humanity, the small farmer, is very important, and it comes ahead of the soil.

Mrs. BENSON. I agree with him. I am a field hand, you know, out on the farm.

The CHAIRMAN. Do not interrupt the lady.

Mrs. BENSON. Lady and gentlemen, I am a field hand. I am a real farmer's wife, and I heard the other gentlemen talk about their wives went out to work. Daddy won't let me work; besides, I don't know how to do anything. Here is what worries me: I feel my children are entitled to a college education like the doctors', lawyers', and big farmers' children. Well, it is almost impossible to do that on our family-sized farm. My daughter is in college and she wants to study medicine. We hope she is able to fulfill her great ambition. The only way she can stay in college, she is doing laundry for a family of five people, cooks meals for five people, has to keep a house spotless and clean. She is making a straight

B average. I don't think it is fair, whenever we work, 10 and 12 hours a day, tobacco farmers, cotton farmers, cow farmers, there is no time of the year that there is any extra time. There is no time of the year where I can see where a farmer's wife can go off and draw a dollar an hour, and, boy, I would like to have a dollar an hour.

Don't you think you can supplement the farmer's wife? And I will guarantee there won't be overproduction.

Mr. BENSON. We use it up.

Mrs. BENSON. We use the money.

In my community there are women like me, and there are school teachers, and they have other professions. And another kick I heard so much about brought out today, about the doctors and all buying up land.

Here is the thing about the money people going out and buying the farmers' land: The small farmer doesn't have the money to run in competition with the doctor.

Now we are farmers. Pop was a preacher, and it took me 21 years to learn how to farm, with State college ideas, but daddy was a dirt farmer, and he tried to put in his idea of farming. Anyway we haven't gone broke, or haven't gotten rich, either.

Then the News and Observer started printing the horoscopes, and I started reading it and farming through their advice.

We did well, but we are no match for the hurricanes, if they had not hit us three times last summer.

I think we do just as well as the State college theories. I shouldn't talk all of this — people will see how ignorant I am — but I still think the major thing and most important thing is helping the family farm, because we do teach our children early in life a sense of responsibility, and I am going to brag a little further.

When we send our farm children to school, they are the ones that get down to business and really make the fine men and leaders, because they have been taught leadership and responsibility from birth. [Applause.]

The CHAIRMAN. That is a splendid statement.

I understand, that you attach more faith to the News and Observer horoscope than you do the Department of Agriculture?

Mrs. BENSON. That and the almanac. At least it tells us when it is going to rain.

The CHAIRMAN. Now that the lady has finished, you may proceed, sir.

Mr. BENSON. With, say, 4 or 5 dry years, and the recent wind-storm, we have suffered, and if it weren't for the horoscope, I guess we would have left the farm.

The CHAIRMAN. It all comes down to this: If you could get an adequate price for the things you produce, you could stay on the farm and educate your child and would not do the thing you are doing now.

Mr. BENSON. That is it.

Mrs. BENSON. Absolutely.

The CHAIRMAN. The same thing goes back to what Mr. Aber-nethy said. If you do not have money to put in the bank, you are not going to be a very successful farmer.

Mr. BENSON. That is true.

I would like to say something else in regard to the soil conserva-tion. It is a wonderful program, and I receive parity from the soil-conservation project, and here the other day I read in the News and Observer ——

The CHAIRMAN. Still reading that News and Observer, are you?

Mrs. BENSON. Yes, sir.

Mr. BENSON. Our President of the United States, Mr. Eisen-hower, predicts we are going to put out 25 million diverted acres, in grass and trees. Well, then the day after — maybe 1 day after — I read the News and Observer where it hasn't any seed, any trees, and where Mr. Benson did away with the nurseries.

The CHAIRMAN. You do not mean "Cousin Ezra?"

Mr. BENSON. I am no cousin, but I am speaking about the nurseries — I am a Benson — and I understand he made a boner — I guess I made one today, too, but I am proud to be here. I am enjoying this. I am off the track.

Mrs. BENSON. You see, nature provided the grass seed.

Mr. BENSON. Back on this conservation of seed and tree business, it was passed in Washington, where there wasn't any more money appropriated for the nurseries. I am proud of that, because it is foolish to spend any money, in my way of thinking, and taking the ceiling price off the grass seed.

Well, we probably need that. I am not going into that, because I don't have the figures on it.

Here is what I want to come out and bring to you: We don't need the trees. We need the seed. We have good leaders, in other words, we have everything we wish for — we have leaders, in other words, to show us how. I wouldn't know how to go out and sow pine seed or poppy seed, or anything, but I get the information. If our soil grows the trees, it would produce the trees, sprout the trees. That nursery proposition, I don't see it is necessary for that for the grass seed — my farm will produce the nature grass and preserve the soil. In other words, in 5 months I guarantee it will be knee high in grass, head high in weeds, without any grass seed.

And, instead of appropriating a lot of conservation money for this soil bank ——

Mrs. BENSON. All we need is the money.

Mr. BENSON. For the soil bank, I think we should have the farmers' bank, or maybe the small-tenant bank, subsidize him so he can get the surplus moved off so our crop will rise to the point where it pays.

I want to bring out another point about surplus.

I don't see any need in the world for a farmer to produce something he already has.

It would be very foolish for me to go down to the service station and put a tank of gas in a car when it already had a tank of gas in it. In other words, it would be wasted. That is what we are doing today. We are just wasting — think about the use of oil, gas, tractors — to put 25 million acres in trees and grass. Think about all the labor, all the sweat and everything you have to do. Let nature take its course, and we will have the trees and have the grass, and we could have this appropriation for our people at home, the little farmers.

The CHAIRMAN. Thank you very much, Mr. and Mrs. Benson.

Mr. THOMPSON. Thank you very much for your statement.

Mr. BENSON. Thank you very much.

Mrs. BENSON. Thank you.

[. . . . .]

THURSDAY, NOVEMBER 14, 1957
Fergus Falls, Minn.

Statement of Ole A. Moe, Solway, Minn.

Mr. MOE. Mr. Chairman, I should like to read my statement and, perhaps, there will be a few comments I should like to make on various points in the statement. Is that all right?

Mr. THOMPSON. That is all right.

Mr. MOE. Hon. Coya Knutson, members of the House Agriculture Committee at its hearings at Fergus Falls, Minn., on November 14 and 15, 1957, with the permission of the members of the subcomittee of the House of Representatives I wish to submit a statement relative to some of the problems confronting the family farms in this part of Minnesota, particularly Beltrami County.

First, I must state that the family farm as we knew it a few years ago is rapidly disappearing from the scene. A few weeks ago I attended a church meeting at which this very problem was discussed and it was forcefully brought out that this erosion of the family farmer was affecting the church organizations to such an extent that realignments must be made in order to keep some congregations alive. We are also aware that this same problem is now affecting the business and professional people in the towns and cities. I note that in the past few months some of the business establishments are advertising liquidation sales and going out of business.

We may safely assume that under present policies this trend will continue and that the family farm which has been the bulwark of rural America for hundreds of years is now in the process of being replaced by an alien system which is commonly referred to as agricultural feudalism.

This trend started back in 1947 or 1948 when all price controls were abandoned and our pricing system became a free-for-all markup scramble and the prices to the farmer which is and has not been managed in his favor was left far behind.

[. . . . .]

My point is that in our complex economy a certain amount of price control will sooner or later become absolutely essential because we cannot have one segment of our economy pricing its goods and services higher and higher while another segment, such as the farm prices, fall through the cellar floor.

In my opinion, it is this pricing system that is at the bottom of the distress the family farmer finds himself today rather than the problem of surpluses.

This morning, on my way down, I ordered a little bacon with my breakfast, and I tell you, ladies and gentlemen, if I could have received that kind of price for my hogs that I sold a few days ago, I could go to Florida and live high for the rest of the winter.

Mr. THOMPSON. You could go to Texas, too.

Mr. MOE. Yes, by the way, to the gentleman from Texas —
I was rather hesitant to come here when I found he was the chair-

man because I have heard that people from Texas are rather tough. In fact, in the old days they used to take on a war by themselves and lick the Mexicans; but when I heard actually that he was born in Minnesota I felt better.

In order that the farmer may be able to pay his fixed costs of operation, such as taxes, interest, and the ever-increasing cost of the things he must have in order to stay in business and the increasing cost of living, he must endeavor to produce an ever-increasing amount of things to sell. This in turn increases the amount of surpluses and there is no end in sight.

Some time ago I read an article on rationing in the Capper publication, published in Kansas, and they had a very good article. It was the contention that rationing is practiced now practically by everybody in dispensing food. That came to my mind, particularly, a few days ago when my neighbor went to town and had lunch; and at the time he was culling his potatoes because he could not sell them, he asked for a little more potatoes and the waiter said they could not give him any additional potatoes. And potatoes were then selling for about 80 cents a hundred in my area. You might remember that when you go to the dinner today whether you get that many potatoes for 80 cents.

[. . . . .]

My concluding point is that when the farmer takes his produce and livestock to market he is losing three ways in the manner in which things are priced. First, he is the loser because he has no bargaining power in the market place and, therefore, the price he receives is too low; secondly, he loses because by the time his merchandise is handled and processed, the price to the consumer is so high that it has a tendency to set up consumer resistance to these prices and the purchases are smaller than they may otherwise have been, and, third, when the farmer repurchases the things he sold in the first place he must pay these higher prices and thus adds to his cost of living.

It is my opinion that regardless of any effort that may be made to alleviate the farm problem any plan must have a price-control feature built into it in order to work. The old concept that the law of supply and demand will automatically adjust supply and demand is as outdated as the horse and buggy as compared to the present fast automobile. The law of supply and demand simply is not working and will not work so long as most products are priced by the processors and manufacturers without much regard to the cost of the

raw material. This leaves the family farmer at a great disadvantage
at every turn.

[. . . . .]

Statement of Leroy Bach, of Fergus Falls, Minn.

[. . . . .]

Now the standards of living for the family wife; in 1954
there was a survey made in Otter Tail County; 313 farm families
were visited. Thirty-eight percent of the farm homes had bathroom
facilities, otherwise 62 percent are now living below the standards
of the slums of many big cities. There are two solutions. The
Government could start a rural bathroom association just like the
REA. The man on Main Street would be subsidized, when the
farmer would buy bathroom fixtures just like he was when the
farmer bought electrical appliances when REA was formed. Or
just give the family-type farmer his fair share of the national income. Fourteen percent of the farmers took a beating in the last
6 years, to keep the Nation's economy stable.

Let us put the shoe on the other foot. The last few years all we
have heard is people say, "There are two Cadillacs in every garage
on the farm." Here is what the 1954 survey shows: Of the 313
farms in Otter Tail County, the number of cars, there were 9.6
percent who had none; 1 car, 89 percent had 1; 2 or 3 percent had
more.

Model of cars — 1949 or older, 45 percent; from 1950 to 1953
there was less than 48 percent, and in the 1954 to 1955 models there
was just a little over 7 percent.

In the price range there were 86.5 percent in the low range,
medium was 11 percent, and on the high range, it was 2.5 percent.

I do not think you will find many Cadillacs in Otter Tail County.

[. . . . .]

Statement of Bob Moses, Chippewa Falls, Wis., Chip-
pewa Falls Farmers Union Local

Mr. MOSES. Madam Chairman and members of the committee,
I wish to state that I am no farmer. I represent the Wisconsin
Farmers Union, and I am very happy to have the opportunity,
through Congresswoman Knutson, to testify today.

Almost 2 years ago, the brother newspaper columnists, Joseph and Stewart Alsop, wrote:

The decay of Rome quite certainly began when the hardy farm citizens whose valor had made Rome great ceased to be able to maintain themselves and their families by farming their small holdings. In hardly more than a generation, over great areas of Italy, the family-sized farms were swept away. They made way for vast, consolidated, slave-operated, absentee-capitalist holdings that were the equivalent in those days of what we now call industrialized farms.

The Alsops continued in their March, 1956 nationally syndicated column:

The warnings of history need to be remembered, at the moment, for the rather simple reason that there would be no really grave American farm problem if it were not for the plight of the family-sized farms.

So write the Alsop brothers, Joseph and Stewart, on the subject of family farming in the United States and in the days of the Roman Empire.

Speaking for those who firmly believe in strengthening and saving the family farm in America, it is hoped that this very fine congressional subcommittee will return to Washington in 1958 with singleness of purpose: to write the kind of legislation that will produce unwavering, official United States Government family farm policy. For, as the Alsop brothers suggest, in that we have always looked back into history to judge the possible mistakes of the present and the future, it would not be completely unrealistic to state that what happened in Rome 500 years after Julius Caesar could also happen in the United States 200 years after George Washington.

The many threats to our family-farm agriculture in America have been related many times. We have heard the need for strengthening the family farm expressed on many occasions: by people of both political parties, by the farm organizations, and the farmers. Untold resolutions have been passed affirming methods to eliminate the threats to family farmers, on one hand; and to strengthening family farmers, on the other hand. Reports on the family farm have been published, such as the brilliant study by Marshall Harris and Robert Rohwer for the National Planning Association. The Agricultural Committee of the House of Representatives has even established a special subcommittee, which has held previous hearings, and is in Fergus Falls, Minn., today to help determine the needs of the institution of family farming that is as "American as the 4th of July and Thanksgiving," as Harris and Rohwer so eloquently described family farming in their NPA report.

Republicans and Democrats can defend the family farm from now until the next five presidential elections; we can pass countless resolutions and publish scores of reports; yes, the House Family Farm Subcommittee that is here today can continue to hold hearings all over the country. All of this can be done and we will still not have solved the problem. For until the Congress of the United States writes into legislation a sound, workable family farm policy, and until that policy can willingly be administered by the executive branch of our Federal Government, it will be virtually useless to continually talk about saving the family farm.

Today, our United States Government is supporting not 1 type of American agriculture, but 2. The question I put to this subcommittee is: How much longer will our Government continue to foster and help expand the corporate "factory in the field" type agriculture while at the same time supposedly fostering and helping to expand the kind of agriculture manned by family operations?

[. . . . .]

This past August, a newspaper in your State of Texas, Congressman Thompson, the DeKalb News, editorialized on the family farm:

We think that America will be a stronger Nation, and a greater one, as long as the individual and his family can farm a small area, living with the soil and keeping in touch with the earth in this fashion.[. . .] If the farmer were getting his fair share of the income and profits derived from farm products, there would always be room in this country for the one-family farm. We hope there will always be.

The National Catholic Rural Life Conference, at its 1956 convention, had this to say:

Communities in which family farms predominate are characterized by an equality of opportunity and position, by a recognition of the rights and dignity of persons, and by emphasis upon individual initiative and responsibility. This is the atmosphere in which wholesome family life, Christian ideals, and democratic principles thrive best.

I could also cite what fewer family farmers do to our factory workers and to our small towns. In my State of Wisconsin, the number of farm operators dropped from 199,000 in 1935 to 137,000 in 1956. From 1954 to 1956, the Wisconsin falloff in farm operations was 16,000 farms, a little better than 10 percent. The United States

Census Bureau recently estimated that the American farm population has dropped by almost 2 million persons, from 22 million to 20 million in just 1 year, from April 1956 to April 1957. The seriousness of these statistics is borne out in rising unemployment in the automobile and farm machinery industries, and in reduced farmer buying in rural America.

There's a bigger reason why city workers are jobless and small town cash registers aren't ringing with the same regularity in 1957 as they were in 1947. United States per capita farm income is down to less than $900 ($889 in 1956) compared to nonfarm per capita income last year of over $2,000. As Missouri farm leader Fred Heinkel looked at it not long ago, if farmers had parity of income with nonfarmers, "our cities and towns would thrive because farm customers would have money to spend." Like others, Heinkel was disturbed because this parity of income had dropped to 44 percent in 1956.

So much for the need to place entire Government emphasis on family farm type agriculture in this country. The threat to the family farm is clear and unmistakable. It is Arizona cotton farmer Jack Harris who nicked Uncle Sam for a check for $209,000 in soil bank subsidy this year, and then bragged that he went after the subsidy to show how ridiculous the Government programs were. The threat to the family farm is the big farm operators in California and other Southwest states who bring in cheap, imported farm labor from other lands to compete with United States family farmers. The threat is the aforementioned Delta Pine & Land Co. of Mississippi, which annually collects over a million dollars in price support subsidy, and all other big business farm operations.

[.   .   .   .   .]

What are the alternatives? What must be our program? Life magazine, a sister news publication of Time, supplied part of the answer in an editorial last February 4, when it suggested that Congress

might do well to resurrect a measure, which died last year in committee, to put a $25,000 limit on the farm subsidies any single farmer or corporation can receive.

Henry Luce, editor and publisher of Time and Life, is a loyal supporter of virtually all Eisenhower Administration policies and could lend valuable assistance to a Congress with inclinations to limit Government financial farm support to family farmers.

The $25,000 farm subsidy cutoff idea is not new. It has been ad-

vanced in the past by Senator Hubert Humphrey of Minnesota, and
by former Agriculture Secretary Charles Brannan. And speaking
of Minnesota, in a recent article in the religious magazine, the
Lutheran Herald, Rev. Maynard E. Stokka, of Hawley, Minn., suggested that:

It might just be worth our effort to invest in our future, to insure the one
great source of freedom by seeing to it that family sized, owned, operated
farms get full parity and complete crop loans privilege, and that anything
above family size acres be graded off so that production over $25,000
receives no support.

Almost 2 years ago, the New York Times, a very influential newspaper, reported that the Eisenhower Administration was

actively considering a ceiling on farm price support loans (which) would
limit loans to producers below a specified gross income.

This idea should deserve the closest attention of Congress in 1958.
[.   .   .   .   .   ]
So that there can be the full force of the United States Government behind obtaining a strengthened family size farm agriculture
in America, it is proposed that the Department of Agriculture
create a Family Farm Administration (headed by an Assistant
Secretary of Agriculture).

Included in this Department of Agriculture family farm setup
would be such regular department features as the rural development program and the Farmer Cooperative Service. The new
Government family farm agency would have as its sole purpose
the "selling" of family operated farming to America, and the world.

It is suggested that, through a Family Farm Administration,
funds be increased substantially for the Farmer Cooperative Service. The Government should spend many times more than $500,000
each year, the sum it now spends on this Service. Overall expenditure on the Family Farm Administration need not be large,
but should be sufficient to administer and to promote United States
family farming here and abroad.

This job of "selling" the family farm by the United States Government would be done through various means: speeches, pamphlets,
the press, radio, television, and other audio visual devices. It would
need no large administrative bureaucracy under which to operate.
The Family Farm Administration would work very smoothly with
already existing Agricultural Extension apparatus across the coun-

try, with the farm organizations and the farm cooperatives; and would maintain close liaison with the churches and schools and with civic, labor, and business organizations in the United States.

Perhaps through the added punch the Family Farm Administration would bring to the American farm co-ops, we might eventually arrive at what Senator Humphrey talked about last week at the National Milk Producers Convention in Cincinnati: "collective bargaining" through producers' cooperatives. As many in agriculture look at this picture, farmer to consumer producer cooperatives may have to come about as the ultimate.

Given the tools to help them back on the economic road to prosperity, family farmers might some day even come to be the owners of their own processing companies. But all of these tools hinge on placing the full resources of our American Government behind the family-operated units in United States agriculture. We cannot have the subsidy payment cutoff, the direct payment plan, and other Government or cooperative programs without having a family farm course well charted out for our Government to follow.

The Family Farm Subcommittee of the House of Representatives can launch the ship, it can guide the rudder, it can chart the course. The Family Farm Subcommittee can help save the American family farm, but there's not much time to waste. Time is running out. You must act now.

I thank the committee very much for allowing me to be here today.

Mrs. KNUTSON. We thank you, Bob Moses, for that very excellent and complete statement.

Are there questions from the members of the committee at this time?

Mr. THOMPSON. I would like to make a comment, Madam Chairman. The Family Farm Subcommittee in their final report of August 1, 1956, recommended just exactly the Administrator that you have in mind within the Department of Agriculture. It is a very unfortunate thing that was not done, but I think it is a sincere difference of opinion on the part of some in authority. We find it in the Republican administration and we find it in too many who are high in the Democratic Party — there is a very sincere belief that the only successful family farmer is one who has a job in town, works in industry or something like that, and farms part time. We do not subscribe to that opinion on this committee.

We believe that every family farmer who knows his business and who wishes to earn his living for himself and his family by that means should have an opportunity to do so.

I do not define for you the committee definition – I did not tell you that – of the "family farm." We had to know, of course, just what type of operation we were talking about. This is it: It does not depend on the number of acres farmed. In some lines of farming it may be 200 acres. In others it may be 500 acres, depending entirely on what it is. But it is any operation which in normal times has been successfully operated by a farmer and his family. I do not mean that if he hired somebody in planting season or harvest season to help, that rules him out.

That is the kind of operation we are talking about. Certainly, I think the members of this committee would agree with everything you said as to the plant. We do encounter stumbling blocks among those who at present have the power to stymie any such move as this. They insist that the answer is to let farming be an adjunct of industry, one way or another. Possibly they would deny it, but that is it. They say, "If you cannot make a living on the farm, go and get a job in town" – forgetting entirely what happened during the great depression of the late 1930's.

Now I find myself making a speech and that is not intended from any committee member.

I might, also, comment on an interesting thing we discovered about the Government policy toward farms at home and abroad. I have a copy of an interesting hearing that we held with Dr. White, who is Acting Director of the Office of Food and Agriculture in the International Cooperation Administration, the organization that reaches out abroad and spends our money trying to develop foreign economy. I have no criticism, certainly none at this time, of the effort to strengthen our friends. That is not the purpose of making this remark.

The purpose of it is to point out that abroad we are doing, in the name of the Government, exactly what this committee and this group is trying to do here at home. In Spain, for instance, we are trying to stabilize the family farmer. We are trying to cooperate with the authorities in Spain. We are trying to fix it so that the family farmer over there can prosper, and the reason is – and it is all reflected in the hearing – that that is the only way you can stabilize the political economy of those countries.

We all harbor the hope that that same policy will spread in our country. We are doing it abroad.

Mrs. KNUTSON. Thank you, Mr. Moses.

Mr. MOSES. Thank you.

Mrs. KNUTSON. The next witness on the list is Mr. George Helmstetter, Roosevelt, Minn., near the Canadian border.

[. . . . .]

Statement of George Helmstetter, Roosevelt, Minn.

Mr. HELMSTETTER. Madam Chairman and members of the committee, first, I would like to extend my appreciation to the Subcommittee on Family Farms for coming up into this area and getting first-hand accounts of the problems of we farmers. We, certainly, have them at this time. I am not going to take any more time than I feel necessary. I will enter into what I have jotted down immediately.

My name is George Helmstetter from Roosevelt, Minn., and I farm, in partnership with my brother, about 500 acres of cropland. Our major crops are wheat, flax, barley, and beef.

The one main problem in agriculture, we can all agree, is the low net income of family farmers, and we farmers at this time are receiving a net income amounting to less than half that received by nonfarm people. That is, the income of the family itself.

But this is not the whole picture when you consider the hours of work required to earn these wages. There is no such thing as a 40-hour week on the farm. The average is closer to 70 for the farmer himself, and many of the farm women will be found out in the fields during the busy season driving tractors, trucks, taking care of dairy herds, poultry flocks, and almost any task that must be done.

Add to this the many jobs done by the farm children that contribute to the operation of the farm, you will find that the wages per hour are almost nothing.

In contrast to this, the people in the cities are earning more or less hours of work, and we see corporation earnings on investments increasing each year while ours go down.

We see the average individual worker who has nothing invested in his job, who hardly has to think to do his job, earning 2 or 3 times the income we do.

Yet, in my case we have about $40,000 and half a lifetime invested in the farm.

We are confronted each day with many management problems, and at the present time because of the cost price squeeze these problems become almost insurmountable.

I do not think that most farmers hope or desire to become rich. They feel it is necessary to have an income equal to that of the city workers, because there are certain things about farming, as a way of life, that makes up for a small loss of personal income. But there are many things that in these modern times are considered almost a necessity which are not possible for the family farms to have, such as annual vacations, modern plumbing, automatic heat, and so forth.

We, also, must consider the education of the farm children. Because of the limited opportunities in agriculture these young people must be trained for a different life. College education is expensive when they must be paid for out of 75-cents-an-hour wages.

[. . . . .]

Statement of Harry T. Burau, Fergus Falls, Minn.

Mr. BURAU. Madam Chairman, and members of the committee, my name is Harry T. Burau. I own and operate a 300-acre farm in Dane Prairie Township, in Otter Tail County. I am married and have two sons. I am a township supervisor, secretary of soil-conservation district supervisors, treasurer of local telephone company, and a member of many other boards of directors of various organizations.

I wish to make the following statement in regard to the family-farm problem in this area:

THE FAMILY FARM IN OTTER TAIL COUNTY

Is there a problem of the family farm? If there is, what is it and what can be done to remedy the problem?

First of all, what is a family farm? Family farms cannot be defined in terms of acres, in numbers of livestock, or size and value of equipment, a family of 2 people may well find 80 or 160 acres adequate in size to give them a satisfactory income while a family of 5 sons may find 2,000 acres entirely too small for efficient operation. Type of farming that is followed, size of family, efficiency of operation, availability of finances, and productivity of the soil all help determine how large or small the family farm shall be.

The problem in the cases where there is a difficulty is largely one of obtaining a unit of sufficient size to be economically efficient and at the same time to have sufficient capital to adequately machine, stock, and house the operation and make it successful. Whether we like it or not, farms must gradually become larger in a majority of cases. In the first place farming is changing from a way of life to a business, and in the second place the overhead costs in machinery and equipment make larger farming units in most cases a necessity.

Here in Otter Tail County we have some areas, because of the topography, where farms are small. The soil in some of these areas is not the best. In many cases the cropland available is low, and cannot be easily or cheaply increased. Income per farm is low.

Should the solution in these cases be direct production payments to supplement these people to the point where income is adequate to supply their needs? Such a problem as this with such a solution becomes a permanent problem and the solution is no solution at all. The result is the first step in the socialization of American agriculture.

I would suggest a solution that could go far in solving this problem and also solving another of which you must certainly be aware. Today we have a concentration of industry in small areas close to metropolitan centers. This, of course, is a highly dangerous situation and should be corrected. My suggestion would be that industry and manufacturing be scattered over the country as a defense measure and that smaller units be set up in agricultural areas where those farms do not provide adequate income. In this way farm people who cannot expand operations to an economically sound basis could supplement their earnings by doing factory work, and the country would be safer as well.

In those areas where farms need to be expanded to a unit of efficient size and the area is such that lends itself to such expansion, I would suggest that adequate low-cost long-term financing always be ready to help young farmers get started.

We have passed through an age of diversification in agriculture and are entering an age of specialization. The more specialized we become, the more profitable a farming operation may become and also the more risk may be involved.

Many people are highly concerned today over large-scale feeding operations of poultry and livestock by packing companies and groups of individuals. The same concern used to be felt toward chainstore operations in relation to individually owned stores. Independent merchants found ways to meet competition and family-size farms will find ways to meet competition of these larger feeding operations.

We sincerely believe that there is one other way in which the family farm can be helped to continue to be a part of our economy. Your committee should do something to stop inflation. Every day we see union labor asking for wage increases as their contracts are renewed, and every day the things we buy continue to rise. Labor should realize that this economic squeeze will in the end hurt them as our buying power dries up and the things they produce do not sell.

In conclusion I would say your committee can help preserve the family-type farm by:

1. Providing adequate low-cost longtime financing.
2. Providing for decentralization of industry and locating factories in places where part-time farmers could do factory work to supplement their income.
3. Help to stop inflation by stopping labor's demands for increased wages every time a new contract is signed.

I believe that the family farm in Otter Tail County is going to change but most certainly is going to remain as a part of our economy.

Mrs. KNUTSON. Thank you, Mr. Burau. That is a very fine statement.

Are there questions by the committee?

Mr. MCMILLAN. I note that you state that you have two sons. Are you going to be able to make farming attractive enough to keep them on the farm?

Mr. BURAU. I certainly hope so. They both go to agricultural school and will graduate next year. One is already planning to take over and farm. The other is going into some other line of business.

Mr. MCMILLAN. We are having great difficulty in my State in keeping young men on the farm. They find much better pay in the factories, war plants, and so forth.

Mr. BURAU. We find it a hard job trying to convince this one boy of mine that he cannot find a better place to make an income than he can on that farm out there.

Mrs. KNUTSON. Would you be in favor of keeping the family farm as a way of life and a business as well, so that we do not separate the two. I am quite concerned about the family farm as a way of life.

Mr. BURAU. I think they will go together. I think we have to remember that farming has changed from just a way of life. In the beginning we must admit that it was a way of life. Now it is a business, and we need to recognize it as a business. It will be the farmer's way of life, of course, to live on the land, but the way of life has to be a way of life that is on the same level as all other segments of the economy. We cannot just have one level for the farmers of the country and another level for all of the other segments. They are all going to have to be on the same level, but I think that the two will go together.

Mr. THOMPSON. Let me ask a question, Madam Chairman, please.

Your plan to have industry move out into the country is being carried out in a great many instances. It is one of necessity. In many cases we see the beginning of exactly what you have in mind; namely, that the man works part time in industry, part time on the farm.

What this committee has been trying to figure out is where are we going to draw the line; and if we go too far, if we take that as the only cure to the problem that is troubling us today then we are going to hit the point where family farming will be an adjunct to industry. That, I do not think, is what we are trying for. We do not want anything to interfere with the independence — and I think that is what keeps a great many here present this morning on the farm, struggling along until times get right — it is the independence, the good, clean life that you have in the country, and that you do not have in a like degree in the city. That is the problem that we are trying to thresh out.

We appreciated very much what you have said. If at some later time we can sit around together and discuss that phase of it, fine. I do not think it would ever satisfy any of us to be an adjunct to industry. In my own part of the country there are many places we find women working part time in the closest town, boys working in the cities, and papa staying home struggling along, looking forward to the time when he can be independent again on his farm.

Mr. KRUEGER. I would like to compliment Mr. Burau for his very plain, concise, and sensible statement as presented. I appreciated it very much.

Mrs. KNUTSON. We thank you very much, Mr. Burau.
Mr. BURAU. Thank you.

[. . . . .]

FRIDAY, OCTOBER 7, 1955
Hallettsville, Tex.

Statement of Eugene Hermes, Sweet Home, Tex.

Mr. HERMES. Honorable Congressmen, businessmen, and fellow farmers, I am considered a small family sized farmer. I have a 57$\frac{1}{10}$ acres in cultivation. My cotton allotment is 8½ acres.

With lots of pleading with the county committee, I was granted 2 additional acres. That gives me a total of 10½ acres.

I have 3 boys in high school, 1 boy in elementary school, and me and my wife to feed, clothe, and educate on 8½ acres of allotted cotton.

My land needs terracing and needs it bad. The soil-conservation people say how in the world can I terrace any land on 8½ acres cotton allotment?

When me and my wife first married, 19 years ago, we were on the place that we are on today, and we worked, we always planted from 15 to 18 acres of cotton annually. Now my boys are big enough to help me and I have nothing for them to do.

I have a neighbor south of me who is moving to town this year, and one north of me moving to town.

Fellows, that is where I am going to have to go, and I will be dissatisfied, unhappy. I know no other trade but farming. I was raised on a farm and I must stay there if I am going to risk making a living.

To be honest with you, gentlemen, I am not making a living. I am just existing. Two of my boys desire to be farmers. That is their ambition. They want the free life that we have on the farm, but they cannot see it. The oldest boy will graduate this year. He told me through cotton-picking time, "Daddy, I would like to farm, but how am I going to farm? You can't give me a start. You can't help me."

When I was a boy and a young man I got 45 acres of cotton to help me get started. What is the boy going to do? If he goes to the city I can't give him an education. He would have to be a common laborer, and, fellows, you have plenty of common laborers in the cities, as you probably know.

I think I covered my situation as briefly as possibly. I thank you, gentlemen. [Applause.]

[. . . . .]

Mr. ABERNETHY. Mr. Hermes, how many acres did you have in cotton in 1950?

Mr. HERMES. I will tell you — I couldn't go back to that without my record book.

Mr. ABERNETHY. What about 1951, do you remember that?

Mr. HERMES. I have an idea what it was. As I have stated previously, I had planted from 15 to 18 acres. When I was under an allotment, under allotted years, I planted what my allotment was.

Mr. ABERNETHY. In 1952, do you recall that?

Mr. HERMES. No, sir. I could tell you by looking in my record book.

Mr. ABERNETHY. This is the reason I am asking the question: This does not altogether hold true, but the allotment for 1955 was based first on the average planting on your farm in 1952–54. Now, I believe you stated that you had about 17 acres in 1953, but I did not get what you had in 1952 and 1954.

Mr. HERMES. Well, in 1954 I had 10 ——

Mr. ABERNETHY. Ten and a fraction.

Mr. HERMES. Yes, sir.

Mr. ABERNETHY. And there was a further cut in the national allotment in 1955 and you were cut about two more?

Mr. HERMES. Eight and a half — an acre and a half.

Mr. ABERNETHY. An acre and a half?

Mr. HERMES. Yes.

Mr. ABERNETHY. Now, did you vote in the referendum?

Mr. HERMES. Yes, sir. I never failed voting.

Mr. ABERNETHY. I want to commend you for that. You know, it is so often, that we, in democratic America, where we have a right to vote, but do not vote.

Did you also vote in the elections when they elected the county committeemen?

Mr. HERMES. Yes, sir; and I had the honor of serving on the Lavaca County Committee.

Mr. ABERNETHY. You were elected yourself?

Mr. HERMES. Yes.

Mr. ABERNETHY. Good for you. What is your general attitude

with regard to a controlled program for cotton? Do you feel that controls are essential to keep cotton, the production of cotton, in line with the demand? Is it your feeling that that is essential?

Mr. HERMES. Yes, sir. I honestly feel supply and demand will doctor the thing.

Mr. ABERNETHY. Then you are against the control program?

Mr. HERMES. No. We have to have a control. But still — while I don't know, I am just a little bit on the side to think that we have been hurt too bad, the small family farm.

Mr. ABERNETHY. I am not differing with you on that. I am just trying to test the people in this section. The general objective is to try to bring the cotton in line with the demand.

Now, the question of allocation and distribution of acreage, that is something else.

Mr. HERMES. Yes, sir.

Mr. ABERNETHY. As I understand you, it is your feeling, in order for the Cotton Belt to keep its production in line with demand that the control program is essential?

Mr. HERMES. It is essential. The way it seems is as if we could meet by going to it gradually, lowering our parity rates, and going into it gradually.

Mr. ABERNETHY. Now, when you say lower your parity rates, do you favor the so-called flexible program that has been fostered and promoted in recent years?

Mr. HERMES. Yes.

Mr. ABERNETHY. Then you think it would be advisable to reduce the price-support level on cotton from 90 percent to 75 percent of parity?

Mr. HERMES. Well, we would have to have a few more acres or we can't exist.

At the same time, if cotton was a dollar a pound and we don't get the acres, we can't exist. We have to have consideration to have acres back to us.

I know that is not your question, but if we are cut to 75 percent of parity with our small allotment, we will be in worse shape than we are at the present time.

Mr. ABERNETHY. Do you think you could clear more money on 15 acres of cotton at 75 percent of parity than you could on 8, 9 or so acres of cotton at 90 percent of parity?

Mr. HERMES. Yes.

Mr. ABERNETHY. Have you ever figured it out?

Mr. HERMES. No, sir; I haven't.

Mr. ABERNETHY. You would be surprised to see what the result would be. When you reduce the price, you do not reduce the
cost of production. You reduce your profits, and all of the reduction will come off the profits. None will come off the costs. The
cost will remain stabilized.

[. . . . .]

4.

The City Problem

URBAN RENEWAL INVOLVES FAR MORE THAN SLUM CLEAR-
ance. Removing blights and restoring urban neighborhoods is a tremendously complex task that includes countless
human problems as well as legal, financial, and construction
activities. Many studies have traced the natural history of
cities from first settlement to metropolis. The progression
from fine residential section to slum as buildings age and commercial centers expand is well known. But the social engineering of relocating people whose homes are being demolished
and then admitting large numbers of families to the newly
constructed units, all during a time of general housing shortages, requires consideration of many problems not so widely
understood.

During the decade after World War I, moving regularly
from apartment to apartment seemed almost a social norm
in urban centers. It was easier to move into a new apartment
than to have the old one repainted. Since World War II the
shortage of available dwellings has limited the shifting of
residence severely. Dwelling inadequacies are recognized,
but moving seems to represent pulling up roots that people

don't want to disturb. This phenomenon may well be contingent upon the state of tensions in the world at large rather than a fundamental and universal desire for a permanent shelter. Nonetheless, the emotions aroused by threats to the continuity of occupancy of particular housing are powerful instigators of behavior of resistance and protest.

In addition to the problems revolving around relocation, urban renewal brings to light a number of interesting conflicts between urban and rural areas within a state. The common conception of the hierarchy from local neighborhood through larger community to county, to state and then to the federal government level does not seem to be completely valid as a description of sympathetic loyalties. City managements seem to feel the need to bypass the state level and proceed directly to the national legislature in order to get proper understanding of their problems. This attitude raises a number of problems concerning the hierarchy of allegiances and standards of control that need exploration and clarification.

Suggested Discussion Questions

How do you account for the urban-rural conflict in state legislatures and the apparently unrepresentative character of the legislative bodies? Why do cities feel they can get more sympathetic understanding of their problems at the national than at the state level? Why does it take about two years for low-income families settled into newly built dwellings to learn to live appropriately? Why do individual families resist being relocated? What are some of the special relocation problems of groups which are discriminated against? Review and analyze the special problems of middle-income families in connection with the renewal programs. Discuss the differences in "ethics" of the legislative inquiry and report as compared with that of the social worker. How can you account for these differences?

URBAN RENEWAL IN SELECTED CITIES

HEARINGS *before the Subcommittee on Housing of the Committee on Banking and Currency, United States Senate, 85th Congress, First Session*

MONDAY, NOVEMBER 4, 1957

Chicago, Ill.

THE SUBCOMMITTEE MET, pursuant to call, in room 209, United States Courthouse, 219 South Clark Street, Chicago, Ill., at 9:30 a. m., Senator Paul H. Douglas presiding.

Present: Senator Douglas.

Also present: Robert A. Wallace, staff director, Committee on Banking and Currency; Jack Carter, staff director, and Milton Semer, counsel, subcommittee on housing; James B. Cash, Jr., staff member. and Donald L. Rogers, counsel of the Committee on Banking and Currency.

Senator DOUGLAS. The subcommittee will come to order.

The chairman of the Senate Housing Subcommittee, Senator John Sparkman, of Alabama, has assigned to me the responsibility for conducting the hearings which are about to begin here in Chicago. With these hearings, the subcommittee opens a series of inquiries to be held this fall in Midwest, South, New England, and Middle Atlantic cities.

All these subcommittee sessions should develop information and proposals for use during the next legislative session. Earlier this year, the Congress increased the urban renewal grant authorization by $350 million, which was widely regarded as sufficient financing for 1 more year. During the 1956 session a public-housing program of 70,000 units was enacted on a 2-year basis. Thus, next spring, both the urban renewal and public-housing programs are scheduled for major congressional review.

The Chicago hearings represent a specific inquiry of the Housing Subcommittee, and should not be construed as general legislative hearings. During our Chicago sessions, the subcommittee will seek data on the operation of the Federal urban-renewal and public-housing programs at the local level. With the exception of one representative of the regional office of the Federal Housing and Home Finance Administration, all witnesses will be mayors. General legislative hearings on all housing programs will be held next spring in Washington.

The mayors of our Nation's cities are the nerve center of Federal slum-clearance activities. They feel the desires of their constituents on the one hand, and direct the operations of the city-planning technicians on the other. They must chart the course of their cities' housing policies between political realism and planners' dreams.

[. . . . .]

I shall ask Mr. Carter, staff director of the Housing Subcommittee, to read Senator Sparkman's statement.

Mr. CARTER. This is a statement by Senator John Sparkman, chairman, Senate Banking and Currency Committee's Subcommittee on Housing.

(The statement referred to follows:)

[. . . . .]

IV. Relocation

Relocation is the most delicate and explosive area of the whole urban-renewal program. Relocation, which in this sense includes the acquisition of properties, particularly through the exercise of eminent domain, deals with the homes, businesses, and the very lives of those unfortunate people who live in areas to be cleared.

I have long felt that if we were not required to deal so intimately with human lives in this program and need only deal with money and materials, our difficulties would be substantially reduced. However, we must deal with human lives and human values, for the very basis of this program is our desire to improve the conditions under which human beings must live.

Nevertheless, the fact that we must condemn an individual's home and exercise the force and majesty of the Federal Government to take an individual's property prompts us to move with extreme caution and requires us to lean over backward in being fair to that individual. There is a statutory requirement that the urban-renewal plan of a community provide adequate housing for those who must be moved. A thorough discussion of the community's relocation program, its results, its deficiencies, and its problems would be of the utmost benefit to the subcommittee. Such a discussion should include some evaluation of the recent amendments to the statute providing for relocation payments for both businesses and individual families.

V. The Relationship Between the Urban-Renewal Program and the Federal Highway Program

If we are sufficiently intelligent to recognize the highway program and the urban-renewal program as twin tools to accomplish the objective of providing a better, healthier, and more prosperous community, we can devise methods of coordinating these two programs so as to achieve community objectives more speedily and at a reduced cost. Both of these programs can and have been used to clear undesirable slums.

The highway program, in addition, may result in the demolition of some adequate housing. Unlike the urban-renewal program, and the public-housing program, it appears that the highway program provides no adequate safeguards for dislocated families and businesses. There is, for example, no relocation payment. There is no statutory requirement in the highway program for relocation of displaced families. Obviously, these families must be relocated, particularly families which rent.

No provision is made to help those businesses which operate under a short-term lease. Their loss under the highway program is comparable to the loss they would suffer if they were affected by the urban-renewal program, and yet no comparable safeguards or benefits exist.

Have there been local efforts to coordinate the activities of the highway program and the urban-renewal program? Should all displaced families be entitled to the same benefits, regardless of whether they are displaced by the urban renewal or the highway program?

VI. Public Housing

The impact of the urban-renewal program and the highway program is now sizable, and will continue to grow in force and velocity. More and more families will be displaced as a result of these two programs. In Washington, D. C., the Chairman of the Board of Commissioners has already stated that lack of public housing will tend to slow down the District of Columbia urban-renewal program. Is this true in other communities?

Records indicate not only that communities are requesting few public-housing units, but that those communities whose applications for additional units have been approved are not undertaking construction promptly. As a result, a backlog of units, both requested but not authorized and authorized but not under construction, is building up. Local comments on this situation would be of assistance to the subcommittee.

In closing, I would like to express my appreciation to the members of the subcommittee for undertaking these hearings, and to witnesses who will appear voluntarily in an effort to contribute the benefits of their knowledge and experience to our efforts to improve the urban-renewal program.

Senator DOUGLAS. I should like to place various materials in the record, and then we shall begin.

(The material referred to follows:)

THE CHURCH FEDERATION OF GREATER CHICAGO,
Chicago, Ill., November 5, 1957.

Senator Paul H. Douglas,
    Acting Chairman, Senate Subcommittee on Housing,
                                            Chicago, Ill.

DEAR SENATOR DOUGLAS: On the authority of the federation's department of citizenship education and action, we are sending to you an expression of our concern that the housing needs of Chicago be given serious consideration by your subcommittee and by the Government in Washington.

This is undoubtedly one of our greatest social problems, and must be attacked in a much more vigorous way than has heretofore been the case if we are to meet the primary needs of Chicago people.

Enclosed is a copy of our most recent policy statement, entitled "An Address to Christians and the Churches Concerning Race Relations," which has a section to be found on pages 8, 9, and 10. This is a subsection under the general heading, "Tension Areas and What the Churches Can Do About Them." You will find this portion of the document marked in red.

Very sincerely,

John W. Harms,
EXECUTIVE VICE PRESIDENT

(The excerpt referred to follows:)

TENSION AREAS AND WHAT THE CHURCHES CAN DO ABOUT THEM

Housing

The acute housing shortage in Chicago and the surrounding metropolitan area has created keen, even bitter, competition for available housing. Racial prejudice and animosity, already present, are greatly stimulated by this competition and are especially directed toward those minorities which are most easily distinguished. The Negro community in Chicago is literally bursting its bounds. Sheer pressure of population has forced expansion. It is estimated that upward of 10,000 new Negro families are moving into the Chicago area each year, and that $2\frac{1}{2}$ more blocks each week are added to the number of blocks with at least 25-percent Negro occupancy (Real Estate Research Corp., 1956). Population movements of this size, involving different racial and cultural groups, almost inevitably kindle suspicion and tension.

The situation is further aggravated by some real-estate owners and

operators, white and Negro, who for a long time have exploited the perennial housing shortage by dividing buildings into 1- or 2-room apartments
which frequently lack proper sanitary facilities or sufficient privacy. A
survey in 1 area revealed that 3,580 families, plus 646 roomers were living
in dwelling units built for 1,127 families. Such overcrowding and intensive use are responsible for deterioration of the physical condition of the
property, abnormally high incidence of disease, juvenile delinquency, and
crime. These social and economic conditions then tend, mistakenly, to be
identified with the particular minorities occupying the property.

A factor of major importance in improving housing conditions for
minority groups in Chicago has been the work of the Chicago Housing
Authority, which provides homes for low-income families without discrimination as to race. In the past 21 years, this governmental agency has completed 29 housing projects, and now has 4 others under construction.
Together, these projects supply 18,447 dwelling units. In the design and
land-purchase stages are 28 additional projects, which will provide approximately 9,000 more dwellings. About 80 percent of this housing is
occupied by Negroes and, currently, Negro tenants are in all but 1 of
these projects.

The Chicago Land Clearance Commission, which also operates in part
on the basis of Federal loans and grants, in its 9 years of existence has
cleared, or is clearing, 474 acres of slum dwellings. Most of this space
has been on the South Side in the Negro district. Housing redevelopments
on this land are required to be open on a nondiscriminatory basis. In these
developments, care should be taken to see that political consideration and
special interests do not produce a new condition of housing segregation.

There is general acceptance of the idea that a program of public housing
is needed to supplement private efforts, if people are to be adequately
sheltered. But it is not generally recognized that people in the under-
privileged areas which are not included in such housing projects are
equally entitled to protection through the enforcement of housing, building, and zoning codes, as well as to public services such as policing,
garbage collection, street lighting, and educational facilities for their
children.

The old argument that if Negroes move into an area property values will
fall is being disproved in numerous situations. While it is true that whites
sometimes become panic stricken and quickly sell their homes, thereby
under-cutting property values, eventually real-estate values return to their
earlier level or even rise above it. And the whites who remain often revise
their earlier opinion. As one woman, who was formerly very hostile to the
inmovement of Negroes, remarked: "My new neighbors are more quiet
and the children are more respectful than those who used to live here."
The pastor of a Lutheran church and parochial school in Englewood states
that 2 years ago, when the area was occupied by whites, his school had a

window-breakage bill of $170, but there has been no breakage since the block "changed hands."

Important to the whole question of housing for racial minorities is equality of opportunity in financing, either the building or the purchasing of a home. The prospective minority-group homeowner has great difficulty in obtaining a loan, and may be compelled to pay higher rates of interest, and his insurance rates may also be higher.

It is, of course, obvious that, under current real-estate practices, racial minorities may not buy where they choose on an open market.

What the Churches Can Do   Local churches can begin by encouraging their members to study the housing situation in their own vicinity. Especially where Negroes and whites are living in the same or adjoining communities, committees from their churches should study and work together on the problem.

The churches can make a large contribution by educating their total membership concerning housing and its influence on race relations in the Chicago area. Members who are property owners should be urged to refuse to join restrictive "gentlemen's agreements" or exploit racial prejudice even for their own financial advantage.[1] The churches can act affirmatively by challenging their members, whether owners or tenants, to remain in an area when its racial composition begins to change, and to assist in building a stable, cooperative, democratic neighborhood. A local church can properly stimulate pride in the local community. One such organized a cleanup campaign and even arranged to secure paint at wholesale prices to make it more available for persons willing to improve the appearance of their houses. At Christmas time, through the efforts of the interracial block committee (also organized by the church), each of the 38 houses in the block had a lighted tree in its front yard.

Property owners, white and Negro alike, should be alerted to the fact that it is unchristian to select tenants on the basis of race. A real-estate operator who capitalizes on the fears of white people in a changing area and on the desperate need of Negroes for housing, sins against God and his fellow men. Real estate dealers in city and suburbs should be helped to realize that the desire of the people in any given neighborhood is to maintain the fine residential qualities of that neighborhood, and should be persuaded that these qualities can be maintained by a careful selection of purchases regardless of their race, color, creed, or national background.

---

[1] A conspicuous example of church action in this regard is the advice given to Presbyterians by the General Assembly of the Presbyterian Church, U. S. A., in 1956, to wit: That in the sale of residential property Christians should practice nondiscrimination.

Gentlemen, I am Paul Iaccino, executive secretary of the Cook
County Industrial Union Council with 250,000 members. We asked to
be heard by your committee because of our grave concern with the slum
clearance and urban renewal programs as they affect this metropolitan
area. We may not have new facts for you, but we feel sure that our emphasis on a few of these facts should have your careful attention.

Chicago, as you know, is making use of the Federal aids to slum clearance and rehabilitation, and we in labor are convinced that without such
aid, Chicago would quickly fall behind in its race against decay and the
evils of overaged neighborhoods. We want to go further and state that it
is our firm belief that the only possible successful alternative to Federal
aid, financial and program planning, would be a drastic upheaval and
overhaul of the entire building, financing, and management industries of
this area to attain lower costs, revised planning standards, and a new concept of human relations in our city such as would enable our second most
needy group of citizens, the middle-income people, to afford out of their
own pockets, to do the renewal and rehabilitation which needs to be done
where we live. We are not too hopeful you, or our city will manage this
alternative, and we therefore urge that the Federal program continue, but
we also urge that it be altered in some degree to avoid so many new problems for us.

Chicago has not had the housing it needed in the lifetime of most of its
citizens. In a market in which there are more bidders than there is good
housing, we have a constant problem of housing our poor and our low-paid
people. We need more public housing, and will need more for years to
come, until we have no more unhoused low-income people, or the unex-
pected miracle of the low cost, privately built housing unit comes into
being. You should plan on more public housing.

Next to our poor, the most hard-pressed group in Chicago are our
middle-income group — our union members and our small-business and
professional people who receive no subsidy but are expected to pay their
way in the market. Several points in our experience we feel we must
emphasize are: 1. Most new private housing built on land cleared with the
aid of Federal funds is almost as high priced as strictly private new construction. This housing is in the main small units, unsuited for a family
with children, and units large enough for a family rent at levels far beyond
what middle-income people can sensibly afford. The result is, slum clearance and rehabilitation in Chicago is a process of removing working people
from their old neighborhoods, with no prospect of ever returning unless
or until decay again reduced the cost to our levels. This aspect we do not
approve, yet it is the prospect we face in Hyde Park and the fact in such
places as the New York City project. 2. The new roads and public build-

ings, the reduced density of housing in cleared areas, means that the middle-income family must relocate itself, with its own resources, outside the central areas of the city. Thousands of individual homes have been sold to this class of our population, at the edges of the city, and in our suburbs. There are almost no Chicago builders who build homes for the economy of this class. Instead these families undertake mortgages often 3 to 4 times their annual total wages. They are meeting the payments of principal and interest in a large percentage of cases by having 1 wage earner hold 2 jobs, or by having 2 wage earners in the family.

This situation must be a stern warning not only to your committee, but to the city of Chicago. If a recession should occur, a nasty situation will be created here. Many of these mortgage loans will be defaulted. But we believe as well, that many Chicago area building and loan associations will be in trouble, when their assets become foreclosed real estate, and they are unable to meet all the demand of their depositors for cash withdrawals.

Unless you can assure yourselves that a recession will never occur in our area, you should, we believe, anticipate this tragic possibility by action in the next session of Congress. 3. Forcing the workingman into the outlying areas compounds our traffic and travel problems. These people, who must travel to their jobs and from the job each day, put new and heavier loads on roads, and public transportation, where such exists. This leads to a demand for more roads, and more land withdrawn from housing in the city. There must be a better way. We suggest that better coordination between the planners of roads and urban renewal may help some.

Obviously the situation of the middle-income family in our area is a major concern. He is the victim of the current convenience of city planning and urban renewal. He is not the beneficiary of any class planning or subsidy, since he is supposed to be able to pay his own way. In our area he is offered housing in quantity only in price levels that bleed him almost to poverty. He lives on the edge of disaster. The real-estate industry or Government will some day have to take the pressure off this big body of people. We prefer, because we are supposed to pay our way, that industry solve our problem of reasonable housing security, but we suggest that industry will never make a sincere attempt to do so, except to meet the competition of government, or to beat off its intervention.

We therefore urge the Congress to give this problem of the middle-income citizen its proper weight and significance in the national planning. We know that some members of your committee have realized better than we, the seriousness of the situation we point to, and we appreciate your past efforts. We also urgently and insistently ask that there be some action to solve the problems.

[. . . . .]

Senator DOUGLAS. We are very glad to have as our first witness to open the Chicago hearings the distinguished mayor of Chicago,

Richard J. Daley, who has been making a magnificent record in all respects, but a particularly magnificent record in the field of urban renewal and neighborhood improvement. We are very glad, indeed, to welcome you, Mayor Daley, and we will await with interest your statement.

Statement of Richard J. Daley, Mayor, Chicago, Ill.

Mayor DALEY. Senator Douglas and representatives of the Housing Subcommittee of the Senate Banking and Currency Committee, I have with me Ira J. Bach, commissioner, department of city planning; Phil A. Doyle, executive director, Chicago Land Clearance Commission; Clifford Campbell, deputy commissioner, department of city planning; and D. E. Mackelmann, consultant, department of planning.

You will recall that I appeared before this subcommittee in Washington on April 2, 1957. At that time I joined with several mayors throughout the Nation who were concerned with continuing Federal aid for the urban-renewal program of our American cities. Congress recognized the urgent needs of the people and later authorized $350 million for this program. The people of Chicago are thankful to the Members of Congress for this action.

[. . . . .]

The city of Chicago, as you know, Senator, has been a pioneer in the vital program of urban renewal — a program to rebuild and revitalize the neighborhoods and communities of Chicago.

[. . . . .]

Our public-housing projects continue to be the major resource for relocation housing of low-income families displaced by slum-clearance and public-improvement projects. There is, therefore, a continuing need for public low-rent housing as a vital part of our urban-renewal program.

[. . . . .]

Our planning activities have been strengthened by the organization of a new city planning department and of a metropolitan planning commission. In short, we have developed and are carrying out a workable program of city building and rebuilding.

Last June the voters approved a $113 million bond issue, which included $20 million for urban renewal and $10 million each for slum clearance and community conservation. The services and facilities included in the bond issue, in addition to urban renewal, were sewerage, street lighting, fire protection, recreation, mass transportation, and garbage disposal.

The city of Chicago now has some 10 years of experience in the program of redevelopment and conservation. You will recall that last April I suggested a 3-year program of Federal aid at $250 million a year. I pointed out the need and the necessity for a continuing program. Perhaps it would be wiser now to think in terms of a 10-year program, so that we can count on continuity and plan our work on a longer-range basis.

You will note that I assume continuing Federal aid for urban renewal. I said in April, and I would like to repeat, that:

I am sure I speak not only of Chicago's aspirations, but also of those of other cities, when I urge that the Federal Government continue its aid on a scale large enough to cope with the problem of urban blight so that the aroused interest of the municipal governments and of the people will not lessen, but rather grow as the program of urban improvement goes forward.

The limitations imposed by the Federal Government on the funds authorized by Congress for urban renewal, therefore, are quite unrealistic. It is my understanding that the commitments already made by the Urban Renewal Administration and the applications already pending in its regional and Washington offices, will exhaust the $250 million which the Administration proposes to release in this fiscal year out of the $350 million authorized. We are, therefore, coming again to a period of uncertainty as to the future of the program as we experienced earlier this year, when no funds were said to be available.

Therefore, I urge that steps be taken immediately to release the additional $100 million authorized this year.

May I also call your attention to the fact that of the $500 million authorized in 1954, $100 million have not yet been released. The release of these two $100 million funds already authorized would assure continuity of the program until Congress in its next session can review the overall program.

It seems to me we ought to approach the question of making our cities better places in which to live and work with the same courage and with the same scope with which we approach the national ex-

pressway program, both in terms of the period of time over which
the program is to be carried out, and in terms of the funds that have
been authorized for this particular program.

[.   .   .   .   .]

This is our basic purpose, and it is worth reiterating: This is a
program for all of the people of the country. You cannot separate
juvenile delinquency, crime, and health from these programs. Certainly, we all recognize the need to economize and reduce the Federal budget, but there can be no intention to economize on human
needs, nor should there be. It would be false economy to interrupt a
program now just well started and essential if the inventory of
housing is to be protected and if the land of our city is to be used
efficiently and productively, and if the present and future generation
is to live and grow in an environment which promotes good citizenship and a strong nation.

Present here this morning are the operating heads of the city
governmental agencies administering the urban-renewal program.
They will be happy to answer any questions and provide any information you may desire.

May I thank you very gratefully for the opportunity of appearing
before you and this fine subcommittee.

Senator DOUGLAS. Thank you, Mayor Daley, for your very
fine statement.

[.   .   .   .   .]

Mr. WALLACE. I would like to direct a question to the group
as a whole, and whichever one wants to answer, that will be fine.

I have a copy of the Urban League Newsletter for September–
October 1957, quoting Mr. Kenneth Green, research head of the
Urban League. The article reads as follows:

NEW MAP PINPOINTS EFFECT OF CITY "RENEWAL"
ON NEGRO HOUSING

It is quite obvious that most forms of urban renewal tend to increase housing shortages. Not widely realized however, is the startling
extent to which such land clearance, in Chicago, affects the housing supply
of one group — the Negro community. Says Kenneth Green, Urban League
research head, "It seems critically necessary to focus attention on three
largely neglected aspects of problems related to urban renewal:

"First, the alarming degree to which renewal projects are so located
that they displace Negro homes.

"Second, the extent of the load which this displacement will add to the
already intolerable overcrowding in Negro housing.

"Third, the fact that Chicago's overall planning gives little or no explicit consideration to this problem."

Because of the need for information on these points, the Chicago Urban League has developed a graphic presentation of the situation, in map form.

The Urban League's new map shows the coincidence in location of Chicago's renewal projects and the location of Negro population. While Negroes constitute 20 percent of the population, they bear more than 60 percent of the brunt of such demolition.

Specifically, according to the Housing and Redevelopment Coordinator, 1948–56 saw 86,000 Chicagoans displaced; 66 percent were Negro. For 1957–58, the South Expressway alone will displace about 12,000, and other projects already approved will displace at least 50,000. To this over-all total of nearly 150,000 displaced, many will inevitably be added in the years just ahead.

Where Will They Live?

Says William E. Hill, housing authority and long-time Urban League board member, "With displacement affecting Chicago's Negro population so heavily, the resultant housing load falls on those parts of the city which are already the most overcrowded. And with residential segregation limiting free movement of Negroes, the population density in the already overcrowded areas keeps soaring."

Planned relocation of displaced families, offered as a solution, is admitted to have failed quite generally, according to a recent report by the city planning commission.

Actually, the housing strains due to renewal activities are "only one part of the desperate picture," according to Urban League authorities. "Add the housing needs caused by normal population growth, plus immigration," says a league spokesman, "and we see that at least 100,000 additional housing units, available to Negroes, will be needed in the next 6 or 7 years, just to keep residential density at its already staggering level. What plans does Chicago have to provide these houses?"

According to Dennis O'Harrow, executive director, American Society of Planning Officials, "There is no stated plan by the city government looking toward a greater Chicago." The lack of such a plan makes it almost impossible to predict and control such social consequences of urban renewal as population displacement.

(The map referred to will be found in the files of the committee.)
Perhaps Mr. Bach will be the one to answer this.

Mr. BACH. I will start off, if I may, Mr. Mayor.

The overall program of the city of Chicago has been one, as was pointed out, directing attention to conservation as well as clearance, and a good deal of code enforcement, and so forth, is included in this overall program. There has been a considerable amount of

Negro population within some of the slum areas. However, this has been carried out in an orderly relocation pattern. To our knowledge, at least in the first instance, every family that has been relocated has had their habitation improved. In many instances they have been moved to public housing where, of course, their housing has been improved enormously. But in many instances the relocation pattern has been such that the improvement has been direct and in the first instance.

As to the future program, as I mentioned a moment earlier, the stress is on conservation as well as on clearance. This is why we need the continuity to the program, so that we can plan over a 10-year basis and balance our relocation with adequate housing not only in the low-income field, but in medium- and low-medium income housing as well.

I believe we have proven this because our records indicate families that have relocated under our slum clearance are better housed now.

Senator DOUGLAS. Can you prove that?

Mr. BACH. We have checked a number of areas and find these families have in the first instance. Mr. Doyle might add to that.

[. . . . .]

Mr. DOYLE. [. . .] The real difficulty is that we disrupt an area and uncover every social ill that ever existed, from drunkenness to physical disability to old age and senility and income problems. Actually, it is the old pensioner who has a room and is sharing facilities with a family, and that kind of problem, which creates the biggest relocation problem.

So it seems to me it is a matter of not only paying attention to an increase in the housing supply in the middle-income brackets in addition to the low-income brackets, but also that a city should develop a breadth of social services which would take care of these problems which very often get public recognition. A lot of these problems I think exist in areas that you do not clear but, you never uncover them because you don't clear them.

Senator DOUGLAS. There is one obvious problem, of course, and that is the fact that the areas which have been primarily cleared are the outlying areas close to the business district on the southwest and north sides. These have throughout the last 75 years been regions where successive waves of low-income people have lived. In recent years they have been the areas where the Negroes have lived. Now the Negroes face a difficulty which the previous nationality low-income groups did not face, namely, that when they move out into the areas farther removed from the center of the city, they encounter a large degree of local prejudice.

Do you think that there is sufficient leeway in the city so that you can clear these areas and yet these people can still find satisfactory accommodations elsewhere?

Mr. DOYLE. I do, sir. I think the rate at which, to speak very frankly about it, the Negro is improving his economic position, has as much to do with this as anything else. Increasingly you see some very striking figures recently on the numbers of Negro members who have seniority now and have a kind of security that guarantees them.

[. . . . .]

Mr. CAMPBELL. Mr. Chairman, I would like to turn to the question of relocation. I submit it is one of the most sensitive and delicate problems in the whole program of urban renewal. Some of us who have some knowledge of the historical pattern out of which Chicago developed know full well that by and large Negroes live in those areas which are most in need of some sort of urban renewal treatment, but I think there is much more on the plus side than appears on the surface. I would certainly not be critical of those organizations which point up the need for more sensitivity in terms of relocating people. I think they are necessary as a catalytic agent to keep a sharp focus on the problem. I am reminded, and I use it as a very typical example of positive action in this area, that as late as 1948, out of some 49 high schools in the city of Chicago, there were not more than 5 or 6 where there were Negro students. Today we find no more than 5 or 6 where there are not Negro students. That would, in my judgment, indicate there has been an orderly movement of people to all sections of the city.

However, I would submit that we recognize that we are not batting 100 percent on this question of relocation. It is a sensitive area and will call for our best judgment and thinking and planning to remove and eliminate as much as possible human suffering where we go into an area for slum treatment and urban renewal.

Senator DOUGLAS. Thank you very much.

[. . . . .]

TUESDAY, NOVEMBER 5, 1957
Chicago, Ill.

Senator DOUGLAS. We are greatly honored this morning by the presence of the distinguished and able mayor of St. Louis,

Raymond R. Tucker, who has made a magnificent record as chief executive of that great city. Mayor Tucker, we appreciate the interest which you are taking in this matter in coming all the way from St. Louis to testify.

Statement of Raymond R. Tucker, Mayor, St. Louis, Mo., Accompanied by Charles L. Farris, Executive Director, St. Louis Housing Authority and Land Clearance for Redevelopment Authority

Mayor TUCKER. Thank you very much, Senator, for your most gracious remarks. Shall I proceed?

Senator DOUGLAS. Yes, please.

Mayor TUCKER. As mayor of the city of St. Louis, I wish to make a short general statement. The views of our city with respect to the slum clearance, housing, and urban renewal programs will be presented in more detailed form by Mr. Charles L. Farris, executive director of the St. Louis Housing Authority and Land Clearance for Redevelopment Authority of the City of St. Louis.

We welcome the opportunity to appear before your subcommittee at this time. The city of St. Louis is in the midst of a great effort to destroy the decay and blight in its very center. Our citizens have voted to spend over a hundred million dollars for capital improvements during the next few years. We are not sitting by idly and waiting for things to be done for us.

But, the total cost of rebuilding our city is simply beyond our present financial resources. This is the problem which challenges your subcommittee today, and for which an answer must be found: How can the Federal Government, which has the major tax resources in our country today, cooperate most effectively with our large cities in the renewal of their residential, commercial, and industrial areas?

The future of all social-welfare programs is uncertain in our present political climate. Yet the need for such programs was never greater. The American people are moving by the millions each year from rural to urban centers. Despite this, there are indications of a deemphasis of Federal programs designed to alleviate the problems resulting from this migration.

We, who live and work in the cities, appreciate the great work you have done over the years. We are thankful for the work of your subcommittee's members and staff. You make us feel that our investments of effort in the future of our city are well made. It is in this spirit that we are here to present our views and to exchange views with you.

Senator DOUGLAS. Thank you very much.

Mayor TUCKER. May I present Mr. Farris now?

Senator DOUGLAS. May I ask you this, Mayor: You say that the city of St. Louis has approved bond issues amounting to approximately $100 million?

Mayor TUCKER. $110 million to be exact.

Senator DOUGLAS. To be spent over how long a period of time?

Mayor TUCKER. We have at the present time a 5-year program for spending at the rate of $12 million a year. At the end of this 5 years we will be able to sell the whole bond issue if we so desire and be able to finance it.

SENATOR DOUGLAS. You mean the additional $50 million?

Mayor TUCKER. That is right.

Senator DOUGLAS. So you are roughly planning to spend $12 million a year for 9 years.

Mayor TUCKER. That is right.

Senator DOUGLAS. For what purposes is this money being expended, Mayor?

Mayor TUCKER. We have appropriated there $10 million for urban renewal, $4 million for neighborhood rehabilitation, and the rest is divided between hospitals, recreation, parks, expressways, and things of that kind — $18 million.

Senator DOUGLAS. Have your projects been approved by the Federal agencies?

Mayor TUCKER. All of them as yet, no; but our expressways are now underway and have the approval of the Federal organization.

Senator DOUGLAS. Has the urban-renewal program been submitted to the Federal authorities yet?

Mayor TUCKER. We have one to start and one in the planning stage.

Senator DOUGLAS. Has there been a reservation of funds by the Federal agency?

Mr. FARRIS. There has been a reservation of funds, Senator, on all three projects.

Senator DOUGLAS. That is, urban renewal is making a total reservation of approximately $22,700,000?

Mr. FARRIS. That is correct, sir.

Senator DOUGLAS. I congratulate the city of St. Louis. Mayor Tucker, do you find much opposition to urban renewal in the city of St. Louis?

Mayor TUCKER. Not that I am aware of.

Senator DOUGLAS. Is there much support for it?

Mayor TUCKER. I think the best evidence of that is that they voted for it by 5 to 6 to 1, that is, the citizens did.

Senator DOUGLAS. It is very hard to get a bond issue approved.

Mayor TUCKER. Yes. It requires a two-thirds majority but it carried by 5 to 6 to 1, which would indicate their approval.

Senator DOUGLAS. In the past St. Louis has been very conservative in approving bond issues. Is that not true?

Mayor TUCKER. I would say that is true.

Senator DOUGLAS. Mayor Tucker, there is quite a strong movement on, as you know, to take the Federal Government out of slum clearance and urban renewal and public housing and turn these issues over to the States. What in your judgment should be done about that? Would you feel happy at the Federal Government getting out of this picture?

Mayor TUCKER. I would feel it would be most unfortunate if it were channeled down to the State governments.

Senator DOUGLAS. Why do you feel that way, Mayor?

Mayor TUCKER. Experience has taught me that the State governments, as a rule, do not have a sympathetic attitude toward the urban centers.

Senator DOUGLAS. Missouri is gifted with two great cities, Kansas City and St. Louis. Both of them are great cities. Cannot Kansas City and St. Louis get anything from the Missouri Legislature which they want?

Mayor TUCKER. I think Kansas City is perhaps a little bit more successful than St. Louis, but neither one has any degree of success of which they are proud.

Senator DOUGLAS. Will St. Louis and Kansas City be underrepresented in the State legislatures?

Mayor TUCKER. They are.

Senator DOUGLAS. Control of the State legislatures is in the hands of the small——

Mayor TUCKER. The rural areas.

Senator DOUGLAS. The rural counties?

Mayor TUCKER. That is right.

Senator DOUGLAS. They are not very alert to the needs of the huge metropolis?

Mayor TUCKER. I think that is a correct statement, Senator.

Senator DOUGLAS. Lacking adequate representation in the State legislatures, you feel, therefore, that you must make your appeal to the Federal Government?

Mayor TUCKER. I would prefer, under the existing circumstances, to do that.

Senator DOUGLAS. Then what would you say to the people who declare that slum clearance and these other matters should be turned over to the States? Would you say, first, put your system of representation in order and give the cities adequate representation in the State legislature?

Mayor TUCKER. I think that is a very desirable answer to whether or not the Federal Government should turn over these programs to the States. I do believe, however, that the taxing power of the State and the cities would be unable to support these programs.

Senator DOUGLAS. Because you are limited in your local taxation to the general property tax?

Mayor TUCKER. Yes.

Senator DOUGLAS. The State is largely restricted to the sales tax?

Mayor TUCKER. To a great extent.

Senator DOUGLAS. You have a limit on your bonding capacity?

Mayor TUCKER. Yes. We have. It is 10 percent of our assessed value.

Senator DOUGLAS. Have you about reached that?

Mayor TUCKER. We are within about $25 million, and we should have that reserve in the event of an emergency of any kind.

Senator DOUGLAS. This is a very important question. Some of my friends who are on the Kestnbaum Commission started out with a great prejudice in favor of turning these programs over to the States. The more they studied the sources of revenue which the localities and the States had, on the one hand, and the gross underrepresentation of American cities in State legislatures, on the other hand, they were driven against their will to the belief that, unless and until the representation in the State legislatures was altered, and better allocation of revenues between Federal Government and

State government provided, the cities would have to turn to the
Federal Government for assistance.

It is difficult enough in the Federal Government, because, in the
House of Representatives, as you know, the congressional districts
are laid out by the various State legislatures, which are themselves
overrepresented in the country districts. If you will examine the
boundary lines of the various congressional districts throughout the
country, I think you will find that there are some 20 or 30 seats
which, on the basis of contiguity in population, you would expect to
be urban counties but which are largely dominated by the rural
and suburban groups.

For instance, the city of Rochester, N. Y. There would seem to
be a compact congressional district there, but, nevertheless, it is
split right down the center at the river, and each district has tied
to it a series of rural counties which, in practice, means that the
rural counties and the suburbs will dominate the city. The city of
Rochester has not had full representation.

Much the same situation exists in Buffalo, and a Brooklyn district,
I think, is notorious, and some of the California districts are notorious.

Do you have any complaints in Missouri?

Mayor TUCKER. Of course, I think that is the common attribute
of all of us. We believe that we are grossly underrepresented, too.
We have 3 Congressmen from the city of St. Louis, out of 17 in the
State.

Senator DOUGLAS. Thank you very much, Mayor Tucker. Mr.
Farris.

Mr. FARRIS. Senator Douglas and members of the staff, I wish
to thank this committee for the opportunity to appear before it
and to present our views on the urban-renewal and public-housing
programs. Mayor Raymond R. Tucker has already spoken to you,
and the mayor has asked me to present to your committee a more
detailed statement of our views.

As Mayor Tucker told you, my name is Charles L. Farris, and I
am executive director of both the St. Louis Housing Authority and
the Land Clearance for Redevelopment Authority of the City of
St. Louis. Both programs are administered under one executive head
and a combined staff in St. Louis. Mo.

[. . . . .]

I think it is time for people interested in the housing field to recognize one specific point. We cannot say that you can take people

from the slums and put them into decent, safe and sanitary housing and that automatically this changes their whole attitude and method of procedure whereby they live. People have to be worked with over a period of 2 years, we find, before you elevate their standards and living habits to accommodate the kind of quarters they are living in.

Senator DOUGLAS. That is, there is an improvement?

Mr. FARRIS. Yes, sir.

Senator DOUGLAS. But not as great an improvement as you would like?

Mr. FARRIS. That is right. On that point, Senator, there is one other aspect I should like to mention. At the present time the Public Housing Administration, and this is very recent, has just issued a directive which makes it possible finally for us to hire people to work with these families. Up until very recently they had an unwritten policy which prohibited it. We have, through a waiver of this unwritten policy, for about 8 months been working with these families in terms of the kinds of people who could be the most good to them in elevating their standards and living habits.

Senator DOUGLAS. Garbage disposal?

Mr. FARRIS. Garbage disposal and just internal methods of cleanliness. Stove cleaning and little pieces of handiwork that need to be done that you do not want to call in a maintenance man for. These aids are equipped to do that kind of thing and assist them in terms of personal problems, like methods of budgeting and dealing with children.

The people we have hired are women whose families have grown up and who have been through this whole process themselves and who can be extremely helpful to these families. I think it is time we get back to some of the basic concepts originally contemplated in the 1937 housing bill, namely, that we want to increase the standards of the families we want to bring in, with the ultimate objective of these families moving from public housing and going into the private industry field. May I continue?

Mr. WALLACE. I think for the sake of the record I would like to make a point and see if you do not agree with it. It is not that any group of persons are better trained than any other group of persons. Is it not really, instead, the fact that many families in a low-income group have deep family difficulties, that is, they have lost the head of the household? For example, many of them are women who have to work and have 3, 4, or 5 children. It is very difficult to maintain the proper supervision over these children when they have to work to make a living for them and there is no breadwinner in the family. Problems of that type. So it is really mostly a situation where you have deep family problems rather than differences in one group of people or another group of people.

Mr. FARRIS. I would certainly agree with that, Mr. Wallace. I would like to add to that, however, one other point. You must remember the families that we are relocating are families taken from slums. With all its implications, and without talking about what it means, you must remember in most instances these are families that have had to double up with limited facilities, and so on and so forth. Consequently, this is the only manner of life they are familiar with. They have lived like that for years and years. To take them from there and put them in decent and sanitary housing does not mean that automatically they will change overnight.

We know there is intense pride on the part of these families in terms of the new dwellings they occupy after we have had an opportunity to work with them. It would be most interesting, and I would like very much the opportunity of taking you around, letting you see some of the families we have in our projects. I think you would recognize this point as a very familiar one. [. . .]

May I make a couple of additional comments, Senator?

Senator DOUGLAS. Yes.

Mr. FARRIS. I think it is rather interesting to note that the actual expenditures in 1956 for the slum-clearance and urban-renewal program were less than the money spent on fish and wildlife in 1956.

Senator DOUGLAS. You mean, by the Federal Government?

Mr. FARRIS. By the Federal Government. Yes, sir. I would also like to observe expenditures for annual contributions for low-rent housing and capital grants for slum clearance and urban renewal combined represent but 2 percent of all Federal domestic grants-in-aid in 1956. More significantly, they were less than one-fourth the Federal expenditures for aid to dependent children. I will not go into the fact that many of these dependent children who live in our projects are certainly living in slums that ought to be eliminated.

Obligational authority for the urban-renewal program is but one-thirtieth of that for the Federal highway program at the present time. So I think these are significant factors that have to be weighed in terms of ribbons of concrete as opposed to people.

Senator DOUGLAS. I quite agree with you. I have always marveled at the way in which it is very popular to build roads and very unpopular to build schools. How it is thought to be more important to get from one place to another than it is to have decent homes to start out from or come back to at night. I have marveled at the sense of social values which the community seems to exhibit.

I can only say it is easier to get $40 billion for a national system of highways than it is to get $40 million for housing for low-income groups. Why this should be so I do not know. Mayor Tucker, I hope you can release this man so that he can go around the country for a month or two talking to interested groups, just as he has been talking to us this morning, because I think he might make some converts.

Will you consider the possibility of a leave of absence with pay?

Mayor TUCKER. When he completes those projects we are interested in.

[. . . . .]

Mr. FARRIS. I would like to make another observation I think is extremely important, which the mayor and I have discussed. We would like to recommend very strongly that there be created a Department of Housing and Urban Affairs. We feel that cities and communities must have representation at Cabinet level in order to insure a proper participation in administration policy decisions. The Administrator of the Housing and Home Finance Agency, as the agency presently exists, by not being at Cabinet level is so far down the line that by the time the tax dollar is split up that he comes in for his piece through the mechanism of people who are in staff capacities as opposed to being a member of the Cabinet where he would be able to make his direct statement and his position felt in terms of what ought to be done as it relates to cities.

I am not just talking in terms of housing, and I use the term "urban affairs" because I do not want the concept to become limited only to existing housing programs as administered by the Housing and Home Finance Agency.

Senator DOUGLAS. The cities are the Cinderellas of American life anyway. The major portion of the people live in the cities, but we are underrepresented in the State legislatures, we are underrepresented in the National Congress, we are underrepresented in the Senate.

Mr. FARRIS. And we are underrepresented in the administration.

Mr. WALLACE. But we are Cinderellas without a glass slipper.

[. . . . .]

Senator DOUGLAS. Mayor Zeidler we are very glad indeed to welcome you. We know what a magnificent record you are making up in Milwaukee and we are very proud, as midwesterners, of your achievements and accomplishments. We also appreciate the fact that you helped to father the world championship baseball team. You have had much better luck with your Braves than we have had with the Cubs or White Sox.

Generally we agree with you highly, Mayor Zeidler, although we have great differences on lake diversion, but we will not let it disturb the testimony this afternoon. You may proceed in your own way. You are a great mayor of a great city.

Statement of Frank P. Zeidler, Mayor, Milwaukee, Wis.

Mayor ZEIDLER. Thank you, Senator Douglas. I am extremely complimented to hear that come from you, because I regard you as one of the shining lights of the Senate.

Senator DOUGLAS. We now bandy compliments back and forth.

[. . . . .]

Mayor ZEIDLER. I presume that earlier you caught my expression that when you move people out of slums, you ought to have other communities prepared to receive them. That means you prepare satellite communities or allow the central cities to expand to put them in there.

Senator DOUGLAS. And suppose the communities do not want to receive them?

Mr. WALLACE. And suppose the people do not want to go to them?

Mayor ZEIDLER. This is where English law is superior to ours. You can create it. But when you move them out of an area like you did on the South Side of Chicago, you have to have some place for them. What happens to a lot of them is, they go into existing housing and pile up. Some studies made recently in the Chicago area indicate that there is a tremendous amount of piling up here, largely because you cleared out areas but did not provide adequate replacement housing for them. As it stands now, title I seems to be very lucrative to big builders and has evoked much interest, but not enough thought has been given to the people being thrown out.

[. . . . .]

Mr. WALLACE. It is a very real problem in moving people out of these areas when many of them lived there for 30 or 40 or 50 years, and are used to an established community, which by our standards is not too pretty. But they are still human beings and it is awfully difficult administratively and humanely to pick up a large segment of our population and move it from one place to another. That is especially so when you have no programs for providing housing for a large group of them.

Mayor ZEIDLER. I have no quarrel with you, but I think it is a defect of the existing program. I know how difficult it is to move people out of areas because that burden falls on my office. However, I believe they are not so much attached to the particular kind of house they live in as they are attached to their church and their neighborhood and their butcher and their shoemaker.

Under the present existing plans you put the shoemaker and butcher out of business and you only put houses back. You forget the small-business man. So there is a defect at the present time in our concept of planning. This was very carefully pointed out in the first article of the municipalities which appeared recently in Fortune magazine, where the planning is deficient because we do not think of the small-business man.

Senator DOUGLAS. The shopping center replaces the neighborhood store.

Mayor ZEIDLER. Yes. And it is not adequate because not every neighborhood store can go into a shopping center. It is not an incubator.

[. . . . .]

One of the big problems of cities is that although the city code enforcements are very tough, when they go into the courts the courts give extension after extension to the owners, who systematically milk properties.

Senator DOUGLAS. You say that happens in Milwaukee?

Mayor ZEIDLER. Ah, yes.

Senator DOUGLAS. I thought this was peculiar to Chicago.

Mayor ZEIDLER. I can show you, Senator, a building in Milwaukee which some years ago the fire chief noted and called me to look at. There was a group of old men living on the third floor and the roof was so slanting you could not stand up straight. There was no heat in the building and we found there were 36 separate actions by the city against the owner to try to take that building down, but it was still in existence. The building was built in 1876.

The third floor is not now occupied. This building probably returned a value of 100 percent of its assessed valuation each year to the owner. We have still been unable to get complete code enforcement, because they could take us into the courts and get delay after delay.

Somehow the courts seem to favor, in most places in the United States, those owners who systematically seek to defeat the intent of the building codes. Whether they do it intentionally or are leaning over backward to protect property owners, I do not know, but this is one problem which has led to Federal Government support to clear out whole districts.

Senator DOUGLAS. You mean you want the Federal Government to cure the cities of their own moral weaknesses?

Mayor ZEIDLER. I said one of the reasons why the cities have gone to the Federal Government has been that they have been unable to deal with some of these districts on an individual basis by dealing with the landlord. So they decided to buy them out.

My own feeling, of course, is that there is a problem involved here as to whether or not it is morally right to spend money under title I to reward slum landlords. That is what we are doing. At the present time it is the only way we have of getting rid of some of these districts on a wholesale basis.

Senator DOUGLAS. Part of the regular law of the country and really part of the Constitution is the principle that the State government shall not take property without due process of law. Due process of law carries with it merely the payment of market value. There should be no confiscation of property values.

It is different in England where they have the right to take property if decent housing prevailed. That is the English law, but that is not the American law, and we have to work with American law.

Similarly, on your suggestion that we have the Federal Government permit cities to annex territory adjacent to them, and denounce the system with the States as the intermediaries between the local government and the Federal Government, where localities are the creatures of the State and not of the Federal Government, because of the Federal nature of our Government, which is not a dominion, the Central Government cannot have those powers that it has in England. So whatever our desires may be, it is just impossible for us to proceed anywhere along that line which you suggested.

Mayor ZEIDLER. Except as I said in my testimony that by the

carrot-and-stock philosophy you can encourage States to do that which they are failing to do now, namely, to deal adequately with their great metropolitan centers. As a matter of fact, in many places States are encouraging the fragmentation of these metropolitan centers by setting the suburbs against the central city. Of course, the Federal Government cannot look at it with indifference, because part of the national strength of the Federal Government is to be found in these urban areas, so the Federal Government does have a direct interest.

Senator DOUGLAS. I find myself in great sympathy with what you say, but there are not many United States Senators who come from urban areas. We are in the main in a very small minority and are more or less looked down upon because we do come from the urban areas. Yet the Senate is more friendly to the big cities than is the House. The House is largely dominated by rural districts, and the rural population is overrepresented in the House of Representatives because the State legislatures lay out the congressional districts and they themselves have an overrepresentation of the country districts.

So while the population is moving citywise there is no accompanying increase in strength of the cities either in the States or in the National Government. The National Government is far more friendly to the cities than various State governments are.

Mayor ZEIDLER. May I say this, in a slight amendation of your remarks: The Congress and many State legislatures are not necessarily dominated by rural people. In terms of agriculture and the farmers, they are dominated by smalltown people who presume to speak for the agricultural States and the farmers. It is a very subtle but nice distinction which ought to be recognized, because you will find many people come from incorporated areas who presume to speak for farmers around the area.

Senator DOUGLAS. In other words, it is the county seat which will speak for the countryside?

Mayor ZEIDLER. Yes. I at one time suggested that the State of Wisconsin have a special department dealing with the cities of the State, but this encountered hostility not only from the rural areas, but also from many smaller towns that felt it was an invasion of home rule.

Under the Canadian system of government, as in the case of the Province of Ontario, there is a department of municipal affairs. The department was powerful enough to effect the federation which is known as the Municipality of Metropolitan Toronto. We have nothing similar here.

I believe Mayor Daley yesterday or the day before suggested a Department of Urban Affairs in the Federal Government. A lot of us have supported this particular idea. I do not think it is necessarily an invasion of home rule, but I do think since so many people now live in incorporated areas, that a Department of Urban Affairs in the Federal Government is fully as justified as the Department of Agriculture is, for instance.

Senator DOUGLAS. Thank you very much, Mayor Zeidler.

[. . . . .]

THURSDAY, DECEMBER 5, 1957
Portland, Maine

THE SUBCOMMITTEE MET, pursuant to recess, in the main courtroom, United States Courthouse, 156 Federal Street, Portland, Maine, at 2 p. m., Senator Joseph S. Clark presiding.

Present: Senators Clark and Payne.

Also present: Jack Carter, staff director and Milton Semer, counsel, Housing Subcommittee; and Donald L. Rogers, counsel, Committee on Banking and Currency.

Senator PAYNE. Ladies and gentlemen, we will officially open these hearings.

First I want to say that it is a great privilege for me to welcome my distinguished colleague, Senator Clark of Pennsylvania, a member of the Subcommittee on Housing, to Maine, and to Portland in particular, along with members of the staff. Senator Clark is seated at my side. Donald Rogers, counsel to the full committee, is on my right. To the other side of Senator Clark is Milton Semer, a Maine man, coming from Auburn, who is a counsel to the Subcommittee on Housing. Over further, standing up and taking care of the press problems, is Jack Carter, who is the staff director of the Subcommittee on Housing of the Senate Banking and Currency Committee.

[. . . . .]

The relocation of displaced families is one of the most serious problems encountered in the urban renewal program. At the outset I should like to emphasize that the subcommittee has no desire whatsoever to get involved in the pros and cons of whether or not public housing is needed in Portland. This is a matter for the citizens of Portland to decide under the procedures established by the Maine Legislature. Public housing is only one of the tools authorized by Congress to assist in relocating families displaced by urban renewal projects. Another alternative is the very liberal terms for FHA mortgage insurance on homes acquired by persons forced to relocate provided in section 221 of the National Housing Act. Extension of the provisions of that section from 1-family houses to 2-, 3-, and 4-family houses has been suggested, and this is one of the matters we wish to explore further in these hearings.

[. . . . .]

I am delighted to welcome the subcommittee to Portland and to participate in these hearings. I am particularly pleased that my distinguished colleague, Senator Clark, is here to preside. In his home State of Pennsylvania he has both great metropolitan areas and many smaller cities, and I know from his work on the subcommittee that he shares my interest in the urban renewal problems of medium and smaller sized cities.

[. . . . .]

Senator CLARK. Thank you very much, Senator Payne, for your kind words and your warm welcome to Portland. I know that I need not tell you how very happy I am to be here and to have the privilege of serving with you on this subcommittee, whose immediate task it is to determine what urban renewal, urban redevelopment, and housing conditions are in Portland; what your problems are; and what assistance you ladies and gentlemen believe, if any, the Federal Government can give, in the solution of these problems.

[. . . . .]

Portland is the second of six cities in which the Senate Subcommittee on Housing is holding hearings this fall on the general topic of urban renewal. Portland was selected at the suggestion of my distinguished colleague, Senator Payne, who feels, as I do, that, there is much to be learned from the experiences of small- and medium-sized cities in attempting to clear slums and arrest the growth of blight.

[. . . . .]

At the present time, the program is on a year-to-year basis and for all practical purposes the authorization for this fiscal year, which ends on the 30th of June 1958, is already exhausted. There are various reasons for this and I will state them.

Two factors have led to the present situation. First, the program has begun to pick up speed all around the country; and, second, the national administration has impounded about 30 percent of the funds authorized by the Congress. The result is that cities which are ready to start on their local plans for renewal are faced with costly delay, and many cities which already have received approval for their projects find that they are frozen in their present status without the flexibility to revise them in accordance with changing local needs.

Another aspect of urban renewal — in many ways the most important of all — is the problem of relocation. This is the human side of slum clearance and urban redevelopment. It is the most delicate part of the whole program. It must be well planned and administered with justice and compassion.

Federal law requires that an urban renewal plan, before it can be approved, must provide for the relocation of displaced families into decent, safe, and sanitary housing that is financially and geographically accessible. We would like to have the benefit of your thinking as to how you propose to do that in Portland, not only with respect to your pending redevelopment project, but with respect to those which I surmise, after a tour of the city this morning, will be on your capital improvement program in the foreseeable future.

I personally am particularly interested to know, although I realize that this is in some sense a rather hot potato in Portland, how you think you can do it without a substantially expanded program of public housing. That is a matter of some concern to us because the public housing question will be a very critical one in the 85th Congress, on which members of our committee have quite different and varying views. I am not at all sure that my good friend Senator Payne and I will see alike on that subject. Time alone will tell.

We would benefit greatly by a thorough discussion of your relocation program and its problems. We should like to know in detail where displaced families are being relocated, what plans, if any, are being made to provide public housing for those families who could qualify, and what the housing conditions are for those displaced families whose incomes are too high to qualify for public housing but too low to buy into the new dwelling units being constructed in this area. The latter is often referred to as the problem of housing for middle-income or moderate-income families.

There are many other subjects which we want to discuss with you — the progress of your program, the financing of the projects, Federal-local relations, rehabilitation, and something about your plans for re-use of cleared land. We are eager to learn from the officials and private citizens of Portland all that we can about the progress you have made so far in renewing your city, the problems that confront you in carrying out existing projects, and what your plans and hopes are for the future.

I would like also to raise this point: We are faced with a threatening international situation in which I think almost all Americans are in accord that very large sums of Federal money, raised by taxes paid by you and the other citizens of the United States, must be allocated and appropriated to modernize and support our defense system, particularly in the fields of missiles, our foreign-aid program, and perhaps our educational program. The sums of money in my judgment will not be available for all those things without an increase in taxes, unless we cut back on some domestic programs.

Would it be your feeling in Portland that you would rather maintain the present tax level and give up your urban redevelopment, or would it be the thinking of your leaders here that you would want to go ahead with this program and would be prepared to reelect your Senators and Representatives who voted for the increased taxes which were essential to make the program a reality? I feel that we cannot continue to live in a dream world.

This program costs money, and it is going to cost more money. The needs of the country generally are very acute and we have a hard choice to make. I think it would be of great benefit to Senator Payne and to me and to all of the other members of the committee if we knew how deeply you felt about this. Is this something in which you are glad to have a Federal handout and where you pay your one-third share, or is this something to which you are deeply committed, and which you feel you are prepared to make further sacrifices for?

With that preliminary statement I would like to call on the first witness, Mr. Carleton Lane, the outgoing chairman of the Portland City Council, to give us a preliminary statement and view on behalf of the city administration.

Councilman Lane.

Statement of Carleton Lane, Chairman, Portland, Maine, City Council

Mr. LANE. Thank you, Mr. Chairman and Senator Payne. It is with considerable pride and pleasure that the city of Portland welcomes members and staff of the United States Senate's Sub-committee on Housing. We welcome the opportunity to represent the Nation's smaller metropolitan cities in this examination of our common effort to renew the Nation's urban centers.

[. . . . . .]

You were introduced to the city of Portland on the bus tour this morning. A few facts and figures will serve to underscore your visual impression. The population of Portland, for example, increased only nominally between 1920 and 1940, while in the decade from 1940 to 1950 the Portland metropolitan area, including this city and its closest neighbors, South Portland, Westbrook, Cape Elizabeth, and Falmouth, grew considerably. Whereas the total population of Portland is today estimated at 80,300 — a 6-percent increase over 1940 — its suburbs have grown from 33,000 in 1940 to approximately 44,000 at present: an increase of nearly 30 percent. Portland, in other words, is a mature city, evidencing the same trends of suburban growth as the Nation, but at a slower rate.

[. . . . .]

The city of Portland has been working to improve its housing conditions since World War II. Following an intensive study by a citizens' group, we decided to inaugurate a program of inspection and rehabilitation, and also to participate in the then new national program for urban redevelopment. You have seen today the visible evidence of our progress in our first project: the Vine-Deer-Chatham redevelopment project, which you saw this morning. You have also seen the areas in which we are about to go forward with the urban renewal program. You will hear from our administrative personnel the details of the planning and programing of the first of these projects, Bayside Park.

[. . . . .]

Senator CLARK. Thank you very much, Councilman Lane, for your very clear and illuminating statement.

Do you have any questions, Senator Payne?

Senator PAYNE. No, except to direct your attention to the question, or to one of the questions, that Senator Clark raised during the course of his discussion — you being particularly interested in the financial field — as to whether or not your thought is that this program is of a type that is so important that the Congress should go forward with it rather than curtail it as one of the phases of economy, in the event that economy has to be practiced in order to live within a balanced budget.

Senator CLARK. Without an increase in taxation.

Senator PAYNE. Right. Without an increase in taxation.

Mr. LANE. I think if I knew the answer to that I would try for Congress. I think that we all look at a problem of this sort from a purely local point of view. For me to try to apply what I feel about Portland to a national situation I find extremely difficult to do because I realize that the large cities are in an entirely different position than cities our size. I feel it impossible for me to make any valuable contribution along that line.

I would be delighted, however, to talk about Portland, and how I feel about Portland in this connection.

Senator CLARK. I think that is all we meant.

Senator PAYNE. That is right.

Mr. LANE. Senator, as you know, or as you may know, I am financial vice president of a rather large lending institution. We operate nationally. Therefore I do have some knowledge of situations elsewhere.

From a lender's point of view I believe that urban renewal is an extremely valuable development. I think that it is essential, if we are going to maintain downtown real-estate values, to do something about the encroachment of depreciating buildings. They can do nothing but drag down the values of those adjacent to them and, as they do that, more and more areas depreciate adjacent to the declining ones.

Therefore, I feel that so far as communities like ours are concerned, that it is tax money well spent, if it is spent at the local level on this particular program.

So far as the other question is concerned which you propounded in your opening statement, Senator Clark, I think we here in Portland are very anxious to solve this problem with our own facilities if it is at all possible and to the extent it is possible to do so. I think we in this area of the country are reluctant to lean on public housing any more than is necessary.

I think that a great many people in our community, however, have come to much the same conclusion as I — and now I am speaking very personally — that the accomplishments which are possible are so valuable that we will give up a little of our free enterprise desires if we cannot do the job with free enterprise, and use the public housing route to make it possible.

Senator CLARK. Just one more question, Mr. Lane. I won't detain you any longer than that.

Would you say there would be any possibility of going ahead with the urban renewal and redevelopment program here in Portland if the Federal Government were to withdraw its support, which amounts, as you know, to $2 for every $1 you put up?

Mr. LANE. I think that that is economically impossible.

Senator CLARK. Thank you very much, sir.

Anything more, Senator Payne?

Senator PAYNE. No. The only other thing I would like to have you discuss, Mr. Lane, if you will, because of your experience in the lending field, is this: Do you believe from your knowledge that there are sufficient dwellings for tenants available in the price range that the people in the low-income brackets can afford?

Senator CLARK. Standard housing.

Senator PAYNE. Standard housing.

Mr. LANE. I don't think I am in any very good position to answer that because that is not within my experience. When we are considering properties from a lending standpoint we are always considering full ones and not empty ones.

Senator PAYNE. Yes.

Mr. LANE. So that while we do give consideration to the amount of vacancy that may be in an area, I don't think it is from the point of view you are thinking of.

In the first place, as I think you well recognize, lending institutions are reluctant to locate in areas such as we are considering for urban renewal. We are very reluctant to do it. Therefore we know comparatively little in detail about that. That is the point I tried to make before.

If this continues it just makes larger the area in which lending institutions are reluctant to engage. So, I have not answered your question, and I realize that, but I do not think I can.

Senator CLARK. Would I be overstating your position, Mr. Lane, if I suggested that you felt that this urban-renewal program was a necessity rather than a luxury for Portland?

Mr. LANE. I think not only for Portland, but for any community in which the blight is extensive.

Senator CLARK. Thank you ever so much.

[. . . . .]

Mr. Orr, would you place in the record, the figures which you told us about on the tour this morning with respect to the number of inspectors and their salaries, the number of dwelling units they have inspected, and total number of dwelling units in the city.

Do you want to wait and have one of your colleagues do that?

Mr. ORR. I would like to have Mr. Martin answer that more specifically, if he gets here. If he does not, I can answer some portions of it all right.

We do have 4 inspectors with a housing inspection supervisor, who is Mr. Martin, so that there is a total team of 5 working on that. Mr. Martin gave you their entrance salaries as $56 a week. The top would be somewhere about $66 or $68, or somewhere in there.

Senator CLARK. I think you did tell us also, did you not, that your policy was to put those housing inspectors in areas where, in your judgment, rehabilitation was possible, rather than sending them down to these blighted areas where, in your judgment, you could not rehabilitate them, but would have to relocate them?

Mr. ORR. Yes; that is correct.

As I started to say, the program has been on an area-improvement basis. We tried to block out, with the joint operation of the planning staff and the health department staff, a section of the city where we feel that some real results can be obtained from this kind of program. There is no point in sending them into the worst areas. We want to put them in areas where what is there can be conserved through the enforcement of the code.

Senator CLARK. I want to emphasize again, and I think you will agree with me, that the reason you do not put them into the bad area is because it will immediately give you a relocation problem which you could not cope with.

Mr. ORR. That is certainly part of the problem. I think it is also true that those areas are simply so bad that if it were possible to enforce the housing code to require a standard number of baths and toilets and that sort of thing, it still would not change the nature of the neighborhood very much. They have gone too far.

Where we have tried to use this program is in the areas where blight is beginning to show; where the first evidences of blight appeared.

Senator CLARK. I am not saying this in any critical sense at all. Personally I agree with your program. But the net result is to favor the slum landlord, is it not, as opposed to the landlords or owner-occupants in better areas who are forced to make improvements?

Mr. ORR. No. I certainly could not agree with that, Senator, and I think we have more drastic treatment involved in the future for the slum landlord, rather than this area.

Senator CLARK. When?

Mr. ORR. Just as soon as we can get to it.

Senator CLARK. Maybe as soon as the Federal Government makes it possible for you to get to it.

Mr. ORR. There is always the possibility that assistance from that direction will help us to speed it up.

Senator CLARK. Mr. Weaver, if you want to say something, please feel free to do so.

Mr. WEAVER. I was wondering. Probably waiting for Mr. Martin is the thing to do.

Senator CLARK. All right.

Mr. ORR. I think Mr. Weaver suggested that I mention the fact that through another phase of this program, which I will come to in a moment, one of the largest holders of slum properties has within a relatively short period of years had his holdings cut about 75 percent; whereas when we started out he had a long list of properties which were giving us constant trouble. Through the enforcement of the code and through the operation of our coordinating committee we have cut his holdings way down. So I would not say he is no longer a problem, but we have certainly not favored him in the operation of this program.

Senator CLARK. What has happened to the 75 percent which is no longer a problem? Have they been condemned?

Mr. ORR. Many of them have been demolished. Yes; and they have been torn down as a result of city prodding.

Senator CLARK. Was that a geographical problem? I understood you were not moving into these redevelopment areas. Did it just happen that there were some isolated properties in other areas where you cracked down, or was it a complaint situation?

Mr. ORR. No. I think perhaps I have oversimplified it a little bit. The major effort of the inspection program is on this block-area basis, but we do have a complaint program as well and we do go in wherever we receive a complaint to try to correct the situation in that specific dwelling. We have, through the inspection program and through the work of our coordinating committee, done a great deal even in this area which we pointed out to you this morning as being the worst; but we have not been able to go in there on a block by block conservation program, because there is not much left to conserve. That is the best way to put that.

Senator PAYNE. Before you get away from your discussion on Bayside — and you are probably not anywhere near through that —

so the record will be very clear, how many families would be affected in the so-called Bayside area?

Mr. ORR. Affected in what way, Senator?

Senator PAYNE. In other words, if that area were going to be redeveloped, how many families will have to be relocated?

Mr. ORR. How many families will have to be relocated?

Senator PAYNE. Yes.

Mr. ORR. Can you answer that, Mr. Dickson?

Mr. DICKSON. I am William Dickson, senior planner of the city of Portland.

We anticipated a total of 173 families to be relocated from the Bayside project when it is in process, and out of that total we estimate the number eligible for public housing should we decide to relocate using that medium will be 110 families.

Senator PAYNE. I am glad to have that figure in there because that was going to be 1 of my next 2 questions.

First, how many of those 173 families are those that let us say are presently receiving old-age assistance? Do you know that?

Mr. DICKSON. No, I cannot answer that now, Senator. I could find it out for you because we have that information.

Senator PAYNE. Do you have it on the basis of how many of those are presently receiving public assistance, either under aid to the blind or old-age assistance, or aid to dependent children?

Mr. DICKSEN. On a very rough estimate I would say 15 percent, probably, of that total. I know in the Bayside West area, the worst area, we went through that many.

Senator CLARK. This is the area not included in the present project?

Mr. DICKSON. It is not included in the Bayside Park project, but it is the neighborhood area. Last year 20 percent of the people living in that area received public assistance.

Senator CLARK. Of one form or another?

Mr. DICKSON. Yes. Of one form or another.

Senator PAYNE. This may be aside from the point, but has any study been undertaken in the city with reference to the providing of housing for the aged? For instance, let us take that area.

A person under old-age assistance, and let us be fair about it, with the amount of grant that he will have available, just cannot find a place to live unless he can live with a son or daughter or somebody. He cannot find a place to live in in decent surrounding and exist under a certain standard with the money that is available.

Mr. DICKSON. Yes sir.

Senator PAYNE. That area is uphill and downhill; is it not?

Mr. DICKSON. Yes, sir.

Senator PAYNE. Nothing in the world could be worse for poor old folks than pulling themselves uphill and downhill trying to get to a store or somewhere else.

Also it looks to me as if they would have to go up some pretty steep steps. What I am getting at is, has there been any study undertaken in Portland or any place that you know of in this vicinity — I know it has been in Boston — of housing for the aged that would make use of side railings, for instance, which an aged person could take hold of to help himself along and where the housing would be constructed on a ground level? That would give them a chance to enjoy the declining years of their lives in a little bit more pleasant surroundings and without all of the difficulties they have to go through at present, with most of them up on the third, fourth, and fifth floors. Why? Because the rent up there is cheaper.

Senator CLARK. And they are walkups.

Senator PAYNE. They have to walk up and walk down. That is a problem for them and I am just wondering if some study has been made of it.

Mr. WEAVER. May I make a statement on that?

There is a concern locally and one of the witnesses tomorrow morning I think will have a statement where there will appear some recommendations from the child and family services group about housing for the elderly. There is some concern. There has not been a definite study as yet of the problem or program, although it is foremost in the minds of this particular group, and they will have something to say about it tomorrow, I am sure.

            [. . . . .]

Mr. ORR. [. . .] Mrs. Moore is here from the child and family services, who handles our relocation problems.

As you know, and perhaps we should have brought it out in our report, and it may be buried in there somewhere, we do employ the child and family services to do our relocation casework and have the advantage of a professional case work agency on a contractual basis for handling that problem. We have found it most helpful. I do not know how unique we are in that regard, but it certainly works in Portland.

Senator CLARK. If you are not unique you are pretty unusual.

As I understand it, Mrs. Moore, and correct me if I am wrong, this

is the retaining of a nonprofit charitable agency on contract by the
city to do this relocation work.

Mrs. MOORE. Yes.

Senator CLARK. Senator Payne.

Senator PAYNE. I have nothing further.

Senator CLARK. Do any members of the staff have any questions they would like to ask Mr. Orr?

Mr. SEMER. Mrs. Moore, where is the other place that does it that way?

Mrs. MOORE. The Family Service of Delaware County.

Senator CLARK. Pennsylvania.

Mrs. MOORE. That is the only other private agency in the country, I believe. The Delaware County redevelopment in the Hook Road area.

Senator CLARK. Thank you, Mrs. Moore.

Mr. SEMER. I understand, Mrs. Moore, that you have written an article setting forth the experience you have had in Portland. It probably would be very helpful, Mr. Chairman, if we could insert it into the record at this point. I read the article and it tells the relocation story in Portland from the point of view of how to coordinate the relocation efforts and the welfare efforts.

Senator CLARK. Could I see it, Mrs. Moore?

Mrs. MOORE. Surely.

Senator CLARK. I would like to ask that Mrs. Moore's article entitled "The Social Worker — Social Workers Take Over Relocation," which appears in the October 1957 Journal of Housing, be made a part of the record.

(The document referred to follows:)

SOCIAL WORKERS TAKE OVER RELOCATION

By Louise S. Citrine and Catherine B. Moore, both of Child and Family Services, Portland, Maine; adapted from a presentation at the 1957 National Conference of Social Welfare

In the early daylight, an enormous crane was reflected against the sky as it maneuvered great lengths of structural steel. The trailer truck that was being loaded completely filled the narrow alley between the plate yard and a row of houses. Proceeding along the uneven path beside the truck, a barefooted 3-year-old was pushing a well-worn stroller. His nightshirt indicated a surreptitious departure earlier from the tumbled-down building to which he was returning. A partially eaten green apple was riding in the stroller. He showed no concern for the swinging crane overhead nor for the possibility of his family's disapproval. With eight brothers and sisters clamoring for breakfast, they might be glad he had "eaten out" this morning.

This scene was enacted in Portland, Maine, in 1955. Today it would be a long walk from this toddler's new home to the steel yard.

Background to Renewal

Portland, like many cities, large and small, came through World War II to find its housing in an extensively neglected state. The influx of military and defense workers by the thousands during the war years had used — and sometimes abused — every available dwelling unit, with supply the primary concern. Materials for improvements were scarce. There had been no planning to stem the approach of widespread blight.

In 1947, the city planning board began surveying the situation and some of its findings were brought forcibly to community attention by newspaper pictures and stories.

In 1949, the city manager appointed a Citizens Housing Committee representing a cross section of community interests. The details of the report this committee developed were publicized through presentation at a general meeting of the voluntary community welfare organization, namely, the Council of Social Agencies.

In 1950, a housing code was adopted and an inspection service established under the health department to administer the code and work with owners and tenants toward rehabilitation of salvagable dwellings to meet the standards.

In 1951, State legislation and a municipal referendum established the slum-clearance and redevelopment authority, authorized to survey and plan for a slum-clearance program that would be jointly financed by the city and the Federal Government. The social agencies and central welfare planning body of the city were active in supporting these moves.

Two hundred units of federally owned public housing built to meet wartime housing needs were obtained by the city as a relocation resource for possible clearance projects. But the State legislature had not approved additional public housing, in the face of the opposition of builder and realtor lobbies.

Social Agency Role

Throughout this period of increasing concern for attacking housing blight, there was close liaison and mutual cooperation between the community welfare planning organization and municipal bodies and administrators. The correlation between poor housing and vulnerability to social difficulties and hazards to health to which social agencies could attest — as well as the effective presentations these agencies made to community and legislative groups — played a decisive part in developing citizen understanding and acceptance of the program.

In planning for the city's first slum-clearance project, the planning board requested the Council of Social Agencies to administer a program of relocation housing for the families affected. Believing that this important phase of the redevelopment process involved many of the techniques of family casework, the Council of Social Agencies referred this request to Child and Family Services, a private, multiple-function casework agency.

Relocation Contract

The contractual agreement between the slum-clearance and redevelopment authority and Child and Family Services included specifics in relation to actual relocation, staff requirements, and the basis of financial remuneration. Functions of the relocation service as set forth in the agreement were:

1. To interview and register all project occupants and to keep a record of the particular needs of each.
2. To promote and compile satisfactory listings of available and suitable vacancies.
3. To inspect or have inspected every unit listed and to place all vacancies of acceptable quality on the accredited register of listings for referral.
4. To encourage site occupants to seek accommodations for themselves.
5. To escort families to approved vacancies when necessary.
6. To interview each family after relocation to ascertain whether their needs had been adequately met.

The agency's location within three blocks of the area proposed for clearance made it readily accessible to the site occupants.

Site Survey

The first step in relocation was the site occupants survey conducted in November and December 1955. The initial interview, at which the factual data were obtained on family composition, housing needs, income, location preference, etc., was also used to establish rapport between fieldworker and family. Where there was hostility, it was important that opportunity be given to express this feeling. Some evaluation of the social situation seemed called for if relocation were to be more than simply taking a family's problems into a new dwelling unit.

Some of the relevant facts from the survey:

1. Large proportion of families were Italian (50 percent) having lived in area from 4 to 50 years; 77 percent of resident-owners were first generation Italians.
2. While 12 percent of the residents had lived in the area less than 1 year, 18 percent had been there more than 15 years.
3. More than one-quarter of the families were eligible for public housing.

4. Eighteen percent of the families were receiving some form of public assistance.
5. Seventy percent of such families were known to one or more health and welfare agencies.
6. One or more members of 26 percent of the families had been involved with the courts.
7. Eighteen percent of the homes were "broken."
8. Thirty-seven percent of the families or individual householders had health problems.

"Attitude of Relocatees"

Portland's first clearance area had been selected because it was small — a little less than 100 families and individual householders were involved. The area was near the waterfront, surrounded by industry. It was to be redeveloped for commercial and industrial use. The group reaction in the area was almost complete rejection of the plan. The neighborhood was not cohesive but the crisis brought it together. Throughout the preliminary planning, publicity, and public hearings, the connotation of the word "slum" was bitterly resented. Some individuals reacted, as might be expected, by displacing personal problems to relocation and to the worker directly involved. In some instances, the impact of the situation on family interrelationships was marked. In certain families, the stress of having to plan for a move and actually to relocate played into already established family discord.

As has been noted, the owner occupants, in many instances, were first generation foreign born to whom property ownership achieved by hard work, personal thrift, and sacrifice meant a great deal. Relocation to them was a real uprooting. These families demonstrate clearly that, while redevelopment spells progress and benefits the community as a whole, it may actually be painful for some individuals.

To the second generation of foreign born, trapped by their culture into remaining with the parents, usually as tenants, relocation in many instances, meant release. Under Veterans' Administration and Federal Housing Administration mortgage programs, they were able to continue the tradition of home ownership, but in a much better residential area of the city.

To some individuals, the neighborhood was a necessity, either economic or psychological.

Members of minority groups, especially nonwhite, were accepted there.

The restrictions by landlords in other neighborhoods against large families were not prevalent here.

The low rents met the needs of those with marginal income, as well as those reluctant to spend a reasonable proportion of income for shelter. Some preferred "being lost" in a crowd, so to speak, either for social or legal reasons.

The church (Italian-Catholic) within two blocks of the area was the center of living, particularly to older members. In many instances, they were comfortable in, or adjusted to the neighborhood. Some were here by choice, others through force of circumstances.

The meaning of the neighborhood was strikingly demonstrated by almost complete rejection of public housing, which is located on the outskirts of the city, several miles distant from the redevelopment area. While this distance may have presented transportation problems in relation to employment, there was a subtle distrust of the totally different and unfamiliar setting.

Basic Approach to Relocation

As social workers, we first recognized that, whatever the reasons for the people's residing in the neighborhood, they were now faced with the external pressure to move. Some resentment and hostility were inevitable. We were offering our services, rather than having the area residents seek our help after an unpressured decision to move. Although our assistance was termed "voluntary," we could not help but be identified with authority. We felt it was important to respect the dignity and individual worth of every person contacted. Responsiveness on our part as to how each person viewed what was happening and as to his desires in moving was basic to cooperative planning. Meeting the people where they were, in their own attitudes, was the first step in helping to build confidence in the relocation worker, permitting the family an opportunity to test out our interest.

Some might say such an approach would encourage delay. Within the limits of the time we had available to plan, we felt this approach not only evidenced basic human consideration, but was also a sound move toward the goal of relocation. Readiness for relocation needed to be assessed family by family, recognizing that some people were willing and able to move ahead independently.

Out of our concern for the people came an appreciation of the backgrounds and experiences of the area residents: an essential in an individualized approach to relocation. Otherwise, the worker could easily have created misunderstandings by being "judgmental" or could have been trapped into setting artificial goals for families. Respect and sensitivity toward cultural patterns, especially those of the Italian group, not only enrich the relationship between the worker and the residents, but also helped the staff evaluate realistically the needs and the strengths people develop through different cultural heritages. (The fieldworker is now the proud possessor of a recipe for an interesting Italian dish that is used as an alternate for the traditional New England Saturday night baked beans.)

The concentration of our efforts was with families who needed practical help in finding and moving to new quarters, as well as those who psychologically needed to accept change and be enabled to mobilize themselves for a move. Careful evaluation of what was appropriate focused toward the goal of relocation, was made on an individual casework basis. In mobilizing families, the processes most used were: understanding, suggestion, guidance, clarification of alternatives, support, encouragement, and practical assistance.

The agency felt that the personality of the caseworker was very important and is proud of the excellent relationship established under circumstances of pressure for both the worker and the residents. Patience, a genuine feeling for people, the capacity to work with many variations of personal adjustment, an ability to accept hostility without becoming frustrated nor fighting back [. . .].

Relocation Begins

The original plan was to effect relocation in stages of approximately 6-month intervals, over a 2-year period. The procedure of purchasing property from the owners by direct negotiation rather than via total condemnation of the area changed the timetable somewhat. There was reluctance, and in some cases refusal, to accept the inevitability of the project's completion. With no time limits for relocation set in the early months, mobilizing the families to move presented a problem. As each building was purchased, the fieldworker again contacted the families, obtaining current factual data. As might be expected, we found numerous changes in family situation — such as a new baby, unemployment, or change of employment.

The families were encouraged to use the unit listing at the agency. Some families found their own units and moved quickly. Others used the agency listings on a simple referral basis. And still others required more continuous contact and planning with the field worker. Regardless of condition of the site unit, in fact the worse it was, the more "particular" some families seemed in approving a new unit.

When actual demolition began in August 1956, relocation was given some impetus. With some families, only a court order eviction brought action.

One influence in getting the occupants to move was financial assistance, given in the form of moving expenses, first month's rent, or abatement of rent by the redevelopment authority, on the basis of need. This form of assistance has recently been changed to moving expenses alone, under a revised contract with the Federal agency, reflecting 1956 legislation. This change in method of providing financial help to move has created some problems. There is more to relocating than the cost of the moving van; e. g., utility changes, appliance installations, furnishings that fit new windows and floor space.

A few acts of God mobilized some families when all else had failed. A psychotic man who had not left home for 10 years was unmoved by demolition all around. His family had a conflict of feelings about his illness.

They had resisted hospitalization, believing in their own adequacy to "handle things in the family." Although concerned and eager for a move, they were not able to face the basic problem of his illness. In the bitter subzero weather of New Year's Eve, the water pipes froze and burst. This man packed his personal belongings immediately. His wife, happy at last to be able to move, did not even wait to call their son, in whose home they were to have an apartment. She summoned a police cruiser and completed relocation in about an hour — after weeks of unsuccessful planning on our part.

"Plus Values"

Beyond actual relocation, help was given to meet some families' needs by referral to other community resources, as well as to Child and Family Services. For example:

Mr. X is blind. He came from his native Italy in 1907. As he became unable to work on the railroad, he had moved from one boarding arrangement to another. Four years ago he moved in with Mr. W, another Italian, who owned property in the redevelopment area. Mr. W decided to return to Italy and tried to persuade Mr. X to go with him. Through an interpreter, it was learned that Mr. X has warm feeling for his adopted city and country. After long searching, a home was found where Mr. X can live, receive the proper diet as treament for an ulcer, and be part of the family. Here he enjoyed his first "family Christmas" since coming to this country.

A 17-year-old girl, with employment counseling, obtained her first job and aided her family in affording a better home.

Arranging for old-age assistance to supplement social security moved an elderly couple out of a dark, dilapidated building into a sunny larger unit.

Mr. Y married a widow with a large family. He was working out of State at the time the family relocated. When contacted later, he had become unemployed and the marital situation was at a crisis. Mr. Y, rejected in this his second marriage, was threatening to go to court and prove Mrs. Y an unfit mother. Housing had become the displaced target of Mr. Y's hostility. Counseling has helped to ease some of the tensions in this family and can be continued.

Teeth extractions and new dentures gave a teen-age boy in a broken home the confidence to continue his high school education.

Vocational rehabilitation was instrumental in easing the anxieties in a family where uncertain employment had made them fear assuming the increased rental of better housing.

In all, 28 percent of the site occupants used supplementary services to effect improvement of the family situation.

Followup

Within a month following relocation, the families were visited by the fieldworker to appraise their unit, if self-located, and determine the general family situation and attitude toward relocation. In some cases, this occasion was used as an opportunity for further contact or referral to community agencies. Where the housing was substandard, the worker offered additional referrals of standard units or contacted the landlord about meeting standard requirements. This latter move had to be carefully taken, as the relationship between landlord and tenant is often tenuous at best. Upgrading is by small steps, in most instances. The large majority of site occupants moved into better housing, although some chose substandard units either because of location or low rent. In one case, standard housing made the family uncomfortable. Conforming to the neighborhood in the matter of housekeeping alone was a cause of hostility and apparent dissatisfaction. This family is among those where continued contact beyond relocation may be helpful in family adjustment.

Thirty percent of the relocated families resettled near the clearance site; i. e., in the immediate adjacent area where the church continues to be the center of interest. Others, because of employment on the water front, remain within walking distance. Only one family has moved into public housing. This rejection of public housing was due primarily to geographical location in relation to employment.

Results

While there have been obstacles, two pictures reflect what housing can mean to people.

A large family with eight children moved from a crowded second floor in a building surrounded by only sidewalks and pavements to the spaciousness of the city outskirts. Although they are renting a one-half duplex, they reseeded the lawn and built a white picket fence. Mowing that lawn is not a chore, but a privilege to a different member of the family each week.

An elderly lady, with her eyes shining — and her difficulty with English requiring many gestures — hurried the worker through her large apartment, exclaiming "sun, the sun, I have all day." Thirty years in a tiny building crowded in between two taller ones had allowed her a brief few minutes of pale sunshine each morning and that was all. There would be more windows to clean and she was 73 years old, but for her it would be a pleasure.

Public Relations

As the first redevelopment project in the city, the program came under the close scrutiny of the public. The press had an interest in keeping the community informed on progress, with an understandable desire to highlight the human interest aspects of the program. The protection of the families' privacy and maintenance of confidentiality posed problems when the publicity spotlight became focused on them. The community's right to know came into conflict with personal desires for anonymity. In some instances, publicity had a decidedly negative effect on families and added another barrier to be surmounted in working through their problems on continued contact basis.

When the city contracted with a private social agency to engage in relocation service, an enlarged group of citizens became involved through the agency's board of directors and special committee on housing. The study that went into the agency's decision to accept the contract was an informative one. It provided a basis of understanding and support on what was involved in community planning for better housing and subsequent plans for expanded programs under urban renewal. (Bear in mind that the issue of public housing has not yet been settled in Maine. The enabling legislation passed in May 1957, permits the construction of public housing in redevelopment areas — but requires that each project be subjected to a referendum.)

Our experience as a voluntary social agency engaged in family relocation under an urban renewal program has shown the effectiveness of cooperation between public and private agencies — working together for a common goal and utilizing established skills and resources available in a community. We have seen the varied responses of people to change under pressure and the need for sensitive understanding in helping families to move under time-limited circumstances. In the planning, as well as the action, stages of urban renewal, the social agency can make a definite contribution in focusing on parts of the program directly affecting the residents.

Mr. ORR. Mr. Martin reminded me of one more thing in our program here. We have not had too much experience with it, but we are rather proud we started it, at any rate. With the success of our coordinating committee on housing we decided we needed a similar committee on the problem families who live in some of these areas. We have recently started a series of regular meetings of representatives from the school department, and the police department, and the welfare department, and the housing department, and the health department, where we are taking specific families that seem just to have problems in every direction, and see if we can bring all of these agencies together with the private agencies in the community to bear on it, and see if we can work out solutions for their problems. Although that is not perhaps directly related to housing and renewal, yet it is certainly the matter that this program is built around and we think we have something there in the future.

Senator CLARK. Thank you, Mr. Orr.

[. . . . .]

THE SUBCOMMITTEE MET, pursuant to recess, in the main court-room, United States Courthouse, 156 Federal Street, Portland, Maine, at 9 a. m., Senator Joseph S. Clark presiding.

Present: Senators Clark and Payne.

Also present: Jack Carter, staff director and Milton Semer, counsel, Subcommittee on Housing; and Donald L. Rogers, counsel, Committee on Banking and Currency.

Senator CLARK. Good morning, ladies and gentlemen.

The committee will be in session.

Our first witness this morning is the Honorable Catherine I. Hendricks, representative, House of Representatives, State of Maine.

Mrs. Hendricks, it is very nice to have you with us. We appreciate your help.

Statement of Catherine I. Hendricks, Representative, House of Representatives, State of Maine

Mrs. HENDRICKS. Thank you. I am very grateful for the opportunity.

Senator CLARK. Will you proceed in your own way, please?

Mrs. HENDRICKS. I feel that the city is not relocating people according to Federal specifications. The reason why I feel that way and the reason why I feel the city has not been relocating people according to Federal specifications is because of a tour I made a year ago last November, when a man by the name of Mr. Asali, whom I did not know at the time, called me up and told me there was going to be a legislative tour of the relocated families.

Senator CLARK. Is that the same Mr. Asali who testified here yesterday afternoon?

Mrs. HENDRICKS. I did not see him.

Senator CLARK. I think it was, and I would like the record so to note.

Mrs. HENDRICKS. What I saw on this tour I was really disgusted with. People were moved into bug-infested houses and into houses they were unable to heat, and they had to buy several stoves to try to heat the places. Later on I understand these people who were relocated made complaints to the authorities who relocated them elsewhere.

Just last Saturday I made another tour and that was a year later, practically, after the first tour.

Senator CLARK. Excuse me 1 minute more.

Mr. ORR, I think it would be helpful if you and Mr. Weaver and your people were able to hear this testimony. Can you hear back there all right? Perhaps you can come forward a little bit. I want to be sure what Mrs. Hendricks says is heard by those of you who are responsible for the relocation program here, so if you have any comments to make later you will be able to do it.

Excuse me for interrupting you, but I thought we should have everybody here to hear it who ought to hear it.

Will you go ahead, please?

Mrs. HENDRICKS. Last Saturday I thought I was going to come in and testify at this hearing and thought I should make one more check to see how the relocation picture was at the time. So last Saturday night I called Mr. Asali and told him I felt I would like to make a tour of the slum area. I call it that because I feel the people who were relocated were put into another slum area.

[. . . . .]

The family I am thinking of is a family by the name of Langley. It seems to me the reason why I first visited that family a year ago last November was that it was nearest to the Lee Recreation Center where the group met to begin the tour.

I talked with Mrs. Langley along with the other legislators and she told me she found her house so cold that a basket of apples froze in the front room. She said she just did not know how she was going to continue to heat the place in the winter. I believe she was receiving State aid at the time.

Senator CLARK. What type of heating apparatus was there in the house?

Mrs. HENDRICKS. Just ordinary stoves.

Senator CLARK. Coal, or oil, or kerosene?

Mrs. HENDRICKS. I believe it was coal. I am not quite sure, but something like that.

Senator CLARK. How big was the house? How many rooms were there?

Mrs. HENDRICKS. She was moved from Middle Street, from a 5-room apartment with a bath, to a 5-room apartment on Federal

Street, but there was no hot-water connection and she was paying $20 a month first, and then she had to pay $32 a month. There are 6 people in the family, but when she was moved to this place there was 1 room less that she could use, so actually it only gave her 4 rooms.

Senator CLARK. Was there a bath in the new house she moved into? Was it a house or an apartment?

Mrs. HENDRICKS. It was an apartment. That is another story about the bath. The bathtub was in what I call a closet. It was right off the kitchen and in order for anyone to prepare for the bath they had to do so in the kitchen and get into the bathtub and open the door and step out into the kitchen again.

Senator CLARK. Did I understand you to say there was no hot water?

Mrs. HENDRICKS. None connected.

Senator CLARK. There was a flush toilet?

Mrs. HENDRICKS. That was in another closet off the bedroom, with no ventilation whatsoever.

Senator CLARK. Are you generally familiar with the housing code of Portland, enough so that you could tell us whether the apartment they moved into was a standard or substandard dwelling under the housing code?

Mrs. HENDRICKS. I am not familiar with the housing code of the city of Portland, but it seems to me I read the Federal specifications and it said they were supposed to have a bath and it was supposed to be in sanitary condition, and so forth. I also feel that Federal specifications require that it be a similar place to what they lived in previously, and I do not feel that was so in this case.

Senator CLARK. You said, Mrs. Hendricks, that the apartment was very cold. Were you able to determine the cause for that?

Mrs. HENDRICKS. I believe it was an old house and there were high ceilings, and there was no central heating system, but just stoves that they used. I do not believe at the time there were any storm windows. As far as I could see it was a place that was let go.

Senator CLARK. You actually went into the house?

Mrs. HENDRICKS. Yes; I did.

Senator CLARK. What was the condition of the roof and the floor and the ceilings? Do you think it was rainproof?

Mrs. HENDRICKS. I feel perhaps that particular one was.

Senator CLARK. But you felt it was a dilapidated slum dwelling?

Mrs. HENDRICKS. I did. I felt so. The halls were dark and if an elderly person walked downstairs I believe they would fall down, because it was so dark in the hall.

Senator CLARK. What was the size of this lady's family?

Mrs. HENDRICKS. There were children there.

Senator CLARK. Children or grandchildren?

Mrs. HENDRICKS. Children. I believe Mrs. Langley has 5 or 6 children.

Senator CLARK. What age groups?

Mrs. HENDRICKS. I would say most of them were under 15.

Senator CLARK. Would you say she was getting old-age assistance?

Mrs. HENDRICKS. No; I believe she was getting State aid — $108.

Senator CLARK. Aid to dependent children, probably?

Mrs. HENDRICKS. Probably.

Senator CLARK. Were these children of both sexes?

Mrs. HENDRICKS. I can't remember. I believe they were. It seems to me there was a little boy there and I know there were little ones. They were not all in the house at that time. The husband was lying on a couch in the room at the time we entered. I believe he was dying at the time, because he died 2 weeks ago. He was suffering from shock.

Senator CLARK. Do you mean shock or a stroke?

Mrs. HENDRICKS. The wife said shock. She said my husband had quite a shock, but whether she termed it rightly I do not know.

Senator CLARK. He was not employed, obviously?

Mrs. HENDRICKS. No; he could not talk or anything at the time. He did not say anything, and she said he was very badly off.

Senator CLARK. Would you mind keeping your voice up, please? It is a little difficult to hear.

Mrs. HENDRICKS. Yes.

I had started to tell you about the facilities there. The toilet was in what I called a small closet off a small room, supposedly a bedroom, and I would say there were very unsanitary conditions.

Senator CLARK. That perhaps might have been the fault of the family, do you think, or do you think it was impossible to keep it clean?

Mrs. HENDRICKS. I believe it was bad because there was no ventilation in there. I think the toilet should have been in a room where it was large enough to have windows.

Senator CLARK. I think that is pretty universally required in sanitary codes throughout the country.

Is that the end of your story on that particular house?

Mrs. HENDRICKS. I wanted to tell you that we talked to Mrs. Langley about it, and she said that Mrs. Moore told her she would find her another place, because she didn't feel it was sanitary there. Later on we had a meeting at city hall with the city officials, and the people that relocated these families. I spoke to Mrs. Moore about that again. I spoke to her about it then, and she said she did intend to try to find another place for these people.

Senator CLARK. How long ago was that?

Mrs. HENDRICKS. I believe that was a little less than a year ago, and it was probably 2 or 3 months after we had visited.

Senator CLARK. At that time how long had the Langley family been in this new dwelling, if you can recall?

Mrs. HENDRICKS. I cannot recall how long they had been there, but after the meeting we had at city hall with city officials and relocation officials I just waited to see what would develop. Then I noticed in the paper this hearing was going to be held, so I contacted your committee. I did not want to stir up anything, because I wanted to do all I could to help the situation out. So I just kept quiet about it to see when an opportune time would arise.

Just before the hearing I decided I had better check again to see how the situation was shaping up. I asked Mr. Asali if he would take me to where Mrs. Langley lives now, because I would like to talk to her. He took me there, and she was not in, but one of the children ——

Senator CLARK. Excuse me a minute so we get this straight. This is a different dwelling from the one you had been to before?

Mrs. HENDRICKS. Yes.

Senator CLARK. Where was this located?

Mrs. HENDRICKS. On India Street.

Senator CLARK. In the same general neighborhood?

Mrs. HENDRICKS. Yes.

I talked to Mrs. Langley after one of the children went out and brought her to the house. I said, "Mrs. Langley, what has Mrs. Moore done for you?" I said, "Did you move here on your own, or what is the story now? There is going to be a Federal hearing, and I would like to find out where I am so I can testify about it."

She said, "Well, Mrs. Moore never did anything about getting me another place."

I said, "Where did you move when you moved from Federal Street?" She said, "I could not stand it any longer so I went out and looked for a place on my own and moved to Smith Street, which is in about the same area, but Smith Street was so full of rats we could not stay there, so we moved from there."

Senator CLARK. Excuse me a minute. Is Smith Street also in the same general area?

Mrs. HENDRICKS. About in the same general area.

So she stayed there as long as she could until she could find another place, and then she moved to India Street, which is the place I saw her.

Senator CLARK. That is where she is now?

Mrs. HENDRICKS. Yes.

In the course of the conversation I said, "Have you seen Mrs. Moore and did she try to get you a place, or what is the story?" She said, "Well, I had met her on the street several times but she hasn't been to visit me for that specific purpose. But she did come to visit me today." That was last Saturday.

I said, "You mean after about a year or so she did come and talk to you? What did she talk about?"

She said, "She told me she may be able to find me an apartment, but if I am moved to another apartment I will have to pay the charges."

In my opinion I felt that if these families were relocated and were relocated unsatisfactorily — the city paid to have them relocated but it was unsatisfactory — I feel if the families are moved again they should be paid the moving charges.

Senator CLARK. Mrs. Hendricks, do you know who paid the moving charges the first time?

Mrs. HENDRICKS. I understand that the people who were responsible for relocating did.

Senator CLARK. But on both of the other moves which were initiated by Mrs. Langley, is it your understanding that she paid her own moving charges?

Mrs. HENDRICKS. Yes, because I do not believe anybody knew she moved.

Senator CLARK. Do you know anything about the rent she is now paying on India Street?

Mrs. HENDRICKS. Yes. She is paying $9 a week.

Senator CLARK. About $40 a month?

Mrs. HENDRICKS. Yes.

Senator CLARK. With or without heat?

Mrs. HENDRICKS. Without it.

Senator CLARK. In what sort of shape is the apartment that she is now in?

Mrs. HENDRICKS. I just talked to her.

Senator CLARK. You did not go inside?

Mrs. HENDRICKS. Yes. We just went in one room, which I believe was probably the living room. There was very little furniture in it, but it was very neat and clean.

I want to bring out that the Langley family is a very clean family and if they had a decent place I know they would keep it that way.

Senator CLARK. Did you have any impression of your own as to whether the India Street apartment in your judgment is a standard apartment and an adequate apartment, or is it also substandard?

Mrs. HENDRICKS. I really cannot say because I did not look at the bath, or the toilet, or anything like that. I just talked to her in that one room and had a very limited time to talk to these people, because it was a Saturday night and I didn't know we were going to make the rounds that night. I did not know myself until I decided.

Senator CLARK. Is this the end of your story on the Langley family?

Mrs. HENDRICKS. Yes, I believe it is.

Senator CLARK. Is the area which we have been discussing in your legislative district?

Mrs. HENDRICKS. Yes. I represent all of the city of Portland.

Senator CLARK. Senator Payne, I wonder if you would think it appropriate procedure if we interrupted Mrs. Hendricks' testimony at this point and asked Mrs. Moore, and perhaps some of the city people, to let us have their version of the story, so there would be continuity when we read the record?

Senator PAYNE. There is one thing I think ought to be in the record here, although I may have missed it.

Did you have an opportunity, Mrs. Hendricks, to inspect and observe the property that the Langley family occupied in this previous area?

Mrs. HENDRICKS. In the Vine-Deer-Chatham area?

Senator PAYNE. Yes.

Mrs. HENDRICKS. No, I did not.

Senator PAYNE. So as to be able to make any comparison between that and the property they were moved to?

Mrs. HENDRICKS. No, sir.

Senator PAYNE. So you have no knowledge of what that situation was?

Mrs. HENDRICKS. No, I do not. Only what she told me.

Senator PAYNE. What did she tell you?

Mrs. HENDRICKS. She told me she was satisfied with the place she was in. It was not hard to heat like this place was.

Senator PAYNE. Did she say anything about sanitary facilities?

Mrs. HENDRICKS. They were satisfied.

Senator PAYNE. I wanted that in the record.

Senator CLARK. Mrs. Moore, I wonder if you would mind testifying now to tell us what you know about the Langley family and the situation which Mrs. Hendricks just testified about.

Statement of Catherine B. Moore, Field Worker, Child and Family Services, Portland, Maine

Mrs. MOORE. I would like to preface this by saying that in a very real sense as the representative of a casework agency I am reluctant to speak. In a sense the information that we have on these families and the work we have done with them on their family problems, and so on, we have considered as confidential; but I do feel it is important, although in a sense it is my interpretation of what that family referred to has said and done and worked with me, and it does contradict.

Senator CLARK. Mrs. Moore, let me make it very clear that we are not urging you to say anything you do not want to say. If you feel as a matter of professional ethics that you should not say anything, that would be quite all right with me, and I assume it would be with Senator Payne too; but we have here now on a public record a statement which is damaging.

Mrs. MOORE. That is why I say I am reluctant.

Senator CLARK. I am going to leave it to you and to your agency and to your city as your contractee as to what you would like to say. So you say anything, or nothing, as you think wise.

Mrs. MOORE. I will say to begin with the place this family was in was one of the worst buildings in the area. The family first of all was eligible for public housing. They could have gone to Sagamore and I tried very hard to encourage them to go to Sagamore.

Senator CLARK. Would you mind telling us in a little more detail than Mrs. Hendricks was able to what the family consisted of, if you know?

Mrs. MOORE. It was a somewhat fluctuating family, as far as composition is concerned — Mr. and Mrs. and a teenage daughter who was in and out of the family, and three smaller children.

Senator CLARK. Of both sexes?

Mrs. MOORE. A boy and two girls.

Senator CLARK. Had the husband been ill for quite a while?

Mrs. MOORE. Yes.

Senator CLARK. And therefore unemployed?

Mrs. MOORE. This was a public-assistance family — both A, B, and C — and we were able to help them get aid to the disabled, which they did not have until the relocation problem came up, because all families which were eligible for public assistance were contacted very shortly after the site survey was made in November and December of 1955.

This family along with others was contacted to make application to Sagamore. All those who were eligible did so, so that should a place become available in Sagamore they could take advantage of it. I believe this family was contacted in February of 1956.

Senator CLARK. Let me interrupt you a moment to ask you whether the lady was employed.

Mrs. MOORE. No.

Senator CLARK. There were no wage earners in the family?

Mrs. MOORE. The 17-year-old at the time I think was employed off and on.

Senator CLARK. Intermittently?

Mrs. MOORE. And has been in and out of the family.

Senator CLARK. A daughter of the family was employed intermittently?

Mrs. MOORE. That is right. They did not want to go to Sagamore. I urged them to make an application.

Senator CLARK. Were there then vacancies at Sagamore?

Mrs. MOORE. There might not have been at that particular time.

Senator CLARK. But there would have been in a reasonable period of time?

Mrs. MOORE. That was why they were urged to make application. None of the property had been purchased by the redevelopment authority at this time. That is why we were trying to foresee that when it became time for them to move there might be a vacancy.

Senator CLARK. Did Mrs. Langley indicate to you why she did not want to go to Sagamore?

Mrs. MOORE. She wanted to be near where they had lived. That was in most cases the reason why families did not want to go to Sagamore — because it is quite a distance from the city, although from an employment point of view, you see, it was not really a problem.

Senator CLARK. This was a fundamental attraction to a place which she had always lived in. Is that correct?

Mrs. MOORE. That is right.

Senator PAYNE. I think it is pretty natural, too.

Senator CLARK. I think it is very natural.

Senator PAYNE. Right.

Mrs. MOORE. So the next thing was that they came to ask if there were places available, because the place was getting so dirty where they were. The water had frozen.

Senator CLARK. Excuse me. I am a little confused.

Mrs. MOORE. This is in Vine-Deer-Chatham.

Senator CLARK. Have they made the first move yet?

Mrs. MOORE. No.

Senator CLARK. All right.

Mrs. MOORE. So they came saying they would like to find a place.

Senator CLARK. Even though they did not yet have to move?

Mrs. MOORE. That is right. The authority had not purchased the buildings.

So we took them to see several places, but they were farther away. This landlord where they moved had a place, but when they got there it had been taken. So they contacted them about this one into which they did move. I said, "Do you not want to wait until you find something better?" No; they wanted to move right then.

Senator PAYNE. About what time was this?

Mrs. MOORE. That was in February.

Senator PAYNE. Of 1956?

Mrs. MOORE. Of 1956, or March of 1956.

I had been in contact with them quite regularly. A married daughter moved to an apartment above them. A married son moved into an apartment on the other side of the building. I have seen Mrs. Langley in the office because she had come regularly. We have been working around a number of problems in this family besides this. I was very distressed. I took them to see some other places. We got to one and they did not even want to go in because they had decided it was probably too far. They still wanted to be near.

When I learned the place they had found on Smith Street was ——

Senator CLARK. Excuse me, Mrs. Moore. Do you mind if I take you back a minute and ask you if you can make your comments on the condition of the place which they first moved to, which Mrs. Hendricks just testified about somewhat critically?

Mrs. MOORE. Yes. High ceilings, hard to heat; bath was in a closet, but it was not substandard to be in a closet, in a sense.

Senator CLARK. I am sorry. We cannot hear you.

Mrs. MOORE. The bath was in a small room. It is one of these things probably they do in housing where they have to put in a bath, and they took a corner off a room and put in a bath.

Senator CLARK. Was there any ventilation in the bathroom?

Mrs. MOORE. No.

Senator CLARK. Did you hear Mrs. Hendricks comment about the dressing facilities? Was that accurate?

Mrs. MOORE. That is right. It was just a small place.

Senator CLARK. How about the toilet?

Mrs. MOORE. In a small room. There was a window into a rear corridor, with a window outside. It was not an outside window. It is not good.

Senator CLARK. Is the apartment standard or is it substandard?

Mrs. MOORE. Actually from that point of view I expect it would be substandard.

Senator CLARK. They had no central heat?

Mrs. MOORE. They had no central heat. Hot water is a responsibility of the tenant. The landlord is not responsible for connecting it. They could provide a hot water tank. The tenant has to connect the hot water from a stove to the hot water tank.

Senator PAYNE. In other words, there is a coil in the stove?

Mrs. MOORE. That is right. But that is not the landlord's responsibility.

Senator CLARK. Was there a hot water tank in the apartment?

Mrs. MOORE. That is right.

Senator CLARK. But it was not connected with the coil on the stove?

Mrs. MOORE. No.

Senator CLARK. And that was the Langleys' responsibility?

Mrs. MOORE. That is right. We had given them financial assistance.

Senator CLARK. I am sorry, but we cannot hear you.

Mrs. MOORE. Some of these families where they have had financial needs beyond what relocation payments were due we have found ways to get them additional financial assistance, which we did.

Senator CLARK. Not out of the budget of the city of Portland?

Mrs. MOORE. That's right.

Senator CLARK. Private assistance?

Mrs. MOORE. That is right. And we have continued to be in contact with the family regularly. They have other problems, as I said before.

Senator CLARK. I understand that this family does have other problems, and for very appropriate and proper reasons you do not want to discuss them. I think we can bring a little bit of experience to bear on what might be the problem there.

But now, Mrs. Moore, is that about all you want to say about this family?

Mrs. MOORE. I think so, except that they have moved a number of times.

Senator CLARK. Would you consider this a typical relocation case or an exceptional one?

Mrs. MOORE. An exceptional one.

Senator CLARK. Am I overstating the situation if I say that there is good reason to be discontented with the relocation potential in the city of Portland for these people, or do you feel that there are adequate relocation houses and apartments available for all of the people?

Mrs. MOORE. If they will accept them.

Senator CLARK. If they will accept them?

Mrs. MOORE. There is self-determination, which is the final decision in each case.

Senator CLARK. Of course, self-determination is one of the great New England virtues.

Mrs. MOORE. You can try very hard to encourage them to go to other parts of the city, but if they do not want to move into another part of the city you cannot do anything about it.

Senator CLARK. What I am trying to get you to tell me, and please do not tell me if you do not want to, is whether as a professional social worker you are content, at least for the time being, with the relocation possibilities here in Portland. In other words, is your work manageable. What I am really driving at is what are your views on the necessity for public housing in Portland?

Mrs. MOORE. I am sure it is needed.

Senator PAYNE. In other words, you do not feel that there are adequate facilities available for what we term the low-income family, which either might be on public assistance or of very low earning power, to be able to find what we would call good and satisfactory rentals at prices they can afford to pay, particularly in connection with future relocation problems.

Mrs. MOORE. There are units available.

Senator PAYNE. Are they within the price range?

Mrs. MOORE. There are some. These are the things that can be done. A do-it-yourself technique. A landlord may rent at a moderate rental and allow a tenant to make repairs in lieu of rent. They may supply materials so that the tenant may do the work, or some of these possible arrangements where they can keep the rental down. The number that will be needed and what they can afford to pay I think we have had in the study that has been made. We have found sometimes it is the location that keeps the rental down. It may not be a place where many people would want to live. It could be standard housing and not be — well, I would not like it for children. But they still might take it because they would rather pay that rent.

Senator PAYNE. Just to go back 1 minute, so I am absolutely clear in my mind about it and so the record is clear, am I to understand when that family made the move from the Vine-Deer-Chatham area, that they made that on their own and not as a matter of relocation?

Mrs. MOORE. That is right.

Senator PAYNE. Am I to understand they were paid the $100 at that time?

Mrs. MOORE. No. They moved at the time when we did not have the relocation payments.

Senator PAYNE. So they made that on their own. When was the first time that the relocation people came in to help to move them? Did they step in at all to help move them from one area to the other? I understood they went to Middle Street first. Is that right?

Mrs. MOORE. That was in the Vine-Deer-Chatham area. That was where they lived.

Senator PAYNE. That was in that area, and then they moved from there to India Street?

Mrs. MOORE. Yes.

Senator PAYNE. And they did that on their own, and before the relocation took place at all?

Mrs. MOORE. That is right.

Senator PAYNE. I just wanted to get it clear. That is all.

Senator CLARK. That is quite helpful.

Mrs. HENDRICKS. Let me say there is conflicting testimony.

5.

Civil Rights

THOUGHTFUL CITIZENS HAVE OFTEN WONDERED WHY THERE is so much controversy over "civil rights" when practically everyone endorses them in principle. In thinking about this problem it is helpful to remember the principle of general psychology that stimuli are responded to, in part, in terms of the context in which they are presented. Objective study of discussions of civil rights legislation readily discloses that such proposals are generally seen in different contexts by the participants, and consequently the discussions do not present opportunities for direct confrontation of opposing points of view.

The issues associated with federal civil rights legislation in recent years are varied and many. However, a most important recurrent theme relates to the issue of "state's rights." Because of our loyalty to the *United* States and the evident unity of the nation, it is at times hard to remember that there are some issues about which the different histories of the various regions of the U.S. would lead to significant cleavages. We recognize the importance of such historical differences in discussions of international relations, but we are often slow to appreciate equivalent factors in intranational relations. Regardless of our own particular social and political philosophies, it is important to understand the nature of the resistance of those who do not agree with us.

The concept of prejudice as "what the other fellow says when he disagrees with me; I have facts, opinions, beliefs" is hardly helpful to objectivity. Men of integrity, intelligence, and education are to be found on both sides of our current controversies. Similarly, there are men of good will and high moral standards in all sections of the country. To resolve disagreements, we need analyses which provide "more light and less heat."

Suggested Discussion Questions

Make an inventory of the variety of issues that seem to be involved in these hearings. For what audiences do the various speakers seem to be talking? Is the chairman always "neutral" in handling a session? When is a question not a question? On what bases might one expect Messrs. Patterson and Taylor to agree with Messrs. Wilkins and Scull on legislation in this field?

CIVIL RIGHTS PROPOSALS

H E A R I N G S *before the Committee on the Judiciary, United States Senate, 84th Congress, Second Session*

WEDNESDAY, MAY 16, 1956

Washington, D.C.

THE COMMITTEE MET at 2:35 p. m., pursuant to notice, in room 424, Senate Office Building, Hon. Olin D. Johnston presiding.

Present: Senators Eastland, Johnston, Hennings, McClellan, O'Mahoney, Wiley, Jenner, Watkins and Dirksen.

Also present: Robert B. Young, professional staff member, and Richard F. Wambach, assistant to counsel.

Senator JOHNSTON. The Committee on the Judiciary will come to order.

We have met today to start the hearings on the civil rights bills. I have been informed that we have 16 bills dealing with civil rights. Our first witness today is the Attorney General of the United States, Mr. Brownell.

Mr. Brownell, you may testify and proceed as you see fit in regard to what you have to say, either by following your paper or by discussion. If you don't want to be interrupted, we won't interrupt you. Or if you don't mind, we may interrupt you along the way if we have a question we want to ask.

Statement of Hon. Herbert Brownell, Attorney General of the United States

Attorney General BROWNELL. Thank you very much, Mr. Chairman. I appreciate the opportunity to be here this afternoon to testify on this important series of bills which the chairman has rightly designated the civil rights bills.

220

In his State of the Union message, President Eisenhower said that his administration would recommend to the Congress in this session a program ——

Senator O'MAHONEY. What was the date of that message?

Attorney General BROWNELL. In January, the regular State of the Union message.

To advance the efforts of the Government, within the area of Federal responsibility, to the end that every person may be judged and measured by what he is, rather than by his color, race, or religion. On April 9, 1956, I transmitted to the President of the Senate and to the Speaker of the House our proposals in this area. I am grateful for the opportunity to appear before this committee to discuss these proposals and, if the members wish, to comment as well upon other proposals relating to this same subject which are also pending before this Committee.

My letters to the President of the Senate and to the Speaker of the House recommended congressional action on four matters: First, the creation of the bipartisan Commission on Civil Rights to implement recommendations made by the President in his State of the Union message; second, creation of an additional office of Assistant Attorney General to head a new Civil Rights Division in the Department of Justice; third, amendment of existing statutes to give further protection to the right to vote and to add civil remedies in the Department of Justice for their enforcement; and fourth, amendment of other civil rights laws to include the addition of civil remedies in the Department of Justice for their enforcement.

[. . . . . .]

Senator HENNINGS. Mr. Chairman, with the permission of the committee, as I happen to be chairman of the Subcommittee on Constitutional Rights, I would like very much if the Attorney General would indulge me to inquire into some of these matters.

Mr. Attorney General, this is the first time, is it not, that the Justice Department has seen fit to transmit to the Congress any suggestions as to legislation relating to civil rights or cognate matters?

Attorney General BROWNELL. We have commented on bills that were introduced, in response to requests from Congress.

Senator HENNINGS. But you have come up with no program during your 4 years, until last month, I believe, April 1, was it not?

Attorney General BROWNELL. Let me say that might lead to a very misleading answer. I know you don't mean to do so.

The program the Department of Justice has carried on in this area in the past few years I would characterize as, and I hope you would agree with me, the most vigorous in the Department's history.

Almost the first day I was down here, we had the Thompson Restaurant case, which was in the courts then, on which we filed a brief, and got a favorable decision from the courts, which laid the groundwork for doing away with discrimination here in the nation's capital, specifically in the restaurants. I can't exaggerate the importance that has had nationwide.

Then we have had 2 years of steady litigation in the Supreme Court on school segregation, which took a great deal of time. You know the results there.

Furthermore, we worked closely with the President's Advisory Committee on eliminating discrimination in employment and contracts. We did the legal work on abolishing discrimination in the armed forces.

All of those things we have been active on. In addition to that, we have had great success in carrying our cases forward in elimination of peonage, stopping a revival of this Ku Klux Klan in one of the States, and as I mention in my prepared statement, we are now getting to the point where we are participating in some of these civil cases. I wouldn't want your question to imply we haven't been awfully busy on this.

Senator HENNINGS. You may know that I haven't any intention of being misleading. You know these were initiated in the preceding administration.

Attorney General BROWNELL. A great many of them, yes.

Senator HENNINGS. It has not been initiated, and I don't mean to bring this into the realm of politics, except to indicate perhaps insofar as being a knight in shining armor, and we welcome you, indeed, to that fold, and hope you will continue your good work in the prosecution of these good cases.

Attorney General BROWNELL. I am not here as a knight in shining armor today. I read your speech in which you pointed out your 20 years of activity in this field.

I have tried throughout my private and public life to do the same thing. I do want to say I am not here today except in my capacity to carry out the President's program, and I claim no personal credit whatsoever.

Senator HENNINGS. I just wanted it clear that many of the

things that this administration has done have been initiated in preceding administrations.

Attorney General BROWNELL. I think there are men of good will in both parties, who want to see these objectives attained.

Senator HENNINGS. Certainly I can agree with you on that. If you will forgive me, I think that we should have the record clear on some things.

Attorney General BROWNELL. I agree with you on that.

Senator HENNINGS. We welcome your suggestion, for example, that there be a Commission on Civil Rights in the Department of Justice. At my request on March 22, 1955, this letter was addressed to you, signed by the late Harley Kilgore, former chairman of the Committee on the Judiciary. The letter reads as follows:

DEAR MR. ATTORNEY GENERAL: Attached herewith are copies of S. 902, S. 905, S. 906, and S. 907, concerning the protection of civil rights, amending and supplementing existing civil rights statutes, and establishing a Commission on Civil Rights in the executive branch of the Government.

These four bills are now pending before the standing Subcommittee on Constitutional Rights which intends to schedule hearings on all of the above mentioned measures within the very near future.

Accordingly, it will be appreciated if you will submit to the committee as soon as possible individual reports on each of these measures.

With kindest regards, I am

Most sincerely yours,

Harley M. Kilgore,
CHAIRMAN

Now, as relates to the question of the Division of Civil Rights.

Attorney General BROWNELL. It is all in the Congressional Record if you haven't it there.

Senator HENNINGS. There was no reply in our records of the subcommittee, no reply from you whatever over a year ago relating to the establishment of a commission or a division, I should say, of Civil Rights in the Department of Justice. We have no record of your ever having replied to that request.

Attorney General BROWNELL. I hesitate to say there, but the fact is I discussed the matter with the then chairman of the committee. He was unable to get together on a hearing on the subject.

You are undoubtedly correct that there is nothing in writing in answer to that.

Senator HENNINGS. Did you want to testify on the subject?

Attorney General BROWNELL. If a hearing could have been arranged, I would have been glad to.

Senator HENNINGS. But you did not thereafter request that a hearing be held.

Attorney General BROWNELL. I discussed it with the then Chairman of the Committee.

Senator HENNINGS. That would be Senator Kilgore.

I don't recall that you ever discussed it with me.

Attorney General BROWNELL. I don't recall that I did.

Senator HENNINGS. These bills are lodged in the subcommittee of which I happen to be chairman.

Attorney General BROWNELL. Didn't you read the letter that came from him?

Senator HENNINGS. You will recall that last fall, we made a number of efforts to get you to testify before the subcommitttee on Constitutional Rights.

Attorney General BROWNELL. That was on a different subject.

Senator HENNINGS. On a number of subjects.

Attorney General BROWNELL. Yes.

Senator HENNINGS. You wanted to know what subject it would be, and we said it would cover a multitude of things. We were unable to persuade you to come.

Attorney General BROWNELL. I remember that.

Senator HENNINGS. Now, then, Mr. Attorney General, on July 27, 1955, some 9 months ago a letter was addressed to you as follows:

The Judiciary Committee is herewith transmitting S. 903 for your study and report thereon in triplicate.

To facilitate the work of the committee, it is urgently requested that your report be submitted within 20 days. The committee should be formally advised in writing if any delay beyond this time period is necessary.

Most sincerely yours,

Harley M. Kilgore,
CHAIRMAN

On September 8, 1955, the following letter was received by the then chairman of this committee, Senator Kilgore, which letter reads as follows:

DEAR SENATORS: This is in response to your request for the views of the Department of Justice concerning the bill (S. 903) to protect the right to political participation. [. . .]

The purpose of the bill, as stated in its title, is "to protect the right to political participation." This purpose is a laudable one with which the Department of Justice is in full accord. Whether this particular measure should be enacted constitutes a question of policy concerning which the Department of Justice prefers to make no recommendation.

The Bureau of the Budget has advised that there is no objection to the submission of this report.

Sincerely,

William P. Rogers,

DEPUTY ATTORNEY GENERAL

So at that time, the Department of Justice had no recommendation. Would you like to look at this letter to see that it is an accurate copy?

Attorney General BROWNELL. I am sure that must be an accurate copy of the letter.

Senator HENNINGS. I'll be glad to hand it to you for your verification.

Attorney General BROWNELL. I am sure it must be accurate. If it weren't, I am sure you wouldn't be reading it.

Senator HENNINGS. I usually make sure that I have accurate copies to read from.

Senator O'MAHONEY. Would the Senator yield for a moment?

Senator HENNINGS. Yes, surely.

Senator O'MAHONEY. Does the Attorney General mean to suggest that through a letter written by Mr. William P. Rogers, it did not reflect the view of the Department of Justice at that time?

Attorney General BROWNELL. No such implication as that. Quite the contrary, Senator.

Senator O'MAHONEY. Thank you.

Senator HENNINGS. Now, then, pursuant to the letter of March 22, which I undertake to call to your attention — at that time, on the matter of the so-called right to vote provision, and on the so-called S. 907, which relates to protection of civil rights of individuals by establishing a commission on civil rights in the executive branch of the Government — as long ago as March 22, over a year and some months or so last past, there had been at that time, until April 1, no expression from the Department of Justice upon any of this legislation.

Had there, Mr. Brownell?

Attorney General BROWNELL. I think, Senator, that letter that you read is right. I think no hearings were held, however, by the committee at which we had a chance to give oral testimony.

Senator HENNINGS. I am speaking now of the letters that were written to you asking for your advice and guidance.

Attorney General BROWNELL. As far as I know, those are the only letters on those subjects.

Senator HENNINGS. And you had no advice, and indeed you had no guidance to give this committee on that subject at that time.

Attorney General BROWNELL. I wouldn't say that, because we were never invited up to a hearing before.

Senator HENNINGS. But you didn't answer the letter.

Attorney General BROWNELL. The letters will speak for themselves.

Senator HENNINGS. If there is no letter, it can't speak for itself. There is one letter I read in which you said that is a matter for Congress to determine. The words in the letter were, "whether or not such a measure should be enacted constitutes a question of policy concerning which the Department of Justice prefers to make no recommendation."

This was as of last September 1955. At that time, you had no recommendation to make upon any of these subjects.

Attorney General BROWNELL. Congress wasn't in session then, was it, Senator?

Senator HENNINGS. Well, the committees were functioning. We had a Subcommittee on Constitutional Rights sitting here. We extended a number of invitations to you to appear before that subcommittee, up to December 1, commencing on October 15.

Now, then, on S. 908, relating to the commission on civil rights in the executive branch of the Government, as indicated by the letter which I read, on September 8, on that same date, and in that same letter. This relates to S. 903. I have another letter here, also dated September 8, 1955, relating to S. 906. In both cases, on page 2, the conclusion of Mr. William P. Rogers, the Deputy Attorney General, is that

whether or not this measure should be enacted constitutes a question of policy concerning which the Department of Justice prefers to make no recommendation.

In the accompanying letter relating to S. 903, to protect the rights of political participation, you say

whether or not this measure should be enacted constitutes a question of policy concerning which the Department of Justice prefers to make no recommendation.

Now, then, you of course are aware, Mr. Attorney General, that on December 3, 1955, I wrote to you — rather, I should say Senator Kilgore wrote at our request — the following:

DEAR MR. ATTORNEY GENERAL: Attached herewith is a list of bills on which reports previously have been requested but, according to records of the committee, have not been received.

It will be appreciated if every action is taken to insure the receipt of the requested reports so that these bills may be processed for presentation to the committee before the beginning of the 2d session, 84th Congress.

With kindest regards, I am

Most sincerely yours,

— — —,

CHAIRMAN

Now, then, that was way back in December 1955, December 3, to be exact. In an attachment to that letter are listed S. 902, S. 905, S. 907, and I should say a total of 28 bills upon which the Department of Justice had not given either the full committee or its subcommittee the benefit of its impression.

Does the Attorney General remember this correspondence?

Attorney General BROWNELL. You refreshed my recollection. I am sure that also is accurate.

Senator HENNINGS. Now, then, of course, on February 24, I had written this one:

DEAR MR. ATTORNEY GENERAL: The Subcommittee on Constitutional Rights of the Committee on the Judiciary has scheduled a hearing on S. 902, a bill to reorganize the Department of Justice for the protection of civil rights, on March 2, 1956, at 10 a. m., in room 424 of the Senate Office Building.

By letter dated March 22, 1955, the Committee on the Judiciary requested the views of your department on this legislation, but, as yet, no answer to the letter of March 22 has been received. Inasmuch as this measure directly concerns your department and its functions, the subcommittee hopes that you will be able to present your views on this very important matter at the scheduled hearing. If for any reason, you cannot appear on the scheduled date, would you please suggest a date and time within 10 days of that date when it would be possible for you to appear personally and present your views.

Then, on February 28, 1956, I sent a telegram to you as follows:

With respect to my invitation to you of February 24 to appear and testify before the Subcommittee on Constitutional Rights on Friday, March 2, with respect to bill S. 902, I respectfully wish to advise you that the hour of the meeting has been changed from 10:30 until 11:30 to permit committee members to attend the funeral services of our distinguished colleague, Senator Kilgore. The committee is exceedingly desirous of learning your views with respect to S. 902 and we are looking forward to your being with us.

Does the Attorney General remember any of these communications?

Attorney General BROWNELL. It sounds right to me.

Senator O'MAHONEY. Will the Senator yield for a minute?

Senator HENNINGS. I'll be glad to yield.

Senator O'MAHONEY. I direct your attention to page 5 of your statement, Mr. Attorney General. The first two sentences of the first paragraph.

We have observed that S. 902 would also provide for a Civil Rights Division in the Department of Justice. I believe, however, that bill is more detailed than is necessary.

I have looked at both of these bills, which are in the folder of the Assistant Attorney General, Mr. Rogers, who has kindly loaned them to me, and I find that S. 3604, which is the bill you recommend, was introduced in the Senate on April 11, 1956, by several members of this committee and several other members of the Senate, all of whom happen to be Republicans.

S. 902 was introduced February 1, 1955, by Senator Humphrey of Minnesota for himself, Mr. Douglas, Mr. Lehman, Mr. McNamara, Mr. Langer, Mr. Magnuson, Mr. Morse, Mr. Murray, Mr. Neely, and Mr. Neuberger.

The first section of S. 902 deals with the exact subject of the bill S. 3604, which you endorsed. It contains 80 words. Your bill contains 69 words.

Attorney General BROWNELL. A little on the side of economy there.

[.   .   .   .   .]

Senator O'MAHONEY. [. . .] Section 2 of the bill, the one which you now say is more detailed than you think is necessary, has the provision — I am now referring to the second section of S. 902, which reads as follows:

The personnel of the Federal Bureau of Investigation of the Department of Justice shall be increased to the extent necessary to carry out effectively the duties of such bureau, with respect to the investigation of civil rights cases under applicable federal law. Such bureau shall include in the training of its agents appropriate training and instructions to be provided by the Attorney General in the investigation of civil rights cases.

Now, you have already answered that question by saying that that is the section to which you objected when you said S. 902 went into more detail than is necessary. Do you object to the Assistant Attorney General having the assistance of the Federal Bureau of Investigation in investigating civil rights cases?

Attorney General BROWNELL. No.

My point is rather this, Senator, if I am permitted to put it on the record. The experience in the past has been that it is inadvisable to try to pin down by statute, investigative jurisdiction of the FBI. That has always been left to the discretion of the head of the FBI. We felt it would be advisable to drop this entire section 2 out because plenty of authority exists under the present law.

Senator O'MAHONEY. Then why didn't you say that back in 1955, when this bill was introduced, instead of waiting until today to say in these few vague words you have used?

Attorney General BROWNELL. I came up here today in the frame of mind to be all the help I could be today, and if I have made errors in the past, I am sorry.

Senator HENNINGS. I think it only appropriate, Mr. Attorney General, and I really mean it when I say that we are not trying to put you through the mill up here on some of these things.

Indeed, you did come out with what you heralded as a new administration civil-rights program. At the time you did that, there were three bills that had been reported out — four bills, indeed — by the subcommittee of this standing committee of the Senate, the Subcommittee on Constitutional Rights.

I don't think that you could or would want to say to me that I have not made consistent and protracted efforts to get your views on this legislation before this committee met.

Senator O'Mahoney will bear witness that I did that a number of times. We put some thought into these matters. Perhaps we are not as expert or have the great legal precision or the legal craftsmen or technicians that you may have at your command, but we on the subcommittee did the best we could on this legislation to bring that out. We did bring it out way back in February.

I wrote you this letter on April 9, following up some of the other letters of 1955. If you will indulge me, I would like to read that, as indicative of the fact that the Standing Subcommittee on Constitutional Rights of this Committee on the Judiciary was not sitting here doing nothing; that we were working on this legislation; that in the preceding Congress, there were only two meetings held on that subcommittee when Senator Hendrickson was chairman of it, and that we immediately commenced to think about this and many other matters which I know are of sincere concern to you. I want to say, too, that I don't question your good faith. I think you believe in this sort of thing. I am satisfied you do.

Attorney General BROWNELL. Thank you, Senator.

Senator HENNINGS. But I do want to know and I think I am entitled to know why we were consistently by-passed, why our letters were ignored, why we were given no assistance or help from the Department which later unveiled with considerable publicity a new civil rights program.

Now, on April 9, I took the liberty of addressing this letter to you, and I hold a copy of it in my hand:

DEAR MR. ATTORNEY GENERAL: Before leaving for Missouri more than a week ago, I dictated a letter inviting you to appear tomorrow morning before the Senate Subcommittee on Constitutional Rights, to give your views on civil rights legislation. I find that through inadvertence, this letter was not dispatched in my absence. Notice, however, had gone to the other two Senators on the subcommittee that a meeting would be held tomorrow at 10:30 a. m. The subcommittee would appreciate very much your appearance before the House Judiciary Committee which I understand meets tomorrow morning at 12 noon.

Recent newspaper stories have indicated that you desire to present to Congress a three-point program on civil rights comprising proposals for a Civil Rights Commission with subpena powers, a Civil Rights Division within the Department of Justice, and a bill to protect every citizen's right to vote by providing for civil action in the Federal courts.

You are undoubtedly aware that the subcommittee reported favorably on February 9, 1956 on four civil rights bills (1) to establish a Civil Rights Division in the Department of Justice, (2) to protect the voting rights of all citizens in Federal elections and primaries, (3) an anti-lynching bill, and (4) a bill to protect members of the Armed Forces against bodily attack.

As you will recall, the subcommittee requested your views on two of these bills last year. These were S. 902, a bill to establish a Civil Rights Division in the Department of Justice; and S. 903, a bill to protect the rights of all citizens to political participation. You replied to our request for your views on S. 903 that since this bill concerned a matter of policy, you preferred to make no recommendation; and to our request for your views on S. 902, although this bill concerned the creation of a new division in your own department, you had made no response up to the time the subcommittee reported the bill on February 9.

In view of the recent statement of President Eisenhower and the newspaper reports that you will present the administration's civil-rights program to Congress, we would again like to give you the opportunity of presenting your views on this legislation. Even though these bills have been reported, we feel that your appearance and testimony would assure bipartisan support which is necessary to their enactment, and would at this time assist in their early consideration by the full Senate Judiciary Committee.

As you also undoubtedly know, there are presently pending before the committee other civil-rights legislation. The subcommittee would very much like to have your views and recommendations on this important legislation. These bills are:

S. 904, a bill to tighten criminal provisions relating to peonage and slavery.

S. 905, a bill to amend and supplement existing civil rights legislation.

S. 906, a bill to create a permanent Commission on Civil Rights to gather and disseminate information on developments affecting civil rights.

S. 907, an omnibus bill incorporating the principal provisions of S. 902, S. 903, S. 904, S. 905 and S. 906.

We are particularly interested in your recommendations concerning S. 906 to create a Civil Rights Commission since it has been mentioned in the press that this is a proposal that has administration backing. We are most desirous of having the administration's recommendations on this proposal, and feel that you as the proponent of the administration's three-point program, are in the best position to give us these views.

I would appreciate it if you would notify me whether you will be able to appear before our Subcommittee following your testimony before the House Judiciary Committee.

Sincerely yours,

Thomas C. Hennings, Jr.,
UNITED STATES SENATOR

We have no record of any reply to that letter.

Now, all of this may seem, Mr. Chairman, collateral. All of it may in some respects be subsidiary to the principal issues in some of these bills. But some of us who have been engaged in the preparation of this legislation believe that we were entitled to the assistance of the Attorney General, just as the Attorney General comes before our committee with his nominations for the Federal judiciary, for additional district judges, for various other related matters where we seek and enlist your cooperation.

But on these measures, I think it fair to say, and I think you will agree with me, that we had no cooperation. [. . .]

I am going to conclude now.

I am sure we are all very glad that you are evidencing this interest in this very important field. I wonder if you could tell me, Mr. Attorney General, why you did not see fit to reply to these numerous requests for advice and counsel; why you didn't answer?

Attorney General BROWNELL. In order to make an answer on that, I would have to consult with my staff, because I know there was a great deal of telephoning and correspondence on it. Very often in a situation of that kind we will talk to members of the staff or the chairman of the committee. I would have to check with my own staff on that.

Senator HENNINGS. Some of these letters were written by me, and some of those wherein I listed the numbers of the bills to which you gave no answer or no guidance. I know for a fact that you and I didn't talk about those things, nor was I called by telephone to discuss it.

Attorney General BROWNELL. That is my recollection also.

Senator HENNINGS. Then you don't remember exactly why these letters were not answered?

Attorney General BROWNELL. No; I don't, Senator.

[. . . . .]

Senator JOHNSTON. Are there any other questions?

Senator DIRKSEN. No; but I would like to make a little comment. And I make this with the utmost respect for my colleague, because I have served with him on the Civil Rights Committee of the 83d Congress, and I know how diligent he was in seeking to achieve some action.

But I point out that in the 82d Congress there were quite a number of civil rights bills introduced, all of which got to the subcommittee stage, and no further.

And then I point out that in the 83d Congress there were some bills introduced, I introduced a bill on the civil rights and FEPC. It was a rather all-inclusive bill. My good friend from Missouri will remember that we had a few hearings on that, and we did report it out of the subcommittee, but it never got out of the full committee.

Senator Ferguson introduced a bill on antilynching, I don't know whether it got out or not.

Senator HENNINGS. We have one that is out at the present time.

Senator DIRKSEN. I am speaking about prior.

And there was a bill to set up a Civil Rights Division, introduced in 1954, and it was pending at the time, and no further action was taken.

Now, certainly since I can remember — I think Senator O'Mahoney will remember and Senator Hennings will remember that on five occasions we passed an antipoll tax bill in the House, and it got over to the Senate side, and no action was taken.

In the last 12 years we have had 6 bills dealing with fair employment practices, and evidently no action was taken on this side — some action was taken on the House side, as I recall it.

And then we have had bills in the last 8 years in every Congress that create some type of commission to deal with the problem.

I allude to it, Mr. Chairman, only for this reason, without for the moment commenting on the omission of any public servant with respect to correspondence between the executive branch and the legislative branch. But I sincerely hope that now there is an opportunity to get some action, now that the time and circumstances and interest and everything are somehow combined to set the stage for action, I sincerely hope that we can go ahead.

I am not insensible to the fact that probably on occasions I may have been fallible enough to think in terms of political credit. It could be that others have thought in terms of a little political credit. But whatever our derelictions and sins of omission and commission were in other days, I hope now that we have come to this point where the issues have been pretty well dramatized not only by the Congress but by the Attorney General and by the Supreme Court, I hope that we can now address ourselves to the substance of the thing that is before us, and go through regardless of the consequences.

Senator o'MAHONEY. With neither political credit nor discredit.

Senator DIRKSEN. I am just a frail human casting ember, I admit to my own sins, and I feel — I am still anxious, of course, to get some action. And now that we have ventilated the record I trust that we can put all that to one side and devote ourselves to what is before the committee.

Senator HENNINGS. In reply to the distinguished Senator from Illinois, having served on this committee I know that we have sought at all times to get guidance. I believe it was 2 weeks ago that the Senator from Illinois introduced the administration bill, or the Attorney General's measure, into the Senate.

Senator DIRKSEN. And if my good friend will permit a comment, we went back to look at the record the other day, and I introduced an anti-poll-tax bill in January of 1945 in the House, also an antilynching bill, and an FEPC bill. I have continued from that day to this.

So I think the record will add up to a claim that I have had a sustained interest in it.

Senator HENNINGS. I believe that you and I introduced our first antilynching bills when we were together back in 1935 in the House of Representatives, and every year after that.

Senator DIRKSEN. It could well be.

Senator HENNINGS. And other legislation.

Senator DIRKSEN. Yes.

Senator O'MAHONEY. Mr. Chairman, I would like to make just a little historical addition to what the Senator from Illinois has said.

Before my leave of absence in 1952, I was a member of the Judiciary Committee, and I remember very well that Senator Borah of Idaho was also a member of that committee. Senator Borah, I believe, thought that the anti-poll-tax bill and antilynching bills were unconstitutional, because they were an invasion of the rights of the States, and that the only sensible way to proceed under such laws, to gain such objectives by law, would be to amend the Constitution.

Following his suggestion, I introduced a constitutional amendment — I drafted it myself, believe it or not — and introduced it to amend the Constitution so as to make the levying of the poll tax illegal.

Well it rested in the cubby holes of the committee. And then when the 80th Congress came along I was startled and surprised when the late Senator Murray introduced my amendment in his own name. And it lay in the cubby holes all the time in the 80th Congress, too.

So we can forget the political credit and discredit and go to work.

Senator JOHNSTON. While everybody is getting on the record in regard to it I had better get on the record, too. If you will search the records of the House you will see where I was taking the opposite view, and I would get everybody I could to really stand up for State rights at the time.

Senator MCCLELLAN. Mr. Chairman, I am sure that no one

was ever suspicious that this issue was tainted in the least degree with politics.

Senator JOHNSTON. Not a bit.

Senator MCCLELLAN. We have wasted a lot of time, but I would like now to suggest that our distinguished friend talk a little bit about something substantial.

Senator DIRKSEN. Would you permit the intrusion of one more historical postscript?

Senator MCCLELLAN. Yes.

Senator DIRKSEN. It comes about — it is not of the caliber of the distinguished Attorney General and my friend from Missouri — but I think you will bear me out that while we were sensible of the fact that constitutional issues were involved here, and that people did not always agree as to whether it could be controlled by statute or whether constitutional amendments were required, the bills upon which action was taken in the House so often came over to this very deliberative body, and I have a recollection that we felt terribly ignored over on the other side that we could not even get an expression from the Senate as to whether they were opposed or indifferent on constitutional grounds.

So this issue simmered. Those bills found a nice, comfortable dark pigeonhole, and they seemed to stay there. So there has been a sort of an impasse as to this issue for a long time.

So now, as I say, we have washed out all the petty little things in the spirit. I think we are now prepared to go ahead and devote ourselves to it.

[. . . . .]

FRIDAY, MAY 25, 1956
Washington, D.C.

THE COMMITTEE MET, at 2:35 p. m., pursuant to notice, in room 424, Senate Office Building, Hon. Thomas C. Hennings, Jr., presiding.

Present: Senators Hennings (presiding), Jenner, and Dirksen.

Also present: Robert B. Young, professional staff member, and Richard F. Wambach, assistant to counsel.

Senator HENNINGS. The committee will please come to order.

I must apologize to the witnesses who have been kept waiting. I was erroneously advised that the meeting this afternoon would start at half past 2. And I went to the floor of the Senate and had just returned from there, when I was advised, Senator Dirksen, that you had called, and Mr. Young had called.

I am very sorry about any delay or inconvenience I may have caused any of you.

This afternoon we have as our first witness Mr. Roy Wilkins, who is the executive secretary of the National Association for the Advancement of Colored People.

Would you like to come forward, please, Mr. Wilkins? Sit where it is most convenient. Perhaps right here. Would you suggest, Senator Dirksen, Mr. Wilkins might sit there?

Senator DIRKSEN. Yes, indeed.

Mr. WILKINS. Thank you, Senator.

Senator HENNINGS. You may proceed, Mr. Wilkins.

We are very glad to have you here this afternoon to add to our information, I am sure, and our enlightenment upon the subject under consideration. And you may, if you will, proceed in any manner you please.

Statement of Roy Wilkins, Executive Secretary, National Association for the Advancement of Colored People

Mr. WILKINS. Thank you, Mr. Chairman.

My name is Roy Wilkins and I am executive secretary of the National Association for the Advancement of Colored People. Joining our association in this statement are the organizations listed on the attached sheet which, through authorized spokesmen, have consented to the use of their names as endorsers of this testimony.

And, with your permission, I would like to call the names of them and I think some of the representatives are here, and may identify themselves.

The American Council on Human Rights.

The American Jewish Congress.

The American Veterans Committee, Mr. Andrew Rice.

The Americans for Democratic Action, Mr. John Gunther.

The Brotherhood of Sleeping Car Porters, which was not able to have a representative here.

The Catholic Interracial Council.

The National Union of Electrical, Radio and Machine Workers, AFL-CIO, Mr. Peterson or Mr. Hartland.

The Jewish Labor Committee.

The National Alliance of Postal Employees, Mr. James Cobb.

The National Association for the Advancement of Colored People, of course, I am representing.

The National Council of Negro Women.

The United Automobile Workers of America, AFL-CIO, Mr. Paul Sifton.

The United Steel Workers of America.

The Workers Defense League.

And the Women's International League for Peace and Freedom.

Senator HENNINGS. I am sure that we are very glad, and that Senator Dirksen joins me in welcoming all of you representatives of these groups to these hearings. And with that, you may proceed, if you please, Mr. Wilkins.

Mr. WILKINS. Mr. Chairman, all of these groups through authorized spokesmen have consented to my speaking in their behalf, in this testimony.

Because of the short notice a number of other national organizations could not be reached for definite authorization, although in the past these have also supported the legislation under consideration, as reference to past committee hearings will reveal.

The Constitution of the United States guarantees full equality of rights and opportunities to Americans of every race, color, religion and national origin. Legislation to secure for every American his constitutional rights has been repeatedly presented for enactment by the Congress, thus far, unfortunately, without result. Chief among these proposals have been measures to:

1. Wipe out interference with the right to register or vote in primary or general Federal elections, and to abolish the poll tax.

2. Create a Civil Rights Division within the Department of Justice, headed by an Assistant Attorney General, with authority to protect civil rights in all sections of the country.

3. Establish a permanent Federal Commission on Civil Rights to make continuous appraisals and to recommend action with respect to civil-rights problems.

4. Set up an effective Federal FEPC to prevent discrimination in employment.

5. Make lynching and other assaults by public officials or private citizens, acting either in concert or individually, on persons or property because of race, color, religion or national origin, a Federal crime.

6. Eliminate remaining segregation and other forms of discrimination in interstate travel.

The organizations subscribing to this statement endorse all these measures and have repeatedly called for their enactment into law. But what has happened to these proposals in the successive Congresses in which they have been introduced?

With respect to the right to vote, legislation to outlaw the poll tax has passed the House five times, but has never come to a vote in the Senate.

In four instances since 1942 the filibuster kept poll tax bills off the Senate floor. In more recent years the mere threat of a filibuster has prevented action on this measure.

With respect to civil-rights enforcement, responsibility for the enforcement of existing civil-rights laws is vested in a nonstatutory Civil Rights Section of the Criminal Division of the Department of Justice. It has been proved to lack the resources or the authority necessary to cope with increasingly flagrant civil-rights violations.

Legislation to establish a Civil Rights Division in the Department of Justice, with sufficient authority and appropriations to prevent civil-rights violations has been before the Congress continually since 1948. No such legislation has ever been brought to the floor of either House for debate and vote.

As for a Federal Civil Rights Commission, in a democratic society, the systematic, critical review of social needs and public policy is a fundamental necessity. This is especially true of a field like civil rights, where the problems are enduring and range widely.

Yet, nowhere in the Federal Government is there an agency charged with the continuous appraisal of the status of civil rights and the efficiency of the machinery with which we hope to improve that status.

Bills to establish such a Commission have been pending in the Congress since 1948. No such bill has ever been brought to the floor of either House for debate and vote.

FEPC bills have been before every session of Congress since 1944. Committees have reported FEPC bills favorably in the past six Congresses.

Yet, no FEPC bill has ever been allowed to come to the floor of the Senate for debate and vote. In 1946, the vote to break the filibuster and take up an FEPC bill was 48 to 36; in 1950, the votes were 52 to 32 and 55 to 33, all for taking up FEPC.

Yet the filibusterers blocked the majority will because rule 22 required a two-thirds vote to break a filibuster.

Security of the person: Legislation to make lynching a Federal crime was killed by filibuster in 1922. 1922, I repeat. This matter has been before Congress continually since that time but has not been brought to a vote in the Senate.

On interstate travel, the Supreme Court has ruled that segregation in interstate transportation is a denial of constitutional rights. However, there is no adequate machinery to protect these rights, with the result that segregation and other discriminatory practices persist.

Legislation to provide specific penalties for those who impose segregation in interstate transportation has been before the Congress, Mr. Chairman, continually since 1948. None of this legislation has ever been brought to the floor of either House for debate and vote.

During this same period significant advances have been made in safeguarding the civil rights of American citizens through the courts, through the acts of State legislatures and municipal bodies, through administrative and executive actions and through the efforts of voluntary organizations. Only the Congress has stood still. No Federal civil rights legislation has been enacted by the Congress for 80 years.

In recent years there have been frequent declarations that the judicial and executive branches of the Government were acting on civil rights in areas and in ways which are alleged to be more properly the responsibility of the Congress. But those who so contend are the very ones who have consistently denied the Congress an opportunity to express its will on civil rights.

Let them now permit the Congress to record its view. Let them allow the democratic process to work. Let them now at long last, after reasonable debate, permit civil rights legislation to be brought to a vote.

Mr. Chairman, while the organizations submitting this statement endorse all the measures referred to above and believe that their enactment is long overdue, developments during the past year have especially highlighted the need for legislation to guarantee security of the person, to protect the right to vote and to provide the Justice Department with adequate enforcement powers.

Thus, while lynching has changed in character over the years, protection of the person is still a problem. Organized mob violence and terror of the Ku Klux Klan variety, often in collusion with local enforcement officials, are reappearing in new forms. The present-day lynchers arrange economic reprisals or bombings, as well as acts of personal violence, against individuals who do not conform to established community patterns.

The poll tax is still a substantial barrier to voting in 5 states. Where it does not suffice, discriminatory administration of voter qualification tests serves to bar many who should be allowed to vote. When these have failed, threats, intimidation and even murder have been used with great effectiveness.

Flagrantly and systematically, the right to vote has been denied colored citizens in many parts of the South.

I offer the committee a sample of the kind of ballot used in Alabama elections which have just been concluded. You will note that the ballot carries a rooster and the declaration of white supremacy. It is fantastic that in America at the polling booths there would be such open flaunting of theories of racial superiority.

Mr. Chairman, I pass this for your inspection, sir.

Senator HENNINGS. Mr. Wilkins, would you not like to have this made a part of the record of these hearings?

Mr. WILKINS. I would, sir.

Senator HENNINGS. Without objection, that will be so ordered.

[. . . . .]

Mr. WILKINS. In Alabama the opposition to voting by colored people is not merely symbolic. Macon County, for example, is the seat of Tuskegee Institute — a world famous institution of higher learning. In Macon County colored citizens have had a long hard struggle to obtain the right to vote. The latest effort to keep many of them from casting a ballot has been most effective. State officials have simply refused to appoint a full board of registrars. At least two members are necessary for the board to function, and at present there is only one.

An interesting commentary on the Macon County, Ala., situation is that State Senator Sam Inglehart, who hails from that county, and who is a State senator, by reason of the fact that many thousands of colored citizens in his county cannot vote, Senator Inglehart is the state chairman of the White Citizens Council in Alabama, which organization is now busily engaged in trying to keep still more Negroes from voting, not only in Macon County but throughout Alabama.

Because there has been a steady increase in the number of qualified colored voters in Louisiana, an organization known as the White Citizens Council has started a campaign to purge as many of these voters from the books as possible.

In Monroe, La., representatives of the councils have actually invaded the office of the registrar of voting for the purpose of purging colored voters. It is estimated that at least 500 colored voters have been taken from the rolls because of this activity. At one point the action of those who oppose voting by colored people became so flagrant that a former Governor of Louisiana, Mr. Knowles, went to the office of the registrar to challenge the proceeding. A near fist fight ensued.

It should be noted here that this is an illustration of one of the conditions that would be corrected by a section of the legislation before this committee. These citizens in Louisiana who were summarily purged from the polls a few days before election had no chance to get themselves back on the rolls.

There was no machinery, there was no law, and the Federal Government, the Department of Justice, had no law under which it could proceed. The result was that in 10 days or 2 weeks, after the summary action against them, an election was held and they were denied an opportunity to participate in it.

An Associated Press dispatch from Baton Rouge, La., dated May 14, 1956, reported that Governor Robert Kennon had announced the dismissal of a woman registrar of voters in Webster Parish after complaints from members of the White Citizens Councils that she had failed to enforce voter registration qualifications.

After criticism [says the Associated Press dispatch] Mrs. Clement (the registrar) applied the law uniformly to both races and disqualified 24 white persons.

For this, of course, she was dismissed.

She contended, "What's fair for one race is fair for the other."

It is an interesting commentary on this situation to interpolate, this woman who saw such fairness in administering the law without discrimination, has been restored to her post, a few days after a new state administration took office in Louisiana. Presumably the new administration regards the fair administration of the voter registration laws as not cause for dismissal from office.

Mississippi has run the entire scale from economic reprisal to outright violence in preventing colored people from voting.

The following is a quote from an issue of the State Times of Jackson, Miss., in March 1955:

An offshoot [says the paper] of a meeting of Mississippi circuit court clerks Tuesday was a suggestion that the clerks seek information of citizen's councils in their counties to halt an overload of Negro voting.

Earl W. Crenshaw, circuit court clerk of Montgomery County, said the councils are very effective. He spelled out their method of operations as follows —

And I quote again:

The council obtains names of Negroes registered from the circuit court clerk. If those who are working for someone sympathetic to the council's views are found objectionable, their employer tells them to take a vacation. Then if the names are purged from the registration books they are told that the vacation is over and they can return to work.

A dramatic illustration of how the program of fear works comes from Humphreys County area of Mississippi. Prior to May 1955, there were approximately 400 colored voters in this county. By May 7, 1955, the number of colored voters had been reduced to 92. On that day, the Rev. G. W. Lee, a leader in the register and vote effort among colored people, was fatally shot in Belzoni, Miss.

Today, Mr. Chairman, there is only one colored eligible to vote in Belzoni, Miss. He is Gus Courts, who once ran a grocery store in the community. On November 25, 1955, he was shot and seriously wounded while in his store, but has since recovered.

I offer the committee a photostat of an envelope and a threatening message mailed by persons unknown in Columbus, Miss., July 30, 1955, to Caleb Lide, one of the few registered Negro voters in Crawford, Miss. The message reads:

Last warning. If you are tired of living vote and die.

I submit the reproduction of the envelope and of the message, Mr. Chairman.

Senator HENNINGS. Without objection it will be admitted into the record and made a part thereof.

[. . . . .]

Mr. WILKINS. The need for minimum safeguards to civil rights along these lines is reflected in the volumes of favorable testimony at congressional hearings, in the many favorable reports of committees of the House and Senate, in the platforms of both political parties, and in the sponsorship of such legislation by Republicans and Democrats alike.

The House Judiciary Committee, after reviewing all the bills now before this committee, has reported out H. R. 627, a measure which combines the proposals submitted by the administration with those previously introduced by the Democratic chairman of the committee.

As reported, H. R. 627 had the support of both Democrats and Republicans in the House committee. It would provide for (1) the establishment of a commission in the executive branch of the Government to hold hearings and make inquiries on problems of discrimination; (2) the establishment of a Civil Rights Division under an Assistant Attorney General in the Department of Justice; (3) the protection of the right to vote; and (4) the strengthening of existing civil-rights statutes.

H. R. 627 will meet in a small but substantial and worthwhile degree the most immediate needs of the American people in terms of justice for and protection of millions of American citizens who have been and are still today treated as second-class citizens.

The present session has less than 90 days to go. In the light of past history, protracted hearings at this time or the reporting out of a bill which will later require conference between House and Senate, must be interpreted as delaying tactics designed to prevent action in this session. A sincere desire to enact legislation calls for prompt reporting out of a Senate measure identical with H. R. 627.

What is involved here would add no new civil rights but calls merely for provisions to protect rights established 75 years ago.

Is this going too fast? Both parties have endorsed these principles. Sincere nonpartisan effort can assure enough votes for passage in this session. Give the voters in 1956 a chance to judge by performance rather than words.

We urge your committee and both Houses of the Congress to put H. R. 627 and its Senate counterpart on President Eisenhower's desk before adjournment.

Thank You.

Senator HENNINGS. Thank you, Mr. Wilkins.

Senator Dirksen, have you any questions?

Senator DIRKSEN. No; I have no questions. I have just one observation. I am sure that the chairman was in the House when I was there. We were voting on antilynch bills and antipoll tax bills and sent them over a long time ago.

Senator HENNINGS. Twenty years ago.

Senator DIRKSEN. I think we have endeavored ——

Senator HENNINGS. More or less.

Senator DIRKSEN. By action in order to get something accomplished in this field. I just wanted to make that statement.

Senator HENNINGS. I am sure that is true of my learned friend of Illinois. Some of us have been doing that.

[. . . . .]

Statement of David H. Scull, Friends Committee on National Legislation

Senator HENNINGS. We will be very glad to have you proceed in your own manner. Do you have a prepared statement?

Mr. SCULL. I thought I would try to condense my written statement a little bit in order not to take up the time of this committee.

Senator HENNINGS. You are very considerate, sir. We do have some other duties this afternoon and evening. We will be very glad to hear from you, sir, in any manner that you are pleased to convey your thoughts.

Mr. SCULL. My name is David Scull. I am a businessman, from Annandale, Va., and am representing today the Friends Committee on National Legislation — not as an official spokesman for our Society, but trying to convey the idea that our religious belief has something to say on such vital questions of legislation as this.

I think on this legislation we are discussing today, the views we are presenting are widely shared by American Quakers, and indeed by religious-minded Americans generally.

We are supporting particularly the four bills, S. 3717, S. 3718, and S. 3604, and S. 3605, but I understand these bills embody some of the provisions previously included in the bills introduced by today's chairman, Mr. Hennings, and we are happy to have his support.

We do urge that this question be considered in the light of the highest morals and religious standards we know. This is pretty much in the tradition of our Society of Friends, although we know that even among our membership there are many, as in other churches, who are not always able to live out all of the beliefs that they profess.

Anyone approaching this task, whether in the Government or not, has to do so with a profound sense of humility, and with the recognition that these problems are not limited to any one area, or confined to relations between just two racial groups.

The South wrestles with its problems, but northern communities have their own difficulties, and there is no room for smugness or complacency or for pointing the finger of shame or blame at any area.

The southern legislator or leader of opinion whose conscience might lead him to differ with the white majority in his State has a special problem. He will often be tempted to compromise with his conscience lest, in the end, he lose influence to a more extreme leader. Yet, there is an irreducible minimum which he may not compromise, and I believe that, in the program endorsed by the administration and being discussed today, we have such a minimum program.

There are three points we would like to make, and I will try to keep this brief. There are three points in connection with the Commission, which is an idea we heartily endorse.

We would like to see, in addition to the three responsibilities given it in the bill, Mr. Chairman, a fourth responsibility, to study and to publicize ways in which communities are successfully increasing understanding, allaying tensions, and generally playing a constructive role.

Rather than giving it a merely defensive role, we feel that it should look on its duties, not as essentially punitive or coercive, but with the emphasis on persuasion education, providing a forum in which divergent views can be heard or discussed.

We would like to see the bill amended in that respect, or the committee's report cover that additional point.

I would like to point out especially the importance of the governmental policy, and even more of a Presidential appointment in this connection.

Now, ordinarily volunteer groups can be very successful in exploring new areas of social problems. But in much of the South today, even the prominent individual may face ostracism if he announces voluntarily that he is openminded on this question. But the same person, if he is offered an appointment to an official body, could often accept that, and not meet the same degree of opposition and criticism from his neighbors.

So that, it is not only the Commission itself which may be of value, but there is a provision for advisory committees in section 4 of 3605. We would like to have your committee's report show that you intend that provision to be, in fact, used, and advisory committees set up in order to give this status of official appointment to additional people, and bring more of them into this whole process.

On the point of the duration of the Commission, 2 years should be able to bring forth a valuable contribution. But if these constructive aspects are stressed, and leadership is shown, we feel that its continuation for a further period might very well prove to be in the national interest.

So that we would also like to see your committee's report take cognizance of the possibility of extending the life of the Commission, if at the end of 2 years it has proven to be useful, and mindful of the Attorney General's statement before your committee, that no agency now in the executive branch of the Government has the legal authority to exercise such powers as this Commission would possess in the study of matters relative to civil rights.

I think I need not go into detail to say that in regard to the voting provisions, or protection of voting rights, and so on, we endorse these other measures, 3717 and 3718, and 3604, to support the appointment or authorization of an additional Attorney General.

My previous experience leads me to believe that if the committee's report is perfectly explicit as to the purpose for which such an officer is authorized, that is pretty much binding on future executive officers in the Department of Justice, and that would, in fact, be used for the purpose you intend.

Just a closing word. We are fully aware that justice is not established nor laws enforced in a social vacuum. There are frequent predictions of dire results if the social pattern in the South of white dominance is too rapidly or too drastically changed as a result of Court decision or Federal law enforcement.

But where one group has had special advantages there are not going to be changes without some sacrifices being made. We hope that in the Senate and the House may be found the kind of wise leadership which realizes that that is necessary, but will see that it comes about through equity and with restraint, rather than another outburst of violence.

Some 200 years ago John Woolman, one of the greatest of American Quakers, said these words, in language which is a little old fashioned, but I think takes a meaning for us today:

My mind is often led to consider the purity of the Divine Being and the justice of his judgments; and herein my soul is covered with awfulness. I cannot omit to hint of some cases where people have not been treated with the purity of justice, and the event hath been lamentable. Many slaves on this continent are oppressed, and their cries have reached the ears of the Most High. Such are the purity and certainty of His judgments that He cannot be partial in our favor. In infinite love and goodness He hath opened our understanding from one time to another concerning our duty toward this people, and it is not a time for delay. Should we now be sensible of what He requires of us, and through a respect to the private interest of some persons, or through a regard to some friendships which do not stand on an immutable foundation, neglect to do our duty in firmness and constancy, still waiting for some extraordinary means to bring about their deliverance, God may by terrible things in righteousness answer us in this matter.

Senator HENNINGS. Mr. Scull, we thank you very much for your exceedingly fine statement and your contribution to the deliberations of this committee. We appreciate your coming.

Mr. SCULL. Thank you, sir.

[. . . . .]

MONDAY, JUNE 25, 1956
Washington, D.C.

THE COMMITTEE MET, pursuant to call, at 2:30 p. m., in room 424, Senate Office Building, Senator James O. Eastland (chairman) presiding.

Present: Senators Eastland (chairman), A. Willis Robertson, and Langer.

Also present Robert B. Young, professional staff member, and Richard F. Wambach, assistant to counsel.

The CHAIRMAN. The committee will come to order.

The first witness is the Honorable Joe T. Patterson, the attorney general of the State of Mississippi.

Mr. Patterson, we would like to have your views, sir, on the desirability and the constitutionality of these bills.

Statement of Joe T. Patterson, Attorney General of the State of Mississippi

Mr. PATTERSON. Thank you, Senator Eastland, and gentlemen of the committee. First, I would like to express my appreciation to the committee for affording me an opportunity to appear here in opposition to these pending bills.

I can fully appreciate how busy this committee is at this time at this session of the Congress, having been an employee of the Senate here a good many years ago myself and, for the sake of brevity, I shall address my remarks to the recent proposals submitted to the Congress by the United States Attorney General Brownell and the bills that have been introduced in support thereof, and what I propose to say with reference to the 4-point civil rights program, as it has been designated, of course, is equally applicable to all other bills of similar import.

Viewing the "4-point civil rights program" as proposed by the United States Attorney General, as a whole, and taking into consideration the guiding question that should control in the consideration of such far-reaching legislation — that is — whether such legislation is needed to accomplish the stated purpose of same? We can come to only one conclusion, and that is, that all 4 proposals are wholly unnecessary, in addition to the fact that all 4 proposals strike once again at the rights reserved unto the States by the 10th Amendment, and constitutes another broad step toward the centralization of power in the Federal Government to the exclusion of the rights of the State.

1. Let us view the first proposal, and S. 3605 — "To establish a bipartisan Commission on Civil Rights in the executive branch of the Government." The duties of the Commission as set forth in the bill are far beyond the capacity of 6 members to accomplish in 2 years, which is the life of the Commission according to the bill. In my humble judgment, the task assigned to this 6-member Commission by the bill could not be accomplished by 6 men, regardless of ability, in 8 or 10 years. Having served two terms in the legislature of my State, and having observed a similar trend in Congress, I learned long ago that the creation of a "temporary" commission or bureau by a State legislature, or the Congress, is in fact the birth of another permanent commission or bureau.

Every duty imposed upon the proposed Civil Rights Commission can now be accomplished under existing Federal or State laws.

Practically all of the duties imposed upon the proposed Commission are properly the prerogative of Congress and State Legislatures, and not of a commission in the executive branch of the Government.

Moreover, the creation of this Commission for the stated purposes would set up in the executive branch of the Government a source of harassment to the States in the administration of their laws, and a constant source of harassment to the executive branch of the Federal Government by those who are going to feel that this Commission is being provided for their sole benefit, to the exclusion of all others. At the very beginning, if the President does not appoint members of this Commission who have previously demonstrated complete sympathy and accord with the views and wishes of those well-organized groups that are responsible for this proposed legislation, he will immediately have the wrath of these groups brought down upon his head, and be accused of not being in sympathy with his own recommendation.

Regardless of party affiliation, regardless of the party in power, I think we can all agree that the creation of this Commission, for the purposes stated in the bill, will be the establishment in the executive branch of the Federal Government one of the greatest sources of political harassment that the Executive has ever had to contend with, and in my opinion it already has more than its just share of that to contend with.

The CHAIRMAN. What is the point in it? Our people are law abiding are they not?

Mr. PATTERSON. Definitely so, Senator.

The CHAIRMAN. And races get a square deal, do they not?

Mr. PATTERSON. This would just be a source of harassment to those States that the record shows are law abiding, which I shall attempt to point out briefly as I go along, with my statement.

The CHAIRMAN. Proceed.

Mr. PATTERSON. 2. The second proposal: "Creation of a new Civil Rights Division in the Justice Department, under an Assistant Attorney General, to facilitate enforcement of civil-rights statutes. The Attorney General said he anticipates a flow of litigation from the Supreme Court's ban on race segregation in public schools."

As I understand this proposal, it would create in the Department of Justice a "new Civil Rights Division" under an Assistant Attorney General appointed by the President, which would give to this Division the status of being one step from that of cabinet rank.

The proposals that follow the recommendation of the creation of
a new Civil Rights Division in the Justice Department clearly show
that it is the desire of the Attorney General to completely take over
the supervision and enforcement of all so-called civil rights legislation.

The CHAIRMAN. Does it not also show that he desires to move
in on the States?

Mr. PATTERSON. Yes, sir, definitely.

The CHAIRMAN. And the expression of State sovereignty?

Mr. PATTERSON. Under the recent decisions on the question of
supersession, I presume they would strike all of the State legislation on all such matters.

The creation of a Civil Rights Division in the Justice Department
under an Assistant Attorney General, and amending existing laws
to give to this assistant the power and authority as recommended,
would create an even greater source of harassment to the States and
their law-enforcement agencies than the creation of a Commission
on Civil Rights.

The creation of a new Civil Rights Division in the Justice Department, clothed with the authority that is requested, presupposes the
fact that the United States district courts throughout the country,
and especially the State courts, have wholly failed to take proper
cognizance of the civil rights of its citizens, regardless of race, and
have not and will not see to it that the constitutional rights of its
citizens are properly protected. After all, so-called civil rights cannot
rise any higher than those rights conferred upon a citizenship by the
Constitution of the United States and the constitutions of the respective States. The records of the United States district courts and
of the State courts do not warrant any such assumption.

3. The Attorney General proposes an "Amendment to existing law
to make it a crime for any person to use intimidation, threat, or
coercion to deprive anyone of his rights to vote for candidates for
Federal office. At present, Federal statutes aimed at preventing
deprivations of voting rights reach only State officials and not
private individuals."

That is the statement of the United States Attorney General.

In the first place, existing Federal and State statutes are fully
adequate to protect the citizen against "intimidation, threat or
coercion to deprive anyone of his right to vote for candidates" for
both Federal and State office.

Section 1985 of title 42, United States Code Annotated, affords full protection of the right of a citizen to vote for President, Vice President, and Members of Congress of the United States.

It is wholly unfair to the United States district courts and the United States district attorneys throughout the country to assume that they have ignored this statute and have wholly failed to enforce same. Moreover, every State in the Union has statutes making it a crime "for any person to use intimidation, threat, or coercion to deprive anyone of his right to vote for candidates" for any office, State or Federal.

The CHAIRMAN. Those statutes are enforced within the States?

Mr. PATTERSON. Yes, sir.

As far back as 1848 the State of Mississippi had statutes making it a crime to intimidate electors in seeking to exercise their rights to vote.

Section 2032 of the present Mississippi Code of 1942 provides:

Whoever shall procure, or endeavor to procure, the vote of any elector, or the influence of any person over other electors, at any election, for himself or any candidate, by means of violence, threats of violence, or threats of withdrawing custom, or dealing in business or trade, or of enforcing the payment of a debt, or of bringing a suit or criminal prosecution, or by any other threat or injury to be inflicted by him, or by his means, shall, upon conviction, be punished by imprisonment in the county jail not more than one year, or by fine not exceeding one thousand dollars, or by both.

Section 2106 of the present Mississippi Code of 1942 (Annotated) provides:

If any person shall, by illegal force, or threats of force, prevent, or endeavor to prevent, any elector from giving his vote, he shall, upon conviction, be punished by imprisonment in the penitentiary for a term not exceeding two years, or in the county jail not exceeding one year, or by fine not exceeding five hundred dollars, or both.

We submit that it is wholly unfair to the courts of Mississippi to assume that they will not enforce the above-quoted statutes. However, the request of the Attorney General that "he be authorized to bring injunction or other civil proceedings on behalf of the United States or the aggrieved person in any case covered by the broadened statute," and his further surprising request "for elimination of the requirement that all State administrative and judicial remedies must be exhausted before access can be had to the Federal Court," is to assume that State administrative and judicial processes have broken down and wholly failed to meet their responsibilities under the law.

If it is to be assumed that State courts have so completely failed in the field of civil rights, then it is reasonable to assume that they have at least partially failed in their responsibilities in all other matters, and if the proposed legislation creating a Civil Rights Commission in the executive branch of the Federal Government, and a Civil Rights Division in the Justice Department of the Federal Government, has become necessary on account of the failure of the State judges and other court officials to live up to their solemn oath of office, then it is reasonable to assume that they have failed all up and down the line in the discharge of their duties, and have, therefore, ceased to accomplish their mission; and in order to correct this, another commission should be created in the executive branch of the Federal Government and another division created in the Justice Department of the Federal Government, to investigate, supervise, and direct on behalf of the Federal Government, or the individual concerned, in all matters that might come under the jurisdiction of State courts.

4. The fourth proposal of the Attorney General to amend "existing statutes so as to give the Attorney General power to bring civil action against any conspiracy involving use of hoods or other disguises to deprive any citizen of equal treatment under law," so as to "allow the Attorney General to bring proceedings on the Government's behalf," is wholly unnecessary and places the Federal Government in the courts as the complaining party instead of the aggrieved person, who certainly should properly bring his own suits.

Why should all the power and prestige of the Federal Government be thrown behind just one particular type of litigation on behalf of an aggrieved person? Isn't it reasonable to assume that if an aggrieved person really has a just cause of action that he could stand on his own in Federal or State court, without the Federal Government taking over for him? I again repeat, if the Federal Government is to take over so completely in this particular field commonly called civil rights, then is it not reasonable to assume that the precedent has been set for the Federal Government to take over in any other field of law enforcement that it might deem expedient to do?

Such a course is bound to culminate in virtually the entire field of law enforcement being taken over by the Federal Government, and in reducing the State courts to mediocrity. Certainly, no justification for such a course can be found in the Constitution of the United

States. Certainly, no such course can be justified if the States are to continue to be recognized as sovereign States.

I think it is reasonable to assume that the "Four-point civil rights program" as recommended by the United States Attorney General, is aimed directly at one section of the United States; however, I think that it would be well to consider the effect that such broad and sweeping authority conferred upon the Department of Justice might have upon every State in the Union, because the authority and power conferred upon the Department of Justice by these proposals can be exercised and brought to bear upon the people of the States of New York and California as well as upon the people of Mississippi and Georgia.

The right kind of thinking people in every State, regardless of location, concede that members of so-called minority races are entitled to have their rights as guaranteed to them by the Federal and State constitutions properly protected; however, I have never found anyone from any State in this Union — and from $3\frac{1}{2}$ years in the Army, I had the opportunity to know and be with boys from every section — I never have found one yet that felt that the so-called minority groups had paramount rights to the exclusion of the majority.

Speaking for the State of Mississippi and its fine people, the record wholly fails to show where the people of Mississippi have ignored the civil rights of the Negro race, which up until only a few years ago constituted 50 percent of its population, and in some particular localities the Negro population exceeded the white population as high as 10 to 1.

A spirit of understanding and good will has existed between the white and colored races in the State of Mississippi for more than 100 years, and each race has prospered and gone forward side by side in an atmosphere of sympathy, understanding, and good will.

The charge of economic pressure being brought upon members of the Negro race by the people of Mississippi is unfounded and wholly refuted by the number of prosperous business and professional members of the Negro race in Mississippi. If an unbiased investigator wants to get at the truth of this charge of economic pressure, he has only to go to the banks, the mercantile establishments and other leading businessmen and make inquiry as to the credit rating of these reliable and well-to-do members of the Negro race.

An unbiased investigator has only to look at the farms and different business enterprises owned exclusively, and operated by, members of the Negro race, to arrive at the conclusion that a member of the Negro race can prosper in the State of Mississippi and be protected in his right to do so.

As heretofore stated, the request of the United States Attorney General "for elimination of the requirement that all State administrative and judicial remedies must be exhausted before access can be had to the Federal Court" presupposes the failure of the State courts to recognize, and properly protect, the constitutional rights of its citizens, regardless of race, color, or creed.

The unbiased mind has only to review the decisions of the supreme court of the State of Mississippi, beginning many years ago, long before the present agitation and crusade for so-called civil rights was commenced, to come to the conclusion that the supreme court of Mississippi was jealously and carefully guarding the constitutional rights of its citizens, regardless of race, color, or creed, long before the present crusaders came upon the scene claiming for themselves to be the redeemer and savior of constitutional and civil rights for certain groups.

I will not burden this committee with a lengthy and detailed review of the numerous cases decided by the supreme court of the State of Mississippi, wherein the constitutional rights of a member of the Negro race have been so forcefully upheld; however, I do call the committee's attention to the case of *Richardson* v. *State*, decided by the supreme court of Mississippi on May 8, 1944, and cited in 196 Mississippi page 560, 17 So. 2d 799.

The defendant was a Negro man who had been convicted and sentenced to death upon a charge of rape, alleged to have been committed upon a 20-year-old white woman.

It is interesting to observe extracts from the opinion of the supreme court of Mississippi in reversing and remanding this case. In passing upon the testimony in the case, the supreme court of Mississippi said:

The entire record of the testimony has been read by, or in the hearing of, every member of the court. Fifty years ago in *Monroe* v. *State* (71 Miss. 196, 13 So. 884), the rule, and the philosophy thereof, for the guidance of bench and bar in such cases was laid down, and that rule has never been departed from. It was reaffirmed in the recent case, *Upton* v. *State* (192 Miss. 339, 6 So. 2d 129). In these cases it was said that it is true that a conviction for rape may rest on the uncorroborated testimony of the person alleged to have been raped, but it should always be scrutinized with caution; and where there is much in the facts and circumstances in evidence to discredit her testimony, another jury should be permitted to pass thereon.

A critical and cautious scrutiny of the record of the testimony discloses that in not less than four material, and in fact decisive, particulars the testimony of the prosecutrix is so highly improbable as to be scarcely believable —

that is the supreme court of the State of Mississippi, passing on a case where a Negro was convicted and where the prosecutrix was a white girl, saying that her testimony was wholly unbelievable —

except, of course, to one who would simply prefer to believe it, and that when the four are considered together there arises such a doubt of the truth of what she has said on the stated crucial issue as to render the evidence hardly equivalent to a preponderance much less that which must carry conviction to an impartial and unbiased mind beyond all reasonable doubt. A majority of the court are of the opinion, in this respect, that without the so-called confession of appellant he would be entitled to a peremptory charge.

In the same case the supreme court of Mississippi, in reversing and remanding the conviction of its own accord, on the question of due process, in that the defendant had not been properly represented by counsel, stated:

It is desired by some members of the court that mention be made of the fact that there hovers in the background of this record the broad issue of due process. The record does not disclose whether the attorney who appeared for the defendant was employed or whether appointed by the court; but, however, that may have been, candor compels us to admit that he made only a token defense. We are entitled to take some knowledge of the members of the bar of the supreme court, of whom the attorney in this case is one, and we may assert with some confidence that he possesses both ability and energy. Why, then, did he make only a token defense, as to which see *Powell* v. *State of Alabama* (287 U. S. 45, 53 S. Ct. 55, 77 L. Ed. 158, 84 A. L. R. 527)? There must arise, therefore, more than a suspicion that there were such circumstances surrounding the trial, such a pervading atmosphere of prejudice engendered by a probable popular assumption of guilt with the resultant and revolting reaction of outrage, that it was deemed wiser by the attorney to make no more than the defense he did with a hope of life sentence, and that later, time would come to the relief of the helpless defendant. Such a situation involves due process, the protection of which, above the interest of the accused in his own life or the prosecutrix in her own vindication, is the supreme duty and responsibility of the court, and both in the trial court and here.

That is the record of what was laid down by the Mississippi supreme court in these cases that so often attract so much attention.

I submit that no court throughout the United States, Federal or State, could more clearly and forcefully express its belief in due process, and its determination to see that a member of the Negro race was accorded the full benefit of due process, than is set forth above.

I would like to call this committee's attention to the fact that in the celebrated case of *Willie McGee* v. *State of Mississippi,* a case that was seized upon by certain radical groups outside the State of Mississippi and made a cause celebre throughout the country. The seeds of hatred and discord were sown, which whipped the crowds to fever pitch, and then at the psychological moment, the hat was passed around for funds to save Willie McGee from an alleged legal lynching. All of this took place after Mr. Emanuel Block, of New York City, took charge of the defense, and who, incidentally, was later chief counsel for the Rosenbergs, wherein the same tactics were pursued as in the Willie McGee case. But in spite of all of the adverse criticism heaped upon the courts and other officials of the State of Mississippi in the Willie McGee case, the fact still remains that the conviction of Willie McGee was reversed and remanded twice by the supreme court of the State of Mississippi, and not by the United States Supreme Court, and that his third conviction and sentence to death was affirmed by the supreme court of the State of Mississippi and certiorari denied by the Supreme Court of the United States.

I would call the committee's attention to the recent case of *Bell* v. *State* decided by the supreme court of Mississippi on November 14, 1949, and reported in 207 Miss. 518, 42 So. 2d 728.

The defendant, Bell, was a young Negro boy around 20 years of age, who was charged with the killing of a white plantation manager in Coahoma County, Miss. Upon arraignment, Bell advised the court that he was without counsel and had no money to employ same. The court immediately appointed two of the ablest members of the local bar to defend Bell. Bell was found guilty and sentenced to death, and his appointed counsel appealed his conviction and sentence to the supreme court of the State of Mississippi, where they appeared and argued same.

And, incidentally, I handled the case as assistant attorney general in charge of the criminal docket.

The supreme court of Mississippi in its opinion setting forth the holdings of the Supreme Court in construing the law of self-defense for many years, held that Bell was

not guilty of any crime but acted in his reasonably necessary self-defense.

And further held:

In our judgment, appellant was entitled to have had the directed verdict for which he asked; and to acquittal, on the ground of self-defense, as convincingly demonstrated in appellant's fine brief.

It further stated:

We therefore reverse the judgment of the lower court, and direct the discharge of appellant from custody.

In the case of *Cockrell* v. *State* (168, So. 617, 175 Miss. 613), decided by the supreme court of Mississippi on June 8, 1936, a Negro was convicted of murder. The proof showed that he had killed a white boy when found in adultery with his wife, and had burned the body of the deceased. The supreme court reversed and remanded the defendant's conviction of murder and held the defendant to be guilty only of manslaughter, if anything.

In the case of *Coleman* v. *State*, decided by the supreme court on October 12, 1953, the defendant Coleman, a Negro, was convicted of murder for the killing of the town marshal of the town of Doddsville, in Sunflower County, Miss., Senator Eastland's home town. The proof showed that the town marshal had ordered defendant to leave town during the early hours of the night, and that later, upon discovering the defendant in town, proceeded to bump and shove the defendant, informing him that he had told him to leave town. The defendant turned upon the town marshal, stabbing him one time with a knife, which resulted in his death. The supreme court, in reversing and remanding the defendant's conviction of murder, held that the defendant could not be guilty of more than manslaughter, if anything.

At the recent term of the supreme court of Mississippi, on March 9, 1956, the court had before it the case of *Willie Mabry & Oscar Mabry* v. *State* (86 So. 2d 23). The two defendants, brothers, were young Negroes, jointly indicted, tried and convicted of an assault and battery and intent to kill and murder a white man with two alleged deadly weapons, one being an iron wrench in the hands of Willie Mabry and the other being an iron pipe in the hands of Oscar Mabry. Each defendant was sentenced to serve a term of 5 years in the State penitentiary. The court, in concluding its opinion, said:

The appellants contend that under the proof they should not have been convicted of assault and battery with intent to kill and murder, but at most they were guilty only of a simple assault and battery, and we think this contention is well-taken. [. . .]

citing many previous opinions of the supreme court of the State of Mississippi in support thereof. The court reversed the conviction and sentence and remanded the cause for proper sentence for a conviction of simple assault and battery, which is a misdemeanor, and carries with it only a fine and a probable short jail sentence.

The supreme court of Mississippi has, throughout the years, jealously guarded against deprivation of the constitutional rights of one charged with crime, regardless of race or color, by refusing to permit any conviction to stand wherein the records show that an appeal had been made to racial prejudice.

In the case of *Harris* v. *State* (50 So. 626), decided by the supreme court of the State of Mississippi in 1909, the supreme court said:

> The language to the effect that he murdered a white man in the house out there he did not deny is direct comment upon the failure of the defendant to testify. It is impossible for us to see any other construction to be given this language, and under repeated decisions of this court this is a fatal error. But, aside from this, it certainly needs no argument to show that these remarks of the district attorney, the representative of the State, in his closing argument to the jury, were a direct appeal to race prejudice, and are of such a highly inflammatory character, and so manifestly transcend any legitimate bounds of argument, as to necessitate reversal of themselves, if there had been no other error. Every defendant at the bar of his country, white or black, must be accorded a fair trial according to the law of the land, and that law knows no color.

I could cite some 13 or 20 more other such cases, decided by the supreme court of Mississippi, wherein the court has condemned an appeal to racial prejudice in equally as forceful language as above quoted, but I will not do that here.

I wish to say again to this committee that if the State and Federal courts are to be permitted to continue to function in their respective fields as intended by the Constitution of the United States that such legislation as proposed by the United States Attorney General in the bills here under consideration should not be enacted into law.

We already have a situation in the courts with reference to habeas corpus proceedings wherein defendants who have been convicted in State courts and certiorari denied by the United States Supreme

Court, have taken refuge in the Federal courts under petitions for habeas corpus, and hereby delayed their conviction and sentence indefinitely; in many instances, over a long period of years. The judges throughout the country have taken cognizance of this deplorable situation and the Habeas Corpus Committee of the Conference of the Chief Justices of the United States, in its report to the 84th Congress recommending legislation that would put a stop to such unwarranted procedure and abuse of the writ of habeas corpus in the Federal courts, stated that their recommendation:

Meets virtually every situation that can be reasonably expected to arise under our system of dual sovereignty; and will insure to State courts — whose judges are just as sincerely desirous of protecting an accused against the invasion of constitutional rights as are the judges in the Federal system — that no longer will a criminal be able, upon a trumped-up or groundless claim, or one supported by new evidence not presented to the State court, to delay, unreasonably the execution of his sentence by invoking the jurisdiction of an inferior Federal court.

The proposed legislation under consideration here would open the gate to those who would go around and foment strife and confusion among the races for a flood of litigation in the Federal courts on behalf of the Federal Government, whereas, if the Federal statutes are permitted to remain as they are now, such will not be the case.

Certainly, it is not reasonable and fair to the States to assume that the judges of the State courts are not

just as sincerely desirous of protecting an accused against the invasion of constitutional rights as are the judges in the Federal system.

The principle of States rights goes further and deeper than just civil rights:

The United States Government can never be any stronger than the 48 States that comprise it. The stronger and more independent the individual State, the stronger and more forceful the Federal Government.

It was Thomas Jefferson who stated:

It is not by the consolidation or concentration of powers, that good government is effected. Were not this great country already divided into States, that division must be made, that each might do for itself what concerns itself directly, and what it can so much better do than a distant authority.

In later years, President Calvin Coolidge said:

It is too much to assume that because an abuse exists it is the business of the National Government to provide a remedy. The presumption should be that it is the business of local and State governments. Such national action results in encroaching upon the salutary independence of the States and by undertaking to supersede their natural authority fills the land with bureaus and departments which are undertaking to do what it is impossible for them to accomplish, and brings our whole system of government into disrespect and disfavor.

The Nation is inclined to disregard altogether too much both the functions and the duties of the State. They are much more than subdivisions of the Federal Government. They are also endowed with sovereignty in their own right.

I believe that if these words of wisdom uttered by President Calvin Coolidge will be applied to the pending legislation under discussion that all bills of this nature will be very promptly defeated in this committee.

Very recently another prominent public figure who now occupies an exalted position in the Federal judiciary, in speaking of the rights of the State, said:

We operate this State on the premise that in government every problem capable of solution on the local level ought to be solved on that level. [. . .] Similarly, everything that can be solved by the State should be solved on that level. [. . .] We want decentralization of authority because the strength of the Republic depends largely on the virility of the State and local governments.

That sound philosophy of the right of the State to solve its own problems; that sound philosophy advocating decentralization of authority on the ground that strength of the Republic depends largely upon the virility of the State and local governments, was advanced by Gov. Earl Warren, of California, then Republican candidate for Vice President of the United States.

I submit that if this sound philosophy of Government advocated by the then Governor of California, and then candidate for Vice President of the United States, who now is Chief Justice of the United States Supreme Court, is applied to the bills here under discussion, and all others of similar import, that such bills will never get beyond this committee.

The enactment of the "four-point civil rights program" under consideration here, and all other similar legislation can serve no good purpose for the future welfare of this Nation and especially of the Southern States.

The same well organized radical groups that have demanded and brought about the introduction of this proposed legislation will be just as militant in their demands that they be permitted to select or approve the appointment of the membership of the proposed bipartisan Commission and of the new Assistant Attorney General who will supervise the enforcement of the proposed laws. They will be just as militant in their demands that the Commission and the newly created division of the Department of Justice permit them to formulate the policy and direct the course they will pursue in administering the law. This can only result in a widening of the breach between amicable Federal and State relations between the Federal Government and the States against whom this legislation is directed. The Federal Government can be no stronger than the States that support it. The history of the Southland shows without contradiction that it has contributed its part toward the progress and development of this great Nation. The young manhood of the South has always been among the first to answer the call to arms whenever the security of this Nation has been threatened. The records of World War I and II will show that the Southern States were among the first to oversupply their quota of men, and the military records of the soldiers from the Southland clearly shows that the people of the South are a sincere and patriotic group of people. Sincere and patriotic soldiers are not born to, and raised by, parents who are not equally as sincere and patriotic. The Federal Government needs the cooperation and support of the Southern States, and certainly the Southern States need the cooperation and support of the Federal Government; neither can go its way alone.

I believe that the Director of the Federal Bureau of Investigation of the Department of Justice, and its many investigating officers, will tell you that one of the greatest contributing factors to their outstanding success has been the cooperation and services rendered them by State, county and local law-enforcement officers. This is as it should be. However I state to this committee, not by way of threat, but as a fact, that the Department of Justice cannot reasonably expect the cooperation and assistance of State, county and local law-enforcement officers when it goes into those States to administer laws designed to harass and intimidate the people of that State for the gratification of well-organized radical groups beyond the borders of that State who are really not interested in peaceful and harmonious relations between the people of different races of that State, but who in fact prefer to stir up hatred, strife, and discord between the races of the States toward whom the bills under consideration, and all others of like import, are directed.

Thank you, Senator Eastland, so much.

The CHAIRMAN. Thank you, Judge Patterson. You have made a very able and a very fine statement, and I know that it is going to be very influential with the committee.

You have put your finger exactly on what the problem is here. In my judgment, the Attorney General's proposals are political and an attempt to divide the people of this country at a very crucial time, and I should think that he could better take up his time in helping correct the pro-Communist decisions of our present Supreme Court.

As chairman of this committee, and as chairman of the Internal Security Subcommittee, I have never gotten adequate cooperation from them in correcting these far-reaching pro-Communist decisions that would destroy the American system of Government.

I want to thank you, sir, for a very able and very fine statement. Senator Langer, any questions?

Senator LANGER. Mr. Chairman, I am glad that this gentleman is here, because I have received a great many letters about one case which, apparently, has aroused a lot of interest in a great many of the States. I do not know the name of the boy but the Chicago boy that was killed in Mississippi. He was 13 or 14 years of age. Are you familiar with that case?

Mr. YOUNG. The Till Case.

Mr. PATTERSON. Yes, sir.

Senator LANGER. Will you just tell us about it?

Mr. PATTERSON. Under the procedure in Mississippi, Senator Langer, the attorney general of the State does not handle prosecutions at the local level. That is handled by the county prosecuting attorneys and the district attorneys.

The Till case, as it has been referred to, was prosecuted by a most able district attorney, an able county prosecuting attorney, and the attorney general of Mississippi did that which he does not usually do, he employed special counsel to go down and assist the district attorney in the prosecution.

The accused killers of Till were indicted by a grand jury and were tried in the courts, and a very forceful and able prosecution of the case was made.

The jury did acquit them — of course, that could happen in any State of the Union and does happen just as frequently as it does

Civil Rights Proposals 263

in the State of Mississippi — in fact, more often in some States than in the State of Mississippi.

I might say this. There was lacking circumstantial evidence. However, the judge permitted it to go to the jury, but it is nothing unusual for any case wherein the evidence is based entirely on circumstantial evidence, it is certainly not unusual for a jury to acquit the defendant; but I think the State of Mississippi showed its good faith when a grand jury promptly indicted the two parties accused, when the district attorney and county attorney, and, in addition to that, the attorney general employed special counsel to go in there and vigorously prosecute those men ——

Senator LANGER. You were not attorney general at that time?

Mr. PATTERSON. I was assistant attorney general at that time; yes, sir.

The CHAIRMAN. Isn't it true that the hostile papers who were there very heartily stated that it was a fair trial?

Mr. PATTERSON. Those who were there, who went down — and, of course, I don't think there is a State in the Union that would have a murder committed therein and have a bunch of outsiders say, "We will go down into that State and see that you try and convict those men"; I don't think any State in the Union would tolerate such an attitude from outside sources.

However, they came down and reviewed the trial and announced at first that it was a very fair and impartial trial and they were satisfied.

But, of course, when they went back home, they wanted to continue and make it a cause celebre, and a whipping post throughout the country, why, then they changed their minds and had other things to say about it.

I will say now that it was a very unfortunate occurrence, but one that could happen in any State of the Union, and does happen.

The CHAIRMAN. Mr. Young, do you have any questions?

Mr. YOUNG. Yes, sir.

[. . . . .]

Mr. YOUNG. I would like to direct your attention to the subject matter that Senator Langer brought up, this famous Till case.

Now, there has been a great deal of publicity concerning that, has there not?

Mr. PATTERSON. Yes, definitely there has.

Mr. YOUNG. And it has gotten its greatest national publicity through an original article in Look magazine — have you read that article?

Mr. PATTERSON. I did, sir.

Mr. YOUNG. That was an article with pictures, was it not?

Mr. PATTERSON. Yes, sir.

Mr. YOUNG. That was an article with suggestions, was it not?

Mr. PATTERSON. Yes, sir.

Mr. YOUNG. It was a racial article, was it not?

Mr. PATTERSON. Definitely so.

Mr. YOUNG. It was an antisouthern article, was it not?

Mr. PATTERSON. Definitely.

Mr. YOUNG. Was it a factual article?

Mr. PATTERSON. I don't think it was.

Mr. YOUNG. Well, you know the case. Would it stand up to the facts in that case in Mississippi?

Mr. PATTERSON. I did not participate in the trial of the case. I have never read the record of the trial of the case, so, therefore, I have my information from those who had attended the trial and who participated in the trial, that it was not factual; but, for myself, I did not participate.

Mr. YOUNG. Would you say that Look magazine is known as a southern or a northern magazine?

Mr. PATTERSON. Well, I think that it is definitely anti-South.

Mr. YOUNG. You know it is, don't you?

Mr. PATTERSON. Yes.

Mr. YOUNG. It is antisouthern — no question about it?

Mr. PATTERSON. Yes.

Mr. YOUNG. And the article was picked up and reprinted by the Reader's Digest magazine.

Did you happen to read the reprint in Reader's Digest?

Mr. PATTERSON. No, sir; I did not read the reprint.

Mr. YOUNG. Do you know the Reader's Digest magazine?

Mr. PATTERSON. Yes, sir.

Mr. YOUNG. Is it a magazine of general circulation?

Mr. PATTERSON. Yes, sir.

Mr. YOUNG. Is it a magazine that reputes itself to be without prejudice?

Mr. PATTERSON. Oh, yes, sir.

Mr. YOUNG. Is it a magazine that reputes itself to transcribe facts and to take prejudice out of stories and have little homey items and be pleasant reading for the women and children of America?

Mr. PATTERSON. Yes, sir.

Mr. YOUNG. Is it a magazine that prides itself on checking the authenticity of its sources?

Mr. PATTERSON. I had always understood that.

Mr. YOUNG. Does it not advertise that?

Mr. PATTERSON. Yes, sir, and that is why I had accepted it as such, and I had subscribed to it on that basis. However, my subscription was discontinued sometime ago.

Mr. YOUNG. Have you heard the rumor, a very interesting one, that they will not hire a Jewish writer? Have you ever heard that?

Mr. PATTERSON. No, sir.

Mr. YOUNG. But it will reprint many articles by minority groups; you have heard that?

Mr. PATTERSON. Yes, sir.

Mr. YOUNG. It is published where, the Reader's Digest?

Mr. PATTERSON. In New York, is it not?

Mr. YOUNG. Yes, in New York.

Do you happen to know the name of the town in New York?

Mr. PATTERSON. No, sir. Rochester, isn't it?

Mr. YOUNG. No, sir; it is not quite that far north. It is a little town up near the Connecticut border.

Do you know who wrote the articles for Look magazine and Reader's Digest on the Till case?

Mr. PATTERSON. I do not.

Mr. YOUNG. You do not know the names of the writers?

Mr. PATTERSON. I have a copy of the article in my desk, in my office, right now.

Mr. YOUNG. Have you ever heard of a free lance writer by the name of William Bradford Huie?

Mr. PATTERSON. No, sir.

Mr. YOUNG. Would it be enlightening to you if I said that William Bradford Huie wrote the Look magazine article?

Mr. PATTERSON. Yes; it would. I paid no attention to the writer's name. I read the article a couple of times and stuck it in my desk, and it has been there since.

Mr. YOUNG. Well, it would be news to you that Mr. Huie was not a reputable free lance author, it would throw some light on the Till case, wouldn't it?

Mr. PATTERSON. Well, I judge from reading about the Till case, he came to Mississippi, if he came, for a purpose, and he seemed to have accomplished his purpose.

Mr. YOUNG. What was that purpose?

Mr. PATTERSON. To write an article which would fan the flame of fury and hatred between people.

Mr. YOUNG. Well, did he pay any attention to facts?

Mr. PATTERSON. From what I learned of the Till case, no, sir.

Mr. YOUNG. Have you ever heard of a book known as The Revolt of Mamie Stover?

Mr. PATTERSON. No, sir.

Mr. YOUNG. Would it surprise you to know that a man by the name of William Bradford Huie wrote that book?

Mr. PATTERSON. I know nothing about that.

Mr. YOUNG. Do you know what the plot of the book was?

Mr. PATTERSON. No, sir.

Mr. YOUNG. Well, Mr. Huie wrote that book.

Would it surprise you to know that Mr. William Bradford Huie has written for the Saturday Evening Post athletic articles dealing with professionalism in college athletics? Would that be news to you?

Mr. PATTERSON. Yes, sir.

Mr. YOUNG. Have you ever seen an article in the Saturday Evening Post apologizing for a previous article which they published, by Mr. Huie, on athletics in the University of Alabama?

Mr. PATTERSON. No, sir.

Mr. YOUNG. In which they categorically stated Mr. Huie had not paid attention to any facts, that he was not an assistant coach in the University of Alabama while he tattletaled on their little activities there, and made a special apology; would that surprise you?

Mr. PATTERSON. Yes, sir; it would. As a matter of fact, I don't read the Post.

Mr. YOUNG. Are you acquainted with the fact that Mr. Huie has a reputation as being a nonfactual writer, a sensational writer, a writer who delves in pornographic type of materials such as this Mamie Stover book shows? Are you acquainted with that?

Mr. PATTERSON. No, sir.

Mr. YOUNG. Are you acquainted with the fact that the Reader's Digest has not ever followed up with an article of Mr. Huie's since the reprint of the Till case?

Mr. PATTERSON. No, sir.

Mr. YOUNG. Do you think that the Reader's Digest would reprint another article by Mr. Huie, from what you have heard me discussing here?

Mr. PATTERSON. I am sure they would not, if they intend to live up to that which they hold out to the public, that they are.

Mr. YOUNG. Do you think it would be interesting if this committee had Mr. Huie here to testify before it, under oath, as to where he secured the facts for the Till case in Mississippi, which he presents as an eyewitness, does he not?

Mr. PATTERSON. Yes, sir.

Mr. YOUNG. It is all in the ego, it is in the first tense, isn't it, "I was there," and "I saw it" and "I heard it" and "I did everything." Don't you think it would be a grand thing if he came and showed us where the "I" was?

Mr. PATTERSON. I do. I think that we would go further than that. I think that if he would go down there and show those people those facts that he purported to see in that case, they would appreciate it very much, because he brought out facts that nobody seemed to know but him.

Mr. YOUNG. It was "I" all the way through?

Mr. PATTERSON. Yes, sir.

Mr. YOUNG. "I was there." And he led you to believe in reciting that, that there was something odd, and there was a third person there besides the two men, and that it was covered up, didn't he? He writes with a great deal of realism.

Mr. PATTERSON. He just portrayed it as a whitewash by the courts and everybody else.

Mr. YOUNG. All right. That is all.

Mr. PATTERSON. I would like to say this in that connection, Mr. Young, as to this unfortunate case. The embittered things that have been directed toward the State of Mississippi because of the Till case — which, as I said before, is certainly unfortunate, but could happen in any State in the Union ——

Mr. YOUNG. Let me ask you another question on the Till case. The Till case failed, did it not, on the identification of the defendants?

Mr. PATTERSON. That is right, sir.

Mr. YOUNG. And there, like any case, we have to have an identification, do we not?

Mr. PATTERSON. The supreme court of the State of Mississippi, as well as the supreme court of every other State of the

Union, has held that for conviction on circumstantial evidence, that that circumstantial evidence has got to be positive to the point of and to the exclusion of every other reasonable doubt, and that is the rule, and that is not only the rule in Mississippi, but the rule under the entire American jurisprudence. It is an ironclad ruling that people cannot be convicted of a crime on circumstantial evidence unless it is so strong that it excludes, as the courts say, every other reasonable hypothesis.

Mr. YOUNG. Well, would it surprise you to know that Look magazine sells 10 issues in the North to 1 in the South?

Mr. PATTERSON. No.

Mr. YOUNG. Would it surprise you to know that the Reader's Digest sells 8 issues in the North to 1 in the South?

Mr. PATTERSON. No, sir.

Mr. YOUNG. Would it surprise you to think that the editor of this magazine would play up to the northern approach more than to the South, knowing the respective percentages of issues?

Mr. PATTERSON. They would not at one time, I understand, that they were more concerned with news than playing one group against another.

Now, Mr. Chairman, may I make one statement?

The CHAIRMAN. Yes.

Mr. PATTERSON. About this adverse publicity that came my way with reference to the Till case and the remarks that so many men in prominent life have seen fit to make about it in places like the State of Illinois and other places, and that is this: that I think that it is just as fair or that it would be just as fair for Senator Eastland or myself or anyone else who has been honored with high office at the hands of the people of Mississippi, to come along and say that all of the good people of the city of Chicago and the State of Illinois condone the ruthless murders that take place there at the hands of mobs every year, mobs who go out and deprive people of their civil rights, just as much so as people are deprived of their civil rights anywhere else when they are put on mob rule, it would be just as reasonable for Senator Eastland or I to say that it is indicative of the great State of Illinois and the people's thinking, as it is for them to say that the Till case is typical of the people of Mississippi.

I read an article only a short time ago where a good citizen, I believe, of Cicero, Ill., was beaten by baseball bats solely because he opposed the mob rule in his city.

When a grand jury of Mississippi indicted the perpetrators of the Till crime or the alleged perpetrators, and when a district attorney and a special assistant attorney general went into the courts and prosecuted him for having committed the crime, that is far more than has been done to those mobsters that beat up that good citizen in Cicero, Ill.

The CHAIRMAN. You mean gangsters when you say "mobsters"?

Mr. PATTERSON. Yes, sir; mobsters, gangsters, whichever one you want to call them.

So I say this thing can cut two ways. People have civil rights all over the country, as well as Mississippi. But I think the record of the courts of Mississippi will show that perhaps we go a little further in protecting people in their civil rights than they do in some of those localities where so much criticism is directed at us.

Even right up here in New York only a few weeks ago, some gangsters go out there and throw acid in the eyes of that fine newspaper reporter, Mr. Riesel. No one has been indicted or even arrested for that. But certainly it would be unfair for me to sit here and say that is typical of the people of New York, because I know it is not.

But if I did say it was typical of the people of New York, I would be just as truthful as those who say these great unfortunate occurrences down our way are typical of all the people of Mississippi.

[. . . . .]

FRIDAY, JULY 6, 1956
Washington, D.C.

THE COMMITTEE MET, pursuant to adjournment, at 2:40 p. m., in room 424, Senate Office Building, Senator John L. McClellan, presiding.

Present: Senators McClellan and Dirksen.

Also present: Robert B. Young, professional staff member, and Richard F. Wambach, assistant to counsel.

Senator MCCLELLAN. The committee will come to order. The witness is Mr. Taylor. Come around, please, sir.

All right, Mr. Taylor, you may proceed. I believe you have a prepared statement, have you?

Mr. TAYLOR. Yes, sir.

Senator MCCLELLAN. Do you wish to read it?

Mr. TAYLOR. Yes, sir.

Senator MCCLELLAN. All right, sir, you may proceed.

Statement of Tyre Taylor, General Counsel, Southern States Industrial Council, Nashville, Tenn.

Mr. TAYLOR. I appear on behalf of the Southern States Industrial Council, the headquarters of which are in the Stahlman Building in Nashville, Tenn. My own address is 917 15th Street here in Washington.

The council was established in 1933. Its membership is comprised of industrial and business concerns in the 16 southern states including Maryland, West Virginia, Missouri, and Oklahoma. This membership represents all lines of manufacturing and processing, mining, transportation, and related industries and accounts for very substantial employment throughout the region.

On January 6, 1956, in his State of the Union message, President Eisenhower said:

> It is disturbing that in some localities allegations persist that Negro citizens are being deprived of their right to vote and are likewise being subjected to unwarranted economic pressures. I recommend that the substance of these charges be thoroughly examined by a bipartisan commission created by Congress.

That was the extent of the President's recommendation.

On April 9, 1956, the Attorney General wrote the President of the Senate and the Speaker of the House submitting four proposals in the field of civil rights. In addition to the study commission already recommended by the President, these included:

1. A proposal to create a Civil Rights Division in the Department of Justice;
2. A proposal to give additional Federal protection to the right to vote and to provide civil remedies in the Department of Justice for its enforcement; and
3. The addition of civil remedies in the Department of Justice.

As I understand it, this is the program now before you and that is the administration program, and to it I shall address my remarks.

Of course the Executive already has the power to appoint a civil rights commission. President Truman did in fact appoint such a commission. The reason why the administration wants a commission created by Congress was explained by Mr. Brownell in his appearance before this committee on May 16, 1956. He said:

For a study such as that proposed by the President, the authority to hold public hearings, to subpena witnesses, to take testimony under oath, and to request necessary data from executive departments and agencies is obviously essential. No agency in the executive branch of the Government has the legal authority to exercise such powers in a study of matters relating to civil rights.

So, what you are asked to create is a Federal commission with full subpena powers which would investigate not only the matters referred to by the President in his State of the Union message, but in the words of Mr. Brownell to this committee:

It will study and collect information concerning economic, social, and legal developments constituting a denial of equal protection of the laws. It will appraise the laws and policies of the Federal Government with respect to equal protection of the laws under the Federal Constitution.

That, gentlemen, would seem to be about as broad a delegation of authority as even the NAACP could want. Under it, the Commission could require persons to appear before it and produce records in Washington or any other place the Commission might choose to hold hearings.

If past experience is to serve as a guide, most of the voluntary witnesses would be representatives of the NAACP, the American Civil Liberties Union, Americans for Democratic Action, and similar left-wing organizations. And as a minority of the House Judiciary Committee has pointed out — it is a well-known fact that more unreasonable complaints are made in the field of civil rights than in any other field. A study by Tom Clark shows that in 1940, 8,000 civil rights complaints were received, with prosecutions recommended in 12 cases, including Hatch Act violations. In 1942, 8,612 complaints were received, with 76 prosecutions. In 1944, 20,000 complaints were received and 64 prosecutions undertaken, but it is not known how many were convicted.

There is no indication as to what this Commission will cost the taxpayers. It is to be provided with a paid staff and the Commissioners themselves under most of the bills are to be paid $50 a day.

So much for the proposed Commission. It would appear to be merely another Federal agency designed primarily for harassment and propaganda purposes. And it goes without saying that its primary interest and activities would be directed at the South.

The provision for an additional Assistant Attorney General and the creation of a Civil Rights Division in the Department of Justice is a further invasion of a field which has been traditionally reserved to the States.

The approach here is the usual one by which bureaucracy expands and proliferates.

First, a Civil Rights Section of the Criminal Division is to be expanded into a Civil Rights Division. The Attorney General in his statement to his committee said this was necessary because the Justice Department had been obliged to engage in activity in the civil rights field which is noncriminal in character. In support of this proposition, he cited the case of where the Department intervened

to prevent by injunction unlawful interference with the efforts of the school board at Hoxie, Ark., to eliminate racial discrimination in the school in conformity with the Supreme Court's decision.

Of course, if — as is proposed in other parts of the Attorney General's recommendations — the United States Government is to become the legal guardian of all the groups covered by this legislation and is to invade the states and localities and become the enforcer of all the Supreme Court decisions and decrees of recent years relating to integration, education, primary elections, and so on, then not only is an additional Assistant Attorney General necessary, but he will require the help of a veritable army of lawyers, investigators, hearing examiners, and clerical staff members.

Mr. Maslow, general counsel of the American Jewish Congress, said last year in the hearing before the House Judiciary Committee that this division should have 50 lawyers in it. In view of the enormous scope of the duties to be assigned to it, this would seem to be a conservative estimate.

We hear — and you have heard — a great deal about the overworked Federal judiciary, the backlog of cases, sometimes extending back for 3 years, and the need for additional judges. All I can say is that if you provide that the Attorney General can, without exhausting State judicial and administrative remedies and with or without the consent of the complainant, go into the Federal courts on behalf of the private parties in interest, then no one can estimate how many additional lawyers and judges will be required at the taxpayers' expense.

The Attorney General's third recommendation is that section 1971 of title 42, United States Code, be amended by:

First, the addition of a section which will prevent anyone, whether acting under color of law or not, from threatening, intimidating, or coercing an individual in his right to vote in any election, general, special, or primary, concerning candidates for Federal office.

Second, authorization to the Attorney General to bring civil proceedings on behalf of the United States or any aggrieved person for preventive or other civil relief in any case covered by the statute.

Third, express provision that all State administrative and judicial remedies need not be first exhausted before resort to the Federal courts.

The purpose of these recommendations is crystal clear. It is to permit the Federal Government to enter into a field which heretofore has been reserved to private persons and to do this without complying with the usual requirement that State administrative and judicial remedies be exhausted before resort to the Federal courts.

How would this operate in practice? Let's take the Lucy case. In that instance, the complainant sought to enter the University of Alabama under a court order obtained for her by the NAACP. All the expenses of this proceeding were borne by the State of Alabama and the NAACP. However, if the Attorney General's proposal had been law, we can imagine then what would have happened.

The NAACP would have been camping on the doorstep of the Department of Justice seeking direct intervention — at the expense of the taxpayers — just as was done on the Hoxie, Ark., school case.

This would relieve the NAACP of a large part of its present expense and release funds for fomenting other cases in which the United States would be called upon to intervene.

At the same time, the cost to the States for legal services and litigation would be greatly increased. In practice, this added cost would, of course, fall mainly on the States of the South at which this legislation is aimed.

However, taxpayers everywhere should be interested in this effort — in effect — to subsidize the NAACP by making the Department of Justice its enforcement arm.

The Attorney General's final recommendation is that he be authorized to institute a civil action for redress or preventive relief whenever any persons have engaged or are about to engage in any acts or practices which would give rise to a cause of action under the present provisions of the law. He says that such an amendment would provide a procedure for the enforcement of civil rights which would be far simpler, more flexible, more reasonable, and more effective than the criminal sanctions which are the only remedy now available.

Granted that the right to vote is one of the most important rights of any American and that all the Attorney General says about the virtues and advantages of a civil action is true, the question nevertheless remains as to the propriety of the Federal Government entering this field at all.

Up to now the right to vote has been controlled by the States. If this historic principle is to be abandoned and additional broad powers to regulate elections are to be vested in the Federal Government, surely this should be accomplished by a constitutional amendment as the President recognized in his recommendation that 18-year-olds be given the vote.

As a minority of the House committee observed:

[. . .] Assuming, for the sake of argument, that the Supreme Court would overturn recognized constitutional doctrine and uphold (such an) expansion of Federal power, this is no reason for Congress in the first instance to fly in the face of the traditional and historical American policy of leaving the control of elections to the States and to the people.

In conclusion, may I raise a question that troubles me? Why all this unfriendly Federal preoccupation with the South? Or to put it another way, why is it that some northerners — not all or even the majority, but some — seem to hate the South and to be determined to destroy its civilization and way of life?

I don't think this hostility is a hangover from the Civil War. After all, that war is almost a full century behind us. Furthermore, the North won the Civil War and it is not in American character to hold a grudge against the losers — as witness our generous and continuing aid programs for our late enemies, the Japs and the Germans.

Nor do I think this hostility can be attributed to the South's great industrial advances of recent years and the fact that, in many fields, it is a tough competitor of the North.

I say this for two fairly obvious reasons: One, ordinary business competition does not engender — at least it does not normally engender — animosities of the kind that are here involved; and two, the South haters do not include more than a corporal's guard of northern businessmen who are the ones who would feel this competition most severely.

Could this animosity perhaps arise from some sort of inferiority complex — or possibly unconscious envy of the South's milder climate and gentler, less pushing and less ruthless way of life? Or could it be a product of resentment of the South's conservatism and a knowledge on the part of the northern so-called liberals that on this, the South is eternally right and will be proved so by history?

I don't know. It is a problem that both bothers and fascinates me. I think it would be a good subject for a research project by the Fund for the Republic or some other equally unbiased foundation or organization. That concludes my statement. I thank you.

Senator MCCLELLAN. Senator Dirksen, any questions?

Senator DIRKSEN. No questions.

Senator MCCLELLAN. You appear here as attorney for this organization, I believe?

Mr. TAYLOR. Yes, sir.

Senator MCCLELLAN. And has the organization passed any resolution opposing these bills?

Mr. TAYLOR. Yes, sir.

We held a board meeting in Ponte Vedra, Fla., in May and reaffirmed a resolution that they had on this very subject.

Senator DIRKSEN. Generally speaking, Mr. Taylor, you are opposed to any Federal action in this field?

Mr. TAYLOR. That is correct.

Senator DIRKSEN. That sums up your position in a nutshell?

Mr. TAYLOR. Right.

Senator MCCLELLAN. Any other witness?

Mr. YOUNG. No.

Senator MCCLELLAN. Thank you very much, sir.

The committee is adjourned.

(Whereupon, at 2:55 p. m. the hearing in the above-entitled matter was adjourned.)

6.

Juvenile Delinquency I

JUVENILE DELINQUENCY IS A PROBLEM THAT RANKS high in public concern and has engaged the attention of research workers for many years. Currently specialists believe in "multiple causation" rather than that delinquency is caused by this or that factor, even though at any given time and place or with a given individual, some one factor may be more important than others. However, we must be wary of overgeneralizing any such findings. The problem has been approached from many points of view and all have contributed to our understanding. Precisely what should be done, and how, however, has not as yet been specified to everyone's satisfaction.

Many analysts emphasize the social factors contributing to delinquency. We commonly hear the phrase "delinquency of individuals simply represent a delinquent society." Just what such a phrase means, when the number of delinquents is but a small minority of the total number of our youngsters, is not easy to elucidate. Certainly there is much validity

in searching for the dislocations in society which
bring the individual under the cross-pressures
of conflicting value systems, in determining where the
system of rewards and punishments is ambiguous.
Social forces work through individuals. Once a socially
common standard is interiorized by an individual,
it becomes his personal standard. Technological developments have made available to modern youth
a far larger variety of social norms than ever before;
and in our rapidly changing society, the integration of these different patterns is far more difficult
than it was formerly.

Suggested Discussion Questions

To what extent does juvenile delinquency represent
a byproduct of general historical social and
technological "progress"? Consider the pros and
cons of Mr. Shaw's proposition that a major aspect
of the problem is the breakdown of communication within the family, and of Judge Bailey's
proposition that a major aspect of the problem is the
improvement of communication (transportation) in
the semirural community. Evaluate the woodshed concept of dealing with delinquents.

TO COMBAT AND CONTROL
JUVENILE DELINQUENCY

HEARINGS *before the Subcommittee on Special Education of the Committee on Education and Labor, House of Representatives, 84th Congress, First Session*

TUESDAY, MARCH 19, 1957

Washington, D.C.

THE SUBCOMMITTEE MET at 10 a. m., pursuant to call, in room 219, Old House Office Building, Hon. Carl Elliott (chairman of the subcommittee) presiding.

Present: Representatives Elliott (presiding) and McGovern.

Staff members present: Fred G. Hussey, chief clerk; and Mary P. Allen, subcommittee clerk.

Mr. ELLIOTT. The Subcommittee on Special Education will please come to order.

The subcommittee has before it for present consideration 10 bills dealing with the subject of juvenile delinquency. Most of them express briefly in their title that they are bills to provide for assistance to and cooperation with States in strengthening and improving State and local programs for the diminution, control, and treatment of juvenile delinquency.

[. . . . .]

Mr. ELLIOTT. . . . I think we are ready to begin now, and our first witness for today is Mr. Elliot L. Richardson, Acting Secretary, Department of Health, Education, and Welfare.

Are you ready to proceed, Mr. Richardson?

Mr. RICHARDSON. I am, Mr. Chairman.

I would like to ask Mr. Schottland, the Commissioner of Social Security, and his assistant, Legislative Reference Officer of the Social Security Administration, Mr. Hawkins, to come up with me.

Mr. ELLIOTT. We will be happy to have Mr. Schottland and Mr. Hawkins.

Mr. Hawkins, are you with the Legislative Reference Service?

Mr. HAWKINS. No. I am in the Office of the Commissioner of Social Security.

Mr. ELLIOTT. Yes, sir. And I assume you may want to testify somewhere along the line here —

Mr. HAWKINS. Probably not.

Mr. ELLIOTT. Or contribute to the discussion in some way. You may proceed, Mr. Richardson.

Statements of Elliot L. Richardson, Acting Secretary, and Charles I. Schottland, Commissioner of Social Security, Department of Health, Education, and Welfare

[. . . . .]

Mr. RICHARDSON. The Department believes that the control of juvenile delinquency is primarily a matter for States and local communities and that many of them have made outstanding contributions. However, a more intensive attack is needed, and this attack must be nationwide in scope.

With the mobility of population, the expansion of suburban areas, and modern transportation, juvenile delinquency can no longer be thought of as being confined within the boundaries of neighborhoods, local communities, or even States.

The continuing rise in juvenile delinquency extends throughout the Nation. It is not confined to any one group of States. Nor is it confined to any one geographic area. Rural and urban areas alike are confronted with this problem.

Because of the seriousness and extent of juvenile delinquency throughout the country, it has become a problem on which the States and localities require the help of the Nation through assistance and stimulation with Federal funds. This is not to minimize the efforts being made by States and local communities, public and voluntary agencies, civic groups, religious organizations, and many other groups and individuals. Only through their unrelenting efforts have they been able to develop the resources and services we now have for helping delinquent youth. But I am sure that during the course of your hearings, you will receive from them, as the Department has already received, extensive evidence of gaps in programs, the reservoir of unmet need, the incalculable unhappiness of the many delinquent youth for whom too little comes too late to restore them to normal, happy, and productive lives.

For all of these reasons, the Department is convinced that more direct encouragement and help, in the form of grants to the States and for the other purposes I have mentioned, is essential. Consequently, the Department has proposed a 5-year program of grants, as set forth in H. R. 5539. In the light of experience with the rate of development of other new programs, we have attempted to establish a level of authorization that is reasonably related to expenditures for comparable programs. While the amount of money proposed is modest, we are convinced that it would have the effect of stimulating improvements whose value would be many times greater than the Federal dollars involved. We believe this bill would greatly advance the welfare of the children of our country. We urge your favorable consideration of this legislation.

I would like to ask Mr. Schottland, Commissioner of Social Security, to tell you more about the nature and extent of the problem of juvenile delinquency which we are facing today and to describe in more detail some of the major provisions of H. R. 5539.

Mr. ELLIOTT. Thank you, Mr. Richardson.

Mr. RICHARDSON. Thank you, Mr. Chairman.

Mr. ELLIOTT. Mr. Schottland, we will be happy to hear from you.

Mr. SCHOTTLAND. Mr. Chairman and members of the committee, I am happy to appear before this committee in support of H. R. 5539. This bill is designed to carry out the recommendations of the President, and I would like to explain briefly the problems involved and the content of the administration's proposal.

First, I want to speak of the mounting tempo in juvenile delinquency. Based on the statistics available to us for the seventh consecutive year juvenile delinquency continued to rise in 1955, the latest year on which we have information. In that year, there was a 9-percent increase, over 1954, in juvenile delinquency cases coming to the attention of the juvenile courts. The overall increase in these cases since 1948 was 70 percent. During this same period, the child population of juvenile court age, generally 10 through 17 years, increased only 16 percent, which is shown on the chart.

Mr. Chairman, at this point may the chart be made a part of the record.

Mr. ELLIOTT. It may be included in the record.

(The chart follows:)

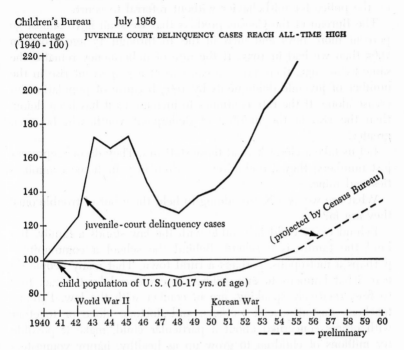

Children's Bureau   July 1956

percentage   JUVENILE COURT DELINQUENCY CASES REACH ALL-TIME HIGH
(1940 - 100)

Mr. SCHOTTLAND. As shown on the chart, the number of delinquent youth appearing in juvenile courts is at an all-time high — greater even than the peaks reached during World War II.

Mr. ELLIOTT. Is that a proportional chart, in proportion to population?

Mr. SCHOTTLAND. This line here is the child population age 10 to 17, and this is juvenile court cases. It is a proportional chart.

Mr. ELLIOTT. Do I see from that chart that juvenile court cases were on the downward trend during the period of the war maybe and immediately after the war, but then about 1949, or so, they took a very sudden rise, which threatens to run completely off the top of the chart? Is that correct?

Mr. SCHOTTLAND. That is correct, Mr. Chairman.

The Federal Bureau of Investigation reported an 11-percent increase in police arrests of juveniles under 18 in 1955 as compared with 1954.

In 1955, roughly 2 percent of the 20 million children 10 through

17 years of age were involved in delinquency cases coming before juvenile courts. Several times more children were handled by the police for misbehavior without referral to court.

The Bureau of the Census predicts that we shall have almost 50 percent more boys and girls in the 10 through 17 age group in 1965 than we had in 1955. If the rate of delinquency remains the same as in 1955, therefore, we can expect a 50-percent rise in the number of juvenile delinquents by 1965 because of population increase alone. If the rate continues to increase as it has been doing, then the rise in the number of delinquent youth will be even greater.

Let us take a closer look at these statistics. They do not represent just numbers; they are children, children in your home communities and mine.

What are we as a Nation doing to help them out of trouble once they are in?

Behind every child in trouble with the law stands a family. Behind the family is a school. Behind the school a community — perhaps a metropolis, perhaps a rural town. That many people do care what happens to our children is evidenced by the fact that so few, relatively speaking, are in conflict with the law. Parents, teachers, pastors, social workers, and doctors, alone or together with others concerned about a particular child, make it possible for millions of children to grow up as healthy, happy youngsters and take their place as responsible adult citizens of our communities. But the number for whom this is not true, small as it may be as a statistic, is still much too large and the price society pays much too costly in human misery and in adult crime.

GAPS IN PROGRAMS

Why is this so? Because the gaps in our programs for delinquent youth are great, so great that these children do not secure the care and treatment they need when they need it. Services for the location, diagnosis, and treatment of delinquent youth are inadequate throughout the country; and our mounting toll of juvenile delinquents testifies to this inadequacy.

[. . . . .]

TRAINING SCHOOLS FOR DELINQUENT YOUTH

Mr. SCHOTTLAND. About 40,000 delinquent children are committed by the courts to training schools for delinquent children each year. Few training schools have the mature, experienced, and professionally trained staff needed to offer a genuine treatment program that these children must have if they are to return to their communities as responsible citizens. Less than two-fifths of our State public training schools for delinquent youth have a psychiatrist on their staff, either on a full- or part-time basis; two-fifths have no psychologists on a full- or part-time basis. Almost two-fifths of these training schools do not even have a social worker on the staff.

LACK OF COORDINATION

Too often we fail to make the best possible use of the resources we have for the treatment of delinquent children. Coordination among State and local public and voluntary agencies and organizations working in behalf of delinquent children is generally inadequate. Responsibility for State services for the control of juvenile delinquency is often divided among State departments of welfare, health, education, institutions, or corrections, State youth authorities, and State youth commissions. Certain services, such as juvenile courts, probation, police, and detention care, are usually entirely local and not represented at the level of the State government. Facilities and services provided by voluntary agencies may or may not be coordinated with the public programs.

In most States provisions are lacking for assuring continuity in planning and providing care for individual delinquent youth. This is perhaps the most serious result of lack of coordination. You have probably been concerned, as I have been, over the relatively frequent newspaper stories about adolescent youth involved in serious acts of violence — murder, rape, or aggravated assault.

Have you noticed how many times the adolescent involved had shown serious difficulties and a need for help long before his situation became so acute that he or she resorted to a serious act of violence?

Have you noticed how many times the adolescent did not receive the help he needed at the time his problems became apparent and, instead, the situation was allowed to grow from bad to worse until it was too late?

These are the situations that cry for coordination of effort in communities and in the State. If more communities had a plan and a mechanism for coordinating their efforts in behalf of individual children in trouble, it is my firm conviction that fewer children would find themselves involved in serious acts of violence and fewer would find themselves in the ranks of adult criminals for whom prison is the only possibility.

Responsibility for an individual child often shifts back and forth from the courts to public or voluntary child-caring agencies, clinics, schools, local and State institutions, and other State departments or institutions. In many States and communities, there is little, if any, continuity in treatment of the child. While in many instances certain avenues of cooperation between agencies and departments have been established, the procedure is often devious and slow. As a result, many delinquent children do not receive proper care and treatment at the time when it would be most effective.

SHORTAGE OF TRAINED PERSONNEL

Serious shortages exist in personnel serving delinquent youth. More people are needed who have had professional training in social work, education, law, psychology, psychiatry and other health services — all fields in which the demand is already far greater than the supply of trained personnel. This calls for enlarging the pool of trained personnel available for employment in the juvenile delinquency field. It also calls for more in-service training programs to improve the quality of services of personnel already employed in serving delinquent youth, both professional as well as nonprofessional personnel.

We are not using the new knowledge we have effectively enough. In addition, better approaches and improved methods for the control and treatment of juvenile delinquency need to be developed.

[. . . . .]

Statement of Hon. Edith Green, A Representative in Congress from the State of Oregon

Mrs. GREEN. Thank you very much, Mr. Chairman, and my apologies for the delay here. I had a group of students from Williams College that I had promised to meet with, so I left to be with them a few minutes.

I appreciate the opportunity of appearing here this morning in support of the provision of H. R. 652 — and of the similar bills before this subcommittee — for a program of assistance to and co-

operation with States in strengthening and improving their own
and local programs for the diminution, control, and treatment of
juvenile delinquency.

At the outset, I must make clear to you and to the other members
of this subcommittee that I do not pretend to be an expert on the
subject of juvenile delinquency. My lack of expertness, however, is
not a mark of any lack of interest in this important subject. I approach the subject as a teacher, as a mother, as a legislator, and as
a person who for years has worked for community betterment
projects of deep concern to the continued well being of the people
of my State.

You have already had appearing before you experts who have
testified as to the nature and scope of juvenile delinquency in the
United States today. I will not repeat to you the statistics they have
given you as to the shocking rise in the incidence of juvenile crime
for the seventh successive year. As a matter of fact, you do not need
my repetition of these facts to underscore the seriousness of the
present situation. You have but to listen to the radio, read your
daily papers and periodicals, or see and hear your television programs. This public concern with the problems of juvenile delinquency is not out of keeping with the seriousness of the problem. It is a reflection of what this continued rise in delinquency
portends for the future — for the future welfare of millions of children and youth.

Neither does this public concern about juvenile delinquency
evidence an unawareness of the fact that the number of children
who get into trouble with the police is but a small — a very small —
percentage of the total number of children and youth in the United
States. As I have said repeatedly before, and as I shall continue to
repeat, the majority of the young men and women of our Nation
are fine, decent, upstanding young citizens who will, one day, be
worthy of assuming their rightful place as citizens of our country.

But while we should not overemphasize the problem of juvenile
delinquency we should not, by the same token, underestimate the
problem.

I need not remind you, Mr. Chairman, or any of the other members of this subcommittee, that the original resolution authorizing
a Senate subcommittee to investigate juvenile delinquency in the
United States was passed almost 4 years ago. As that investigation
proceeded, during that period, the number of youngsters getting
into trouble with the law continued to rise. The time has come

for congressional action. We cannot longer sit idly by while the States and localities are losing their fight against juvenile delinquency.

There can be little room for doubt but that this is a matter of vital Federal concern. The vastly increased mobility of our population is testimony to the fact that the delinquent who is not given the needed treatment in State X will end up in State Y, hundreds of miles away, at the cost of thousands of dollars annually to State Y. We can no longer treat delinquency as an isolated problem of concern only to the State or locality where the delinquent by chance commits the delinquent act.

It is sheer nonsense to say that the Federal Government has no concern with programs for the prevention and treatment of juvenile delinquency. Can we say that the Federal Government is concerned with research into plant and animal disease and pest control — but that when it comes to the question of researches into the latest techniques for the control of juvenile delinquency the Federal Government is not concerned? We authorize Federal research into hoof-and-mouth diseases of animals. Are we reluctant to authorize Federal grants for demonstration projects for juvenile-delinquency prevention?

Why is hoof-and-mouth disease any more of a Federal problem than our problem children? We make grants to the States for teachers of agriculture and industrial subjects, and for the training of teachers of these subjects. Are these subjects any more important than training personnel to work with boys and girls who are in trouble, and are we less concerned, or is it any less of a Federal concern?

I cannot subscribe, Mr. Chairman, to any notion that there is anything forbidding about Federal jurisdiction in matters of human welfare which, by the same token, is the less forbidding when we talk about the health of hogs or poultry or cattle. If we are not even more concerned about the future welfare of our children, we should at least be as concerned about it as we are about stopping the spread of hoof-and-mouth disease.

I shall not belabor this point. I raise it because it has come up before and will come up again, and it seems to me we must, therefore, dispose of this perennial charge once and for all.

The Federal Government has a legitimate concern with its children and youth. That concern is great, whether they are crippled children for whom the Federal Government has expressed its concern tangibly for over 20 years now, or whether they are delinquent children — for whom the Federal Government will express its concern in the near future, I hope, by the adoption of a program such as the one I propose to assist States and localities in their efforts to control and prevent juvenile delinquency.

[.   .   .   .   .   ]

Mr. ELLIOTT. Mrs. Green, before you get into that I would like to volunteer this observation about this matter. We are speaking about the role of the Federal Government. The Federal Government has, by the nature of the powers granted it and by virtue of the fact that it has pretty well taken over the major sources of revenue in the country, the responsibility, I feel, to help States and local communities do those legitimate functions that they cannot do well for themselves. And it is with that feeling that I agree with you wholeheartedly that the Federal Government has a role in aiding the States and local communities toward the solution of this problem. I personally wish it were possible that the Federal Government did not have many of the responsibilities that it has under the situation that we live in. I wish it were possible that the communities were able to do many of these things for themselves that they talk to us about helping them do. But as long as we are getting the revenue, the huge taxes, that we are getting from the people, I think it is in the nature of fairness that we help them out.

I might go farther and say in the southern part of the country now we are besieged — and your reference to the hoof-and-mouth disease reminded me of this — we are besieged with a terrible plague of the so-called fire ants which is about to eat us up, and we are appealing to the United States Department of Agriculture to help us out in correlating a program to get rid of those fire ants. We are asking the Federal Government to help us a little bit not only in the correlation of a program but in the financing of what it will take to get rid of them.

I just wanted to say, before you passed into the more complete detailed analysis, that I am in complete agreement that there is a Federal concern here greater than for hundreds of purposes for which the Federal Government spends money.

Mrs. GREEN. Thank you, Mr. Chairman. I am delighted to hear the opinion you have just expressed. I must say I get concerned at times when, as you say, the Federal Government moves in right away when you have these biting ants — is that what you call them?

Mr. ELLIOTT. Fire ants.

Mrs. GREEN. And you do not hear anything about whether it is a Federal problem or not, they just move in. But when you have a problem about girls and boys, you have all these cliches and arguments about whether or not it is of concern to the Federal Government.

For example, last year we tried desperately to get an appropriation of $100,000 for the Children's Bureau for more trained consultants in this field, and we could not get enough funds. Yet, with comparative ease, we vote $1 million to Agriculture for the study of diseases of plants, animals, pigs, and chickens. I cannot help asking the question: How important are our children to us?

Mr. ELLIOTT. In the same connection, it seems to me the angle of preventing juvenile delinquency is worthy of spending some money. Mr. Hunt, whom we have just heard, said it costs about $3,800 in Maryland to rehabilitate a juvenile delinquent in one of the institutions up there. We are fairly willing to spend that $3,800, whereas if we spent a few $3,800's before the delinquent acts occurred, we might save a great deal of money by way of prevention. That thought has occurred to me many times in this connection, and I am sure it has to you.

Mrs. GREEN. That is true, and I do not think the term "diminution of juvenile delinquency" can be said to rule out prevention.

Mr. ELLIOTT. Mrs. Green, you have studied these bills and are the author of one of the leading bills here and have given a lot of thought to it. How might the program envisioned by you be used to prevent juvenile delinquency? I want to get that in the record.

Mrs. GREEN. There are three main provisions. The first part is to strengthen the local and State programs and secure greater coordination. Then you have the grants-in-aid for training personnel. Then you have demonstration projects. Those are really the three divisions of the bill.

I think one of the saddest things is the lack of trained personnel, and back of that is the lack of schools or places in this country where people can secure the training they need in this field. In the schools themselves, if we had more psychologists and more social workers who would recognize early in a child's life the warning signs, the danger signals, and do something about this youngster who might later on become a delinquent, it would be a great step forward. We do not have nearly the amount of information we should have. We need research into it. There is a great deal of feeling that youngsters who become delinquent at the age of 15 and 16 show signs of it in the second grade. How can you expect a teacher who has 50 youngsters in her classroom to know her youngsters well enough to recognize these signs? And a lot of our teachers have not had training in that field, either. It seems to me that is one area.

To go back to the police officers that were mentioned a few moments ago, I said one of the sad commentaries is that we do not have police officers who have had any training in working with juvenile delinquents, and you know as well as I do that we have a lot of police officers who have had no training at all. In some towns they are there by political appointment. We can do a great deal by getting personnel that recognize the danger signals and do something about it early.

There are some demonstration projects.

Mr. ELLIOTT. Right there, Mrs. Green, I would like you to expand on that a little bit. What are some of those demonstration projects?

Mrs. GREEN. I am vaguely familiar with some of them. There, again, Mr. Chairman, I do not pose as an expert on this at all, and I would like the experts to give the testimony on this. But I am aware of one project that will get underway soon, and that is small cottages, places where you could have 10- or 12-year-old youngsters who are predelinquent. They cannot go back to their homes, there is trouble there, and they certainly are not youngsters who should be placed in reform schools or in training schools. This is a project to see what could be done with these 10-, 11-, and 12-year-old youngsters in as nearly a home environment as possible with trained workers. This is an expensive job, and it is being done on a demonstration basis.

Then, of course, there is a great need for some kind of a home for the youngsters who have been in a training school and who cannot go back to the home from which they came. Where do they go? Do you send them to some penal institution? The foster homes are not able to take care of them. There is some experimentation needed to provide a suitable setup for the youngsters who are on probation or parole.

I am sure as we get into it there will be many other areas, and the experts could give you a better idea of some of these projects.

Off the record, Mr. Chairman.

(Discussion off the record.)

Mrs. GREEN. Both of the proposals, the two major ones before the subcommittee, have four objectives:

1. Greater coordination at the Federal level of the programs dealing with the prevention, control and treatment of juvenile delinquency;
2. Grants-in-aid to the States for strengthening and improving such State programs;
3. Grants-in-aid to the States for training personnel engaged in providing services to delinquents; and
4. Grants-in-aid to the States for demonstrations of new techniques for the prevention, control and treatment of juvenile delinquency.

There is, then, substantial agreement on the objects which any Federal program in this field should seek. There is also, in my view, substantial agreement on the methods by which the Federal Government should seek to attain these objectives. There are, I will admit, some differences between the two proposals but they are differences which I sincerely believe can be reconciled, given the will and the desire to do so.

[. . . . . .]

WEDNESDAY, APRIL 3, 1957
Washington, D.C.

THE SUBCOMMITTEE met at 10 a. m., pursuant to recess, in room 356, Old House Office Building, Hon. Carl Elliott (chairman of the subcommittee) presiding.

Present: Representatives Elliott (presiding), Nicholson, Wainwright, and Green.

Staff members present: Fred G. Hussey, chief clerk, Kennedy W. Ward, assistant general counsel, and Mary P. Allen, subcommittee clerk.

Mr. ELLIOTT. The subcommittee will be in order.

Our first witness today is Mr. G. Howland Shaw.

Will you come around, Mr. Shaw?

Mr. Shaw represents the National Association of Training Schools and Juvenile Agencies.

Is that correct, Mr. Shaw?

Statement of G. Howland Shaw, Representing the National Association of Training Schools and Juvenile Agencies and the National Probation and Parole Association

Mr. SHAW. Yes, Mr. Chairman, but in addition to that I am representing the National Probation and Parole Association.

Mr. ELLIOTT. The National Probation and Parole Association. Is your testimony in writing, Mr. Shaw?

Mr. SHAW. No, sir. Written statements will be submitted later on.

Mr. ELLIOTT. We are happy to have you, Mr. Shaw, and you may proceed.

Mr. SHAW. Thank you, sir.

I am representing those two organizations, the National Association of Training Schools and Juvenile Agencies and the National Probation and Parole Association. I am representing the National Association of Training Schools and Juvenile Agencies because the present president, Mr. Hyman Stalk, who is head of the youth authority in California, cannot be here. I am a former president of that organization. I am also representing the National Probation and Parole Association. I am a member of their board of trustees and chairman of their law committee.

Mr. ELLIOTT. Where do you live, Mr. Shaw?

Mr. SHAW. I am a resident, Mr. Chairman, of the District of Columbia.

In the first place, let me say that both of these organizations are heartily in favor of the proposed legislation that is before you.

I am going to address my remarks to H. R. 652, which I take it is the document that is currently before you. Specifically, we are strongly in favor of the Federal advisory council which proposed in that legislation, first, because we feel that that will make available to the Department of Health, Education, and Welfare the best professional opinion outside of the Department, and then we are interested in another provision which says that persons representing the general public shall be represented on that advisory committee.

Now I think all of us who have had anything to do with the problem of juvenile delinquency, realize that our greatest failure has been in the education of the public. There has been a group of professional persons, on one side, who had a good many of the answers, and then, on the other side, there has been the public and there has been a great gulf between them. And I say that as somebody who has worked in that field for now some 20 years. I think that is our greatest failure. Therefore, I attach very special importance for the representation of the general public on this advisory committee.

I take it for granted that the committee — the council, rather, of course, will be geographically representative. So I just mentioned that as it has been mentioned previously by the National Association of Training Schools and Juvenile Agencies.

Now, title 2, which provides for grants to the States to strengthen and improve programs and which has also a subdivision, I think, on research, we emphatically endorse. I think we realize that while there is a great deal of talk about juvenile delinquency — in my opinion too much talk — there is very little or far too little getting down to brass tacks and finding what exactly are the facilities in any given State or in any given locality of a State, and then coordinating the program.

Way back in, I think it was, in 1946, I was a member of the Attorney General's Conference on Juvenile Delinquency, and that was the thought that we tried especially to stress. We cannot solve the problem of juvenile delinquency in Washington. It has to reach out through the States and through the States it has to reach out to all the localities in that State. We can formulate standards here in Washington, we can give all sorts of data, but we cannot solve the problem of juvenile delinquency in any one locality. Therefore, the emphasis which is placed in the proposed legislation on surveys and coordination seems to us a very great importance.

And then when it comes to title 3, which provides for grants for training personnel, I think we have reached the stage in the treatment and prevention of delinquency where we realize that it is not something that a well-intentioned individual can go in for — there must be training, and training, really, means saving not only lives but dollars and cents.

I think we know perfectly well that if a juvenile court, for instance, has an adequate number of well-trained probation officers, the community is going to be saved in terms of lives and in terms of dollars and cents. In other words, training is essential.

And the lack of trained personnel throughout the United States in all aspects of the prevention and treatment of juvenile delinquency is, to my mind, one of the most depressing facts in the whole picture.

Then we come to title 4, grants for special study projects, demonstrations, and in that connection I refer back to section 401 and section 402 (e) where there is provision for research.

I think all of us, and I know both of the organizations that I am representing before this committee, feel very strongly that we need research under two headings: First, we need evaluation of what we are doing now. To give you an illustration I will take our contemporary training school. Now, there are 129, I think, State training schools. How many private training schools for delinquents there are I am not prepared to give you an accurate figure. The per capita cost of those State training schools runs between $200 to $3,000. The most expensive private institution which deals with a very small number of delinquents and with a very high percentage of professional personnel is costing something like $6,000 and $7,000 per capita. Contrast that with the 1920's when the most expensive institution was something like $1,180 and the average was running at $518.

Now, the public, the taxpayer, and the private donor has the right to know what results are being obtained from that expenditure of money, and it is going higher and higher all the time. As things are today we can give him very little information. We can say that we think that we are getting 70 percent success and yet we are very much disturbed by the fact that something like half of the inmates of our adult institutions have had experience in juvenile institutes. In other words, we need an evaluation of what we are doing in the training field.

And then, besides evaluation of what we are doing now, we need money for experimental projects, demonstration projects.

Yes; we have, in the last 50 years, learned a great deal about how to deal with human behavior. There is no question about that. The psychiatrists, the sociologists, the anthropologists, and all the rest of the people have contributed importantly. We do know more about how to deal with youngsters in trouble than we did 20 years ago. But we are still in a position where there is a lot to be learned. We need experimental projects.

I can give you two examples. One is in New York.

Some 10 years ago New York City was very much disturbed by gang activities. In this particular summer, which I recall very well, 9 boys had been killed in gang warfare. Some of us who were interested in the problem thought that we ought to get busy and do something about it. So the Welfare Council, which is the coordinating agency of all social and health welfare agencies in the city of New York, got a committee together, and we came up with the idea that all of the existing agencies, when it came to dealing with this particular type of boy, were failing. The police could not put enough officers in the conflict areas to control things. The adult sponsored youth organizations, such as youth clubs, were not able to get next to this boy at all. In fact, if that type of boy got into a boys' club he would do his best to wreck it. In other words, we felt that we were dealing with what is now called the unaffiliated boy. So we started out with a hypothesis, that if we could get the right sort of individuals, who would hang around the street corners, we could perhaps accomplish something. We got enough money — it was $175,000 — for a 3-year project, and that project has been reported on in an important publication of the Welfare Council, and has been the basis of a nationwide approach to this particular type of boy, especially illustrated by the work of the youth board of the city of New York. Now that is one example of the importance of research.

Another one is a project which has not been very much publicized, the Highfield project in New Jersey. That is a very small project which deals with only 25 boys at a time. It takes a boy that the judge of the juvenile court does not dare put on probation and does not want to send to the open reformatory. And we are going to publish pretty soon a book which will demonstrate that with the kind of an approach that we have in this very small setting. For this kind of a boy we can accomplish something more after 3 months' residence better than can be accomplished by sending that boy to the reformatory at a very considerably greater cost.

Now, these are two examples of the importance of research and the importance of demonstration projects.

I would like to emphasize that particularly, Mr. Chairman, because that is the way that we are going to make progress in this very difficult and complicated problem of dealing with juvenile delinquency. I know that we have a tendency to try and reduce problems to one cause. Just now, of course, the cause is the family, and now we are busily denouncing the family, while disregarding the fact that the family is the product of all sorts of forces that are in effect at the present time in American life.

I think, Mr. Chairman, that is about all I can say in behalf of these two organizations other than to express the earnest hope that this legislation will be enacted into law.

Mr. ELLIOTT. Thank you very much, Mr. Shaw.

I think you made some very excellent statements and very helpful statements.

There was one statement that you made that impressed me, and that was that there was too much talk about juvenile delinquency. I wonder, however, how we are going to conduct these hearings and get a solid base upon which we can enact a law without doing lots of talk about it.

Mr. SHAW. I did not intend my remark to be in any degree critical of persons who are seriously engaged ——

Mr. ELLIOTT. I understand that.

Mr. SHAW. In trying to deal with the problem. But in my own case, I have learned that if you get a reputation of being able to talk on the subject of juvenile delinquency you can talk every evening and usually at luncheon, and that is the kind of talk that I rather deplore, not what is going on before this committee.

Mr. ELLIOTT. Mrs. Green.

Mrs. GREEN. Yes.

I am aware of the very active role that you have played in trying to get work started on the street gang in New York. Are you familiar with any efforts being made in other cities?

Mr. SHAW. I think that the detached-worker technique has had a very considerable influence not only in the United States but even in England, because that book, which you probably have seen, the report of the Welfare Council, has been very widely read all over the country and I think it has had a tremendous impact.

I think now the persons responsible for the more conventional adult-sponsored youth organization are beginning to do a lot of thinking. For instance, the Boys Club of New York, as you probably know, now has workers out in the street to get the boys in. The old fashioned idea that you had a fine boys club with all sorts of facilities and the boys flocked in, I think has now been definitely established as inadequate to our present-day needs. You see we have various radiations of boys and that means grades of boys. We have the boy, for instance, who goes in to Boy Scouts. That tends to be one group. Then we have below that the Boys Club type of boy. Then way below that we have this unaffiliated boy, who has — we had a demonstration of that here in Washington with our junior police and citizens corps, which is essentially nothing more than a conditioning organization. We deal primarily with very tough boys, boys who break street lamps, boys who are doing all kinds of things they should not do. Now, thanks to the genius of Officer Cowan of the Metropolitan force we brought these boys into our organization. After a year or perhaps less than a year, those fellows will go into boys' clubs, but they have to get out of their systems that hostility. In every big American city you have a lot of boys and girls who hate everything that you and I stand for. They just hate it. They want to destroy it. Now that boy and girl has to be approached not through the conventional things that we think function 100 percent but through a specialized technique. I think we have evolved that technique now and it is working. We can deal with these fellows.

When the Welfare Council stated this hypothesis, which was nothing more than a hypothesis when we started out with this experiment, we did not know it was going to work at all. We started out with five of the toughest gangs in Harlem, and we were able to get next to them. Now it took time. It takes a special kind of person. It is not a question of a fine building. Whenever we think of these problems, we think of a building. We do not think of a person. That is one of the pressing things in this whole field of prevention of delinquency and the treatment of delinquency.

I might have mentioned in research projects one that is of special interest to me. I think we know that the most powerful rehabilitative factor for a youngster who is in trouble is an adult who cares for him. What kind of an adult is that? If you study training schools, as I have because I have been connected with 3 of them now for 20 years, you will soon discover there are certain individuals that the boys are really influenced by. I have talked with a lot of my boys that I have known in training schools and sometimes, unfortunately, they have gone on to adult institutions; and sometimes, fortunately, they have not.

Some years ago I conducted a very unscientific and very informal inquiry.

I said to them: "Why did you suddenly get the idea of going straight? What did it?"

Every single boy mentioned an individual, nobody ever mentioned a program — an individual and the kind of individual. It was not the professional staff. It was not the psychiatrist. It was the foreman in the automobile repair shop, it was the cottage father and more often, especially with a certain type of boy, the cottage mother who did that.

Now what is it? That is 1 of the research projects that 3 or 4 of us have been talking about a lot, but we have not been able to get enough money to go ahead with it so far.

Mrs. GREEN. I have one other question, Mr. Shaw, that I would like your comments on. Do you see any possible friction among the various State agencies under this type of legislation when it comes to the distribution of funds?

Mr. SHAW. Well, one of my colleagues on the National Association of Training Schools and Juvenile Agencies feels that an entirely independent — I think I am doing justice to his thought — agencies should be set up; that if, for instance, the money should be turned over to a department of welfare, which itself would be interested in getting some of the money and at the same time there would be the mental health department and perhaps the educational department, and other departments would be interested, that that would create a situation which would be unfortunate; and that it should be set up as a completely independent agency representative of all the various disciplines involved, but nevertheless not a beneficiary of the money.

Mrs. GREEN. Do you see any possible friction of the administration's bill when it refers — I have forgotten the section — to a single State agency?

Mr. SHAW. That is the thought that I was trying to express in behalf of this particular member of our executive board; that it should be an entirely neutral agency that would not receive itself any of the funds.

Mrs. GREEN. I think that is all, Mr. Chairman. I am certainly very happy that Mr. Shaw, who is a former Assistant Secretary of State and one who had a great deal of experience in this field, took the time to come and give testimony before the committee.

Mr. ELLIOTT. Yes, I agree. We are fortunate to have his fine interest in this subject matter.

The gentleman from New York, Mr. Wainwright.

Mr. WAINWRIGHT. No questions.

Mr. ELLIOTT. The gentleman from Massachusetts, Mr. Nicholson.

Mr. NICHOLSON. I suppose that human nature has not changed very much since Biblical days; has it?

Mr. SHAW. Basically I suppose not.

Mr. NICHOLSON. They had the same problems that we have here now.

Mr. SHAW. Yes, but in quite different degree and form.

Mr. NICHOLSON. Well, King Solomon said, "Spare the rod" — or did he say spare the rod?

Mr. SHAW. I do not know who said that.

Mr. NICHOLSON. It is in the proverbs anyway, and he was an author.

Mr. SHAW. The back of the woodshed concept in dealing with delinquency is still with us.

Mr. NICHOLSON. Now we do not allow schoolteachers to shake up one of these brats; do we?

Mr. SHAW. In most States we do not.

Mr. NICHOLSON. Of course, I am interested in this because a great many of us, most of the public, I guess, believe that the fault lies more or less in the family life. The boy talks back to his mother. These things do not happen in well-regulated families because he gets a slap if he does. I mean those things lead to delinquency. He has not any respect for authority.

Mr. SHAW. I agree, but then I think you have to take into consideration the terrific change in American family life. Now when you had a bunch of boys growing up on the farm or in the small town, that was one thing. Now you have youngsters growing up in apartments or tenements. You have the father working. You have more and more mothers working, now. So when junior comes back from school 3 or 3:15, there is nobody home. Therefore, junior goes out on the street. That applies not only in slum areas, it applies in the more privileged areas of our big cities, the suburbs; you have the same situation. One thing that is of special interest nowadays is delinquency is not confined to the slum. Some of the worst delinquents I had anything to do with come from privileged families. There is a breakdown in American family life.

One of the great problems on which I think we ought to do a lot of thinking is how to restore communication between parents and children. It is broken down to a large extent. The home is a place where we have breakfast, where you raise Cain with Dad because he does not want you to use the car tonight. You have television. What does television do? The youngster watches television. Dad is reading the newspaper, Mom is upstairs or in the kitchen. There is no communication.

Mr. NICHOLSON. What are you going to do with this boy from half past 3 to suppertime?

Mr. SHAW. That is just what we are worrying about. What are we going to do with him?

Mr. NICHOLSON. There are the probation officers. A boy that comes under the supervision of some person a great deal depends on who that person is.

Mr. SHAW. Yes.

Mr. NICHOLSON. If he has not any respect for the probation officer he is even worse. Maybe he is thinking up new schemes.

Mr. SHAW. But, sir, I know lots of probation officers. I work with them. Consider his situation. He is loaded down with far more cases than he can effectively handle.

Now I worked with a certain number of juveniles and older fellows both in and out of prison. My caseload is what? In the District of Columbia at the present time I have about what — a dozen youngsters, that I am working with. I know if they are really getting into trouble. I may have to see them every single evening, and I may have to see them not for a genial 15 minutes but for 3 hours.

What probation officer can do that? They cannot.

You see one of the discouraging things in this whole business is that we know what a probation officer should do, we know the kind of training he should have, we know how many cases he should have, but there is scarcely any jurisdiction in the United States of America where that standard is even approximated, and the same applies for parole. Most of my work is with parolees.

Mr. WAINWRIGHT. Will the gentleman yield?

Mr. NICHOLSON. Yes.

Mr. WAINWRIGHT. Do you think this is primarily a local problem that should be handled by the locality, the community or the city, or do you think it is primarily a Federal problem.

Mr. SHAW. I think it is primarily a local problem, with a good hard push given from the Federal side, but it has to be handled right down at the local, community level.

Mr. WAINWRIGHT. I agree.

Mr. SHAW. Definitely.

Mr. WAINWRIGHT. You have very erudite and scholarly testimony without the benefit of a prepared statement. But, to start, I may have misinterpreted you because you tended to debunk the current trend to put most of the blame on the family, as such, and then you have, in the last 10 minutes, completed a very worthy case for the family as the core of the problem.

Mr. SHAW. Yes. Let me see if I can make my point clear to you. I suppose I have in the last 20 years gone over a good many thousand case histories of delinquents and adult criminals. I would be embarrassed if you asked me to cite to you a case where the delinquent or the criminal came from a happy, well-organized family.

Mr. WAINWRIGHT. To use a sociological term, an adjusted family.

Mr. SHAW. No; I like the term "happy" better. It included adjusted but it adds a little bit to it.

Now, with that fact which I think anybody will stand for, we have gone on to the idea that the family is to blame and that we should, as has been proposed in some jurisdictions, punish the family. It is that that I protest against.

Mr. WAINWRIGHT. You would rather educate them.

Mr. SHAW. Yes. Because what has made the family what it is?

Mr. WAINWRIGHT. You have answered that by saying it is the change in the American way of life, with the woman out of the home, and I read in the Sunday New York Times ——

Mr. SHAW. After all, when you come down to this whole problem of delinquency, what is it in the last analysis? It is the pathology of the contemporary life. It is the negative side of American life. It is what we pay for the kind of life we lead in the United States in the year 1957. Now that is exactly what it is.

Now you start investigating, for instance, a 14-year-old boy here in the District that has been stealing. What do you get into? You get into housing. You get into the efficiency of the school system, you get into his family situation, you get into the whole picture of conditions as they exist in the District of Columbia. And we know what we ought to do. We know that the front line of defense against delinquency is the elementary school. We know that the important thing is to have teachers, who are skillful enough to detect these early symptoms of trouble. And we know, besides that, that we have to have resources, in the community to do something about it.

Take, for example, some of the tragedies that have happened in the District of Columbia or nearby the District of Columbia. There is the case of the 15-year-old boy who killed a 15-year-old girl. What developed? He had been in a mental hospital. He had been diagnosed as it was essential that he have institutional treatment. The father could not afford it. The community had not a clinic. Therefore what happened? Tragedy.

Mr. WAINWRIGHT. Of course, you are raising the point that has bothered me while listening and reading this testimony, and that is with regard to the funds that we seem to be cutting on the floor today — with all due respect to the very intelligent and capable authors of these bills — I wonder whether we should not be fighting for better housing in slum areas and for better welfare programs ——

Mr. SHAW. We need both.

Mr. WAINWRIGHT (continuing). Because those are really the sources for all juvenile delinquency that have been pointed out.

Mr. SHAW. I think the thing that is worrying most of us that are concerned in this field now with the future in mind is the situation of our schools. We know that unless something pretty terrific is done about schools, we are going to have a big crop of juvenile delinquents in 15, 20, 25 years from now. It is inevitable.

How many careers of delinquencies start with truancy. It is characteristic — truancy, then small stealing, and then it goes on and on and on.

And we have to recognize that there is a considerable number of youngsters who cannot make the grade and who need help. Philadelphia, for instance, has done a magnificent job in school-work programs. We want to do much more of that kind of thing. We want to develop special facilities. Here in the District we have something like 4,000 dropouts. Half of them we estimate have not any jobs. There are 2,000 potential delinquents.

Mr. NICHOLSON. Excuse me.

Mr. WAINWRIGHT. That is all right.

Mr. NICHOLSON. But you have now things that we did not have when we were boys, vocational training. I remember when I went to grammar school there were boys there that never got any further than the grammar school. If they had vocational training perhaps — they were not delinquent, those boys were not — they just did not have enough I. Q.

Now, in most States, I suppose they have vocational training and in the last year of the high schools there is always a course.

Mr. SHAW. That is not covered in the bill.

Mr. NICHOLSON. It keeps their minds on something except deviltry, I guess.

Mr. SHAW. I am chairman of the youth employment commission youth council and I spent 2 years now digging into that problem. We do not worry about the boy that is going on to college, to law school and medical school; we do not worry about the boy that is going to become a plumber, an electrician, or a carpenter. We are worried about a great group, and it is a very big group, who are never going to attain to that vocational status, who are going to be what — short-order cooks, stock boys, elevator boys, what can we do for them. That is a problem that I am going to talk about this afternoon with one of the commissioners. It is a big group.

Most people think that all boys and girls fall into two categories. Either they go through high school and perhaps on to college or else they qualify for vocational education. Now, the standards of vocational education today thanks in large measure to labor unions, are just about as high as the standards for academic work. But both of those categories leave this other big group, and that is the group that is furnishing a large number of delinquents. Now, the employers do not like them. The labor unions do not like them, nobody likes them.

I had luncheon not so long ago with a group of employers to talk about this person. They said: "We don't want to have anything to do with them. They have no sense of responsibility, no sense of time, nothing. Why do you want me to take them on?"

Now that is a very serious problem, and I am not prepared to come up with any solution to that problem.

Mr. NICHOLSON. Your organization wants the National Government to go into the States and establish schools so that the probation officers who are going to be connected with these cases get their education, is that it?

Mr. SHAW. Yes, sir. We want the probation officer and the parole officer to be professionally adequately trained. That is what we are shooting for and we want him to be a high-grade kind of individual, and our thought is if we can get enough of those we can save the taxpayer expenses in juvenile institutions and adult institutions.

Mr. NICHOLSON. Well, of course, lots of people think that these things ought to be done near the local level as possible.

Mr. SHAW. I agree.

Mr. NICHOLSON. In the first place, they want to see whether or not the family life is there, whether the children obey the parents, whether they do not, and then they get into the school system, because these children show those signs when they are 4 or 5 years old.

Mr. SHAW. That is right.

Mr. NICHOLSON. Maybe sooner than that.

Mr. SHAW. That is right.

Mr. NICHOLSON. Then they go to school and instead of the kind of correction we received, a slap with a strap or a ruler or something, they are not allowed to discipline them that way. Then of course when they are out of school there is nobody to look out for them but themselves.

Mr. SHAW. Yes.

Mrs. GREEN. Will the gentleman yield?

Mr. NICHOLSON. They have not had any restraints that would maybe change the whole course of their life. Yes.

Mrs. GREEN. You are not suggesting that the whole problem of juvenile delinquency could be solved if every delinquent got a slap or a shaking up at the proper moment?

Mr. NICHOLSON. I certainly do not but I know in a great many cases a slap helps out. I will give you an illustration if I may, Mr. Chairman.

Mr. ELLIOTT. You certainly may.

Mr. NICHOLSON. My sister was a schoolteacher and she took the place of a lady that the boys used to bat around, and it was kind of tough. So she went teaching school when she was 19 years old. The first kid that started it, she took every button off him shaking him. She did not have any more trouble. The rest of the kids realized that they had somebody there that was going to make them mind.

Mr. SHAW. Let me introduce you verbally to a boy who I was dealing with not so long ago. He was 13 years of age. His father had beaten him routinely every single day for about 1 year with the result that he embarked on a serious career of delinquency.

Mr. NICHOLSON. I do not blame him. The trouble was not with the boy there; the trouble was with his father.

Mr. SHAW. Yes. The father was a chronic alcoholic.

Mr. NICHOLSON. He was chronic something or he would not be beating the boy every day.

Mr. SHAW. That is what you run up against.

Now, I agree if you are dealing with a 6-, 7- or 8-year-old boy in a sound family setting it is a good plan to give him a spanking once in a while, it is good, because he knows that his father loves him. Now, the spanking is disagreeable, but he has no doubt. But we run into so many cases that the spankings are given not because the father loves the boy but because he hates the boy. Then we run into the problem of corporal punishment in training schools. I am strongly against it because he who beats up a boy in a training school, and it is frequently a question of beating up, not corporal punishment, the boy knows that that man does not like him, and the effect is totally different. Now I do not think spanking in a well-organized family is a solution to every problem, the less spanking there is the better, but occasionally it is a very desirable thing to do in a well-organized family. But in a training school; no. And where the family is disorganized and the father does not know what to do to deal with this youngster and he just wallops him, I am against it.

Mr. NICHOLSON. I think most everybody is.

Mr. SHAW. Yes.

Mr. NICHOLSON. Thank you, Mr. Chairman.

Mrs. GREEN. I had one other question, if I may take the time.

Mr. ELLIOTT. Mrs. Green.

Mrs. GREEN. I would like to have you comment on one other thing, that is, the difference between the two bills: one carries a matching fund under training of personnel and one does not. Would you care to comment on that?

Mr. SHAW. One requires matching by the State in training of personnel. Here, I am talking just off the cuff, in my own personal opinion. I would rather favor matching by the State.

Mrs. GREEN. Now there is matching in some parts of the bill. But on the training of personnel, the reason for one of the bills — which happens to be mine — not requiring the matching is the feeling that if you have certain schools, that will train personnel, those people will not stay within the State.

Mr. SHAW. Yes.

Mrs. GREEN. And therefore it would be more of a Federal responsibility.

Mr. SHAW. I see your point.

Mrs. GREEN. Because if you set up a school, for instance, in New York, for training of personnel, there is nothing that would indicate that those people, with our dearth of trained people, will stay in New York.

Mr. SHAW. They probably will not. At least a percentage of

them will not. I see your point there. I do not think in my opinion on that — I am always in favor of getting the State to do as much matching as possible.

Mrs. GREEN. I agree.

Mr. SHAW. I am talking about in principle.

Mrs. GREEN. Matching is required for the grants for the co-ordination of the plan within the States.

Mr. SHAW. I am not taking into consideration the important point that you set forth. I agree that is an important point.

Mr. ELLIOTT. Mr. Shaw, your testimony has been most helpful and we thank you very much.

Mr. SHAW. Thank you very much, Mr. Chairman.

[. . . . .]

TUESDAY, MAY 21, 1957
Washington, D.C.

THE SUBCOMMITTEE MET at 10 a. m., in room 429, the Old House Office Building, Hon. Carl Elliott (chairman of the subcommittee) presiding.

Mr. ELLIOTT. The Subcommittee on Special Education of the Committee on Education and Labor of the United States House of Representatives will be in order.

Our witnesses today are Judge Eugene V. Bailey, Mr. Clarence W. Boebel, and Mr. Jacob W. Zang.

In our audience today we have Mr. Kenneth Rose of Bryn Athyn, Pa., and with him there is a group of seniors from his high school. They are from the district represented by the gentleman from Pennsylvania, Mr. McConnell, who is the ranking member on the minority side of this committee.

Our first witness today, and one I am very happy to welcome to the committee, is an old and long-time friend and associate and classmate of mine, the Hon. Eugene V. Bailey, a judge of the juvenile and domestic relations court of Tuscaloosa County, Ala.

He appears here for himself and for his county and for the people interested in the problems of youth throughout his area.

Judge Bailey was invited here primarily because he has very excellent knowledge and experience in the field of dealing with juvenile delinquents from the rural areas of his county, which I think is fairly representative of the southern part of the country at least.

We are happy to have you, Judge Bailey, and we have your statement which has been made available to all concerned, and with what I have said as a background you may proceed in any manner you see fit.

Statement of Judge Eugene V. Bailey

Judge BAILEY. My name is Eugene V. Bailey and I am judge of the juvenile and domestic relations court of Tuscaloosa County, Ala.

Mr. Chairman, I am very grateful and flattered in being invited to come before your committee. I assume that in being here I represent a locality, a society, and a type of community which perhaps has not had a vast number of representatives testifying before this committee. To use a trite political expression, I think we could aptly say that I come from a situation close to the grass-roots of the delinquency problem as it exists in a semirural county in the Deep South. It is my assumption that a great portion of your testimony has come from authorities in the large cities as well as well-known authorities in education and institutions directly associated with or related to the field of juvenile delinquency or child problems. My observation and analysis of these things are based on my experience as judge of the juvenile court in a county of 100,000 population which is equally divided between the city of Tuscaloosa and the county of Tuscaloosa, Ala.

We are, naturally, interested in the matter of juvenile delinquency as it relates to rural or country life and what, if any, progressive manifestations are being exhibited by our rural society and its children in this connection. In its earlier history in my section of the United States the matter which, for the lack of a better title, is known as juvenile delinquency, was almost nonexistent. This, I think, was due to a number of reasons which I shall discuss briefly. One of the outstanding factors was the traditional family structure in which the father and husband was head of the house as well as the supreme authority. In an average family the father did not assume the supervision of every minor detail of family activity or discipline, but the father was the supreme authority in the family. In a final decision of a matter his word was the law. The pursuit of his occupation, his social life, his entertainment, and his religion was confined to his family and the surrounding community not more than 3 or 4 miles away. There was a constant, close, harmonious association in the family circle.

By our present standards, life may have been somewhat slow and perhaps a little dull. It was, however, the life the family knew and enjoyed and children were contented and happy. Their economical, social, and psychological needs were met in the home. I think we all know that, more than ever today, one of the surest immunities to juvenile unrest and delinquency is to be privileged to live out in the open with plenty of space, plenty of trees, growing crops, and a blue sky overhead surrounded with good clean, fresh air flavored with the smell of honeysuckle. In the present age of our society this is not available to every child. It is not available to every adult. Even in the minds of us country boys, now too long removed, it only exists in a nostalgic recollection. I recall in the days of my own youth that teenage boys were imbued with a heritage derived from many generations of forefathers which permitted him the minor deviation of "slipping" one of his neighbor's watermelons and a few peaches, pears, and plums, but stealing a bicycle, horse, money, merchandise, or things of value was as far from his mind as the end of the world.

The social age in which we now live has made a change in things in the nearby rural areas. The great network of farm-to-market, paved roads, and the ever-increasing prevalence of automobiles has made a different culture. Every family, regardless of economic circumstances, has some type of car. The advent of the various means of communication, such as the daily newspapers, the radio, and the television has brought reform to the rural life as well as the ancient customs and traditions of family life. The city is now the center of entertainment, and social activity. The old-fashioned community general merchandise store has disappeared. Our county is the second largest in area in Alabama. The city can be reached by automobile within 30 minutes from any community in the county. Actually, the rural area is now not much more than a figure of speech.

The great economic change in our way of life, the great movement of industry into the South, and the great trend toward mass operation in agriculture has rapidly diminished the number of citizens who rely on small farms for livelihood. These circumstances are draining away the people who live on small farms and radically changing the whole economic and social structure of their lives. This is occurring in two very well defined categories. One is the great movement of the more impoverished rural citizenry into the suburban and slum areas of the city. These people are lured by visions of economic successes. Cash rather than crops and the glitter of city life as against the drab rural life poses as economic and social progress. The children in these families living in deteriorated and fringe areas of the city create one of the greatest juvenile problems. Families in the other principal category, particularly the offspring, continue to live in the country and while the land lies idle or in pasture they commute, over paved roads, to the industrial plants in the city or to business and professional pursuits.

This has brought a substantial change in the juvenile society on the rural areas. Eleven years ago when I became judge of the juvenile court, delinquency was almost unknown in the rural areas. In the last 12 months, 30 percent of the 255 referrals in my court for delinquency were rural cases. The disturbing thing is that a disproportionate increase is being manifested in the rural areas. As I stated earlier, our population is divided on a 50–50 basis between the city of Tuscaloosa and the county of Tuscaloosa. The rural areas are increasingly taking on the social aspects of the urban society. This, in my judgment, will be manifested in the social behavior of the rural children. The father being away from home a major portion of his time in pursuit of his occupation, and the children going to town in pursuit of entertainment, has broken down the closely knitted family life.

Of course, this does not give a picture of the statewide situation in Alabama in connection with rural communities. This only applies to a limited number of counties in the State which have the largest cities. There are only 4 counties out of the 67 counties which have separate juvenile and domestic relations courts. In 60 counties in the State the juvenile and domestic relations cases are handled by the probate court. In three counties these matters are handled by misdemeanor courts having criminal and civil dockets as well. My court is one of these three. The probate judge is the head of the county government and is burdened with financial affairs of the county, roads, buildings, machinery, bridges, and all other county governmental functions. He presides over the commissioners court or the board of revenue which is the agency that handles the funds of the county. By the very nature of things, he is a very busy man. The qualifications for probate judge do not require any legal training or training in social problems which, of course, includes juvenile delinquency. About 55 of our counties are agricultural communities. The county seat is the principal town. It is the focal point for social, political, and economical activity. Not only is there no separate court to deal with delinquency of children but there is no probation staff, there are no facilities for handling juvenile offenders, and there is no county employed agency for making prehearing investigations. The judge has no information in advance of the hearing.

As the result thereof he is not familiar with the background of the family's social, intellectual, or economical circumstances. He has no personnel, trained in fields of social work, attached to his court. He has no supervisory authority for his probationers after hearings. What investigation and reporting, if any, as well as post-hearing supervision, must be delegated to an agency of the State department of public welfare which at most only affords one worker in the rural counties who is already pressed by a heavy load of public assistance, neglected and dependent cases as well as adoptions and miscellaneous responsibility. The State welfare department has less than 10 percent of its personnel with educational qualifications required for probation officers. As a result of this we find that in the State of Alabama during the year of 1955, 24 of the 62 counties not having a probation staff sent from one-sixth to two-thirds of their juvenile referrals directly to the State training school without benefit of probation services. Thirteen counties sent from 50 percent to as high as 100 percent of their referrals to the State training school without benefit of probation services.

In many of these counties there are varied types of economics. Some of the counties are entirely agricultural, but are generally on mass-production basis with much of the work being performed on day wage basis. Other counties have a diversified economy. Lumbering, pulpwood, textile milling, concrete production and other industries are mingled with agriculture. This, of course, brings about many mill villages, mining camps, sawmill communities and other groups of settlements of low-paid industrial workers who, as a general rule, have large families. This in recent years has tended to produce an increasing number of juvenile referrals in these rural counties.

The rural counties are seriously in need of trained personnel, for family counseling, for social investigation, for prehearing reporting, and for posthearing supervision for children placed on probation. It is a sad thing indeed when almost all of the children referred to the family court in any country are promptly committed to the State training school without even an opportunity of adjustment and rehabilitation in his own community. The fact is that the poor economic circumstances, inadequate living standards, and the broken and disturbed homes are now beginning to show themselves in a proportionate ratio to that of urban society. Juvenile delinquency is definitely and progressively becoming a matter of concern to the rural counties and the establishment of adequate facilities to deal with the problems is an inevitable thing of the future. Our society throughout the State is in desperate need of a general overhauling of its family court system. It is my judgment that the rural counties are now experiencing as great a need for trained personnel to deal with its social problems as the urban counties are. The tensions, economic pressures and social disruptions which have heretofore prevailed in our urban life are rapidly extending into rural society and as a result of this the attendant social problems are beginning to show. The bills before the House of Representatives, in my judgment, provide an answer to the desperate need, not only in Alabama but throughout the Nation. There is a destitution in the field of qualified social workers in Alabama. Qualified personnel is urgently needed throughout the State and is not available. Practically every social agency authorized to hire qualified personnel has a vacancy and in some instances several vacancies. We are simply failing to provide training for our young people who are interested in the field of social work. We are not able to attract them under the prevailing circumstances.

The truth of the matter is that we have not made the necessary provisions in our institutions of learning to make social work training available to our interested students. There are many different phases of planning which must be done in order to effect some control of this rapidly increasing delinquency problem. Without a doubt the greatest of them all is the training of personnel for work in the field of delinquency control. The provisions of these bills which provide grants to institutions for training personnel in this field is absolutely essential to the ultimate success of the program to combat and control delinquency. The University of Alabama is located in my home county. There are a wealth of students enrolled in the university who are very much interested in this work. We use a number of these students, who are majoring in sociology, for voluntary workers in our social investigations for our court. Some of the best work, and the best reports I have ever seen have come from these students. There is, however, no accredited school of social work in the State. It is my judgment that the greatest accomplishment that could come from grant-in-aid money would be to provide a school of social work in the State and in addition thereto provide some compensation for in-service training for these students and permit them to be attached to juvenile courts. They could work while learning and the courts would be wonderfully benefited. This, I believe, is a vital factor.

Only three counties in the State have detention facilities. The other 64 use the county jail for detaining children. In many of them, segregation of juveniles from adults is very difficult. The number of counties having separate court facilities for juvenile hearings is very limited.

Indifference, both public and private, has always been a factor in the slow progress which we have experienced. Only recently have people in any sizable numbers begun to show real concern about the problem. We have been prone to treat the matter as though it did not really exist or if it did exist, if you would ignore it, it would go away. This has also been more or less true in political circles at all levels. As far as I know, there has been no important legislation, with state-wide application relative to juvenile matters in the last quarter of a century. I am afraid that we have been prone to treat it more as a tolerated nuisance than as a reality. One can discuss it in a group of average citizens numbering a hundred and receive a hundred different versions as to causes of delinquency and an equal number of remedies for the cure. The public is oblivious to the reality of the thing and generally consider recognized methods of child rehabilitation as coddling.

It is surprising how many people in high places that agree with them.

I am told that Alabama ranks seventh in the Nation in the number of its prison population. I am told further that over 50 percent of our prison population is 25 years of age or under and that the trend toward youth is rapidly increasing. It is alarming to study the records of automobile thefts in our county; 70 to 80 percent of these cars are being taken by teen-age boys. An alarming number are taken by adolescent children.

Millions are spent annually on adult convicts, but as yet my State and most of her sister States have appropriated trivial sums for juvenile control. Our State training schools are so overrun with children that it is necessary to keep boys 14 and 15 years of age in jail for as long as 9 weeks. There is a waiting list at our girls' training school. It takes from 3 to 6 months to get a girl admitted. Often, by the time she can be taken, the purpose has been defeated by pregnancy or a child marriage. It can all be summed up by saying the States have failed to meet this issue and it has now become a real threat to our national social order. The reason always advanced is inability to pay for the program prescribed by learned authorities on the subject. This being the case, our greatest hope is the enactment of a bill such as is now before the Congress to provide some financial assistance to the States to combat this growing menace before we are so far in that it will take a generation to dig out.

Ultimately bigger and better institutions will have to be provided in Alabama. We are paroling our juveniles now in 9 to 12 months, whereas, formerly they stayed twice that long. This is being done to make room for those being held in jail. This defeats a rehabilitation plan, particularly in view of the fact there is little or no aftercare.

It is my judgment that a qualified probation officer working with the offender and his family before, during, and after the court hearing can accomplish more in control of juvenile delinquency than 10 prosecuting attorneys can accomplish.

No one knows all the causes or cures for delinquency. In our court, we have made some deductions which I believe are fundamental. We have found that delinquency stems from maladjustment in the family circle. It may be physical, psychological, financial or one of a hundred other kinds of disruptions but is always there. We have found that the majority are starved for love and recognition as individuals. Most of them respond to a trained probation officer. We have found delinquency quitting the slums and moving into fashionable residential areas, where the economic rat race for security and prominence upsets the orderly processes of the family circle. The high standard of living and the attending cost plus the hysterical urge to keep up with the Joneses has changed family values which directly affects the children. One instance I think of is the prevalent feeling among high-school boys that they are unsuitable for girls unless they have a car. This thing alone leads to thousands of automobile thefts.

Before we had a probation officer, the number of repeaters ran very high in my court. Since we hired a probation officer, our repeaters have been reduced to about 10 percent. Since we can no longer rely on the proper cooperation of parents in juvenile cases, the Nation must now look to machinery to deal with and appeal to the child himself, in spite of his parents. Money to train and pay for personnel to adequately staff the courts and other agencies dealing with the subject is our immediate and desperate need.

I hope Congress will pass a bill in this session. I hope the Congress will not skimp on the money necessary to hobble this, greatest of American, social problem. To do so would be to extend the type of thinking so long prevalent in the States — that is, that juvenile delinquency is only kid stuff — and of little concern.

Money to aid the States in research is equally important.

Mr. ELLIOTT. Thank you, Judge Bailey. This is a very excellent statement, I think, on the rural aspects of this problem, particularly in areas where, as you pointed out, and it is true in Tuscaloosa, the population is about 50–50 as between the principal town in the county and the county itself.

I was surprised to learn from your statement on page 12 that

since we hired a probation officer our repeaters have been reduced to about 10 percent.

Then you state:

Before we had a probation officer the number of repeaters ran very high in my court.

You have seen from your own experience, evidently illustrated there in Tuscaloosa, Ala., the great advantage and benefit to be derived from probation services. Could you elaborate just a little on that, Judge Bailey?

Judge BAILEY. Mr. Elliott, before we had our probation officer a major portion of our delinquency was by boys committing recurring acts. It was like rolling a snowball, picking up new ones all the way around. Since we got Mr. Shofner with us, and I think he is unusually qualified in every respect, our repeaters have been very largely eliminated. We are much more concerned now with the new ones that come in rather than those we already have, because his work has reduced the inclination on the part of those who already have been to the court to get back into delinquent acts in violation of the law again.

Mr. ELLIOTT. So you would say one of the really great needs in this field is many more trained probation officers, would you not?

Judge BAILEY. Definitely. So far as I am personally concerned that is the biggest need.

Mr. ELLIOTT. How many probation people would it take, Judge, to adequately man a court such as you have? What would be your judgment? Can one person do it? I believe you said you had 255 referrals last year?

Judge BAILEY. Yes, 255 referrals in a 12-month period.

We had what they referred to as a walk-through survey made by an agent of the National Probation Parole Association and according to their standards we should have 5, and we should have 5 percent of the police department trained in juvenile work, which of course we do not have. We have none.

I think five would be mighty fine, but if we had one more man and one woman we certainly would be in fine shape as compared to what we have now.

Mr. ELLIOTT. Did I understand you to say that the University of Alabama does not have an accredited school for social workers?

Judge BAILEY. That is correct, there is not an accredited social workers school in the State. Most of our people, those I know who pursue this on into postgraduate work, as a general rule go down to Tulane University. That is the nearest they have so far as I know.

What other States have accredited schools I do not know, Mr. Elliott.

Mr. ELLIOTT. Somebody came before this committee since we started these hearings who said that many scholarships in this field were going begging. Do you know of any scholarships in that shape?

Judge BAILEY. I really do not know about that. I have not taken the opportunity to hear whether that is true or not in our State, but I feel certain that we do have a good many students who would pursue it but are not enthused enough to go on down to another State because that entails a lot of additional expense and being away from home and those things which deter them. By the time students are ready to graduate they are thinking of making a living, and if it entails a lot of additional trouble and expense they get sidetracked off to making a living and that is the end of that.

Mr. ELLIOTT. Judge, I wonder if you ever thought about the proposition that most of our living today is being constantly gauged to the urban outlook rather than to the rural outlook which I knew 35 or 40 years ago. Every time we take some action in this country now we talk about its contributing to the efficiency of Government and reducing the budget and all that sort of thing, and we abolish post offices that have stood 100 years in these little rural communities and we take away that standard of stability which is so important.

The reports I see on the churches are that the rural churches are being closed down. We give no benefits that I know of to encourage rural living today as it has been known in years gone by. We do not even allow a man a tax exemption for driving his automobile from his rural home 30 or 40 miles into a job in the city, but instead we encourage him to tear himself loose from his rural moorings and to move into the cities. I think that tendency is going on all over the country. I know it is throughout the South.

I am glad to hear you mention the fact that it is in these areas that the people move into these days, seeking employment and other things, where you have the greatest influx of people into the city which causes the greater problems of juvenile delinquency.

Is it your idea that the sudden change from the rural environment to the city environment and the sudden new competitive atmosphere in which the people live, the adjustment they are trying to make, and the more time-consuming work they have to perform than they did when they lived in rural areas and did things which fit into that picture, which help bring about this problem that you speak of pertaining to the rural aspects of this problem?

Judge BAILEY. That is very true. To put it in a simple country-boy statement, all the country folks are trying more and more to live like city folks. The country community atmosphere has disappeared. It has gone to town. There is no community activity in the way it used to be.

As I said before, nearly everybody has gone to town to work, and the result is that the family now, instead of being of very closely knit family life that it was out in the farm of yesteryear, is scattered just like townfolks. We all know townfolks are scattered because in nearly every pursuit in our economy now folks work during the day and most of them are then called on to go out a great deal of the time at night for social, civic, church meetings, and so forth; so the family does not live at home any more. They sort of live at home in shifts, or else they sleep there.

The kind of family life that used to prevail when we were both young and living out in the country just does not prevail any more.

You can leap into your machine and be in town in 15 or 20 minutes and enjoy the city entertainment, and the type of rather crude and what I think was rather wholesome entertainment out in the country is nonexistent. What you get in scattered churches is about what is left of social life.

As strange as it might seem, many of those people are driving into the city to go to church.

The thing that impresses me, and as you know, when we were young out in the country if we had gotten into trouble with the law our father would have had trouble sleeping all night so he could get down to see the judge at the crack of dawn, and there would be an understanding about the matter as soon as they could possibly get together.

Nowadays in my section I have the fathers calling in before breakfast and saying: "I have to work today but I will send my boy in. I hope you can do something with him. I don't seem to be able to do anything with him."

That is the biggest factor that is involved in this whole thing. I think every person that knows something about juvenile work in the whole Nation will agree with that.

Mr. ELLIOTT. Judge, we read these articles by these people who profess to give advice about juvenile delinquency, and I read one the other day which stated that unless we could restore this closely knit family relationship that we knew that our problems in the field of juvenile delinquency would be compounded.

However, how on earth in the midst of the things you mention are we going to be able to restore as a society and how are we going to be able to bring about again this closely knit family unit when everybody has an automobile and is going in a half dozen different directions, as you put it, and people are using their homes as a place to sleep and to live there in shifts, as you said?

It seems to me we will have a great difficulty in restoring that closely knit family unit.

When I grew up I went to work with my father and we worked in the fields all day. We ate breakfast together and we worked to lunchtime and ate lunch together, and we worked throughout the afternoon and at night we ate supper together, and I had a lot of association with him because we worked in a common endeavor and a common enterprise.

I know a large number of families today, outside of the few remaining rural families today, which have that opportunity for association and the closely knit lives we speak of, and at which time we did not have much juvenile delinquency.

Is there any opportunity in modern America to restore that kind of living, in your judgment?

Judge BAILEY. I hate to answer a question that sounds so bad, but I do not think so. I think this situation is here to stay, delinquency is here to stay, and I think parents are not going to be of any more help than they are now, and I think we will have to set up machinery to deal directly with the child.

When a man says, "I have to work today but I will send my boy in and I hope you really give him a going over," you have a situation there that if it remains you will have him sent in as long as there are people, and I believe, as much as I hate to say so, somebody will have to supply the association and the companionship and the love and affection and respect and trust that they are not getting in the family circle.

That certainly is so in my section. I am not an educated man academically in this field but I have looked a lot of them over in the last 11 years, and the greatest factor I find, of course, whether it is rural, city, or whatever it is, is that a child for one reason or another has lost his standing in the family as an individual.

It may not be known to him personally, and his parents probably are the last people to ever find out, but a child wants to be recognized as an individual.

I used to have a little story I told in my speeches. When my boy was little I went somewhere so much at night that he asked his mother who that fat man was that left about sunrise every morning. That is the only time he ever saw his father.

That is really almost literally prevailing in millions of families.

That is just human. If a fellow doesn't know his "old man" he doesn't think much of him. How could he? He doesn't know one way or the other.

Many of us are being reduced to a class of Chester A. Rileys, anyway. We just bring home the bacon and otherwise do not contribute much. If we do not contribute anything we will not get much.

That is the biggest problem, and I think this: I am not advocating it but it is here to stay. If we do not set up some machinery to deal with the child directly and supply some of these things that he cannot wheedle out of his father and mother, we will have this situation.

The average age in the Alabama Penitentiary now is about 23 years, and old Frank Lee down there predicts by 1970 the average age will be about 19 or 18 years, somewhere along in there.

I have kids down there all the time that go on these red-hot carlots with flags flying in the breeze and they use the cars 2 or 3 hours and put them back. When I talk to them naturally I will ask the question, "Why?" and I never heard that question answered adequately yet. They will say, "How are you going to get a girl without a car?" They are 13 or 14 years old. They cannot even drive legally in Alabama until they are 16. Of course we have a lot of wealthy people down there that buy their children cars when they are 13 or 14 years old, anyhow.

He says, "You cannot get a girl without a car." He feels subdued and discriminated against if he cannot go see his girl in a car. He is 13 or 14 years old and he feels he must have a car to go see his girl. Sometimes that urge is so irresistible that he borrows one from old Honest John, and brings it back after his date. We have had 10 or 12 cases like that.

Mr. ELLIOTT. You have had 10 or 12 cases like that?

Judge BAILEY. Yes. One boy did it regularly every time he went to see his girl for 8 or 9 weeks until they caught up with him. And they did not catch him taking it then; they caught him putting it back.

I think if our fathers had caught us taking one of the neighbor's A models there would have been a very serious conference between the neighbor and our fathers. But these things happen and parents come in and sit down with me, and of course they are always friendly as a general rule and I am friendly with them, but the parents are prone to say, "Judge, I can't understand it. This boy never indicated to me he would do a thing like this. I think you ought to talk to him."

I say, "Have you ever talked to him?"

They will say, "No; I haven't yet, but I hope you will give him a good talking to."

That sentiment is one of the most damaging things we have. I had a man call me and ask me to advise with his boy because, as he put it, he had lost control of him. When I asked how old the boy was, he said seven. He had lost control of his seven-year-old boy and wanted me to advise the boy to pay attention to his father.

The great factor involved here is not with the kids themselves any more but with the parents. Parents just don't have time any more. They like to have good children and they always believe they really have, but they always tell me when these things happen that it amazes them, and if they had time they would have sort of supervised that boy a little better, but they never had time. They are engaged in the process of making a living and many urgent things like taking care of their civic responsibilities, community projects, and so forth, and 2 or 3 times a week going to the church, so that they just don't have time.

To make a little humorous suggestion, you know how we are always talking about all the automatic gadgets we have now. Well, I am advocating if somebody can come up with an automatic child raiser, that would be the most wonderful thing society could have.

Mr. ELLIOTT. Sort of a child-raising Univac, I guess?

Judge BAILEY. That is right; push a button and it will take care of the child for 18 hours. The child would be dressed and fed and loved ——

Mr. ELLIOTT. And put to bed.

Judge BAILEY. And put to bed and admonished and taught and all of that.

Mr. ELLIOTT. Judge, what you are saying is that in this age in which we live our society will have to recognize, and not only recognize but grapple with the solution of some of these problems that manifest themselves as what we call juvenile delinquency.

Judge BAILEY. That is right.

Mr. ELLIOTT. And you think these bills or some modification of the bills before the committee might help in getting this train of circumstances started. I refer now to research, and I refer to the training, through scholarships and otherwise, of people to do the work and to lead the way; and I refer to demonstrations of projects in communities that have done a good job.

You think those things, modestly proposed by this bill, might be something that would help us find our bearings, so to speak, in this difficult field?

Judge BAILEY. Of course, naturally we would like to have the States provide their needs, whatever the need is. That is always the first premise in any matter that involves social problems, financing and all of that. But the States are not meeting the need; certainly the States I know about are not. There are many good reasons why they are not, of course, which I do not propose to discuss because I do not know, but the fact remains they are not meeting the need. Therefore, the problem is very rapidly becoming very serious. The States are not meeting the need and the reason advanced is always money; that they just are not able.

The fact that the States do not have the money or are not spending the money, even assuming they are not doing their duty, is not going to change the fact that this great wave of antisocial activity is advancing on the whole Nation and if somebody does not do something about it there will be a terrible situation by the time these kids are able to have children of their own.

That is the reason why I certainly advocate the Federal Government participating in it, because whether the States should or should not, the States are not doing it, and these people belong to all of us, you know, and somebody has to do it and it has to be done pretty soon.

I guess I sound a little more alarming than the average man on the street, but the reason is I know more about it than the average man on the street.

Mr. ELLIOTT. You are in daily contact with the situation.

Judge BAILEY. That is right.

Mr. ELLIOTT. Judge, one of the troubles we have, of course, is the fact that the Federal Government has usurped or taken over the sources of revenue to such an extent that there is not a great deal left in these States when you get past the proposition of the sales taxes and income taxes, tobacco taxes, gasoline taxes, and all these fields in which the State has already levied. It is getting hard to find a place to get the money to do the things we ought to do. Even if we want to do them, yet there is a limit to what we can do.

Let me ask you about this problem. Do you have a good many kids coming into your jurisdiction and committing offenses against the law that are from other States and areas? Somebody made the point here in testifying a day or two ago that the situation had gotten so bad that California runs a train across the country and lets off these children when they get to their homes. Do you have much, shall we call it inmigration or outmigration of juvenile offenders in the jurisdiction of your court?

Judge BAILEY. We have, I think, our proportionate share, but our city being only a 50,000 population city, these children who are traveling don't stop with us much, they go on to Birmingham with a half million population. We do have a number of them. We have quite a few boys that come through our county and take automobiles and continue on their way. And of course we have our proportionate share of those we pick up who have left their homes in other places and we discover them in our town and send them back. We, I guess, run probably, combined between the 2 types I have just mentioned, between 35 and 40 a year. We send quite a number back that are intercepted in our county or stop off in town.

One of our great problems about stealing vehicles is our boys decide to run away from an unhappy home, and they find a confederate who is in similar circumstances, and they steal somebody's car, generally the next door neighbor's whom they know very well, and they run away from home. They will go as long as the thing will run, and when it stops they usually flag a ride back home or get picked up by the police. You do have quite a number of those.

Mr. ELLIOTT. Judge, do you think the fact we do not have detention homes to keep these youthful offenders in is a real drawback to your rendering justice in these cases?

Judge BAILEY. Yes, I do. Of course the detention home is a remedy; it is not in my judgment a preventive, but a remedy. It is one of the facilities you would use in treating rather than in preventing. But the absence of a detention home is very serious and it does contribute to the affirmative side of it very definitely. I do not think you help the future personality or attitude or conduct of any child by incarcerating him in a dirty, dilapidated jailhouse, and sometimes that is necessary. As a matter of fact, it is becoming increasingly necessary.

Mr. ELLIOTT. Jails are being used more and more for that purpose in these days?

Judge BAILEY. That is right. A jail is not a place to advance culture, and I don't see how they could be put in those places without damage. One of our boys who is a pronounced psychological case might pick up some steam while he is in there with some of the boys who have had a lot of experience.

Mr. ELLIOTT. The gentlewoman from Oregon, Mrs. Green.

Mrs. GREEN. I think you have covered the subject pretty well. Judge Bailey, could you make some general observations about parents in this connection? Do you think the parents of today love their children any less than in previous years?

Judge BAILEY. That is a difficult question. I think parents

love their children, but I think they do not have the same almost acute concern about them every hour of the day that they did when I was 5 years old. Out in the country where I lived, if I had been missing at the age of 12, we will say, and unaccounted for for 3 or 4 hours, it would have prompted a community-wide search. I find kids today that are missing for 24 and even 36 hours without the family getting too concerned.

Mrs. GREEN. Is that not the exception, though? You do not think all or most parents are that indifferent, do you?

Judge BAILEY. Yes, I think that is the exception. I think the families of delinquent children are still, fortunately, the exception in society.

Mrs. GREEN. When I think back over the years when we had sweatshops and child labor and nobody was concerned about it, it seems to me that the parents of today are far more concerned about the children and are trying to make sure they have the best possible kind of environment.

Judge BAILEY. I agree with that. But I think the parents are primarily concerned with economic security. In fact, I think most of us are bordering on hysteria on that point, and I think that in itself is contributing to a loss of association with the children which puts them on their own more or less at a very early age.

Mr. NICHOLSON. Will you yield? I have to leave because somebody wants to see me very badly.

Mrs. GREEN. Certainly.

Mr. NICHOLSON. All through the time I was going to school, I do not remember any parents finding fault with the teachers because they gave the kids a licking. I got plenty myself and I ex- pected it if I got caught. But today in my State they have laws that teachers cannot touch children at all. We had a case in the superior court not long ago because one of the teachers slapped this boy or girl. Now the school committees are getting complaints all the time in my State about the treatment that the children are getting from the teachers. We have laws the teachers cannot lay hands on the children, and the children get wise to it in primary grades when they are 6 years old.

Do you not think if teachers were allowed to punish these chil- dren it would do some good?

Judge BAILEY. Mr. Nicholson, we have a concept in Alabama that is right in line with that, and we still have the law on the books in Alabama that the teacher can punish as long as it is not cruel and inhuman. It is not resorted to a great deal because in many cases in our State the parents gets involved. If a teacher whacks a child a few times, the parents go up and whack the teacher, and for that reason it does not work so good. When I was a youngster and when Mr. Elliott was a youngster, the rule was if we got a licking at school we got another one at home.

MR. NICHOLSON. That was the rule in my day.

Judge BAILEY. I think that would cure a lot of school delinquency, but now the parents will go back with the child and transfer the licking to the teacher instead of to the boy when he gets home.

Mr. NICHOLSON. About probation officers, do you have 2 probation officers, 1 for adults and 1 for children, or do you handle the children yourself?

Judge BAILEY. I only handle children's cases. I do not handle adults that are on probation. We have a State probation system that furnishes a probation officer for adults. We have one now that we have had for a year, in fact a year the 15th of April, for children. Of course you can readily understand with 255 referrals in a year, one man, if he can get to each one once, he is doing pretty good.

Mr. NICHOLSON. One thing that enters into it is whether he is merely trying to hold his job or whether he has a way with children so that they will think twice before they do it again. You cannot get for $2,500 a year a man of the caliber that is needed. I think a great deal of our trouble is because we do not spend enough money on the right kind of probation officers. Most normal children ought not ever to get into court, whether it is on an automobile violation or anything else, if it is impressed on them they are an enemy of society if they take a car, as you say they are doing, and are caught bringing it back.

This bill to me seems to smack of getting more people into the Federal Government doing a job that in the first place should start at home, and if it does not it should start in the village or in the State before it gets to the Federal Government. If it gets to the Federal Government, it will be just a job — no love and affection or anything.

Judge BAILEY. I certainly hope we do not ever have that type. I think the qualifications for a probation officer for children is 85 or 90 percent native instinct and inclination and about 10 percent education.

Mr. NICHOLSON. These social workers may not be good probation officers — the ones that go around to see that the family is bringing up the children right, things like that. They have a feeling of distrust for those people. They are not neighbors and friends. Perhaps if we could put it on a neighborhood basis we could do more.

Judge BAILEY. I see your point. I certainly would not ever want an arrangement where the Federal Government or the State or anybody else just assigned people who were interested in a job and nothing else.

Mrs. GREEN. I would like to ask both of you gentlemen if you can show me any place in either of these bills where that could be done?

Mr. NICHOLSON. No, except as I understand the bill we are asking the Federal Government to appropriate a certain amount of money.

Mrs. GREEN. Yes, but in no case do we envision sending a social worker to the States. The money is for research and training. These people will return to the States after their training.

Mr. NICHOLSON. Our experience with aid to dependent children and old-age assistance and things like that is that the Federal Government makes rules and regulations we have to live up to, otherwise we do not get Federal aid.

Mrs. GREEN. You are not opposed to the aid to dependent children, are you?

Mr. NICHOLSON. Of course not; I am very much for it; but I think it can be done locally better than the Federal Government making rules and regulations about how long you have to be a social worker before you can take an examination to be one of these visitors.

Mrs. GREEN. Is that in the Federal law?

Mr. NICHOLSON. It is in the rules and regulations of the Department, because I went to the department of public welfare in Boston years ago when the Federal Government first went in that field, and the commissioner told me they had to abide by the rules and regulations that the Federal Government made, otherwise we could not get the money. That is what he said to me. I was inquiring about a girl who had been working for the board of health and welfare department but she could not get a job because she had not had 2 years of social welfare experience behind her. Without that she could not take the civil service examination for the job of visiting those on old-age assistance.

Mrs. GREEN. Yet the testimony of witnesses before this committee has been that in various States they have had to hire just anybody they could get for social workers in their areas; there were no qualifications in many cases. That seems to me to indicate not rules and regulations that the Federal Government has laid down, but rather a real dearth of people trained in the field.

Mr. NICHOLSON. This girl had 2 or 3 times more experience than she would have had had she gone to a social welfare school, but we have none of those schools. I should say we have one here and there, but we need more people to go among the children and impress them.

I am sorry I took so much time. I have to run along now.

Mr. ELLIOTT. We are happy to have you take as much time as you want, Mr. Nicholson.

Mrs. GREEN. It seems to me it is awfully easy to oversimplify things. I am a little bit concerned about equating juvenile delinquency or, with poverty and low-income groups, with the fact that in our public schools we cannot have physical punishment. Do you not think that is not getting to the heart of the problem?

Judge BAILEY. I certainly do and I, for one, do not go along with any of those theories. I try not to be disagreeable about it with anybody. One of the concerns I have in my area is that juvenile delinquency is moving into the fashionable areas.

Mrs. GREEN. Do not statistics show that for a long period of time juvenile delinquency has not been confined to any particular economic group or to any particular educational level or to any particular stratum of society, but that we have as many juvenile delinquents who come from wealthy families and families who are well educated as from families less well off?

Judge BAILEY. I think that is very true. I do not think that has literally been true in my section until recent years, but I think it has always been true.

Mrs. GREEN. Could one of the answers be that the wealthy family has sometimes been able to make private arrangements with the courts so that the statistics do not accurately reflect the facts?

Judge BAILEY. I think that is true all over the country. It is getting less true now because, for one thing, a lot of those children are with us before their parents even know about it now. Something occurs and they are in juvenile court before the parents find it out.

Mrs. GREEN. On page 9 of your statement you say:

As far as I know, there has been no important legislation with statewide application relative to juvenile matters in the last quarter of a century.

Are you referring to Alabama?

Judge BAILEY. Yes, ma'am.

There is something I would like to mention before I leave that Mr. Nicholson made me think of. There is hardly a month that passes but that the Federal Government probation officer does not try to give me one of these boys. Maybe I should clarify that. We have 13, 14, 15, or 16 who have been guilty of multiple automobile thefts, and the Federal Government is so hard pushed for rehabilitation facilities, apparently, that the probation officers and the Federal courts are constantly conferring with me about transferring a child either back to me or transferring one I have not had to me for rehabilitation under our own methods.

Mrs. GREEN. Wouldn't that really be better?

Judge BAILEY. It sure would, but the reason I thought of that was in connection with Mr. Nicholson's remarks about the Federal Government getting into the thing. They are already in it.

Mrs. GREEN. Do you know how many boys from Alabama are here in the National Training School?

Judge BAILEY. I do not.

Mrs. GREEN. What do you think about the situation where children are taken away from their family environment?

Judge BAILEY. I am strongly for the proposition of rehabilitating children in their own homes and their own families, but it cannot be done without personnel. I do not think there is a better place in the world to rehabilitate a child than in his own family if you can organize the proper material in that family. As you all know, there are some families you cannot ever develop into a family place to rehabilitate a child. I think family first, community next, and State next. I think the Federal training school is the last resort.

But even the Federal court is being hard pushed with their juvenile delinquents, apparently. I am stating that from the fact I am constantly being offered one of my boys back or offered one I have not had because they say things are getting pretty crowded. I find them very delightfully inclined to let us have our boys back if we will take them, which indicates they are having their own problems in the Federal system.

Mr. ELLIOTT. Thank you very much, Judge Bailey. Your

statement has been very helpful. We appreciate the fact you have traveled a long distance to bring it to us.

Judge BAILEY. As I stated earlier, I appreciate the opportunity and it has been a very delightful occasion. I hope eventually, and not too far away, that something will be accomplished.

As one last parting statement I would like to say — I do not think I emphasized it enough a while ago — people throughout America all belong to us, and whether the States do this job or do not do it, they are all citizens of the United States of America and whatever they are, we as Americans in the whole United States will have to live with them, and I think it is the responsibility of the Federal Government.

Mr. ELLIOTT. In other words, you feel that the solution of this problem is more important than quibbling about who will do it?

Judge BAILEY. Who bells the cat is not the question. The question is, the cat needs the bell.

Mr. ELLIOTT. Thank you.

Our next witness is Mr. Clarence W. Boebel, executive secretary, the Tennessee Commission on Youth Guidance, Nashville, Tenn. We have a statement from Mr. Boebel that has been made available to the subcommittee and other interested parties.

Mr. BOEBEL. I am sorry. I do not believe you do.

Mr. ELLIOTT. Excuse me. You may proceed in any manner you desire.

Statement of Clarence W. Boebel, Executive Secretary, the Tennessee Commission on Youth Guidance, Nashville, Tenn.

Mr. BOEBEL. I would prefer, in order to save the time of the committee — and I know in holding your hearings you have heard much testimony on delinquency — I thought I could best serve your committee by sharing with you some of our thinking in Tennessee, what we see in terms of need for Federal legislation.

Governor Clement instructed me rather warmly to give his greetings to the committee and to tell you that we are interested in doing anything we can in Tennessee to move forward in this direction of youth guidance. Also, he wanted me to say that had the hearings been scheduled without some of the delays that I know were necessary, the members of our Commission, particularly Mr. C. Howard Bozeman, the chairman, would have been here themselves to testify, but it was unfortunately impossible for them to come at this late date.

I would like to tell you briefly what the Tennessee Commission on Youth Guidance is. It is composed of nine persons or citizens selected by the Governor from across the State of Tennessee to serve a varying length of time. The Commission is directed to study, to advise, to make recommendations, and to coordinate the activities in all areas relating to the welfare, health, education, and recreation of children in the State of Tennessee.

Over the past 2 years we have worked very closely with the State correctional schools for juveniles and with the juvenile courts in Tennessee. At the last count we had 101 juvenile courts.

Mr. ELLIOTT. Are those State or county courts?

Mr. BOEBEL. By law the county judge becomes the juvenile court judge except in those municipalities where, by private act, they have created their own juvenile courts. We have seven juvenile courts created by private acts. Otherwise, the county judge serves as the juvenile court judge.

Mr. ELLIOTT. Is that what we call in Alabama the circuit judge?

Mr. BOEBEL. No. The county judge has no judicial function except as county auditor or judge of the juvenile court.

Mr. ELLIOTT. Is he trained in the law?

Mr. BOEBEL. Unfortunately or fortunately, in Tennessee the only requirement you can make of somebody elected to the bench is that he have attained a certain age and that he has been a resident for a certain length of time. You cannot require that he be a lawyer to be elected. I think the same is true of the Supreme Court. By law a member of the Supreme Court need not be a lawyer, although in practice he usually is.

Mr. ELLIOTT. What percentage of the judges are lawyers in Tennessee?

Mr. BOEBEL. We have it completely charted as to those judges who have law degrees and those that do not. I think the interesting point is that approximately 23 of the 195 counties have judges with law degrees, but those judges serve better than 75 percent of the child population.

Mr. ELLIOTT. Do your 100 or more county courts in Tennessee have probation systems in connection with them?

Mr. BOEBEL. That is what I would like to talk about, and I

would like to make this illustration, although I know it is not fair to the committee.

We have in the room some lawyers, maybe some judges, certainly members of the press, and social workers. I happen to be a social worker. I worked 6 years in Knoxville as a social worker with low economic groups, and I have also worked in Cleveland, Ohio, and Buffalo, N.Y., as well as having served a hitch with the Navy in the South Pacific. But Johnnie is the same in Alabama, Tennessee, New York, or Philadelphia. Johnnie is 13. His family just moved into town. We do not like him very much. We really do not know him. Johnnie is outside the window — assuming we are on the first floor — and he has a brick in his hand and he wants to throw that brick through the window. I suggest there is no way we can stop him from throwing the brick. We can shoot him — and I am not being facetious. In London as late as 1890 it was legal to decapitate a juvenile for a delinquent act. That eliminated a few kids but did not eliminate delinquency.

So you can shoot him. Or, if I threaten him that I will whale his bottom until he cannot sit down, he may not throw the brick. Of course, he might come slash my tires tonight. Or I can bodily take him away and retain him, and if I retain him until he dies, I will solve it; otherwise, he will come back if he has a mind to and still throw the brick. There is no way you can stop him unless you find out why he wants to throw the brick. That is the whole complex, compound picture of delinquency.

In Tennessee this is our concern with Federal legislation for delinquency. I think we learn much by history. I do not think parents have gone to the dogs, and I do not think children have. When you have 25 children sitting in the back of the room as they were this morning, they haven't. They have problems, yes, and we have to find answers.

We did a rather intensive study in Tennessee — and this is one I will leave with you, if you like — and on the basis of that study we sold to the Tennessee Legislature, with the help of the PTA and other interested groups, a statewide probation system. Our legislature, a few months ago, appropriated $275,000 for a probation system, and this is hard to get. So we are going to have a probation system. It will start in July.

The question arises, Where are you going to get 43 trained persons in Tennessee? Where will we find a trained chief of staff? I do not know. We will find one, but it will be difficult.

The people in Tennessee, when we can sell them a program —

and we have moved into most of the rural communities in Tennessee and worked with the PTA's, the Future Farmers of America, and other groups, and when we say, "This is a program we need and we must have X dollars," they come up with it, because the people are concerned. But we have never historically, either in Tennessee or Oregon or Massachusetts or Alabama, been able to sell local people an idea to support a program that is experimental. There are too many demands.

If you will look back in your history you will find your welfare department, even during the depression when there was a crying need, did not get moving until there was Federal legislation. This is a professional job. We have to have trained people. You set up grants-in-aid, you allow some free money to experiment, then you can sell the program back home after you prove its worth.

Look at mental health. I knew a person in an institution in Knox County who had a bed with his name on it. He had been there 20 years. As far as they were concerned, that bed was reserved for him until he died. He is an outpatient now. Tranquilizers. We have a new department of mental health that is 4 years old. That is because the Federal Government took the leadership. My degree cost as much as a degree in law, and it took equally as long to get it. It is expensive to get that training, although the return afterward is not as high. It is harder to get people to go in the field.

In the area of delinquency, as far as I know, in the field of correction this is the only State service serving people directly that has no Federal participation whatsoever to help in experimentation, in research, in study, or in grants. Welfare has it; mental health has it; rehabilitation has it; and all down the line. This is the crying need.

As far as I am concerned — and I cannot speak for the Governor, but our commission is responsible to the Governor and to the legislature — I do not think Tennessee or any other States are looking for a handout. We are not looking for Uncle Sam to come in and say, "We know the answer and will put on a program." But we really need help, because we have never been able to sell research or to sell grants-in-aid or a new program.

7.

Juvenile Delinquency II

⚜ MUCH OF THE EMPHASIS IN ANALYSIS OF DELINQUENCY
is, of course, on the factors in the personality
of the delinquent that steer him on his course.
Some individuals are delinquent because they are
accommodating to delinquent norms, others are
rebelling against law-abiding norms. The remedial
programs required obviously must be geared to accurate
diagnoses.

The interrelation of personal and social factors can
be seen rather readily in studies of delinquency.
War is a social process. World War II drew millions
of American men into the armed forces and
caused the relocation of countless others as workers
moved to new industrial centers. The impact of
these dislocations on the emotional development of very
young children would be represented as a personal rather
than a social factor. Clearly a sharp line cannot be drawn
between the two. Is it not likely, however, that such personal-
social factors have contributed to the delinquency of
youth in recent years?

The materials selected for inclusion in this chapter,

though focused on the problem of delinquency,
reveal many facets of the dynamics of the group process.
The influence of a group on the individual in changing
norms and standards and the difficulty of intro-
ducing changes in a cohesive group are interestingly
revealed. On a small scale, there is also the reflection of the problems of leadership and the age-old
controversy of students of history: do the times
make the man or does the man make the
times?

Suggested Discussion Questions

What are some of the personal factors in determining
that an individual becomes delinquent? How does
the peer group provide satisfactions for youth
not available through other channels? Compare the
concepts of leadership emphasized by Senator
McNamara (in discussion with Jersey Joe Walcott) and
Saul Alinsky. Could the street club worker be
thought of as a leader? How would you answer the
questions at the end of the presentation of working
with a street gang?

TO COMBAT AND CONTROL
JUVENILE DELINQUENCY

HEARINGS *before the Special Subcommittee on Juvenile Delinquency of the Committee on Labor and Public Welfare, United States Senate, 84th Congress, First Session*

WEDNESDAY, JULY 6, 1955

Washington, D.C.

[. . . . .]

Chairman LEHMAN. The hearing will come to order.

Our first witness is Mr. "Jersey Joe" Walcott, special investigator, bureau of juvenile delinquency, department of police, for the city of Camden, N.J.

Mr. Walcott, I am very happy indeed to welcome you here to-day. I have had the pleasure of seeing you in action many times, and I greatly admire you for your courage in the kind of life which you have followed and for the contributions you have made as an example to the youth of this country in your successful career. I am particularly happy that you are here to testify, because I have a strong feeling that in order to combat juvenile delinquency it is not just a question of what the Federal Government is going to do or what the State is going to do, or even of what the city is going to do. To be successful in this program requires community effort, a truly community effort and a cooperative effort of all the elements that are involved. And I know of nothing that is more important in the handling of young people than having them led by men and women in whom they have respect, in whom they have faith, as an example they wish to emulate. And you have been a shining example of that. The boys of your community, the boys of

333

any community, especially those who know you and follow you, have great respect for you, and so I know of the important work that you have done and can continue to do.

I am very happy indeed to greet you here today, and I thank you for coming.

Now, you have a statement. If you wish to read it and if then you wish to enlarge on it in any way that seems desirable to you, please feel free to do so.

Mr. WALCOTT. Thank you, Senator Lehman and members of the subcommittee.

Statement of "Jersey Joe" Walcott, Special Investigator, Bureau of Juvenile Delinquency, Department of Police, City of Camden, N.J.

Mr. WALCOTT. I am very happy to come here to Washington and act as a witness in this most important task we have of juvenile delinquency.

I have a prepared statement I would like to read, and if I sound nervous, please forgive me.

You know, this is a new role for me. I have been a fighter all my life, and fighting has been my business. I promised God when I finished fighting that I would dedicate my life to the youth of our country, hoping that some little thing that I may do, or the way that I live, may inspire some boy to live a clean American way of life.

Now, as to my statement, the more often I hear the words "juvenile delinquency," the less I think they fit the situation. Actually, and to a larger extent, what we have to deal with is parent delinquency.

In the city of Camden we have our share of trouble with unruly, headstrong, and irresponsible youngsters. Fortunately they are but a small percentage of all the children in the community. In my opinion, most of them would not get into trouble if they had the right sort of home life. Let me explain by personal reference.

I was born and raised in an area often described as "the wrong side of the tracks." It was a tough neighborhood with plenty of tough kids in it. There were times when my brothers and I thought we could ape the bad boys and get away with it. Fortunately we had parents blessed with understanding. They were severe but fair. When we threatened to get out of hand, pa and ma stepped in and stopped the smart aleck conduct before it had fairly started.

Each had a different method. Pa's actions were direct. They called for a trip out back to the woodshed and a dose of what, in those days, was called "strap oil." It was painful but effective. It taught us the result of wrongdoing. Ma never interfered, but when it was all over used to gather us by her side and explain why what we had done was wrong, and why boys who pushed aside the rights and properties of others, broke windows, or beat up smaller boys could expect to be punished. Sometimes she used to say a little prayer that we would break off bad habits and become better boys. Pa and ma were a perfect team. Whatever they did was for our good. We need more old-fashioned fathers and mothers.

I know that there are many good parents who have to work hard to make ends meet, just as there are careless parents who neglect their children no matter what. I hold that all of them, anywhere, and under whatever conditions, can find time enough out of the day to make their youngsters face up to a knowledge of right and wrong; to make sure that evil will be punished; that no particular reward ought to be expected from just behaving yourself; that each of us makes his own future and that the beginning of it starts with the things we learn at home. And, in my opinion, while I believe that bad children ought to be punished and not coddled, it is the parents who fail in their duty to their children who rate severe punishment.

Neglect children, let them get into bad company and they follow a pattern. Without home training, what has a youngster to go by, but the example of others. To be sure there are churches and schools and organizations, all good and all trying, but all together they cannot replace a knowing, helpful father and mother.

In Camden, as in many other places, most of our trouble stems from teen-age gang wars, a tendency to vandalism and a strong flavor of alchohol on the side. We have no difficulty with narcotics. That evil is well under control. Runaways are few and far between. What with one thing and another our boys and girls can find enough mischief at home without hunting for it in far-off places.

As may be expected, when youngsters are taken into custody the first to complain at the arrest are the same parents who failed to keep their children straight. They accuse police of persecution, insist in spite of evidence that their boys and girls are good children, and make dire threats against the arresting officer. As for the teen-agers themselves, they laugh at us and ask what we intend to do about it.

Our laws provide that children under 18 must have special treat-ment. They may not be hauled off in a patrol wagon; no publica-tion may be made of their names; no matter what their known record, officially they have no criminal record and may not be treated as criminals; they must be kept in a special place of deten-tion and have special hearings with no publicity. The juveniles know all this as well as we do. They have no fear of laws which cannot touch them. It is about time we stopped coddling habitual offenders.

Since I have been engaged in juvenile work following my retire-ment from the ring, my observations suggest several recommenda-tions:

First, hold parents personally responsible for payment of damage done by their children to property or individuals. Make it impos-sible for such payments to be evaded. A few digs into the family pocketbook will affect all concerned.

Second, more severity in dealing with the actual wrongdoer. A crime is a crime no matter who commits it. The shock to society remains the same.

Third, stricter enforcement of legislation against the sale or gift of alcoholic beverages to minors with harsh punishment meted out to procurers.

Fourth, immediate adoption by constituted authority of whatever additional laws are needed to put teeth into acts for the suppression of crime by juveniles.

Fifth, provision by communities to drain off the pent-up energy of youth by substitution of wholesome activities to replace the excite-ment of wrongdoing.

Regarding the last-named recommendation, we have recently set up, in Camden, a youth council. It is operated entirely by teen-agers, 14 to 18, themselves. They elect their own leaders and make their own rules of conduct based mainly upon respect for property and the rights of others. It has divided the city into six units each with a potential of several thousand teen-agers. In its 3 months of existence it has developed basketball and softball interdivisional competition. Classes in handicrafts are in operation. Meetings with growing attendance are held weekly in housing projects about town. Dances are held in schools. Each member receives 10 tickets and is held personally responsible for the conduct of guests. The council has stimulated an interest in leadership and responsibility. It has developed sportsmanlike competition. There is a growing pride in contributing to the welfare of the city. These teen-agers have their own committees on behavior and if a boy or girl gets out of hand they are dealt with accordingly. There are no arguments. Either a regulation has been broken or it has not.

In summing up for the so-called delinquency problem, I, for one, would say that its correction is not an impossible task. I will admit it may be a long pull. It has been a long time growing. You do not correct that situation overnight. It takes time and patience and understanding, a willingness to see good in youngsters given the right start, and to do your part in guiding them toward a happy and useful destiny.

Chairman LEHMAN. Thank you very much indeed.

Mr. Walcott, will you tell us how did you come to be a special juvenile-delinquency investigator for the city of Camden, N.J.?

Mr. WALCOTT. Well, Senator, the mayor, George E. Brunner, and Commissioner of Camden, N.J. — because I suppose of my reputation of trying to live cleanly and trying to be helpful to youngsters — selected me to be the head of this organization, and they thought perhaps that my reputation as a former champion could add some influence in helping boys and girls to go in the right direction of American citizenry.

Chairman LEHMAN. You refer in your statement to this youth council which has been set up in Camden. How is that youth council selected?

Mr. WALCOTT. Well, we have another investigator named Clarence Johnston and we have an officer named Louis Walls, and together, we went into 6 sections of the city, into the different churches, and asked the leaders of the churches to select 6 reputable boys and girls to head this committee, and we have 6 boys and girls from each particular section to act on this committee, and they in turn have their regular weekly meetings to arrange and set up programs of activities throughout the city.

Chairman LEHMAN. Are these youth councils composed of different groups, regardless of race, color, or creed or nationality? Do they represent the youth of the community? I am asking you that because I am very much interested.

Mr. WALCOTT. I am very happy and very proud to say that in Camden we believe in the American way of life, and this is an integrated group. We are trying to build good, clean, honest Americans. We live in a democracy and we are trying to practice what we believe in, and the committee consists of groups of all kinds.

Chairman LEHMAN. Well, how do they reach a decision? That is to say, they make the rules of conduct, but how do they enforce those rules? I mean, is it purely voluntarily set by their example for the other boys and girls in the district who undoubtedly number many hundreds, if not thousands?

Mr. WALCOTT. Well, as I said in my statement, sir, boys and girls do as they see others do, and in all of our affairs when a situation arises when a boy wants to get out of line, when he comes in contact with the members of our council, due to the respect he has for those others and the conduct of the others, he doesn't take it in his head to do wrong, but he is influenced to be a good gentleman or lady.

Chairman LEHMAN. I assume that you have been particularly interested and active in the development of athletic programs?

Mr. WALCOTT. Very definitely, sir.

I, as a boy, as I said in my statement, grew up on the wrong side of the tracks, so to say, and I sincerely believe and honestly say from the depths of my heart, there aren't any really bad boys. When I was a boy some people would say I was a delinquent, but through proper guidance I turned myself into right directions. My parents insisted that I go to church, took me to church, and gave me the best they had to offer, and gave me faith to go forward in life, and I tried to grow up to live in better surroundings.

Now, since I have been fortunate enough to have the success of being the champion, I think it is no more than right that fellows like me and others throughout the country should turn back and do whatever they can to help to build boys into better Americans.

Chairman LEHMAN. Do you find in setting up athletic programs that often juvenile delinquent or problem children stop being delinquent and problem children and become good members of their groups?

Mr. WALCOTT. Very surely. You see, once you get boys or girls within your confidence and give them something they like to do, and show that you are interested in them, they will take a turn for the better. As you know, all persons like to know that they are wanted, and once a boy or girl knows they are wanted, that there is a place for them and they are loved and feel that someone is concerned about them, then they are not too apt to go astray.

And I might mention that some of the parents are more or less delinquent. In a meeting one night a parent got up and asked: "Mr. Walcott, do you have a curfew here in the city of Camden?" I remember he was a man weighing about 200 pounds. I said: "Yes, 10 p. m." He asked since I am now doing this work, "Is that curfew being enforced," and I said "I hope we can get together and enforce it." He said, "I certainly hope so, because I have a 12-year-old boy that stays out to 2 and 3 o'clock in the morning."

I mention that to bring out the point that there is the problem of delinquent parents. He feels as though it is not his responsibility to see that his boy returns home at a proper time, but he is waiting for the police department to enforce the curfew law to make the boy stay in the house.

Chairman LEHMAN. Mr. Walcott, how important do you think adequate recreation facilities are?

Mr. WALCOTT. Very important, sir. I do think that any type of recreation or athletic program plays a very, very important role with our boys and girls.

Chairman LEHMAN. Mr. Walcott, I have always felt that way very, very deeply and I feel that way today. I feel that there is a direct relationship between juvenile delinquency and inadequate recreation facilities such as in the form of facilities offered by settlement houses, by gymnasiums, and by adequately supervised parks. Here recently some of our sociologists have maintained that the parks, even though adequately policed and supervised, really encourage juvenile delinquency because they offer an easy place for the meeting and planning of these teen-age gangs. How do you feel about that?

Mr. WALCOTT. Well, as I say, being a former athlete myself, I can honestly say that any type of recreation is very necessary and very badly needed. If you give a boy or girl some outlet to use up his or her energies, that boy or girl is not apt to go astray and visit such places as pool rooms or corner gangs and create disturbances. Yes, I sincerely say and I sincerely hold that not only the Federal Government, but the State and the cities also should provide opportunities for proper recreation. In Camden the city commissions have programs and playgrounds throughout the city so that everywhere you go you find playgrounds and recreation places for boys and girls to play, and that is the reason that we have very little of the problem of juvenile delinquency in the city of Camden.

Chairman LEHMAN. I am glad to hear you say that as it has been my point of view for a great many years.

Let me ask you, how much effect do you think poor housing, substandard housing, has on the problem of juvenile delinquency?

Mr. WALCOTT. Senator, I think that plays an important part. Everyone likes to feel as though they are advancing from day to day and that they are living like normal people. Of course, in the city of Camden we have quite a few housing projects, and it is noticed that in those areas where these projects are built, juvenile delinquency is cut down to a minimum.

Chairman LEHMAN. Do you think poverty has a great effect on this problem of juvenile delinquency?

Mr. WALCOTT. Well, I think that poverty plays a small part. Again, if I can make a personal reference, as I came from a community of poor people, I know something about it. My family was extremely poor, so poor that many nights I have seen my mother, after my father passed away, sit down and cry because she was unable to feed us and because the sheriff was putting a sign on our home to sell it because we couldn't afford to pay for it, and still, under that situation that existed there were 10 of us who grew up to be fairly respectable citizens; and I think it is entirely up to the parents and the individual. If the boy or girl is directed into the right direction I am sure that poverty or nothing else can stop him from being an honest citizen and a good American.

Chairman LEHMAN. I notice in your statement that you have some criticism of the handling of children by parents, and you quoted the guidance your own parents gave you, and that is fine. Now, I agree with you that one of the very important, if not the most important factor in bringing up children, is the example of parents in the way they deal with their children. But suppose you have parents who have no sense of responsibility for the taking care of their children, and you have children who are put in foster homes where there is no great sense of responsibility directly although there are some good ones too, how would you enforce the proper attitude on the part of those people?

Mr. WALCOTT. Well, I think that there is where you talk about the trained personnel. When unfortunately you have broken homes, that is where trained personnel comes in to take in hand these boys and girls and try to teach them to take the right road. In my own family, this is what I find is the most important thing. I have 6 children, and each child to me is an individual problem.

You can't take any of the 6 and do the same to each and expect to get the same results.

Each one has a different disposition and a different temperament, and it's a parent's job and duty to study the child, like the child today studies the parent, and again as I say, I have six. I have a boy who is 21 and I have a girl of 19, and on down to a girl of 10. I know that my boy of 21 smokes, and I tell him, "You are 21. Don't hide your smoking. I know you are smoking." He shows respect to his mother and myself. He doesn't go in poolrooms and he doesn't hang around on corners, and that isn't because I stand over him with a baseball bat, but because when he was small I instilled in him right from the wrong and the things that were expected from him if he wanted to grow up to be an upright citizen.

Chairman LEHMAN. You are a member of a minority group as many of us are ——

Mr. WALCOTT. Yes, sir.

Chairman LEHMAN. And I want to ask your opinion as to what part discrimination, racial, national, or religious, may play in delinquency, because I do think that it plays a part.

Mr. WALCOTT. Well, it plays its part, Senator, but again I say that it is up to the individual. Some people would say or some would have you believe that if you are born of a certain denomination that you have two strikes against you — but that may have been years back, because today it is a little different story. It is up to the individual. If you have something, and if you have faith in God, and if you have the will to persevere, you can be successful, whatever the circumstances may be, whether it is a boy growing up in poverty or whether it is a man trying to be successful. If you have perseverence, faith in God, and you are ambitious you can be successful regardless of what denomination you are, or what minority group you belong to.

Chairman LEHMAN. Do you think that segregation plays any part in the attitude of some of the boys now?

Mr. WALCOTT. Yes, sir; very much so. It is heartbreaking sometimes, and it affects in lots of ways and lots of times the things you want to do. It is heartbreaking that simply because you were born of one denomination that you have to be punished or you have to be pushed aside. People should realize that none of us, regardless of our race, creed, or color, asked to come here in any particular way, but it is God's will that we come here what we are, and it is His will, and people should think of it that way.

I have had no doing in coming here as a Negro, and none of us had any doing coming into any race or creed. But that plays I would say a very, very important part in delinquency problems. When boys grow up they want to do different things and because they are one race they are turned back or pushed aside.

Chairman LEHMAN. Let me ask you just two further questions: You have come in contact, and you are in constant contact with different groups of boys, those who are in minority groups and those who are not in minority groups — Jewish boys, Negro boys, Puerto Rican boys, and Anglo-Saxons. Do you feel that boys and girls who are made to feel inferior by reason of race, creed, or color, are more likely to express their resentment by delinquent conduct? I am sure that isn't true in all cases, thank God, but do you find that it is true in some cases?

Mr. WALCOTT. Yes, sir; not in all cases is it true, but in some cases, it is so. When a person feels that he is rejected or not wanted, then he gets bitter and resorts to anything to get even with, seemingly, the world.

Chairman LEHMAN. One final question: What part do gangs play in delinquency?

Mr. WALCOTT. Well, that plays a terrific part in delinquency, and in the city that's where most of our trouble arises, from the corner gangs, one gang resenting the other gang; and when they go to parties and dances or different affairs, they get together and something starts, and gangs are our biggest source of trouble with juveniles in the city of Camden.

Chairman LEHMAN. You do think that is quite a problem?

Mr. WALCOTT. Yes, sir.

Chairman LEHMAN. Senator McNamara.

Senator MCNAMARA. Thank you, Mr. Chairman.

I first want to express my appreciation for Mr. Walcott's being here. I am sure he has already made a real contribution to the affairs of the committee, and I am sure that he has done a good job in the field in which he has selected to make his livelihood, and I believe he is headed for a great career in that field.

I think that people in your category who have been nationally successful in any sport, such as you certainly have, can make a great contribution to the problems we are considering here today.

You mentioned gangs as being part of the problem we have here, as they certainly are; I think you are in a unique position to teach the youth of the nation that sportsmanship as against cowardice is what is most needed, and that probably goes to the roots of modern juvenile delinquency. Wouldn't you agree that it is cowardly for boys to have to get into gangs so that they can attack smaller numbers? We find the youth of today in such situations armed with clubs, blackjacks, knives, and even guns. When you were a child you were taught that it was cowardly to attack somebody with these weapons, and you have had a wonderful chance to prove what real sportsmanship is. By your example you can show that sportsmanship does not allow the use of these weapons, that these are the tools of the thugs and not of good Americans. I think you are in a unique position to get across to these boys and girls the fact that they just have to be good sportsmen, and I don't think we stress that enough in this problem.

Mr. WALCOTT. Well, Senator, again I have to refer when I was a boy to some of my good neighbors in my community. I will have to admit, as I said before, that some people would have said I was a delinquent. But I was a boy who loved to fight, and if I was with some boys whom I didn't particularly like, there was a fight. Some of the people in the neighborhood said to me: "Seeing that you like to fight, why don't you come along with us and we will take you to the gymnasium in Camden, where if you are going to fight, you can make something out of your fists." So from there, they took me to the gymnasium, and the first thing I was taught in the gymnasium was to respect others. I was told: "If you want to fight, here is where you do it: Keep your hands up and live clean."

As you say, there is not too much stress laid on that, but I would like to say to the youth of the country that living clean, serving God, being a good citizen, will pay off.

I was 37 years old when I won the championship, and I was a fellow who for 21 years tried to climb upward. Lots of times I was hungry and lots of times I had to put my children to bed without food or fuel in the house, but I never lost faith, and I never stopped praying, and I never stopped working, and after 21 years God answered my prayer and I became heavyweight champion of the world; and if the American boys have any ideals or any ambitions, if they will see a little bit of my life and will try to pick some of the good up, not all, but some of the good, they too can become champions if they will try to live clean, have faith in God, and continue to pray.

Senator MCNAMARA. Certainly what you have said has been

very well said, but I note that too frequently the youth we are talking about idolize the fellow who has got to be in the position of a gang leader, even though he gets there by using brass knuckles, knives, and guns and such things as that. They should be taught to idolize as their heroes those who have fought their way upward by living clean, as you have, rather than those who try to get some place by jumping each other, or using clubs and knives or other tools of the gangster. The point I was making is that you are in a position, a unique position, to show them that the real leader is the one who comes by what he has through sportsmanship rather than by the tools of the gangster, which are really signs of cowardice.

Mr. WALCOTT. It answers for itself. It is cowardice when 3 or 4 boys jump on 1 boy, or when 1 boy will take a stick or bat or knife or gun or what have you to use on another boy of practically the same size. That in itself spells nothing but cowardice.

Senator MCNAMARA. I don't think we stress that enough, the cowardice of the gang leader in using his methods against the sportsmanship of persons like yourself who have worked for your success, and I think you are in a position to make the youth of our country conscious of that.

Chairman LEHMAN. Senator Purtell of Connecticut.

Senator, may I apologize for recognizing Senator McNamara before I did you. It was an inadvertency on my part, Senator Purtell, and I am sorry.

Senator PURTELL. It is quite all right.

Mr. Walcott, I am going to call you Joe out of a feeling of affection for you and a very deep respect, because I think you are doing what more men should do. You are setting an example, and certainly I think your influence on the youngsters that you come in contact with immediately is greater than even you imagine; and, Joe, you remind me of a little bit of philosophy I was taught and took a liking to many years ago. It goes like this:

> Isn't it strange that princesses and kings,
>   And clowns that caper in sawdust rings,
> And common folk like you and me,
>   Are builders for eternity.
>
> To each is given a bag of tools,
>   A shapeless mass, and a book of rules,
> And each must make ere life has flown
>   A stumbling block or a stepping stone.

And you, Joe Walcott, I believe, are making a lot of stepping stones for a lot of people. I want to thank you for it as a father and as a citizen and as a Senator. I want to ask you this, Joe: You have set an example and youngsters look up to you and idolize you. I know I also as a kid had my heroes. I, too, was born on what you call the wrong side of the track, and when we are young we look for somebody in our impressionable years that we can sort of idolize, and kids idolize you, and of course to the extent that you have such an effect you have a grave responsibility. You recognize it as a grownup, and you are living so that your example is a living example. I would ask you, do you find there are many grownups that are willing to do what you are doing, Joe?

Mr. WALCOTT. No, sir, Mr. Senator.

Senator PURTELL. If more would set an example, wouldn't we have less of a problem of juvenile delinquency?

Mr. WALCOTT. Less of a problem and much better country to live in.

Senator PURTELL. We talk a lot but do little as grownups for these youngsters to look up to. Have you found many men in Camden that are willing to devote some of their time to these youngsters who need some guidance?

Mr. WALCOTT. Not too many.

Senator PURTELL. Has there been any indication to you throughout the country, and I know that you have done a lot of traveling, that grownups realize that one of the ways to solve this problem is by actively taking it upon themselves to set an example and to be of guidance to the youngsters they contact? Have you found much response to that?

Mr. WALCOTT. Well, that is what is needed above all, for parents and for citizens to show more love and more consideration and to spend more time with our children. If you take some of the parents today, for instance, if you go to a house today, you may see a mother sitting down and talking over the phone about some affair at some nightclub or some gathering or dance that she had been to, and a little 8- or 9-year-old boy stands close by and listens to some of our conversation of things of that sort, and a mother sits up and smokes with her dress not properly down and children lose respect for the parents, and the sooner the mothers and fathers will start taking into their minds and hearts the fact that they must show respect to their children before they can ask it, the better off we will be in solving this kind of problem, and we will avoid a lot of cause for delinquency.

Senator PURTELL. Don't you think, Joe, that if more business-men and other groups of adults in various clubs and organizations were more cognizant of this problem and were willing to get out and spend a night or a week, let us say, with some of these boys, for example, some of our business leaders would do this, who by their example would be an inspiration to kids, don't you think if we did more of that that we would have less delinquency?

Mr. WALCOTT. I think so, and I think it is a combined job, not only for businessmen or for any particular group or organiza-tion but I think it is a job for the whole community, the churches, the schools, and the organizations that exist in the community. I think if they would all band together and work together on this we would eliminate a lot of our problem.

Senator PURTELL. I notice, Joe, that in your suggestions here, they all go down to the grass roots, back into the home and the local community, and you feel that this job has got to be done there, don't you?

Mr. WALCOTT. Yes, sir; I think that a child is like a tree. If you plant a tree you can make it grow anyway you want it. You can grow it crooked or straight, this way or that way, and I think raising the children is the same, that the same thing applies. You can raise the child almost the way that you want him to grow.

Senator PURTELL. How many champions are you going to develop down there in Camden, Joe? Those kids are taking up boxing.

Mr. WALCOTT. Quite a few of them.

Senator PURTELL. God bless you, and thank you.

Chairman LEHMAN. Thank you very much indeed. You have been very helpful. We all appreciate very much your coming here.

Mr. WALCOTT. Thank you very much.

[. . . . .]

FRIDAY, JULY 8, 1955
Washington, D.C.

Chairman LEHMAN. The hearing will be resumed. The last witness is Mr. Saul Alinsky, representing the Industrial Area Foundation.

Mr. Alinsky, will you take a seat. We are very glad you were able to come. I understand you came all the way from Chicago to testify.

Mr. ALINSKY. I have.

Chairman LEHMAN. We are anxious to hear you. Do you have a prepared statement?

Mr. ALINSKY. I do.

Chairman LEHMAN. Do you wish to read it, or do you wish to speak from it.

Mr. ALINSKY. Well, sir, I would like to do both, Senator. I will be brief as possible.

Chairman LEHMAN. Will you proceed, Mr. Alinsky.

Statement of Saul D. Alinsky, Executive Director, Industrial Areas Foundation, Chicago, Ill.

Mr. ALINSKY. In these days of concern about becoming engaged in "controversial issues" or being labeled as "controversial" the issue of juvenile delinquency is extraordinary in its uniqueness as being probably the only completely noncontroversial social issue today. Everyone on this planet is opposed to it. In a significant sense its lack of the goading spur of controversy may well be a factor in the Alice in Wonderland panorama which confronts any student of prevention and treatment of juvenile delinquency.

Every year, every conference, in every part of the country, whether city, State, regional, or national, has its share of reports of particular delinquency prevention and treatment projects and each one concludes with figures showing drastic reductions of delinquency. And yet, the national rate of delinquency climbs on.

Every year the same panaceas with a slightly different twist or emphasis, or dressed in new verbalism makes similar claims. Military terms have pervaded the field, and now everything is called Operation Saturation, Operation Dilution or just plain Operation Prevention; and the claims are the same until the end of the year, when the national rate is revealed as still climbing.

Every year we find the fund-raising literature of nearly all agencies dealing with youth making the same claims directly or indirectly. Everyone in this field is armed with a foolproof formula which is veritably a heads-I-win, tails-you-lose proposition. Statistics are used here, as has been once said, as a drunk uses a lamppost, not for light but for support. They work in a community and if the delinquency rate goes down, they did it. If the rate remains unchanged, they held the line. If the rate goes up, think how much higher it would have gone up if they hadn't been there. And at the end of the year the national rate keeps mounting.

Call it Alice in Wonderland, or call it what you will, but in the vernacular of the people in Chicago's back-of-the-yards area one can properly raise the question, Who's kidding who? I am afraid that the answer is that we are kidding ourselves.

One of the purposes of both bills, S. 728 and S. 894, is to promote research and surveys designed to aid us in the control of juvenile delinquency. Again, may I on this point indulge in a back-of-the-yards idiom, "If there is any truth to the saying that the road to hell is paved with good intentions, then there sure must be a 36-lane boulevard to hell paved with surveys."

I cannot say to you with sufficient earnestness that the problem is not that we do not know what to a major extent are the causes of delinquency; because we do. The trouble is that we shy away from doing what we know must be done. We persist in programs of cosmetic coverups, instead of the required social surgery. It is almost impossible to find the criminology study or textbook which does not begin and end with the findings that in the main delinquency and crime arise out of inadequate, substandard housing, disease, economic insecurity, inadequate educational facilities, discrimination, and a series of social ills which combine to foster and relate to each other in a vicious circle with each feeding into the other so that frustration, demoralization, and delinquency mounts.

And what do we do about it? Do we attack the causes? Do we do as the medical profession did when they discovered the etiology of malaria, drain the mosquito-breeding swamps? We do not. We avoid the causes and go in for supervised recreation, leisure-time activities, handicraft, summer camps, and something mysterious called character building. These approaches may be good in themselves for whatever their objectives may be, but they certainly are not aimed at coming to grips with the recognized major causes of delinquency and crime.

The issues of delinquency prevention are to a large extent to be found in your legislation or lack of legislation, in the area of housing, economic security, health, education, and nondiscrimination. This does not mean that good housing, good educational facilities, relative economic security, adequate health care, and the disposition of discrimination will automatically dispense with the problem of delinquency. But it does mean the necessary supporting steps to the revitalization of that essential unit of our society, the local community where people live. It is here at the level of their family life, their schools, their churches, their community where the issue of prevention and control of juvenile delinquency will be resolved. Make no mistake about that; the job is not here but out there.

It is a job of breaking through the silence barrier of apathy, anonymity, of the feeling that they don't belong, that nobody cares for them and that therefore they don't care. It is difficult even for the family to continue as a vital, integrated unit in this morass of demoralization. The job is one of community organization, so that our citizens will have a medium through which they can actively participate, assume the obligations, responsibilities, and rights of citizenship, have roots of stability, of belonging, a feeling of status and identification as persons. This kind of aroused, articulate, and mobilized citizenry will attend to those issues which threaten the welfare of their children and themselves. Let us also remember, what we too often forget, that having a belief in the democratic way of life means having faith in the ingenuity, resources, leadership, and power of the people to solve their own problems if given the opportunity to mobilize their spirits and resources.

These are not words or theories. These are facts. Facts such as Chicago's Back of the Yards, known as Upton Sinclair's Jungle, which today is one of the best neighborhoods in Chicago and getting better by the day. Ask the Chicago Police Department, the juvenile court, the churches, or better yet, the people who live there, as to just what has happened to the issue of delinquency in Back of the Yards. Ask them what they have done and are doing to meet this problem. Look at Los Angeles' Boyle Heights, the former battleground of the zoot-suit riots, and check your results there. There are other areas in America where this citizens' movement in their community is well underway. With it goes a popular understanding by the local people that delinquency is just one facet of a series of social ills, and cannot be isolated or attacked by itself.

Current studies in causes of juvenile delinquency cry out for this kind of citizen participation. Recently we had the Epstein report in New York City:

[. . .] This is a job to be carried on, in the last analysis, by the neighbors themselves although outside help can play a constructive role. [. . .] It is simply not possible to put too much emphasis upon the potentials of activity along these lines. [. . .]

This holds true for just about every other report that is made in every other city.

The purpose of my comments to this point has not been to indulge in special pleading for a particularized procedure but primarily to present certain facts in order to emphasize the limitations of any legislation with reference to the prevention and treatment of juvenile delinquency. This does not mean that there are not certain positive contributions which can be made, but it does mean in simple language that we cannot and should not peg any extraordinary expectations as to constructive results in this field from any piece of legislation specifically targeted on the prevention and control of juvenile delinquency.

S. 728, Delinquent Children's Act of 1955, carries within it a number of positive potentials which merit encouragement by legislation. There is the degree of recognition of the function of voluntary agencies and the fact that it is from this area that you may expect the major contributions. We realize the practical considerations involved in any legislation which enters the area of financial and functional relationships with other legally constituted public authorities. We urge the recognition, if not the emphasis upon, the role of community organization, particularly as in section 202, where there is reference to special projects. Similarly, on this point it must be accepted that that kind of community activity cannot be initiated or developed by public authorities and that this fact should be clear in the thinking of the Secretary, so that any special projects on community organization initiated under title V should be free of any State body supervision or administration, at any rate as free as possible.

There is a broad flexibility in the character of the provisions of S. 728 which impresses us as being more elastic than parallel sections of S. 894, Juvenile Delinquency Control Act. One also gets the feeling from reading both bills that the statement of purpose implicit in S. 728 as well as other characteristics tends not to view the delinquency problem as specialized and insular as was the feeling which we have gotten from S. 894. There is also a greater recognition of the role of the voluntary agencies in meeting this problem in S. 728 than appears, at least on the surface, of S. 894. For this and other reasons we strongly favor S. 728 over S. 894.

An additional argument for our support of S. 728 over S. 894 is that the reasons cited in terms of flexibility, of a recognition of the functional relationships of those issues which are the cause of delinquency and of a recognition of the role of voluntary agencies, all lead to a belief that there are more potentialities for the developing of a broader program in the future from the actual operations of S. 728 than there are in S. 894. The possibilities for future development is very much in our mind for the simple reason of our previously stated convictions, that the present legislation has definite limitations.

Before commenting on S. 1832 I would like to make some last remarks on both S. 728 and S. 894. Both of these bills place considerable stress upon the issue of coordination, and coordinating activities. I have already expressed my opinion of the alleged need for research (which both of these bills also stress) and may I in all humility on the issue of coordination repeat a statement made to me some years ago by a group of Frenchmen who were touring this country and examining our work in the field of community organization and the prevention and treatment of juvenile delinquency:

> The most extraordinary thing which we have found in America is that every place we go everybody is coordinating, everybody we meet is a coordinator — we have great trouble trying to find the work or the people who are doing the work which is supposed to be coordinated.

On S. 1832, the National Youth Rehabilitation Act, we take a positive and supporting position. This proposed act is sound and good for a variety of reasons, not the least of which is the fact that anything is better than the present disposition of such cases: This bill provides for the kind of activities, services and programs which we have no question but would be a positive contribution. We cite one suggestion for S. 1832: That its personnel include the kind of trained, talented counselors who can establish a personal relationship with these boys and use this informal confidence in trying to help them work out their personal problems. It is this kind of informal personal relationship which presents a real opportunity for the reshaping of attitudes rather than formal instruction on [. . .] the privileges, duties and responsibilities of citizenship, [. . .]

If we are going to have hope of getting the right answers we must be willing to propose the right questions. This is a human problem which must be looked at — not down, as from a bird's-eye view, or up, as from a worm's-eye view, but straight ahead on the level, from the human point of view. People live in communities. The welfare of the family, the schools, the churches, the children all reflect the state of the community. Juvenile delinquency is a problem which must be coped with in the community. The state of the community is in fact the state of the Nation. This issue greatly transcends the point of juvenile delinquency, for with the surrender of daily active participation on the part of local citizens in the sharing of the making of the multitudinous decisions of daily living — with the sinking into apathy, anonymity, not caring, and the feeling among people that they don't count and don't belong, that here is to be found the core of the problem — the delinquency of democracy.

Thank you very much for your patience, Senator.

Chairman LEHMAN. Thank you very much, indeed. I found your statement most interesting.

I want to point out that I, like you, have a very strong suspicion that if we are going to make any real headway in this thing, we have got to make this a community, or area, responsibility.

I could go further, as you have gone, in saying that the situation, to some extent, affects the state of the Union, the state of mind, the state of alertness, the state of concern that exists in the Nation as a whole.

I realize, of course, that what we are trying to do with this legislation will be limited in scope, that we must have the fullest cooperation, the fullest teamwork, within the communities and areas themselves, people who live in the communities, or we are not going to be able to make it really effective as we should.

Of course, what is intended in these bills is not a cure. We who have studied this situation carefully realize that. The cure lies with the people, the attitude of the people, the point of view of the people, the morals of the people and, above all things, with the interest of the people.

But it does seem to me that this legislation can serve as an encouragement, and can serve as a stimulant to the States, the municipalities, and also to the communities and to the voluntary agencies, the different agencies, that make up the community.

Therefore, I think legislation of this sort is very worthwhile, as you do, although as you very, very freely pointed out, the possibilities must necessarily be very limited.

I know you are connected with the Industrial Areas Foundation, and I also note in your statement that you referred to the Back of the Yards organization.

Mr. ALINSKY. I was a cofounder.

Chairman LEHMAN. Which was a community activity?

Mr. ALINSKY. That's right.

Chairman LEHMAN. And I think it would be very interesting to my colleagues and to me for you to describe in some little detail just what is included in the Chicago Back of the Yards movement. I think it might serve to bring into focus what really is meant by community effort and what can be accomplished by community effort.

Some reference was made to this in the testimony of Monsignor O'Grady, who appeared before us the other day, but he did not go into any detail in explaining just what was covered by the term "Back of the Yards Youth Movement."

Will you give us a statement on that?

Mr. ALINSKY. Well, I will try to. I am the cofounder of the Back of the Yards Council. The Back of the Yards Council preceded the Industrial Areas Foundation. At the time of the organization of Back of the Yards, I was employed as a criminologist by the State of Illinois, and criminology was my profession at that time. Apparently it still is, rather reluctantly on my part.

Through my years in the field of criminology, I found myself encountering the problems mentioned in this paper, to wit, that you could never get involved with any of the causes of crime, although everybody assumed in the field of research that the causes of crime were, as I indicated in this statement, housing, education, discrimination, disease, slums, et cetera.

Nevertheless, the moment you entered those fields, you became involved in areas of controversy. The moment you entered the field of housing, you got caught in the fight between private real-estate boards and public housing, and I might add in those years public housing had not achieved the respectability that it has today.

The moment you got into the area of economic insecurity, you were caught in the arena between organized capital and organized labor. The moment you got into the field of health, you were caught between the American Medical Association, and the proponents of health insurance. Similarly, every single cause of crime was, and is, a controversial issue.

You were told to stay out of controversy, most particularly if you were employed by a public agency. If you were employed by a private agency you had a board of directors to be concerned about, as well as your financial donors.

Hence, all activities were, and are, pretty much centered in so-called noncontroversial areas.

Back of the Yards was begun on a simple premise, and it was begun, I might add parenthetically completely independently — as a matter of fact, my job was in jeopardy within a week of the time the Back of the Yards Council began. The Back of the Yards Council was begun on the premise which was somewhat revolutionary in those days.

They have a statement of purpose which is sort of enshrined, like the Declaration of Independence, in their headquarters in Chicago. The general ideas were as follows:

1. We and our fathers and our grandparents have lived in this neighborhood for 50 or 60 years, and many people have studied and written books about us. Many theses have been written about Back of the Yards.

Relatively few students got a doctor's or master's degree in sociology in Chicago in the schools of that region who hadn't made a study in the Back of the Yards area. This is the Jungle, the highest rate of delinquency in town.

It was called a 4–D area — dirt, disease, dependency, and delinquency — an area teeming with about 16 nationality groups, about 92 percent Catholic.

Chairman LEHMAN. I am glad to see Monsignor O'Grady back here. He just entered the room. I believe he will be very much interested in your testimony.

Mr. ALINSKY. There was tremendous controversy and complete disunity.

And what I refer to as the so-called revolutionary ideas are the following:

1. I use their own words on this in their so-called declaration of independence:

We, our families, and so on, have lived here for 50 years in all of this — deterioration and at the end of this time we still have the same conditions.

For 50 years all of these do-gooders have come in from the outside and told us, "After we got through with this" we would be better for it, and after all this we are still living in this same deterioration. We know now that if there is to be improved conditions for our children, we are going to do it, and nobody else.

That was the first idea. The second idea was and is that no outsider can possibly have the interest in our problems that we have. When we talk about children we are talking about our children. When we talk about our rotten housing, we are talking about the housing we have to suffer in. When we talk about low pay, we are talking about the jobs we are working on. And we have more interest in those issues than anybody else could possibly have.

And, thirdly — and the third thing caused sort of an explosion in Chicago. It was two ideas: one which brought down on our heads the coals of fire of just about every professional agency in town and through the country, and still crops up from time to time.

That we feel that we, the local people, have as much intelligence as anybody else has, and that, if given the opportunity, we can resolve our problems as good or better than anybody else can.

This was interpreted as an attack against professional training, which it wasn't. It was just simply their position and how they felt about the situation. The Back of the Yards Council uses their own trained people. The other idea was that we reject the idea of philanthropy. We believe that the only things we are going to get is what we can get. And on that basis we started to work.

They accepted fully the idea of pressure. The Back of the Yards Council has been charged as being a pressure group, and we say, "Sure, democracy is a system of government which responds to different pressures of people, and the people who are undemocratic and lax in discharging their democratic functions, are those people who are not part of a pressure group, who are not pressing to tell their representative what they want."

They also followed their own leadership, and their own leadership was quite different from that leadership which outsiders defined as leaders.

For example, a common mistake of professionals in the search for so-called leadership, is that being possessed, as all human beings are, of an ego, they start looking for people that are somewhat like themselves, think as they do, who have the same kind of educational background, and so forth.

For outsiders to accept the kind of leadership which the people themselves want just isn't done generally. In the first place, the outsider has nothing to say about it. And, in the second place, the outsider may well disapprove of the character of the people who have leadership roles in that area.

The same thing holds true on the issue of their program. They are well aware, as people in most communities are, that the usual kind of community council comes about when a group of well-meaning people purporting to have some interest in the community proclaim a community council and themselves as leaders. It may be true that nobody in the community even knows that they are alive, let alone accepting them as leaders in the community, but the community being completely disorganized, does not challenge that assumed position.

Furthermore, there is no challenge because nobody even knows that this development has taken effect. Then these self-appointed leaders decide what is a good program for the neighborhood, instead of the community itself developing its own program.

The fact is that a community can only develop its own program through getting organized around its own leadership.

That as people start getting together on the basis of a series of common agreements, and as these agreements continue to increase, then the sum of these common agreements become the program of the people.

Since it is their program and since they are not fronting for anybody, they will fight, they will do everything, they will finance their own organization.

And this is an acid test. If the people in the community are really interested in a community organization, if that community organization really represents them, they will foot the bill for it. They will pay for it. It is theirs, and it is worthwhile paying for it.

It is important to note here that this kind of community organization does not originally arise because of appeals to idealism but rather because of appeals to self-interest. Nobody came into the Back of the Yards Council on the basis of an altruistic ideal in the beginning.

And I say that advisedly, regardless of the character of all the organizations, even in the cases of, let me say in getting away from Back of the Yards in making this a general statement, in cases of religious institutions. Here the situation was clearly presented that if they wished to continue to have any kind of a leadership role in the community, they had better join in with this civic organization, which was including all other kinds of organizations, if for no other reason than to simply protect their particular vested power interests.

The union came into this because it wanted to have a means for getting public support behind it in various times of crisis. Other organizations came in for exactly the same reasons from their own point of view.

I cannot think of a more realistic or a sounder reason for people to get involved, at least in the first stages of it.

And then what happens is a very curious thing. It is this extraordinary business of what occurs when two people get to know each other, and a personal relationship develops.

If I may be so blunt as to attempt to explain it this way, let's assume that just as about 11:30 or 12 o'clock today when you were considering hearing me, you suddenly got a report stating that the plane I was coming in had crashed, and that I was no longer here.

Now, what would be your reaction to it? I don't think I am being unfair, Senators, when I say I think — Senator Lehman, who has met me, and because of the involvement of that personal factor would have one but I think in the minds of both of you other Senators there would be a feeling of distinct relief. Why? Because there would be no personal reason to feel disturbed and besides you would have one less witness to listen to; it is Friday afternoon and you have got an awful lot of things to do, and you want to get going. I don't know what your procedure is here, but you might pass some kind of a statement of regret, and that would be the end of it.

Senator PURTELL. I hope your conclusions as to the rest of your testimony are more accurate than that one is, sir, because that would not be my reaction.

Mr. ALINSKY. All right; but I am talking generally, Senator. I am glad to hear you take that reaction.

Generally, I would say that unless there is a personal relationship of some kind of identification, the reaction is more on a transitory basis with people — let me put it that way.

Senator PURTELL. I would say this: that as far as the personal equation goes, certainly that is true. I don't know about you, but as far as coming here as a witness to help us in our determination, I would regret very much that that evidence would not be available.

Mr. ALINSKY. Well, I am glad to hear you say that, Senator.

Senator MCNAMARA. I think we can go a little further than that. You know, we are not tied to these chairs. We don't have to be here. We are quite free to move around, so I think your statement is so erroneous that you hurt your case, and I believe you are presenting a good case, except for this last statement.

Mr. ALINSKY. Let me apply this case, then, to other situations outside of the United States Senate.

I would say that once a personal relationship is developed, an entirely new situation with radically different reactions comes into being. Let me give you an example.

The Back of the Yards Council got a large section of land from
a major railroad, which runs through the community in Back of
the Yards. We could have had certain public projects come in and
level off this land. This land was filled with hummocks and had
been used as an old dumping ground.

Instead of doing that and having that section of land prepared
in 60 days so that the community could use it, the community organization decided to spend 2 years having local groups do the
physical work themselves, and the actual leveling of this land.

And deliberately, groups which were hostile to each other were
placed in adjoining sections, so that as they were working on a hot
day leveling this land, usually on a weekend or a late afternoon,
they began to call each other by their first names. They stopped
to have a glass of beer together. They began talking about problems. And an entirely new relationship developed.

Today it is now one of the largest recreational centers on the
south side of Chicago, completely manned and supported by the
local community, completely equipped by the local community.

It is the old situation you know, and without laboring the point
any further, the kind of person who says, "All people in such a
field are rats, they are no good, they are this, they are that, this one,
this one, this one, this one," then he comes down to a certain name
and says, "Now this fellow is a little different. I had lunch with him
one day and he isn't such a bad guy when you get to know him."

How often have you heard that expression, "not such a bad fellow
when you get to know him"?

This has been the big push in the Back of the Yards movement,
getting people to know each other and to know their problems.

Now there is no point in going on into a detailed discussion of
how they financed themselves. They have. They have been in
operation now for 15 years.

They are infinitely bigger and stronger than they were when
they began. They are well known through the city and the Nation.
The record which they have established for themselves is an outstanding one, and I believe that many of your colleagues are
familiar with the Back of the Yards Council in other areas of interest which they have come to Washington on from time to time.

Now I am going to stop for one reason, because if I continue
talking about Back of the Yards, one thing leads to another and I
could go on here all afternoon.

But suffice to say that beginning on a personal self-interest basis, these personal relationships are made, and when I say "personal relationships" that includes institutions. Too often we simply look at an institution as an organization coldbloodedly representing a certain policy, and deal with it on that basis. In the community organization they approach that situation from a different point of view.

They know the leadership of institutions as human beings, as persons, and so institutions which are in the last analysis people. They deal with institutions as people and the institutions respond and throw everything into a common community basket. This has happened in the Back of the Yards Community.

Let me give you an example of what this means in the field of delinquency. I remember being present at one meeting of the delinquency committee of the Back of the Yards Council. They have their own social worker, a girl who the council had helped with her tuition and helped pay her expenses through graduate work in social work, with the understanding that after finishing her training she would return to Back of the Yards and work for the Back of the Yards Council for at least 3 years at a salary the equivalent or better than that prevailing among private agencies.

I might add that person is still there and will probably always be there. And the reason for it is this. She works in a unique organizational structure where she has available the powers to get the job done. When you have the kind of organization set up and with the organizations so interdependent upon each other, you have this situation. A boy is arrested, let us say for shoplifting. Children who are arrested in Back of the Yards are no longer taken to the police station. They are taken to the Back of the Yards Council by the arresting police officer.

Immediately a meeting is held. This meeting will include not only the plaintiffs in the case, but the police department and the various authorities involved, the priest or the minister of the child's family's church, a member of the father's fraternal organization, a member of the father's national organization, a representative of the mother's societies that she belongs to, and representatives of the labor union that the boy's father belongs to, and so on. You get a complete array of everything in that community life.

I was present at one meeting where this took place. In the course of a discussion it was decided upon that one major factor involved in this boy's delinquency was that the mother was working as well as the father, and there was nobody at home.

As the talk went on, it became clear that the reason the mother was working was because the father wasn't making enough money, at which point we brought in the employer, and discussed the situation.

The employer was perfectly willing to go ahead and upgrade the employee, the father, which would have meant just enough extra money to permit the mother to stay home. The employer, however, had certain obligations with other groups which made it very difficult.

We called in the other groups. A question of seniority came up.

It was explicitly pointed out that every group from time to time came to all the other groups in Back of the Yards and asked for assistance for their particular problem, and it certainly would not be a wise thing for any one group to raise an issue of seniority which might bounce back at them at a time when they might need help.

There is — and this has made some people view the situation with some alarm — a constant pressure pattern between the different organizations, but all tied to a mutual social objective.

Following Back of the Yards, there were a great many demands made from people in different parts of the country for assistance and guidance in helping to show them how to do this work. What had happened, you see, was very interesting.

We got letters from people, people living in Kansas City, who said their cousins who lived in Back of the Yards in Chicago had written them about this and "Could we help them on this."

Churches would write, saying they happened to meet this priest or minister at such and such a place and they learned about this work. "Could we come out and show them how to do this work?"

We were getting requests from churches, unions, and just rank-and-file citizens. We had no facilities to answer these requests and thus the IAF came into being. We didn't and don't feel that we have any particular formulas. Basically what it comes down to is a sensitivity to the use of issues in breaking through this feeling on the part of people that they just don't care and that nobody cares for them.

This is a very important feeling. I can't tell you how standard it is. Any community you enter greets you with the first question, "What's your angle? What is your gimmick? You are not interested in us except what you can get for yourself."

And it takes some time before this issue is worked out.

As a result of all these requests from these different groups through different parts of the country, the Industrial Area Foundation came into being in 1940 for only one purpose: To provide the kind of staff that was trained in the back-of-the-yards situation, to be able to go out and help in terms of experience and also to learn.

We knew that what applied in Back of the Yards in many cases would not apply to other communities, but we also knew there were certain universalities in the situation.

Its personnel on the original board of trustees consisted then as it does now of prominent Republicans, Democrats, Catholics, Protestants, Jews, leaders in big business, and leaders in big labor unions. It is a not-for-profit, voluntary agency. This has been our function for the last 15 years.

A large part of our work has taken place in California. We go in, we help, we get out, and we have nothing further to do with it.

At the point that we get out they are self-financed, they have their own leadership. They are rolling like Back of the Yards is.

Let me make one last remark, and then I will finish, because I think that this will explain the degree of importance that we place to the issue of financing.

Usually I am asked to come out to one of our local community organizations after we have been working with it for about 4 or 5 months. At that point they have reached the point of having a set of bylaws or a constitution. They read this at the meeting. It continuously emphasizes their independence and the fact that they have complete autonomy.

I am always asked to say a few words, and I always give the same talk. I say: "I have listened to your constitution, and I think it is a wonderful document. You talk about your independence and you talk about your autonomy. Well, now let me tell you one thing. As long as the Industrial Areas Foundation is in here paying the bills for your organizers, so long in actual fact you don't have any autonomy or independence, regardless of what you have got written down on that sheet of paper."

At which point there is a long silence. Somebody gets up and says, "But the Industrial Areas Foundation has never dictated any policy. We know from Los Angeles, we know from Fresno, we know from this and we know from that."

And I say, "Sure, but I would appreciate it if you would just shut your eyes for about 30 seconds and try to think of the names of those people that 2 or 3 years ago you would have been willing to bet would never do certain things which they have done since. And how do you know that that might not happen with us?"

I must say that their eyes usually aren't shut as long as 30 seconds. They can remember awfully fast. Then I just say:

"If you want independence and if you want autonomy, you get rid of our people. You get self-financing and you pick up your own tab, and when you are picking up your own tab nobody is going to be able to tell you what to do."

That is the reason why in this discussion I keep laboring the self-financing. Now, Senator, I feel that I have wandered around the ˙mulberry bush.

Chairman LEHMAN. It has been very interesting indeed, and I do thank you very much. We are very grateful to you for coming from Chicago to speak to us.

We, were so eager to hear you that my colleagues and I, after having heard the last witness prior to you, were very glad to recess for a time to await your coming. I want to express my appreciation to you for being here. I found your statement extremely interesting.

I need not tell you that I am in full agreement with the emphasis that you have laid on the need of community organization and community effort. In my opinion it is the only way to deal with this and with possibly many other subjects.

There are 1 or 2 questions, however, that I want to ask you. How long has this Back of the Yards movement been in existence?

Mr. ALINSKY. It started around November 1938. At that time, in 1938 for the first 6 months of organization, it was about a twentieth of its present size. It has gotten to be about 20 times stronger, bigger in every way, during the past 16 years. It has been in existence 16 years.

Chairman LEHMAN. When you say 20 times larger, you mean the size of the council or the size of the people who are taking an active part in this work?

Mr. ALINSKY. Both.

Chairman LEHMAN. Let me ask you this. You have emphasized two things. One is that there is nothing altruistic in the attitude of the people who are carrying on this work.

Mr. ALINSKY. In the beginning.

Chairman LEHMAN. Well, there is a change?

Mr. ALINSKY. There is a change; yes.

Chairman LEHMAN. That of course answers in part at least one of my questions, because you did emphasize so strongly that there was nothing altruistic in this movement, that it was based exclusively on self-interest.

You quoted, and I think very graphically, the point of view of these people. I cannot quote you exactly, but the implication was that they said, "These are my children, this is my home, this is my house, these are my jobs," which is a very natural thing and a healthy thing I think, if it is coupled at least to some extent with the feeling of altruism, with the feeling of community responsibility, rather than individual responsibility.

Now in the working of this plan, has any political self-interest entered into it to any great extent?

The reason I asked that is that in a situation of an organization self-created, based as I understand you to say not at all on the altruistic grounds, there is always a possibility of some ambitious man or group of men capitalizing and exploiting it for sinister political motives or opportunities. Now have you observed that in this experiment?

Mr. ALINSKY. No. You have raised two questions, and I think I can answer both in about two sentences apiece.

First, on the issue of altruism, I believe that I have labored the issue of self-interest against altruism, because I have an idea that you have been listening to altruism all week from most witnesses. Maybe I am trying to overcompensate a little bit the other way.

But let me say that altruism in the actual field of power relations or community organization here it seems to me becomes perfectly consistent with the self-interest of families or individuals. It works its way through in this kind of an organization so that they begin to realize that in order for them to take care of their children, they have to take care of next door's children and children on the next block. This becomes an extension of self-interest, and it may well be altruism.

In other words, being concerned about the other fellow's welfare, because basically in the last analysis his welfare is your welfare. I would say that is altruism or enlightened self-interest.

Now on the issue of this type of organization being exploited for sinister political purposes, there are two ways I can answer that.

First, this was a question, Senator, which disturbed me a great deal in the very beginning of this organization. At that time I went along on the simple rationale that anything worthwhile carries within it a risk. You just can't get away from that.

But then, as the organization began working its way onward, it became quite obvious that this kind of a situation was not going to come about, and the best proof of it is the fact that it hasn't.

There is no way for the Back of the Yards Council to either endorse a Republican platform or a Democratic platform in any of our local elections, because both parties run on the back-of-the-yards platform, because these are all the people in the community with all their institutions, and they are in common agreement.

The only question candidates raise is that they feel they can carry out the platform a little better.

We did have an issue in 1943 with a leading political figure who became terribly concerned that Back of the Yards covered what was known as the so-called machine wards in Chicago, and here suddenly people were no longer turning to precinct captains, they were turning to their own institutions, and the Back of the Yards Council, for various services.

There was a deadly war that lasted for about 4 months, and was over the front pages of every newspaper in Chicago. We won.

Elsewhere in the California situation, if an active leader in one of these local community organizations decides to run for political office, he has to resign from his office in the organization, and he cannot use the organization. It has become a part of the tradition.

To do otherwise is to do one of the most immoral things you can do in the eyes of the community organization, and the community just won't stand for it.

Now, I am in a very fortunate position of not just being here to say, "No, this kind of thing doesn't happen." I can't predict the future, but from the past it probably won't happen.

Back of the Yards now has gone on for 15 or 16 years. It has not happened. The LACSO has gone on now since 1947, it hasn't happened. And similarly elsewhere. I think that is the best answer I can give to your question.

Chairman LEHMAN. That is an answer. I was trying to get a statement from you as to the experience over the last 16 or 17 years.

I want to make it very clear that I don't think there is anything unhealthy at all in political differences, but quite the opposite. I think it is part of our democratic way of life.

I have seen that some of these organizations that have started with high purposes later develop into a medium by which one man or a group of men could come into control, not of the politics of the city or State but of the district.

I think you have come a long way from a bad situation in the last 25 to 40 years. My recollection goes back much further than that, and I have seen some of these organizations that were based on high purposes. That is the reason I asked that, and I am very glad to have your answer that that is not happening in this case.

Now may I ask you just one more question.

What is the ethnic and religious makeup of this district that you are talking about? I am not acquainted with Chicago. If this was a district in New York, I probably could answer the question myself.

Mr. ALINSKY. You mean, specifically the Chicago "Back of the Yards" district?

Chairman LEHMAN. Well, what do you mean by "Back of the Yards"? Is that a political district, such as an assembly district?

Mr. ALINSKY. No.

Chairman LEHMAN. Or congressional district?

Mr. ALINSKY. It covers five wards in Chicago. It is a district which got that name because it was back of the stockyards and was the district in Chicago that was the other side of the tracks; just like such areas as Hell's Kitchen in New York got a dramatic, colorful name in terms of the kind of life there, "Back of the Yards" was that way in Chicago.

The ethnic composition is practically a little Europe, and some Pan-American in it. It is heavily Polish, Slovak, Lithuanian, Czech, Croatian, Russian Orthodox, a large population of Mexican-American, Irish. You name them, and we've got them. We've got about 17 there.

Senator MCNAMARA. Would you say, generally, first generation?

Mr. ALINSKY. No; not now.

Senator MCNAMARA. I mean when you started.

Mr. ALINSKY. Yes; I would say that this community ——

Senator MCNAMARA. Every city has the same composition, in general.

Mr. ALINSKY. That's right.

Senator MCNAMARA. I think that would describe it.

Chairman LEHMAN. At the beginning of your statement, I understood you to say — I am not sure, because I did not hear everything that you had said, very distinctly, but I understood you to say — that years ago, maybe 30 or 40 years ago, this was largely an Anglo-Saxon community?

Mr. ALINSKY. No. If I said that, I misstated it.

No; this community, like almost every other low-income area, was heavily inhabited by the particular groups that were coming in during certain periods of immigration.

At one point it was almost exclusively German. Then the Irish came and then the Swedes and then the Poles and the Ukranians and the Slovaks.

Each group, as the changes occurred within the community, did not leave in toto, so that finally by about 1930 or 1929 you had this kind of a composite population in the area. It probably would have continued to change, just as it had through the years, if immigration hadn't been shut off at that time.

Chairman LEHMAN. Again, I must apologize for asking this question because you may have answered it, but as I pointed out, I was not sure that I heard you.

To what extent does this group or council — did you call it a council?

Mr. ALINSKY. Yes.

Chairman LEHMAN (continuing). Concern itself with general civic affairs?

Mr. ALINSKY. To a complete extent. Its program is anything which relates itself to the welfare of the people, and as they have gone ahead in their own self-educational programs, almost everything has started to somehow or other get related.

I have picked up papers and seen where the Back of the Yards Council has been in Washington, struggling to get the release of Father Rigney from China. I have seen them leading in the fight for the Federal hot-lunch program.

And again this comes back to the self-interest basis. They realized that in order for them to have the hot-lunch program in the Back of the Yards, the whole country has to have it.

And then after they finished in Washington on this one issue, they carried the fight to Springfield, our State capital, to get the enabling legislation for the rest of the State, because otherwise Back of the Yards couldn't have had it.

As they realize the functional tieups and relationships of one issue to the other and of one part of the country to the other and of one part of the city to the other, their concern has included every kind of issue.

Chairman LEHMAN. In other words, while fundamentally based on self-interest, self-interest which every citizen should have, it is not confined to a specialized interest in a narrow sense?

Mr. ALINSKY. That's right.

Chairman LEHMAN. Senator Purtell.

Senator PURTELL. I want to thank you, Mr. Alinsky. I have enjoyed listening to you.

Of course, we are here to discuss mostly this legislation, or proposed changes in it, or any other legislation that might be proposed. I am glad you cleared up this question of selfishness and of selfish interest, or selfish self-interest, because I got the impression that you felt for a while there that there wasn't any such thing as altruism.

I am sure you don't now, because you cleared it up. Obviously with our crippled children's hospitals and the support of such things as the National Foundation for Infantile Paralysis and many other institutions of a like character that have been supported by the people, there is a great deal of altruism.

We can remotely connect that with selfishness if we want, by saying, and it is true if we want to stretch it that far, that the better off all people are, the better off we are in this country. But I still like to call it altruism. I think it is, and I hope we never get rid of it.

In relation, however, to these two bills that we are here to discuss, or other bills or proposals, I would judge from your testimony, Mr. Alinsky, on page 2, that you have some objection, do you, to the further research and surveys that these bills provide for.

Mr. ALINSKY. Well, I did try to point out in that statement that I have, let me say, reservations about the undue emphasis on the need for research and coordination.

I don't believe, in the field of delinquency, that those two areas need so much attention, that we do know pretty well the job to be done. And the thing to do is to start applying ourselves to that job.

Senator PURTELL. Now, you did say one of the purposes of both bills — and I am not trying to confuse this thing, I am trying to get my own confused thinking on it, after listening to you insofar as your attitude goes, I want to get that cleared up.

One of the purposes of both bills, S. 728 and S. 894, is to promote research and surveys designed to aid us in the control of juvenile delinquency. Again, I might indulge in a Back of the Yards idiom, "if there is any truth in saying the road to hell is paved with good intentions, then there sure must be a 36-lane boulevard paved with surveys." But you are not against surveys, as we have provided in this bill; are you?

Mr. ALINSKY. No. I don't know exactly what the surveys are going to be.

Senator PURTELL. You studied the bills?

Mr. ALINSKY. Yes.

Senator PURTELL. You passed an opinion upon these bills very strongly, I might say.

Mr. ALINSKY. I did study the bills.

Senator PURTELL. Fine.

Well, we do provide, of course, for surveys. And, of course, we feel, as the bills indicate, that what the Federal Government's place in this picture should be is to point the way, because the money is provided in there to carry out a program that will reach down into the grassroots and do the job at that level, so that we must have surveys, we must have information, we must have information channeled in here that in turn can be evaluated and channeled down to the states for their use, and that can only come, can it not, from surveys, information of that nature?

Mr. ALINSKY. Yes.

But may I ask you a question, Senator?

Senator PURTELL. Sure; go ahead.

Mr. ALINSKY. Let's assume that you have a survey that goes into community X, which has a very severe and chronic problem of juvenile delinquency lasting over a period of time, and your survey then determines that among some of the basic things that have to be corrected here is the issue of housing, is the issue of more schools, the issue of better health treatment, and after your survey has that, where are you going from there?

Senator PURTELL. I think if it were an individual case and applied to only one individual community, that would receive that weight. If it was a result of a survey made that those were some of the reasons that prevailed throughout very many states, that would be a part of the result given to those states, too, for determining what action they would take at the state level in meeting this need.

Mr. ALINSKY. Well, the Wickersham crime survey, under President Hoover in 1930, determined that in about 18 major American cities, in your slum areas you had the same factors operating in creating delinquency, the factors that we have mentioned here and which, I am sure, have been mentioned all week.

Senator PURTELL. Those are some factors, they are not all.

Mr. ALINSKY. No; but they are very key factors.

Senator PURTELL. They are factors; yes.

What I am trying to say is this:

I want the record to show this because we read this, and many of the members that will have to act on the bills before us, the full committee, will obviously want the information in there.

Your testimony indicated that you might feel that there was very little value to surveys, and I wanted to establish whether you did feel that way or not.

Mr. ALINSKY. I feel that there are surveys that are important. I feel that there are also a great many surveys that are undertaken that are needless.

Senator PURTELL. In this field?

Mr. ALINSKY. In this field, I am perfectly willing to have the record show that I believe that these surveys can point out the areas that you have mentioned.

Senator PURTELL. That is what I wanted to know.

Now, one more thing. I may be confused again, but will you tell me about the Industrial Areas Foundation. Is it a parent to these back-of-the-yards movements, or is it the movement itself?

Mr. ALINSKY. The Industrial Areas Foundation was born out of Back of the Yards. Back of the Yards came first. The Industrial Areas Foundation was then set up as a not-for-profit organization.

Senator PURTELL. How is it supported?

Mr. ALINSKY. It is supported by private contributions and by grants from other foundations.

Senator PURTELL. Do you have a large staff?

Mr. ALINSKY. Not particularly.

Senator PURTELL. Would you have a substantial budget?

Mr. ALINSKY. In terms of other groups, no. Our budget I would say, runs about $120,000 a year, $150,000.

Senator PURTELL. And you are engaged in establishing these back-of-the-yard movements in various cities; is that correct?

Mr. ALINSKY. That's right.

Senator PURTELL. What is the function of the foundation?

Mr. ALINSKY. The function is to respond to requests of representative local groups in different communities in the country who

ask for us to come in and to show them how to develop this kind
of a citizens' organization in their own area.

Senator PURTELL. And do you also seek out places in which
to operate, or do you wait until you are requested to go in, or do
you perhaps encourage that request? I am trying to get the picture.

Mr. ALINSKY. Yes.

The only reason I am hesitating is because my answer at different
times would be different.

Right now we have so many places after us that my answer
would be, "No," we certainly do not seek them out. We try to
avoid them, actually. We have so many commitments.

If you had asked me that 4 years ago, I would have given you a
different answer. I might well have said that there are certain areas
we do encourage, yes.

Senator PURTELL. So actually, right now your function is to
respond to these requests that are generated at the grassroots rather
than by encouragement through your foundation; is that correct?

Mr. ALINSKY. That is correct.

Senator PURTELL. That is fine.

Thank you very much.

Chairman LEHMAN. Senator McNamara.

Senator MCNAMARA. I was interested in the testimony, too.

Something impressed me in former testimony today that had not
been under consideration. One of the witnesses pointed out that
a great many problems develop from idleness or lack of employment after children drop out of high school in the 16-to-18-year-
old age groups.

This person pointed out that boys were having much more
trouble in finding employment in these age groups than girls were,
and as a consequence that was one of the contributing factors to
the comparatively small rate of juvenile delinquency among girls
as compared with boys.

These people recommended that we try to institute a CCC program to bring about employment for these young people. There is
in one of the bills, not in either one of the two just mentioned but
in another one, a proposal for something like the CCC.

Have you given consideration to that phase of the problem?

Mr. ALINSKY. No. Any comments I would make would just
be in terms of our general experience in the community.

I did think along the lines of the Watkins bill on the rehabilitation corps, that the only thing unfortunate in it was the fact that

while it was a so-called CCC in a significant sense, it was limited only to those boys who had gotten involved in delinquency. In other words, it was sort of an eternal penal extension.

I would much rather see delinquent boys placed with a group of boys who have not gotten involved in delinquency, so we would not have that kind of a segregated situation. I think it would be better in terms of hopes for social adjustment.

As far as an argument for CCC in terms of unemployment of that age group, I do not know the facts or figures on that. I would say that probably youngsters of the age of 17 fresh out of school would have some difficulty which they did not have 10 or 15 years ago. I say this for two reasons. One reason being the external one, that industry might be more loath to hire them since they are going into selective service very shortly. The other reason being inwardly on the part of the boy, that since he is going into the Army in a couple of years, there is no compulsion to start getting stabilized on an economic basis.

I don't think I could contribute much more than that to you, Senator.

Senator MCNAMARA. The way you sum it up, the state of mind of the youngster plus the fact that industry is not interested in him because he is going into the Army, seems to justify the thinking that a CCC program would help if it doesn't incidently just accept delinquent boys who have gotten into trouble, but also boys who want to be employed in that manner. It would really be helpful and I think your conclusion justifies the thinking that it would be well to have that done.

Mr. ALINSKY. I would hesitate to go on record for that, for one reason.

I think that the Watkins bill is important and I think that the moment you start turning it over into the kind of thing that we have been discussing, your financial considerations jump so completely into almost another world on that kind of a project that it may kick around 3 or 4 years and not have anything.

Senator MCNAMARA. You mean it would not be worth the financial expense, is that your conclusion?

Mr. ALINSKY. No, not at all, but I think it is important that this bill be passed.

Senator PURTELL. Will the Senator yield? I thought you ought to know this because this happened.

I don't know if the papers have gotten it. While Senator Watkins has not abandoned S. 1832, he did suggest, and I think the chairman will bear me out, he did suggest further study. Certainly it seems to me, Mr. Chairman, any suggestions Mr. Alinsky or anyone else has as to how that bill could be improved upon I am sure would be welcomed by the chairman.

Chairman LEHMAN. We certainly would be very glad to have it, but we do not intend to consider that at this particular time, because Senator Watkins, while he has not entirely withdrawn his bill from further consideration, felt further study should be made.

Senator MCNAMARA. Just one other thing. You laid great stress on the racial-religious conflict in the Back of the Yards area in 1938, was that the year?

Mr. ALINSKY. Yes.

Senator MCNAMARA. No doubt the program that you have, this back-of-the-yards program, has contributed a great deal to the elimination or lessening of that racial-religious strife.

Mr. ALINSKY. That is correct.

Senator MCNAMARA. I think that fact that now we have second generation rather than first generation children to deal with also contributes a great deal. Percentagewise will you estimate how much progress you have made? Is it 100 percent or 90 percent?

Mr. ALINSKY. I am very glad you asked that question because there are just too many claims being made by everybody, and not deliberately.

Now if you study the delinquency rate of the Back of the Yards Council, you will find that it took a terrific nosedive. I could sit here and I could say to you, "Look, this is the work we have done — just examine the results!"

But there are certain very important factors that enter the picture, factors over which the Back of the Yards Council had nothing whatsoever to do with. One was a war which caused full employment. A war also in its own way met the problem of youth. Our youth just were not around through that period.

Second came the issue of full employment which followed the war, as we started up on an economic plateau. These are things over which the community organization had nothing to do with, and how are you possibly going to measure the effect of one and the other.

I would say that the most extreme statement that any honest

person in this field can say is that we have reason to believe that what we have done has made a contribution in this direction. We know that.

But to say that we take the credit for this, we may take the credit in some small areas, but to take the full credit that we are responsible for delinquency prevention would be just kidding ourselves, Senator.

There are all kinds of outside factors over which you don't have control that come in and operate one way or the other. For example, the packinghouses were organized for the first time actually in our history. If you examine the differences on the wage rates and the working conditions of the workers in the slaughterhouses from 1939 up to the present over what it was before, it is enormous. I think that there is a greater spread than any major industry in America.

Now the union did that, the United Packinghouse Workers of America–CIO. And when you start pointing your finger at economic security as one issue, this is not the Back of the Yards Council.

It is true that the Back of the Yards Council did say to the union as one of its constituent members, "Economic security is an important thing, this is your jurisdiction. We will support you in your particular stand over here."

But for any organization to take the credit on these things is just kidding yourself.

Take the issue of participation. I assumed that this community back-of-the-yards was so mobilized that the expression they had was that "It was hopping." The actual participation on the part of the people seemed to be engaged in by the overwhelming majority. If you would have asked me that under oath here in 1942 or 1943, I would have told you that at least 50 percent of the people back-of-the-yards were actively engaged in this kind of civic activity.

I began to make a study of it in spite of my aversion to surveys, Senator — I do make one every so often — of this so-called degree of participation, and my first study showed we had approximately between 5 and 6½ percent of the people participating, 94 percent were not.

The criteria I used were simple. I would talk to people. I would ask them if they belong to the Back of the Yards movement, and they would say, "Certainly."

I would ask, "How do you belong to it?"

They would answer, "My church belongs to it, my labor organization, my nationality group. I belong to it in 15 different ways."

I said, "Well, now in any of these groups that you belong to, you have an agenda at your monthly meeting and part of that agenda concerns Back of the Yards counsel work. Have you ever volunteered for it?" They said, "Well, no, but I have been behind it."

On that basis he was chalked down as nonparticipating.

I ran another study along this same line and came out with a 5- to 7-percent participation, and I could not believe these figures because everyone assumed this community was so organized, that at least 80 or 100 percent were participating.

My next study came out with the same finding, about 5½ and 7 percent. Then I began to examine the other institutions.

I examined the Catholic Church. This community happens to be heavily Catholic, and I applied the same criteria. The fact that somebody went there for mass about once a month or so, or communion, was not the test. The test was whether he belonged to any of the religious societies, or whether he was active in any of the work of the parish at all.

And on that basis the Catholic Church, percentagewise, was infinitely lower, let me say, than the Back of the Yards Council.

I then checked ——

Senator PURTELL. You made a lot of surveys there, I might say, Mr. Alinsky.

Mr. ALINSKY. Yes; but I needed them. They were important for what was going to happen afterward.

The CIO's sampling rang about one-half of 1 percent.

Then I checked the Kelley so-called machine, because we were the so-called machine section, and the participation rate there was about one-tenth of 1 percent.

After all, what do you have in a precinct? There are 300 people there, and you have 1 precinct captain. The chances are he isn't a jobholder. There aren't enough jobs around town for every precinct captain. He has got a couple of cousins that only start work once in every 4 years just 3 weeks before election. That is 3 people out of about 300. Then I realized that 6 or 7 percent was a tremendous number. Then I ran across a statement of a report that in Moscow, where the Communist Party has literally life and death power over citizens, jobs, housing, everything else, that there the

Soviet Government was boasting about having about 50 percent participation in so-called projects.

This business of participation is not what we think it is. Actually there is so little participation in the American scene that when you get citizen participation up to 2 percent in any area you have got a machine on your hands.

Senator MCNAMARA. My question was, since this experience from 1938 up to 1955, or whenever your last survey was, there must be a tremendous improvement because nationally we have had tremendous improvement in what you pointed out as conflict, race and religious conflict, from the early days?

I was asking you if it was more marked in that area than in the rest of Chicago, or places where your efforts weren't so concentrated as in this back-of-the-yards area.

Mr. ALINSKY. Yes; I could point out to you, Senator, in great detail, a series of these areas, particularly in the field of race relations, where there have been marked changes, which I could say, to a major extent, were due to the Back of the Yards Council.

Senator MCNAMARA. That is a definite thing you can really analyze and compare with the rest of the city. Thank you very much.

Chairman LEHMAN. Mr. Alinsky, I want to thank you again and make one observation: I know too little about the Industrial Areas Foundation to express any opinion as to the manner in which it is administered. Therefore, this is not intended to represent an endorsement on my part with regard to that particular organization, but I do want to say that I think your conception of American citizenship and the duties of American citizenship is sound, in that you are trying to stimulate, as I try to stimulate, the feeling of responsibility in a community or an area, a relatively small community, a relatively small area, not only in this particular matter which we have got before us today, juvenile delinquency, which I think is extremely serious, but in all civic activities.

I think your organization is on the right track when it tries to stimulate community organization as you have expressed it, and I am quoting you now:

The job is one of community organization so that our citizens will have a medium through which they can actively participate, assume the obligations, responsibilities, and rights of citizenship, have roots of stability, of belonging, a feeling of status, and identification as persons. This kind of aroused, articulate, and mobilized citizenry will attend to those issues which threaten the welfare of their children and themselves. Let us also remember, what we too often forget, that sharing in a belief in the democratic way of life means having faith in the ingenuity, leadership, resources, and power of the people to solve their own problems if given the opportunity to mobilize their spirits and resources.

You have referred to the fact that housing, economics, security, health, education, nondiscrimination, and other subjects affect the issue of delinquency, and they do, but you also point out that that is not the sole answer to it.

But I can say to you that if we can stimulate and encourage sufficient interest in the community, every community, not a great city like New York as a city, because there there are a few people speaking for 8 million people, but the people themselves in Philadelphia, Chicago, Detroit, or Hartford, I think we will get these things: We will get good housing, economic security, improved economic security, at any rate, better health measures and a better education and further steps toward nondiscrimination.

I will say to you, Mr. Alinsky, that if I were not an incorrigible optimist, I, by this time, would be much discouraged by the failure of the Congress to act effectively on many of these subjects.

They are not going to act effectively on some of these subjects at least until and unless there is an aroused grassroots sentiment for it and then they will because we are all in favor of the sentiment of the people we represent, and the people of the Nation, as a whole.

So I want to thank you for coming here and say that I think your exposition of the importance of community effort, which I think is the answer to this thing in a large way, has been very useful. Thank you very much.

Senator PURTELL. I want to thank you for coming, too.

Mr. ALINSKY. Thank you very much.

NOVEMBER 16, 1955
New York, N.Y.

[. . . .]
Chairman LEHMAN. Ralph W. Whelan.

Mr. Whelan, have you a prepared statement?

Mr. WHELAN. Yes; I have, Senator. I want to say it is an honor to be invited to appear before you and a privilege to be asked to present my views with respect to Senate bill 728.

Statement of Ralph W. Whelan, Executive Director, New York City Youth Board

Mr. WHELAN. I want to preface my remarks by saying the opinion I express in regard to this bill is the opinion of myself and several colleagues and not the opinion of the members of the youth board.

This bill has not been considered formally by the youth board as yet. [. . .] I would express the hope that this bill will result in truly dynamic programs using new and experimental techniques which in our opinion are necessary for the diminution, control, and treatment of juvenile delinquency.

We believe this can be partially achieved particularly through the proposed provision for training. In addition to providing more personnel, we hope that schools will prepare candidates for this field in helping them meet the realistic problems they are faced with in working with resistive and hard-to-reach young people and their families.

This requires reaching out and bringing services directly to people wherever they are rather than waiting or expecting that they will seek services on their own.

It means actually working in the market place if you will, whether or not it is with teen-age gangs or unaffiliated young people, or families and children who are too deteriorated and immobilized to ask for help.

Training for work with citizen groups on neighborhood and grass roots levels should also be provided if we hope to bring about improvement and permanent changes in the environment of so many of our young people, at the same time that we help them to resolve their psychological or emotional problems.

Rather than superimpose change, we can assist communities to help themselves in fostering healthier climates and conditions of living in which children and youth grow. We will then be implementing fully the social work concept of helping people to help themselves.

Chairman LEHMAN. Are there any schools that train people specifically for this kind of work or are they usually people who have been trained in social work who are then enlisted in this kind of work?

Mr. WHELAN. The tendency over the last decade or two in the schools of social work has not been in this direction, but rather towards training in psychologically oriented concepts with the principle of self-determination. This means that the client must ask for help and have sufficient anxiety and sufficient concern about his problems to go to a social agency. We therefore find that many of the workers we get on our staff have to be reoriented in their thinking since we would like them at this point to bring their services to the people whom we know need help, and to offer services to them, and to work through any resistance they have for help.

The social workers on our staff are gradually coming around to this point of view, and I understand that some of the schools have picked up this concept and are beginning to develop workshops and institutes around this philosophy. They are training workers to move out into the communities away from their desks, and to offer assistance to people before their problems reach the point where they require much more intensive work and where the children are already involved with the law-enforcement agencies.

I express these convictions as a result of our experience in working for 8 years with the most difficult individuals and groups who make up the hard core of the delinquency problem. For we found that it was necessary to reorient our workers to a more reaching out philosophy if we were to deal effectively with these children and youth who are very often inaccessible to existing services in the community. It is our belief that in just such reorientation of thinking and actual on-the-job training that more dynamic and successful approaches to the problem will be achieved.

[. . . . .]

Chairman LEHMAN. You feel, don't you, that this must be a community approach. It can't be solved by any 1 or 2 or 5 agencies — the schools, the churches, the homes or recreational activities and things of that sort?

Mr. WHELAN. Yes, sir.

Chairman LEHMAN. It must be a truly community attack. Does the youth board try to mobilize all the resources, moral and otherwise of the community, of an area?

Mr. WHELAN. Yes, sir. As a matter of fact this is carried out in the composition of the membership of the youth board itself. We have 28 members. Of that membership of 28, 18 are lay people and 10 are ex officio members on the basis of their official position with the city government. There alone we have coordination. We have the commissioner of health, the chief justice of the court of special sessions, the chairman of the New York City Housing Authority, the presiding justice of the domestic relations court, Dr. Jansen, the superintendent of schools, the police commissioner, the commissioner of corrections, the commissioner of welfare, the commissioner of parks and the chief city magistrate, all sitting on our board in an ex officio capacity.

The other 10 members are appointed and selected by the mayor on the basis of their contribution over the years to this whole problem of delinquency. [. . .]

I think you are familiar with the youth board program from previous testimony by Judge Kaplan but perhaps I may just describe how we work in one area.

Chairman LEHMAN. I will be glad if you will.

Mr. WHELAN. You will then get an idea of how the program operates in all areas. The core of the youth board program in each area is what we call a referral unit. This is a detection center for locating children with behavior and personality problems through the school system before their problems become so great that they become involved with the law. Each referral unit is manned by a trained social work supervisor and 4 or 5 trained social workers. Their job is to concentrate on the elementary schools in the area. They discuss problems with principals and teachers. They locate youngsters who are presenting problems in the classroom and whom the teachers know are also presenting problems in the community, they discuss the problems with the child and his family and quickly refer that child and his family to a treatment agency serving that area which is best equipped to help them.

This brings into play all of the agencies — family counseling agencies, child-guidance agencies, group work agencies and others which offer services in this particular area and based upon the judgment of the referral unit worker and the supervisor, the agency is selected and the child referred to the proper kind of help.

We reach children at an early age. We go right down to the first grade, for in this way we help to forestall the development of delinquency not only with that child but probably with his brothers and sisters as the family grows. [. . .]

Chairman LEHMAN. Mr. Whelan, are you acquainted with the "Back of the Yards" movement in Chicago?

Mr. WHELAN. Yes, I am. I am very well acquainted with it.

As a matter of fact we have a project that we are now operating which is conducted on a similar basis to the "Back of the Yards" movement. We have a neighborhood self-help project in Staten Island which we instituted about a year ago that has shown great progress. There we sent in a community organizer as in Saul Alinsky's organization.

Chairman LEHMAN. Mr. Saul Alinsky testified with regard to what had happened in the "Back of the Yards" movement, and Monsignor O'Grady also testified before us. I was very greatly impressed with the possibilities of that kind of a project. I am not passing judgment now with regard to the quality of a particular project. What you described as the work of the youth board here is of tremendous importance. The activities will all flow down from the top to the bottom. They are all more or less official activities, whereas this "Back of the Yards" movement is really a grassroots movement. It is a community movement. As one of the witnesses said in his testimony before this subcommittee, in that area, which was one of the toughest, I imagine, in Chicago — 30 or 40 years ago — many, many of the citizens felt that the problem of controlling juvenile delinquency as well as other problems was their problem.

As it was described, "It is my children that we are dealing with. It is my job that I am dealing with." It becomes a community problem and as it is a community problem, the vast number of people in the district are acquainted with what is sought to accomplish and also take a part in it.

I am glad to know that you are testing it out on Staten Island.

Mr. WHELAN. Yes, sir.

Chairman LEHMAN. Do you feel that kind of movement is practicable in many of the areas in the city and of other cities?

Mr. WHELAN. Yes, sir. I am thoroughly identified with that approach. I think that it has great value and I think that if we are to have lasting impact on this whole problem of delinquency we have to mobilize the neighborhoods to do something about their own problems.

I have this reservation about it and I would like to express it because I think it is a very real one. I have questions about a public agency sponsoring this kind of a program for these reasons. Obviously and inevitably as you mobilize a neighborhood to do something about their own problems, it involves additional funds. When additional funds are mentioned particularly where a public agency is in there organizing the community, the neighborhood says all right, you get us the funds; or they go to city hall looking for the money from the public agency or from the agency which can do something about their problem.

In that event if a public agency is the sponsor, it has to either become an apologist for the city administration or a defender of the city administration.

In my opinion an approach such as the "Back of the Yards" and a community organization neighborhood self-help approach is better carried on under complete voluntary auspices rather than under public auspices.

Chairman LEHMAN. Isn't that the fact with the "Back of the Yards" movement?

Mr. WHELAN. It is a fact.

Chairman LEHMAN. It is purely voluntary.

Mr. WHELAN. That is why I have my fingers crossed about my project. [. . .]

Chairman LEHMAN. From your experience, what effect has poor housing on juvenile delinquency? Has it a serious, substantial effect?

Mr. WHELAN. We feel that it is a very important factor, one of the very important factors that contribute to delinquency.

As we move around the 14 high delinquency areas, we have youngsters who come from families which I have described as deteriorated, very unhealthy family situations, where the mother is having difficulty or has to work because the father is a chronic alcoholic or unemployable and so forth. We have areas where the congestion is so great that the street is the only playground for these youngsters.

We have housing conditions where every room has to be a bedroom, where families attempt to curtain off parts of the room so that youngsters can sleep and so forth.

When these conditions exist, naturally the youngsters are not going to stay around the house. They are going to stay out until it is time to go to bed. It is just a sleeping place for these youngsters. As they stay out and get involved in the streets, particularly where there is a lack of recreational facilities or a lack of places where they can go to get some guidance, they are no longer spending time with their family which is the natural, normal setting and they gradually get into difficulties.

I am not saying that housing is the prime factor. I am saying if you take these family conditions, and a poor neighborhood and a neighborhood with lack of recreational facilities. You take these youngsters that are mixed up with a lot of gang kids and put these factors all together you get the problem you have.

Chairman LEHMAN. You lay great stress as I do, I assume, on the relationship of adequate recreation facilities ——

Mr. WHELAN. That's right.

Chairman LEHMAN. To this whole problem, adequate recreational facilities for youngsters, particularly in high delinquency areas where the housing conditions are poor and where they need a substitute for their own home living room.

What effect have you found as a result of discrimination, whether discrimination on the ground of color or race or religion, or national origin. Has that played much of a role? Does that play much of a role in your opinion?

Mr. WHELAN. In my opinion it is not so much of a racial problem, so far as New York City is concerned. It is a problem of newcomers coming into the city and pushing out oldtimers. We notice this particularly on the peripheral areas of the different places where we are working. As newcomers come into the city or move about the city into new neighborhoods, the people who have been there for a generation or two resent the newcomers. It takes quite a while for the newcomers to be integrated into the neighborhood life and to be accepted by the oldtimers and for the newcomers to accept the oldtimers. We find as an actual fact that when a new housing project goes up we experience a rise in delinquency rates on the periphery of the housing project until integration takes place between the newcomers in the project and those living in the area around them. I might add that one of our greatest needs, as we see it, is a crew or staff of people to help newcomers integrate into an old neighborhood and to help the old neighborhood accept them.

Until something can be done about that and we can work through those problems, we are still going to have that problem around the peripheral area because of the mobility of these people.

Chairman LEHMAN. I should think that when a child lacks security because of discrimination shown against him on the grounds of race, color, or creed, it would be quite a factor in developing juvenile delinquency.

Mr. WHELAN. It definitely is. There is no question about it, particularly if their skin is tan and they find it difficult to get employment. They find it difficult too when they go into a new area where they have not been accepted. The tensions naturally increase.

Chairman LEHMAN. Just to ask two more questions.

Have you made any study, or has any study been made, with regard to the intelligence quotient of children of juvenile delinquents? Is a child with a very low intelligence quotient more likely to be a juvenile delinquent or otherwise?

Mr. WHELAN. We have made no specific studies in that regard, Senator. The institute at Harvard probably would have some information on that rather than we. We would say generally speaking that a child with a low IQ is more easily influenced in the path of delinquency than the child with a high IQ. But at the same time you can have a child with a high IQ who is very emotionally disturbed who can get into delinquency much faster than one with a low IQ.

[. . . . .]

Chairman LEHMAN. I have pointed out that there is one school of thought, which does not happen to be mine, which holds that juvenile delinquency is just getting more publicity and is not actually increasing.

What is your impression about that?

Mr. WHELAN. My impression is that it is getting more publicity but that it is also increasing. I think it is both.

I think that we are much more aware and alert to the problem than we were a few years ago because of the publicity we are getting but we are also getting much more serious situations with regard to juveniles than we had before.

It is our thinking that the offenses in which young people are engaged these days are of a much more serious nature than they were 10 years ago. There is no point in going into the causes and factors of this, but there seems to be a lessening in terms of a young person's respect for the dignity of life itself.

They are using regular guns, zip guns, and knives, and so forth in their battles with one another. Years ago we used brickbats and sticks and stones and so forth. We seem to be getting an increase in the seriousness of the type of offense these days over what we had 10 years ago.

Chairman LEHMAN. You say that part of this is due to lack of respect for life itself, but to what extent is it due to lack of respect for the law and the way the law is being administered?

Mr. WHELAN. I think that, too, is a very important factor. I think some of us have become confused a little bit by the development of our psychological and psychiatric concepts in the treatment of people. We have become a little confused between that treatment and also the enforcement of the law as it should be enforced. I am a little concerned that there has been a tendency for young people to lose their respect for authority, and it seems not only to permeate the home in terms of the parents who I think have been carried away by these progressive ideas of rearing children, but who also seem to have lost their respect for teachers and their respect for other people whose job it is to enforce the law on the outside.

[. . . . .]

Mr. EDELSTEIN [chief of legislative staff to Senator Lehman]. Could you supply for the record — it would be very illuminating, sir — some case studies of this really radical work you are doing — which I don't believe is going on in many areas of the country — going into the market place and working with these gangs to try to turn them in a constructive direction?

Mr. WHELAN. We have some very interesting cases.

(The information referred to follows:)

WORKING WITH A STREET GANG

(Delivered by Kenneth E. Marshall, street club worker)

You have been given an idea of some of the ways we went about contacting our groups. Since I did not know anyone who could introduce me to the gang leaders, and since I learned that the Boppers, the gang I'd been sent out to work with, did not frequent regularly any of the few community centers in the area, I elected to use the hanging around method. After a few nights in the neighborhood, I was able to pick out a candy store, a restaurant, and a street corner where an unusually large number of boys seemed to congregate at all hours of the day and the night. I gradually found that many of these boys were members of the Boppers. I installed myself as a fixture in these places. I listened openly, with a friendly air, to the boys' conversations and it was not too long before some of the friendlier ones would nod to me, or look over in my direction to catch my smile when they had made a particularly biting or humorous contribution to the conversation.

The restaurant had a jukebox and I used it to help me get to know the fellows. I would put in a couple of nickles and ask the nearest boy to punch in the numbers he wanted to hear. I was thus able to start a casual conversation with him about the latest hit song. My expression would not change when a boy surreptitiously changed a number I had picked to one more to his liking. After awhile, although the majority remained suspiciously aloof or indifferent, there were 2 or 3 boys with whom I had become quite friendly. Our conversations, at this early point, had to do with the coming baseball season, basketball, popular music, the newest dance step, the mambo and such things.

During the first weeks I realized that there were definite cliques in the neighborhood, and that I would be likely to see a certain boy only in the company of certain other boys. Some of these cliques I saw only fleetingly, coming and going and I was not able to find their hangouts.

As soon as the boys realized that I was not going to take out a badge and say, "Let's go," the first time one of them pulled out a pair of dice, I learned that such things as the hijacking of bakery and soda trucks, the rolling of drunks, and joy riding in stolen cars were their behavior pattern. Three boys were sent to jail for stealing and wrecking a car before I'd had a chance to know them very well. I was shown zip guns and was assured that they would work. I was invited to partake of some of the loot of a rifled candy truck. One night, one of the boys was waylaid and badly beaten by members of a rival gang.

While the antisocial activities of the Boppers were dramatic, it should be noted that they represented a very small segment of the time and activities of the Boppers. Actually, the most significant characteristic of their lives was the fact that it was aimless, disorganized, and unproductive.

The average boy had no job and was out of school. He slept late, met his friends on the corner and moved back and forth from the corner to the candy store, the poolroom and back to the corner. He ate snacks with his friends in the luncheonette and returned home only to sleep, usually in the early hours of the morning.

The fellows themselves were aware that their activities were limited and monotonous. One boy once told me, "Now, for example, you take an average day. What happens? We come down to the restaurant and we sit in the restaurant, and sit and sit. All right, say–er–after a couple of hours in the restaurant, maybe we'll go to a poolroom, shoot a little pool, that's if somebody's got the money. O. K., a little pool, come back. By this time the restaurant is closed. We go in the candy store, sit around the candy store for awhile, and that's it, that's all we do, man."

In spite of the pattern described above and the fact that one of the chief but destructive activities of the boys when together was a form of scapegoating – a bantering or tossing back and forth of personal insults known as "ranking," they however, gained a very real sense of belonging and status from their associations with each other.

After about a month in the neighborhood, I had my first opportunity to explain something of my role when I heard two fellows discuss their interest in finding jobs. I offered to help them and I used this situation to invite the boys to the project office. Meanwhile, I established contact with a vocational guidance agency which specialized in finding jobs for hard to place teen-agers. While they were at the office, we not only discussed employment opportunities but also explored some of their other interests. They told me that they belonged to a social club which wanted to throw dances and I indicated that I would be interested in helping them. This opening into the boys' social life later proved quite productive. Fortunately, the employment agency placed these boys almost immediately. In rapid succession, several other boys approached me about jobs and the agency was able to place them also. While in the eyes of the boys, I became the "job man," this situation deepened my relationship and gave me the opportunity to further structure my role.

Shortly afterwards I got another break. One afternoon the boys were hanging around and a crap game started. I decided it would be strategic for me to participate so that I might get closer to them. During the course of the game one of the fellows turned to me and said, "say, man, you're supposed to be out here to change us and it seems like we're making you like us instead." Actually there was real significance in his words because the boys were beginning to understand that I accepted them as they were and in turn their acceptance of me was growing.

At this time I had been working in the neighborhood for almost 3 months. During that period there were times when I was not sure of where I was going. Like in any situation involving work with people I sometimes felt that I was taking two steps backward for every step forward. Gradually, however, the various pieces of information and knowledge of the gang that I had acquired began to fall into a meaningful pattern. I learned that the Boppers were a loosely knit federation of small social clubs and cliques who came together as Boppers only in time of conflict. These subgroups varied in size, activities, interest, degree of organization, and the extent to which they participated in antisocial activities. I decided I could have more impact on the gang as a whole if I devoted my major efforts toward working with a social club which I felt had the greatest potential for positive development. It was my feeling that if the prestige of this group was enhanced through activities such as dances, parties, athletics, trips, and other social events, the other clubs and cliques making up the Boppers would also be influenced positively.

The group I selected was known as the Angels. It was one of the largest of the local clubs in the gang. While the leaders of the Boppers were not members of the Angels most of them were active on the fringe of the club. I showed interest in the activities of the club and was soon invited to sit in on their meetings.

The club was under the rather rigid control of a taciturn president, a very serious minded young person. Club meetings tended to be solemn affairs having to do mainly with how much each member owed the club.

My immediate objectives with the Angels were to foster more democratic participation, broaden the membership, and expand their interests. Because dances were important to the members of the club, this was my first point of concentration. Previously the club ran their dances in homes of the members. These parties were poorly organized and unsupervised. There was considerable wine drinking, mauling of the girls, and stealing of clothing. A typical session attracted over a hundred young people many of whom were the members of rival gangs. The crowding that resulted frequently created tense situations out of which gang fights often developed. Work with the club around dances was a slow process, in fact one that is still going on. Gradually, certain positive changes took place. There is a greater degree of advance planning, members assume responsibility for policing the dances, and there are fewer fights at the dances.

In addition there are two other interesting developments which grew out of our experience with the dances that I feel are significant. The first was that the club held a large successful hall dance from which they gained not only considerable prestige in the neighborhood, but a sizable sum of money for their treasury. This in turn they used to purchase jackets which again further increased their status. At the present time the group is planning a second hall dance and is interested in running this type of dance on a regular basis. When they reach this point, the session type dance I previously described may be discontinued.

The second development occurred when the members expressed an interest in obtaining a clubroom of their own where they could meet regularly and hold a variety of social functions. This became a reality when one of the members obtained permanent space for the club in his home.

Gradually their activities broadened and at the present time include in addition to dances, a newspaper, and a weekly movie. In regard to the films, it is interesting to note that along with the usual films, psychological and educational ones are included which often provoke stimulating discussions. These discussions explore important subjects, such as, relations with girls, and problem of nonunderstanding parents, jobs, and life ambitions. In the congeniality of the clubroom, these discussions can be guided by the worker and are more purposeful and without the interruptions that are encountered on the street corner.

The Angels became one of the top prestige groups in the neighborhood. Gang members who had previously been either on the fringe or who were uninterested began taking considerable interest. Sometimes, after a club meeting, we would find them on the stoop anxiously waiting to hear what had transpired in the meetings. As time went on, several of them applied and were admitted into the club.

Significantly, the president of the Boppers, who was previously on the periphery, became a regular member. Prior to his joining, I had the following conversation with him while I accompanied him to court: "You know, Kenny, if I get out of this mess, you know, if I don't have to go to jail or anything [. . .] now that I have a job [. . .] I'm really going to straighten out [. . .] try to get into the club if I can [. . .] straighten up in general." As with this boy, work with gang members when they were involved with the law such as contacts with the police, visiting them in jail, attending court hearings, etc., not only was helpful to the members involved but also did much to strengthen my relationship with them.

The boys began to use meetings for discussions of other program and promotional ideas that would bring the club additional reputation. As the members' interest increased, so did democratic participation. For example, the president really allowed them to take a greater part in the running of the club. Also, a member whom he had put out of the club was reinstated when the members made known their opinion that he had been unfairly abrupt in putting the fellow out. Democratic participation increased. At the suggestion of the vice-president, secret balloting was instituted. The leader of the Boppers, who incidentally is content to be merely a member of the Angels, on one occasion voted against one of his best friends on a disciplinary matter, informing him later that friend or no friend, he had wronged the club and should be censored.

It is interesting to note that as the activities of the club broadened and democratic participation increased, the membership of the club broadened and by December, it included almost all the active Boppers.

In regard to gang conflict, at an early meeting of the Angels, I had the opportunity to further interpret my role. The question of fighting under the name of the Angels came up. One of the boys said, "Look, if we don't be careful, we'll be back bopping right where we started." There were several nods of agreement to this and I seized the chance to tell the group that one of the reasons I had been sent to the area was because the boys had engaged in gang fights and that I would try to do all I could to help them in their resolve to put down fighting. In this regard with the assistance of one of our workers assigned to work with a rival gang, I was able to help the gang mediate a conflict by having representatives from the Boppers and the rival gang sit down together and resolve their differences peacefully.

Generally speaking, with the development of constructive interest and increased status through the social activities of the club, their need and interest in maintaining "rep" through street fighting diminished. This was borne out when a Bopper not in the Angels came bearing rumors that "we" meaning the Boppers are fighting the Jaybirds, a rival gang. He was told in no uncertain terms first of all, "we" aren't the Boppers; we are the Angels, and the Angels ain't fighting nobody. Fighting now is not only bad business, it is bad for business. When a fight is in the offing, many of the girls and some of the fellows will stay away from the dance that weekend — the club will lose money. Another time when the Deacons, also a rival gang, threatened to come down and turn out a party, several of the boys readily acceded to my suggestion that we get police protection. They agreed that it was foolish to risk getting into trouble by taking it upon themselves to deal with the other gang. They also agreed that it was foolish to risk having the party poorly attended because there was no protection. Later when some of the less socialized members of the club expressed aggrieved amazement that we had called in the police, several of the majority who were for the move were able to convince most of the boys and silence the remainder with the soundness of their reasons. On the next occasion when trouble threatened, the leader of the Boppers himself, in no uncertain terms suggested that we call the police, went with me and stood by prompting me while I put in the call.

The total effect of our work with the Boppers cannot be completely evaluated at this time. There have been some significant changes in both group and individual behavior. Street fighting and weapon carrying has decreased. When fighting has occurred it has been entirely defensive in nature. Through the activities of the Angel social club, a beginning code of behavior has emerged. A member may not wear his jacket unless he is otherwise neatly dressed; he may not get drunk while he's an official representative of the club at a dance or other social function; only one girl may wear his club jacket, and he has to take responsibility for the care of the club facilities. Mainly, boys have learned to accept the give and take of group life, developing new interests and learning democratic skills.

In regard to individual behavior, all of the boys who expressed an interest in work have been helped to obtain jobs. Others have been stimulated to seek work and are now gainfully employed. A few of the boys through their participation in the group and their relationship with me have developed a deeper understanding of themselves and their environment. There is still much to be done with the Boppers. Some boys still drink excessively; there is much mauling of girls and sexual promiscuity. Ranking or scapegoating continues to torment many boys. In addition, there are certain boys with deep-seated personality problems who need individual treatment. They are not yet ready to use such service. However, I am working with them in this direction.

Finally, I would like to relate one incident which I believe not only clearly demonstrates that my role is understood by the Boppers, but also that there has been a change in their attitude toward gang fighting. Recently when I introduced a new worker who had been assigned to work with a particularly troublesome nearby gang, one of the fellows exclaimed to him, "See what you can do with those cats, man, get them off our backs. We have no time for them."

WORKING WITH A STREET GANG MEMBER

(Delivered by Vincent A. Riccio, street club worker)

I work with the Rumblers, a street gang which during the past few years has been in conflict with several rival gangs. My work with this group follows the general pattern previously described. In addition to working with the gang as a group, I have worked intensively with a few boys who need special help. Shorty is one of these boys.

About a year ago I met Shorty, he was thin and undernourished with a sickly pallor. Even though 17, his short frail build gave him a very childish appearance. I learned that his mother died when he was in infancy and according to information secured from relatives and agencies, his father, a chronic alcoholic, whose whereabouts were unknown, had abandoned him when he was 7 years old. Shorty was placed in a series of child-caring institutions, and for many years this environment was the substitute for family life. He soon established a pattern of running away from these institutions. I learned that for the last year his home had been subways, hallways, automobiles, and "hand-out beds." Shorty was a quiet kid who used to like to sit around and listen to the bigger fellows brag about their exploits. The fellows liked him and even though he was small they felt he had a lot of guts. He was easily led and whenever some gang activity was planned, Shorty was the first to follow along. He participated actively in gang wars, robberies, assaults, lineups, and was a narcotics user. In a word, Shorty was a seriously disturbed and unhappy youngster.

In my early contacts with the group Shorty viewed me with extreme suspicion. After many weeks on the street corners, in poolrooms, community centers, cellars, and hallways, my relationships with the group developed. As various fellows accepted me, Shorty followed suit and began to accept me, too, as someone genuinely interested in him.

On one occasion, Shorty came to the office greatly upset and seemed anxious to talk to me. He told me he was in trouble — that the police were after him. While he was with me I contacted the local police precinct and found that Shorty's fears were based on rumor and that there was no warrant out for his arrest. Shorty was greatly relieved. I used his readiness to talk at this time to explore some of his other problems. He related that when he was 16, he was involved in an auto theft and was apprehended by the police. He was tried in adolescent court and placed on probation. He violated probation almost immediately and for the past year has been evading his probation officer. When Shorty left he was much relieved. This contact went a long way toward strengthening our relationship.

Shortly after, at a dance sponsored by the club, I learned that Shorty, and some of the other members of the gang were users of heroin. When Shorty realized that I knew about his using drugs, he began to speak to me freely about it and several times he described how "booting up" made him feel happier. He said, "When I don't use the stuff, Rick, I don't care if I die, but when I'm 'high' everything seems better." Another time he said, "I don't care if it kills me [. . .] my life is all messed up anyway."

Shorty and I talked frequently and freely about his problems. I always had the time to let him talk and it was always with deep interest that I listened to what he had to say. I was understanding, and supportive when he revealed things to me about which he felt guilty. One time when he was talking, he stopped suddenly and said, "I wish I was dead." We talked further until I felt that I had at least lifted him temporarily out of this depression. I stuck as close as possible to him during this period, seeking him out every day when he did not come to the office. I was always around, and when I thought it important, I had a half a buck for cigarettes or a show and often when I thought he hadn't eaten all day I would say, "C'mon Short-Stuff, I'm hungry and I want some company."

When the boys "ranked" him, I would take his side to give him status and show the group that I liked and respected him.

Gradually he began to depend on me. On a planned basis, I allowed this dependency to develop so that Shorty could gain the security he needed from having an adult he could count on. For weeks, Shorty was depressed, withdrawn, and talked much about dying and not caring anything about the future. Gradually, I was able to use my relationship to help him understand himself a little better and begin to face his future more realistically. He talked about working and being tired of running all the time and using the subways and abandoned cars as his home. One day, he came to the office and asked me to get him a job. I said that I was interested in his wanting to work, but explained that there were many things that he would have to straighten out before I would be able to help him. I reminded him that he had no working papers, he was wanted as a probation violator, and that he was well on his way to serious drug addiction. We discussed these problems at length and agreed that I would help him with them. However, Shorty was unable to face these problems at this time. Instead, he went out and got himself a job and was able to stay at it only 1 week.

During this trying period for Shorty I continued to stick close to him. In August, Shorty became acutely ill. He was frightened and thought he had withdrawal symptoms. Three of the boys took him to a hospital. His illness was diagnosed as appendicitis and he had an operation. During his convalescence, I saw Shorty almost daily. This was a reflective period for the boy. He talked a great deal about his problems, particularly about his desire to give up drugs. His deep concern about this was expressed to me one afternoon at the hospital. While we were eating some ice cream, he said, "Hey Rick, get a load of this — Lulu was up here today and wanted to give me a 'cap'; he thought I needed the stuff — you know when I get out of here I'm really going to kick the habit this time."

When he got back in the neighborhood, Shorty tried to stay off the stuff. It wasn't long, however, before he was back on the habit. He continued attendance at club meetings and the sense of responsibility that the group was developing toward some of their problem members showed itself in their attempts to persuade him to "kick the habit." Initially they tried by ridiculing him and calling him and his friends "junkies." Later, they became less punitive and more sympathetic as I was able to help them understand how their actions affected Shorty.

One evening Shorty and two of his cronies arrived as a club meeting closed. He had been using narcotics and the symptoms were very noticeable. He called me aside and asked again if I could get him a job. I told him I would talk to him about the possibilities the next day at the office. Shorty was stung by my answer. He broke down, cursed me and shouted at the top of his voice, "I hate you. I don't need your help, drop dead. I got pride. I don't want your help."

Though startled I concealed my feelings and just listened. I understood that through his emotional outburst, he was really saying, "I need you. I want you to help me more." Following this, my contacts with Shorty were similar to that of a worker who is trying to reach an unfamiliar gang boy. Anytime I approached Shorty, he would walk away. If I entered the candy store, Shorty would leave. If I tried to talk, he would not answer me. This continued for about 2 weeks. In the meantime, the fellows were trying to make him realize that I was really interested in him.

A change came one evening at a club meeting. He sat apart and did not participate. At one point the group was discussing how a sum of $7 was to be delivered to a local YMCA the next day as a deposit for our dance. Tony, one of the leaders asked for volunteers to make the trip to the Y, but each member gave excuses. Noticing this, I saw a splendid opportunity to indicate to Shorty that we trusted and needed him.

I said, "Shorty, I was wondering — if you are free, would you take the seven bucks to the Y? It's very urgent that we get the money there tomorrow."

Shorty's face lit up. I could see that he was surprised and happy to have this recognition from me. He said, "Yeah, I'll go." At the close of the meeting, he walked up to me and said, "Rick, I wanna tell you I'm sorry for the way I been acting. Ya know, I've been trying to get off the habit and I haven't touched the stuff for the last week. Ya know, Rick, I act that way when I 'boot up' and I fight and argue with everyone. Look, Rick, I wanna give myself up. I'm sick and I need help. Would ya help me?" I reassured him I was not angry, that I understood, and that I would certainly help him. We discussed what Shorty wanted to do. He felt that he first wanted to see a priest he knew. He asked me to go along and I agreed. He told the priest everything, and the priest agreed that Shorty was doing the right thing in giving himself up.

A few days later, when Shorty was ready, I met him in the neighborhood and accompanied him to the probation office. En route, Shorty was frightened and apprehensive. I reassured him that we both knew that he was now taking an important step toward straightening himself out.

Shorty's probation was revoked and he was remanded to the city prison pending hearing. I visited him at the prison. I found Shorty ambivalent. Although he was relieved that he was no longer being sought as a probation violator, he was fearful of the consequences he might have to face. I reassured Shorty that I would stick by him, that he had taken the correct step and regardless of the immediate outcome, in the long run things would work out for the best.

At a conference called by the judge and attended by the assistant district attorney, a representative of the Youth Counsel Bureau, his probation officer, and the worker, it was decided that the best plan for Shorty would be that he be remanded to Kings County for a complete physical and psychiatric examination. Further, pending the results of the examination, it was agreed that if there was going to be any possibility of Shorty remaining in the community a stable home environment would have to be found.

On one of my visits to Shorty at the hospital, I talked with him about his aunt whom I had met when he was previously hospitalized for his appendectomy. He did not seem to feel very close to her, but told me about another aunt who lived in New Jersey, whom he liked. We discussed the possibility of his going to live with her when he is released. He reacted favorably to this possibility. Later I visited this aunt. She expressed a real interest in Shorty. I was careful to clearly point out not only his need for a good home, but the severe problems he was presenting. After discussing the situation with her family, his aunt agreed to appear in court at the time of Shorty's next hearing and offer him a home with her.

In the interim the gang reaction to Shorty's decision to give himself up can best be illustrated by an excerpt from a letter written by the president of the club. It reads as follows:

"HELLO, SHORTY: We're dropping you a line to let you know that we're thinking of you. Even though we miss you around the neighborhood, we feel happy and proud of what you did. Rick and the rest of us feel that everything will turn out for the best this way. We're sending you some money to help you along until you get out.

"Luck.

"*Johnny* (writing for all the gang)."

While awaiting the final hearing, I informed Shorty that his aunt would like to take him into her home if the court approved. We both understood that if this worked out, Shortly would still need additional help with his problems. He agreed to this saying, "Yeah, Rick, I know what you mean. A guy like you — only he could understand better, and help me some more, huh?"

Incidentally, for some time I recognized Shorty's need for more intensive individual treatment, but felt that the time had not arrived for a transfer in light of Shorty's great need for a consistent relationship with the same adult.

Last week at the court hearing Shorty was placed in the custody of his aunt. Followup psychiatric treatment for the boy to facilitate his adjustment to his new environment was recommended. I agreed to assume responsibility for arranging for this service.

Shorty, his aunt, and I left the courtroom together. As we walked down the street I felt that they would get along. I stated that I would like to visit them when Shorty was settled. He said, "Gee, I hope you'll come soon, Rick." His aunt also voiced her agreement. As I left, she was taking him into a clothing store to buy him a new suit.

All of Shorty's problems are by no means solved. He still has a hard long road ahead of him. He does, however, have a fresh start and we are going to do all we can to help him make the most of it.

Study Outline for Working with a Street Gang Member

The Gang Member   1. The gang provides for its members a security they do not find within themselves.

2. Members usually have experienced severe physical and emotional deprivation.

3. They have a disrupted relationship with adults and more particularly with adults in authoritative positions.

4. Most gang members and their families present a pathology of many years' duration. Usually they have been known to the full gamut of social services and have come away from these services unhelped.

Workers Approach   1. As the group has become acquainted with the worker some of their suspicions have been diminished, and in the unity of the group there is apparent acceptance of the worker. A greater personal security, however, is necessary before individual members feel free enough in coming to the worker for help with their more basic individual problems. Often the worker has to show them concrete evidence of his desire to help, before they will relate intimate information.

2. In the interim, the worker must reach out to them in an accepting, nonjudgmental, friendly, adult manner.

3. In working with individuals the work capitalizes on crisis situations utilizing the boys' involvement with the law, situational anxiety, etc., as the means for demonstrating direct help; at other times he may be asked for help with some more superficial request such as employment.

4. Boys have almost insatiable need for demonstrated acceptance on the part of the worker. Therefore, the client is constantly alert for anything which might indicate rejection. Obviously, this infers strong guilt feelings and feelings of unworthiness.

5. Need for consistent identification with an accepting male shows itself during this period by overly strong identification with the worker. This regressive over-dependency in many cases is a prerequisite for further growth on the part of the client.

6. Worker endeavors to help client to accept the realistic limitations of society as opposed to the temporarily more comfortable escape which he has formerly taken.

7. Hostility: These boys have great hostility and at times focus it on the worker. As he places limits, or withholds his own giving, the boys may demonstrate this hostility, for these limits reinforce their own feelings of

unworthiness. However, the setting of limits is a necessity if the boys are ever going to realistically accept their responsibilities as members of society or more immediately if they are ever to be able to accept help.

8. Based on the relationship which is developed and the growth in security on the part of the client, he may then be able to accept another agency for other treatment.

9. Worker is aware of and able to use the resources provided by the community.

Additional Point   Although treatment may be needed for many, with most the task is one of support and in general holding the line through the process of maturation. After this point and with the positive experience with the worker most boys are able to accept their responsibility as adult members of society without further treatment. Whether or not they will once again regress when faced with serious stress at a future time, is a question which would bear interesting research in the future.

> *Questions for Discussion of Working with a Street Gang Member*
>
> 1. The worker permits strong dependency to develop on the part of Shorty. Why did he feel this was necessary?
> 2. The worker does much in terms of environmental help. Of what importance is this to Shorty?
> 3. Why did the worker continue to work with Shorty over so long a period of time? Could he not have referred him to a treatment agency much sooner?
> 4. Shorty has a violent reaction to worker, around the job request. What are the components of this reaction?
> 5. At the point where Shorty gives himself up to the probation officer why does the worker not sever his responsibility?
> 6. What part does the group play in the running story of this boy's life?

8.

The Klamath Indians

ALTHOUGH MAJOR NATIONAL CONCERN IN "MINORITY group" problems has recently focused on the Negro, events are moving so rapidly with respect to this group that it is preferable for our purposes to turn to another group which has had at least as long a history of discrimination in this country, the American Indian.

In recent years there has been general recognition that the American Indian in the United States has received other than just treatment. Though steps have been taken to remedy matters, at least in the present (since history cannot be changed), the problem of integrating Indians into the larger community is still with us. The "Indian problem" is complex, and the Indians cannot be treated as a single group. Reservations range in size from about one-half acre with one person to over 15 million acres with more than 80,000 persons (Navajo); economic assets range from almost $60 per family (Sisseton in North and South Dakota) to over $750,000 per family (Agua Caliente); educational levels vary from those unable to speak English to university graduates with doctoral degrees, and cultural assimilation shows an equivalent range.

There seems to be widespread agreement on the desirability of terminating federal supervision of the American Indians and integrating this minority group into the general community. The essential questions relate to how this might best be done with proper regard for the rights of the Indians and the responsibilities of the government. On the economic side, there is the question of how to dispose of tribal assets so that those members who wish to withdraw from the cooperative community may take their just share and enter the larger community as individuals.

The Klamath Indians form one of the wealthiest groups in the United States. Their major wealth, in economic terms, are the timber resources of the reservation. (For those not familiar with lumbering practices, it may be worth noting that there are two forms of utilizing such resources. These two forms are often compared to mining and farming. In the first form, "clear-cutting," all the timber is cut and the supply is exhausted in one operation; this is commonly recognized as an uneconomic practice, wasteful of the country's resources. The second form involves selective cutting, "sustained yield lumbering," so that year after year the prime lumber can be harvested; this is the preferred form but is usually not profitable for small units.)

Suggested Discussion Questions

Identify the major problems noted in the hearings, separating them into two lists, one for economic and one for psychological problems. With respect to the psychological problems, how might one develop the information needed to permit the congressional committee to assess the facts? Make whatever assumptions concerning these facts that seem reasonable and outline a program for termination that would properly implement the intentions of the legislators. Where the assumptions concerning the "facts" seem dubious, prepare alternative programs if necessary.

AMENDMENTS TO THE KLAMATH TERMINATION ACT OF 1954

HEARINGS *before the Subcommittee on Indian Affairs of the Committee on Interior and Insular Affairs, United States Senate, 85th Congress, First Session on S. 2047*

OCTOBER 2, 4, 1957

Klamath Falls, Oregon

THE HEARINGS CONVENED at the county courthouse, Klamath Falls, Oreg., at 10 a. m., Senator Richard L. Neuberger presiding.

Also present: James Gamble, chief clerk, and Robert Wolf, forestry consultant, Subcommittee on Indian Affairs.

Senator NEUBERGER. May we come to order please?

[. . . . .]

In my capacity as chairman of the Subcommittee on Indian Affairs, I would like to begin these hearings by welcoming all of you in attendance today. I think it would be proper for me to make a short statement explaining some of the recent developments which have brought the Senate Subcommittee on Indian Affairs to Klamath Falls at this time, in order that the record may be clear.

One year ago we held hearings in this very room on the subject of the Klamath Termination Act of 1954. At that meeting the Management Specialists charged with the responsibility of carrying out Public Law 587, 83d Congress, brought to our attention the need for amending the law to provide additional time in which to solve the many complex problems that had arisen in connection with termination. They pointed out that a large percentage of the Klamath Indians probably would elect to withdraw from the tribe, and that such action could result in the wholesale liquidation of the timber assets of the reservation. Mr. Watters, in his testimony before this committee on October 18, 1956, stated:

After studying the basic qualities of each proposal the Management Specialists now believe that the most feasible method for terminating the Federal Government's present trust responsibility in a manner that will safeguard the long-term welfare of tribal members as well as the economy of the community is through the purchase of the Klamath tribal property by the Federal Government.

We were also told by the Klamath Executive Committee that Federal purchase of the tribal assets appeared to be the only solution that would prevent the destruction of the Klamath forest property. The testimony furnished us by Mr. Watters and his associates, members of the Klamath Tribe, conservationists, church groups and individuals was forceful and cogent, and made a deep impression on subcommittee members.

At the outset of the 85th Congress, I introduced for Senator Wayne Morse and myself a bill, S. 469, to defer the sales of tribal assets, extend the final termination date to 1961, and provide for full reimbursement to the tribe for all termination costs. The bill also made certain other desirable changes in Public Law 587. We succeeded in having this proposed legislation passed by the Senate on March 8, 1957. Following consideration by the Indian Subcommittee of the House of Representatives, S. 469 passed the House on June 21, although in amended form. Because there were two versions of the bill, it was necessary for the two committees to confer to work out our differences. In my judgment, the Senate had passed a more equitable bill, a more fair bill, and I tried to convince our colleagues that the Senate bill provided a more realistic approach to the existing problem. However, the House members were adamant in their position, and in order to obtain a bill of any sort we agreed to their language. S. 469 was signed by President Eisenhower on August 14, and is now referred to as Public Law 85–132.

I mention this sequence of events to show the difficulties I have encountered in attempting to restore some order to this situation. I want to take this opportunity to state for the record my deep appreciation to Senator Murray, the chairman of the Senate Interior Committee, and the members of the Indian Subcommittee for the understanding and assistance they have given me in my efforts to find a workable solution to the Klamath problem. I regret that the other members of the subcommittee could not be here today, but they have informed me that other commitments prevent their participation.

Many of you may wonder what the Congress had in mind when Public Law 132 was enacted, and what we hope to accomplish through this hearing. Let me quote to you from the Senate report which accompanied my bill, S. 469, when that legislation was reported to the Senate:

The primary purpose of S. 469, as amended, is to delay the sales of tribal property belonging to the Klamath Indians until the end of the 2d session of the 85th Congress. Such a delay period will afford Congress an opportunity to consider alternative means of protecting the economy and preserving good conservation practices in the Klamath Basin.

By the terms of Public Law 132, we now have approximately 11 months in which to come up with these alternative plans for preserving the forest on the reservation. That leaves very little time in which to hold hearings, sponsor legislation, move it through the legislative process and have it signed by the President of the United States. Therefore, I have scheduled these hearings in Klamath Falls and in Portland — and I wish to say that I apologize for scheduling these hearings on World Series day, but they were scheduled prior to the time we noticed the start of the World Series — for the purpose of receiving recommendations and suggestions from the members of the tribe, the Management Specialists, and other interested groups on how we should proceed. I feel it is absolutely essential that we in Oregon, both Indian owners of these lands and private citizens, build a record at this hearing that will serve as a guide to Congress in formulating a program that will be fair in all respects to the Klamath Indians in giving them a fair return on their property, and yet afford an opportunity to retain the timberlands under a form of sustained yield management.

As you know, I have introduced a bill, S. 2047, which would provide for Federal acquisition of the reservation timberlands, and management of these assets by the United States Forest Service. It would also provide for the purchase of the marshlands, and management of that area by the Fish and Wildlife Service. Senator Wayne Morse, the senior Senator from Oregon, is cosponsor with me of this legislation. [. . .]

This proposal is only one possible method of preventing the gutting of the ponderosa-pine forest and preserving the feeding and nesting grounds for the waterfowl following the Pacific flyway. There may be other means of accomplishing this end, such as purchase of the reservation by the State of Oregon, and I have suggested to State officials that they give us their reaction to this alternative at our Portland meeting on October 4.

In letters dated August 21 and August 29 I requested that the Secretary of the Interior and the Secretary of Agriculture provide our committee with departmental reports on S. 2047 by October 2. I have received a tentative report addressed to me from Secretary Seaton dated September 26, 1957.

I want to introduce Mr. James H. Gamble, who is chief clerk of the Senate Indian Affairs Subcommittee, who is with us today, on my left, and Mr. Robert Wolf, forester for the committee, who is here on my right. And, Mr. Gamble, I think it is sufficiently important that you read into the record, so that the people here may hear it directly, Secretary Seaton's views on S. 2047.

Mr. GAMBLE. This letter is dated September 26, 1957, addressed to Senator Neuberger as chairman of the Senate Subcommittee on Indian Affairs:

DEAR SENATOR NEUBERGER: In recent conversation with Mr. H. Rex Lee, Legislative Associate Commissioner of Indian Affairs, and again in a letter dated September 9, 1957, you asked that the departmental report on S. 2047, relating to Federal acquisition of the Klamath Indian Forest, be submitted prior to the scheduled hearings in Oregon on October 2, if possible.

We appreciate your interest in the subject, and shall cooperate fully in the effort to provide for the conservation of the timber resources of the reservation in a manner that recognizes and safeguards the property rights of the Indians. We regret that it will not be possible for the Department to have ready by October 2 a final report on S. 2047, but we can outline for the benefit of the committee some of our present thoughts on the subject. You will understand, I am sure, that these thoughts are tentative and are still under active study. We, as well as your committee, are still seeking the most feasible solution to the problem.

We believe that the conservation of this timber resource is of primary importance to the economy of the area and to the welfare of the public generally. In recognition of this fact, Congress has deferred and sales of tribal forest lands until after the end of the 2d session of the 85th Congress in order that Congress may determine whether further legislation with respect to the forest will be enacted.

Congress has determined by the act of August 13, 1954 (68 Stat. 718), that a continuation of the Federal trust over the property of the Klamath Indians would not be in the best interest of the Indians. As would be the case in any group, however, certain individuals may not be qualified to handle a large capital asset with reasonable prudence, and the 1954 statute requires the Secretary of the Interior to safeguard the interests of these individuals by arranging for the appointment of guardians through the State courts or by such other means as he deems adequate, which could include, for example, the establishment of individual involuntary private trusts for them.

The essence of the 1954 act is that the Klamath Indians shall be freed of all Federal restraints applicable to them because of their Indian origin, and that they shall be placed in the same status as all other citizens, subject to no special restrictions or rights. Inasmuch as existing Federal and State laws do not require the owners of large forest resources to maintain them intact and to manage them on a sustained-yield basis in the interests of conservation, the Klamath Indians should not be subject to any such restrictions when the Federal trust is terminated.

The manner in which the Klamath Reservation forest area is managed in the future, however, will have a vital impact on the life and economy of the entire Klamath River Basin.

Kept intact through continued management according to conservation principles of sustained yield, the forest will remain a perpetually productive source of ponderosa pine and other commercial species. Such management would also assure continuation of its important function as a watershed. The large numbers of migratory waterfowl for which it now provides nesting and feeding grounds would be protected, as would the deer and other species of wild animals that now find sanctuary within its boundaries. Further development of the forest's recreational potential would be made possible.

Were sustained-yield management to be abandoned and the forest broken up and disposed of in small individual tracts to bring the highest price, it is our belief that all these values soon would be lost.

We believe that the likelihood of the forest's being dissipated in this fashion is a matter for genuine concern.

Section 5 of Public Law 587 provides that each adult member of the Klamath Indian Tribe shall be given an opportunity to withdraw from the tribe and have his interest in the tribal property converted into money and paid to him, or to remain in the tribe and participate in a tribal-management plan. Inasmuch as the forest resources represent approximately 90 percent of the total value of all Klamath tribal property, it is probable that a major portion of these resources must be sold in order to pay those members who elect to withdraw from the tribe. Based on the findings of a survey conducted by the Stanford Research Institute among tribal members on the Klamath Reservation during August and September 1955, it appears that approximately 70 percent of the members may elect to withdraw from the tribe. If this were to happen, as much as 2,660 million board-feet of tribally owned timber might have to be sold from the reservation lands prior to August 13, 1960, in order to comply with the provisions of section 5 of the law. This sales program would be carried out concurrently with the removal of restrictions from allotted timber which, in itself, will make approximately 225 million board-feet available for purchase during a period of approximately 2 years in an economic area with an installed capacity that can cut, at the most, 400 million board-feet per year.

It is doubtful whether sustained-yield management would be continued on a very large portion of the timber area if it is sold without restriction in small economic units. The Management Specialists, who have responsibility for the sales of these units, are obligated under the law to obtain on behalf of the withdrawing members the greatest possible return from these sales. This obligation means that a sizable portion of the area to be sold would have to be sold in small-sized units in order to obtain the greatest amount of competition possible. It is doubtful that such small units, within themselves, can furnish a sustained cut for even the smallest of sawmills.

In this connection, it should also be noted that State laws do not require sustained-yield management by private operators.

The tremendously disruptive influence that cutting over of the Klamath Reservation forest lands would have on the economy of the basin is not difficult to contemplate when it is realized that 40 percent of the area's economy is based on timber production. The importance of the reservation timber to the Klamath economy is evident from the fact that it includes about 26 percent of the total commercial-forest area and 26 percent of the sawtimber volume in Klamath County.

Other values of the forest as a management unit, while less tangible than timber, are of significant importance and must be considered in the public interest.

In the fall, waterfowl by the millions, following the Pacific flyway, pour into the upper Klamath Basin to rest and feed before continuing southward to their wintering grounds. The marsh on the Klamath Reservation is the most important marsh to waterfowl that is left unprotected in the Nation. This nesting area has been one of the mainstays in keeping up the supply of redheads, canvasbacks, and ruddy ducks in the Pacific flyway. Deer and other wild creatures also find year-round habitat in the forest.

The influence which the Klamath Reservation forest has in reducing flood crests and stabilizing the flow of streams throughout the year should, in itself, warrant measures being taken to prevent the timber from being cut to the minimum specifications of the State law. Approximately 303,000 acres of irrigated farmlands are dependent on streams that head on the forest slopes of the Klamath Basin.

Further, the maximum development of waterpower on the Klamath River cannot be realized without the protection of its headwaters. A large part of the extensive water resource of the Klamath Basin originates in the many large springs found on reservation lands. Cutting over of the Klamath Reservation forest well might jeopardize the farm production and the waterpower developments dependent on the watershed protection provided by this forest.

Too, denuding this area of its forest cover would destroy its scenic and recreational appeal, and the slash left from hurry-up logging operations would tend to increase the fire hazard.

When it is considered that this 745,280-acre tribally owned forest area, described as one of the finest of its type, now is contributing so vitally to the general welfare of the Klamath River Basin and to the Nation it must be concluded that any action that would, in the long run, diminish or eliminate those benefits should be avoided.

This Department believes that only through sustained yield management of the forest can its timber, water, wildlife, and recreational resources be maintained forever, and that further legislation for that purpose is desirable.

The two problems confronting both the Federal Government and the State of Oregon are protecting the property rights of the Klamath Indians on the one hand, and providing for the sustained yield management of an important natural-resource area on the other. Public ownership would accomplish both of these objectives. If there is any reasonable alternative to public ownership which would accomplish the same results, we believe such an alternative should be thoroughly explored.

It is our purpose to cooperate fully with your committee, and the Congress, in the successful application of the Termination Act in a manner which will accomplish the objective of protecting the values existing in these lands for the benefit of the Klamath Indians and, at the same time, protecting a resource important to the Klamath community, the State of Oregon, and the Nation.

The views expressed in this letter are tentative. We shall, however, have a departmental report and recommendation ready for the consideration of your committee early next session.

The Bureau of the Budget advises us that it has no objection to the submission of this report.

Sincerely yours,

Fred A. Seaton,
SECRETARY OF THE INTERIOR

[. . . . .]

AFTERNOON SESSION

Senator NEUBERGER. Will we please come to order? Before we hear from the first witness this afternoon, I should like to say that it is my hope that every future witness will be as brief as possible and, yet, at the same time, will make such statement and provide such information as he or she deems necessary.

I have a resolution adopted by the Central Labor Council of

Klamath Falls, Oreg., signed by H. W. Waits, Jr., president; Alma Sweetman, secretary; and C. D. Long, delegate; which deals with the attitude of the Klamath Falls Central Labor Council on this question. They have not asked to read it or present it, but wish that it appear in the hearing record, and without objection it will appear in the hearing record at this point.

(The document referred to follows:)

CENTRAL LABOR COUNCIL OF KLAMATH FALLS, OREG.,

Klamath Falls, Oreg.

Senator Neuberger,
   Senate Investigation Committee,
      Klamath Termination Act,
         In Session at Klamath Falls, Oreg., October 2, 1957

Whereas the Congress of the United States has passed an act to terminate the Klamath Indian Reservation as such and portends to appraise the assets of the Klamath Tribe of Indians; and

Whereas this act provides further that the Indian agency be discontinued after a certain date specified in the act and its amendments; and

Whereas this action on the part of the Federal Government will place this tribe of Indians on its own to manage its affairs as individuals; and

Whereas a sale of the assets of this tribe would net a large sum of money per capita, estimated at approximately $50,000 each, man, woman, and child; and

Whereas this sum of money placed in the hands of these Indians would be a target for unscrupulous persons who would use to every advantage, the inexperience of these people in money matters; and

Whereas this sudden influx of wealth on the part of the Indian and the immediate acquisition of the timber growth on the tribal lands within the reservation would cause a serious upset in the economy of Klamath County and to the State of Oregon as well as to the lumber market in the entire Northwest: Therefore be it

Resolved by this Klamath Falls Central Labor Union, AFL–CIO, That we issue this statement of policy and send a copy to the Senate Investigating Committee in session in Klamath Falls, Oreg., October 2, 1957, to wit: We, the Central Labor Union, AFL–CIO, urge the Congress of the United States to consider very carefully the subject matter contained in this particular act and if it feels that termination of the Klamath Indian Reservation is an absolute necessity, then they empower the Federal Government to purchase the entire reservation and to make proper provision for adequate protection of the funds paid to the Indians and, further, that timber sales from this tract be handled in such a manner as to be fair to the small operators who may wish to purchase for cutting on a sustained-yield basis. We feel further that such small operators be recognized as part of the free-enterprise system of the Nation's economy.

We especially wish to call to your attention the necessity of continued supervision of the funds paid to the Indians. While we recognize the fact that many of these people are wholly capable of managing their own affairs and finances, we also feel apprehensive of the fact that many of them are not capable of handling any large sum of money and will become the prey of "sharpies," "swindlers," "con men," and others of their ilk. Then, after the Indian and his money are separated, what is to be his final fate — a county or State charge for the balance of his days and even his descendents will have no recourse but to become also State and/or county charges.

Further, we, as a labor council, are requesting that the Federal Government do purchase the reservation outright and that it dispense the funds to the Indians in such a manner that is properly safeguarded from those who would take undue advantage of the inexperience of these former wards of the Government.

Failing in this, we urgently appeal to you to return the Indian to his former status and repeal the act in its entirety.

Respectfully submitted.

KLAMATH FALLS CENTRAL LABOR UNION, AFL–CIO
By *H. W. Waits, Jr.*, PRESIDENT
Alma Sweetman, SECRETARY
C. D. Long, DELEGATE

Senator NEUBERGER. I have a telegram from the distinguished Member of Congress from the Second Oregon District, who represents this area in the House of Representatives, and I should like to read it:

Regret that previous commitments prevent me from joining your subcommittee for these important hearings.

You and I agree that it is imperative that legislation be enacted changing the present untenable termination formula. It is only by doing so that Indian rights can be protected and the great reservation resources preserved.

Consequently, I believe that your hearings and the forthcoming visit of the House Indian Affairs Subcommittee on which I serve are of inestimable importance to the formulation of a sound termination program.

My thanks for your kind invitation and my best wishes for a constructive hearing.

Congressman Al Ullman

In addition, Mr. Elnathan Davis, who, with Mr. Jackson and Mr. Kirk, represented the Klamath Tribal Executive Committee before our subcommittee this morning, has made a request of me. Mr. Davis has asked particularly that a study by the Klamath Management Specialists dated December 19, 1956, entitled "Some of the Social Implications of Public Law 587" be included in the hearing record. It is a rather long document, but I have looked it over and because Public Law 587 is very much at issue here, I agree with Mr. Davis that it should be included in the hearing record, and, without objection, it is so ordered.

(The document referred to follows:)

Klamath Management Specialists, Klamath Falls, Oreg.

SOME OF THE SOCIAL IMPLICATIONS OF PUBLIC LAW 587

Accompanying the proposed Klamath terminal legislation when it was submitted to Congress in January of 1954 was a letter from the Office of the Secretary of the Interior which contained the following statement:

"Through intermarriage with non-Indians and cooperative work and association with their non-Indian neighbors, such as adult education and technical assistance programs, education in the public schools over an extended period of years, and employment in gainful occupations within and without the reservation, *these people have been largely integrated into all phases of the economic and social life of the area.*" [Italic supplied.]

It may be assumed that this statement was made in reference to that group of adult Klamaths living on the reservation in Klamath County, Oreg., as Klamath agency welfare personnel have stated that only recently has any appreciable amount of information been gathered concerning the approximately 40 percent of the tribe that is scattered over the rest of Oregon and 19 other States. Our factual information necessarily pertains to the majority group of the tribe, i. e., that group living on the Klamath Reservation which comprises approximately 60 percent of the total adult tribal population. Reference to Klamath tribal members in the body of this report apply to those still on the reservation, the majority of the tribe.

While our duties as management specialists under our contract with the Secretary of the Interior have to do with the physical resources of the tribe and the economic implications of Public Law 587, we cannot ignore the basic social implications of this legislation. Of national importance is the question of what will happen to the Klamath tribal forests and lands under the terms of Public Law 587. Of equal importance is the question of what will happen to the 2,000 human beings who are directly affected by this law. The management specialists do not presume to have the answer to that question. However, as we have become increasingly familiar with the situation on the reservation, and as we have studied the documents and statements that were submitted to Congress along with the original legislation that became Public Law 587, and as we have become more familiar with the contents of the transcripts of the hearings that were held relative to Klamath terminal legislation, we have become convinced that Congress acted on the basis of inaccurate information concerning the majority of Klamath tribal members. It is most important that the facts be made known to all concerned with Klamath terminal legislation. The Klamaths are entitled to consideration in the light of valid factual information. The decision to terminate Federal supervision over the property and affairs of the Klamaths, to bring to a halt practices which have been in effect longer than the span of memory of the oldest living tribal members, is an important decision. Such a decision, and the legislation for implementing it, must necessarily be based on facts.

The Secretary of the Interior has called for a review of the entire Klamath termination picture with the objective of making certain that termination of Federal supervision is brought about without harmful effects. It is essential, therefore, that he also have access to the facts which are so fraught with both economic and social implications, and that he give them careful consideration.

We are in favor of terminal legislation for the Klamath Tribe. We feel that an indefinite continuation of the present situation is undesirable, and that there is more than ample evidence to support the conclusion that the Klamaths will not realize their potential for becoming responsible, respected, and self-respecting citizens under continued Federal supervision. It is our contention that Congress intended that the carrying out of the mandate contained in House Resolution 108 be based on nothing less than factual information. Consideration may well be given by the Secretary of the Interior and by Members of the Congress to the information contained in the remainder of this report.

Management of Affairs

One concept held by the members of the Committees on Indian Affairs would seem to be that the Klamaths are, and have for a long time been managing their own affairs. The fact of the matter is that the Klamaths have never managed their own affairs as a group since the establishment of the reservation and there is a large group of the Klamaths whose members do not manage their own affairs as individuals. Historically the Klamaths have never practiced unity in any true sense of the word. The lack of unity is reflected in the present state of tribal affairs in that many times in recent years the tribal general council has been unable to convene at a scheduled meeting for lack of the necessary quorum of 100 eligible members or has been unable to complete the deliberation of items on the agenda because of the failure of the quorum to remain at the meeting. Many adult members of the tribe do not attend the meetings of the general council, either because they are disturbed by the general bickering and dissension within the tribe, or because they are not sufficiently motivated by interests in their own affairs. Many members have expressed the opinion that the function of the general council has degenerated to such a point that attending the meetings is merely an empty gesture.

Every major decision of the Klamaths, expressed through the general council of the 10-member tribal executive committee, is and has been subject to veto by the Bureau of Indian Affairs. Such financial matters as the budget for operation of the Agency sales of tribal timber, and distribution of per capita payments are either planned by the Bureau and submitted to the tribal general council for approval, or, if they are initiated by the general council or the tribal executive committee, must be proposed to and approved by the Bureau before planning may proceed.

A typical example of the control which it has been deemed necessary to exercise over the affairs of the Klamaths is the Federal regulation requiring approval by the Bureau of Indian Affairs for any loan in excess of $3,000 which the tribal loan board proposed making to a tribal member. This fact fails to bear out the conclusion voiced by many witnesses at the various hearings that the Klamaths are and have been successfully managing their own affairs as a group. Also inconsistent with this conclusion is the fact that only 15 of approximately 70 permanent employees of the Klamath Agency are Klamaths and none of these 15 hold major administrative or finance positions.

The picture involving individual management of personal affairs is not promising. One month after the passage of Public Law 587, 240 adults were considered by a local committee to be incompetent to handle their own personal funds, and the funds of 600 minor tribal members were held at the agency for supervision. This means that almost 50 percent of the adult Klamaths then living on the reservation were not considered competent to handle their own funds at the time Public Law 587 was passed. We have been advised that there were at that time practically no records pertaining to those tribal members residing away from the reservation.

Records disclose a number of case histories of individuals who have received substantially large sums of cash at various times and have dissipated those sums with no apparent increase in their standard of living. Three of the more recent examples of this type involve a 40-year-old male Klamath who received $2,180 in a lump sum in December of 1955 and did not have money for food 2 weeks later, a 50-year-old female tribal member who received close to $70,000 during the summer of 1955 and who is currently borrowing money and a middle-aged male Klamath who received more than $11,000 in February 1956, and by midsummer had spent more than $8,000 with no perceptible increase in his standard of living.

Since 1949, and even prior to that time, many Klamaths have received sums of money in excess of $10,000 and only a very few have had the protection of a guardian. Some of these persons have used their funds judiciously, but they would seem to be in the minority. At any rate, the records show a sufficient number of these people who have dissipated large sums of money with no apparent increase in their standards of living to cause concern and to serve as a warning that any terminal legislation should contain proper safeguards for the future security of all tribal members.

Background of Education, Training, and Experience

Information furnished to members of the Committees on Indian Affairs indicates that the Klamaths have received an education in the public schools comparable to that of all other citizens. The fact is that in the school year 1953–54 the schoolwork of 40 percent of the 225 Klamath Indian children enrolled in Klamath County public schools was not sufficiently satisfactory to warrant their being promoted to the next grade. Another fact is that during the 13-year period from 1934 through 1947, only 10 Klamaths were graduated from Klamath County high schools. This is particularly unfortunate in view of the fact that one should expect this latter age group to assume control over tribal affairs and to provide management personnel for any post-termination legal entity.

Public schools have been available to these people since 1927 but only a few have been interested in securing an education. Not until 1953 could State authorities enforce school attendance and the manner in which enforcement has been attempted since 1953 has lacked the vigor and consistency which the situation appears to demand.

In general the Indians on the Klamath Reservation have received a very poor education. This has been attributed chiefly to the prevailing attitude of the Klamaths themselves — an attitude which has reflected apathy, or outright opposition on the part of many of the parents toward their children's schooling. Circumstances under Government supervision appear to have bred a philosophy which fails to place proper emphasis on either the need for or the value of an education.

A study of the available statistics leads to the following conclusions:

1. The Klamath Indians do not nearly measure up to their non-Indian neighbors in terms of educational background, and

2. There is no statistical support for the thesis that the Klamaths have the necessary education, business experience, or unanimity of purpose to manage their assets under a corporate entity.

Insofar as experience in business management is concerned there is at present one tribal member who appears to be successfully operating a service station and store on the reservation and a few Klamath Indians who are operating ranches with varying degrees of success. To what extent these Indian ranchers would be successful in a competitive situation in which they were required, without benefit of per capita payments, to pay the same grazing fees as the non-Indian ranchers in the area, and to raise or buy their winter feed, is a most serious question.

Work Record and Potential

While it is known that a number of Klamaths both on and off the reservation have established good work records, generally the work record of the Klamaths leaves much to be desired and the future is not bright. It appears that more than two-thirds of the 270 able-bodied male Klamaths on the reservation between the ages of 18 and 63 either do not work at all or work only off and on. The majority of this group live, so to speak, from one per capita to the next.

The manager of the Klamath County office of the Oregon State Employment Service has stated that almost without exception the employers in the Klamath Basin will not hire a Klamath Indian if they can possibly avoid doing so. This attitude is attributed to the want of a sense of responsibility and the lack of dependability on the part of a great many of the Klamaths. It must be kept in mind that upon termination of Federal supervision these people, the majority of whom have no special skills or training, and less than an average amount of public-school training, will be injected into a local situation in which there is a surplus of common labor during all but a few weeks of the year, and in which the annual unemployment figure averages 16 percent of the employable population in the local area.

An example of the attitude of many of the Klamaths toward employment is to be found in the fact that virtually all the Klamath veterans who are entitled to Federal unemployment insurance upon their return from service lose the benefits within a few weeks through their failure to meet the requirements that they (1) actively seek employment, and (2) accept any suitable employment that is offered.

Tribal Loan Board as an Example of Management Ability

The existence and functions of the Klamath tribal loan board have been cited as an example of the adequate business and management ability of the Klamaths as a group. When viewed in the light of the facts, this example proves otherwise, as the records show that at the time of the passage of Public Law 587 the affairs of the tribal loan board were in a sorry state. Klamath Agency personnel familiar with the functions of the loan board have stated that the primary result of the function of the board has been to give the Klamaths negative and improper credit training and experience. The great majority, estimated to have been as great as 90 percent of the loans that were made by the loan board to tribal members were nonproductive loans. It became the common practice to allow a tribal member whose loan had become due to borrow enough to pay the loan currently due and have some to spare. Eventually, when some payment had to be made, the Bureau personnel simply decreed that the individual's per capita payments were to be automatically applied to the delinquent loan. Thus we see that it became the major function of the Klamath tribal loan board to make advances on per capita payments and there was little or nothing in the situation to imbue the tribal members with any sense of financial responsibility or realization of the value of a desirable credit record.

We have been informed that during the period of operation of the tribal loan board only two applications for a loan to be used to purchase land were made by tribal members.

Record of Social Adustment

One indication of the degree of social integration of any group is the record of how well or how poorly that group manages to live within the laws of the local community. The experience of the Klamaths in this respect is very poor. Court records within Klamath County indicate that a substantial majority of the local adult Klamaths have been arrested and convicted during the past 10 years for offenses other than traffic violations. The number of convictions ranges from 1 to more than 100 per individual. There appear to be substantially greater proportions of convictions for misdemeanors and felonies among the Klamaths than one finds in the general population.

Another indication of satisfactory or unsatisfactory integration and adjustment is to be found in the quality of the domestic relations within a group. Here, again, the Klamaths fall short of a desirable record, with the reported number of desertions, illicit unions, illegitimacies and extra-marital relations appearing to far exceed that of the public at large. We do not presume to pass judgment on that segment of the tribe whose moral code differs from that of the general public, but merely point out the existing difference. The record also shows that the Klamath Indians whose numbers in Klamath County comprise less than 3 percent of the county population, are accounting for almost 50 percent of the child dependency cases requiring county welfare services.

Predicted Exploitation

We share the opinion of many persons who are participating in the Klamath terminal program that concerted efforts will be made by certain tribal members and by non-Indians to exploit the Klamaths and relieve many of them of their wealth. One such effort by a tribal member, a direct violation of section 4 of Public Law 587, is a matter of record.

We suggest a very careful review of the provisions of section 15 of Public Law 587 and the manner in which those provisions are being implemented, as the broad provisions of this particular section give rise to many of the social implications of this legislation. Certain developments, such as the unprecedented costs to the Klamath people of the required guardianships, do not seem to be consistent with the intentions of government officials as expressed at the hearings nor with the trust relationship existing between the Federal Government and the Klamath Indians. The adequacy of the protection afforded under Oregon laws to Klamath minors, incompetents, and others in need of assistance in conducting their affairs is open to serious question. This basic issue warrants a careful reconsideration by all persons responsible for terminating Federal supervision over the affairs of the Klamaths.

The Klamath Indians have been described to Congress as one of the most advanced Indian groups in the United States. To substantiate this has been offered a description of their material possessions and references to the absence of Indian customs and dress. We suggest that a more reasonable criterion than the extent to which the Klamaths have shed the blanket is how well the majority of them have acquired the skills and attitudes necessary for the assumption of the responsibilities in a non-Indian society which they will be required to assume upon termination.

Senator NEUBERGER. Our first witness this afternoon is Mrs. Dorothy McAnulty. Mrs. McAnulty, we will be pleased to hear from you at this time.

Statement of Mrs. Dorothy McAnulty, Member of the Klamath Tribe

Mrs. MCANULTY. Mr. Chairman and visitors, ladies and gentlemen, I am a member of the Klamath Tribe and a former member of the executive committee. I wish to state here, as I have stated before, that I have never been in accord with Public Law 587. It seems to have so many things in it that are not understandable; and when I was on the executive committee we felt that it still should be given — that some amendments should be made.

I felt at first when it came out that we should repeal it. In the very beginning, as I understood it, when we worked on it, it was to have a withdrawal bill for those that wished to withdraw, and I have never felt that the way we were under the supervision of the Government was ever going to mean any advancement for us any more than we would if were under the Indian Bureau supervision for another hundred years, if we lived that long. We would still be the same as we are now.

It would seem to me that they should have been instructing our members of the tribe to stand on their own feet and manage their affairs. However, that is past, and it seems now we are in a position where there is no turning back, and something must be done; and, when the honorable Senators and the different ones find the difficulties, they can readily understand the position that the members of the Klamath Tribe are in, where it is very difficult for them to understand how to work out a solution to this difficult problem.

As I see it — the public bill as it is written — there are a lot of things that are not mentioned. One of them is subsurface rights, which we have never been able to find out, not being able to stand on our own feet and do the things that we might do to investigate to find whether we have any mineral resources that are worth investigating and finding out about. We have never been in a position to do it. In other words, it is an undeveloped resource. And no mention is made for preserving for the Indian people in the future the subsurface rights that may eventually be uncovered.

There is no mention of it with the carrying out of Public Law 587 for the loss of our hunting and fishing rights. In addition to that, there is no other provision made; there is a provision made for those that have their personal property, individually owned property, the subsurface rights; so it was not something they didn't think of at all, but it was not made on the tribal lands owned by the members of the tribe.

We do know that we have had titanium on the reservation. We know that there are valuable timber resources; and when the termination came up, I felt that it meant the end of the supervision of the Government over the Indians, and, since they were competent to handle their own affairs, that they would then be able to take over their reservation and operate it themseves. The things that they did not understand, surely, with the expense of going out, they could have hired competent people to have managed different things.

We had our pumice; we had our timberlands; we had our grazing lands that the nonmembers of the tribe have been getting wealthy on. We could have bought with our funds in the reserve. A lot of people felt that Mr. Crawford when you offered the proposition before the people it was turned down because I imagine he was the instigator of it, but he did have a wonderful plan that was put before, we wanted to put it before the people, whereby we could have all banded in together and made something of our reservation. But it was a plan that would have worked.

Now, the plan that they have for the remaining members of the tribe, I have never wanted to withdraw. However, the plan that as I see it now, and understand it, that is put before us, I see no future to it. It seems very inadequate and very lame and I suppose there is no reflection on the management specialists because I realize they have had a very difficult task to try to carry out Public Law 587. Because, as I see it, the little piece of land that is reserved for the supposedly 20 percent of the people that remain, there is nothing set up whereby more, it could be carried on. In other words, it is just sell and sell and sell until there is nothing left to sell. Then if the timber should drop and the market should go down, for every dollar, as I understand it, it would be a loss to each member for every member of $33. I believe that was the amount.

Then we have no assurance that the timber market is going to remain up, especially if the other timber is sold to pay off the withdrawing members. Why would they go and pay a big price for this other timber and in the meantime while they are selling all this other, this land, as I see it on the map is isolated away from railroads, or any roads, or any water, and it is going to be hard to get at, and where they have got all this other land, why would they go in and cut that little bit of land for the remaining members? And if this should drop down to — well, each time that would mean a loss of $33 for each member on every dollar, that is $350; isn't it? Or $350 if the $33, if it is $33. In a year's time if it should drop down to the amount where I had it all straightened out here, but I'm not going to take the time to look it up. But we have no assurance in the timber that it will not drop clear down to where it used to be years ago, and in that case, as I figured it out, it would amount to about $350 a year for each remaining member.

Well, how could they exist on such a thing? Then it brings out the fact that if in order to keep up a livable amount they would have to sell the land that this timber was cut off of. Well, if they sold the land and kept on doing that, how long would those people have anything? What is there to remain for?

Then we are told again if we withdraw that our timber would be put upon the market if the Government doesn't buy it and it would be bought at a price that these big lumber companies or whoever bought it would want to pay. What is there to stop them from all going in together and bidding a certain amount and just taking it that way?

I can see no future for it at all. I don't see anything that — they talked about the saving of it for the watersheds and the preservation of this land for the wildlife and fish. But what about the people? Does anybody give any thought to the people?

What is a fair price that the Government is supposed to pay? Who is to set the fair price, and how do we know what is a fair price, and if it goes on for another 2 more years, who knows what the market will be at the end of 2 years?

Senator NEUBERGER. Mrs. McAnulty, let me ask you this question so we come to some conclusion. What do you recommend that the Congress do?

Mrs. MCANULTY. Well, it is so late in the day, I say, Senator, we have been kept in the dark as to even what is going on. We, the people that are to be terminated, know nothing about these things.

Senator NEUBERGER. Mrs. McAnulty, I think you have to address yourself to something that is within the province of the Congress of the United States.

Mrs. MCANULTY. Yes; I understand that.

Senator NEUBERGER. You understand that?

Mrs. MCANULTY. Yes; I do.

Senator NEUBERGER. There are only certain things that we can even try to do. This is not a situation of our doing; it is a situation of our inheritance. Now, what do you suggest we do at this point? What policy would you propose that we follow?

I want to say this: I think you have made a very good recommendation as to subsurface rights. That is the purpose of a hearing, to find out some of these things. Now, I haven't gone into it fully with the committee staff, but I believe we might very feasibly try to recommend this Federal purchase bill so that the subsurface mineral rights on the reservation lands be held for the Indians for a period of, let's say, 25 or 50 years, and I am going to look into amending the bill in that respect. But what other policy do you advise us to follow?

Mrs. MCANULTY. Well, I feel this way about it, Senator Neuberger: I have never felt that we should ever at any time break up the reservation. Our people have considered it home. I have always stated that no matter how. But as Mr. Davis said this morning, they talk about the things that are going on down in the South now, but are the people in Klamath County going to welcome our people into the homes? I know of instances where they won't even rent to an Indian, and the termination isn't going to make white people out of them. They are still going to be Indians and treated as such.

What about that? What is their money going to be good to them for if they can't buy a home and they have to live in a place where they don't want to live? Now I am speaking of all of us together. I am not just speaking of 2 or 3 that have always had homes, maybe. I am speaking of all of us. I am putting myself in it as one of the people on the reservation. Are they going to be treated like people should be treated? No. I can answer that truthfully now. They are not. It is wonderful as long as they have money. When the money is gone they are just Indians.

Now, those are the things that my people are going to have to face.

Senator NEUBERGER. Why did your people favor termination?

Mrs. MCANULTY. I don't believe they did.

Senator NEUBERGER. In 1954?

Mrs. MCANULTY. I don't believe they did understand it any more than they understand this now.

Senator NEUBERGER. Let me say this: This is what puzzles me. You know I have only been in the Congress 2½ years. I came there after termination had been effected, and it was the law of the land. But the thing that has puzzled me ever since I first went on the Indian Affairs Subcommittee is that I have met hardly any members of the Klamath Tribe who have told me they favored termination. And yet it is my understanding, and I would like to check this with Mr. Gamble and Mr. Wolf, who have been with the Federal Government longer than I have: Isn't it true that, when the termination bill was put through in 1954, the Klamath Indian Tribe was officially on record in favor of the bill? Is that right or wrong?

Mr. WOLF. That is what Mr. Jackson testified.

Senator NEUBERGER. He did testify to that this morning, and that is a fact of record, isn't it?

Mr. GAMBLE. It is.

Senator NEUBERGER. That is what puzzles me and perplexes me.

Mrs. MCANULTY. Termination and the selling of the reservation was definitely not understood. I know that it wasn't. I worked on different committees, and I worked there, but I didn't even understand it. How would the people that are out on the reservation, that know nothing about these things, know that their homes and everything around them, and the reservation itself was to be because of the termination of the supervision, Government supervision over the Indian? Now that is something I didn't even understand.

Senator NEUBERGER. I realize that Secretary McKay and the

group around him favored termination, and yet I have never felt that President Eisenhower would have signed Public Law 587 if he had felt that the Klamath Tribe as such was opposed to it, or if representation had been made to the President by the Klamath Tribe, and I am puzzled why now there are some of you who say what a great mistake termination is. I am inclined to agree with you in many respects, but why was that not said in 1954 when the law was passed by Congress and the President signed it? That is what I don't understand.

Mrs. MCANULTY. As near as I can explain it, Senator, the withdrawal bill and the termination, the supervision of the Government over the Indian and the $250 per capita, the payment which the Indians needed so badly, is your answer.

Senator NEUBERGER. You mean that $250 per capita payment?

Mrs. MCANULTY. That was merged in with it. That is your answer. A lot of those people were destitute.

Senator NEUBERGER. You remember I asked a question earlier this morning.

Mrs. MCANULTY. I am answering it in plain words. Some of the people were destitute and they needed this money, and all they could see, a lot of them can see now, is this $50,000, or $40,000, that they are going to get when the timber is sold. Now, there is your answer.

Senator NEUBERGER. Let me ask you this, Mrs. McAnulty; we must get along. What would you recommend? You were here this morning, I think, when I discussed alternatives with Mr. Jackson and his associates. Of all the alternatives you heard mentioned, which would you prefer?

Mrs. MCANULTY. Well, there isn't much choice in any of them. I don't prefer any of them because if — I would prefer the Government paying for it, buying the timber at a price, but I would like to know what that fair price was. Is it going to be a special price made for the Government to buy, or would it be a fair market price?

Senator NEUBERGER. Well, I think you heard Mr. Jackson recommend that my bill be amended to eliminate the appraisal method set out in the bill, and that the appraisal being worked out by the Management Specialists be accepted as final. I think that was Mr. Jackson's recommendation. Would you think that was agreeable?

Mrs. MCANULTY. Well, I don't know whether I would or not. I don't know who is making the appraisals; whether they have a special appraisal. Who appointed the other appraisers besides the ones that the Management Specialists were making? Was that done by the Government?

Senator NEUBERGER. It has been done under the direction of the Management Specialists, it is my understanding, and that was what Mr. Jackson had reference to.

Mrs. MCANULTY. I think whatever appraisal they arrive at, and it is a fair appraisal.

Mr. WOLF. If the appraisal that the Management Specialists hope to have on October 21, were satisfactory to you, would you then say that you would be in favor of Federal purchase?

Mrs. MCANULTY. Yes; I would.

Mr. WOLF. And, if it weren't satisfactory, what would you think should be done then?

Mrs. MCANULTY. Well, if repealing the law would mean going back under the Indian Bureau, I would say that we wouldn't be any better off than we were before.

Senator NEUBERGER. There was a figure used last night in an article, I believe, on the front page of the Klamath Falls newspaper, the News and Herald, which gave an appraised figure of $113 million. Would you think that was a fair appraisal?

Mrs. MCANULTY. I would say so. But I still feel that, if they could repeal the law in such a way so as to let the Indians themselves make the plans that they wanted to make, it would be fine for whatever they wanted to do, but to repeal it and put us back under the Indian Bureau, where you can't even cut a tree on your own land without a lot of red tape, why, I can't see where we would be any better off. And I do feel, though, that if the State was, if the Government didn't buy it and the State did want to buy this land, I believe that something could be worked out on that, since they are going to put it, if ample security was made for the children's funds, since they are not going to allow the children to have any way instead of putting them under all these guardians that are going to charge such exorbitant prices for guardianship, if they would put sufficient security to see that these children receive their money when they reach majority, and then pay the adult members the amount that they were supposed to receive for the sale of their timber, I believe that would be a sensible way for the State to retain their resources that they are worried so much about, and their fish and game and wildlife deal, and nobody would suffer from it. I believe that could work out.

Senator NEUBERGER. Mrs. McAnulty, thank you very much

for coming, and I think you have performed a very useful service in calling to our attention particularly the subject of subsurface rights, and I am going to see to it that an amendment is prepared to S. 2047 dealing with that. Thank you so much.

The next witness will be Mr. Orth Sisemore, attorney of Klamath Falls, and I believe he is accompanied by Mr. Nelson Reid for a citizens' committee. I understand from Mr. Gamble that you are appearing in place of Mr. Sisemore, is that correct?

Mr. NELSON REID. I believe so, yes.

Senator NEUBERGER. Mr. Reid, we are pleased to see you today.

Statement of Nelson Reid, Representing Klamath Falls Citizens Committee

Mr. REID. I have a petition that has been signed by some 430 people, not only of this immediate area but also some from adjoining areas such as Bend, Medford and Ashland. I would like to read it.

Senator NEUBERGER. All right.

Mr. REID (reading):

PETITION TO THE SENATE SUBCOMMITTEE ON INDIAN AFFAIRS IN REGARD TO PUBLIC LAW 587

We, the undersigned, have given much thought and careful consideration to Public Law 587. There appears to be three possible basic plans for the termination of the Klamath Indian Reservation:

1. The immediate sale of the tribal timber lands in relatively small tracts to the highest bidder.
2. The sale of the tribal timber lands to the State of Oregon, to be cut on a sustained-yield basis.
3. The sale of the tribal timber lands to the Federal Government, to be cut on a sustained-yield basis.

We are definitely opposed to plan 1. To offer the timber for immediate sale in relatively small tracts would certainly result in a "boom-and-bust" economy, not only for this but for adjacent areas. It would glut the already depressed timber market to the point where the Klamath Indians could not hope to receive stumpage prices comparable to the prices they have been getting. Worst of all, purchasers of relatively small tracts could operate under State of Oregon forestry regulations which could mean practically "clear cutting." Relatively small tracts of timber cannot be harvested economically on a sustained-yield basis over a period of years.

The "clear cutting" of much of the reservation would result in great damage to the water resources of this area upon which our agriculture and power depend. The principal streams that feed Upper Klamath Lake, that great reservoir for our irrigation and power development, all flow out of the Klamath Indian Reservation. To denude this great forest area could easily result in damaging erosion and a disastrous water shortage in dry years. It would hurt our economy, not only immediately but for years to come.

We are opposed to plan 2, to have the State of Oregon purchase the reservation because of practical economic and political problems involved. We do not believe that the people of Oregon would be willing to vote a bond issue for such purchase where the benefits to most of the voters are so indirect. Such a bond issue today would have to offer a 5-percent coupon in order to sell. Marketed on a sustained-yield basis, the reservation timber could not possibly bear that rate of interest, presuming that the purchase price would give a fair return to the Klamath Indians.

We feel that the only solution that offers a fair return to the Klamath Indians and that will protect the watershed and economy of this area, is plan 3, purchase by the Federal Government. It is experienced in the long-range management of large timber tracts on a sustained-yield basis. While many of us are opposed to Government ownership of any more of this area, we see no other solution. The Federal Government is already trustee for the Klamath Indians. It has an obligation to them by treaty. Purchase by the Federal Government should provide for a fair price to the Klamath Indians. These people should not be required to subsidize continued sustained-yield management. Marsh areas now owned by the tribe could be made more productive of pasture with a minimum amount of reclamation. Those areas more suitable for wildfowl should be left undisturbed except that a provision should be made for public shooting on a fair proportion of the reserve.

We believe that the Congress was wise in decreeing the termination of the Klamath Indian Reservation by Public Law 587. For over 50 years, we have seen the ever-increasing deterioration of the moral fiber of the Klamath Indians. The per capita payments have become nothing but a dole. They have destroyed the initiative and ambition that many of the Klamaths once had. We believe that some system of payment to the Indians after the purchase by the Federal Government can be worked out, so that minors and those incapable of handling large sums of money because of inexperience, can be paid off in serial coupon bonds. Those capable of handling sizable amounts of money should be offered the option of taking their share in a lump sum at a reasonable discount, so that they may have the opportunity to go in business for themselves or invest the money as they see fit. Some method can surely be evolved to encourage initiative and ambition which the present system has certainly destroyed.

The Federal Government does not hesitate to spend a hundred million dollars for the economic and social welfare of foreign countries, with small chance of any direct return. Why should it hesitate to invest a like amount in the welfare of an American community where it already has a treaty obligation and it will have an excellent chance to get back its investment in hard cash and indirect benefits?

We therefore recommend to your committee the Federal purchase of the Klamath Indian Reservation.

Respectfully,

The Undersigned

(The complete exhibit containing 436 signatures is a part of the committee's file.)

Senator NEUBERGER. Thank you very much, Mr. Reid. Are there any questions you would like to ask Mr. Reid? I just have one question. I noticed you referred to public shooting on a portion of the marsh. That isn't incompatible in your mind, is it, with the provisions in S. 2047 that would include some 70,000 acres of the marsh in a waterfowl refuge under the Fish and Wildlife Service?

Mr. REID. No, I don't think it is incompatible. I don't believe that there is much over 20,000 in the marsh that is not privately owned. I think there are some 20,000 acres that are still tribal lands. I could see no objection to public hunting. I know it is a wonderful nesting area. I lived up there for two summers. I don't believe that hunting in the fall has any bad effect at all on the nesting part of it. I think in all our reserve areas a certain proportion should be set aside for public hunting.

Senator NEUBERGER. What is the situation on areas like the Malheur refuge and others? Do they allow hunting?

Mr. REID. I don't know what proportion. I believe there is some area over there. We have limited public hunting areas down here in the reserve across the California line in Tulelake and in the lower Klamath.

Senator NEUBERGER. Mr. Wolf, you have been with the Interior Department conservation agencies. What are the rules with regard to hunting on wildlife sanctuaries and reserves?

Mr. WOLF. I have never had any experience with the Fish and Wildlife Service, but I think we could ask them to supply for the record what their policy is.

Senator NEUBERGER. I would like to have that. Mr. Sigler, would you get for us from the Fish and Wildlife Service a comprehensive statement governing hunting in and along the reserves and waterfowl sanctuaries?

Mr. SIGLER. Yes, I shall.

Mr. REID. Senator, I think some representatives of sportsmen's associations will probably discuss that.

Senator NEUBERGER. I appreciate your calling this to our attention, too, and thank you very much, Mr. Reid.

(The following information was subsequently submitted:)

DEPARTMENT OF THE INTERIOR,
OFFICE OF THE SECRETARY,
Washington, D.C., October 31, 1957

Hon. Richard L. Neuberger,
    Subcommittee on Indian Affairs, Committee on Interior and Insular
    Affairs, United States Senate, Washington, D.C.

DEAR SENATOR NEUBERGER: During your recent subcommittee hearings in Klamath Falls, Oreg., on October 2, 1957, you asked for information about hunting and fishing on wildlife refuges administered by the United States Fish and Wildlife Service.

Migratory bird and wildlife refuges fall into three general categories:

1. Refuges established under the Migratory Bird Conservation Act of February 18, 1929 (45 Stat. 1222, 16 U. S. C. 715), as amended. Under section 5 of that act, the refuges are inviolate sanctuaries for migratory birds. Inviolate sanctuary means that the birds are to have undisturbed use of the lands.

The Migratory Bird Hunting Stamp Act of March 16, 1934 (48 Stat. 451, 16 U. S. C. 718), supplements the Migratory Bird Conservation Act by providing funds for the acquisition of areas, but it does not change the status of the refuges as inviolate sanctuaries.

2. Areas acquired with duck stamp funds under the act of August 12, 1949 (63 Stat. 599), which was an amendment to the Migratory Bird Hunting Stamp Act. Under section 4 of this act, the areas acquired with duck stamp funds become parts of inviolate sanctuaries under the 1929 act, but "in the discretion of the Secretary of the Interior not to exceed 25 per centum at any one time, of any area acquired in accordance with the provisions of this Act, may be administered primarily as a wildlife management area not subject to the prohibitions against the taking of birds, or nests or the eggs thereof, as contained in section 10 of the Migratory Bird Conservation Act of February 18, 1929 (45 Stat. 1222; 16 U. S. C. 715i), as amended, except that no such area shall be open to the shooting of migratory birds when the population of such birds frequenting the area or in the migrations utilizing such area is on a decline, nor prior to July 1, 1952, or the date upon which the same has been fully developed as a management area, refuge, reservation, or breeding ground, whichever is later."

3. Wildlife refuges created by special act of Congress or by a withdrawal of public lands where hunting and fishing is permitted in accordance with rules and regulations of the Secretary of the Interior.

Sincerely yours,

Ross Leffler,
ASSISTANT SECRETARY OF THE INTERIOR

Senator NEUBERGER. As long as this matter has been raised, I am going to read a very brief telegram from a gentleman who was to have been a witness here today, but cannot be here. State Representative Joseph S. Crepeau, of Lane County, has been quite well known as a conservationist and, if I am not mistaken, I think has a small cabin himself somewhere near the agency lake. It is addressed to me as chairman of the subcommittee:

Matter of extreme urgency prevents my testifying in Klamath Falls but I would appreciate your placing me on record. Together with any other sportsman I feel that the preservation of the 68,000 acres of upper marshlands should if possible be preserved as a waterfowl sanctuary. This area is eight times as large as Summer Lake shooting grounds, and contains many thousand more geese and ducks. It is probably the largest waterfowl congregating place on the Pacific coast. I cannot urge too strongly that preservation of this area is a must. Sorry that I cannot be with you in person.

J. S. Crepeau

Our next witness is Mr. William Ganong, Jr., representing the Chamber of Commerce of Klamath Falls, Indian Affairs Committee. Mr. Ganong, we are happy to have you here.

Statement of William Ganong, Jr., Indian Affairs Committee, Klamath Falls Chamber of Commerce

Mr. WILLIAM GANONG, JR. Mr. Chairman, in order to save the time of the committee, the Klamath County Chamber of Commerce has prepared a written statement of its position for inclusion in the record.

Senator NEUBERGER. I just want to say at this point that without objection the entire statement presented by the chamber of commerce will appear in the hearing record.

[. . . . .]

Mr. GANONG. Thank you. Briefly, the Chamber of Commerce

unreservedly recommends that the Federal Government purchase the Klamath tribal properties so that it may continue the scientific sustained-yield management of the forest under the appropriate Government agency. This position has not been easily or quickly reached. The great majority of our members are businessmen who sincerely are opposed to Government ownership or control except in those cases where no other alternative exists. In the present case, we have reluctantly reached the conclusion that there is no alternative to Government ownership. If the Government does not purchase the tribal forests, they will be destroyed.

Senator NEUBERGER. We thank you very much. Are there any questions of Mr. Ganong?

Mr. WOLF. I have one. I notice that very often when we have representatives of local chambers of commerce before congressional committees, they take a position which is diametrically opposed to the national chamber. You will get local chambers in favor of Federal acquisition in this case and the national chamber may take the opposite side. You may get local chambers in favor of something down in the TVA area, the national chamber is opposed. Now, how do you think the Congress ought to reconcile this constant situation where a local chamber comes in and says "We are in accord with national objectives everywhere but here"?

Mr. GANONG. I am afraid I can't give the Congress much advice on that point. That is one where they have to draw their own conclusions.

Mr. WOLF. Then how does national chamber policy come into being when we constantly have these local situations that call for a differentiation from the national policy?

Mr. GANONG. I believe the national policy is formulated through the board of directors of the national chamber, of which the individual chambers are members. In other words, I imagine they would be sort of compared with Congress. The Congress represents the Nation as a whole, where a legislator or a county court or a city council represents a local area.

Senator NEUBERGER. Mr. Ganong, I would like to ask you a question. How long have you lived here in this community?

Mr. GANONG. I have lived here all my life; 35 years.

Senator NEUBERGER. The whole purpose of my question was to find out if you were here when Public Law 587 was passed, and obviously you were. This is what puzzles me. This question has come up before pertaining to the Indian community. Now it comes up pertaining to the local non-Indian community.

I read your statement earlier today and I think it is a very fine statement. I won't say I agree with the way you crossed every "t" and dotted "i," but I think on the whole it is a very ably drawn and well written and comprehensive statement. But on page 4, for example, I want to read one paragraph and then tell you what really perplexes me about the background of the bill.

The Congress substituted for section 5 of Senate bill 2745, the present section 5 of Public Law 587 which eliminated the period of further study and planning substituted a crash program, for the sale of tribal assets. This was done without the knowledge of the people of Klamath County. In fact, the Klamath County Chamber of Commerce was unaware that this amendment had been made until after the bill had been enacted and signed by the President. There was absolutely no advance warning ever given the people of this county that Congress intended to make this change and radically depart from the bill upon which hearing had been held in this county.

This is what perplexes me. Wasn't the local sentiment aware of what was in this bill that went to the very crux and core of the economic and social life of this county when it was passed by Congress and signed by the President of the United States?

Mr. GANONG. Not insofar as section 5 was concerned.

Senator NEUBERGER. That is the meat of the coconut in the operation of the termination.

Mr. GANONG. With which we are vitally concerned. The Senate bill 2745 was fairly well known. In other words, it had been discussed in our own chamber and the hearing had been held at Klamath Agency on it. But, of course, that was, I would say, a radically different bill than the law that became Public Law 587.

Senator NEUBERGER. Weren't you informed by the representatives of this State in the Congress about what was in this law when it went through the Congress and went to the White House?

Mr. GANONG. No. We were unaware that this change had been made in section 5.

Senator NEUBERGER. You were unaware that the entire operation of the termination program had been substantially changed?

Mr. GANONG. That is correct.

Senator NEUBERGER. Thank you very much.

[. . . . .]

Statement of Chester L. Langslet, Klamath Sportsmen's Association

Mr. LANGSLET. Senator Neuberger, members of this committee, we have a short resolution passed by the Klamath Sportsmen's Association, which states:

Whereas Federal supervision of the Klamath Indian Reservation is about to be terminated; and

Whereas acquisition by private ownership would limit access for hunting, fishing, and other recreational purposes; and

Whereas denuding the area of timber would disastrously affect the streamflow necessary for fisheries; and

Whereas the forest cover is mandatory for game, waterfowl, and wildlife habitat; and

Whereas it is necessary that the timber be marketed under a sustained-yield program in order to afford maximum protection to fisheries and wildlife: Now, therefore, be it

Resolved, That the Klamath Sportsmen's Association, Inc., recommend the purchase of tribal lands by the Federal Government.

Respectfully,

KLAMATH SPORTSMEN'S ASSOCIATION, INC.

Senator NEUBERGER. Thank you very much. The resolution will appear in full. I just want to ask you one question, if I may. You heard Mr. Reid's very interesting presentation of the resolution signed by some 400 citizens. What is your feeling about this question of shooting of game birds in this area?

Mr. LANGSLET. Well, Senator, I think you are familiar with the program that we have outlined here for fish and wildlife, in which we are in hopes that they will acquire title to approximately 105 square miles of land in this area for public shooting and refuge purposes. Now, I have heard this figure of 70,000 and many other thousands of acres mentioned as marshland up there. I was up to the reservation, and talked to several people up there, and as near as I have been able to determine, there is actually only 15,000 acres of marsh. The rest is grazing land. And, as I understand it, there is only around 22,000 acres that are actually privately owned.

Now, I don't think that the people in this community would hold still for the acquisition of that additional private land to make it a 70,000-acre refuge, and take that additional land off the tax roll.

[. . . . .]

Statement of Mr. and Mrs. Wade Crawford, Members of Klamath Tribe Executive Committee

Mr. CRAWFORD. Thank you, Senator. Senator, Mrs. Crawford and I, we appear here before your committee, as you know, representing the people that enrolled on the Klamath Reservation that want to withdraw from Federal supervision. I think that has been a matter of record over a period of years, and I think that the record shows before this Congress that we are the official representatives of the 75 percent of the Indians that want to withdraw from Federal supervision. There is a petition filed before the different committees of Congress to verify that. So, we speak for 75 percent of the Indians that are interested in withdrawing from Federal supervision.

Senator NEUBERGER. By what machinery is that decided? Were you elected by 75 percent of them?

Mr. CRAWFORD. We were; that was by petition of the Indians that are enrolled on the reservation, speaking for them and their families.

Senator NEUBERGER. In other words, by petition you are representing 75 percent of the Indians?

Mr. CRAWFORD. That is right. That is, let's put it this way: We represent the Indians that want to, that have stood to withdraw from Federal supervision, and your survey by the Management Specialists through the Stanford Research and their own survey shows that from 61 to 75 percent of those Indians want to withdraw from Federal supervision as individuals.

Senator NEUBERGER. What is the title of Mr. Jackson and Mr. Cook and Mr. Kirk? What title did they have, with respect to Indian representation?

Mr. CRAWFORD. They are members of the executive committee.

Senator NEUBERGER. How were they chosen?

Mr. CRAWFORD. They were elected by the secret-ballot vote of the Indians that lived on the reservation. They were not elected; they were not elected by the Indians that were entitled to a secret-ballot vote on and off the reservation. Jackson, the council records show that they opposed, were in opposition to give the Indians a right to vote for the executive committee by absentee-ballot votes, and we have Indians living in 18 states besides Oregon, and those people were denied of a vote to elect someone to represent them on handling their tribal affairs and representing the tribe as a group. And the record shows that.

Mr. GAMBLE. Mr. Crawford, are you a member of the tribal executive committee?

Mr. CRAWFORD. Mrs. Crawford and I both are.

Mr. GAMBLE. Were you elected by the tribe, both by absentees and by those living on the reservation?

Mr. CRAWFORD. Not from absentee ballot. We were elected the same time Mr. Jackson, Mr. Kirk, and the present executive committee were elected.

Senator NEUBERGER. In other words, you were elected by the same procedure?

Mr. CRAWFORD. By the same procedure, which we opposed. We don't think it is proper representation because we have got over, well, we have Indians living in 18 states and throughout the adjoining towns of the reservation that didn't have an opportunity to elect someone to represent them.

Mr. WOLF. Mr. Crawford, just to clarify in my mind who you represent, you say 75 percent of the Indians wish to withdraw?

Mr. CRAWFORD. That's right.

Mr. WOLF. That is as shown by the Stanford Research Institute?

Mr. CRAWFORD. And by the Management Specialists' own survey.

Mr. WOLF. Did 75 percent of the Indians elect you to represent them?

Mr. CRAWFORD. No.

Mr. WOLF. How many elected you to represent them on this matter, on withdrawal?

Mr. CRAWFORD. I think if you will examine the petitions you have in your files and the record, I think there are 225 of the adults which represent about possibly 600 or 700 children.

Mr. WOLF. In other words, 225 adults have petitioned you to represent them but it is not by an election?

Mr. CRAWFORD. That is right. We were denied an election last year and so that was the only way the Indians had to get representation before this last Congress.

Mr. WOLF. Who sent them the petition?

Mr. CRAWFORD. What do you mean who sent them the petition?

Mr. WOLF. Who sent the petition to the people to ask you to represent them?

Mr. CRAWFORD. The Indians carried it around themselves.

Mr. WOLF. Various people?

Mr. CRAWFORD. Yes.

Mr. WOLF. Who were also associated in withdrawal?

Mr. CRAWFORD. That is right.

Mr. WOLF. But this doesn't constitute an election in any sense.

Mr. CRAWFORD. No, it doesn't.

Senator NEUBERGER. Is there a tribal constitution of the Klamath Tribe?

Mr. CRAWFORD. Yes, there is, but it never has been approved of by the Secretary of the Interior, which formally the constitutions require the approval of the Secretary of the Interior.

Senator NEUBERGER. Does the constitution provide for absentee balloting?

Mr. CRAWFORD. No, it doesn't. But it was a form that was used in prior elections that absentee ballots be used and it was the decision of the Secretary of the Interior, Clarence A. Davis.

Senator NEUBERGER. He was Under Secretary?

Mr. CRAWFORD. Yes, he was Under Secretary. I will read you his decision in this matter. It is very short.

Senator NEUBERGER. Just do it by reference.

Mr. CRAWFORD. It is pages 3 to 5 in the hearings before the — joint hearings — before Congressman Chudoff's committee, and we placed it in the record at that time.

Mr. WOLF. Those were hearings on Federal timber sale policy?

Mr. CRAWFORD. Yes. November 15, 1955. In here Mr. Davis wrote a letter of instructions to the members of the Klamath Reservation instructing a decision to be made by the members. I will have Mrs. Crawford read it. It is real short.

Mrs. WADE CRAWFORD (reading):

To the voters of the Klamath Tribe: Section 23 of Public Law 587 which provides for the termination of Federal supervision over the property of the Klamath Tribe states that the Secretary of the Interior may in his discretion provide for tribal elections on matters pertaining to management and disposition of tribal assets. Section 5 of the same law directs that the Secretary retain Management Specialists to deal with the appraisal of disposition and distribution of tribal assets as well as to prepare plans for the management of tribal property in order to carry out these functions without waste of time, effort, and money. It is imperative that the Management Specialists be given the opportunity of working closely with representatives of the tribe.

I am unwilling to designate any particular person or group of persons to represent the tribe in this important matter without first being assured that such persons are the choice of a majority of the tribal members. I am fully aware that it has been the custom of the Klamath people to meet in general council to discuss and take action on matters of interest to the tribe as a whole. Also, I recognize that this Department in the past has taken action on recommendations of the general council as well as recommendations of the Klamath executive committee to which the general council has delegated authority to act for it in certain matters.

However, it is not convenient for all the adult members of the tribe who have an equity in the tribal assets to attend meetings of the general council and I deem it to be of the utmost importance that all members be given an opportunity to express themselves in the matter of the termination of Federal supervision over the assets of the tribe.

In order to accomplish this, I have requested the area director of the Portland area office to hold an election by mail for the purpose of selecting representatives to serve on a committee to represent the tribe in working with the Management Specialists. I urge that you take advantage of this opportunity and indicate your choice on the enclosed ballot and mail it to the superintendent of the Klamath Agency as soon as possible. Signed, Clarence A. Davis, Acting Secretary of the Interior, April 21, 1955.

Senator NEUBERGER. May I ask just one thing? It refers to an election in here and in Secretary Davis' letter. Now, was such an election held?

Mr. CRAWFORD. Yes, it was.

Senator NEUBERGER. And who was elected?

Mr. CRAWFORD. Laurence Witt and Seldon Kirk and myself.

Senator NEUBERGER. And then what happened? Were you authorized by the Secretary to speak for the tribe in these matters?

Mr. CRAWFORD. We spoke; we were authorized and functioned for about 6 months after that election. In fact, they had two elections. They had a first election, then a runoff election, so we were elected twice under the same procedure, and then we acted for about 6 months until the Secretary of the Interior and the Commissioner of Indian Affairs arbitrarily cut off the use of tribal funds to pay us.

Senator NEUBERGER. Why did they do that?

Mr. CRAWFORD. One of your dictators. You ask them why they did it.

Senator NEUBERGER. Well, now, this was done by Commissioner Emmons and Secretary McKay. These are the people you are referring to, I presume?

Mr. CRAWFORD. Yes, that is right.

Senator NEUBERGER. Did they have any reason? Did they give any reason?

Mr. CRAWFORD. The only reason they gave us was that it required the approval of our budget, required the approval of the general council of our budget.

Senator NEUBERGER. All right. Please go ahead.

Mr. CRAWFORD. But I just wanted this, it is important.

Mr. WOLF. Wouldn't the general council approve your budget?

Mr. CRAWFORD. We never submitted it to them.

Mr. WOLF. Then they never had a chance?

Mr. CRAWFORD. Well, listen here, Mr. Wolf.

Mr. WOLF. I am not making a statement; I am asking a question.

Mr. CRAWFORD. Here, under the law, under Public Law 587, the Secretary of the Interior could approve of our budget without being referred to the council. He has complete control over it. They approved of the Management Specialists' budget without submitting it to the general council.

Mr. WOLF. That is what I wanted to get.

Mr. CRAWFORD. That certainly is true.

Senator NEUBERGER. Let's go ahead.

Mr. CRAWFORD. I think it is important, Senator, that we go into this just a little bit further here, for this reason: You are here to find out the attitude of the Klamath Indians regarding your bill S. 2047, and you want to get, fair and square, the facts regarding the Indians and the management of this forest, and when you come to the Indians to find out their attitude, who is their spokesman? Why, they are their spokesmen. That should be substantiated by the record. And on page 305 of that same hearing, I will read you one short paragraph. Senator, may I have your attention now please? It was expressed here this morning by three members of the executive committee that they favored Federal purchase of the tribal timber and stating they spoke with authority to represent the tribe. I will read you the authority that they are acting under.

In August 21, 22, 1952, in general council at Beatty, Oreg., the resolution that the Klamath General Council assembled on this 21st day of August do hereby delegate to the executive committee for the promotion of their general welfare and the regulations of our tribal affairs, constitutional powers to act in the name of the general council when circumstances so warrant it.

A vote was taken on that and the vote was 21 to nothing. Now, in our constitution, it requires 100 present before any business can be transacted. And the constitution also requires 50 percent or more for the voters to decide any subject that would represent the action of the council. So 21 people voted for this resolution in that general council and that is the authority that the executive committee sat here this morning and told you they represented the Klamath Indians. And that is certainly not true. It is not official. This was a resolution passed in 1952 and has nothing to do with Public Law 587. Public Law 587 doesn't give you one section of the law that requires the executive committee to speak for the tribe.

Senator NEUBERGER. Mr. Crawford, let's get down to cases. Who is authorized to speak for the Klamath people?

Mr. CRAWFORD. As I interpret the law, Senator, it is the individual speaks for himself, because each member of that tribe, they speak for themselves and their families. The adults speak for their children. I think this law is very clearly carrying out the intention of Congress to terminate all Federal supervision with the Indians and put the Indians on their own as citizens of this country.

Senator NEUBERGER. Why don't you then give us — you are speaking for yourself then — why don't you give us the benefit of your views on S. 2047?

[. . . . .]

Mr. CRAWFORD. Well, Senator, I am looking — Mrs. Crawword, she will speak for herself — but I am looking at it with an open mind. I didn't come here with the idea of opposing the bill, in general, of the Government buying this timber and putting it into the national forest, until, I mean unless, you can show me something different than it is. We are opposed to the bill as it is written. I don't want to be put in the position that because we are advocating the carrying out of Public Law 587, that because we advocate private enterprise and the lumber companies buy this timber, that we are in for destroying the forest.

Now, we are conservationists, I think as well as anybody else.

Senator NEUBERGER. Let me just ask this. The lumber companies buy timber from the national forests, don't they? Isn't that correct?

Mr. CRAWFORD. That is correct, but regarding your bill here, for me to say that I favor your bill, I would say "No."

Senator NEUBERGER. Do you oppose it then?

Mr. CRAWFORD. I oppose it for this reason: because I will not agree to sell the tribal lands to the Government when I don't know what the Government is willing to pay for it, and furthermore, I haven't been able to get the report from the Management Specialists as to the inventory and the appraisal they have made so we don't know exactly what our resources amount to.

Senator NEUBERGER. Let me ask you this, then: In other words, if you are opposed to the bill, then ——

Mr. CRAWFORD. I am opposed to it for that reason, because we don't know our assets.

Senator NEUBERGER. In other words, you are willing to have the Management Specialists start next August, after the adjournment of the 85th Congress, to start to sell the timber? Are you willing to have that happen?

Mr. CRAWFORD. I don't want you to put words in my mouth, Senator. I will speak for myself.

Senator NEUBERGER. Then what do you think should happen if you don't favor this bill? After it is defeated, if you get your wish, what do you favor then?

Mr. CRAWFORD. I favor carrying out Public Law 587.

Senator NEUBERGER. Public Law 587, if it is carried out, requires that the Management Specialists start with the sale of the assets, does it not?

Mr. CRAWFORD. Certainly they will.

Senator NEUBERGER. Then is that what you favor?

Mr. CRAWFORD. Absolutely.

Senator NEUBERGER. Do you know what you will get for those?

Mr. CRAWFORD. Well, I know one thing, that I am going to — that the timber will go on the market and get, there will be competitive bidding and we will get the highest price that is offered on these different units.

Senator NEUBERGER. Were you here earlier this morning when the letter from the Secretary of the Interior was read in which he commented upon what a depressing effect on timber values might be caused by putting all that timber for sale on the market?

Mr. CRAWFORD. Oh, I have heard that, yes, and I have heard a lot of other people say a lot of things. I want to say this, Senator: Now, when you talk about putting this timber on the market and a fire sale, you have heard that expression, which sounds very good. Devastating forest, destroying watersheds, and so on, because the land is in private ownership. I think that people are predicting and accusing a lot of people of a lot of bad things and I don't think they have got no right to do it. Because somebody goes out — this timber will be put on sale, for sale, and people will buy it. We know of some lumber companies, 7 or 8 big lumber companies as big as Weyerhaeuser can come in here and buy this timber, any one of them. We know that. If they come in and put this $150 million into this forest, they are not going to cut their own throats. They are business people, to protect that forest. They own timber in other parts of the United States, we know that. They are not cutting their throats because they own $200 million, $300 million worth of timber; they are not having fire sales there.

Now, that is a ridiculous statement for anyone to make, the Secretary of the Interior or anybody else, to say that because a man buys $100 million worth of timber that he is going to go out and have a fire sale and destroy the forest.

Now, we know, too, Senator, that the Government is subsidizing these big lumber companies throughout the United States. And they are practicing as good forestry as the Forest Service is practicing, or any other Government agency. So Mr. Seaton is absolutely wrong, and anybody else is that will make a wild statement like that.

Now, is the Weyerhaeuser Lumber Co. here now devastating the forest? Look at the property they own. I have been out on the Weyerhaeuser cuttings and they are cutting their timber there and practicing sustained yield.

Senator NEUBERGER. Have you knowledge that if Mr. Weyerhaeuser and his company purchase this timber that they are going to pay a competitive price to the Indians for it?

Mr. CRAWFORD. Well, if they are interested; if they are not, there are other people that are.

Senator NEUBERGER. Then, you said there are other people that are. Who are these other people if Mr. Weyerhaeuser won't pay the competitive price? Who are the other people?

Mr. CRAWFORD. Well, put it on the market and find out. I don't care to reveal these companies' names, but I do know them.

Senator NEUBERGER. And they are going to pay the Indians a competitive price for it?

Mr. CRAWFORD. Why, certainly. They are interested in buying

it. Any day that you put this timber up on the market, tomorrow morning you will find them interested in buying it. So that is just wild talk that you are going to ruin this forest.

Now, there is a lot of privately owned timber in Oregon. Why don't you say to those people here throughout Oregon that own their timber that the Government should handle it under the national forest or some other Government agency? You're not doing that. No, but Indians, you want to say, "Well, you've got to put your forest under the national forest in order to protect and have it cut on sustained yield."

Now, the people are cutting it on sustained yield besides the national forest and the O. and C. people.

Senator NEUBERGER. Some of them are clear cutting it, too.

Mr. CRAWFORD. Yes, I know that. Some of the smaller operators, I realize, Senator, are doing it.

Senator NEUBERGER. These sales will not be to smaller operators then?

Mr. CRAWFORD. Well, they are going to be put up for competitive bidding. I understand there are 140 units, 130, 140 units in different sizes, and if the lumber companies are interested, they will buy it on competitive bidding.

Senator NEUBERGER. Do you want to sell it to the small operators or not?

Mr. CRAWFORD. I don't care who buys it. We are interested in getting the most for it, but what I am afraid of in your bill here is, as to the reason I won't accept it, because I don't know what our values are now. We don't know the value of our forest. The Management Specialists have not completed their appraisal and until I know that, then I am willing to sit down with you and say that I am willing to sell my property.

Senator NEUBERGER. Well, is your interest then in the private enterprise forestry you are mentioning, or in the maximum price, which?

Mr. CRAWFORD. I am interested in the maximum price.

Senator NEUBERGER. And you will sell it to anybody who pays the maximum price?

Mr. CRAWFORD. Certainly I will. And just because somebody buys it, that is no reason why you should accuse me that they are going to ruin the forest.

Senator NEUBERGER. We are not.

Mr. CRAWFORD. That's what people have been doing, and the

newspapers have been full of it, and you have heard it before this committee today and you will hear it from now on. It has been the propaganda that has been poisoning the minds of the American people here and the people in this country.

Senator NEUBERGER. Some of the allotted timber of the reservation has been sold?

Mr. CRAWFORD. Yes, it has.

Senator NEUBERGER. What happened to it?

Mr. CRAWFORD. Well, I think some of it has been cut and some of it not.

Senator NEUBERGER. What kind of forestry has been practiced on it?

Mr. CRAWFORD. I haven't been out there. That is their individual business. I have got more than I can do to take care of my own business without going out.

Senator NEUBERGER. It is right on the reservation you are speaking for. Have you examined the forestry that is being practiced on there?

Mr. CRAWFORD. Listen, I make it my business, Senator, to look after the tribal affairs, not any neighbor's affairs. What some individual does on that reservation is not of my business and I don't intend to make it my business.

Mr. WOLF. On October 21 of this year the Management Specialists hope to have the appraisal; is that correct?

Mr. CRAWFORD. That is what I understand.

Mr. WOLF. If the price that is set by that appraisal satisfies you, would you then be willing to consider S. 2047?

Mr. CRAWFORD. I would give it some thought.

Mr. WOLF. If it satisfies you?

Mr. CRAWFORD. I say I will give it some thought, but this bill of yours, Senator, requires a great deal of study, more than the few minutes that the executive committee acted upon it there yesterday. In 3 minutes they passed that resolution to adopt the Federal purchase and the machinery that should go with this bill, there should be more written in here. I would like to have a little time to go into it with you, in putting time, dates in it, and a few other things, if I was interested in the price that the Management Specialists were going to report.

And another thing, just because Management Specialists report the timber is going to be worth so much a thousand for the different species of timber, I am not so sure that the Government will pay it. I have had a little experience with the Government in buying this timber. For about 6 years I had a bill in Congress. I wrote it myself. It is known as S. 1222 and S. 1313 for Federal purchase, and I went down to the Department of Agriculture to inquire if the Government was interested in purchasing it and they said they were interested in purchasing it at a fair market value, and what I wormed out of them that fair market value means about half what the timber is worth — was worth at that time. So I am not so sure that the Congress will go along with you to buy this timber for the appraisal of the Management Specialists put on it.

Senator NEUBERGER. Do you know of any lumber companies that will buy this timber?

Mr. CRAWFORD. I certainly do.

Senator NEUBERGER. Would they testify before our subcommittee?

Mr. CRAWFORD. I don't know whether they would or not. I can't speak for other people. I can speak for myself.

Senator NEUBERGER. It seems to me this is extremely important, an issue involving the future of your people and of this area, and if there are some lumber companies that will buy this timber and pay the Indians a competitive price for it, which you say you are interested in ——

Mr. CRAWFORD. That's right.

Senator NEUBERGER. Would they appear before this committee?

Mr. CRAWFORD. I don't consider their business. Now, you can take the Indians' business and make it a public business, which you have been doing, and our business has been too much politically handled; we have been kicked around here for the last 90 years politically, and we are sick of it, and I don't think that other people will stand for it, and most people that have got money won't stand for it, and I don't think you could drag them before a committee and handle their property like you have been handling ours. That's why I want to caution you without any further delay in handling our property. I wish that you would use — be careful and use a little bit more judgment about it, because under the amendment that you made last year it is going to cost the Klamath Indians over $3 million in money besides the losses in timber in the overmatured, the windfalls, fire-killed timber, and you are the cause of it.

Senator NEUBERGER. What amendment do you refer to, delaying termination?

Mr. CRAWFORD. That is right, delaying the termination. Otherwise the law would have been carried out, if you hadn't interfered.

Senator NEUBERGER. Do you realize that the community sentiment expressed to me was nearly overwhelming?

Mr. CRAWFORD. Are you going to settle this thing to the interest of the community or the Klamath Indians?

Senator NEUBERGER. I heard from many Klamath Indians in favor of postponing Klamath termination, too.

Mr. CRAWFORD. Did they give you any reason? Certainly I know Mr. Jackson would like to stay on the payroll here for the next 15 years, and carry on like he has been carrying on, go to an executive committee in the morning, and maybe show up there around 11 or 12 o'clock, 1 o'clock, put in his time for $20, $32 a day. He has been doing it for years.

Senator NEUBERGER. Are you on the executive committee?

Mr. CRAWFORD. Certainly I am. And I know; I have been and I have seen how it is operated. I tell you, it is a racket, Senator, and you should correct it if you are going to look out for the interest of the whole of the Indians.

Senator NEUBERGER. Have you ever drawn any funds from the Indian tribal funds?

Mr. CRAWFORD. Certainly I have.

Senator NEUBERGER. Why do you condemn Mr. Jackson?

Mr. CRAWFORD. Because — I don't condemn him, only in this way: I condemn him here, that you show up to do a job, you call a meeting for 10 o'clock in the morning; you don't show up until 11 or 12 o'clock, or start at 1 o'clock, then put in your bill for $32 a day, or $20 a day. That is a little chisel game that has been going on here for years. Mr. Jackson has had his feet in the tribal trough here all these years and he don't like to take them out and get out and make an honest living — take a pick and shovel like the other Indians have to do.

Mr. WOLF. Why doesn't the Bureau put a stop to this?

Mr. CRAWFORD. That's what I wonder. I can't conceive the Department of the Interior to protect the tribal funds that belong to the individual members of this tribe and allow a thing like that to continue. And we have sent in our protest and protest and we have protested before every committee we have ever appeared before.

Senator NEUBERGER. But you have drawn tribal funds yourself?

Mr. CRAWFORD. But I earned them, too.

Senator NEUBERGER. Well, he didn't. Is that it?

[.   .   .   .   .   ]

Mr. CRAWFORD. What I wanted to tell the Senator there: the reason why we opposed the million dollars to be used of the taxpayers is because we didn't want the time extended 2 years, which you advocated. Now, what you did, you asked for a million dollars of the taxpayers' money to continue this thing to pay the Management Specialists their thousand dollars a month with all their expenses. Then in addition to that, it was costing the Klamath Indians 3 million while the taxpayers were wasting a million by continuing and extending this time. If the time had not been extended you would have saved the Klamath Indians a million dollars and you would have saved the taxpayers a half a million dollars which there was no need of spending.

But on your insistence that the time be extended, you put the taxpayers and the tribal funds to be poured down the trough and for no good reason, which you are going to come to in the end to sell this timber to private enterprise. And by your delaying and stalling this thing off, you don't know, Senator, realize how you are hurting these Indians individually and tribally.

Now, you are hurting them more ways than one. We have got all these cases being held up here that the court won't act in probating their estates and settling up their estates. You have got your amendment in this last Congress which the Indian Service now is screening these Indians to the extent that very few of them are going to have control of their own funds. Going to be put into these trust companies.

I tell you, you ought to look into the record a little bit and you are setting up some history here that the Klamath Indians and the American people are not going to forget very long, that's going to take them a long time to outlive.

And I'd say great stress has been made about these Indians that are going to stay in and not withdraw and form some management plan. And have certain lands set aside for them here to manage. Now, I have the management plan here, the preliminary plan here for these Indians who have been telling Congress all the time that they want to stay in. Listen ——

Senator NEUBERGER. You are critical of me on this ——

Mr. CRAWFORD. I want to tell you this, Senator.

Senator NEUBERGER. Let me finish this statement. You think that the Bureau of Indian Affairs, the Oregon Council of Churches, the Secretary of the Interior, and the Management Specialists, all of whom favored extending the termination date, were likewise wrong?

Mr. CRAWFORD. I certainly do. I certainly do.

[. . . . .]

Statement of George Weyerhaeuser, Representing Weyerhaeuser Timber Co.

Mr. WEYERHAEUSER. Thank you very much, Senator Neuberger. I would like to say that our company appreciates the opportunity to present our opinions on this very important matter.

Senator NEUBERGER. If I am not mistaken, I think — correct me if I am wrong on this — isn't the Weyerhaeuser Timber Co. the largest timber company operating in the area where the Klamath Indian Reservation is located?

Mr. WEYERHAEUSER. Yes, I believe that is correct.

Senator NEUBERGER. And you have the most extensive operations and timber holdings in that area, if I am not mistaken, of any private company.

Mr. WEYERHAEUSER. That is correct.

Senator NEUBERGER. Thank you.

Mr. WEYERHAEUSER. I would like to say before I begin my remarks that with regret I am replacing our manager of forestry land and timber, Mr. Dave Weyerhaeuser, because of illness, and if in the questions or throughout the testimony any pertinent questions arise that I can't answer, we will attempt to get our expert witness' opinion on that matter.

Senator NEUBERGER. If there are questions which you cannot answer, you will have an opportunity to answer them later on in writing before the hearing record closes, and I hope you will extend to Mr. Dave Weyerhaeuser our best wishes for a complete and early recovery.

Mr. WEYERHAEUSER. I certainly will.

Senator NEUBERGER. Please go ahead with your statement.

Mr. WEYERHAEUSER. As a longtime neighbor and customer of the Klamath Indians, Weyerhaeuser Timber Co. is interested in the effects of the prospective termination of Federal supervision over the property of the Klamath Indians. We appreciate the opportunity to express our views about the disposal of the Indian timber. We hope that what we have to say may contribute to the solution of a problem of paramount importance to our Northwest timber economy.

By way of background, we should like to describe briefly our own operation in the Klamath Basin. We have owned lands and timber in the basin for more than half a century. Since 1929 we have operated a sawmill and related manufacturing facilities.

We manage our timber in accordance with sustained-yield principles so that we will have a continuous and permanent supply of raw material for our mills. This involves selective cutting of mature pine stands and management of residual stands so that growth equals cut. This supply is about half of what we need to operate our Klamath mills at their full capacity of 200 million feet per year.

In recent years we have reduced our production rate to about two-thirds of capacity to conform to the allowable cut on our own lands and the limited amount of timber available for purchase from public agencies. While reducing the amount of lumber we produce, we have substantially expanded our facilities for remanufacturing and finishing rough lumber, some of which we purchase from others. Also, we have built a hardboard plant that utilizes defective white fir and sawmill waste for which there is no other use. In this way there has been a substantial increase in the number of jobs, based upon a given quantity of raw material. For example, in 1942, our peak production year, we employed an average of 1,176 persons. Today, in producing less than two-thirds as much lumber as in 1942, we employ 19 percent more people, or a total of 1,396. Thus the level of employment has increased while the drain on local resources has been decreasing. Because of our adherence to sustained-yield forest management, it has been possible to increase the stability of this higher level of employment.

The importance of the Indian timber to the general area can be appreciated only if we consider briefly the timber resources and utilization facilities in the general area. (We define the general area as Klamath, Lake, and Deschutes Counties.) The commercial timberlands in this area are owned as follows:

	Acres	Percent
Federal agencies:		
U. S. Forest Service	2,480,000	54
Bureau of Land Management	117,000	3
Indian Service	779,000	17
All non-Federal ownership	1,221,000	26
TOTAL	4,597,000	100

The mills in Klamath County require about 365 million board-feet of logs annually to maintain their present level of operations, which is less than capacity. Those in the 3-county general area now use more than 600 million board-feet of logs annually.

Half these requirements are met by the present allowable cut from all Federal lands, including the Indian lands, which comprise about three-quarters of the total commercial-timber acreage. The annual allowable cut from Federal-agency lands, including 80 million feet on Indian lands, is 175 million board-feet for Klamath County and 325 million board-feet for the 3-county area. Thus, non-Federal lands, with 26 percent of the total acreage, are now supplying 50 percent of the logs. Since they cannot do this indefinitely, it is obvious that there already exists milling capacity substantially in excess of the timber available. A substantial overcutting of most private lands has resulted. Because of this overcutting, the problem of excess capacity may get worse in the next few years.

We seem to have come to a turning point in the history of the tribal timberlands. The Klamath Indians are beneficiaries of a policy of sustained-yield management that has been practiced since 1913. This policy has preserved a going business of great value. The latest report of the Management Specialists shows that tribal lands will support an allowable cut of 90 million feet through 1964, and, after that, 76 million feet in perpetuity (Tentative Plan of Management, August 1957, p. 22). This 76 million cut would produce annual net revenues of about $2,250,000 for the Indians. By ironic analogy to the widely publicized situations where people take over a business and then liquidate it, this going timber business appears to be worth more dead than alive. This results from the greater value of timber available for immediate cutting, assuming that a market exists. Consequently, pressures have been building up over the years to liquidate, rather than to continue, the tribal timber operations. This would involve cutting mature stands down to the minimum required by law. A significant part of this current pressure appears to be the widespread belief that the timber must be disposed of in order to permit the Indians to achieve emancipation from their wardship.

On the assumption that the timber will be disposed of, we believe that whatever method is adopted must satisfy the following basic objectives:

1. Sustained yield management of the timber must be continued in the interest of sound conservation, protection of the entire econ-

omy, preservation of watershed values, and for all the other reasons that have induced many forest owners, both public and private, to adopt this principle of forest management.

2. A "boom and bust" cycle for the basin area should be avoided. Mill capacity already exceeds the timber supply. Consequently, the basin may, like other timber-dependent communities, anticipate a moderate decline in forest employment. The Federal Government should not take any action that will inevitably aggravate this decline.

3. There are many small mills in the basin entirely, or almost entirely, dependent upon timber from outside sources. The timber must be disposed of in a way that will preserve for these mills an opportunity to use it in the future.

The achievement of these objectives has been complicated by the widespread disregard of the basic economic premise that is well stated in the old adage that "a bird in the hand is worth two in the bush." In fact, it may take several birds in the bush to equal one in the hand, when we are comparing the value of dollars to be received in the future with dollars in hand today. For example, if we discount future payments at 6 percent, it would take $10 payable 40 years from now — or less than halfway through the cutting cycle — to equal $1 received today. Likewise, it would take almost $2 to be received in 10 years — the shortest period over which the Indian timber could be liquidated — to equal $1 in hand today. Nevertheless, great expectations have been based upon the multiplication of 4 billion feet of timber by the current average retail price of $30 to $35 per thousand.

We assume that this timber will be marketed in an orderly manner, and that during this period the allowable cut from other Federal lands will be offered for sale. On this premise it is our opinion that it would take close to 15 years for the existing mills to liquidate the timber. We can only speculate about the amount of new milling capacity that might be attracted to the basin by the unrestricted sale of the Indian timber. Some new companies might buy timber in the expectation of liquidating it over a 10- to 15-year period. Such an operation would almost inevitably be based upon a limited investment. The number of man-hours per thousand feet of logs would be proportionately small. Following the short boom would be the inevitable "bust."

A dollar payable at the end of 15 years, the period over which the timber might possibly be liquidated, is worth only 48 cents at a 5 percent discount, or 43 cents at a 6 percent discount. Yet this is more than twice as much as the value of a dollar payable at the end of 30 years. This highlights the difference between the value of the timber sold without restriction on the one hand, and timber sold with sustained-yield restrictions on the other.

Whoever purchases the timber cannot afford, as a timber owner, to practice sustained-yield forestry if he is required to pay the present liquidation value of the timberlands.

There are two basic questions that must be answered with respect to the disposal of the Indian timber: (1) How should it be sold? and (2) to whom should it be sold? In order to answer these questions we must distinguish the various capacities in which the Federal Government is operating. The failure to do so has, in our opinion, been the source of much confusion. Let us look briefly at the separate roles in which Government is acting.

First, the Government is the guardian of the property of the Indians. As such, it has a narrow and unqualified duty to try to get everything it can for the Indians without regard to the interests or welfare of any other group. In discharge of this duty, it should sell the tribal timber in a manner that will produce the largest aggregate price for the Indians. Since it will take at least 15 years to cut the timber, the aggregate sales price, reflecting the deferment in recovery of costs, will be substantially less than an amount determined by multiplying retail prices paid over the last 2 or 3 years by the total volume of timber. Moreover, if the timber is sold in a short period, the excess supply will depress prices further. The prices that would be received, or the liquidation value, would probably not be materially greater than the sustained-yield value.

The second capacity in which the Government is acting is as the sovereign. As such it is the Government's function to propound and carry out policies that will be beneficial to all segments of the economy. It is in its sovereign capacity that the Government has spent billions of dollars to protect and build up other areas and other watersheds through reclamation projects, dam construction, and similar projects. Like consideration should lead the Government in its sovereign capacity to require that this tremendous block of timber be managed on a sustained-yield basis in the interests of the basin, the Northwest, and the economy of the entire Nation. Congress started a chain reaction when it passed the Termination Act. Unless Congress controls this chain reaction by preserving the existing limitations on cutting of Indian timber, the economy, the timber resources, and the watershed values of the Klamath Basin are doomed to irreparable injury.

By imposing a limitation upon the cutting of timber, the Government in its sovereign capacity may deprive the Indians of an element of value. This element would be measured by the excess of what they could receive for the lands sold without cutting restrictions over lands sold with restrictions. This would give rise to an obligation on the part of the sovereign to compensate the Indians for the value of this element of their property rights. This obligation relates to those who stay in the tribe and manage their lands on a sustained-yield basis, as well as to those who withdraw and sell their lands to others for sustained-yield operation.

Finally, the Government, as a prospective purchaser of the Indian timber, operates in a proprietary capacity. When the Government buys property in this capacity it should not be expected to pay more for such property than its true value. Thus, if the Government, as a proprietor, buys timber subject to sustained-yield cutting limitations, it cannot be expected to pay more than the sustained-yield value of such timber. In other words, acting in its proprietary capacity, the Government cannot pay any more for the timber than a private operator. Certainly it cannot as a proprietor borrow over $100 million at 4 percent interest, and amortize the purchase price out of annual gross receipts of less than $3 million. In paying an amount greater than the sustained-yield value of the timber, the Government is discharging its obligation as a sovereign, rather than paying a purchase price that it could justify as a proprietor.

The Management Specialists, in considering how the timber should be disposed of, start with two premises. First, the property must be managed on a sustained-yield basis; second, the Indians should be compensated for the reduction in value caused by such restriction. From these premises they draw a conclusion that we do not accept, namely, that the timberlands must be sold to the Government.

This conclusion flows from the following syllogism, which we have modified only by clarifying the term "Government" in each proposition:

1. The Government — as guardian — must obtain for the Indians the liquidation value of the timber;
2. Only the Government — as sovereign — will pay the full liquidation value of timber that is subject to sustained-yield management restriction;

   3. Therefore, only the Government — as proprietor — can buy the timber.

The trouble with this syllogism is that the word "Government" is used in different senses in the premises and the conclusion. We suggest that a more logical syllogism is the following:

1. The Government — as guardian — must obtain for the Indians the liquidation value of the timber;
2. The Government — as sovereign — should pay any excess of liquidation value over sustained-yield value as compensation for a restriction imposed by it for the benefit of all;
3. Any proprietor — whether Government or private — purchasing the timber with sustained-yield restrictions should not pay any more for it than its sustained-yield value. Conversely, any person, including a private enterprise, willing to pay the sustained-yield value has as much right to purchase as does the Government — as proprietor.

We do not accept the conclusion that Government purchase is the only way to provide sustained-yield management of these lands. We see no reason why the Government's present ownership of almost three-fifths of the commercial timberlands in the general area should be increased to three-fourths. Furthermore, we note that doubts have been expressed about the willingness of Congress to appropriate the money necessary to pay the Indians the full liquidation value of their property.

Previous witnesses have assumed that there are only two methods of disposal — to the Government for sustained-yield operation or to private owners for unrestricted cutting. We believe there is a middle ground — that sustained-yield management can be required and private owners can be permitted to bid on the timber.

If this approach is adopted, the Federal Government would be obligated only to indemnify the Indians for any reduction in the market value of their timber caused by cutting restrictions. Consequently, the amount of Federal funds required would be substantially reduced.

We now come to the most difficult question — how should the sale be handled? Any sustained-yield value of the timber should be established by appraisers. This value would reflect the costs during the cutting cycle for interest, carrying charges for the timber, and would also reflect risks of destruction by fire and disease, together

with the risk of economic obsolescence. The appraisers should likewise develop a liquidation value that would reflect all these factors
through the period of expected liquidation. In addition they would
take into account the effect on prices of the sale of the large volume
of timber.

Thereafter, the timber would be offered for sale subject to
sustained-yield management requirements. A minimum price based
upon the appraisal might be established. In the absence of any bids
by private companies, the Government would have a right to bid
in a parcel at the minimum price.

The amount of compensation to be paid to the Indians on account
of the sustained-yield restrictions would be the excess of the appraised liquidation value over the prices actually received.

In order to accommodate the needs of the smaller companies the
timber should be offered for sale in parcels of varying sizes. Some
should be small enough to be handled by any company. As an
alternative, part of the timber might be held by the Government
for periodic sale of the allowable cut.

In considering whether smaller companies might be interested in
buying the Indian timber for sustained-yield management, it should
be borne in mind that there will be a continuous offering of Forest
Service and Bureau of Land Management timber. Consequently, any
particular company would not have to set up a sustained-yield unit
large enough to support an entire mill. Instead, the unit would
merely supplement public timber purchases.

Financing is frequently the principal barrier to acquisition of
timber for sustained-yield operation. A possible way of eliminating
this obstacle would be to offer the timber for sale on alternate bases.
A purchaser could pay cash or, alternatively, pay the purchase price
on an installment basis with a minimum down payment. These installment payments could be used to meet the principal payments
becoming due over the next 15 years to Indian minors upon reaching
their majority. Also, the installment contracts might be an investment outlet for any adult Indian who wished to spread out the
receipt of their share of proceeds.

We have considered thus far only certain economic aspects of the
termination. We are not addressing ourselves to the method of
handling the wildlife resources. We will say in passing that they are
separate from the timberlands so that the public or private purchase
of the timberlands does not require a similar disposal of marshlands.

Finally, we recognize that the problem of overriding importance is the assistance of the Indians in their transition to the status of full-fledged independent citizens. We believe that this committee deserves the highest commendation for the sincerity and industry with which it approaches these problems.

Senator NEUBERGER. Thank you, Mr. Weyerhaeuser. You have certainly presented a thoughtful statement here today, and one which I know is going to receive a great deal of consideration from the subcommittee and from the Congress.

[. . . . .]

Senator NEUBERGER. I want to ask you about the price, because you have referred to that both in your oral testimony and in your written testimony. At the bottom of page 4, you say:

Nevertheless, the great expectations have been based upon the multiplication of 4 billion feet of timber by the current average retail price of $30 to $35 per thousand.

If that price were realized, the sum of somewhere around $120 million would go to the Indian owners of the timber, is that correct?

Mr. WEYERHAEUSER. That is correct.

Senator NEUBERGER. Now, a statement of approximate value appeared in a news article in the Klamath Falls News and Herald the other evening of approximately $113 million. Isn't that correct?

Mr. GAMBLE. That is right.

Senator NEUBERGER. And it is called to my attention, too, that it appeared in the New York Times for October 1. Now, this is what puzzles me: We had some testimony at Klamath Falls on October 2 from some Indians, which indicated even dissatisfaction with the $113 million price. Yet you are pointing out in your statement that great expectations have been based on a price of $120 million, which is not greatly different from the $113 million. Under the proposal which you have voiced to us, what approximately do you think these Indians could realize from their timber?

Mr. WEYERHAEUSER. I will say quite frankly, not only I, nor could our forestry department answer that question because our information concerning the Indian timber is not — we have information concerning the timber we have cut off of Indian land, certainly, but we are not in a position to say what the value of that Indian timber is. We can take the volume figures that are present; we could project what we have cut off in the way of grade off Indian land, but I am not in a position here today to tell you what —

I can't tell you what the original, true retail market value for that would be today, if there were a market existing for 4 billion feet. If I could tell you that, I could then say that is our belief, that is right, after arriving at that retail value, that if that timber were put on the market today and liquidated in the most orderly fashion to get the highest realization from it, that the net effect would be a discount factor of in excess of 50 percent from that value, without sustained-yield cutting restrictions imposed upon the timber, and I say that and I say I believe we have figures to substantiate that premise, based on blockage of timber sold in the Pacific Northwest in the past 5 years.

Senator NEUBERGER. You are assuming that all of this timber is dumped on the market under the provisions of Public Law 587?

Mr. WEYERHAEUSER. No, I am not.

Senator NEUBERGER. You are assuming that Public Law 587 will be amended?

Mr. WEYERHAEUSER. I am assuming that this would be the effect under Public Law 587. I am assuming that not only under that law but under any provision that a prudent manager could dispose of that timber without restriction, that he would have to take on that body of timber with the present, with the milling capacity available, and present economic conditions, the true value of that timber under any conditions is 50 percent discount on current retail market prices which are quoted when you arrive at $120 million.

[. . . . .]

STATEMENT OF OLIVIA N. KIRK

BEATTY, OREG.,
October 29, 1957

Hon. *Richard L. Neuberger,*
Senate Office Building, Washington, D.C.

Hon. SENATOR NEUBERGER: When Congress passed Public Law 587 in 1954 that was one time when the "cart was put before the horse." Ever since then everything regarding the law is going backward. The interest that has been shown by church groups, chambers of commerce, timber companies, and other groups, and the statements I have heard them make leaves no doubt in my mind that the "goose that laid the golden egg" (Klamath Reservation) for the Klamath Basin is going to die a slow death.

Why wasn't all their investigations that are being carried on by different organizations, Senate and Congress done before the bill was passed? Then perhaps a solution could be reached. Now the bill is passed and signed by the President of the United States. Amendments have been introduced and passed by new Members of Congress, and the Klamath termination bill is going no place fast.

I am a member of the Klamath Tribe and along with other members of the tribe voted against termination in any shape or form. Even though we were told by the Commissioner and other members of the Department of the Interior at a meeting at Klamath Agency in 1953, that regardless of what we did or said in our general councils regarding termination we did not have a choice in the matter as we would be terminated regardless. No thought was given to find out who it was going to effect or how.

This law is a good deal for the lawyers in the Klamath Basin. They are sitting back waiting to feather their nests with the fees that they will get from guardianships on our minor children who had no voice in the termination matter. The minors are the ones who will help pay the termination cost, guardianship fees, guardianship bonds, and court costs. By the time a minor reaches the age of 21 there will not be any money left for them to start their life with. The United States Government should be made to pay all of the guardianship costs for the minors.

If the State of Oregon bought our tribal assets, taxes would be raised in the State and Klamath County to help pay for their purchase, and the members of the Klamath Tribes as well as the minors would have to pay taxes to help the State buy our property. The same thing would happen if the United States Government purchased our timber. Federal taxes would be raised all over the United States; and again we the Klamath Indians would be paying into the United States Government coffers; paying for what is rightfully ours.

Should a private company want to buy our timber we would still be on the dole system. As Mr. Weyerhaeuser stated, his company could only pay 50 percent of the appraised price and would have to take several years to pay the balance. A private company could not be made to cut under a sustained yield as the timber would belong to them. They would have to pay for their fire protection and other costs to protect their interests. The United States Government should be made to purchase all of the Klamath Indian timber at the appraised price if we have to sell our timber.

Our duck-hunting rights was taken away from us several years ago by a Federal migratory law. The Klamath Indian Tribes did not sue the Government for this. Our duck-hunting rights was one of our treaty rights. I and many other Indian people purchased Federal duck stamps to hunt ducks in season. Could I not ask the Government to reimburse me for buying duck stamps all these years, when it was one of my treaty privileges to hunt in season or out? Judge Solmon, of Portland, in his district court rendered a decision that the Klamath Indians could hunt anytime. And the word "hunt" means hunting anything to be hunted with firearms. He did not specify what kind of bird or animal.

In all the meetings I have attended no one has yet said who will pay the

Klamath Tribes for their hunting and fishing rights. To purchase our hunting and fishing rights will run into several million dollars; or did Congress expect us to give up all of our treaty rights for nothing? They have already taken our duck-hunting rights from us; now they want to take our proud rights of being a free American Indian from us by putting us in the soup line, on welfare, and in the poorhouse along with our white neighbor.

We have our water rights on the Klamath Reservation, rights that are recognized by the State of Oregon. This water we have that flows from the reservation is worth millions of dollars to the Klamath Basin and northern California. Who will buy our water rights? I believe that our water rights are worth more than the timber on the Klamath Reservation.

There are thousands of acres of tribal grazing land and wastelands on the Klamath Reservation. I have not heard anyone say as to who will pay the Klamath Tribes for this class of land. So far all I have heard is who will purchase the Klamath Tribes timber.

There are the natural resources and mineral rights that should be protected for the Klamath Tribes, also the allottee who sells their allotments to non-Indians.

What guaranty do we have that after termination we receive a sum of money for our reservation, that the Government will not step in and charge us for the Modoc war, fish hooks and plowing implements, and dress goods that was given our ancestors? Or perhaps they may think up some new debts to put against the Klamath Tribes. By the time they get through dipping into our capital we won't have much left. This is what happened when we received money from the boundary suit in 1937. We paid for a war that was forced on the Modoc Tribe by the United States Government. Our Indian people were being forced on reservations all over the United States by United States troops. While Abraham Lincoln was trying to free the Negro from bondage the American Indian was placed in bondage. Forced them from their ancestral homes and lands. Placing them on small reservations by force and they could not leave this reservation without a permit. Why were not the American Indian educated and trained along with the Negro to be free American citizens side by side. Now look at the Negro race they are treated in the most shameful manner. Forced from schools and homes, treated like some wild animal. The very same descendants whose ancestors brought them into this country and sold them and bought them like animals. In a few years after termination the Indian people will be like the Negro. We will be forced out of schools, towns, and cities. We will be kicked from pillar to post. There is already racial prejudice in our city of Klamath Falls in some places of business — prejudice against the Indian. Who is there to judge his fellow man on the face of the earth? There should be but one judge, our Creator.

If the United States Government did not ratify our treaty in the first place we would never have all of this mess we are in now. Therefore, in fairness to the Klamath Tribes, people of the Klamath Basin and State of

Oregon, it is only right that the United States Government buy our reservation, give us every cent we have coming to us in a lump sum and not the dole system. Protect our children and mineral rights and natural resources and not try to shove their obligations and duties off on the State of Oregon or some private enterprise. If this cannot be, leave us alone and do something about abolishing the Public Law 587 even if the Constitution of the United States has to be amended to fit the bill. The United States Government does not have enough money in the United States mint to buy my ancestral home, the Klamath Indian Reservation.

Respectfully submitted.

Olivia N. Kirk

9.

The World Situation

PROBLEMS IN INTERNATIONAL RELATIONS ARE, OF COURSE, exceedingly complex. Foreign policy represents the program for achieving national aspirations and insuring protection against threats to such development. Details have to be seen in the context of the larger wholes. Nevertheless, actions taken on the world scene reflect the decisions of people, be they individuals in power positions or groups of experts.

In today's world, with the availability of rapid communication and world-wide news reporting facilities, all responsible government officials know that any public statement concerning foreign affairs is likely to come before many publics. On the domestic front, supporters and opponents will know what is said; on the foreign fronts, allies, neutrals, and enemies will have the material available. Ideally, all statements will be assessed in advance to estimate their likely effects on these different audiences, and efforts will be made to present material in such fashion as to be maximally effective for the target audiences desired and to be minimally harmful when reviewed by others. Realization that such considerations are usually involved in the statements we hear and read makes interpretation particularly difficult. One of the first problems confront-

ing the analyst of such materials is to determine who the real
target audience is; and second, what effect is being sought.

Recognition of the factors suggested above helps us appreciate the tremendous amount of information that is needed
for errorless diplomacy. Not the least of the needs is the correct assessment of the domestic population, both with respect
to ultimate goals and to the means of achieving such ends.

Suggested Discussion Questions

What seem to be the major audiences for which the two key
statements were intended? What seem to be the effects sought
in each? In the presentation of the late Mr. Dulles, which
parts of the material would be designated as correct by an
official of the Soviet Union, which incorrect? How might competent observers from the other potential audiences, including leaders of the domestic opposition party, react? What are
the major problems in the development of a sound foreign
policy for the Middle East? How are these problems related
to the broader picture described in the Dulles statement?
How might one proceed to solve these problems constructively? What resistances should one expect to encounter?
Where ought one start? How?

BRIEFING ON CURRENT WORLD SITUATION

HEARINGS *before the Committee on Foreign Affairs, House of Representatives, 86th Congress, First Session*

WEDNESDAY, JANUARY 28, 1959

Washington, D.C.

THE COMMITTEE MET in executive session at 10:40 a. m., in room G–3, U.S. Capitol, Washington, D.C., Hon. Thomas E. Morgan (chairman) presiding.

Chairman MORGAN. The committee will come to order.

Now that the committee on committees has met and named the members of the full committee, this is our first full committee meeting.

It is customary at the start of each Congress to have briefings from the Department of State, the military, and Central Intelligence and we also have scheduled for tomorrow the Under Secretary of State for Economic Affairs, Douglas Dillon.

Our first witness is the distinguished Secretary of State and, before we start, Mr. Secretary, I would like to introduce the new members of the committee.

Mr. Diggs.

Mr. Beckworth. Mr. Beckworth is an oldtimer around here. His chief interest used to be interstate and foreign commerce, but now he has switched to foreign affairs.

Next is Mr. McDowell, of Delaware. Mr. McDowell has also served one term.

We have four members who are beginning their service in the House: Mr. Murphy, of Illinois; Mr. Meyer, of Vermont; Mr. Gallagher, of New Jersey; and Mr. Bowles, of Connecticut.

On the minority side, we welcome to the committee a man who carried the burden on the Education and Labor Committee for several years, Mr. Wainright, of New York.

Secretary DULLES. He comes from what used to be my district in Long Island.

Chairman MORGAN. Please proceed, Mr. Secretary.

Statement of Hon. John Foster Dulles, Secretary of State

Secretary DULLES. Mr. Chairman, I am very happy to be here again. This is my seventh annual presentation to this committee, with which I have always had the closest relations and which has been most helpful and constructive in the conduct of a foreign affairs policy which has been bipartisan, or nonpartisan.

I have a prepared statement which I would read if it is agreeable.

Chairman MORGAN. Go right ahead.

Secretary DULLES. Following the statement I understand there will be questions.

It is frequently said these days that so much change is going on in the world that our foreign policy too must be changeable. I myself have often said that, and the sincerity of that belief is shown not just by words, but by deeds.

With a new continent — Africa — opening up, we have, with your help, established the new post of Assistant Secretary of State for African Affairs.

With the peoples of less-developed countries throughout the world stirred with aspirations for development, we increasingly support such international institutions as the World Bank and Monetary Fund. We increasingly supplement private U.S. capital through such institutions as the Export-Import Bank and the economic Development Fund. We join with the other American Republics to organize a regional American development institution, and we have indicated a readiness to assist such an institution for the Near East, if that be desired by our Arab friends.

With the Arctic opening up new and quick routes of communication over the top of the world, we seek to have this area subjected to international inspection so that it will be used for peaceful purposes and not become a new shortcut to sudden massive destruction.

With the Antarctic opening up as a new continent, we propose that it should be subjected to an international treaty which will prevent a competitive scramble there for strategic and material advantages.

With the splitting of the atom opening up immense possibilities for peaceful use, we brought about the organization of the International Atomic Energy Agency and we support through EURATOM and through bilateral arrangements the development of the peaceful applications of this vast new power throughout the length and breadth of the free world.

With outer space now opening up for man's use, we urge that that use be guided by the United Nations.

With 21 new nations, and others at the threshold of independence, we endeavor to help them to retain genuine independence and to overcome the difficulties and dangers inherent in the early stages of independence when, according to Communist doctrine, such states are susceptible of being "amalgamated" into the Communist bloc with the total loss of their independence.

With the Soviet Union and Communist China growing rapidly in military and industrial power, and with the United Nations largely impotent to prevent the violent use of that power, we have extended and strengthened the collective-security arrangements which enable the free world to survive in peace and confidence.

With the growth of free world interdependence, we encourage its practice. This year the policy of the United States to favor a common market in Europe, a policy expressed in the Economic Cooperation Act of 1948, has substantially been realized. Also we seek the evolution of our collective security associations into permanent organs of regular consultation and cooperation in the field of foreign relations. Thus they are becoming constructive political institutions of a new kind and not mere military alliances.

With armament reaching proportions which in cost threaten mankind with impoverishment, and which, if used, would threaten mankind with extinction, we have made new and far-reaching disarmament proposals.

In such ways and many others, we seek to make our foreign policy responsive to the needs of new conditions and to exert an influence on the new evolutions that are occurring in the field of politics, economics, and science.

There are, however, some who seem to think that we should invent new policies that, they say, should "end the cold war."

It would be easy to devise a form of words which could be agreed to between the United States and the Soviet Union and which would give many unwary people a sense of relief, and a feeling that our Nation need no longer make the efforts and sacrifices that are now called for. The Soviet Government has, for a long time, been trying to get that result. It is, however, my deep conviction that the cold war cannot be ended in any such way and that to take that step would merely make it probable that the cold war would end in victory for international communism.

Where lies the responsibility for the cold war? Surely the United States covets nothing possessed by the Soviet Union or any other people. We never had, and do not now have, any substantial differences with the Soviet Union.

The cold war originates in the creed of what Mr. Khrushchev refers to as the monolithic international Communist movement and the fact that this movement controls the policies and resources of some 900 million people and all or a major part of what used to be 15 independent countries.

No one disputes the fact that the Communist Party is the dominant power in these countries; that it dictates who the government shall be and what it shall do. As Stalin used to say:

Not a single important political or organizational question is decided by our Soviet without guiding directions from the party ("The Problems of Leninism," Jan. 25, 1926).

In order, therefore, to ascertain what will be the policy of the Soviet Government and other Communist-dominated governments, it is necessary to ascertain the policy of the international Communist movement.

This policy is nothing secret. It is a policy based upon atheism and materialism and upon the belief that human beings are but animated particles of matter and need to be regulated and controlled by some single directing force: namely, the dictatorship of the proletariat, of which the Soviet Communist Party is the general staff. International communism believes that there will not be peace or maximum productivity unless human beings are forced into a pattern of conformity — conformity of action, thinking and belief — established by the party.

It believes that to achieve this result on a worldwide basis is so essential to peace and well-being that any means are justified to produce this end, whether those means be propaganda frauds, breaches of international agreements, violent subversion, or the threat of war itself.

Therein lies the cold war.

The Soviet Government could end the cold war, so far as it is concerned, if it would free itself from the guiding direction of international communism and seek primarily the welfare of the Russian nation and people. Also the cold war would come to an end if international communism abandoned its global goals, or if, abandoning its methods of force and fraud, it relied on normal methods of persuasion. Also, of course, the cold war would come to an end if the free world ceased to resist and gradually succumbed to international communism.

This last is, of course, the Communist idea of how to end the cold war.

Mr. Mikoyan, as a result of his visit here, seems to feel that there is, on this matter, a gap between the policies of the U.S. Government and the views of the American people.

There is no such gap. The U.S. Government can sincerely express all the generalities which Mr. Mikoyan heard about desire for peace, good will, friendship, easing of tensions, increase of trade, and so forth. And let me say that these are more than polite phrases. They are the ardent aspirations of our Nation. But our Government has to deal with the concrete, not just with generalities. I am confident that in this realm of the concrete there is substantial accord between the American people and their Government.

Every specific proposal that the Soviets have made for promoting an ending of the cold war has been a proposal designed to diminish our will or capacity to resist international communism in the achievement of its worldwide goals.

Take the Soviet economic demands. These would require us to eliminate all control over the movement to the Soviet Union of our strategic goods. They would require us to grant vast credits to enable the Soviet Union to buy in this country what it felt would be useful for its military and industrial development. It would require us to extend most-favored-nation treatment to Soviet goods, which may be sold, for political reasons, at prices which bear no relation to costs.

And there is no suggestion that the Soviet Union might itself free its own trade from political domination. Every kopek of Soviet trade is regimented and directed by the state primarily for political and strategic purposes. Some commercial transactions are made in order to produce needed foreign exchange. But the Soviet Government has never concealed the fact that, in this matter of foreign trade, political and not commercial factors were primary. Thus it would itself maintain the tightest political direction over all its trade while we would be expected to abandon all of our controls.

Berlin and Germany provide another illustration. In 1944–45 there were agreements between the principal Western allies and the Soviet Union on the zones of occupation of Germany. Under those agreements the United States and the United Kingdom, at the close of hostilities, relinquished to Soviet occupancy very large parts of Germany on which their armies then stood. As a part of those same agreements they and France received the right to occupy West Berlin, then a mass of rubble, and to have access thereto.

That rubble has been transformed into a dynamic exhibit of what free men can do. As such, its contrast proves irksome and unsettling to the Communist rule of surrounding areas. So the Soviet Union annuls its agreements with us and calls on us to withdraw the small Western garrison which alone assures the confident independence of the brave people of West Berlin. That, according to the Soviet Union, would be a step toward "ending the cold war."

Another step, according to the Soviet Government, would be for us to accept abandonment of the Soviet agreement that German reunification is a responsibility of the four occupying powers and that Germany shall be reunified by free elections.

This was the principal substantive result of the summit Conference of Heads of Government held at Geneva in July 1955. It was achieved only through the toughest negotiation. But finally the Soviet Government agreed that there was a

close link between the reunification of Germany and the problems of European security, and on the fact that the successful settlement of each of these problems would serve the interests of consolidating peace.

Also the heads of government agreed on

recognizing their common responsibility for the settlement of the German question and the reunification of Germany.

They also agreed on

the reunification of Germany by means of free elections.

The Soviet Union seems now to have concluded that it is not to its interest that there should be a reunification of Germany, and that two Germanies should be perpetuated. Also it has decided that it wants to slough off its share of the agreed common responsibility for the German question and for German reunification and to abdicate in favor of its creature, the so-called German Democratic Republic.

The Soviet Union argues that if we will acquiesce in this tearing up of the summit accord and accept different arrangements more favorable to it, that would be another good step toward ending the cold war.

And so it goes. Never yet has the Soviet Union made any proposal designed to promote ending the cold war except on terms that it calculated would help international communism to win the cold war.

There is, I know, always the temptation to grasp at a form of words which might seem to end the continuing strains, the burdens, the risks, to which we are now subjected. But the Soviet proposals constitute not remedies but drugs which would numb us to the real danger which will then become greater than ever.

Let me make perfectly clear that we are fully alive to the grave hazards in the present situation. Every reasonable and decent effort must be made to avoid needless provocations, to find a modus vivendi, and to reduce the danger of a war which under present conditions would involve a large measure of worldwide annihilation. We have, I think, shown that we believe in such efforts.

We made the Korean armistice which ended the hostilities in Korea.

We participated in the Geneva Conference of 1954 which brought to an end the hostilities in Indochina.

We have sought, and still seek in our Warsaw talks with the Chinese Communists, to assure that in the Taiwan area force should not be relied upon by either side to bring about the reunification of China. And the Government of the Republic of China last October declared its principal reliance on peaceful means, and not the use of force, for restoring freedom to the people on the mainland.

We have joined with the Soviet Union in concluding the Austrian State Treaty which liberated Austria.

We have made, a year ago, an agreement for cultural and scientific exchanges with the Soviet Union.

We have met with the Soviet Union at the summit and indicated a readiness to do so again. But the Soviet Union broke off the negotiations for such a meeting last June when it was made clear we would feel free to talk about some subjects that they disliked.

We are negotiating in good faith for a controlled discontinuance of the testing of nuclear weapons.

We have indicated our readiness to discuss the interrelated problems of Berlin, German reunification, and European security. But so far the Soviet Union insists that we shall only talk about a change in the status of West Berlin — not East Berlin — and about a peace treaty which would be made with the two Germanies and perpetuate the partition of Germany.

The principles of our policy were first announced in 1947. That policy is based, first of all, on our hope of achieving a just peace and on firmness in opposing aggression. Ever since that time the American people and their successive governments have stood by these basic purposes steadfastly and firmly in spite of every kind of provocation.

I assure you that we are as alert and vigilant in seeking every reasonable avenue to achieving a better understanding with those who are hostile to us as we are alert and vigilant in maintaining the kind of strength that will convince them of the folly of aggression.

As President Eisenhower has repeatedly said, there is nothing that we will not do at any time at any place which holds a reasonable prospect for promoting a just peace. But it would be reckless to be intimidated, or lured, into measures which far from ending the present danger would merely increase it.

Chairman MORGAN. Thank you, Mr. Secretary.

Now, for the benefit of the new members, it is our usual procedure here that we operate under the 5-minute rule. The committee being 32 in number, we have to limit each member's questioning to 5 minutes. If the members will keep track of their watches and try to stay within the time limit, it will be appreciated.

Mr. Secretary, do you see any new elements in the policy of Soviet Russia arising from the new meeting of the 21st Communist Congress and the address by Mr. Khrushchev?

Secretary DULLES. We do not yet have the full text of that address. He spoke for 6½ hours, but insofar as we have been able to follow it, there is nothing new.

Chairman MORGAN. Mrs. Bolton?

Mrs. BOLTON. Mr. Secretary, I happen to be a little more alert than I often am because I had to give a talk myself last week about the administration's foreign policy, so I dug into a great many things and was fascinated by what I found.

I am generally enthusiastic about the methods which you employ, about which I knew considerably less than I do now.

I wanted to ask about the suggestion, it is my understanding you made, that there is a possibility that there might be methods other than free elections to change the German situation.

Secretary DULLES. I said in answer to a question at a press conference — the question was, "Is it your position that 'no free elections — no reunification'?"

I said the result we wanted was unification of Germany with freedom. That result, we have agreed upon with the Russians and with the Germans, should be obtained by free elections. That was the summit agreement. If there was any other way to bring it about, we would be glad to explore that way, but before we give up a way which is a good way and the agreed way, we would like to see what the alternative is and we so far have not found any particular alternative.

The Soviet proposals on confederation are not really steps toward reunification at all. They are steps which in the name of confederation would perpetuate the division. The so-called German peace treaty proposed to be made by the two Germanies would be another step to perpetuate the division.

Now, I pointed out in my press conference yesterday that nobody can say that free elections are the only way to achieve reunification. I referred to our own national history.

Our original Union came about through legislative action by the States and not by popular elections. The reunification of 1865 was not by free elections. Even when Alaska became a State, which created a further unification, there was a general election in Alaska but there was no general referendum for popular expression throughout the country.

Mrs. BOLTON. It is not then a weakening on our part. My people have interpreted it in some instances as meaning that we are receding from our firm position.

Secretary DULLES. No. We have this agreement for reunification by free elections. We are adhering to it. Unless and until somebody can come up with an alternative suggestion which would really accomplish reunification in some other effective way. It would have to be a way clearly in accord with the wishes of the people because we don't want to impose something that they don't want, but there is no doubt, I think, but what the German people as a whole do want to be reunified and they want to be reunified in freedom because there is a steady flow of refugees from East Germany to West Germany which I think is convincing evidence of the way they feel.

Mrs. BOLTON. Thank you very much.

Chairman MORGAN. Mrs. Kelly.

Mrs. KELLY. Thank you, Mr. Chairman.

Mr. Secretary, it is always nice to have you with us. I hope if I ask any questions which would seek to divulge negotiations, you will refrain from answering.

Is the United States in complete agreement with our allies on every step of the Berlin situation? Have we complete understanding with our allied nations?

Secretary DULLES. On the basic proposition of standing firm in Berlin, and, if need be, risking a war rather than being taken out of Berlin, upon that there is complete agreement.

It was expressed strongly and vigorously by the four powers — by the four Foreign Ministers when I was at the meeting in Paris last December — and then by the NATO Council and on the basic proposition there is complete agreement.

Now, how you implement that in all possible contingencies that one can think of has to be gone into. Some obvious possible actions we may face are the substitution of G.D.R. people, blowing up bridges, cutting down of trees across the roads, and interference with air flights.

We have not yet achieved full agreement with our allies or I might say even within our own Government as to what we might do in every contingency. The possible courses of action that the Soviets or East Germans might take are very many indeed and we have been studying what we would do under various contingencies. There are studies under way with the Department of Defense, the Joint Chiefs of Staff, and the State Department.

We have been having preliminary talks on these contingencies with our allies, which have been so far in the nature of an exchange of views rather than an attempt to reach an agreement. That attempt will be pushed forward, I hope rather rapidly after our own position is firmed up somewhat more and after the preliminary exchanges are also being considered at a higher level by the British, French, and German Governments.

Mrs. KELLY. On the basic proposition you are in agreement. On those things that are possibly flexible in an approach to meet the problem, there is indecision; is that correct?

Secretary DULLES. I would not say there is indecision.

Mrs. KELLY. Well, the method of meeting them?

Secretary DULLES. There has not yet been decision. I expect there will be decision well before the critical date which will be the end of May.

[Security deletion.]

Chairman MORGAN. Mr. Merrow.

Mr. MERROW. Thank you, Mr. Chairman.

Mr. Secretary, I am glad to see you with us again. I want to take this opportunity to compliment you on the affirmative and positive leadership and statesmanship you are giving in this particularly difficult period. I think you have established a splendid record and I want to congratulate you.

Mr. Secretary, do you feel the Soviet Union will draw the issue in the spring on Berlin?

Secretary DULLES. I believe that they will keep the pressure on until the very last minute. That is their usual tactic. They may not make any concessions in advance. They will keep the pressure on until the very last in the hope that some division will develop, some weakness will develop.

Some people asked, when Mr. Mikoyan was here if he made any indications of concession. I said, "No, and it would not be at all in accordance with their tactics to make any concessions in advance. They will keep the war of nerves, which they are conducting, and they will continue it to the very last to see if our nerves hold. If it doesn't hold, they will gain a great victory."

Mr. MERROW. From your conversations with Mr. Mikoyan and from your observations of what they have been doing recently, do you feel there is any possibility that they may change their line of policy, weaken it or make adaptations that would indicate that it might not be as rigid in the future?

Secretary DULLES. No; there is every evidence that they are becoming tougher and with the growth of their economic and industrial power, their increased military power, I think that is likely to be reflected in a tougher rather than a softer policy line.

The chairman asked me about our reactions to the speech of Mr. Khrushchev. I said there was nothing new there. My advisers who are expert in these matters tell me, based on what they know, that while there is nothing new, the tendency is to be tougher than before, although the general line is about the same.

Mr. MERROW. Are they accelerating to a marked degree their economic offensives in the underdeveloped areas of which you spoke?

Secretary DULLES. Yes. They are now increasing their economic activities quite substantially every year, particularly in the underdeveloped countries.

Their system does enable them to grow economically. You see, capital savings are by and large the difference between what you produce and what you consume. Now, when you have a dictatorship of that kind which on the one hand requires labor to produce at a very rapid rate, with long hours of labor and with labor which largely extends to women as well as men, and if on the other hand you hold them down as to what they can consume, then you get a bigger margin between production and consumption. Your production is up and your consumption is down.

Now, in most of the so-called free countries where labor has greater choice, greater opportunity for leisure and so forth, you get conditions where by and large production and consumption are in balance and when that happens you don't have any capital increase at all.

Normally in a free society you get an annual increment of somewhere between 3 percent and 5 percent in your capital development. The Soviet Union is getting between 5 and 8 percent probably.

Communist China has an even more rapid rate of increase.

Now, out of what they are able to extract from the people, they get the capital for further development for war industry and for economic offensives. They are increasing the weight of their economic offensive, particularly in the less developed countries of the South Asia and Africa.

Chairman MORGAN. Mr. Selden.

Mr. SELDEN. Thank you, Mr. Chairman.

Mr. Secretary, you made the statement that both the Soviet Union and the Chinese Communists are growing rapidly in military and industrial power. If that is correct, do you feel that we are gaining or losing ground in the cold war we are waging against the Communist world?

Secretary DULLES. If you think purely of the material developments such as I referred to, economic and industrial growth and obtaining funds for the cold war, they are gaining more rapidly than we are.

On the other hand, there is developing within the Soviet Union at least — not so much yet in Communist China — but within the Soviet Union there is an internal revolution occurring which I think indicates that they will not be able to carry on indefinitely this type of development which has been characteristic of the first generation of their activity.

More and more the leaders — Khrushchev — are having to promise the people that they are going to get more consumer goods. In the last year or so he has been having to promise the people that they will have more leisure. He now says they are going to have a short working week; have as much leisure as the American workers have.

Now, that shows a growing demand within the Soviet Union on the part of the workers to get more or less the equivalent of what is gotten by workers in the free countries, and that demand has reached proportions so that at least they have to promise to meet it. So far they haven't done much toward meeting it.

They have been talking about more consumer goods for a long time and they provide a small amount of additional consumer goods, but by and large most of the increased production has gone into other things than consumer goods. They have begun to promise shorter hours of work, more leisure, things of that sort. They haven't done anything about it, but there is a revolution definitely going on and so I do not think that this particular threat is one which we shall have to face indefinitely and I think that the situation within the Soviet Union is tending to become more comparable to ours and as it does become so, a rate of growth will be less rapid in relation to ours than it is at the present time.

Mr. SELDEN. In other words, you believe that from a long range point of view we are gaining ground?

Secretary DULLES. Over the long run I am sure that time is working in our favor in that it is working toward a quite different type of society than what was originally conceived as the dictatorship of the proletariat.

Now, over the short run the advantage is not in our favor and it is going to require of us a very considerable effort, sacrifice and determination to prevent losses during this short term period.

If we can hold those off — which I am confident that we can — then I look forward quite confidently to a situation within the next or second generation, you might say, which will alter the complexion of their effort very much, and where the situation will be more normal, more comparable to ours, and where you have a movement away from the conditions where they operate really under conditions of forced labor and imposed austerity.

Chairman MORGAN. Dr. Judd.

Mr. JUDD. Thank you, Mr. Chairman.

Mr. Secretary, it is always good to have you here again and looking so well. Sometimes we read something disturbing that is supposed to be authentic and it is good to get it straight from you without the distortions in the press.

I saw in Time magazine its story of the garbled report of your press conference remark on German unification by elections to which the gentlewoman from Ohio referred. Even Time, which generally is not too critical of other journalistic organs, had to condemn the distortion by certain papers of your very proper reply on that.

I am very grateful for your overall statement here this morning. I think it is one of the best and soundest you have ever made. It will help much with our own people. I have for years been concerned lest, in our efforts to get the support of peoples around the world, we might not pay enough attention to our own people and one day might wind up without the support of our policies by our own people.

You have made a very powerful appeal here to both our people and the people of allied countries, showing that our policy is sound and that what we need now is firmness in support of these principles, while using imagination and flexibility in the application of them to the details of individual situations.

The Communists apparently believe that if they give us a May deadline to come to their position on Berlin — a position that would amount to our surrender under another name — the American people between now and May will force our Government to yield, step by step. There are always some timid columnists who think just one more surrender — called concession — will bring peace. You are showing — unanswerably, I think — why we must not yield.

It becomes a race between the firmness of Western peoples in defense of their freedom and the urge to gain their freedom on the part of the peoples under the Communists. Will their urge become strong enough before our firmness is whittled away by fatigue and the appeasers?

I have but one question: The Communists say that if we won't yield on West Berlin, they are going to turn East Berlin over to the East German Peoples Republic as they call it.

Have we ever said to them that if they do, we will turn West Berlin over to West Germany and support West Germany?

Secretary DULLES. No, we have not made that suggestion.

Mr. JUDD. The Chinese Communists have an aphorism which says "A truce is the military equivalent of the political tactic of coalition." That is a smart sentence. In politics, if you have enough votes to win, then have an election. But if you don't have enough votes, don't permit an election; try to get a coalition as the way to get into power. They say a truce is the military equivalent of that. If you haven't enough power to win a war, then call for a truce — not as a means of ending the struggle but as a means of winning at the conference table what they cannot win on the battlefield. Our people think a truce is a peace move. To them it is a military move.

I am glad that you are considering the possibility that they might back off a bit on Berlin if we would say, "All right, we will turn over to West Germany our portion of Berlin and support West Germany in defense of it." Then they would really be in trouble.

I have no other questions, Mr. Secretary. You have given us a very comprehensive review of policy — past and present. I only wish there was time for you to do your usual job of providing a thumbnail sketch of what is happening in each of the continents, in order to bring us up to date.

Thank you.

Chairman MORGAN. Mr. Fountain?

Mr. FOUNTAIN. I pass, Mr. Chairman.

Chairman MORGAN. Mr. Fulton?

Mr. FULTON. Mr. Secretary, it is always a pleasure to have you here. We think that you are doing an excellent job.

We in the United States have been successful for a number of years in implementing a bipartisan foreign policy. I believe you will agree with me that we should make every effort to continue to work out such a joint foreign policy in every field that we can during the next 2 years. Is that not correct?

Secretary DULLES. I agree.

Mr. FULTON. Now could I question you on several points?

The first is that, since Mikoyan has been to the United States on his visit, there has been no change as a result of that visit in the United States and the Western foreign policy toward the Eastern bloc?

Secretary DULLES. There has been no change.

Mr. FULTON. There have been no secret commitments, agreements, executive or otherwise, made with Mikoyan when he was here, or any promises or guarantees that if certain actions were taken others would follow by this country?

Secretary DULLES. Nothing whatsoever of that kind.

Mr. FULTON. There has been no change in recent weeks of the policy of the United States toward Germany, and there is no contemplated change that there would be any policy taken by ourselves or our allies without the consent of the German people?

Secretary DULLES. That is right.

Mr. FULTON. And, before any change in our U.S. policy on any major European nation would be initiated by the United States or even negotiated for with the Eastern group of nations or any of them, we would, I am sure, through the proper officials of our own Government, check with each of our allies and obtain their agreement?

Secretary DULLES. Such consultation now takes place on a very regular basis, particularly in what we call the Permanent Council of NATO, which meets almost daily; and, as I pointed out in my opening statement, it is becoming more and more an ardent political consultation and it is very useful in that respect, and it does provide a means of quickly bringing matters to the attention of all the NATO governments and getting their views.

That, of course, is supplemented also by diplomatic exchanges.

Mr. FULTON. There is at present really no basic disagreement then on principle or policy with any of our major Western allies in NATO?

Secretary DULLES. No, none whatsoever.

Mr. FULTON. We have had no change of policy recently in the last few weeks in respect to Nasser and the method of negotiating with him, have we?

Secretary DULLES. No. There has been no change of policy. I think that relations have become somewhat better.

[Security deletion.]

Mr. FULTON. Could you have the Department supply me either personally or for the record any evidence of substantial propaganda activities by Nasser, or Nasser interests, in the United States?

(The following information has been supplied by the Department of State:)

The United Arab Republic's informational program in this country is similar to that of many other countries with which the United States has normal relations. Press and cultural attachés are assigned to the United Arab Republic Embassy in Washington. They maintain contact respectively with the American press and with American educational institutions. The United Arab Republic Embassy occasionally issues publications presenting the United Arab Republic's point of view; and Embassy representatives accept various speaking engagements for the same purpose. The United Arab Republic participates with other Arab States at the United Nations in the activities of the Arab States Delegations Office which disseminates information concerning the positions of the Arab countries on various matters arising at the United Nations. The United Arab Republic also participates with other Arab States in maintaining an Arab Information Center which has branches in New York and Washington and which is registered with the Department of Justice under the terms of the Foreign Agents Registration Act.

Mr. FULTON. May I just finish with this thought: When you have been before our committee several times, I have tried to have an impact on one particular matter and that is the country of Albania.

Albania is a country that is separated from the other parts of Eastern Europe by Yugoslavia and by Greece. Macedonia in each of those two countries is the block. Of course, Bulgaria and Russia would probably like to get through by land to Albania and the Adriatic Sea access. When there is the capability to have a submarine base in Albania at a point just above the straits entering the Adriatic Sea, the Straits of Atranto, why don't we try for the defection of a second Communist-dominated eastern European country where it is so isolated and gives the Communists a tremendous advantage of having two submarine bases? One in Egypt for submarines and the other in the Adriatic Sea through the harbor base at Vlônë in Albania?

I believe that gives them a tremendous advantage to have two ports for a submarine base in this area and causes us militarily a tremendous risk in the Mediterranean and the Adriatic area.

Now, my recommendation is, as I finish, that we take affirmative measures to try to get the Albanian people to overthrow the current Government and either move toward Greece, Yugoslavia, or Italy. Our U.S. policy should not get caught in the middle between those three countries, not wanting anything done because they are afraid any one of the others will get an advantage.

That is all.

Chairman MORGAN. Mr. Fascell.

Mr. FASCELL. Thank you, Mr. Chairman.

Mr. Secretary, as I understand the Soviet and the United States obviously have strong military positions from which they cannot retract in the foreseeable future. Is that a statement in which you can concur?

Secretary DULLES. A strong military position?

Mr. FASCELL. Yes, sir.

Secretary DULLES. We both have powerful military establishments. As you know, we are negotiating on certain phases of what is called disarmament. Meetings are in process in Geneva now seeking an agreement on suspending nuclear testing under proper safeguards. The discussions on the problem of surprise attack were recessed in December. I don't know whether that is what you mean or not.

Mr. FASCELL. Well, in general terms; yes, sir.

We both have strong economic offensives with the other peoples of the world and the Russians, as I understand your statement, are stepping theirs up; is that correct?

Secretary DULLES. Yes.

Mr. FASCELL. Also the Russians have for some years enjoyed considerable success, at least from their viewpoint, in the production of hard goods and capital goods?

Secretary DULLES. That is right.

Mr. FASCELL. Now they are saying they will make an effort to shift over to consumer goods. This overall appraisal gives me a feeling that as far as our relationships are concerned, we are reacting to stimuli. What I am interested in is, What are our offensive plans, either short range or long range, to meet the challenge of Russia and the Communists?

Secretary DULLES. Basically, we hope to encourage an evolution within the Soviet world so that they will no longer be a threat to freedom in the world and where they will be concerned with their own affairs and not be concerned with promoting the goals and ambitions of communism.

Mr. FASCELL. Mr. Secretary, excuse me, but that is a very important statement and I would just like to amplify that for a moment. I would concur in the statement but it seems to me at the present time it is completely unilateral. That is, the Soviets are working on this evolution. Is there anything we in the United States can do with respect to bringing about this evolution?

Secretary DULLES. Yes; there is a great deal we can do. That is one of the main purposes of this cultural and exchange agreement made a year or so ago: to bring Russians over to see what our conditions are, and to see the opportunities the workers have, and so forth, and sending more people into the Soviet Union to talk about these things and explain about them.

[Security deletion.]

Secretary DULLES. The example which we are giving to the world and getting across to them is the thing which is compelling the Russian leaders to say to their people, "Well, now, we hope that we will be able to expect — we promise, indeed, that we will give you in a few years, the same advantages that the American workers get.

And their whole purpose — you read their statements — they say, "We are going to have as good a situation as the United States has. We will have as many hours of leisure for the workers as the United States has."

It is our example that has made sufficient impact in the Soviet Union so the leaders of the Soviet Union say to their people, "We are going to follow the American example."

Whenever Khrushchev talks, what does he talk of? He talks to his people in terms of giving them something as good as what we've got.

Mr. FASCELL. Mr. Secretary, you talk in the frame of reference of an evolution that would have some impact within the next generation in Russia.

Is there anything conceivably that we can do to shorten this period of time?

Secretary DULLES. Well, everything we are doing tends to shorten it. I said within a generation. Of course, if anyone tries to measure these things, it is utterly impossible to be precise.

I don't know how rapidly this evolution is going to occur. It could occur to a point where — a significant situation could come about in 10 years, or in 20 years. The rate of development depends somewhat upon what we do, to the extent we get across the image of America, which catches the imagination of the peoples of Russia so that the leaders have to try to realize for their people what we realize for ours.

Mr. FASCELL. Would you agree that there is merit in the suggestion that we could get this image across on a nongovernmental basis?

Secretary DULLES. Yes. It is being done to a very considerable extent on a nongovernmental basis, although the conditions, for example, are worked out as you have to work with the Soviet Government. No private activities can be carried on without the approval of the Government, so we have to work with the Government to get the conditions.

But from our standpoint, the operation of this thing is largely done by private groups, private business.

Private industry now has the opportunity to send some movie films — I hope they pick the right films. If they pick the wrong ones, they can do us a disservice, but the Government can't exercise censorship in these matters. We have to leave it to private industry that has been over there negotiating on this exchange of films, for example.

The exhibits at this fair we are going to put on this summer in Moscow are almost all going to be provided by private industry, labor, and cultural institutions.

I have always said that, when what you are trying to do is to get across to the world the virtues and benefits of freedom, government is the worst one in the world to do it because government is not freedom. In a sense, government is the contrary thing to freedom.

They can demonstrate what government does. We want to demonstrate what freedom does and the best exponents of freedom are the free individuals, the free people.

Mr. FASCELL. The people themselves.

Secretary DULLES. That is right.

Chairman MORGAN. Mrs. Church ――

Mrs. CHURCH. Thank you, Mr. Chairman.

Mr. Secretary, it is always good to have you come and revivify our own determinations. Though I imagine you are as bored as I am with the Mikoyan visit, I would like to follow up a little bit the question Mr. Fascell asked in relationship to that visit: Did the State Department know what was being planned when Big Business decided it would be well to lay the groundwork for this visit?

Secretary DULLES. No; they did not.

Mrs. CHURCH. Do you think this is setting a pattern ――

Secretary DULLES. Because Mr. Mikoyan did not come here at our invitation. He came here ostensibly to call upon and visit the Soviet Ambassador in Washington. That is what he said in the application for visa.

Mrs. CHURCH. I have been rather interested in the comments that have come from certain of the industrialists in Chicago who were thrown in touch with him, as to why they were in touch and how; and I wondered at what stage of the game the State Department became aware that there was being set up perhaps a pattern for non-governmental activity — almost under-the-table diplomacy. Or am I exaggerating what happened?

Secretary DULLES. Well, I don't think it did really a great deal of harm.

[Security deletion.]

Secretary DULLES. I will say at this juncture that the representatives of labor took a position which is, I think, far sounder in the national interests than some of the representatives of business whom he met.

[Security deletion.]

Secretary DULLES. The labor people really stood up to him and gave him a really strong statement of position.

Of course, Mr. Meany refused to meet with him at all.

Carey and Reuther met with him and I guess gave him a clear view of how labor felt.

The State Department was not consulted at all, and there was nothing, I think, that we could very well interfere with.

Mrs. CHURCH. Do you think any pressure will be brought to bear on you, or has been brought to bear on you, in the name of industry to relax our restrictions?

Secretary DULLES. No. There has been very little pressure, and, in fact, none that I am aware of. I think there has been an effort by elements of the business community to try to overcome this.

I know that Business Week, which is perhaps the leading business publication, had a full-page advertisement in the New York Times a day or two ago, on an editorial they were running designed to overcome the impression that all business had been wooed and won by Mr. Mikoyan.

[Security deletion.]

Mrs. CHURCH. Do you think that there was a deliberate plan on the part of the Soviet to go over your head to reach the American people, as the newspapers sometimes put it?

Secretary DULLES. I think they wanted to try to find out to what extent the country was back of our policies or whether there was division in our country — not necessarily along political lines, but whether the feeling was such that the Government would be unable to maintain a strong line.

Now, I think that, in the end, he came to the conclusion that the general line which we have taken, which is certainly a nonpartisan line, and it is a line, which I say here, really Mr. Truman started with his Greek-Turkey Doctrine of 1947, which has been developing since then — I think he went back probably convinced that the Government had enough support to carry it through and that there was not the division and lack of support which may have been suggested.

I don't know just what his state of mind was.

Chairman MORGAN. Mr. Coffin ——

Mr. COFFIN. Thank you, Mr. Chairman.

Mr. Secretary, is this statement going to be released, your major statement?

Secretary DULLES. Yes.

Mr. COFFIN. I would like to mention one difficulty that I think we confront when we state our policy: Virtually everything in the statement is phrased in terms of "anticommunism," and "the Communist threat."

Even that part of your statement which is devoted to helping other countries carries this theme except for one paragraph at the very beginning.

But from what I have heard and read, we would be making more headway if we explained some of our policies as not only based upon the Communist threat in the existence of the cold war, but also on recognition of the fact that even if there were no cold war we probably still would have a policy of helping the underdeveloped countries because, first of all, we believe in freedom, and, secondly, we believe the final permanent conditions of world peace depend upon trade, and trade depends upon fairly well-developed economies.

Is this a correct statement, really, of our basic position?

Secretary DULLES. Well, I think that you are quite correct that many of the things we are doing we would be doing anyway.

When you make a statement like this, you have to alter its emphasis, or decide upon its tenor in the light of conditions at the moment at which you speak.

Now, I have made statements, explanatory of U.S. policy as to why we are doing all these things that had no relationship at all to communism and explained why we are doing them.

At the moment, I am speaking in the aftermath of Mr. Mikoyan's visit and at a time when the 21st Communist Congress is meeting in Moscow, and I am making this statement, having in mind its impact upon that particular situation.

If I had been making this statement as I have in the past made statements under different conditions and a little different environment, I could have put on a different connotation.

Mr. COFFIN. I think to the extent we can phrase these statements not only in terms of being anti-Communist but also being interested in other people's welfare, it would perhaps be helpful.

There is one specific statement that might be misinterpreted at the bottom of page 2, where you say:

We never had, and do not now have, any substantial differences with the Soviet Union.

Now, I assume this means we don't want any of their territory and they don't want any of ours, but it seems to me it is capable of being lifted out of context, and even the context doesn't make it quite clear.

Secretary DULLES. Yes; I think you are probably right about that.

I think perhaps it isn't sufficiently clear. We don't have any national quarrel at all with the Soviet Union.

Mr. JUDD. The Soviet Union as a country rather than as a Communist conspiracy.

Secretary DULLES. I want to say that the trouble is that the Soviet Union is used by the Communist Party for purposes with which we do not agree.

Mr. COFFIN. I have no quarrel with the thought. I merely point out the possibility that it could be lifted out of context.

(Discussion off the record.)

Chairman MORGAN. Are you through, Mr. Coffin?

Mr. COFFIN. Yes, Mr. Chairman. Thank you.

Chairman MORGAN. Mr. Adair ——

Mr. ADAIR. Thank you, Mr. Chairman.

Mr. Secretary, would you comment, please, upon the status of Mao Tse-tung, now, and any significant changes that you see in that Government, and give us your opinion as to what is going on there now?

Secretary DULLES. I do not think that the change in the status of Mao Tse-tung indicates anything of very great significance. He continues on as the head of the Communist Party, which is the really potent power.

As I point out, it is the Communist Parties in these countries that decide really upon what is done, how it is done and who should do it, and he retains that position which is the real post of power.

He has laid down some of the protocol jobs and things of that sort, but I don't attach at the moment any particular importance to the change in Mao Tse-tung's position.

Mr. ADAIR. You see no significant changes in the policies — that is, the international policies of that Government at this time?

Secretary DULLES. No.

Mr. ADAIR. Thank you, Mr. Chairman.

Chairman MORGAN. Mr. Hays ——

Mr. HAYS. Thank you, Mr. Chairman.

Mr. Secretary, this question needs a little background. I was at a dinner the other night at the German Embassy where one of the guests was your sister, and there were some German Members of Parliament there. One of them brought up a hypothetical question which made some sense to me about what might happen in Berlin.

He said: "Suppose the Russians do turn East Berlin over to the East German Government and suppose a convoy of ours goes rolling up the road and the East Germans stop it and say, 'You can't go any further unless you show your documents.' The man in charge says, 'We don't show our documents to you,' and decides to go on."

He said the thing that bothered him is, do the German Government, the British, the French, and the Americans, have a policy, or would the chance of starting a war be decided by a couple of second lieutenants, an East German and an American.

He wondered if you had a set policy as to just about exactly what we would do in the event they do turn this over to the East Germans and the East Germans say, "You can't have access to Berlin any more."

What do we do then?

Secretary DULLES. I assure you we will have a policy on that. It will not be determined on the spur of the moment by some local official.

That is the type of thing being dealt with in terms of this contingency planning which I referred to in answer to Mrs. Kelly's questions earlier. We have a whole series of possible contingencies and are working out what the answers will be and what the position will be if those contingencies occur.

Mr. HAYS. That is all, Mr. Chairman. Thank you.

Chairman MORGAN. Mr. Curtis ——

Mr. CURTIS. Thank you, Mr. Chairman. No questions.

Chairman MORGAN. Mr. Farbstein ——

Mr. FARBSTEIN. Thank you, Mr. Chairman.

Mr. Secretary, would you suggest that there are no differences whatsoever between the Chinese Government and the Government of Soviet Russia?

Secretary DULLES. I expect that there are differences in the sense that the Chinese probably want to get more economic and military assistance and they don't want to pay as much. I have no doubt there are differences of that kind.

There is also apparently a tendency upon the part of the Chinese Communists to be what you might call a little more orthodox, and to resist the trend which I have indicated is occurring, I think, in

Russia toward a somewhat more liberal regime with more con-
sumers' goods for the people and more leisure, and so forth, for the
people. A difference in emphasis.

I don't think there is any difference which is liable to lead to any
serious division at the present time between the two regimes.

Mr. FARBSTEIN. Is there any likelihood or possibility that we
could do anything to promote any of these differences?

Secretary DULLES. I don't think we could do any more than
what we are doing. As I pointed out earlier, our example is setting
up a trend in the Soviet Union which at the moment is contrary
to the prevalent trend within Communist China.

Communist China is moving in a direction of a more severe police
state role, a more complete communization and regimentation of
the people, under more extreme forced labor conditions, with destruction of family life and the like. It is more so than the trend in
the Soviet Union.

I think there is nothing we could do other than we are doing in
that situation.

Mr. FARBSTEIN. Let's go on to another part of the world, following up a previous question which was asked.

Has our policy changed at all with relation to the various countries in the Near East? How about Iraq, with this fellow Kassim?
What is our policy with these countries in view of what has been
happening?

Secretary DULLES. Our policy is to try to encourage as far as
we can the independence, the genuine independence of these countries while not opposing a cooperation in terms of the Arab League,
and the Arab Financial Development Institution, and the like.

[Security deletion.]

Secretary DULLES. We are standing on the basic proposition
that we want to help to maintain freedom and independence of the
area.

Mr. FARBSTEIN. Just one other question, Mr. Chairman, and
then I will be through.

Would you care to give us your opinion on what position we
might take with relation to the Rapacki plan?

Secretary DULLES. The military people — not only our own,
but those of NATO — have considered the Rapacki plan and have
advised us that in their opinion the plan as it stands is militarily
very disadvantageous to the West.

[Security deletion.]

Secretary DULLES. I would assume however, that if there were any plan for German reunification, it would almost inevitably involve some provisions to assure that the reunited Germany would not seem to be a greater danger to the Soviet Union than to the neighboring countries. You could hardly realistically expect reunification except under such conditions.

Chairman MORGAN. Judge Saund ——

Mr. SAUND. Thank you, Mr. Chairman.

Mr. Secretary, some historians have called the First World War and the Second World War "colonial wars," insofar as the major European powers were concerned.

Germany, Austria and Hungary started the First World War because they wanted to acquire possession of colonies, so they could expand.

The Second World War was started by Japan and Germany because they wanted more territory in which to expand and find markets.

It also has been said that the real cause of those wars was the fact that there were certain countries and areas in the world which could be occupied and exploited by foreign powers.

Now, I am beginning to believe that today this cold war between the free world and international communism is an effort on the part of both parties to win the hearts and minds of the millions of people in the underdeveloped areas of the world: Asia, the Middle East, and Africa.

Now, do you care to comment on my thinking?

Secretary DULLES. I think whatever the facts may have been in 1914 and 1939 ——

Mr. SAUND. I am more concerned about the present.

Secretary DULLES. It is demonstrable that the so-called colonial powers have abandoned or are in the process of abandoning a colonial policy and there never in history has been anything comparable to the rapid grant, freely, of independence to nations such as occurred from the West during this past few years, since 1943, when you have 21 nations who have gained their independence, over 700 million people, and where you have got in Africa, 8 or 10 more nations that are on the threshold of independence.

I don't compare that at all with the attitude of the Soviet Union, which is to deny and deprive these countries and peoples of political independence.

The theory of the Communists that has been long expounded by

Lenin and by Stalin is to take advantage of the presumed ill will of what they call the colonial and dependent peoples toward the West, to break the ties there, to create then dependence upon the Soviet Union, and to use that as the opportunity to amalgamate these peoples into the Sino-Soviet bloc. That has been fully expounded by Soviet doctrine for a long time.

Now, I think that you try to maintain the genuine independence of these people, which is quite a different thing and not to be put in the same category as the efforts of international communism, which is to deny them independence.

Mr. SAUND. What I meant to imply was this, Mr. Secretary: The colonial peoples are free now and they are groping to find a way of life where they can acquire a better life and increase their standard of living and acquire things which they would like to have.

There are two philosophies: International communism and democracy. There is a question in the minds of those people, perhaps, as to which will accomplish their objectives better and faster, and the two ideologies are struggling now to win the hearts and minds of those people.

Now, I would like to ask this question: I made a trip through the countries of the Far East, India, Pakistan, and two countries of the Middle East.

Has there been any change in emphasis on the part of the Department of State to direct its efforts to help those people; that is, to put more emphasis on a better public relations job, so far as the objectives of the democratic way of life are concerned, and also to improve the economic conditions of those people, as against the military alliances and pacts that we have in that part of the world?

Secretary DULLES. Yes, I think there is growing emphasis and growing recognition of the importance of that.

Mr. SAUND. That is all, Mr. Chairman.

Chairman MORGAN. Mr. Diggs ——

Mr. DIGGS. Thank you, Mr. Chairman.

Mr. Secretary, I have two questions: Last year there was a report from a committee composed of Mr. Brooks Hays and Mr. Coffin, which indicated a serious deterioration in our relations with Canada.

We in the Detroit area were quite concerned about that and we wondered whether you classify it as surface friction or something more fundamental, and whether or not there has been an improvement in this situation since that report was submitted?

Secretary DULLES. I think there has been improvement. There

has been a very strong effort made at improvement. We have an increasing number of joint committees at the Cabinet level which are working on matters of common concern, to try and iron out the differences that exist, and I have observed myself, I think, a very considerable improvement in conditions over the past year. I would say within a year, yes, a very considerable improvement in conditions.

We have now a Cabinet committee which met in Paris last December, of the Secretary of Defense and Treasury, which deal with common military matters together, and then we have this Cabinet committee which deals with economic problems.

Then there is the effort to establish contact at the congressional level.

I think the irritating points of difference relate primarily to things like lead and zinc, oil, handling of agricultural surpluses, and the like.

I think that there is a growing tendency on the part of the Canadians to play those down rather than to play them up, and the growing ability on the part of both of us by working together to minimize those problems.

Mr. DIGGS. My second question, Mr. Secretary: What offensive plan does the State Department have to firm up our relations between now and 1960 with these emerging African States, especially in consideration of the accelerated Communist activity in those areas?

Secretary DULLES. We now have, as I point out, here, a new Assistant Secretary of State for African Affairs, who concerns himself with those problems particularly and we are training and equipping officers and people to go there.

I think you will find if you talk to our Assistant Secretary of State for African Affairs, that we have a very comprehensive program for dealing with that situation. I don't say it is adequate.

The activities of the Communists in Africa are very intense and pretty effective. They spend a good deal of money there, the propaganda is very effective, and I don't feel satisfied with the result of what we are doing.

We don't get as much money as we would like for these purposes, and one of our troubles is that our funds for this purpose are very largely cut down, very largely cut down, more cut down in the House than they are in the Senate.

If you can do anything about that, we would appreciate it.

Mr. DIGGS. No other questions, Mr. Chairman. Thank you.

Chairman MORGAN. Mr. Beckworth.

Mr. BECKWORTH. Thank you, Mr. Chairman.

Mr. Secretary, I am sure the veteran members of this committee would know the answer immediately to what I shall ask, but what would be the immediate and far-reaching effect if Russia actually got what she wants in Berlin?

You said it would be a great victory for them. I would like you to detail it just a little more.

Secretary DULLES. It would wipe out the most effective exhibit of freedom that there is.

Now we talked earlier about getting across to the Communist world the advantageous of a system of freedom. Berlin, here, is a spot within the Soviet Communist world that everybody sees, and it is one of the most — I don't know whether you have been there recently or not — it is one of the most exciting, dramatic exhibits of freedom that I think can be imagined.

The impact of that is terrific. That is the reason they want to liquidate it. They just can't stand the comparison. If they can liquidate that, they will have destroyed the most effective outpost of freedom that we have, and the most effective exhibit of what freedom can do and can accomplish.

Furthermore, the impact on all of Western Germany, and indeed Western Europe, would be very bad, but the immediate impact would be the snuffing out of the dramatic outpost of freedom.

Chairman MORGAN. Mr. McDowell.

Mr. MCDOWELL. Thank you, Mr. Chairman.

Mr. Secretary, do you believe that the consistent policy of the present Russian Government to insist upon summit conferences is a part of their continuing policy to weaken the prestige of the United Nations and to achieve the end result that the United Nations cannot play a part in negotiations for stable peace in the world?

Secretary DULLES. I think that is a secondary purpose but not a primary purpose.

Let me say first that there has been no recent insistence upon a summit meeting. I am told that while there was an allusion to it in the Khrushchev speech yesterday, there was no plea for a summit meeting.

While Mr. Mikoyan was here, he did not once suggest that. I thought he might suggest that at the White House, talking to the

President. He did not bring up the question of a summit meeting at all.

Ever since they broke off last June, the negotiations and discussions we were having about a summit meeting — because they saw they could not control the agenda and force us to be silent on certain matters — they seemed to have lost interest very largely in a summit meeting.

It is also quite true, of course, that they don't like the United Nations. They have a veto in the Security Council and are trying to get it desperately in the General Assembly through invoking what they call the parity principle.

That means that they will not work on any committee of the General Assembly unless they have enough votes so that they can control or veto any actions taken.

They took that position on the Disarmament Commission that was established, and they are taking it now with respect to the proposed Space Committee, and things of that sort.

So they tend to play down the United Nations and will continue to do so unless and until they get into a position where they think they can run it. Then they will play it up.

Chairman MORGAN. Mr. Murphy —

Mr. MURPHY. Thank you, Mr. Chairman.

Mr. Secretary, may I ask you this: You stated that the Government of Russia has promised the Russian people more consumer goods and more leisure time.

Have they promised them any relief from taxation?

Secretary DULLES. I am not aware of that. Of course, under a monolithic structure such as they have there, the taxation system is not comparable at all to what we have in this country, and the Government gets its revenues from selling goods to the people at a certain price.

It is more, you might say, the equivalent of a sales tax, rather than as a taxation on income, and things of that sort.

[Security deletion.]

Chairman MORGAN. Mr. Meyer ——

Mr. MEYER. Thank you, Mr. Chairman.

Mr. Secretary, I would like to comment a little on one thing that you mentioned and then ask a question.

You spoke about our bipartisan foreign policy, and, of course, I myself, and also I believe almost every person in Congress, do not think in terms of being Democratic or Republican, and I hope that most of the people of the country, and in the organizations in the country will feel the same way.

However, I do think that if are going to speak in those terms, we should also wonder about the policies of the administration and the policies of the Department of State, and if they are bipartisan in the same way in reflecting the wishes of the American people.

I, for one, do not believe they are, and I wonder if you would perhaps answer my question in that respect and say if you believe that the policies will change to more positive lines and to what I consider are the wishes of a large number of the American people.

Secretary DULLES. Well, I believe that our policies do conform to the wishes of the overwhelming number of American people, irrespective of party, so that in that respect I don't feel any occasion for change.

Mr. MEYER. I just happen to disagree with you, and in that respect I will have to follow my own conscience.

Mr. HAYS. Would the gentleman yield?

Mr. MEYER. Yes.

Mr. HAYS. Mr. Chairman, I am interested in the gentleman's questions, because I share his views to some extent.

How much consultation do you ever get from the people in the majority in Congress about the formulation of policy?

You generally bring your proposed legislation up here and lay it down, and we are supposed to go along and be bipartisan about it.

Isn't that about the way it operates?

Secretary DULLES. No; I do not think that is the way it operates. We pay a great deal of attention to what is said in Congress, both at meetings like this and in debate. We read the Congressional Record. We have meetings on a bipartisan basis at the White House with the congressional leaders. I meet often with individual Members of Congress and small groups. We keep in close touch with this committee and with the Foreign Relations Committee. We read the newspapers and the editorials, and I think we have a pretty good idea as to the thinking of the country.

I do think this: I think the job of a government is a little bit more than just trying to find out what the people want and then trying to do it. I believe the Government has a responsibility to give a certain leadership and to point the way.

I think that we are exercising that constitutional responsibility, and I believe that we are doing it in a way which commends itself to the great bulk of the American people.

Mr. HAYS. I would agree with you that the Government has a responsibility to lead, and that is not what I was getting at, but the majority party in the Congress are a part of the Government.

You might be interested to know that one of the leaders on the Democratic side told me he had never been asked anything at any of these conferences at the White House, he had only been told.

And I might say as chairman of the Subcommittee on State Department Personnel, that up until today — I understand Mr. Herter will be up tomorrow — that nobody has ever discussed from your Department a bill with me that is coming in front of my subcommittee, dealing with State Department legislation.

You usually send a bill up here, you get some minority member or some member of my party who might be in sympathy with it to introduce it, and the first thing I know about it, the bill comes before the committee.

Now, I don't care, I operate under the circumstances, however I feel, but it seems to me if you are really interested in bipartisanship you might consult with the chairman of the subcommittee who is going to handle this legislation as to whether or not he is in favor of it, whether or not he would introduce it. That never happens.

Secretary DULLES. I am not familiar with this particular matter. I gather — Mr. Herter will be up here to discuss it?

Mr. HAYS. Tomorrow, yes, and that is the first time — it is a good indication.

Mrs. BOLTON. Will the gentlemen yield?

Chairman MORGAN. Will you yield to Mrs. Bolton, Mr. Meyer?

Mr. MEYER. Surely.

Mrs. BOLTON. I won't be but a minute, but my mind goes back to the day when we had another Secretary of State up here. We had been asking a lot of questions about the point of view of the Executive, and the atmosphere became pretty tense. Finally the Secretary sat very straight and very stiff and used the voice of an old-fashioned sergeant as he told us that we had nothing whatever to do with the foreign policy of the United States, that was the responsibility of the President, and if we got any information from him it was solely because of his courtesy.

Now, that of course has been greatly changed.

Mr. HAYS. Will the gentleman yield further?

Mr. MEYER. Yes.

Mr. HAYS. I might just say if any Secretary of State said that to me, I know how I would operate, because the Congress has the power of the purse, and I don't think they can get away with that.

Chairman MORGAN. The time of the gentleman from Vermont has expired.

Mr. Gallagher.

Mr. GALLAGHER. Thank you, Mr. Chairman.

Mr. Secretary, we seem to gather from Mr. Mikoyan's visit here that the thing which sustains him is his faith in his system.

We seem to place a great deal of reliance on the economic evolution that is going on in Russia today. If it is successful, would not their faith be even greater, and would they not even be a greater problem to us in the future?

Secretary DULLES. It all depends on what they do with their power. There is no way in the world that I know of — unless one wants to engage in what is sometimes called a preventive war, which I am sure none of you want to do, and we do not want to do nor intend to do — there is no way in the world you can prevent, in my opinion the Soviet Union becoming a nation of increasing economic and military power.

The problem is, what are they going to do with that power? If that power is designed primarily to defend the Soviet Union, promote the welfare of the peoples of Russia, we don't have any quarrel with them.

If that power is going to be used to promote the worldwide ambitions of worldwide communism and try to dominate the whole world and make the world conform to a Communist-dictated scheme of things, then it is very dangerous indeed.

I hope and believe that matters are moving in a direction so, as I say, if we can keep the peace, if we can hold the situation for the next few years, there will be an evolution toward using this power in ways that are more compatible with the interests of the United States and with the constitutional objective of preserving ourselves and our posterity under liberty.

However, there is no way we can stop the Soviet Union from developing. It started along that way, it has a big impetus and I don't think we can stop it.

Mr. GALLAGHER. I certainly agree that we must hope that it will be for peaceful means. However, I think we must believe that often their goal is as laid down in the principles of Marxism. If that is so, sometimes we are criticized perhaps for reacting rather than acting.

I note in your statement here today that our policy is responsive to the needs of new conditions. The new conditions are generally created by Russia. I wonder what, if anything, we are doing to create new conditions that would make them responsive to us.

Secretary DULLES. Well, I wouldn't say the new conditions are created by Russia. Russia didn't create atomic energy, we did.

The various things that I described here of what we are doing, Russia didn't create. Russia didn't create this new condition of a growing political freedom throughout the world. The nations of the West did that. The Western nations have done almost everything that is creating a change.

The Soviet Union represents the most reactionary regime there is in the world. It wants to grab more, yes, but there is nothing very constructive about that.

Mr. GALLAGHER. That is not what I am talking about, not that the ultimate goals of freedom are not laid down by us, but they seem to be able to create new crises.

Secretary DULLES. They can create crises; yes. We could create a crisis, too, if we wanted to accentuate the crisis atmosphere. [Security deletion.]

Secretary DULLES. It is our policy to seek a peaceful evolution, rather than violent revolution. I suppose some people — I know there are some people who feel that that is an unsound policy, that we should be more violent in our initiatives and we should seek results through revolutionary processes, rather than evolutionary processes.

We might be commended, perhaps, for more initiative if we were more revolutionary, as the Russians are. But we believe that that path, if you get two regimes as powerful as the Soviet Union and ourselves, each trying to win its way through violent revolutionary processes, then I think a world war is almost inevitable.

I believe that the peaceful processes of evolution are better to rely upon, and while they may be less spectacular they will in the end, I think, be more apt to produce a desired result.

Mr. FARBSTEIN. Will the gentleman yield?

Mr. GALLAGHER. Yes.

Mr. FARBSTEIN. There is only one point in that connection, Mr. Secretary. We depend upon the exchanges of students, et

cetera, to make things difficult for the Soviet Union, making necessary the promise by Khrushchev in this morning's speech or yesterday's speech of what is going to be done for the people.

But it was the initiative of the Russians in starting that — in inviting the young peoples of the world to Russia that caused this
ferment. If they hadn't done that, perhaps you wouldn't have as
much ferment as you have now, and you wouldn't have the boom-
eranging of the youth convention. The Soviets thought the invitation
was for the benefit of Russia. They thought when they invited them,
these young people would naturally lean toward communism, and
hence they would realize the tremendous benefits to be afforded by
Russia.

To a certain degree, it seems to me that the initiative is taken by
the Soviets. They do the inviting. Everything comes forward from
them. Fortunately, here, it boomeranged, as I said before.

Why can't we do something of that nature? I can't think of, at
the moment, what there is we should be doing, but apropos of what
the gentleman just said, that seems to strike me right between the
eyes.

Secretary DULLES. Well, we just talked a little bit about West
Berlin. West Berlin is the most dramatic exhibit of freedom, right in
the Soviet world. That didn't happen by accident. What has been
done in West Berlin is a result of planning, thinking, effort, money
— we have been putting money into it every year.

That is nothing the Russians did. West Berlin — we did it.

Mr. CURTIS. Is not another example of new conditions created
through our initiative and not through Russian initiative to be seen
in our program of technical and economic assistance, which was
copied by the Russians after we had made a good start on it?

Secretary DULLES. This whole business of economic assistance,
technical aid, and so forth is the Soviet imitation of what we have
been doing. It goes back to what President Truman called the
point 4 program.

Mr. CURTIS. One other point, Mr. Chairman, referring to what
the gentleman from Vermont said, Mr. Meyer, about bipartisanship, the most controversial program in our foreign policy that I
have confronted is foreign aid, or mutual security. Isn't it a fact, sir,
that by and large our policies there are a continuation of the Democratic policies which were initiated and got going previously?

Secretary DULLES. Yes, and they got started under bipartisan
auspices at that time, too.

I think the policies, roughly speaking, since 1947 or thereabouts, have been bipartisan. They have had strong support. I know as far as I am personally concerned, when there was a Democratic administration in Congress I worked almost continuously from 1945 to 1953 in support of the policies of the Democratic administration, and I helped make them indeed, and so did Senator Vandenberg and others.

I think they are a bipartisan product.

Mr. CURTIS. And those policies have been continued under your administration.

Secretary DULLES. Continued and I think developed.

Chairman MORGAN. Mr. Bowles.

Mr. BOWLES. Mr. Chairman and Mr. Secretary, I would like to say I am keenly aware of the complexities of your job, and I have often marvelled at your fortitude and the patience you have shown in a very difficult situation.

I don't think that any one of us, regardless of party, questions the urgent need to take extremely firm military positions in various parts of the world, particularly where we are under fire, notably Quemoy, Berlin, and other situations.

What disturbs some of us is the feeling that firmness has become an objective in itself and not a means to an end. By simply being firm we seem to feel we can solve problems which are vast and complex.

Some questions today have hinted at this concern. Some more bluntly than others.

Certainly in Berlin we must stand firm. To be pushed out of Berlin would be disastrous. I believe we should use whatever force is required to maintain our position there.

But our stated military position in that Germany should be armed — presumably eventually with nuclear weapons — as a major military force in the heart of Europe.

At the same time, we take the position in our "liberation" promises that we would like to see the Soviet Army withdrawn from Europe back to its own borders. Indeed the only reason our troops are in Europe at all is because the Soviet is in the center of Europe. It seems to me that these two objectives clash head on.

If I were a Soviet dictator, I would not withdraw Soviet troops from East Germany, Poland, Hungary, and Czechoslovakia in the face of a well-armed, nuclear-equipped Germany, in the middle of Europe.

I do not say here that we should not arm Germany. That is a big subject. But doesn't this objective contradict the promises we have offered of a free Poland, a free Hungary, and eventually a free Eastern Europe?

Secretary DULLES. I don't think there is anybody who suggests there should be a reunified Germany, highly armed, and then the Soviet Union just withdraw.

I have said repeatedly that I don't think that is a realistic thing to do. Actually the proposal that we made in 1955 at the foreign ministers' meeting which followed the summit meeting went very far to make clear that if there was a reunification of Germany we would expect that to take place under conditions which would not carry any increased military threat from Germany to the Soviet Union.

[Security deletion.]

Secretary DULLES. The essential thing is that Germany should be reunified. I think there is a great danger to the peace and to the world if Germany is sought to be continuously divided. On the other hand, I think the reunification of Germany should take place under conditions which will result in increased security for all of Europe and the world.

There is a very large degree of flexibility in our thinking as to how that should be accomplished and we have made that very clear.

Mr. BOWLES. A similar question applies to Quemoy. It would have been unwise to be forced out under fire last summer. But many of us seriously questioned for a long time the wisdom of our being there in the first place.

What are you doing and what can you do, now that the situation is a little quieter, to liquidate what many of us feel is an unrealistic and dangerous situation out of which a major war can start that would gain us nothing which might well bring in the Soviet Union, and which we would fight with no allies or friends outside of Chiang Kai-shek and Syngman Rhee?

Secretary DULLES. There is no way that I am aware of, Mr. Bowles, for the liquidating of the position at Quemoy and Matsu without at the same time liquidating the entire free world position in the Far East, and that would be a pretty expensive price to pay.

[Security deletion.]

Secretary DULLES. Now, whenever the Chinese Communists say we should be expelled from the Western Pacific, it is perfectly easy to see the chain of events which they have in mind.

The first thing would be that we would threaten Chiang Kai-shek to cut off all military and economic assistance to him unless he gets out of Quemoy and Matsu. If we do that, we alienate and antagonize the authorities on Formosa that instead of being friends and allies as they now are, they become violently anti-American, and Formosa becomes an advance post of Communist China against us.

When that happens, there is immediately a grave threat to the position in the Philippines. The Philippines feel that if that happens their position, together with and coupled with the large Chinese population that exists in the Philippines, would be gravely endangered if Formosa falls.

[Security deletion.]

Secretary DULLES. Now, it is perfectly easy to sit and look at a map and say, "It would be a lot better if there wasn't any Quemoy and Matsu," but when you get down to the practical question of evicting our friends from it under conditions which will not set in motion a whole chain of disastrous circumstances, that I have not found a way to do.

Mr. BOWLES. I don't think anybody suggests we should evict Chiang Kai-shek. But I do think it is fair to suggest that he should not be allowed to set our policy for east Asia.

None of us would disagree with you for a moment about the effect of Formosa's fall on the Philippines and our position in east Asia. We can never let Formosa fall into Communist hands.

Yet the administration itself has said it doesn't like our position on Quemoy. I refer to Mr. Herter's statement and others.

Chiang, however, says we can't liquidate this admittedly impossible situation. This seems to me dangerous and weak.

Secretary DULLES. [Security deletion.] From a military standpoint the position in Berlin is even more dangerous and more hazardous than the situation in Quemoy and Matsu. You have a practical situation where, if you try to give them up, and if we tried to force, for instance, the abandonment of West Berlin to domination by East Berlin, it would set up a series of disasters which would probably certainly wreck NATO and the whole Western position in Europe.

It is a comparable position out there. Obviously Quemoy and Matsu are not readily defensible areas. But they are part of what has been held by the Nationalist Chinese from the beginning, and I do not see how we can insist that the reunification of China should be accomplished by turning over to the Chinese Communists ter-

ritory which has always been held, is held, by the Chinese Na-
tionalists who are our friends.

Now, they did get out of the Tachens; they realized that was a
wise and expedient thing to do. If they felt the same way toward
Quemoy and Matsu that would be fine, but they don't feel that way
and there is no way in the world that I know of to get them to feel
that way.

I did go out, as you probably recall, to Taiwan last October and
we discussed the situation and the Generalissimo and his government made a very statesmanlike far-reaching declaration whereby
in effect as far as they were concerned they would not rely upon
force as a means of reuniting China and gaining freedom for the
mainland, but will rely upon the force of principle and example,
upon Sun Yat-sen's principles and the like. We took that to the
Chinese Communists and said, "Are you willing to make an applicable counterdeclaration? If so, we believe the situation in that
part of the world can be stabilized."

They rejected that with contempt. They say, "No, we are going
to reunify China, do it by force and include Taiwan in it."

They won't even talk about settling on the basis of Quemoy and
Matsu. Any such suggestion they reject with contempt. They say,
"We are not really interested in Quemoy and Matsu; we must have
Formosa."

Mr. BOWLES. I would like to say I think the two situations are
alike in that we should not be forced out of either one at the point
of a gun. Moreover our position in regard to Berlin is solid in every
respect and we should maintain it, at least until the whole German
situation can be settled.

But I question strongly whether Quemoy in other ways is similar
to Berlin. That is a big subject and I would be going beyond my
time if I pursued it.

Chairman MORGAN. The Chair wants to state that this is an
executive session.

Last week, there was some criticism in the press of the secrecy of
the hearings over on the other side of the Capitol. We have made
arrangements that after the Secretary edits his testimony to eliminate anything involving the national security, we will release it to
the press.

We have assurance here from the Assistant Secretary for Congressional Relations that that deletion will be made promptly. We ask
the members of the committee to remember this is an executive ses-

sion, and that until this record has been processed, nothing should be made public.

Mr. FOUNTAIN. Mr. Chairman, before he leaves, may I ask the Secretary just one question on a lighter subject.

Mr. Secretary, can you enlighten us beyond what we have been reading in the newspapers about the present situation in Cuba and tell us if there have been any official contacts between our Government and the new regime in Cuba?

Secretary DULLES. We hope to have good relations with the new government. As you know, we are designating a new ambassador to go there. Not but what Ambassador Smith had done an excellent job, but in a revolution as violent as this, it is useful to make a fresh start from the standpoint of diplomatic relations.

We have done that in a number of comparable cases in the world; notably the case of Iraq. The Cuban Government is still in the same process of formation. You have various people who are holding offices. The President, the Foreign Minister, the Prime Minister, and so forth. But much of the actual power is still being exerted by Castro.

I don't think the thing is shaken down yet, but we hope very much that it will be a government which will be responsive to the aspirations of the Cuban people for a government to give more freedom and stability than was the case heretofore.

I think it is difficult to prophesy on the future because, as I say, it is untested.

[Security deletion.]

Mr. FOUNTAIN. Did I or did I not read in the newspaper a statement by you to the effect that we had already been requested to withdraw military forces from Cuba?

Secretary DULLES. Yes.

Mr. FOUNTAIN. We have been requested?

Secretary DULLES. Our mission. I don't know that it went quite as far as that. We got information that they thought they could get along without it, so we decided to withdraw it.

Mr. FOUNTAIN. Thank you.

Chairman MORGAN. This afternoon we have the Secretary of Defense, Mr. McElroy, and General Twining.

If there are no further questions, the committee stands adjourned until 2:30.

(Whereupon, at 12:45 p.m., the committee adjourned.)

BUILDING A WORLD OF FREE PEOPLES

HEARINGS *before the Subcommittee on International Organizations and Movements of the Committee on Foreign Affairs, House of Representatives, 85th Congress, First Session*

TUESDAY, APRIL 9, 1957

Washington, D.C.

THE SUBCOMMITTEE on International Organizations and Movements met, pursuant to call, at 10:35 a. m., in room G–3, the Capitol, Hon. A. S. J. Carnahan (chairman of the subcommittee) presiding.

Mr. CARNAHAN. The committee will come to order.

This morning we have the Honorable Chester Bowles with us, who has recently returned from visiting several countries. We are delighted to have you, Mr. Bowles. We will be glad to hear anything that you have to say to us, and are especially interested in your visit to Afghanistan.

Statement of Hon. Chester Bowles, Former Ambassador to India

Mr. BOWLES. My visit to Afghanistan was really very brief. I was only there a few days. But I went to India; spent 4 weeks there and saw a good deal of their economic growth and development and progress. Then I went on up through Pakistan. Then through Afghanistan, going through the Khyber Pass to Kabul. Then I flew, after an 11-week delay in getting my visas, to the Soviet Union. I flew over the Hindu Kush Mountains into Tashkent, the capital of Uzbekistan. I spent 8 days there; then went on up to Moscow,

Leningrad, back through Poland, where I spent a week, and Yugo-slavia, where I spent another week.

I had an opportunity to talk during the trip to the heads of all of the states with the exception of Poland, where their Parliament was just meeting, where I also think there is a certain reluctance on the part of the Prime Minister and the head of the Communist Party to talk to foreigners at this stage.

However, I talked to various Cabinet ministers. I saw Mr. Nehru in India; Mr. Suhrawady and President Mirza in Pakistan; Prime Minister Da'ud and Foreign Minister Ma'im in Afghanistan; Khrushchev and Gromyko in Moscow; Tito and some of his associates in Yugoslavia.

I was impressed with the strengths of the Soviet Union. I was also very impressed with some of the weaknesses. There is no doubt they have made tremendous progress industrially. There is no doubt that they have built up a very powerful military organization. They have an able military technology. Their educational system has ex-panded, as you know, to an extraordinary degree.

They have some 1,700,000 young people in universities, and they also have these technical schools which are very competent in turn-ing out engineers and other technicians.

They have also developed their resources to an extraordinary de-gree. Their oil, of course, used to come largely from Baku. Now Baku is a relatively minor operation compared with some of the other oilfields which have been opened up.

Mr. CARNAHAN. Regarding education, are they developing an educational system for the masses of people or just for a selected group?

Mr. BOWLES. No, it is for the masses. It is a 10-year ed-ucational system in what we would call elementary and sec-ondary schools. They start at 7 years of age. They run through to 17.

Those students with high marks and good records then go on to the university, where they have 5 years of intensive educational work. They have 5 years of science, engineering, and mathematics before they get into college. They take calculus in their 16th year. They have 5 years of language. About half of them seem to be taking English.

I visited three universities, the University of Samarkand, the Uni-versity of Tashkent and the University of Moscow.

I was also very impressed, however, with the failures of the

Soviet Union in the last few years. I think we are less conscious of those. But I feel they are very important.

First of all, there is the failure of the Communist ideology on a world scale. They are certainly in trouble with the Communist Parties throughout the world. They have tried to tie the destinies of all these Communist Parties so tightly to the nationalistic interests of the Soviet Union that it is a rather rugged life being a Communist outside of Russia as well as within. And many of these Communist Parties are weaker today, I think, by far than they were a year ago.

They also have failed to a much greater degree than I had anticipated in Eastern Europe. I had read the newspaper reports and talked to people who had been there. But, frankly, I had not taken in the extent to which they have fallen down in that part of the world.

They have had 13 years to try to tie those nations to the Soviet Union, and they certainly have failed in that. The people of Poland, for instance, are very vigorously anti-Soviet, and about 90 percent seem to be anti-Communist.

The same thing was true in Yugoslavia, which has a different kind of government, of course. But even there the people were very vigorously anti-Soviet. They have also failed to control their young people or to develop the socialist progress for the future that they have talked about.

There has always been the hope in Communist minds that they could build up an indoctrinated young generation that would pretty much do as the state wanted them to do.

Mr. CARNAHAN. Back to the idea of communism outside the Soviet Union. Am I interpreting you correctly to say that perhaps the Communists outside the Soviet Union are beginning to feel that the international Communist concept only prevails to the extent that it advances the nationalist interests of the Soviet Union?

Mr. BOWLES. Absolutely. And they have become weary of it. Events in Hungary, Poland, Yugoslavia have taught Communists throughout the world that their interest and those of the Soviet Union are not always the same.

The Soviet will always impose its version of what needs to be done.

They have failed, I think, to a large degree to certainly indoctrinate their young people. These young people are asking hard questions.

Mr. CARNAHAN. That is, their own young people?

Mr. BOWLES. Yes. They have assumed, I suppose, that you could teach a man engineering, mathematics, teach him how to think, teach him how to use his mind on certain given problems, and then deny him the right to use his mind on areas which the state feels is not his area. Well, this doesn't work. If a man has a good mind, he uses it wherever he can.

Mr. LECOMPTE. You mean, the young men right in Russia or in the satellites?

Mr. BOWLES. Right in Russia. There is tremendous questioning going on. I don't mean they are going to turn against the state. It is too well organized and too well policed. But they are beginning to ask questions and hard ones.

They are also beginning to want to read better literature. There are great displays of French modern art in Leningrad which they had not allowed a while ago.

They used to say Picasso was a good Communist and a bad artist and none of his works were allowed to be shown in the Soviet Union. Now there is a great display and it is crowded with people.

There is also vigorous searching into new forms of administration. They are trying to decentralize some of their operation. It has been too much centralized, and I think they have felt the stagnation of their centralization. I don't think anyone can tell where this questioning is going to lead. But it certainly is there.

Another failure is that they have failed to make their people hate us. It was difficult to talk to students at this time of year. They are all taking their examinations. Yet one day I went to the library at Samarkand, which is near the Chinese border. There were about 150 students there. When they heard my wife and I were Americans, they crowded around us asking all kinds of questions. I talked with them for an hour or more.

I have three children in college. The Russians wanted to know what they studied, what they are going to do when they get out of college, what they were like, what they wanted, and so forth. The whole tone is one of friendliness and ferment. But I don't think it is ferment that is going to break loose in upheaval.

It would be a mistake to assume that is possible in Russia. Nevertheless I do feel this questioning is likely to open up difficulties for the Kremlin over the years.

They can't very well turn it off, because if they turn it off their industrial growth will stagnate. If they let it go, it may become more difficult for them in the future years.

I was impressed with the extent to which the Russian people are still forced to live in poverty. I knew Russia was a poor country per capita, and all that, but I had no idea of the extent of the poverty or the drabness with which the average family lives. Many of the houses 30, 40, 50 miles out from Moscow are log cabins. I don't mean they leak or were cold particularly, but they are crude.

In Uzbekistan many of them are made of mud as in the Punjab in India. Many of them have radios, but nevertheless they are quite crude.

I don't think an Indian or a Pakistani going into that area would be impressed. He would see less in the way of consumer goods than he would see back in his own country, also less building. That may not be a fair comment because I did go into parts of the Soviet Union where most of the building is going on, the war-torn parts.

Mr. CARNAHAN. You say most of them have radios?

Mr. BOWLES. Most of them do, and I saw 1 or 2 television sets. They had a screen about 4 or 5 inches wide and a big magnifying glass in front of it. If you get in front of it, it blows the image up to look much bigger.

They are paying their people more, but it costs so much to live. The living standards are low. Their farmers, as far as I can figure, are getting somewhere around $700 or $800 per worker. Sometimes there will be three people working in a family. That is at their proper rate of exchange and not the rate at which the visitors pay.

But a normal suit of clothes would cost the equivalent of $300 or $400. It would take a Russian 2 or 3 months' pay to get a suit of clothes.

They are warmly dressed. But there is little to lighten life, to make it easier. The amount of consumer goods is less than in Belgrade or in Warsaw ——

Mr. CARNAHAN. How about food?

Mr. BOWLES. It is plentiful, but it is plain. I think we have made some mistakes in interpreting the agricultural situation in the Soviet Union. Many people in analyzing it point out there are fewer cows and fewer pigs than there were in 1928.

A lot of that is because they had deliberately shifted over to a grain diet. Since all Congressmen have to become farm experts in one way or another, you know that it takes 400 calories of grain at least to make 100 calories of meat. So back in 1928 they shifted from a meat-eating country over to grain. The quality of their food went down as the number of animals went down.

They are now trying to give their people better food, that is, more meat, eggs, butter, and milk. Yet they may be making some grievous errors in opening up some of the colder areas of Siberia for agriculture. Here they will be at the mercy of the weather and will be lucky if they get a good crop 1 year in 3.

What I am suggesting here is the need for a balanced view. We hear a great deal about the power and strength of the Soviet Union. We hear too little of some of the difficulties they face and will face in the future.

The important point politically is that they have failed in Eastern Europe to a greater degree than I think even most of us realize. They now have to put a lot more money into that area if they are going to hold it at all. They have been taking money out; they now have to put money in.

At the same time I would suggest that while they have been focusing a good deal of time and effort on Asia and Africa, we can now expect this effort sharply to increase.

If you study Russian history, as many of you have, you know that there has been a traditional flow back and forth of pressure of both Soviet and Czarist Russia first to the West and then to the East. When they have been blocked in Asia, they have turned back to Europe and vice versa. This has been going on 100 years or so.

I would assume now that they would redouble their efforts in Asia and Africa.

Mr. CARNAHAN. Their efforts in what respect?

Mr. BOWLES. Economic assistance, political effort. I doubt in a military way. I don't think they are going to take big risks in that field as long as we remain strong. But they are going, I think, to turn to Asia with loan programs and technical assistance programs on a fairly major scale. They have many advantages. The amounts of money that are required are relatively small. And because they are loan programs, they get at least something back out of it.

If they devoted 1 percent of their gross national product a year for economic growth and development in Asia and Africa, it would give them a budget of about 4 times or pretty close to 4 times the amount of money we spend now on pure economic assistance to nonallied nations.

Also, they are the only major country that has large numbers of doctors, technicians, and engineers easily available for work abroad. They are graduating, as you know, some twice as many engineers and technicians as we are — and good ones, too.

Many of those engineers and technicians are getting language training. They are also getting training in the culture of these various countries. In Afghanistan, for instance, the Russians whom we saw spoke Pushtu or Farsi, the two major languages; some spoke both.

The average seems to be 3 years of training in the languages and cultures of these countries before they get their assignments.

I met three Russians in New Delhi in the process of getting my visa and all of them spoke fluent Hindi. They had studied it for 5 years. I don't think there are three people in our own setup in New Delhi who speak good Hindi. As far as I can find, most of the Russians going into India speak it well.

As I say, the amount of money needed for a formidable aid program is relatively small against the Soviet national income. They have a great number of well-trained, competent engineers and scientists. Many of them are trained in these languages. They have flexibility. For instance, they can suddenly decide to switch to Afghanistan, as they did, and offer a $100 million loan to meet a special opportunity.

They have also the advantage of a certain rigidity on our part, and I might add a certain lack of imagination, a lack of grasp of the basic issues, problems, and forces which are likely to write the history of Asia and Africa and indeed the world during this coming generation.

Mr. CARNAHAN. Are their technical assistance programs really geared to the needs of the country they are dealing with or pretty well slanted?

Mr. BOWLES. I don't think we know too much about it. They have made some mistakes in Burma, for instance. They found it easy to go into Burma because of various errors that we made there. They then made their own mistakes. In payment for rice they forced a lot of cement, for instance on the Burmese Government that the Burmese didn't really need. A lot of this cement became useless.

As far as I could see and as far as people with whom I talked could see, in Afghanistan they are doing much better. Most of the work that the Russians are doing in Afghanistan is north of the Hindu Kush mountains and south of the Oxus River, where there are 3 or 4 million Uzbeks. These are the same people, speaking the same language as the Russians on the other side of the river. The Uzbeks on the Russian side live considerably better than the Uzbeks living on the Afghanistan side. Most of the Soviet efforts so far in

Afghanistan have been in this area. It is a potentially rich area, about one-third of Afghanistan.

I had hoped to drive through it in a car, but the roads were so blocked up with snow in the mountains that we couldn't get through.

In Kabul itself they have provided dramatic evidence of what they can do. From Peshawar through the Khyber Pass to Kabul, is a 14-hour drive at an average speed of about 12 or 13 miles an hour in a station wagon with a 4-wheel drive, often with no road at all. You go up dry river beds and over the most impossible country. By early evening we were rather exhausted bumping our way up these mountains and down, when suddenly we came out on a completely smooth paved highway.

The driver said, "You have arrived in Kabul." The Russians, I discovered, had paved every street out 3 or 4 miles in the country. These broad highways were completely and beautifully paved. The people of Afghanistan had never seen a paved street. The streets in Kabul were paved better than some of the streets in Russia, but the Afghans don't know that.

The next day we went out to drive around the town. The first thing we saw was a new 10-story building, the only beautiful Russian building I have ever seen. "That," I was told, "is the grain elevator built by the Russians for the Afghans." The Afghans see it as a kind of monument that represents Russian friendliness and power. It is good showmanship.

From what I could gather in Afghanistan the Russians in general are doing well. They are tactful. They are not arrogant. They know a good deal about the past of Afghanistan. This is very flattering to the Afghans because too few Americans or other foreigners who go there bother to learn much about them.

The number of Americans of any prominence who have been in Afghanistan in the last 5 or 10 years is small. I think Mr. Nixon went there. I am not sure that any other major United States official has gone there.

But Khrushchev, Bulganin, and Chou En-lai have each spent several days there. And the Afghans are flattered by the fact that the Russians come, speak their language, know something of their past. As a result of the big Soviet loan they have diverted a good heavy fraction of Afghan foreign exchange into the Soviet Union.

One hundred million dollars in a country the size of Afghanistan is a lot of money. It is going to have a profound effect. This grew, as you know, out of our military agreement with Pakistan, which was signed in 1954. The Pakistani and the Afghans have been having trouble over Pushtoonistan, an area which is in dispute between the two. Many people believe that the Afghans have a poor case. They, nevertheless, think it is a good case.

In any event, when the Pakistani reached a military agreement with us, the Afghans say that they closed the Afghan border for 5½ months. Most of Afghanistan's foreign trade has always gone through Karachi and this was shut off. So they say that they had no place to turn except the Soviet Union.

They were blocked off completely. The roads in Iran are almost impassable. So the Soviet Union was their only outlet. For 5 months even the karakul furs that the Afghans sell in the United States were shipped through Black Sea ports and even around by way of Siberia and across the Pacific.

Following the signing of the United States-Pakistan arms agreement the Afghans also turned to the Soviet for military assistance. The Soviet Union is now training and equipping the Afghan army and air force.

A British soldier once said to me:

I don't know how many young Englishmen died to keep the Russians, in the days of the Czars, out of Afghanistan. But I do know the Russians have made more progress there in the last few years than they have made in the last century, and without a shot being fired.

I am afraid that this is a fact. We sometimes do not appreciate the degree to which our efforts to build a *world* military balance of power critically disrupts *local* balances of power, and thus creates insecurity, when we are earnestly and honestly trying to create security.

I think this is a case of that kind.

Mr. CARNAHAN. What is the situation in Afghanistan at the present time? You said the border was closed ——

Mr. BOWLES. It is now open again. They are now making good progress improving relations between Afghanistan and Pakistan. General Mirza, the President of Pakistan, recently visited Kabul. I think everyone there liked and trusted him.

The situation is somewhat relieved. There has also been talk of allowing not only right of shipment through Karachi for Afghan exports and imports, but special status, warehouses, docks, and sealed railroad cars going right through to the border without custom problems or anything of the kind.

What the Afghans would really like is a port on the Arabian Sea. There is a fishing port in Iran near the Pakistan border that could be deepened. A railroad could then be built through the mountains into Afghanistan. This would give them an open port, an open window on the world, which I think would mean a great deal to them.

This might have been a good investment for us. It may still be. It is important to assure the Afghans that they can look out toward the world, that they can always have free access to the world other than through the Soviet Union. Right now they feel this is the only route they can really be sure of. If I were they, I wouldn't be very sure of that.

Mr. CARNAHAN. Would you care to comment a little further regarding the situation between Afghanistan and the United States?

Mr. BOWLES. The Afghans are in no sense anxious to become a Soviet satellite. They are good, decent people. They are also deeply religious people, perhaps the second most orthodox Moslem country in the world, next to Saudi Arabia. They have a passion to be free. Their neighbors have been trying to control them for centuries and they are tired of it.

Nevertheless they are poor. Like most poor people living in that part of the world, they are in a desperate hurry for progress. So they have been testing out the Soviet Union to see if it is really dangerous to deal with. The Soviets have been handling the situation with skill. Their primary objective seems to be to convince the Afghans that they can work with the Soviet without being gobbled up.

The Afghans are taking an extraordinary risk, but on the evidence as they see it from day to day I don't think they are convinced of that. I think they would like to be friendly to both of us.

In Moscow I asked Mr. Khrushchev what the Soviet objectives were in Afghanistan. He said, "To keep you people out." I said, "Are you sure you don't want more than that?" He said, "No, just to keep you out."

The Russians now have something between 500 and 1,000 technicians in Afghanistan. How many of those are military I don't know. I don't think anybody does.

Mr. CARNAHAN. Mr. LeCompte.

Mr. LECOMPTE. I have only a few questions. Do you think you could tell us — I should know but I do not — what the population of Afghanistan is?

Mr. BOWLES. 16 million, something in that neighborhood. I don't think anybody knows precisely.

Mr. LECOMPTE. It is not growing very rapidly?

Mr. BOWLES. I think it will. It is a country of great resources, as you know. It is so chopped up by mountains that it is very hard to get around. There have been almost no roads. There is some concern in some circles about having it opened up too fast, a feeling that you can somehow hold back the future.

We are working on the Helmand River project there, an American aid program. I asked if they were doing a thorough job of rural development to go along with it. I believe that if you build a dam you must show the people how to use the water, better seeds, fertilizer and all the rest.

The Afghan with whom I was talking shook his head uncertainly. "We don't want them to wake up too fast," he said. But they are going to wake up anyway and this is good.

Mr. LECOMPTE. What is their principal product? They are mostly agriculturists? Farmers?

Mr. BOWLES. Agriculture and hides. What we call Persian lamb, they call karakul. Some minerals are beginning to come out. They are about self-sufficient in agriculture.

Mr. LECOMPTE. The hides of karakul bring in most of their outside money?

Mr. BOWLES. At present, yes. In 1952 when I was Ambassador to India, there were reports of oil north of the Hindu Kush Mountains, on the flat plain south of the Oxus River. As you know, the Russians moved into Uzbekistan in 1868. In a sense this is their colonial area. As the Russians moved south toward India, the British were moving north toward Russia. Afghanistan was the area in which they clashed and struggled indirectly through three Afghan wars.

When the oil possibility developed the Afghans being careful people, having to deal over the centuries with tough neighbors, went to the U. N. for help.

They sent 3 or 4 European geologists to explore the area. But the Russians said: "Get these people out of the country, at least this part of your country. We want no foreigners on Afghan soil so close to our border."

At first the Afghans took a firm position. It is a shame that we did not support them vigorously.

Worse still, the Afghans are convinced that the Pakistanis took this opportunity to slow down the flow of Afghan goods through Pakistan.

The Pakistanis say that it was not deliberate. I am inclined to think they are right. But nevertheless the Afghans thought that their southern border was being closed. So, in a panic they gave in to the Soviet demands and threw the U. N. people out. Here was the beginning of our present problem way back in 1952.

Mr. LECOMPTE. The technicians that you spoke of, are they natives or Russians?

Mr. BOWLES. You mean the technicians now provided by the Soviet Union? They are Russians. Some are their own Uzbek speaking people. They seem to be well trained in engineering and village development work, doctors, and the rest. They come there speaking the language, knowing the culture. It is effective.

Mr. LECOMPTE. Is the country an arid country that needs dams and irrigation, and so forth?

Mr. BOWLES. Yes; it does. We have helped greatly on that. The Helmand River valley project in southwestern Afghanistan is going to irrigate about 700,000 acres. It will mean a great deal.

My concern is that we must use a project of that kind not simply to provide water but to bring roads and fertilizer and better seeds and the things that go to make better life. It has to be a rounded program.

Mr. LECOMPTE. I thank you, Mr. Ambassador. It is nice for you to come up. You have been here before and have always left us a good message.

Mr. CARNAHAN. To whom do they sell most of their export goods?

Mr. BOWLES. I think now probably half goes to the Soviet Union. The other half is divided. We take some. Britain has always been a good customer. Some goes to Europe, generally. Some goes to India.

Mr. CARNAHAN. Dollars don't play a very big part in their economy?

Mr. BOWLES. I don't know what our trade amounts to. If I were guessing, I would put the figure around $20 million, something of that kind, for our purchases there.

But the Soviet has this $100 million credit that the Afghans can draw on.

As I understand, they have earmarked about $20 to $25 million of it so far. That will be in rubles and expendable only in the Soviet Union. What the Soviet Union is getting back for that I don't know.

Mr. CARNAHAN. Mr. Fulton.

Mr. FULTON. I am one of the people on the committee who has admired the work of the Ambassador and am always glad to have him here.

Mr. BOWLES. You are kind. I watch your own efforts in the newspapers with admiration and sympathy.

Mr. FULTON. I am acquainted with both your testimony and your books and find your ideas stimulating and helpful.

When we look at the map, the Indus River is the real trade route into Afghanistan from Karachi, Pakistan. On the Iran side, as to Gwatar, the port I believe you were speaking of, it is just a small river with no railroad access, and it would mean a major development with high expense to develop an adequate trade route to Afghanistan from the Indian Ocean.

In the course of our United States relations with Pakistan, why wouldn't it be a good idea to put some written limitations or conditions on our United States aid program, or else make some requests upon these countries to get together on a regional basis?

This committee has urged that kind of program for southeast Asia for joint economic development. Likewise under the Marshall plan there was joint action. Why couldn't we do something like that in this area?

Mr. BOWLES. We should. I think you have put your finger on the heart of this situation. As a matter of pure security as well as economic development, the only way you can defend that part of the world is through a joint defense program.

As long as Pakistan, Africa, India are at odds the area is indefensible with each nation trying to undermine its neighbor.

If Pakistan fails, India will be disastrously affected. If India fails, Pakistan will be disastrously affected.

If the Soviet Union manages gradually to draw Afghanistan into their area, the Pakistanis will be less secure, the Indians will be less secure.

This is something that the British always understood. So they tried to build a belt of neutral nations, Tibet, Nepal, and to a degree, Afghanistan.

With the best intentions in the world, we have gone out to try to build a purely military defense with a whole string of allies on the periphery of the Soviet Union and China without sufficiently considering the political and economic factors.

Mr. FULTON. Which I question, you see.

Mr. BOWLES. So do I. With our focus on purely the military aspects we sometimes upset the local balances of power, turn neighbor against neighbor, creating all kinds of suspicions and end up with substantially less security than we had in the first place.

When the British left India in 1947, Lord Mountbatten tried very hard to organize a joint defense of Pakistan and India. This was impossible at the time because of the bitterness there.

Now what is happening is that we have focused our attention largely on Pakistan because Pakistan will work closely with us. And the Pakistanis are a great people and a tough people. It is a joy to go there and see the warmth and feeling they have toward America.

But the fact is that in building up Pakistan's military power in comparison to India's we have been destroying the traditional balance that existed in that area, and we have created all kinds of political and economic difficulties.

All these countries are spending far too much money on the military. The Pakistan military budget is something like 60 percent of her national budget. The Indian military budget is pretty near that percentage.

Most of that money could be much better spent in building dams, irrigation projects, roads, schools, and building a more solid economic and political base.

Last year the Indians spent $100 million of their scarce foreign exchange that they had expected to spend in internal development to buy arms in Britain and in France to match the arms that we had given Pakistan.

Congress gave India $50 million last year for economic assistance. But they felt it necessary to spend twice that sum in pounds sterling for equipment to balance up the jets and tanks that we had given Pakistan. I don't know how anyone can expect to create stability, by fostering an arms race between poor countries which desperately need all the money they can get to ease their poverty, yet that is what we inadvertently have done.

In the meantime the Russians come along and say to the Indians, "Don't go to England to buy Canberra planes at $800,000 each.

We will give you good equipment at bargain rates. You can give us some of these rupees of yours and pay us over the years."

The Indians so far have turned this Soviet offer down. They have used their own scarce foreign exchange to build up their own defenses.

But Marshal Zhukov was in Delhi when I was there this winter. I was told that he spoke very effectively to the nervous Indians about what an army with new military equipment would do to one with old equipment.

So, the Soviets are able to play one nation against the other, creating more insecurity. We will get real security only by trying to bring these people together and by helping to ease the economic difficulties in both countries.

The military power that will deter the Russians from aggression in this part of the world is that of the United States. If we are strong enough and willing, if necessary, to use our power we can be sure that that area will be held as far as the military situation is concerned.

But we will only weaken the area by adding on more and more of a military burden to people who can't handle a military burden except by cutting down on their own economic development.

Moreover, we saw what the Egyptians did with all the fancy equipment they had from the Russians. It wasn't used very effectively. If the chips are down we are going to find out that some of our equipment now being sent into the Middle East won't be used very effectively, either.

I do not propose that we withdraw what we have already done. I do favor allowing it to peter out at this level and trying to create some basic security and stability by economic and political means. We are never going to get security here until you bring these people together. Our policy has inadvertently tended to set one against the other.

Mr. FULTON. May I comment on your statement as to the British, Pakistan, and India situation, because when India then used its pound sterling to have Britain produce nonproductive military goods it used Britain's industrial capacity for a nonproductive purpose. This likewise used up the credits that India had had for a long time in the pound-sterling area for a nonproductive purpose. Britain has not, because of her foreign-exchange position worsening, the capital goods to export, and has had to come to the United States and ask for further accommodation and more money and postponing of the British loan payments. So we are really paying in more ways than one for the United States policy.

There is one good thing about this competition between Russia and the United States that we should not forget; that, while each of us suspects the other's motive, it puts the two countries in an economic race to develop the world.

While we are protecting ourselves at home with military goods and buildup, nevertheless out in these disputed areas it means progress for them in the long run.

So that, rather than try to keep the Russians out completely, which from this distance is impossible, and likewise it is impossible for Afghanistan to do so, maybe it is just as wise for both of us to develop Afghanistan. From the Afghan point of view, it is doubly good because they get each of us watching the other so that neither one of us takes over.

Afghanistan couldn't stand against the United States; they couldn't stand against Russia. If they get both countries in and get an economic program from both of us, maybe these so-called natives are much smarter than we think they are.

I think it may be a pretty good thing for the world in general that we are in this competition on an economic development basis to show which system is the most efficient.

Mr. BOWLES. It also has its dangers unless we can muster not only the funds but the tact and the knowledge of these peoples; the willingness to get down in the mud and dirt and work there with them; the willingness to learn their languages, to study their cultures, how they live and want to live.

If we can do that, as well as put up the money, we can do much to help them achieve security.

Mr. FULTON. I see your point. You mentioned the cultures. In this general area, there are the Uzbeks, the Kurds, the Turkomen, all almost completely Moslem. They tie in with the Mediterranean area. Why, then, don't we have a regional economic development, possibly that would include some of these so-called Russian colonial areas, where we jointly develop and try to get some areas of co-operation with Russia to show that we are not just shoving the muzzles of guns in each other's faces all the time?

I am a person who wants to work out a method of living with the Russian people rather than destroying each other.

Mr. BOWLES. My impression in coming back from my recent trip is that the Russians have taken a bad setback in Eastern Europe, but that Asia and Africa offer them all kinds of new advantages. They have the advantage of the color prejudices, of racial antagonisms, the possibility of pitting the impoverished Asians against the wealthy Atlantic nations. All these facets that they can play on; also the skepticism about the workability of democracy in these parts of the world.

They are surely going to make a great effort to pull that area into a closer association with the Soviet Union. Until it is clearly demonstrated that they cannot succeed, that they cannot absorb it, cannot dominate it, my guess is that we will not get very far toward a really meaningful peace settlement on a global scale. I don't mean we can't have regional problems here and there where the tenseness has become so great that the Kremlin fears it will explode. But the lasting peace that everybody prays for will be possible only when it becomes ——

Mr. FULTON. Why not work in local areas of cooperation where we can build jointly? This assures us that even though it is so close to Russia and tied in so closely, like the Uzbeks in background, nevertheless the area opens it up and our program keeps it open. That is greatly to the United States advantage, even though we can't close the area to the Russians and should not, as a matter of fact.

Mr. BOWLES. One more point on the question of the Indian-Pakistan military position. The Indians have always tried to keep the ratio at about 9 to 4. Some people say that is unreasonable. But the Indians have a long border with China, about 1,500 miles. They also have the whole Burmese area to cover.

Others say, "I can't really believe that India, so much stronger, so much bigger, is really afraid of Pakistan." An Indian official once remarked in reply: "I seem to remember that the United States went into a high state of excitement because some Soviet military equipment was shipped into Guatemala in 1954. Are you Americans in a position to criticize our nervousness over our much more powerful neighbor?"

I had nothing further to say. I think every nation has to be a judge of its own security. Certainly we want to be a judge of ours.

Mr. FULTON. We always enjoy you and learn from you.

Mr. CARNAHAN. Mr. Judd.

Mr. JUDD. I was going to bring up the question that you just dealt with, Mr. Ambassador. I am informed that in many fields

the Indians' strength is about 3 to 1 to Pakistan's. First, their territory is much larger. It is in 1 piece where Pakistan is in 2 pieces
and 1,000 miles apart. Second, India's natural resources are enormously greater and their industry and electrical power much more
developed. Third, their military strength is about 3 to 1 and, fourth,
their population is 4 to 1. Yet everybody seems scared for India.
But if India feels jittery about a smaller and weaker neighbor, how
does Pakistan feel with a much stronger neighbor between her two
wings and an infinitely greater giant looking down her throat from
the northwest, able to come through Moslem territory —

Mr. BOWLES. I think it is a little more complicated than that,
if I may say so. There was no outside military threat to any great
degree, and I think if we had encouraged a lower balance of power
between the two there would have been greater security for everyone. Of course nobody is ever happy with their military balance
vis-a-vis their potential adversary. We are not happy with ours
in regard to Russia. But by building a balance at a higher and
higher level, all you do is take scarce resources away from essential
economic growth, and no one finds a means of improving his lot.

Mr. JUDD. It is the same problem we faced in the Middle
East. Israel had enormously greater military strength than the
Arab countries. So the Arab countries felt they had to take resources, which would have been better used for the development
of their people — they had to take those resources and divert them
to arms.

Then when they began to build up, though they never got anything like parity with the Israelis, the Israelis became jittery. We
tried our best to prevent that arms race. The Israelis were unhappy
because we wouldn't send arms to Israel; the Arabs were mad because we wouldn't send arms to the Arab countries. We are in as
much trouble in the Middle East, where we did not send —

Mr. BOWLES. We are doing in south Asia to some extent
what the Soviets did in Egypt. By dumping arms into Egypt the
Soviet created frustrations and fears and the Israeli attack ultimately came. The Israelis are only 2 million people and there are
40 million Arabs. Yet there had been a military balance there, and
no pressing danger of war until the Soviet Union dumped all that
equipment into Egypt. Then the situation became explosive.

The same thing could happen in south Asia. If we can't make
progress toward disarmament with the Soviet Union (and they

have certainly made is impossible so far) at least we can tone down some of these regional arms races. If we don't, they can erupt into war and draw us all in.

We have built up Saudi Arabia, Iraq, Iran, Pakistan with more and more equipment and the Soviet has built up Afghanistan, Syria, and Egypt. If we had a 10-year moratorium on arms shipments there would be no more equipment going to any of those countries and they could all begin to catch their economic and political breath.

If we send more arms to Iraq, they will send more to Syria. If we send more to Iran and Pakistan, there will be more going to Afghanistan and Egypt. I don't see how anybody profits from this. Moreover it is not simply a matter of cost to the American taxpayer. They have to pay their soldiers. Moreover their own scarce technical people are taken away from the work of economic growth and development.

So we have not only the very heavy cost to us, much of which I think is unnecessary, but we undermine their own efforts to build something solid. We take their minds off their real internal problems. Instead of concentrating on building schools and growing food the leaders make angry speeches, and flex their new military muscles, in Baghdad, Damascus, Cairo, Karachi, Kabul, or New Delhi, wherever it may be. As we build up this military power, with each trying to inch ahead of the other, each trying to get their more powerful supporter to build them up at the expense of the other, we take our friends' minds off their real job, which is more food and more water. We take their minds off the big problems of economic and political growth for their people.

The Kashmir issue is tragic for two reasons. First, it has taken Pakistan's mind off its job, which is economic growth and development for its people, getting rid of its abysmal poverty. The second thing it has done is to undermine a good deal of India's moral standing in the world. People have very properly said that India has applied one standard to the world and a rather different one to themselves.

In any event the energies of all these people ought to be building roads, villages, and helping people move ahead instead of wasting themselves in an arms race. The whole Arab world seems to be concentrating now in seeing if they can get a few more jets than their neighbors.

I don't think we can buy the loyalty of people with jets and tanks any more than we can buy it with cash subsidies such as the subsidy the British gave to Jordan. The more we arm one nation the more the Russians arm the other. It is a military merry-go-round. If we really want to start saving money here is a wonderful place to start and a moratorium — if the Soviets will agree to it — is the way to do it.

Mr. JUDD. How do you get them together so you can stop it? You sound as if we started the race. We didn't. We disarmed at the end of the war. The Soviet Union wouldn't disarm. Our arming was the belated consequence of their refusal to do what we did and you want us to do again. How do you do it when the other people won't play ball?

Mr. BOWLES. We have to just ——

Mr. JUDD. Then what is the use of daydreaming?

Mr. BOWLES. I am not talking about our military expenditures. Here I would spend every dime that's really necessary. But the strength that is going to keep the Soviet Union out of the Middle East is not going to be the strength of this Iraqi Army or the Iranian Army; it is going to be primarily the United States Air Force. That is the power that the Soviets understand. That is the security barrier which protects this region.

Mr. JUDD. You are going to give up the thought of local defense on the ground of individual pieces of territory? You would just put all our chips into one bag? Our Air Force striking the Soviet Union?

Mr. BOWLES. Has anyone in the Pentagon told you seriously that the Iranian and Iraqi Armies are going to keep Soviet armored divisions out of the Middle East?

Mr. JUDD. No; they haven't. But there is in Iran a pretty good situation where it wouldn't take an awful lot of strength to hold three major passes long enough maybe to get some help in.

Mr. BOWLES. I do not think that is where an attack would come.

But I wouldn't take anything away from what we have already done. Nor could any moratorium include Turkey which is the eastern anchor point of our whole NATO alliance. It guards southeastern Europe. Turkey must be fully supported militarily. The only way I would consider any change there would be if the Soviet Union would pull their troops out of Bulgaria and Rumania. Obviously they are unlikely to do that.

Mr. JUDD. Turkey is just like Pakistan and India. She is

spending much more of her resources for arms than her economy can afford, and you know that is hard.

Mr. BOWLES. That is so. But the Turks have given great security to this area.

Mr. JUDD. Do you think any of those countries out there or anywhere else trust us enough to turn the defense of their homeland over to the United States, that they have enough confidence ——

Mr. BOWLES. That is what they are doing.

Mr. JUDD. That we would cut loose our power in an all-out atomic attack upon the Soviet Union and thereby bring it upon ourselves?

Mr. BOWLES. I certainly believe we would. If we are not willing to oppose aggression, it will surely come.

Mr. JUDD. You and I might. Do you think they will trust us to do that?

Mr. BOWLES. If we are not prepared to do that, there is no security in the world. If we are not prepared to use our power, there is no security. If America's power is something that we plan to keep unused in a desk drawer, it will be of very little value to free peoples.

But I am talking about increasing the flow of military equipment to Iraq, Iran, and Pakistan.

There are hundreds of millions of dollars going into it that I believe could be put into more constructive work. I am not talking about South Korea or Vietnam or Formosa. I am talking about the Middle East where I think we have gone as far as we can profitably go in piling up locally controlled, high-cost military equipment.

Before you came in, Dr. Judd, I mentioned the fact that when we went all out on our military shipments to Pakistan, the Afghans immediately turned to the Soviet Union and the Soviet Union came through to equip them with arms, loan them $100 million for economic projects, and so began to throw their support behind the Afghans.

Mr. JUDD. But Afghanistan wouldn't have turned to the Soviet Union if she had been able to get arms and help from us.

They talked to us first, and if we had been willing to give them the kind of help they wanted, they would not have gone to Russia and neither would Nasser. Nasser waited 4 months after he was desperate and we wouldn't give arms to him.

Mr. BOWLES. Granted, mistakes were made.

Mr. JUDD. I wish we didn't have to spend a dime for arms. I was a missionary and love to work with people. A missionary came home yesterday from 6 years imprisonment in China and said that missionary work in China is done. It was lost during my period there when people wouldn't do anything about security. We were going to save them just by loving them and bettering their living conditions. We lost them.

Mr. BOWLES. Arms are absolutely essential. But I am for using them sensibly. Before you came in I was pointing out that India, because of the money we gave Pakistan, expended $100 million ——

Mr. JUDD. I got that.

Mr. BOWLES. To buy Canberras and other planes in France and England. That does not give us any more security.

Mr. JUDD. Do you think we should have refused Pakistan's request? We were giving military aid to about 30 countries. Pakistan said, "We feel threatened from the Northwest." How could we have refused to give arms to friendly Pakistan which felt threatened when we were giving them to 30 other countries that felt threatened.

Mr. BOWLES. I do not believe that there has ever been a serious ground force threat from the north through those impassable mountains.

Mr. JUDD. They saw what the Soviet Union was doing in Asia.

Mr. BOWLES. But the result was to push Afghanistan toward the Soviet orbit, to force India to forego some of its essential development work, and today we are closer to an outbreak in south Asia than we have ever been. In the morning paper there is a story that the Pakistanis say they can't hold the tribesmen in check.

Mr. JUDD. And that is true. We talked to the tribesmen in 1955. They don't make any bones about it. They said frankly: We have waited and waited. When is the United Nations going to act on Kashmir? If it isn't going to act, when is the United States going to act? Those are our brothers in Kashmir and we will move.

Mr. BOWLES. We must remember there are 43 million Moslems in India. There are more Moslems in India than in West Pakistan. This often is forgotten.

You put this on a religious basis. Does this mean that the 43 million Moslems should leave India?

Mr. JUDD. No. Some of them might be slaughtered in India.

Mr. BOWLES. I don't think you will see any plebiscite in Kashmir. With some patience and skill and negotiation there may, however, be a semi-autonomous Kashmir Valley; Azad Kashmir going to Pakistan, Jammu and Ladak to India and then building up through gradual negotiation a semi-autonomous area in the valley.

But the thing we ought to do now is to stop handing these angry people military tools with which to chop each other up.

Mr. JUDD. We tried that for years. You were out there, and you are a very winsome salesman and you didn't succeed in getting the Indians to reduce their arms.

Mr. BOWLES. Since then the military budgets have gone way up.

Mr. JUDD. Did you work at that time for the division of Kashmir you mentioned? There were people on the other side, the Pakistan side, who would accept that? Have you been able to get the Indians to agree to it?

Mr. BOWLES. We came within a sixteenth of an inch getting it settled on that very basis in the winter of 1952.

Mr. JUDD. I was out there the following spring.

Mr. CARNAHAN. It is certainly evident that the Russians have given major emphasis to military strength since the end of World War II, and there is considerable evidence that they are going to continue to maintain what we consider a safe military balance. Would you care to comment on whether or not there is a shift on their part toward greater emphasis on the economic aspects of the Russian foreign policy?

Mr. BOWLES. In this whole area there has certainly been a shift. Russia is building a steel mill for India. There is talk of another Soviet loan of about $90 million. They are putting a great deal of money into China. Nobody knows how much. The best estimate I have seen is in the neighborhood of $2.5 billion. The Chinese, of course, pay some of that back in various ways.

Military strength is, of course, vital to our whole global security. But there are two reasons for military strength. One is to prevent an attack. The second is to provide a screen behind which we can conduct constructive economic and political policies. Simply to build a screen and then go away and forget the whole thing is only half a policy.

Behind the military screen we must make sure there is growth, development and a greater sense of belonging. May I emphasize that it is not simply a matter of more economic growth, more rice or more electric power or whatever. I think there has to be three factors present.

First, there has to be more production, of course, but, secondly, the production has to be achieved through a sense of participation by the people and not simply handed to them by the Government. They have to feel they have contributed to this greater advancement.

Thirdly, the greater output must lead to an increasing sense of justice. If the greater productivity goes disproportionately to those who are already wealthy, or in a position of feudal strength and power, you are likely to get more political instability instead of less.

I have talked previously before this committee about the need for tacking some kind of economic conditions to our aid. If you don't put through land reforms, the better seed, the fertilizer, the increased water may double the big farmer's income without corresponding benefit to the others. The result is not more stability, but less.

What we must seek is more output achieved by the people working together, leading to an increasing sense of justice. When you have those three things, you are on the road to political stability. Your military security screen makes it possible to tackle these constructive problems.

Mr. CARNAHAN. We are glad to have the chairman of the Foreign Affairs Committee with us. Chairman Gordon, do you have any questions?

Chairman GORDON. No. I am sorry I was delayed. I am certainly happy to see Mr. Bowles here. You are always welcome before our committee. I have no questions at this time.

Mr. CARNAHAN. Behind this screen, is it your opinion that the Russians are turning more and more to the greatest possible use of economic processes to accomplish their goals?

Mr. BOWLES. That is my feeling. And they are well equipped to do it. I know the number of able Soviet technicians going into India now, for instance, is great. We have on several occasions been asked to send over trained people in medicine, engineering, and other areas. We could not produce them but they could.

Mr. CARNAHAN. Would you give us your opinion as to what we are doing, briefly?

Mr. BOWLES. What we are doing is disappointing in this

sense: When Mr. Truman, in his inaugural address in 1949 outlined point 4, it was an imaginative, creative and bold proposal. Naturally, we didn't know at first how to go about it. It was an unknown area for us. We had to experiment.

Then people such as Brian McMahon and others stepped forward and pressed for a positive program. There was more and more interest. At first, I think too much attention was given in some countries to the technical assistance side. India, for instance, has some able unemployed people with their doctorates in agriculture. What they want most are top caliber people on special problems — a vice president of General Electric or du Pont or outstanding farm experts who can bring them highly specialized skills for a few months at a time.

I hope that some system can be worked out that will provide such expert help perhaps on a management contract basis.

Of course in some countries we need less skilled technical assistance very badly. But generally I would rather have more top people and less of the run of the mill. That doesn't apply to a country like Ethiopia where you desperately need people to take over all kinds of tasks at somewhat lower level. I am talking primarily about more advanced countries like India.

As far as capital assistance is concerned I think Mr. Dulles' statement yesterday was a step in the right direction. But the work done at the International Center at MIT which suggested annual loans of around $1.5 billion a year for a period of years strikes me as close to the amount required. I doubt we could spend more money effectively.

Our farm program with Public Law 480 seems to be a very effective program. People in Asia as elsewhere need so much food to keep alive. But if they get a job they need twice as much food to work properly.

The Indians can now raise enough food to meet their minimum survival needs. But now their people are going to work and working hard. So they need more food to keep them going.

The food almost becomes the means of payment. If you have grain, then you can hire people, put them to work, give them rupees, and they can buy their grain and you don't have inflation. Thus in order to build a dam you have to have more food, as well as more equipment from General Electric and other big companies that provide the dynamos, other electrical gear and all the rest.

Mr. CARNAHAN. You feel then that really an economic development project in one of the underdeveloped countries is going to have to be supported by extra food and fiber, otherwise the economy of the country will be seriously affected?

Mr. BOWLES. That is right. The Egyptians could not have built the Aswan Dam without more wheat and rice. They needed not only the foreign exchange to buy the equipment, the bulldozers, but they needed the food to give to the workers who would be working harder and eating more food; otherwise, they would have had inflation.

Mr. FULTON. That is why I can't understand that the Midwest farm areas of the United States are so opposed to the foreign-aid program, because under Public Law 480, the program is really dumping farm surpluses of the United States abroad. These countries develop into good customers and buy the food with the American dollars that we have lent to them as part of their economic progress and construction costs. So that to me the farm people in this country are some of the best beneficiaries of our foreign-aid programs if they would look into it.

Mr. BOWLES. Dr. Judd knows this subject better than I, but I spent sometime in his area last fall. I found that audiences were bored when I talked about parity and soil banks but they were immediately interested when I began to talk about the hungry people in the world and our capacity to grow more food. If the Russians had 4 billion bushels of wheat, I pointed out that they would be putting it to work. Also, dried milk.

On one occasion I went back to 1932, and at overloaded grocery stores with spoiling food and hungry people walked back and forth in front of the grocery stores unable to buy the food because of what was said to be the iron laws of economics which kept the people and the food from getting together.

Somehow we found the way to break through this iron law of economics and we all profited thereby. The same kind of imagination is now necessary on a world scale to bring our food-producing capacity and the world needs together. I believe that the world economics of 1960 may be as different from the economics of 1956 as the economics of 1936 were from that of 1932.

Mr. FULTON. Could I point out to you how the policy of this country is moving along the lines of the people who feel the world is in for a development generation with education, progress, economic development as the key words, the catchwords of any and all nations.

As you may recall, in 1954, when I was at the Rio Economic Conference, I had suggested to our delegation, headed by Mr. Humphrey, that we come up with a $1 billion United States revolving fund which would be able to finance on a regional basis throughout the world just such projects as we are talking about, which Mr. Dulles has now in his statement endorsed.

For my pains for saying that as an individual I had my dinner invitation at the United States Embassy at Brazil revoked on Thanksgiving afternoon so that neither I nor the two consultants that were with me from his committee were allowed to go to the United States Embassy, for saying something so outrageous.

Yet from November 1954 to 1957, when little bombshells like that go off, they move United States policy, and there is now the statement of Secretary of State Dulles recommending a similar revolving fund of $750 million, and the United States Ambassador to Brazil, Mr. James Kemper, and his ideas have long since departed the scene. How times change.

So may I join with you in saying that we should emphasize economic development, education, working with people, do it on a regional basis, and even do it with the Moslems and Russia in this area where and if real cooperation can be assured.

Mr. BOWLES. If they let you. Uzbekistan could use some help.

Mr. CARNAHAN. Dr. Judd, do you have further questions?

Mr. JUDD. No.

Mr. FULTON. May I say to Dr. Judd that this economic development emphasis, with some deemphasis on the dumping in of regional arms, is not daydreaming.

Mr. JUDD. I didn't say that. I said I am all for greater emphasis on economic development. But to talk about the possibility of doing that in the absence of some cooperation from both sides in being willing to cut down their arms is daydreaming.

Mr. FULTON. Would you please say that again, or explain it further?

Mr. JUDD. If I was misunderstood ——

Mr. BOWLES. I think sometimes when they are talking off the record they have a real awareness of what this military burden ——

Mr. JUDD. I don't think any of them wanted to increase it. But, on the other hand, no government, no self-respecting government that wants to stay in power at home can entrust its own security against its next-door neighbor wholly to the pledged word of another government, even the United States of America.

Therefore they feel they have to have some arms, a tank or two, even if it is a Sherman, to go down the street. They have to have some evidence of local strength.

Mr. BOWLES. All I am saying is: Let's stop at this point at least in the Middle East. What they need most is the kind of military setup that will protect their internal security. That is a different kind of proposition. You don't need 8-inch guns that are capable of firing an atomic shell to stop riots. You don't need jets to stop an uprising in the capital.

Mr. JUDD. India had bought many jets before Pakistan had a single one.

Mr. BOWLES. But at some point you have to freeze the situation without blaming one or the other.

Mr. JUDD. That was my original question. How do you bring them together in order to stop it? We haven't been able to do it with Korea and Japan. We haven't been able to get Sukarno and the Netherlands to deal with the overall situation rather than the local quarrel over West New Guinea. We haven't been able to get the British and the Greeks and the Turks to quit quarreling over Cyprus so as to deal together with the overall threat from the Communists. Or the Israelis and the Arabs to solve the local dispute so as to unite against their common enemy.

It is human nature to be more concerned about the ancient feud with an immediate neighbor right next door than the overall threat. A patient comes in with a boil and we find a cancer. He isn't worried about the cancer, it is the boil that hurts; and if you don't take care of the boil he will go to another doctor.

Mr. FULTON. It wouldn't be a good doctor who listens to the patient in that case.

Mr. JUDD. He won't have him long, unless he tends to the local irritation.

Mr. FULTON. That is what the Ambassador and I feel, that there must be some way to break the arms race that is going on worldwide on a world security basis, but likewise also upset local regional balances. If you could only put the guns in that could shoot one way, on worldwide problems, and not on local issues. They are used for threats locally, when they are put in local hands for general security.

Mr. BOWLES. Or the other people fear they will be.

Mr. JUDD. I am for all you are trying to do. But we haven't succeeded yet in doing one without the other.

Mr. BOWLES. Suppose we said to the Soviet Union: "We will agree to an embargo, a moratorium on future arms shipments to the Middle East. This means that we will ship no more arms to Iraq, Iran, and Pakistan provided you ship no more to Afghanistan, Syria, Egypt, India, or anyone else. We will all agree to stop for 5 or 10 years so everybody can catch his breath." The Russians undoubtedly would say, "How about Turkey," and we would have to say: "No; that is a separate question."

It is still possible that the Soviet Union might accept our proposal. I don't know. If they didn't accept it, we would at least have demonstrated our good intentions that we would like to stop these local arms races.

If they did accept it, we would all be relieved of a dangerous, increasingly explosive competition between neighbors which does not add to the total security of the world. I don't know whether it would work or not.

In Moscow this winter, I asked Khrushchev if he would agree, and I had a strong impression that he might.

Mr. JUDD. I am in favor of trying it.

Mr. BOWLES. You said you wondered about the people in the country and their attitudes toward economic assistance. On Sunday, March 17, the New York Times ran a roundup of points of view on economic assistance. May I quote from it briefly: "Several times in the last 6 years the following question has been asked by various groups: As things are now, which would you say is the most important: To send friendly nations economic aid or send military things like tanks and guns?" Last June, which was the last time the sampling was taken, 71 percent said economic and only 17 percent military. This is in the Times of March 17.

Mr. FULTON. And we certainly had success under the Marshall plan with economic aid programs.

Mr. BOWLES. We did.

Mr. JUDD. Yes, because we had the bomb and the Soviet Union didn't yet have the bomb. We tried that course in Korea. We were going to reduce the military burden and build up economically. We negotiated 2 years and signed an agreement not to increase arms. We kept our pledge and they tore up theirs from the beginning.

Mr. BOWLES. But now in the Middle East we are feeding in arms past the point of a reasonable return.

Mr. JUDD. I just know that cancer generally behaves like cancer, and we are dealing with a malignant process.

Mr. BOWLES. I am thinking of a way to get over it and not kill the patient.

Mr. JUDD. Malignancies don't stop expanding until they are checked.

Mr. BOWLES. I think we must tell these people. You have a good solid American defense behind you. We are going to support you. But now let's turn to the problem of trying to work out these local regional relationships and help people to live better. Then we can begin to make progress. I think a lot of these people are themselves very nervous about the situation as it now stands with the Soviet arming one group and we arming the other.

Just one more point. Congress gave a guarantee to the Middle East that America would become immediately and vigorously involved if there is a Communist action in the Middle East. I wholly agree with that.

Mr. JUDD. If they request it.

Mr. BOWLES. My only criticism is this. I think what we should have said: "It has been American policy since 1945 to oppose any aggression by force by any Communist nation across any border. Congress hereby reaffirms this policy."

Because your congressional commitment was regional it may conceivably weaken our position in other areas. Will Mao Tse-tung in Peiping wonder if this means that the Americans won't support Burma in case he attacks? Will Khrushchev wonder if this means the Americans will not support Yugoslavia?

Our commitment must be global along the whole periphery of the Soviet Union and Communist China. It must be a vigorous commitment. By regionalizing it you did not strengthen the commitment; you may have weakened it. If it had been a global statement, the next day the Secretary would have been asked: "Does this apply to the Middle East?" He would have said, "Of course," and you have what you have now but with no chance of misunderstanding elsewhere.

Mr. JUDD. I think that reaction might have come, but it is our job to explain it was not our intention to reduce our commitment. We had already made it in Europe with the Greek-Turkey program. We had also made it with SEATO, with the Formosa resolution, and now we made it for the Middle East. Probably we should have said in the preamble it was merely an extension of a policy.

I regret the term "Eisenhower Doctrine." No one in the administration used it. The newspapers put it on as a convenient handle. It may have looked like something new. But it was only a reaffirmation for a different area that was now threatened.

I spent some time with President Truman in the late forties trying to get him to apply to the Far East the same doctrine he sponsored in Europe. Nobody has ever stated it better than he did down here in March 1947, when talking about Turkey and Greece. He said that it must be the policy of the United States to support free nations against external aggression and internal subversion. That was a global principle. Wherever aggression threatens, wherever we can help; it must be our policy to do so. But he wouldn't extend his own policy to the Far East at that time.

Mr. BOWLES. I don't want to bring up a controversial ——

Mr. JUDD. That is water over the dam.

Mr. BOWLES. I don't want to bring up a controversial subject in the Halls of Congress. But some time ago Dean Acheson was charged with having drawn a line in the Far East that did not include Korea. When the South Koreans were attacked, it was said it was because he left this door open.

By applying our recent guaranty regionally a great many doors were left open. I would rather have seen a sweeping guaranty.

Let's build a good tough fence and be prepared to defend it. But let's also cultivate the fields behind the fence. To build the military fence and then go away and say that we have stopped communism in its tracks is not an adequate answer. We have to cultivate the economic and political fields behind the fence.

Mr. JUDD. I couldn't agree with you more. But I must add this: I don't think we can effectively give much more economic aid than we are giving. I think in some places we are already choking them a little. I know in one country our people were getting in each other's way when they had about 117 in our various economic programs. We urged they cut it down to the essentials. Now they have 200 people there and the confusion is increased instead of decreased. I don't think you can do it on a quantitative basis.

Mr. BOWLES. There are limits.

Mr. JUDD. You have to ask first, what do they need? That is astronomical.

Second, how much can they effectively use? That is much smaller. Third, how much can they self-respectingly receive? Often that is still smaller. It does not do any good to crowd them to the point of confusion, and sometimes noncooperation.

You said something about if we can learn the languages. Our failure to do this is one of the things that burns me up. We can learn languages. But we don't. I talked recently to a man just back from the university in Kabul, Afghanistan. He said Russians are coming in who speak the language like the natives. They have spent 5 years learning it. We give our people 3 weeks orientation and send them over. No wonder we lose. Dollars are no substitute for knowledge.

Mr. BOWLES. On this question of the amount of aid let me take the case of India, and we all become irritated at some of the positions that India takes in the U. N. Yet history will devote only a few sentences to what Mr. Krishna Menon said at the U. N., while it devotes several chapters to what happened in India, whether India succeeded or not in building the basis for a democratic society.

India is not trying to match China in every field. But it is trying to come close enough so that it becomes clear that there is a valid alternative to communism in Asia.

Most of India's financial needs will be met from her own resources. More will be met by loans from various sources. For instance, they hope the World Bank will give them substantial help on their second 5-year plan.

By these loans and by drawing down their balances of foreign reserves against their currency the gap between their tax income and their minimum capital requirements for the next 4 years comes down to $1 billion.

Now they owe us $190 million for grain that they purchased from us in 1951. This debt soon becomes due and the first payment must be made in June. So this June India is going to start paying us back dollars on that debt.

The fact that they have a $190 million debt to us for this grain means they can borrow that much less from the World Bank. Congress could easily ease this pressure by putting that loan on a rupee basis. That might give India a chance to borrow $190 million more from the World Bank.

Second, during the war, India—and this was during the British occupation — borrowed 180 million ounces of silver from us to support their currency. This silver is now worth $110 million. They are starting to pay this silver back this year. We have no urgent need for $110 million worth of silver, so this payment could be postponed or the debt wiped out altogether.

In this way Congress can easily improve India's financial position by $300 million. That would leave a capital deficit of about $700 million. If this sum could be loaned to them in four installments, it would be put to good use in building a stable democratic society.

I think that Congress would thereby have taken a most vigorous and constructive step toward giving the ideas that we all share, a better chance in south Asia.

It would be $225 million a year for 4 years. There would be no question about that sort of expenditure if it were for tanks or jets. Give it on a loan basis payable in rupees, and you will be building far more security. They don't want a grant. They don't want a gift. They want a loan.

In those three moves you could go a long way in demonstrating that democracy in Asia can challenge Chinese totalitarianism and do a better job.

Mr. JUDD. As for Mr. Menon, he doesn't concern me, except to irritate me. But it seems strange that Mr. Nehru, if he wants to make a good showing against his rival, Communist China, should spend so much time and effort building up the rival. Because who is really master of China will be the strongest power in Asia, no matter whether India has a totalitarian or a democratic system, because the Chinese are a larger and tougher people. Or maybe it is the climate.

Mr. BOWLES. One of the great blocks in the way of the Soviet Union in that part of the world eventually will be China.

Mr. JUDD. One more comment. Mr. Chairman. If my remark on daydreaming was misunderstood, what I said was that to imagine that we can carry out successfully this economic development in areas that do not have security, which in the present situation, because of our inability to get agreement on disarmament can be obtained only by arms, is daydreaming. You have to have the shield of military security to make it possible for people to turn their full energy and resources to economic efforts.

Mr. BOWLES. I agree. But when the Soviet gave arms to Egypt they did not create security for Egypt, they brought on an attack on Egypt.

Mr. JUDD. That is right. We tried to tell the Egyptians that.

The Egyptians waited in vain 4 months to get arms from us, and then they went to the Soviet Union.

Mr. FULTON. I would like to enter my disagreement on one basic phase. When you, Mr. Ambassador, and Dr. Judd were talking about building a fence in answer to the Russian's fence, I believe the world has areas that are essential to the Russian security just as there are areas of the world which are essential to the United States and the free world security. In between, I believe there are areas where neither the Russians nor the United States can physically keep each other out, and the will of the local people is that we neither be kept out but they want us both in for economic development purposes. I think in those particular underdeveloped and uncommitted areas where we in the United States can work with the local people, even in conjunction with Russian economic programs on an overall plan for economic progress, maybe the United States had better try it in certain specific areas. Maybe the best our policy can do is keep the status quo in certain places.

Mr. BOWLES. I mean the fence only in terms of military aggression. A fence is worthless against ideas. A fence can't stop economic penetration. It won't stop trade. I am talking only about a fence against Soviet tanks.

Mr. FULTON. There are certain areas where the United States admittedly cannot maintain military supremacy alone. We won't have the local people joining us. In those areas, then, I say emphasize the economic.

Mr. CARNAHAN. Do you have a further comment?

Mr. BOWLES. No.

Mr. CARNAHAN. I hesitate to bring this to a close.

Mr. FULTON. May I congratulate the Ambassador.

Mr. CARNAHAN. We appreciate your coming. You are always helpful and we always learn from you.

(Whereupon, at 12:17 p. m., the subcommittee adjourned.)

FURTHER DISCUSSION QUESTIONS

CONSIDERING THE SELECTIONS from the various hearings as a whole makes it possible to raise other questions of interest to the student of social processes. For example, what is the role of a legislative committee member during a hearing? What are the variants of this role? What is the role of a witness? How much variability in implementing these various roles was observed? What kind of behavior would conceivably be not tolerable in these hearings?

In addition to questions about roles, one might think of these discussions as samplings of public opinions. What factors seem to determine whether an issue will be perceived? What contributes to the definition of the position taken by citizens on controversial issues? Are there constellations of attitudes in the sense that you can predict from the position taken in one section how the same individual might testify in another section (if we had the chance to check)?

Another general problem might be the common characteristics of individuals who have achieved similar positions on the basis of their own strivings. Thus, what is the composite legislator like as a person? How does the reality compare with the stereotype of the "politician"? How does the senator compare with the representative?

And still another area for study might be the impact of this communication on you, the reader. How did you respond to the various materials presented? Did you respond the same way to materials you agreed with as you did to materials you disagreed with? What was the effect of the various sources of material on the credibility of their presentations? Did you have special difficulty with any particular kinds of materials or people? Has there been any effect on you that is likely to persist? How can you account for this?

INDEX OF PARTICIPANTS

531